The Economic History of Britain since 1700

Volume 2: 1860 to the 1970s

The Economic History of Britain since 1700

Edited by
RODERICK FLOUD *and* DONALD McCLOSKEY

Volume 2: 1860 to the 1970s

Cambridge University Press

Cambridge
London   New York   New Rochelle
Melbourne   Sydney

Published by the Press Syndicate of the University of Cambridge
The Pitt Building, Trumpington Street, Cambridge CB2 1RP
32 East 57th Street, New York, NY 10022, USA
296 Beaconsfield Parade, Middle Park, Melbourne 3206, Australia

First published 1981

Printed in Great Britain at the University Press, Cambridge

British Library Cataloguing in Publication Data
The economic history of Great Britain since 1700.
Vol. 2: 1860 to the 1970s
1. Great Britain – Economic conditions
I. Floud, Roderick II. McCloskey, Donald Nansen
330.9'41'07   HC255   79-41645
ISBN 0 521 23167 1 hard covers
ISBN 0 521 29843 1 paperback
vol. 1 ISBN 0 521 23166 3 hard covers
        ISBN 0 521 29842 3 paperback

To Lydia, Sarah, Daniel and Margaret

Contents

Tables

Figures

Introduction

R. C. FLOUD & D. N. McCLOSKEY

Economic history is an exciting subject, a subject full of problems and controversy. It is exciting because in economic history one is constantly forced to ask the question – why? Why were steam engines brought into use at a particular point during the industrial revolution? Why did so many millions brave great dangers to emigrate to the new world? Why were so many unemployed in the depression of the 1930s? Why do parents today have fewer children than parents two hundred years ago? Economic history is not, therefore, a story – still less a chronological story, for most events in economic history cannot be neatly dated. Instead it is a list of questions; some can be answered, some cannot, but it is the search for answers, and for the best way to seek answers, which gives the subject both its justification and its interest. 'Economic history concerns the dullest part of human life. Sex, art, aberrant behaviour, politics, bloodshed – it is largely devoid of these' (Parker 1971). Yet it is concerned instead with how people live most of their lives, how many people are born and how they die, how they earn and how they spend, how they work and how they play.

At the same time, economic history can be hard, boring and frustrating, both to write and to learn. Simply because it is concerned with how people have commonly lived, and why they have commonly behaved in a particular way, it is often difficult to discover relevant evidence; people, certainly most people, do not record in great detail for posterity what they buy or what they do at work, nor even how many children they have. The historian has to reconstruct the details of such behaviour from scattered and ambiguous evidence, and his reconstruction can often only be imprecise; few of the statements made in this book are, for that reason, entirely free from the possibility of error, and many represent only guesses. They are the best guesses made, when the book was written, by economic historians expert in their subject, but guesses nonetheless. Indeed, part of the fascination of economic history, although also one of the main causes of the controversies which rumble on for years in the scholarly journals of the subject, lies in making new guesses, and in working out what the effect on our knowledge of the past might be if we made different, but still sensible, guesses about the interpretation of evidence.

Even when we know, at least approximately, whether people ate white or brown bread, or at what age they married, they are very unlikely to have recorded for posterity why they ate white bread when their parents ate brown, or why they married at 27 when their parents married at 24. Even if they did so, their records would be inconclusive, for two reasons: first, people are poor at self analysis; second, the factor which they choose as 'the' reason why is usually one among many joint reasons. In any case, the economic historian's interest is not normally in the behaviour of individuals, except as exemplars of the behaviour of society, or large groups within society, as a whole. While a political historian can reasonably hope to understand something of the political history of the nineteenth century by studying the life and thoughts of Queen Victoria or of Abraham Lincoln, the economic historian knows that the behaviour of any one individual has very little or no effect upon, and may even be totally different from, the observed behaviour of society as a whole. The fact that the marriage age in a parish is observed to have fallen from an average of 27 in one generation to an average of 24 in the next does not show that all those who married did so at the age of 24; nor, conversely, does the fact that two people married at 29 invalidate the fact of the fall in the average.

The answer that we give to a question such as 'why did people marry at an earlier age than their parents' cannot therefore stem directly from the memories or writings of those who were doing the marrying. It can stem partly from such evidence, but only because such evidence helps to build up a set of the many possible reasons why people might have decided to marry earlier. This set of reasons, based partly on evidence from those who married and partly on the knowledge and common sense of the historian, is a necessary beginning to the task of explanation. Armed with it, the historian can begin to explore the evidence, and to see to what degree the behaviour which he observes fits best with one reason rather than another. He might begin, for example, with the belief that people are likely to marry if they are richer and can afford to set up house at an earlier age than their parents; if he finds after seeking for evidence of changes in income levels that on the contrary income levels fell at the same time as marriage became earlier, then that belief seems unlikely to be helpful, and another possible reason must be explored.

In other words, the historian uses evidence of the behaviour of individuals to help him to build up an expectation of how people might have behaved, against which he can contrast his observations of how they actually seem to have behaved. The expectation, or model as it is often called, is founded on assumptions about human behaviour, and therefore about the likely response of groups of individuals to changes in their circumstances. At its most simple, for example, the expectation might be that in general people buy less of a commodity as it becomes more expensive. The expectation may not always be correct for each individual, but it serves in general.

We need to have such expectations, or models, if we are to organise our thoughts and assumptions and apply them to the elucidation or solution of problems about what happened in history. If we do not, then we can only flounder in a mass of individual observations, unaware whether the individual behaviour which we observe is normal or aberrant. Models, therefore, cut through the diversity of experience and behaviour which we all know to characterise any human activity, and embody our judgement as to why people are likely to have behaved as they did.

If the models of historians are to be useful in analysing the past, then they must be carefully chosen. The economic and social historian deals in his work on past societies with subjects which are the concern of many analysts of contemporary society: economists, geographers, sociologists, political scientists. It is sensible for the historian to consider whether he may use their models to aid him in his work. In making the choice he must always be conscious that contemporary society is different from past society, and that a model may either have to be adapted to the requirements of historical analysis or, at the extreme, rejected as entirely inappropriate. But if the adaptation can be made then the historian is likely to gain greatly in his work from the insights of contemporary social scientists; these insights help him to expand and refine his model of the past.

These assertions are controversial. Not all historians accept that it is useful to apply models drawn from the social sciences to historical analysis. Not all, even today, would accept that the primary task of the historian is to explain; they would hold, instead, that description, the discovery of the record of what happened in the past, should be given pride of place. Most frequently, critics of the use of models and of the statistical methods which often accompany them claim that models cannot cope with the rich diversity of human behaviour in the past, that they simplify and therefore distort. Even mere statistical description – counting heads and calculating averages – has been attacked for dehumanising history and for replacing people by numbers.

Such attacks are based largely on misunderstanding. It is certainly true that models of human behaviour must simplify; indeed, that is their purpose, to enable the historian to concentrate on a restricted set of possible explanations for that behaviour, rather than being distracted by the diversity of individual deeds. It is also true that models concentrate on expectations of normal or average behaviour; again, this is deliberate and necessary if the normal is to be distinguished from the aberrant. The historian who uses models does not forget that diversity exists; indeed he makes use of the diversity, those different reactions to different circumstances, to help him to frame and then to improve his model. In some circumstances, no doubt, the diversity of the past may defeat the simplifying powers of the historian and the most complex of models, but such circumstances are no grounds for rejection of the use of models as a whole.

A more reasonable criticism of models and their application to history is that they are often themselves too simple, and that they embody unjustifiable assumptions about human behaviour. In later chapters of this book, for example, we make use of models which assume the existence of full employment, or of perfect mobility of labour; such models may lead to misleading results if such conditions do not obtain. Yet to criticise the use of one model in one set of circumstances does not show that all use of models is wrong. It shows simply that the historian, and the reader of this or any book, should be alert and critical and should not make silly errors; the same could be said of any scholarly work.

A third ground of criticism of the use of models and of statistical methods in history is better founded. Many social scientists use mathematical language to express their ideas and to formulate their models, while most historians, and even many social scientists, are not sufficiently familiar with mathematics to understand what is written. They do not appreciate that mathematics is often used merely as a shorthand, and are even less likely to appreciate that it is sometimes used merely to impress the unwary. Very reasonably, someone who does not understand may reject the ideas along with the language by which they are veiled, even though, in truth, the models can almost always be expressed in a language which is comprehensible to non-mathematicians.

This book has been written by economic and social historians who are expert in the use of models and of statistical methods in history, but are conscious of the fears, doubts and misunderstandings which such usage evokes. They wish to show that economic and social history is not diminished thereby but augmented, and that the results can be understood by anyone interested in historical problems. The economic and social history which they write, and which is discussed in this book, is sometimes called the 'new' economic and social history. The novelty of applying the methods of social science to history is by now about a quarter of a century old: it is often 'new' not so much in its aim nor even in its methods, but merely in the language which it uses. The results, however, are of great interest, and for this reason the authors have expressed their ideas in a language which any student of the subject can understand; where they have used a model or a statistical method which may be unfamiliar, it has been explained.

Together, the chapters in this book make up an economic history of England and Wales since 1700. The basic chronology and the evidence on which it is based are discussed, and the book as a whole provides a treatment of the most important themes in English social and economic history during the period of industrialisation and economic growth. Much has been left out, for the authors and editors have chosen to concentrate on the topics which are most problematical and yet where solutions to problems may be attainable. The book is divided into five overlapping chronological divisions, corresponding to the periods from 1700 to 1800, from 1780 to 1860, from 1860 to 1914, from 1900 to 1945, and from 1945 to the present day. Each division except the last begins with a general survey of the period, which is followed by a number of chapters which consider the main problems which have arisen in the historical interpretation of that period; each division except the first and last concludes with a chapter dealing with the social history of the period in relation to the economic changes which have been considered. The period since 1945 is treated as a whole in one, final, chapter. The book is divided into two volumes, with the break at 1860, although a number of chapters in both volumes bridge the break. Each volume has its own index and glossary, and its own bibliography; frequent references to sources and to further reading are given in the text, making use of the 'author–date' system of reference. In this system, books or articles are referred to in the text simply by the name of the author and the date of publication, for example (Keynes 1936); the bibliography is an alphabetical list of authors, with the date of publication immediately following the author's name. Thus (Keynes 1936) in the text has its counterpart as Keynes, J. M. 1936 *The General Theory of Employment, Interest and Money* in the bibliography.

The book has been planned and written by many hands. The Social Science Research Council of Great Britain generously made funds available both for an initial planning meeting and for a conference at which the first drafts of the chapters were discussed. The authors and editors are grateful to the SSRC for its generosity, and to Donald Coleman, Philip Cottrell, Jack Dowie, Malcolm Falkus, Jordan Goodman, Leslie Hannah, Max Hartwell, Brian Mitchell, Leslie Pressnell, John Wright and Tony Wrigley for attending the conference and making many helpful comments. Annabel Gregory, Alan Hergent, Nigel Lewis and Ali Saad gave invaluable help in preparing the manuscript for publication, and Francis Brooke of Cambridge University Press was a model sub-editor.

1

Britain 1860-1914: a survey

R. C. FLOUD

In the fifty years before the First World War Britain lost the unchallenged position which it had gained as the first industrial nation. The loss, perceived at the time and discussed by economists and historians ever since, is the central feature of the chapters which follow. Since it is inevitable that a sense of loss should lead to a search for explanations, and likely that such a search will find scapegoats, much of the discussion of the British economy in the late nineteenth century has blamed one or other facet of the economy. Yet in 1913 Britain was still the world's largest foreign investor, owned most of the world's shipping, provided over 25 per cent of the world's trade in manufactured goods, and headed the largest empire and commonwealth the world had ever known. The British economy had, moreover, continued to grow throughout the period, with only slight faltering, and Britons were on average richer throughout the period than the citizens of any other European nation.

Britain had experienced a period of considerable prosperity between 1850 and 1873, the years sometimes known as the 'Great Victorian Boom' (Church 1975a). This prosperity extended across all forms of economic activity, from foreign trade to farming, as was shown in the first volume, and its benefits were diffused throughout the British population. Although poverty certainly persisted in 1873, and was to persist certainly past the First World War, the standard of living of the population rose unequivocally from 1850 to 1873 and beyond (Pollard and Crossley 1968; Feinstein 1972). At the same time, the economy changed its character as the full potential of such technological changes as the railway, large-scale steel production, and the use of semi-automatic machinery began to be realised. These developments altered the nature of British industrialisation, replacing its earlier concentration on the mass production of textiles and other consumer goods, with a wider range of industries; Britain continued to produce consumer goods in ever growing variety but also made and sold increasing quantities of capital goods – lathes, steam engines, ships, iron rails – for British industry and the world.

After 1873 this trend continued, accompanied by other changes which gradually altered the structure of the British economy and its place within the world economy. 1873 itself was the peak of one of the fluctuations in economic activity which are discussed in chapter 2, but it can serve too as the approximate beginning of a sustained fall in the prices of all kinds of goods, both imported and manufactured at home, which continued until nearly the end of the century (Saul 1969). Within the fall in the price of all goods there was a relative fall in the price of food and raw materials. As is suggested in chapter 3, this change in relative prices favouring European exporters of finished goods was produced by two related events: the peopling of frontier agricultural lands and transport developments which cheapened for European consumers the products of the rest of the world. The changes in world transport, and the growth in the production of raw materials and food throughout the world, were helped by the growth of European investment overseas which is described in chapter 4. The fall in the price of food and raw materials relative to finished goods was therefore an international phenomenon and in altering the international economy and the pattern of specialisation of economic activity it naturally affected Britain. Some activities ceased to be profitable and others became more profitable: a clear example is British agriculture, where massive imports of grain from North America and Russia (an important part of lower food prices) ruined many farmers dependent upon cereal production while their fellows engaged in dairy or meat production became more prosperous (chapter 8). Within manufacturing industry, several of the traditional staple industries such as cotton and coal found that demand for their products suffered temporary declines and that competition from other producers was increasing; profit levels in industry generally declined. For the wage-earner, the fall in prices brought about a sustained rise in real wages – wages adjusted for changes in the cost of living – and an increase in the variety and quality of goods available (although there was also a small rise in unemployment). Britain was not alone in experiencing these changes, bad and good. But Britain was unduly open to them as the world's leading trader and manufacturer; also, unlike Germany and the United States, she held to a policy of free trade and did not attempt to protect her home industries and agriculture from the effects of foreign competition. Chapter 8 shows that this policy benefited the British consumer, but it also made more painful and rapid the necessary adjustment to international conditions.

After the middle of the 1890s the fall in prices ceased and both prices and profits rose gradually until the First World War. International trade continued to expand, but the growth of competition by foreigners within markets which Britain had traditionally served brought fears of national decline and an increase in jingoism and xenophobia. The Edwardian period was an uneasy one for Britain. Wages failed to match the rise in prices, and the fall in real wages produced increasing economic and social tension, exacerbated by the upper classes' delight in the display of wealth and luxury (Dangerfield 1936; Nowell-Smith 1964). Huge differences in relative incomes had survived the increasing prosperity of the late nineteenth century (Pollard and Crossley 1968; chapter 6). Much of the wealth of the rich derived from the investment overseas which had been undertaken from the 1870s onwards and this investment continued to expand in the Edwardian period. In 1913 half of all British investment in fixed capital – machinery, buildings and other productive equipment – was undertaken overseas – and the cumulative results of such investment, worth about £4500 million, were larger than the assets overseas of France, Germany, Holland and the United States combined (Woodruff 1966: 150; Feis 1930).

The question is, how to evaluate this mixture of success and failure. One reason for a preoccupation with Victorian failure, for example, has been that the relative performance of Britain before the First World War seems to anticipate its performance after the Second World War. But the comparison forgets that Britain was in a totally different position within the world economy in the two periods, as a comparison of this chapter with the last chapter in this volume will soon show. Not only was Britain strong industrially, commercially and militarily before 1914 in ways which she has not been since 1945 or probably 1919, but her economy constantly enjoyed a large surplus on the current account of the balance of payments with the rest of the world; thus one of the major causes of instability and of 'stop–go' government policies after 1945 was absent before 1914. Nor was Britain troubled by flows of 'hot money' to other financial centres, since London remained until 1914 the major, if not the only, world money market.

The superficial similarity between Britain in 1900 and in 1960 is a good example of the importance of judging the pre-1914 economy by appropriate standards. Few indicators of the performance of the economy as a whole or of its important sectors show an absolute decline before 1914. What they show is either a reduction in a rate of growth from an earlier higher level, or a rate of growth less than that achieved by Britain's major international competitors. The economic historian has thus to explain not an absolute decline of the British economy, for no such decline occurred, but rather the failure of the economy to attain some target of growth. Unless that target is clearly specified, talk of the 'failure' of the economy or of its 'poor performance' in relation to other nations is meaningless. 'Failure' and 'poor performance' can only be judged in relation to some target that has not been achieved.

It is, however, very difficult to state what such a target should have been, or, in other words, to construct a 'counterfactual' model of the British economy before 1914 against which to contrast the 'factual' achievements of that economy (McClelland 1975). The difficulty lies only partly in the problem of discovering adequate evidence about what the economy was actually like to use as a basis for a counterfactual model, although the limits on our knowledge are considerable. The major difficulty, however, is more fundamental. It lies in the need to agree upon what the targets of the British economy should have been, in the understanding that many desirable objectives for the British economy were either unattainable or contradictory. To fail to achieve an income of £5000 per head in 1900 is not an interesting failure, since that goal was absurdly unattainable. The counterfactual model must therefore be realistic both in relation to what an economy of the late nineteenth century can be expected to have achieved and in relation to its state in 1860. While it might be a pleasant speculation, for example, to imagine what the economy would have looked like in 1900 if the internal combustion engine had been widely adopted in 1870, it will not greatly aid the analysis of economic change. The model must be realistic if it is to be useful.

Many possible definitions of realism have been employed by economic historians studying this period. The major definitions can be expressed as five propositions:

(a) the output of the British economy should have continued to increase after 1873 as rapidly as it had increased before;

(b) the output of the British economy should have increased as rapidly after 1873 as the outputs of the other developing manufacturing nations in the world economy – especially Germany and the United States;

(c) the output of the British economy should have increased as rapidly as was permitted by the resources of raw materials, labour, and capital that were available to it;

(d) the output of the British economy should have responded efficiently to changes in the pattern and growth of world and domestic demand for its products;

(e) the British economy should have used, in its endeavour to increase output, the most efficient techniques available at the time, and should have contributed to further technological advance.

These major propositions do not exhaust the list of targets used, either implicitly or explicitly, by historians. Other dates than 1873 might be chosen, and other measures of growth, for example output per head of the population; all these propositions, in addition, express the growth of the economy in terms of its output, and ignore the distribution of the rewards of economic activity, the standard of living, or the happiness of the population. They are, however, a starting point.

The output of the British economy before and after 1873

Judging whether the output of the British economy increased as rapidly after as before 1873 requires an accurate measure of the growth in output and a decision about which time periods to compare. Neither task is as easy as it appears to be. Since the Victorians themselves did not measure their gross national product (GNP, the market value of all goods and services produced by the nation's economy, including income from foreign investments) nor gross domestic product (GDP = GNP less income from foreign investments) all the measures have been made at later dates, and deserve to be called estimates rather than measures (Feinstein 1972: 8–22). Moreover, there are many gaps in the evidence on which the estimates are based; although there was an increasingly accurate census of population in Britain taken in every tenth year from 1801, no similar census of industrial production was taken until 1907; estimates of the output of goods therefore have to be built up from scattered evidence of varying quality.

One of the many complications of making such estimates is that the growth of industries, of agricultural output, and of the economy as a whole was not smooth. This can be seen from figure 1.1, which gives the best estimates yet made for the movement of gross domestic product over the period. While the long-run movement, or 'trend', of the series is clearly upwards throughout the period, there are clear checks to growth, for example in the late 1870s and in 1892–93. Such slumps or recessions are periods in which the output of the economy ceases to grow, or (rarely) actually falls, and are normally characterised by rising unemployment, because the resources of the economy are temporarily underused. The regularity of the slumps in the economies of all industrial nations in the late nineteenth century inspired observers to speak of them as the 'trade' or 'business cycle' but as chapter 2 suggests this term attributes greater regularity to them than is sensible. Whatever caused the slumps, however, they make it more difficult to measure the output of the economy over a long period. The growth rate of output between 1873 and 1893, for example, is quite different from that between 1870 and 1890: both are periods of twenty years, very close together in time, but figure 1.1 shows that output grew at 1.53 per cent per year in one and 2.05 per cent per year in the other. (This can be seen from figure 1.1 because output has been plotted on a logarithmic scale, on which series of numbers which are growing at a constant proportional rate appear as a straight line, which is steeper the faster the rate of growth; the inset on the figure gives some examples).

The choice of years as initial and terminal dates of measurement is therefore much more than a statistical quibble; it can affect our whole view of the amount or speed of change in an economy and, since economic movements are rarely regular or centred on decades or centuries, it is rarely appropriate to measure, as historians tend to do, from 1860 to 1870 to 1880, or from 1800 to 1850 to 1900 (Aldcroft 1974; McCloskey 1974). It is normal, instead, for the economic historian who is interested in measuring growth over long periods to choose periods which begin and end when the economy is in a roughly comparable state, normally when it is working at full stretch in a boom and almost all the resources of the nation are fully employed – almost all, because as chapter 11 shows, truly full employment of labour never occurs. At other times, for example in recessions, the economy is producing less than it could, since resources of men and machines are unemployed; moreover, some recessions are worse than others, so that measuring from trough to trough will give a less accurate picture of the

6

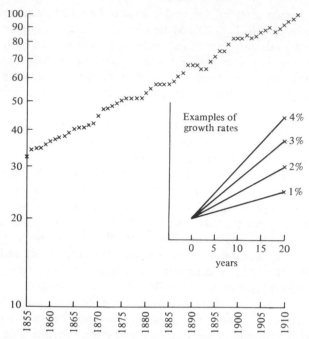

1.1   Index numbers of gross domestic product at constant factor cost (1913 = =100)

long-term trend than will measuring from peak to peak. In our period, comparable dates at which the economy was closest to full employment were 1857, 1866, 1873, 1882, 1890, 1900, 1907, 1913 as can clearly be seen in figures 2.4 and 2.5; measurements are therefore best made between those dates.

One further difficulty in measurement has still to be discussed. We are now used to living in a period of inflation, in which the cost of what we buy increases even if the amount does not. This makes it difficult to measure the growth of output of the economy over a long period, since the value of output will change partly because of increases in the amount of goods produced, and partly because of increases in the money costs of those goods; we have to separate the two causes to produce the 'real' increase in the amount of goods produced, independent of changes in merely monetary costs and independent also (though this is much more difficult) of changes in the quality of the goods.

Today this separation is done by comparing increases in output with such measures as the retail price index, and we have to carry out similar comparisons in the late nineteenth century, even though that period was affected by falling rather than by rising prices. Figure 1.1 shows the results of such a comparison, a series for gross domestic product in real or 'constant price' terms, while table 1.1 presents the estimates as growth rates over various periods.

Table 1.1. *Growth rates of output (gross domestic product at constant 1900 factor cost) and of output per head in the UK 1800–1913 (% increase per annum)*

	Output	Output per head
1856–73	2.1	1.2
1873–82	1.9	1.0
1882–90	2.0	1.3
1890–1900	2.1	1.2
1900–07	1.5	0.6
1907–13	1.9	0.8
1800–31	2.7	1.3
1831–60	2.5	1.3
1873–1907	1.9	1.0

Sources: Figures for 1800–60 from Feinstein (1978: 85); for 1856–1913 from Feinstein (1972): T 18). The earlier figures are for Great Britain, those from 1856 for the United Kingdom.

Britain was not quite able to maintain in the late nineteenth century the rates of growth of output that she had established earlier in the century. Indeed, the figures for the early part of the century suggest that there was a gradual slowing down of the growth of the economy from well before our period begins. There was, it is clear, no spectacular retardation of the economy at any particular period, with the possible exception of the seven years after 1900, although even here the apparent reduction in growth shown in table 1.1 is within the margin of error which has to be attached to these estimates (Feinstein 1972: 20). The so-called 'Great Depression' from 1873 to 1896 which aroused so much interest among contemporaries and later historians is therefore a myth (Saul 1969); it saw part of the retardation, but there was retardation both before and after.

If, then, the test of the performance of the British economy is to be whether the growth rates achieved before 1873 were maintained, then the economy must be said to have failed that test. It is possible, however, that this test is too severe; it might be argued that an industrialising country, such as Britain was in the nineteenth century, and particularly one with such a predominant position in world trade, is unlikely to be able to maintain its earlier rates of growth indefinitely. This is not because the base from which the growth rate is measured itself increases; it does increase, but since the economy is therefore capable of producing a higher output, it has by the same token more resources with which to increase that output still further. Its energies are likely to turn, however, to broadening the economy, diversifying into sectors such as improved retailing or the holiday industries, rather than remaining narrowly tied to the pursuit of higher levels of manufacturing output. Its labour force may choose to take more leisure, or pursue education for longer before starting work (chapter 7). If Britain was in this sense a 'mature' economy, then the realistic expectation of her

Table 1.2. *Growth rates of output for the UK, Germany and the USA (% increase per annum)*

	UK (real GDP)		USA (real GDP)	Germany (real NDP)
1873–82	1.9			1.3
		1869/78– 1879/88	6.5	
1882–90	2.0			3.1
1890–1900	2.1		3.9	3.5
1900–07	1.5		5.2	2.7
1907–13	1.6		2.8	3.3
1873–1913	1.8		4.5	2.8

Sources: For UK Feinstein (1972: T51)
For USA Kendrick (1961: table A-XXII)
For Germany, Hoffman (1965: table 5A)
Comparable French figures are (Mitchell 1976: 797) (real GDP):
  1865/74 –1895/1904   1.3
  1895/1904–1905/1913   2.4.

counterfactual growth should be modified to give a lower target for her growth rate. How much lower is difficult to determine, but one possible guide might be given by examining the growth rates of other maturing economies; this can easily be combined with examining the second counterfactual proposition, that Britain should have grown as fast as other countries in the world economy.

The output of the British economy and of other industrial nations after 1873

Table 1.2, which presents estimates of the rates of growth of output of Britain and her two main competitors, suggests that British output did not grow as fast as that of Germany and the United States during the forty years after 1873. It is hazardous to make comparisons of this kind, since all the difficulties of making national estimates are compounded when such estimates are compared; different economic historians use different conventions, the quality of data differs from country to country, and the dates of cycles may not exactly correspond. Comparisons of growth in total output are misleading when, as in this period, the populations of the countries which are being compared are growing at different rates, so that the output is being produced by, and shared by, populations of markedly different sizes. Table 1.3 giving growth rates of output per head is a more useful guide to the relative growth of the British economy. It shows that Britain was growing more slowly than were her main competitors, but that the difference between them was less than table 1.2 suggested. Of equal

Table 1.3. *Growth rates of output per person employed for the UK, Germany and the USA (% increase per annum)*

	UK (real GDP)		USA (real GDP)	Germany (real NDP)
1873–82	1.0			0.1
		1869/78–1879/88	3.2	
1882–90	1.3			1.7
1890–1900	1.2		1.9	2.1
1900–07	0.6		2.0	1.3
1907–13	0.8		1.0	1.7
1873–1913	0.9		1.8	1.4

Sources: as for Table 1.2.
Figures for France are: 1865/74 –1895/1904   1.0
                           1895/1904–1905/1913   2.0

interest, however, is that table 1.3 suggests that all three countries experienced a similar pattern of growth, although at different levels; stable or gradually increasing growth in the late nineteenth century was succeeded by a period of lower growth in the early twentieth century. This suggests both that the concept of a 'Great Depression' in the late nineteenth century is of little use in historical analysis, and that Britain should not be considered to be peculiar in her experience of growth. There is no reason to be surprised at this, since Britain's economy was so intimately tied to the fluctuations and level of world trade that a close connection of domestic and international trends is to be expected. What still remains to be explained is why Britain's growth should have remained (if we believe table 1.3 and even if we make allowances for likely error in those figures), slightly below the rate of growth experienced by Germany and the United States, and why this disparity should have persisted throughout the period.

The British economy and the resources available to it

The fact that British growth was slower than that of her foreign competitors does not demonstrate that it was slower than it ought to have been. The British economy of the late nineteenth century was not an independent organism, able to grow at whatever rate it chose; its growth was, instead, limited by many factors which it could not control, some within itself and others in the international community within which it traded. Internationally, as was mentioned above, the British economy was more obviously affected than were other economies by changes in the prices of commodities and of transport, simply because of Britain's commanding position within world trade. Such factors affected the growth of British incomes, determined to some extent the pattern of British expenditures, and altered the geographical distribution of British mercantile activity (Saul 1960). Similarly, within the national economy, British growth was constrained and directed by factors which were slow to change and hard to control; among them were the patterns of consumption of the British population and the resources available to the economy, such as the size of the labour force, the amount of natural resources, and the capital invested in plant, machinery and buildings. None of these is impossible to alter and they are not therefore constraints for all time; a country can attempt to alter the resources available to it – immigration can be encouraged, investment can be made more attractive by tax concessions, and raw materials, such as coal and oil can be sought and exploited. Similarly, the consumption habits of the population can be changed by presenting it with new products. Nevertheless, and particularly when international comparisons are to be made, it is important to remember that some countries are better endowed with natural resources than others, some have more labour available, some have built up larger capital resources, some have populations with sophisticated and some with simple tastes, some have larger captive markets and some have political systems more or less concerned with economic affairs. It is because countries do differ in these and other ways that trade and other economic contacts between nations take place (chapter 3).

An individual worker cannot produce whatever he wants; he is limited by his physical capacity and the power of the machine he uses, and by the wishes of those consumers whom he expects to buy his product. Similarly, the output of a nation is limited both by the resources which it has available and by the demand for the goods which those resources can produce. Economists have therefore traditionally examined both supply factors – matters which affect the ability to make and distribute goods and services, and demand factors – matters which affect the wish and ability of consumers to buy those goods and services.

In practice a modern economy is complex because supply and demand are constantly interacting as the prices of goods and services and the amounts of them that are produced and purchased react to both short- and long-term changes in tastes, productive equipment, incomes and many other factors. Both in the short term, in the cycles discussed in chapter 2, and in the longer term, these changes produce the need for adjustments in economic activity – adjustments which are initially experienced as price changes, as unemployment, or as the scrapping and replacement of capital equipment. Since such adjustments can take place as the result of changes in either demand or supply or more often both acting on each other, describing and explaining them is rarely simple. It is for this reason that economists try to simplify by distinguishing between, and examining separately, supply factors, demand factors and other matters which affect them jointly. Armed with this distinction, we can now examine the third proposition, that the output of the British economy should have increased as rapidly as was permitted by the resources available to it. This proposition is concerned with supply factors, while the fourth and fifth propositions are concerned with demand factors and with the efficiency of the economy. None of these is, in reality, independent from the others, but for the sake of simplicity they must be considered to be so.

It is also customary, again for the sake of simplicity, to assume that the amount that an economy can supply is limited by the availability of three main resources, land and raw materials, labour, and capital equipment, and analyses of the economy in this form are extensively used in the first volume of this book. At any one moment, it is assumed, the output of the economy has a feasible maximum, the amount which these three resources can produce when fully used in the most efficient possible combination. Similarly, the output of the economy cannot grow without growth of those three resources unless it finds new ways of combining them more efficiently. The output of the economy can of course be lower than this feasible maximum, by leaving resources unemployed or by employing them at less than full efficiency, as clearly happens when output falls in a slump (McCloskey, 1970).

We can assume that the resources of land and raw materials available to the domestic British economy remained unchanged between 1860 and 1914, but clearly both labour and capital resources changed substantially. As Chapter 7 shows, the British population rose by one per cent per annum between 1861 and 1911. In general, the growth of the total population is an imperfect guide to the growth of the labour force, which is affected by changes in the age-structure, in educational patterns, and in conventions about the employment of women and children. In Britain, as the joint result of these factors, the working population is thought to have grown from 10 520 000 in 1861 to 18 290 000 in 1911, therefore increasing at one per cent per annum, the same rate as the population as a whole. But because of falls in the length of the working week or year, hours worked increased by a smaller amount, perhaps 0.7 per cent per annum. This rate of increase was very similar to that experienced by most other European countries (although in France total hours worked actually fell), but in the United States the massive immigration of the period allowed hours worked to increase by 1.9 per cent per annum between 1870 and 1913, a very rapid rate of growth (Maddison 1964: 36).

The total size of a population, or even of the labour force, is, however, a poor guide to its economic usefulness; Ireland's population grew rapidly before the famine of 1846, without increasing economic growth; India's does today. Equally or more important is the distribution of the labour force between different types of economic activity, together with the agility with which labour responds to economic opportunities by changing its distribution. The distribution in the British economy of 1860 differed spectacularly from the economies of the

12

Table 1.4. *Occupational distribution of the working population* (%)

			Agriculture[a]	Manufacturing[b]	Services[c]
(A)	Britain	1861	19	39	27
	France	1856	52	22	22
	Germany	1882	46	26	16
	USA	1880	59	18	20
(B)	Britain	1911	9	39	35
	France	1906	43	25	28
	Germany	1907	37	29	22
	USA	1910	31	29	35

Refer to figure 7.3 for detailed breakdown for Britain
Sources: Mitchell (1976: 155, 156, 163) for France, Germany, Britain
       Bureau of the Census (1976: 138) for USA
[a] Agriculture, Forestry and Fishing
[b] Manufacturing Industry (excluding Extractive Industries and Construction)
[c] Commerce, Finance, Transport and Communication Services

other developed countries. As table 1.4 shows, a far smaller proportion of her population was engaged in agriculture, reflecting Britain's early industrialisation. British jobs continued to alter down to 1914, as the labour force in agriculture shrank still further, and the proportion in the 'tertiary' or service sector of the economy grew; table 1.4 shows that, unlike any other country, the relative size of the British labour force in manufacturing did not alter during the period. The rise in the tertiary sector reflects a redirection of the British economy, comparable to the rise in the importance of the export of services within foreign trade described in chapter 3. Within the home economy, the distribution of goods became more complex as the growth of national chains of wholesalers and retailers such as Liptons or the Home and Colonial Stores replaced the small-scale distribution networks of an earlier period. An obvious sign of the increase in the distributive networks is the growth of the transport and communications sector of the economy, which absorbed 12 per cent of the labour force in 1911, up from 8 per cent fifty years before; none of Britain's European competitors had nearly so high a proportion of their labour force so engaged.

The shift, in proportionate terms, from agriculture to the service industries is some evidence that the British population was mobile in its search for jobs and in its response to new job opportunities. This is important, because it is thought that industrialisation is aided by transfers of labour from agriculture, which are clearly easier if the agricultural sector is large. Much of this transfer had already occurred, but it continued even after 1860, so rapidly indeed that as many workers were released from agriculture as in France, and almost as many as in Germany, despite their much larger agricultural sectors. Even though part of the rise in the proportion of the labour force in services sprang from a decline of women's work in cottage industry, which forced them into domestic service, the rise in other services such as banking, shipping and insurance where Britain's comparative advantage in international trade was strong (chapter 3) shows that the labour force was flexible enough to move to new types of activity. The amount of internal and external migration also points in this direction (chapter 7). If this conclusion is correct, then it seems unlikely that any deficiency in British growth can be ascribed to labour shortages arising from immobility of labour.

It is however possible that the growth of the labour force in Britain was deficient in another sense, in that the growth in skills and education did not match that of Britain's competitors nor the demands of new, higher technology, industries and service occupations (Landes 1969: 339–48). Britain's preoccupation with empire might have diverted interest and investment from British education (chapter 4). On the other hand, as chapter 7 describes in general, and chapters 8 and 5 suggest for agriculture and industry, there is substantial evidence of improvements both in simple literacy and in the technical training of the labour force in these years. If these developments did not require such dramatic improvements and so much state investment as in several European countries, this may be because Britain was, once again, ahead already and required less effort to maintain itself on a level with its competitors. Thus, although Britain clearly lagged behind in providing higher education in science and technology, the more general charge that it neglected to make improvements in its 'human capital' remains unproven.

In an industrial economy, 'human capital' in the form of a skilled labour force must be combined with physical capital in the form of buildings and machinery. While the labour force is maintained and grows by human reproduction, the stock of capital available to the economy has to be maintained by repair and replacement and increased by the purchase of new equipment. The ability of the economy to make such expenditure is dependent on the expectations of entrepreneurs, on the fiscal policies of governments, and on the willingness of individuals collectively to save and invest resources to maintain and increase productive capacity (rather than to consume them at once). Such saving and investment must take place continuously if the stock of capital is to be increased or, at the least, maintained, and the proportion of the national output which is devoted each year to investment is therefore an indication of the amount of capital which the economy is prepared to supply.

Table 1.5 shows the proportion which capital investment formed of the gross national product of Britain and her main competitors. It is clear that Britain devoted a substantially smaller proportion of her output to investment in the domestic economy than did any of her major competitors, and there is, moreover, little sign of the proportion rising over the period, as table 1.6 indicates. If, however, British investment overseas is aggregated with British domestic investment, and the whole compared with total investment by other

Table 1.5. *Capital formation proportions* (%)

	Period	GDFCF / GDP	GNFCF / GNP
UK	1855–1914	9.0	12.8
Germany	1851–1913	19.8	21.1
USA	1869–1913	21.9	22.1
France	1865–1913	20.2	
Italy	1861–1915	12.5	
Japan	1887–1916	10.9	9.7

Source: Kuznets (1961: 5).
Note: GDFCF (GNFCF) = Gross domestic (national) fixed capital formation. GDP (GNP) = Gross domestic (national) product.

Table 1.6. *Capital formation proportions for the UK* (%)

Period	GDFCF / GDP	GNFCF / GNP
1860–69	8.9	11.6
1865–74	9.1	13.6
1870–79	9.9	13.4
1875–84	9.7	12.3
1880–89	8.0	12.4
1885–94	7.8	12.1
1890–99	9.1	11.7
1895–1904	10.6	12.2
1900–09	10.0	13.3
1905–14	8.2	14.4

Source: Kuznets (1961: 58).
Note: A calculation of GDFCF/GDP from Feinstein (1972: T5) gives the following:
1873–82	8.2%
1882–90	6.5%
1890–1900	8.2%
1900–1907	9.9%
1907–1913	6.8%

countries, some of the disparity disappears. In other words, as chapter 4 shows in detail, the oddity in Britain's investment performance is not just that savings and investment were low, but also that a substantial proportion of those savings was invested abroad rather than at home; in some years overseas investment exceeded domestic investment. Although other countries, notably Germany and France, also increased their foreign investments during this period, none did so on this scale. Indeed no other country, before or since, has invested so much of its resources abroad for such a long period (Woodruff 1966; Cairncross 1953).

Table 1.7. *The components of capital formation*

		Gross domestic fixed capital formation	GDFCF excluding residential construction	GDFCF in residential construction	GDFCF in producers' equipment
(A) As % of gross domestic product
UK	1855–1914	9.0	7.7	1.3	3.2
Germany	1851–1913	19.8	13.8	4.0	5.1
USA	1869–1913	21.9	17.4	4.2	5.3
(B) As % of gross domestic fixed capital formation
UK	1855–1914	100	86	14	36
Germany	1851–1913	100	70	30	26
USA	1869–1913	100	80	20	24

Source: Calculated from Kuznets (1961: 5 and table 13)
Note: UK 1856–1913. A similar calculation from Feinstein (1972: T 88–9) gives the proportions as 82: 18: 42
    USA 1869–1916: a similar calculation from US Bureau of the Census (1976: F98–124) gives 76:24:23

From the present viewpoint there are, therefore, two problems with the supply of capital. The first is whether British growth was constrained by inadequate supplies of capital *in toto*, and the second is whether the supplies were misallocated between home and overseas investment (McCloskey 1970). It must not of course be thought that the overseas capital was wasted, since it and the wealth which it created remained a British asset; moreover, investment overseas yielded higher returns than investment at home (chapter 4). In addition, the actual amount of investment undertaken is the result of the demand for investment as much as of the supply, so that low British domestic investment may reflect low British demand at home, while investigation is additionally complicated by the changing pattern of investment over time which is described in chapters 2 and 4.

Nevertheless, we must accept the fact that investment in the domestic economy was lower, as a proportion of gross domestic product, in Britain than in several other countries. This does not necessarily demonstrate, however, that investment in domestic industry was lower, since so much of domestic investment is employed in residential housebuilding; the proportion which this forms of domestic investment, moreover, varies from country to country and depends very much on the amount of growth and mobility in each country's population. We need, in other words, to discover whether the amount of capital available for industry and in particular for industrial equipment, was lower in Britain than elsewhere. Once again, there is a problem of distinguishing between supply and demand factors, since the amount of capital actually invested (which is all we know) reflects both factors. Table 1.7, however, attempts to distinguish between the main components of domestic investment in three countries. The table shows that, while the amount devoted to producers' equipment was lower in Britain than in the United States or Germany, the gap between Britain and her rivals was very much less – of the order of 2 per cent of GDP – than the gap which appears either in table 1.5 or in the second column of table 1.7. In other words, Germany and the United States were devoting much larger proportions of their total investment to building – of houses, factories, public buildings, and transport facilities – than was Britain, and it is this component of investment, rather than investment in industrial equipment, which mainly accounts for the disparity in Britain's investments. To put it in another way, of the domestic investment which did take place, Britain devoted a much larger proportion to producers' equipment than did the other countries – for Britain the proportion was 36 per cent, for the United States 24 per cent and for Germany 26 per cent (table 1.7).

What might this difference mean? First, it suggests, though it does not prove, that Britain had a different industrial and commercial structure from other countries, and thus had different needs for and uses for capital; this might stem from Britain's 'early-start' in industrialisation and in the development of transport and other parts of the infrastructure of the economy, described in volume 1, chapter 12. It is thus relevant to the question of demand for capital. Second, it is also relevant to the question of the supply of capital. It has often been argued that there was no shortage of capital in Britain, but that the capital was wrongly directed, to overseas rather than domestic projects, and away from manufacturing industry within the domestic economy. The favourite culprit as the cause of this wrong direction is the City of London, which was heavily orientated to the finance of large overseas projects such as railways and gold mines, and is thought to have scorned involvement with dirty industry at home (Cottrell 1975). One implication of the results in table 1.7 however, does not support this view, for it appears from that table that British domestic investment was more heavily orientated towards industry compared with investment by Germany or the United States, rather than less as the traditional view of the defects of the City of London would imply. Taken with the findings in chapter 4 that foreign investment was more profitable than domestic investment, it implies instead that the City was supplying capital to areas where it would obtain the best return, and that it was not biased unreasonably against investment in domestic industry.

It is, therefore, difficult to see any over-riding supply constraints on British economic growth before 1914. Both labour and capital moved overseas in large quantities during the period – often to build up British assets and to use British goods – but it seems unlikely that these movements were irrational or that they starved the domestic economy of resources. Certainly the growth of the labour force, and the growth in capital invested, was low by the standards of other countries, but supply constraints are not the only possible explanation for such a difference. At the very least, it is necessary to examine carefully the other side of the equation, the nature and extent of demand.

Demand and the British economy

Ever since the 1930s and the publication of J. M. Keynes's *General Theory of Employment, Interest and Money* (1936), economists and the politicians whom they advise have been accustomed to view fluctuations in effective demand as a primary source of short-run fluctuations in economic activity. In the long run also, trends in demand both in aggregate and for individual products interact with the ability of the international economy to supply those products; this interaction determines both the rate of growth of world trade and consumption and the mixture of goods and services which is produced. In the late nineteenth century, the British economy was thus affected both by the supply factors which have just been described and by the demands for its products both at home and overseas. The interaction is complex, for two main reasons. First, home demand was not a simple reflection of national income, but was affected by the distribution of that income among different groups in the population, by their different spending habits and propensities to save, consume, and import, and hence by the range of goods available and by their price (chapter 6). Second, as is demonstrated in chapters 2, 3 and 4, demand from overseas for British exports was not an exogenous force, imposed from without, but was endogenous to the complex pattern of international investment, trade and payments in which Britain was a major force: British demand for imports, and British supply of capital, interacted with foreign economic developments to affect the demand for British exports.

The major influence from the demand side in the domestic economy between 1860 and 1914 was the sustained rise in real incomes which was experienced from the beginning of the period until the beginning of the twentieth century. As is shown in chapter 6, this increase had three main components, a rise in output per head and hence in the income per head of those producing that output, a fall in the price of imported goods, and a shift in the structure of the labour force towards more productive and presumably better paid occupations. However, put very simply, this rise in income did not result in a major restructuring or shift of demand in new directions; in income levels, it was as if the British population were arrayed, in 1860, up the side of a mountain and, by 1914, had moved as a body several steps further up. As chapters 6, 7 and 9 suggest, this analogy is too simple, since some groups in the population slipped down to be passed by others, and new groups such as the middle classes became more numerous and coherent. But on the whole the rise in incomes meant that those at the bottom of the file came to be able to consume goods and services which had previously been luxuries or the preserve of the rich, while the rich at the top developed tastes for new luxuries and in particular for the services provided by the tertiary sector. This does not of course mean that there were no changes in the broad structure of consumption, but the changes were of only one or two percentage points and cannot therefore be regarded as being as significant for the pattern of demand as the overall increase in incomes was for the level of demand for the main categories of goods and services (chapter 6). Such changes as there were fit well into the pattern that has occurred in most industrialising countries, as rising incomes and falling family size produce an increase in standards of living and a diversification of consumption gradually towards higher quality and more fabricated goods, and away from food and drink towards manufactured goods, durables, and services. It follows that it is difficult to see the pattern of British domestic demand as being very different from that in other countries, or as providing an explanation for any divergence of the British economy from that of her competitors. It has sometimes been alleged that British consumers were resistant to new, factory-made products and thus did not provide a market for mass-produced consumer goods such as that which emerged in the United States. While it is true that goods such as machine-made hosiery and boots and shoes, and ready-made clothing achieved larger sales earlier in the United States than in Britain, products of this kind were soon made in Britain. It may be that the difference in the speed of diffusion owes more to the wider geographical spread of the American market or to the efficiency of the British retail sector in distributing higher quality goods than to any unreasonable resistance of British consumers to new products. Differences between the two countries in the distribution of income may also have played some part.

In one respect British consumers differed very markedly from consumers in other countries. The British propensity to import, measured by the proportion of imports to gross national product, was much higher than for other developed countries. This trait was particularly marked in the case of foodstuffs, as table 3.1 shows, but particularly towards the end of the period the share of imports in sales of manufactured goods also increased. The reason for the preference of consumers for foreign foodstuffs is clear; in the absence of tariffs such as those enacted to protect French and German farmers, foreign wheat and many other products could be imported at prices well below those of home produced goods. Indeed, it was the fall in the price of imported foods which was a primary factor in raising real incomes during the last quarter of the nineteenth century. If British consumers had been forced to buy home rather than imported food, the higher prices would have absorbed perhaps half the increase in real wages which occurred between 1850 and 1914 (chapter 3). Although British farmers would have benefited, the net loss to the economy would still have been great.

As this calculation shows, it is a serious mistake to assume that it is always better to produce goods at home than to import them. Although it is often less easy to discern or calculate the net benefits of importing manufactured goods than it is to do so for goods such as bananas, the same principle holds that it may be cheaper to buy specialised manufactured goods abroad, paying for them with exports of other products, than to insist on producing them at home at whatever cost. To an economist, this is known as pursuing 'comparative advantage'. The greater propensity to import of Britain than of other countries thus does not show that British consumers made 'wrong' or 'irrational' decisions, particularly since all Britain's major competitors restricted imports by the use of tariffs, while Britain did not. Imports should only be thought of as irrational or damaging if British consumers preferred to buy from abroad what could have been produced at home more cheaply, and there is no evidence that such preferences were of any importance; a liking for French haute couture or Chinese silks is not of significance. There may, of course, be other reasons for preferring to manufacture goods at home; the discovery that all the khaki dye for British army uniforms was imported from Germany caused great alarm in 1914, but this is not an economic reason for arguing that Britain should have developed a dyestuffs industry to rival Germany. A country can practise autarky, or self-sufficiency, for reasons of state, but it rarely makes economic sense to do so.

A policy of restricting imports would also (as chapters 3 and 4 demonstrate) have made very little sense for Britain in the late nineteenth century, since an important component of her wealth came from providing the capital with which countries expanded their abilities to export, and a further part from exporting goods which were paid for with imports to Britain. The description of Britain as the 'workshop of the world' emphasises the importance to her economy of foreign demand, and in particular her increasing role as a supplier of capital goods, railway equipment, farm machinery, machine tools, textile plant, iron ships and the like, in addition to the consumer goods on which the industrial revolution of the early nineteenth century had been based. As the flow of world trade increased, Britain's role in it as importer, exporter, shipper, insurer and banker remained enormously important, as figure 3.4 demonstrates. Nevertheless, within the obvious truth that foreign demand was so important to Britain, the impact of changes in it upon the British economy before 1914 is still much debated. For example, the analysis of the trade cycle in chapter 2 views British exports in the short run as responding to flows in British overseas investment and to exogenous forces abroad, while exports in the long run are seen in chapter 3 as being determined by trends in the prices and quantities of British imports.

It is undoubtedly true that Britain did not maintain the share she had had in 1860 of world trade in manufactured goods; in other words, British exports of manufactured goods grew less rapidly than did world trade in those goods (Saul 1960). Britain had traditionally sent a high proportion of her exports to Europe and the United States. In the late nineteenth century these areas were developing their own manufacturing industries and, under the pressure of intermittent depression and political developments, increasingly adopted protective tariffs both on foodstuffs and on manufactured goods. Tariffs on foodstuffs did not hurt Britain, but tariffs on manufactured goods did, and by 1913 such tariffs were often levied at 30–40 per cent of the price of imports at the frontier (Hawke 1975: Floud 1976b: 96–7). This development was particularly damaging since the countries which imposed tariffs were the countries whose economies were expanding most rapidly and which would in the absence of tariffs have provided good markets for British goods. Since the tariffs were so high, and since they were often intended specifically to exclude British competition, Britain was unable to maintain or increase her exports to those markets, and was faced with two alternatives. The first was to develop new products, and in particular high quality or high value goods in which the tariff made less difference to price and demand; the second was to seek new markets unprotected by tariff barriers. Both policies were followed by private enterprise, leading to a redirection of British trade. In cotton textiles, for example, Britain expanded her exports of cheap textiles to India and the developing world, and also moved 'up-market' to produce higher value goods for the older markets. Although cotton textile exports continued to expand until 1914, this change in structure as the result of changes in foreign demand must have entailed some extra cost for the industry, and for other industries similarly affected, and thereby retarded the growth of exports below what it might have been. Although, as always, many other factors were simultaneously at work, demand deficiency of this kind may therefore supply some of the explanation for the slackening in Britain's rate of growth.

The efficiency of the British economy

The development of any economy is not simply, as we have implicitly assumed up to this point, a passive reaction to increases in the supply of resources and to changes in demand. The growth of an economy will also be affected by the efficiency with which it makes use of its resources, and the speed and efficiency with which it reacts to demand. If, for example, an economy tolerates the existence of pockets of underemployed labour, or persists in manufacturing goods which are unwanted, then it is wasting resources which could be better employed in some other form of activity, and it is thereby retarding growth. If, conversely, it allocates resources to profitable tasks, and moreover encourages the discovery of new and more economical ways of carrying out those tasks, then it will be able to expand its output by more than the increase in resources at its disposal.

Traditionally, changes in the efficiency of production have been measured by calculation of the productivity of labour; this can take various forms, such as the calculation of output produced per head of the population, or of output produced per hour worked, or per person employed. One such measure, therefore, is the calculation of GDP per capita shown in table 1.1 while the inter-country comparisons of table 1.4 are based on calculations of changes in GDP per person employed. Calculations of labour productivity do not, however, take account of the fact that in a modern mechanised economy production is not achieved simply by workers with their hands, but is carried out by workers in conjunction with capital equipment such as machines and factories. Output per worker can therefore be altered significantly by giving a worker a new machine, without any change in the amount of effort which he puts in; a man digging his garden with a spade might, for example, use a mechanical cultivator to speed up the job. Thus any calculation of the efficiency with which the economy uses its resources must include the effects of changes in the amount of capital employed; it is for this reason that economists frequently calculate the capital–output ratio, which is analogous to the calculation of output per man. Instead of output per unit of capital, however, the inverse is calculated, capital employed per unit of output, so that a fall in the capital–output ratio indicates a rise in the productivity of capital. During the late nineteenth century the capital–output ratio in Britain was about 4.0; this can be interpreted as meaning that on average the equipment used in production cost four times as much as the output produced from it each year.

Just as improvements in labour productivity can be achieved by employing more machinery, so a fall in the capital–output ratio could result from employing more men; neither is, taken by itself, an unambiguous indication of increasing efficiency of the productive process as a whole. Such an indication can only be gained by examining changes in output compared with changes in both capital and labour together, rather than either on its own. Such a measure examines how well the economy is using the resources available to it, and it is thus possible to use it to compare the efficiency of two or more countries, such as Britain, the United States, and Germany, whose resources of labour and capital differed greatly. When the measure is calculated in terms of changing efficiency over time it can also make allowances for the fact that, as with these three countries in our period, those resources were altering in different countries at different rates, under the impact for example of migration to the United States.

The measure which has recently been used by economic historians for this purpose (and which is used in several chapters in volume 1) is that of 'total factor productivity', which is intended to compare changes in the output of the economy with an average of changes in all the inputs or resources employed; the average is normally weighted, to take account of the fact that input resources are not normally of equal importance, and the weights used are the shares which the different resources (or 'factors') receive of national income. Although the assumptions underlying this choice of weights can be questioned, the results are not normally greatly affected by different but still reasonable choices. Table 1.8 shows in detail how such a calculation is carried out, while table 1.9 gives the

Table 1.8. *Calculation of growth rates of total factor productivity for the United Kingdom 1856–1913*

	1	2	3	4	5	6	7
			Growth rates of:				Total factor
	Labour	Capital	Output	(1 × 0.52)	(2 × 0.44)	(4)+(5)	productivity
1856–73	0.9	1.0	2.1	0.5	0.4	0.9	1.2
1873–82	0.6	1.6	1.9	0.3	0.6	0.9	1.0
1882–90	1.0	1.1	2.0	0.5	0.5	1.0	1.0
1890–1900	1.1	1.8	2.1	0.6	0.8	1.4	0.7
1900–07	0.8	2.2	1.5	0.4	1.0	1.4	0.1
1907–13	1.1	1.2	1.6	0.6	0.5	1.1	0.5

Source: calculated from Feinstein (1972: T 51).

Table 1.9. *Growth of total factor productivity for the UK, Germany and the USA (% increase per annum)*

	UK		USA	Germany
1873–82	1.0			−0.3
		1869/78–1879/88	2.5	
1882–90	1.0			1.1
1890–1900	0.7		1.2	1.5
1900–07	0.1		1.5	0.7
1907–13	0.5		0.7	1.2
1873–1913	0.4		1.2	0.9

Sources: Feinstein (1972: T 51) for UK
Kendrick (1961: table A-XXII) for USA
Hoffman (1965: table 5A) for Germany

results for Britain, for Germany, and for the United States; it is unfortunately not possible to produce similar results for France or other leading industrial nations.

These tables suggest, as did the results for labour productivity alone, that Britain's total factor productivity grew less rapidly than similar measures for other nations, but that the gap was very narrow given the large margin of error in these 'guesstimates'. The fall in the growth rate around the beginning of the twentieth century, furthermore, was clearly shared by the two other countries, so that none of the three leading industrial nations was improving the efficiency of its production as rapidly after 1900 as it had done before. Although Britain was probably the laggard, her economy was clearly being affected by whatever factors were responsible for producing slower rates of growth of productivity in the developed world as a whole, so that her declining total factor productivity growth rate should not be seen as the result of some peculiarly British form of failure.

The frailty of the calculations in tables 1.8 and 1.9 must be stressed before any reliance is placed on them. The evidence on which they are based is subject to very large margins of error, up to ± 25 per cent in the case of the growth rates of British output and capital input, for example. Secondly, the measure of total factor productivity is a residual; it measures that part of the growth in output which is not accounted for by the combined growth in labour and capital. It is indeed often called simply 'the residual'. As such, it includes within it errors and imprecision in measurement and in calculation, changes in the quality and structure of the labour force and the capital stock, as well as the changes in the efficiency of the economy in using those resources (Gould 1972). To take one example, the reduction in the normal hours of work is not reflected in the series for labour in table 1.8, which is based simply on numbers of men and women employed; as was mentioned above, hours worked grew less rapidly in Britain than numbers employed, so that the input of labour really grew less than is shown in table 1.8. If an adjustment for this were to be made, total factor productivity as the residual would have grown more rapidly than in table 1.8. Conversely, increasing literacy and better general and technical education improved the quality of the labour force in this period, and that should be regarded as an increase in labour input not reflected in the series in table 1.8; if it were to be taken into account, total factor productivity growth in table 1.8 would be overstated. Similar difficulties arise in measuring the capital inputs, where it is equally difficult to assume that capital was homogeneous and unchanging in quality in ways not reflected in the price of equipment.

Assuming that the figures in tables 1.8 and 1.9 give an indication of the performance of Britain, Germany and the United States in these years which is roughly correct, what may account for them? There are really two questions: first, what accounts for the slowing rate of productivity growth common to all three countries particularly after 1900 and, second, why did Britain consistently have a slower rate than her competitors? Unfortunately, the range of possible reasons for changes in the growth rate of total factor productivity is so great that it is very difficult to give a definite or generally acceptable answer to either of these questions. It is possible, however, that the decline in the rate of growth of productivity reflects a slowing in the speed of technological change towards the end of the nineteenth century: the major innovations of steam and steel had by that period been fully applied in most advanced countries to transport systems, to construction, to engineering and to manufacturing generally through the use of powered machinery (Phelps Brown and Browne 1968). The next major innovations, electricity and the internal combustion engine, were only in their infancy in application by the beginning of the twentieth century, and although their final impact on the economy was as pervasive as had been that of the earlier innovations, that impact had not been fully felt by 1914. Similarly, the chemical revolution of the twentieth century had affected only specialised fields of manufacturing by that time. The speed of technological change is, however, very difficult to measure; a theory based on it has to be tentative and imprecise.

Even if the world economy as a whole was experiencing a reduction in the speed of productivity growth, the fact that British growth rates were below those of her competitors requires separate explanation. It might be, however, that Britain had simply exploited the available technology earlier than her competitors, who were therefore 'catching up' and could achieve faster rates of productivity growth while doing so. There were clearly some respects in which Germany and the United States were following a path which Britain had already trod, so that the concept of 'catching-up' might have some validity. In particular, Germany and the United States were following Britain in changing their industrial and occupational structures. By the late nineteenth century, Britain's shift into service industries and the tertiary sector, which in general experience low rates of growth of productivity (where they can be measured at all satisfactorily) may have retarded British productivity growth by comparison with other countries where the major shift was from agriculture to manufacturing industry. Britain had already undergone this latter shift, and thus experienced whatever productivity gains it brought, earlier in the century. In addition, British agriculture undoubtedly became more efficient during the early and mid nineteenth century. If, as chapter 8 shows, it experienced low rates of growth of total factor productivity later in the century, this may be because it was already highly efficient when compared with agriculture in other countries (O'Brien and Keyder 1978). On the other hand, any such theory of 'catching-up' implies a discontinuity in technological progress, such that at some moment a limit was reached at which Britain stopped while others caught up; but there is very little direct evidence for such a theory.

There are, in addition, a number of other explanations which have to be considered. The first, which was that given most often by contemporary observers and which has been frequently repeated by historians, is that Britain was simply unenterprising, conservative and inefficient when compared to other countries. Although this explanation was normally adduced to explain Britain's loss of share in world markets or her slow rates of labour productivity growth, if it were true it would be equally relevant to discussion of total factor productivity. The exact source of the deficiency in Britain's performance has varied, in different accounts, from the malignant influence of trade unions to the debilitating influence of public schools on future entrepreneurs, but there has been general agreement that British enterprise was declining from the high levels of the first industrial revolution. A number of case-studies, discussed in chapter 5, do not suggest that these strictures are justified, even when they have been made sufficiently specific to be adequately discussed. In general, the conclusion of most recent research has been that vague or specific allegations of malaise in the British industrial economy are alike difficult to prove.

Lastly, it is possible that Britain's productivity growth lagged behind that of other countries because of a slower rate of growth of demand for British goods, both at home and overseas, which itself may partly have stemmed from tariffs and other difficulties in export markets which were discussed above. A faster rate of growth of demand and output is likely, if other things are equal, to lead to a faster rate of innovation, as machinery wears out and is replaced by new, and as invention and innovation are stimulated. On the other hand, world trade and British exports grew very rapidly after 1900, at exactly the period when total factor productivity growth in Britain and other countries appears to have been reduced, so the relationship between the growth of output and of productivity is clearly not a simple one.

In general, therefore, we do not know why Britain grew less rapidly than her competitors in this period. The gap was, however, small, and it seems more sensible to see it as stemming from one or some of the explanations which have been given, rather than being content with doom-laden pronouncements about a failure of British enterprise. As chapter 5 shows, such pronouncements have been made repeatedly, though without adequate foundation, about individual British industries; there is no necessary reason why a general condemnation of the British economy should be better founded.

Summary

The treatment of the British economy in this chapter has been an 'optimistic' one, in keeping with many of the chapters which follow and which present the results of research by many economic historians. In essence, its argument has been that although between 1860 and 1914 Britain certainly lost the predominant position which she had held as the leading or only manufacturing nation, this was not because of deficiencies within the British economy. It stemmed, instead, from the increasing complexity of the international economy, and of the national economies within it. This brought to Britain a new role as a pivot of international trade and investment, which demanded adjustments within the domestic economy to enable Britain to carry out that role. Although some of these adjustments were difficult and painful, they were carried out sufficiently well to enable Britain to retain a commanding place in the world economy. As chapter 3 suggests, adjustments would have continued to be necessary, as the old staple industries of coal, cotton, iron and steel and shipbuilding lost their importance and were replaced by a wider spectrum of manufacturing and service industries. The advent of the First World War made it essential for these adjustments to be carried out rapidly, and the pain of the 1920s and 1930s was part of the price.

2

The trade cycle in Britain 1860-1914

A. G. FORD

Introduction: identifying the cycle

The growth of the British economy from 1860 to the outbreak of the First World War may be viewed as the *joint* result of rising effective demand at home and abroad for its products and of a growing ability to supply such products as its factors of production grew in size, improved in quality, and were allocated more effectively. Supply did not create its own demand, nor did supply respond passively to changes in demand. Furthermore, the growth of the economy was not achieved at a steady constant rate of growth of output: in the short run there were fluctuations in output, employment and prices. Indeed, economic fluctuations in the British economy had been noted from the eighteenth century onwards and they continued after 1914.

Figure 2.1 depicts estimates of gross domestic product of the United Kingdom at current and constant factor cost, the gross domestic product 'deflator' (or price index), the rate of unemployment for certain trade unions, export values (visible and invisible), and autonomous spending items (defined as gross home investment *plus* public authorities' current spending *plus* export values). Despite the inevitable shortcomings of the statistical material the uneven growth of the economy in the short run is clear, with the fluctuations more pronounced in product at current prices than in product at constant prices. A similar impression of fluctuation is conveyed by the unemployment rate, and by the export values. After 1880 the price index yields only modest fluctuations.

From these observations it is clear that the British economy both grew and fluctuated, and it is possible to identify (roughly) the years of turning points when output, employment and prices had risen to peaks and other years when they had fallen to troughs. The troughs were slackenings, not actual declines in output. All the time the labour force available was growing steadily so that a slackening in the growth of output continued to bring increases in unemployment in slumps, and an acceleration continued to bring falls in unemployment in booms.

Economists have long been impressed, not to say fascinated, by the recurrent pattern of booms and slumps and have noted for the United Kingdom that the time from one peak to the next is about seven to ten years. Many have been attracted by the notion of regularity and of inevitability, of slump following boom

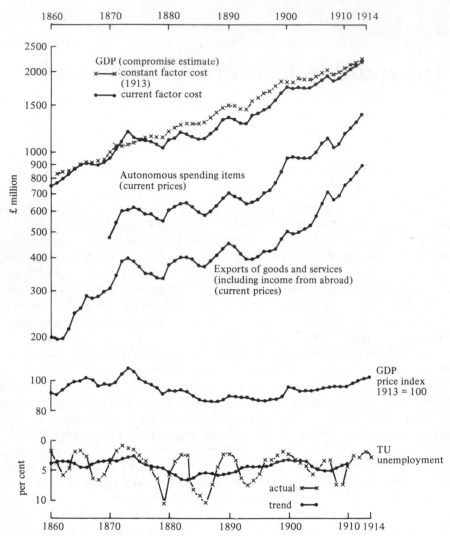

2.1 Gross domestic product, autonomous spending, exports, prices and unemployment in the United Kingdom 1860–1914

to be succeeded by boom again, while others have emphasised that a succession of random shocks could produce the same apparent regularity. The former regard the fluctuations as having a regular periodicity so that they could properly be termed 'cyclical' – the trade cycle or the business cycle – and interpret the behaviour of output in terms of fluctuations about some underlying growth path or trend; the latter believe that a series of erratic shocks (such as wars, gold discoveries, inventions) disturbed the economy and created the illusion of cyclical regularity.

The believers in the cycle have striven to produce theoretical explanations of it that account not only for these fluctuations but also for their regularity and persistence without having to invoke a series of *ad hoc* outside or 'exogenous' shocks (Hicks, 1950; Matthews 1959). With such economic models of the trade cycle, an isolated disturbance sets off a regular series of persistent trade cycles, giving rise to the belief that private enterprise economy is inherently unstable. Such models are attractive, but whether they are realistic – and indeed whether the whole *cyclical* approach is realistic – is another matter, as we shall see.

To explain in the first instance why at times unemployment in Britain was as low as 2 per cent, and at others as high as 10 per cent, and why output and prices fluctuated similarly, one must examine the behaviour of planned spending by people – that is, effective demand. Briefly put, the 'cycle' results in this view from volatile effective demand playing about a steadily growing ability to supply.

Volatile effective demand explains how output or employment comes to rest at a particular level, and will explain how a rise in investment, say, will produce through successive rounds of changes in spending a rise in output. But the rise in investment has to be treated as an external event ('exogenous') to the system. We still have to ask why this change occurred. To those who see the random shock as the cause of fluctuations, the question itself will not be bothersome; it will be to those who see fluctuations as recurrent. In the latter circumstance investment would have to be determined within the system ('endogenously'). For example, one possibility is as follows. Suppose demand for output grew and pressed on existing productive capacity, leading businessmen to expand their capacity by undertaking net investment. Investment therefore would depend on a change in output ('suppose demand for output grew'), and would thus be determined with the system. The distinction between exogenous and endogenous events is central to understanding any historical system, and especially the system of boom and bust.

Whatever the explanation, we must start with the cycle as observed. The way to observe it is to assume that the economy grows steadily at some 'trend' rate around which the economy fluctuates. We then examine the behaviour of the differences between actual values and trend values – deviations from trend – and are able to discern more clearly the pattern of fluctuations. The supposition of a smooth trend could be mistaken: we could be imposing a trend on the series and thus giving the impression of smooth underlying growth even though the basic underlying process of economic growth and development might be uneven.

If that were so, it would make no sense to separate non-existent fluctuations from a non-existent trend, even though the statistical method makes it possible to do this. In the British case the extraction of the trend does indeed pose problems. A straight line trend has a diminishing percentage rate of growth,

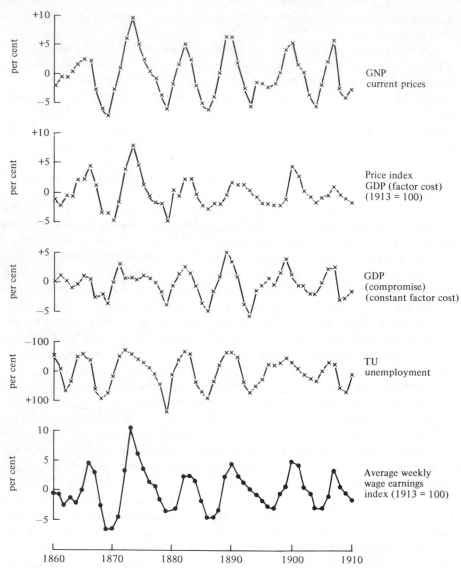

2.2   Relative deviations of gross national product, prices, gross domestic product, unemployment and earnings from a 9-year moving average, UK 1860–1914

while an exponential growth curve has a constant percentage rate of growth. The constant percentage would fit British experience from 1860 to 1900 better, but after 1900 the growth rate in output slows down. And neither trend fits the unemployment or price series.

Table 2.1. *Cyclical peaks and troughs in the United Kingdom 1860–1914*

Peak	Trough
1865–6	1869
1873	1879
1882	1886
1890	1893
1899–1900	1904
1907	1908–9

Source: See text

Table 2.2. *Mean peak and trough relative deviations, UK 1860–1914*

	(1) Mean peak deviation (%)	(2) Mean trough deviation (%)
National product in current prices	+5.78	−5.65
Domestic product in constant prices	+3.18	−3.78
Price index	+3.73	−2.92
Employment (100 minus unemployment percentage)	+2.71	3.84
Weekly wage earnings	+5.25	−3.85

Source: Aldcroft & Fearon (1972)

The device used here therefore is the moving average, calculating nine-year moving averages to isolate the trends. The resultant deviations from trend (actual values *minus* trend values) can be expressed relatively (i.e. as percentages of trend) or absolutely. Relative deviations give a better impression of the volatility of the variables concerned and avoid exaggeration in later years when the magnitudes of income (say) are large, but absolute deviations keep in the correct perspective a series that is highly volatile but small relative to all income (investment in stocks, say). Both will be used here.

Figure 2.2 presents relative deviations of UK gross national product at current prices (income estimates), gross domestic product (compromise estimate) at 1913 prices, the price index, average weekly wages, and the unemployment rate (inverted). Well-defined and parallel patterns of economic fluctuations are clear with the parallelism amongst variables being particularly strong after 1873. The fluctuations in national income at current prices were a product of fluctuations in the volume of output and in prices, and agree closely with the behaviour of unemployment (inverted). Table 2.1 presents the turning points as indicated by the figures and the underlying data, while table 2.2 presents estimates of the mean peak and trough relative deviations of certain variables. The task now is to explain them.

An initial approach to explaining the cycle

Why should such fluctuations in economic activity have occurred? Recall our view that the growth of the economy was the joint result of growing spending and growing supply. It is reasonable to consider ability to supply as growing steadily (as factors of production grew slowly) in the short run, but to argue that spending was more volatile and played about the more stable ability to supply, so that over a cycle the behaviour of planned spending determined the size of output and employment in each time period. Why should planned spending have varied thus? A simple Keynesian macroeconomic model will answer these points. Assume that consumer expenditure, import purchases and taxation are directly related to output (or income) as endogenous variables and move proportionately with output as it rises or falls, while investment spending, public spending, and export proceeds are assumed to be exogenously determined with particular values. Under these conditions the equilibrium position at which planned output equals planned spending will depend directly on the size of these 'exogenous' items (i.e. exports *plus* investment *plus* public spending), so long as maximum attainable output has not been reached. If any of the 'autonomous' or 'exogenous' spending items should change, then a multiplier process will be set in motion until the economy reaches its new equilibrium output position. This multiplier process of a fall in export proceeds, say, will spread the depressive effects throughout the economy, reducing output, consumption, tax receipts, and imports until a fresh equilibrium is established. (The multiplier is defined as the change in output between two equilibrium positions divided by the initial change in 'exogenous' spending which provoked it.)

This, then, is the macroeconomic model which we wish to use to help explain fluctuations in economic activity in Britain with the modification that we are applying it to current price values (when it is usually applied to fixed price values of variables). Fluctuations in output and employment come about because of fluctuations in 'exogenous' items but this does not of itself explain cyclical behaviour.

How large the response of output is to changes in exogenous spending will depend on the size of the multiplier in Britain in this period. As a rough guide to the multiplier, which is defined as the reciprocal of the sum of the marginal propensities to save, import and pay taxation, we calculate as follows: we have in our period consumer spending as 0.86 of gross national product at factor cost, imports of goods and services as 0.30, and taxation on expenditure as 0.07. These average propensities have been arrived at by averaging the figures for 1870, 1880,

1890, 1900 and 1910, while it should be pointed out that the gap between consumption and product at 0.14 will cover both saving and direct taxation as proportions of gross national product. In general the relative marginal propensities to save, import, and pay taxation will exceed the average propensities so that calculations based on the latter will provide an upper limit to the multiplier. The sum of these average propensities is 0.51 ($= 0.14 + 0.30 + 0.07$) and thus the multiplier would be 1.98. More realistically we might suppose the marginal propensity to save and pay direct taxation as 0.20, to import as 0.35, to pay indirect taxation as 0.075, so that their sum is 0.625 and the multiplier 1.60. Hence we conclude that the size of the multiplier was not more than 2 at the very most and very probably around 1.5.

To test this attribution of fluctuations in money incomes to fluctuations in exogenous spending (defined as exports plus investment plus public spending), a regression equation has been calculated which seeks to explain annual changes in UK gross national product, y, in terms of annual changes in exogenous spending, a, in the same time period, and yields over 1870–1914:

$$y_e = 10.27 + 1.02a_t \quad \bar{R}^2 = 0.64$$
$$(1.98)\ (8.83) \quad \mathrm{DW} = 1.64$$
$$(t\text{-values in parentheses})$$

This regression suggests that 64 per cent of the variation in y was explained by the variation in a, but we should be cautious because exogenous spending was an important constituent of gross national product (derived, however, from income estimates). The coefficient of a_t at 1.02 relates to the multiplier process, but cannot be taken as an estimate of the multiplier because the multiplier process is spread out over time and some portion of a multiplied-up stimulus of year one will be felt in year two. The above equation does not capture this, but does provide reassuring evidence that 'autonomous' or 'exogenous' variables make a substantial contribution to explaining variations in output. This relationship is illustrated in figure 2.3, which shows that the cyclical pattern in autonomous spending closely resembles the pattern in output, although this is scarcely odd considering that these items were almost half the value of output.

It is clear that unlike, say, the warlike eighteenth or twentieth centuries public spending in the late nineteenth century was devoid of cyclical activity. Aside from a blip for the Boer War its influences were stabilising. By contrast, exports of goods and services dominate the scene both in actual size and in their violent cyclical pattern. They exhibit remarkable growth after 1895. The last part of autonomous spending, capital formation at home, displays some of the seven-to-ten-year cyclical pattern of 'the' business cycle (and of exports), but far more noticeable are longer cyclical movements of some 18 to 20 years periodicity; known as 'long swings' or 'Kuznets' cycles.

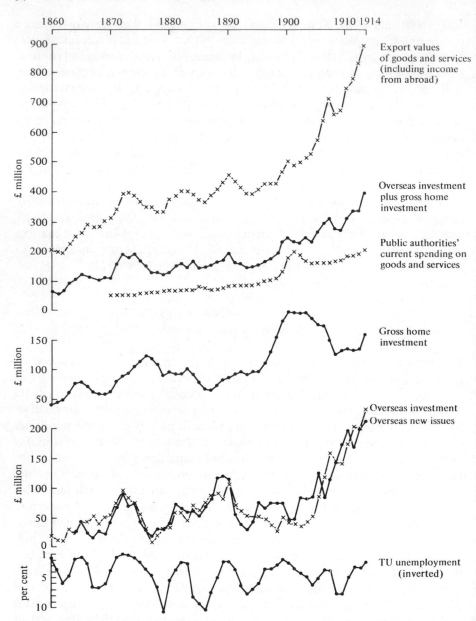

2.3 Exports, investment, current spending by public authorities, overseas investment, overseas new issues and unemployment in the United Kingdom 1870–1914 (current prices)

This last illustrates still another difficulty in describing cycles, i.e. that short cycles might be accidental results of superimposed long ones. The Kuznets cycle is mirrored in the behaviour of the series for overseas (as distinct from home) investment, and for overseas new issues on the London Stock Exchange, the peaks of the overseas swings matching the troughs of home swings and vice versa. Overseas investment took place at the expense of home investment, home investment at the expense of overseas investment, as their relative profitabilities (amongst other factors) varied in the course of world economic development. If home and overseas investment are added together (the second curve in figure 2.3) the long-swing elements are virtually eliminated but seven-to-ten-year fluctuations remain, with their peaks and troughs agreeing well with peaks and troughs in British economic activity, although their agreement is less close than is that of exports. These features have led R. C. O. Matthews to see British cyclical activity in terms of internal influences on demand (represented by home investment) and external influences (represented by overseas investment). He, indeed, concludes 'that the seven-to-ten-year periodicity of fluctuations in national income derived mainly from the existence of two unsynchronised waves, each of roughly twice of that duration, in home and foreign investment respectively, rather than from the existence of a seven-to-ten-year cycle in either taken by itself' (Matthews 1959: 220). D. J. Coppock similarly emphasises a blend of external influences (represented by exports) and internal influences (represented by residential building). He finds the proximate causes of the pattern of the fluctuations to lie in the opposing major secular swings in exports and in residential building. For Coppock, as for Matthews, the UK cycle is a complex affair and 'existed in the United Kingdom after 1870, only as an accidental result of a sequence of turning points in building and exports which have to be explained, substantially, in terms of the repercussive effects of the United States transport–building cycle' (Coppock, 1972: 217).

We shall adopt a different approach and consider the problems of fluctuations in terms of deviations from trend rather than in terms of long-swing interaction. Figure 2.4 presents the main variables in terms of deviations from trend and, although individual cycles have their own particular institutional, industrial and geographical characteristics, a search for common features and consonance of turning points reveals the key role of exports. Indeed, the proximate cause of cyclical fluctuations in the United Kingdom from 1860 to 1914 lay in the behaviour of exports of goods and services, aided sometimes by home investment, especially in the period 1879–1900. Although investment was more volatile than exports in terms of relative deviations, the absolute deviations in exports were some $2\frac{1}{2}$ times those in investment (on average between 1870 and 1914 gross investment formed 8 per cent of gross national product, while exports of goods and services and income from abroad formed 32 per cent), and their turning points accorded more closely with fluctuations in output and employment than

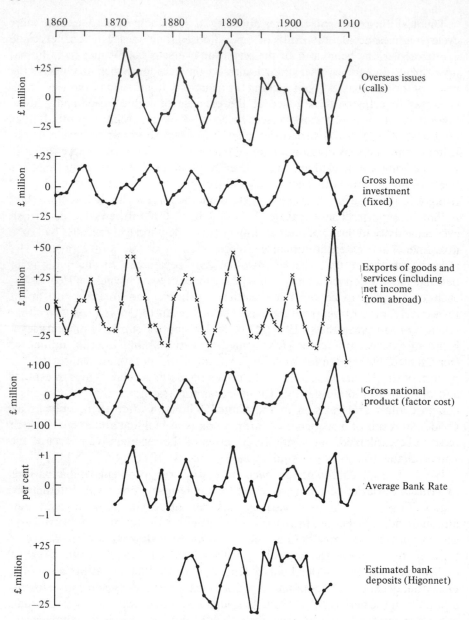

2.4 Absolute deviations of overseas issues, home investment, exports, GNP, Bank Rate and bank deposits from 9-year moving averages (current values) UK 1860–1910

did those of investment. This result is, indeed, not surprising in an economy so committed to international transactions as to be dubbed an export, lending, and rentier economy and which by 1913 still had a sizeable share of world trade.

A proximate cause, however, is not necessarily an ultimate cause. One must ask again to what extent the causes were themselves caused, that is, one must distinguish exogenous from endogenous influences on the economy. Exports were exogenous, determined by the growth of populations and incomes abroad over which events in Britain had little influence. By contrast home investment might well have been influenced by domestic events and might qualify as an endogenous variable. For example, as rising exports brought rising incomes and rising demands for output from British factories, such demands would press on existing capacity and lead to the installation of extra capacity by net investment (the accelerator relationship). This fresh investment would increase home spending via the multiplier and then lead to yet more capacity creation by net investment in a subsequent time period so that the boom might feed on itself – and *vice versa* for falling demand in a down-swing. Economic analysis has suggested various time paths that this multiplier–acceleration interaction might produce in incomes, ranging from a self-sustained explosion through fluctuations to a damped return to the initial position. However, from what we have seen of the British economy in the late nineteenth century, it does seem implausible to expect more than a damped response. Furthermore, we should not expect residential building, public investment or innovatory investment to be influenced by such short-term movements in output, and they formed at least half of British investment.

Nevertheless, a more pervasive influence might be, as Keynes suggested, that in an upswing the cumulative build-up of expectations of profit in an atmosphere of imperfect information and of 'animal spirits' on the part of entrepreneurs and investors would stimulate more investment, both at home and overseas. Exaggerated expectations of gain (which hindsight was to show as grossly bloated) would be pricked by disappointing results and in an equally exaggerated way gloom and revulsion abound with the cumulative collapse of these optimistic expectations. But memories are short, some projects have succeeded, and people recover their nerve to bring about another cumulative build-up.

Each of these endogenous effects on home investment can be brought in to help explain why home investment fluctuations tended to reinforce fluctuations in exports, but they are insufficient in themselves to produce sustained fluctuations. With so much of 'exogenous' or autonomous spending truly exogenous – exports were huge and exogenous – the rewards are low from any model other than that of a (stable) economy buffeted by shocks.

An economy buffeted by exogenous shocks
Shocks from abroad

Some major down-turns are associated with particular overseas episodes – 1872–73 and America, 1890 and Argentina (the Baring Crisis) and Australia. The sharp down-turn of 1907 in particular signalled the growing importance of the United States in the world economy. There is no lack of shocking elements – ranging from gold discoveries, wars, bunched railway construction booms, developmental booms to even sunspots. Particular international shocks could help to explain one major feature of the business cycle – the marked parallelism between Britain, France, and Germany, who were in the same phase of their reference cycles in 83 per cent of all months between 1879 and 1914 (Morgenstern 1959). There were strong trade and money market links between these countries, and infectious changes in confidence. By contrast, adding American experience reduces the degree of agreement to 52 per cent of all months. The American cycle would seem to be shorter in length and perhaps of different character, at least before the all-pervasive influence of 1907.

Of course the European shocks may not have been entirely external to the British economy; the various world shocks may well have been shaped or even initiated by the British economy, in view of its large international role. Indeed, one can see in figure 2.4 that British exports follow one or two years behind the fluctuations of British loans abroad, which are the most volatile of the series depicted. Loans did lead directly to British export sales (Ford 1969; Lewis 1978). Much of the British overseas lending in this period was developmental in character and devoted to social overhead capital formation such as railways, public utilities, port improvements; it was frequently undertaken with the hope of increasing the borrower's capacity to produce and export primary produce (Cairncross 1953). In these circumstances the use made by the borrowers of the funds might be expected to stimulate their import purchases as they used the funds either to import capital goods (British rails for their railways, British machinery for their ports) or to finance extra spending at home, with an ultimate effect of increasing imports of consumer goods (British coal for their houses, British crockery for their tables). In the cases in which strong bilateral trading links existed between the borrower and Britain or where Britain was the major supplier of the required products, we would expect overseas lending by Britain to be followed by increased export sales by British industries. New railway construction financed by such means in India or in Argentina could stimulate activity in British heavy industries just as new home railway construction did. Again, a collapse in British overseas lending would impair the erstwhile borrowers' ability to purchase imports, both directly and through a fall in activity, with the result that British exports after a lag would decline. Table 2.3 illustrates these effects for the episode of heavy British lending to Argentina in

Table 2.3. *How loans led to exports: the Argentinian case 1885–91 (million gold pesos)*

	(1) British new issues for Argentina	(2) British merchandise exports for Argentina f.o.b.
1885	32	23
1886	41	26
1887	77	31
1888	79	38
1889	69	53
1890	30	42
1891	11	21

Sources: (1) *The Economist*, 'New Issues' sections. (2) UK Trade Returns, converted at 5 pesos to £1

the late 1880s, culminating in the Baring Crisis of 1890 for London (an upper turning point in the British cycle) and in economic collapse in Argentina in 1890/91. The one-year lagged reaction in British export sales behind British new issues for Argentina is striking.

Besides such direct links increased purchases by borrowers from other countries would stimulate activity and hence their ability to buy British exports. Even through multilateral links in other words, British exports would be stimulated. This would perhaps provide part of the explanation of rising British exports to Europe on occasions of increased lending abroad even when Europe was not the main borrower. After 1890 the connections between overseas issues and exports became more complex and reflect the growth of alternative suppliers of industrial products (such as Germany, United States, and to some degree France), the weakening of bilateral trading links, and the rise of a more multilateral trading and settlements system. The bilateral links, instanced earlier in the explanation of the sensitivity of British export sales to British overseas lending, have to be supplemented by multilateral links working through continental Europe to help explain the lead of overseas issues over exports.

The correlation between British lending and (with a lag) British exporting might be spurious: some third (as yet unspecified) factor might be influencing both exports and loans, such as rising economic activity and promise in a potential borrower, or gold discoveries, or political stability. In more general terms attractive overseas prospects could be *pulling* both capital funds and goods from Britain, while, equally, poor British prospects in the preceding slump could be *pushing* funds abroad from less attractive home yields and *pushing* manufacturers to seek more urgently new (overseas) markets for their products to make up for a decline in home sales. Problems remain, therefore, in evaluating the role of British lending and in explaining its behaviour. Attempts have been made to explain British lending to specific territories, and these indicate the importance of both pull and push factors (Edelstein 1974: 980–1007; Ford 1971). It might be that to proceed much further a world model would be needed – or at least one explicitly incorporating Britain and the borrowing primary producers; and certainly French and German lending abroad would need to be brought into the reckoning, even though they were not of the same pattern, size, or character as the British. Nevertheless, overseas lending certainly had a distinct role in British economic fluctuations, and its behaviour reinforces the view as to the international character of the trade cycle for Britain.

Home investment behaviour

As noted above, the cyclical correspondence of output with gross home investment was not as close as was the correspondence of output with exports, but there was marked agreement in the period from 1879 to 1901. In figure 2.5 the discrepancy in cyclical behaviour between investment (top graph) and gross national product (bottom) in the 1870s and after 1902 is marked, as is the agreement in the middle period. It is important, however, to examine the different determinants and components of investment. For example industrial profits could influence investment decisions, either by the supply of finance (undistributed profits were an important source of finance for home investment at this time) or by affecting expectations of future profits. Deviations in profits were closely related to deviations in output, with a lead of one year at most peaks and troughs. (This must have reflected full capacity working in upswings, when rising input prices squeezed profits.) Hence both the financial ability to expand capacity and the incentive to do so were present in the upswing. The behaviour of Bank Rate has been included as representative of monetary ease or stringency (various studies have indicated that the influence of interest rates on British home investment was weak or moderate) (Pesmazoglu 1951; Tinbergen 1951; Ford 1962). Bank Rate tended to be high in booms, low in slumps, so that investment and Bank Rate were positively associated, especially from 1879 to 1901. This suggests that investment was playing a following role rather than a leading role in the British trade cycle.

The breakdown in the figure of the total gross investment into its four main components reveals different individual patterns as compared with each other and with the aggregate pattern. The 'ships' component has roughly the same cyclical pattern as output and exports, but investment in 'dwellings' is devoid of any cyclical pattern. 'Plant, machinery and vehicles' does have fluctuations, some of which coincide with, or lag one year behind, fluctuations in output (particularly for 1878–1902), while 'other new buildings and works' displays an

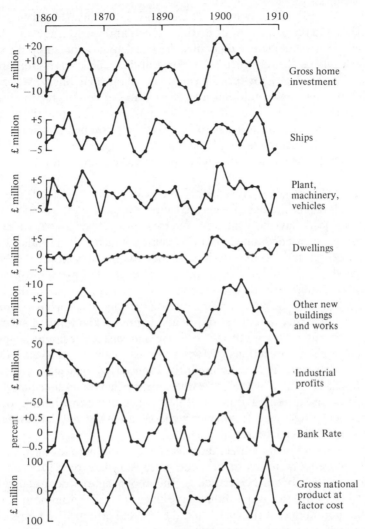

2.5   Absolute deviations of home investment, ships, plant machinery vehicles, dwellings, other building, industrial profits, Bank Rate and gross national product from 9-year moving averages, United Kingdom 1870–1910 (current prices)

interesting and distinct cyclical pattern which consistently lags two years behind fluctuations in output. Over the whole period 1870 to 1914 'ships' claimed 15 per cent of total gross fixed investment, 'plant, machinery, vehicles' 30 per cent, 'dwellings' 18 per cent, and 'other buildings and works' 37 per cent. Building and construction activity, in other words, occupied over half of gross investment. Much of gross investment was replacement, as high as 62 per cent.

A few observations can be made. The behaviour of investment in ships was closely related to the behaviour of British exports and world trade and decisions to expand investment here would meet rising demand for shipping services, particularly given the opportunities for self-finance from rising profits in upswings. The tendency for turning points in 'plant, machinery, vehicles' and especially in 'other new buildings and works' to lag behind turning points in gross national product suggests that in upswings rising activity induced businessmen and local authorities to increase their planned investment, which took time to commission and implement and thus lagged behind activity, while the subsequent downswing scotched some future plans and led to falling investment.

The decline in overseas issues before the peak (recall figure 2.4) might have released funds for the finance of home investment projects. The question remains, did home projects have to wait until overseas projects declined; or did rising activity bring increased planned home investment which pulled funds away from overseas ventures and led to a decline in overseas investment, or did both just happen perchance? Similarly in the downswing the falling home investment made finance available for an early revival in overseas projects, but did overseas investment wait on a decline in home investment, did overseas investment pull funds from home investment, or did it just happen? The implied substitution of investment outlets from abroad to home and *vice versa* might suggest that there were good connections between British capital markets. Overseas investment, however, was predominantly financed by overseas issues on the London Stock Exchange, while home investment relied on undistributed profits, private loans, and a limited amount of new issues, some in London, others on provincial stock exchanges. It is unclear whether an investor would switch easily between these different markets.

Investment spending magnified the effects of export fluctuations in the British cycle, but more work needs to be done to substantiate or refute the various suggestions made above. Nevertheless, the above figures do not lend much support to the proposition that home investment played a dominant role in the cycle in this period or that the cycle should be viewed primarily in terms of waves of innovation and technical progress at home.

The role of money in fluctuations – active or passive?

The British monetary system and the gold standard

So far little has been said about the influences of money and finance. Yet monetary influences were once thought of as the major cause of such fluctuations, and have recently enjoyed a considerable revival in the minds of economists. There are various possible roles for monetary factors, depending on the nature of the country's monetary system and the policies pursued by its monetary authorities. Monetary influences may initiate upswings or downswings; they may aggravate them; on the other hand they may constrain or help to stabilise fluctuations; or the money stock may merely accommodate itself passively to varying demands. Given these roles we must remember that there are various possible interpretations when we find money incomes and the stock of money behaving in a similar fashion. For example, did a rise in the stock of money bring a rise in income, or did a rise in income call forth a rise in the money stock?

After 1821 the monetary unit of Britain – the pound sterling – was defined in terms of gold as 113.0016 grains of gold 9/10 fine, which was the gold content of the sovereign (= one pound sterling). In other words the sterling price of gold was fixed. Under this gold standard the paper currency (banknotes) was freely convertible into its gold equivalent at face value. The money of Britain therefore comprised gold and other coin, banknotes (especially Bank of England notes) and bank deposits – the latter forming the major part of the money supply by the second half of the nineteenth century. The issue of Bank of England notes was strictly regulated by law after 1844, with extra issues having to be backed fully by gold. As Britain was not a gold-producer, increases in the gold coin and bank-note component of the stock of money depended on the net import of gold. The bank deposit component depended on the commercial banks' cash holdings (banknotes and coin and bankers' deposits at the Bank of England), because banks needed to hold a certain minimum of cash against their deposit liabilities so that they could always pay out cash for a cheque on demand. Hence the supply of money and changes in it in the United Kingdom stemmed from international gold movements and the policies of banks. Although the statistics are very imperfect, particularly before 1891 deviations from trend of the money stock display a distinct cyclical pattern (see figure 2.6).

Short-term rates of interest (the London market rate of discount and banks' deposit and advances rates) were influenced by the level of Bank Rate (the rate at which the Bank of England itself rediscounted bills) and by the demand and supply of loanable funds in the market. The long-term rate of interest, as typified by the yield on Consols (that is, the consolidated debt of the government) and on railway debentures, was much less sensitive to the varying pressures of demand and supply and displayed no cyclical pattern. The short-term interest rate and Bank Rate, by contrast, displayed a marked cyclical pattern, being high in booms and low in slumps.

Such as it was, British monetary policy in this period was dominated by the needs of the gold standard. Indeed, the Bank of England regarded as its main policy objective the maintenance of specie payments or the convertibility of its notes for gold at face value on demand, which ensured the fixity of the link between the pound sterling and gold. The pound was not only a national currency, but was widely used internationally as a trading and reserve currency;

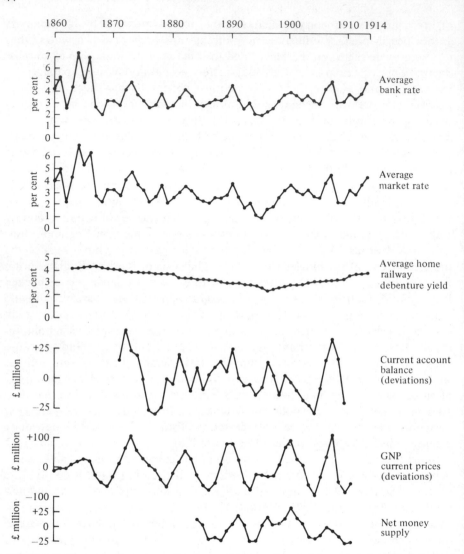

2.6 Bank Rate, market rate of interest, home railway debenture yield, balance on current account, gross national product and money supply, United Kingdom 1860–1914

and the world's major capital and gold markets were in London. To this concentration of finance was added the pivoting of international trade settlement patterns on London and the location of some of the chief commodity markets (e.g. cotton in Liverpool) in Britain (Saul 1960: chs. III, IV). Both domestic and international users of sterling had very high confidence in the currency, and it was the Bank's task to see that this confidence was maintained by ensuring convertibility. This it achieved successfully in the developing and changing economic environment in the fifty years before 1914 despite holding very scanty free gold reserves, amounting in value to only two to three weeks worth of British import payments.

The Bank regulated its monetary policy by watching its 'reserve' (its holdings of gold uncommitted to the backing of notes in circulation) using Bank Rate and the gold 'devices' to protect and replenish its reserve (Sayers 1936; Ford 1962: ch. III). The 'devices' involved raising the buying and selling prices of foreign gold coins and of bar gold (but not domestic gold coins) to deter some demands for gold and to help it acquire more gold. By the twentieth century, however, the major weapon was Bank Rate, which had to be made 'effective' on the London market rate of discount – to ensure that market rate rose following a rise in Bank Rate. For it was the market rate of discount which regulated international and domestic financial transactions, while Bank Rate itself was a technical rate of rediscount at which the Bank of England operated its function as lender of last resort. When the Bank felt that its reserve was strained and inadequate, it would raise Bank Rate and seek to make it effective (Sayers 1936; Ford 1962: ch. III) so that a net inflow of international capital would occur and bring the needed net import of gold to the Bank. When its reserve was ample, Bank Rate would be lowered. The question to be answered is whether such policies smoothed or aggravated economic fluctuations.

Monetary influences in the cycle

Consider the possible cyclical influences on the Bank's reserve. In the upswing of economic activity there would be increased demand for gold coin from people and firms, so that the Bank faced an 'internal' (i.e. domestic) drain; in the downswing the demand for money to carry on business declined and there was an internal reflux of coin to replenish the reserve. These conclusions for internal influences hold irrespective of why economic activity boomed or slumped and are supported by various empirical studies (Beach 1935; Goodhart 1972; Ford 1962: ch. III).

The same cannot be said for external drains or inflows. Here the results depend critically on what forces caused the boom or slump. Consider the 'investment economy' case. If a rise in investment at home brings a boom, then imports rise and gold is sent abroad to pay for the imports. The Bank's reserve is reduced so that Bank Rate is raised while the loss of gold diminishes the monetary base, and monetary influences constrain the boom. Likewise a slump as a result of a decline in investment will be accompanied by monetary ease. The Bank's rigid adherence to a target for its reserves has in this case a smoothing effect on the business cycle.

On the other hand in the 'export economy' case if a rise in exports brings a boom, then imports rise but by less than exports and foreigners send gold to Britain to pay for the goods. If nothing else intervenes – note this qualification – the Bank's reserve is increased, Bank Rate can be lowered, and the inflow of gold has expanded the monetary base. In other words, in this case monetary influences would make the boom more extreme. Similarly an export-induced slump would be accompanied by monetary tightness, making the slump more extreme.

The findings earlier in this chapter would imply that the United Kingdom economy was much nearer to the second case, with export fluctuations providing the main immediate cause of income and output fluctuations; export fluctuations were, in the period 1879 to 1902, aided by similar movements in home investment so that in these years the force of the export economy was modified by the force of an investment economy. Import values display similar fluctuations to exports but are of such a lesser size that the British current account improves in booms and worsens in slumps, the sizes of movements tending to exceed the internal drain in booms, and the internal reflux in slumps. It might be expected then, that booms would bring a strengthening of the Bank's reserve (from the gold inflow) and an easy Bank Rate policy, and that slumps would bring a weakening of the reserve and a tough Bank Rate policy. If exports of goods drove the business cycle, and nothing else intervened, then the gold inflow in booms and outflow in slumps would have Bank policy intensifying the cycle. But in fact Bank Rate was high in booms and low in slumps. Why?

The answer lies in the phrase 'if nothing else intervened'. In a boom the Bank might consider that a higher reserve was desirable while it would also be facing an internal drain. Hence it would be facing strain, while in a slump it might consider a lower reserve more appropriate and there would be the internal reflux of gold to it so that domestic conditions would be easier. Again, and of more importance, the British economy was a lender as well as an exporter, and the flows of gold therefore depended not only on the balance of exports and imports, but also on the balance of loans and repayments. As the discussion of the impact of lending to foreigners on foreigners' purchases indicated, investment abroad tended to lead exports. In consequence the basic balance of payments – the balance of loans as well as current account – tended to move into deficit during booms and in surplus during slumps. The Bank reacted accordingly, raising Bank Rate to offset losses of gold in booms and lowering it to offset gains in slumps. The rise in Bank Rate in a boom attracted so much short-term capital to London that the balance of payments moved into surplus and gold flowed in. In any event, the Bank's policy was not destabilizing.

As noted earlier, the supply of money and its components varied cyclically with output at current prices – if anything, tending to lag behind output – and, despite the earlier mention of the difficulties of interpretation, it does seem reasonable to consider this an accommodating response. Short-term interest rates rise along with output, and fall likewise, in an essentially export-driven cycle. In addition, we find the ratio of bank loans to deposits rising in booms, falling in slumps, as bankers adjusted to the needs of home activity (Ford 1969: 112–14). Goodhart has demonstrated how bankers' balances at the Bank of England rose (or were allowed to rise at the price of higher Bank Rate) in booms to provide the cash support for growing banking transactions and fell in slumps, irrespective of the state of the Bank's reserve. He concludes 'movements of income and the money supply were quite closely associated, but this association was owing to variations in the money supply being adapted to the fluctuations in money incomes' (1972: 219). McCloskey and Zecher, similarly, found that under the gold standard 'flows of gold represented the routine satisfaction of demands for money' (1976, p. 385).

Simple regression equations indicated that annual changes in money incomes (y) are better explained by annual changes in exports (x) than by annual changes in the money supply (m) for the period 1880 to 1913. The so-called 't-values' are in parentheses below each coefficient; the larger they are the better (and note how high – 7.22 – the one attached to exports is):

$$y_t = 15.52 + 1.18x_t \quad \bar{R}^2 = 0.60$$
$$(2.48)\ (7.22)$$
$$y_t = 5.77 + 1.56m_t \quad \bar{R}^2 = 0.22$$
$$(0.47)\ (3.52)$$

From this discussion of monetary factors in the British trade cycle in the period 1870 to 1914 it would appear that the money supply accommodated itself to changes in activity. The other part of the monetary factors, the behaviour of short-term rates, was heavily governed by the needs arising from maintaining specie payments where Bank Rate played a vital role in protecting the Bank's reserve by speedily influencing short-term international capital flows. The contra-cyclical pattern of short-term interest rates was not the result of any conscious stabilisation policy on the part of the Bank of England: it arose in the special British context from gold standard needs. It nevertheless constrained fluctuations a little partly through weak cost effects and partly through altering expectations, damping optimism and alleviating gloom.

There are further possibilities of monetary influence. Overseas issues on the London Stock Exchange always turned down at least one year before exports and incomes, and after Bank Rate had been rising for some two years. Likewise they revived before exports and incomes and after Bank Rate had been falling for at least a year. One strand here is that the rising difficulty of borrowing in upswings may have deterred overseas borrowers and their issuing houses, while ease in downswings may have encouraged them to come forward and seek funds. Rising Bank Rate, in addition, may have influenced adversely the (excessively) optimistic appraisals of would-be lenders abroad and injected more cautious sentiments so that their desire to lend abroad was checked. It is difficult, however, to disentangle this from another possibility unconnected with Bank Rate. Declines in overseas issues may reflect a decline in the marginal efficiency of investment abroad as the more profitable projects had been taken up, while the expectations of British lenders may well have been punctured by disquieting reports from abroad, as for example from Argentina in 1889 as a prelude to the Baring Crisis. But on the whole the business cycle in the late nineteenth century was non-monetary.

Conclusions

The treatment above has concentrated on the behaviour of deviations from trend and has sought explanations in such terms: it has ignored the behaviour of trends and the possibilities of their interaction givng rise to cyclical behaviour. In particular, it has neglected the long-swings of 18–20 years periodicity (or Kuznets cycles) in certain economic variables such as home investment, overseas investment and migration of labour. Indeed, it has been assumed that such trends meshed together to produce a smooth underlying growth path about which 7 to 10 year cycles occurred as a result of the deviation behaviour. In this respect it has differed from two important views of the British trade cycle before 1914 provided by R. C. O. Matthews and by D. J. Coppock, alluded to earlier. External influences – in particular the behaviour of exports of goods and services – were important throughout the period and were linked with overseas lending and with economic development in various countries (not only North America, but also Europe and the empty borrowing primary producers). As D. H. Robertson thought, British industrial fluctuations should be linked with affairs on far off Prairies and Pampas (Robertson 1915). Or, as Beveridge put it, 'one of the main secrets of the trade cycle is to be found, not in bankers' parlours or the board-rooms of industry, but on the prairies and plantations, in the mines and oil wells' (Beveridge 1944). By contrast the role of home investment and in particular of building investment was less important in these fluctuations, while monetary influences were not a significant internal cyclical factor in the United Kingdom.

Appendix: Sources of statistics

This chapter has relied heavily on C. H. Feinstein, *National Income, Expenditure and Output of the United Kingdom, 1955–1965*, Cambridge, 1972 and, in particular, for the following series:
  Gross National Product at current and at constant 1900 factor cost.
  Gross Domestic Product (compromise estimates) at current and at constant 1913 factor cost.

Gross Domestic Product Price Index.
Trade Union Unemployment.
Average weekly Wage Earnings.
Gross Domestic Fixed Capital Formation (and sub-division) at current and at constant
 1900 prices.
Public Authorities Current spending.
Exports and property income from abroad.
Imports and property income paid abroad.
Other sources:
 Merchandise exports (and geographical sub-divisions), B. R. Mitchell with Phyllis
  Deane, *Abstract of British Historical Statistics*, Cambridge, 1962.
 Market Rate of Interest on High Class Bills, B. R. Mitchell with Phyllis Deane, *ibid.*
 Average Bank Rate, R. H. Palgrave, *Bank Rate and the Money Market*, London, 1903,
  p. 33 (1860–1900); *The Economist*, Records and Statistics, 1953, p. 438.
 Bank Deposits, R. P. Higonnet, 'Bank Deposits in the United Kingdom 1870–1914',
  Quarterly Journal of Economics, 1957.
 Stock of Money, D. K. Sheppard, *The Growth and Role of U.K. Financial Institutions
  1880–1962*, London, 1972.
 Railway Debenture Rate, C. K. Harley, 'Goschen's Conversion of the National Debt
  and the Yield on Consols', *Economic History Review*, 1976, p. 106.
 Industrial Profits, C. H. Feinstein, 'Income and Investment in the United Kingdom
  1856–1914', *Economic Journal*, 1961.
 Overseas Issues (Calls) and sub-divisions, M. Simon, 'The Pattern of New British
  Portfolio Investment, 1865–1914', in A. R. Hall (ed.) *The Export of Capital
  1870–1914*, London, 1968.

3

Foreign trade: competition and the expanding international economy

C. K. HARLEY & D. N. McCLOSKEY

The dimensions of trade

In the century before the First World War international trade developed a greater complexity and sophistication than it had possessed in the eighteenth century. By the middle of the nineteenth century Britain had moved to free trade, and many other nations followed the British example in this, though briefly. Industrialisation elsewhere, particularly in the United States and on the Continent, gradually eliminated Britain's lead as workshop of the world. Falling transportation costs, migrations of Europeans unequalled since the dark ages, and the consequent exploitation of new places transformed the supply of raw materials to Europe. Especially after 1870, British lending overseas and a great expansion of Britain's role as carrier, banker and insurer to the world added new dimensions to Britain's international accounts. Multilateral settlements became commonplace, and triangular trades were ordinary facts rather than pleasing myths: American imports of tea from India (say) were financed by exports of cotton to Britain, financed in turn by British loans of money and exports of rails to India. As never before the world was tied together in one great marketplace, with Britain as its centre.

The usual understanding of these events divides neatly at 1870. From 1820 to 1870 the questions asked by the historian of British trade are variants of 'How did foreign trade make us rich?' From 1870 to 1914 they are variants of 'How did foreign trade make us poor?' For fifty years after 1820, and especially during the mid-Victorian boom of the 1850s and 1860s, trade is viewed as the engine of economic growth; after 1870 it is viewed as a brake.

Whether engine or brake, it is viewed now as the activity on which the nation 'depended', just as it was by contemporaries. Wherever one looks in recent summaries by economic historians of the issue of British trade and growth the nineteenth century speaks. John Stuart Mill would find little with which to disagree in the recent assertion by Phyllis Deane and W. A. Cole that 'from the beginning to the end of this story...the British people have depended for their

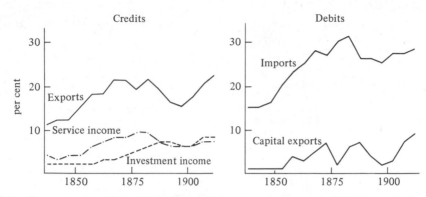

3.1 Components of Britain's balance of payments as percent of GNP, 5-year averages 1836–1913

Sources: Balance of payments: Imlah (1958: pp. 95–8); GNP: Deane (1968: p. 106), and Feinstein (1972: T 18).

standard of living largely on their ability to sell their products in the overseas markets'; nor would Alfred Marshall in their assertion that 'by the end of the nineteenth century the British economy was heavily dependent on world markets and the rate and pattern of British economic growth was largely conditioned by the responses of producers and consumers in the rest of the world' (Deane & Cole 1962: 39, 28). Cobden or Peel might have used Ashworth's recent formulation of the case in proposing free trade to the House of Commons – 'Britain's livelihood depended on international trade and the performance of international services' – as Gladstone or Asquith might have used W. H. B. Court's in defending it from later critics – 'In a century in which economic growth depended very much on international commerce, no country's development had benefited more from world trade' (Ashworth 1960: 256, cf. 138; Court 1965: 181–2).

The correlation between British exports and British incomes lends an air of verisimilitude to this tale of dependence, for as the rate of growth of exports declined after 1870 so too did the rate of growth of incomes. Exports of commodities per head grew 4.4 per cent per year from 1821 to 1873, almost three times faster than the growth of income per head of 1.5 per cent or so per year; but from 1873 to 1913 they grew at only 0.93 per cent per year, rather *slower* than the growth of income per head, itself much slower than its earlier pace. Little wonder, then, that economists of all sorts have assigned a causal role to British foreign trade (Robertson 1938: 501; Haberler 1959: 6; Cairncross 1961: 243; Meier & Baldwin 1957: 228, 257).

Other statistics appear to confirm the impression that trade was important (Crouzet 1979; Saul 1965). After a doubling of its share during the second third of the century, for example, imports supplied 25 to 30 per cent of national income

Table 3.1. *Approximate proportion of imports in domestic consumption of food and raw materials 1913 (per cent)*

Food	
Wheat	80
Meat	45
Dairy products	45
Raw materials	
Raw cotton	100
Raw wool	80
Iron ore	60
Tin	90
Lead	90
Copper	100*

Sources: These are ratios of retained imports to domestic utilisation. The import data are from *The Statistical Abstract of the United Kingdom for 1914*, pp. 126–61 and 214–37. Domestic wheat production and wool clip are from Mitchell & Deane (1962: 87 and 190). The meat data are from Hooker (1909: 332). The ratio for dairy products is composed of butter and cheese imports and the estimate of dairy output in Taylor (1976: 590). Data on the production of metals from domestic ores are from official statistics (*Stat. Abstract*, p. 336). In the case of iron the tonnage of pig iron produced from British ores has been compared with the sum of pig iron produced from foreign ores and the tons of iron and steel products imported. If the comparisons were based only on the pig iron produced in Britain imports would be just under half of inputs. The non-ferrous metals are calculated from the value of domestic output from British ores and the sum of the value of imported ores and metal

* Less than 0.5 per cent British ore

(see figure 3.1): at a minimum one out of every four pounds spent by Britons at the end of Victoria's reign was spent abroad, a higher share than in France or Germany, and much higher than in the United States. Some three quarters of all imports were foods and raw materials, frequently the only or the major source of British supply (see table 3.1). On the other side of the ledger, British exports consisted in the main of the products of a few major industries. Textiles of cotton, wool, and linen, which had contributed nearly three quarters of the value of exports at the beginning of the century, still contributed nearly 40 per cent by its end. Cotton alone, the prototypical industry of the industrial revolution, accounted for 25 per cent of all British commodity exports; iron and steel for 15 per cent and machinery another 7 per cent, smaller figures perhaps than one would expect from the metaphor of Britain as a nation of steam and steel, but nonetheless large. Coal became a major export during the century because industry and transport demanded fuel as they had not before, and Britain was well placed to supply it, earning thereby 10 per cent of all her exports. These 'old' industries of the industrial revolution – textiles, iron and steel, and coal – earned two thirds of British exports of commodities, and were themselves squarely turned towards the outside world. About 80 per cent of the cotton textiles made in Britain were exported, about half the iron and steel, and a third of the coal. With such exports of commodities, not forgetting the growing exports of services, Britain was fed. Of the £530 millions-worth of domestic commodity exports in 1913, nearly 80 per cent were, in the language of the Trade and Navigation Accounts, 'Articles Wholly or mainly Manufactures'. Of the £660 millions-worth of net commodity imports, only 25 per cent were manufactured articles that Britain did not make as well as others did, 33 per cent were raw materials to make manufactures, and the rest, fully 42 per cent, were foods. By means of foreign trade, in other words, Britain produced far more manufactures than it consumed and consumed far more food than it produced. As Clapham put it, 'The countries which fed, or nearly fed, themselves all had a much more even balance of agriculture with manufactures and commerce. A balance – or lack of balance – such as that in Britain had not been known before in the record of great nations' (Clapham 1938: Vol. III, 2).

Furthermore, Britain bulked so large in the trade of the world that events in Britain affecting her trade, such as the move to free trade in the middle decades of the century or the alleged failure of entrepreneurship at its end, might be expected to react on the British economy for good or evil with special force. That Britain was the pivot of international trade in the nineteenth century is apparent in the statistics of world trade in manufactures. In the decade 1876–85, the earliest dates for which usable statistics on the matter are available, Britain's exports of manufactured goods, her chief exports, were about 38 per cent of the world's total, and in earlier years the share had no doubt been larger (Hilgerdt 1945: 157–8). By 1899 her share had fallen, but was still about 33 per cent of the exports of manufactured goods from the industrial countries (Western Europe, Canada, the United States, and Japan) and India (Maizels 1963: 430–1). This position of dominance is unique in modern economic history, approached but not equalled only by the United States, whose share in the manufactured exports of the industrial countries and India in the seven years of Maizels' statistics (1899, 1913, 1929, 1937, 1950, 1955 and 1957) reached its peak – only 27 per cent – in 1950. Only after the First World War did the United States exceed Britain in exports of all kinds (with American wheat and British coal included in the accounting) and only after the Second World War in total exports of manufactures (Maizels, place cited; and pp. 10–11 in his 'Corrections').

Why Britain did not 'depend' on trade

Britain and the world, then, appear to have been mutually dependent. But 'dependent' suggests that removing foreign trade would have impoverished Britain. In particular, the statistics of 'dependence' suggest that removing trade would have cut national income by 25 or 30 per cent and would have cut British wheat consumption (for example) by 80 per cent – after all, these were the shares of foreign supplies in national income and in wheat consumption. The volume of a trade, however, is a poor guide to how much the economy's prosperity depends on it. You may hire a professional house painter to paint your house, but were you denied his services you would not lose all their value, because you would paint your house yourself, or spend the resources on the next best project. A Britain denied imports of wheat, similarly, would grow its own, albeit at greater expense than wheat from the fertile plains of Illinois or the Ukraine, or would shift resources to other, homegrown foods. The loss to British happiness would not be the whole value of the wheat imported.

The reasoning here is characteristically economic, focusing as it does on the alternatives to acquiring imports by trade. The more usual reasoning is non-economic, making exports, not imports, the thing-to-be-desired. One hears it said, for example, that Britain had to import corn and timber and wine in order to give foreigners the wherewithal to buy British. A person or nation fully employed, however, yearns to acquire goods, not to get rid of them. Exports are an unfortunate sacrifice that people or nations must make to acquire imports for consumption. As Adam Smith remarked in his attack on the mercantilist doctrine that an excess of exports over imports should be the goal of policy, 'Consumption is the sole end of and purpose of all production...The maxim is so perfectly self-evident, that it would be absurd to attempt to prove it' (Smith 1776: 625). If Britain's foreign trade can (as it must) be viewed as a way of acquiring imports, then the question of the extent of British dependence on trade reduces to a question of how well Britain would have done had this way to imports been blocked.

The answer has little significance in itself, for no historical issue turns on the literal abandonment of British foreign trade. Finding it, however, is useful as background to more modest experiments in counterfactuals and as a check on exaggerated opinions of Britain's dependence on trade. The answer proceeds as follows. Foreign trade can be viewed as an industry producing imports, say wheat, in exchange for sacrifices of exports, say cotton cloth. The 'productivity' of this industry is the rate at which quarters of wheat exchange for yards of cloth, i.e. the 'terms of trade'. The price of Britain's exports of cotton cloth, iron, coal, shipping services, and so forth divided by the price of imports of wheat, lumber, tobacco, raw cotton, and so forth is the terms of trade, and has the same relevance for British welfare as does a man's real wages. His money wage for his hour of work (what he exports) divided by the price of what he consumes (what he imports) is his real wage, i.e. the physical amounts of consumable goods he can buy per hour of work. The effect on national income of a change in the productivity of Britain's foreign trade (the terms of trade) depends on the importance of the foreign trade 'industry' relative to other, domestic industries. That is, it depends on the ratio of exports (or imports) to national income, which rose from about 0.12 early in the century to about 0.30 by its end. If the terms of trade rose by 10 per cent early in the century, therefore, national income would rise on this account by (10 per cent) × (0.12), or 1.2 per cent.

Table 3.2. *The terms of trade 1820–1910: a price index of exports divided by a price index of imports* (10-year averages; 1860 defined to be 100; for United Kingdom).

1820	170
1840	130
1860	100
1880	110
1900	130
1910 (8-year average)	130

Source: Imlah (1958: 95–8); rounded after averaging

This matter of concept settled, the remaining question is the counterfactual one of how much in fact the terms of trade would have moved had Britain insisted on growing all its own wheat, and by the same token consuming all its own cotton cloth. Clearly the price of now-abundant exportables like cloth would have fallen relative to the price of now-scarce importables like wheat. In other words, the terms of trade would have deteriorated. How much? The actual course of the terms of trade over the nineteenth century, shown in table 2.2, gives some guidance. The massive fall from 170 in 1820 to 100 in 1860 was a consequence of Britain's own ingenuity in making exported cotton cloth cheaper and of the push of population in Europe against supplies of grain. The small rise thereafter was a consequence of the full application of steam and steel to the making and, especially to the shipping of imports to Britain. In view of these 70 or 30 per cent rises and falls in the terms of trade we should be wary of supposing that the change in the terms of trade for self-sufficiency in say, 1860, was much lower or higher. But where exactly is difficult to say. Not much of a rise in the price of German toys relative to British clocks, perhaps 10 per cent, would have been necessary to stop shipments of either into or out of Britain. But quite a large rise would have been necessary to stop wheat coming in or textiles going out, so powerful in these goods were the forces of specialization. A tariff of fully 40 per cent was necessary to stop foreign corn from entering Britain in years of good harvest under the Corn Laws; a doubling of the price of cotton cloth exports during the cotton famine caused by the American Civil War abated demand by only a third, although the experiment is inconclusive because the prices of Britain's competitors in this market went up as well. All in all it would appear that a prohibition of trade might have reduced the price of exportables relative to importables by, say, 50 per cent at most. The share of imports in income to multiply the 50 per cent would be half of the way from zero, under the prohibition, to the 25 per cent that actually occurred in 1860. Self-sufficiency in 1860, then, would have cost Britain only (50 per cent) × (0.125) or about 6 per cent of national income.

Six per cent of national income looks small beside the bold metaphor of

Britain's 'dependence' on foreign trade. Indeed, the calculation is worthwhile only to loosen the grip of the metaphor (for other attempts see Kravis 1970; Crafts 1973; Kravis 1973). It seems likely that the gains from trade increased as British population grew and limited agricultural resources strengthened the comparative disadvantage in food production but even if the gains were twice those suggested above the conclusion remains that even on the quite absurd premise of no foreign trade at all Britain would have survived. True, had Britain suddenly been denied all trade by strike or edict the immediate effects would have been larger (cf. Crouzet 1958 and 1964; Olson 1963). The experiment relevant to all the history of this period except for times of war and blockade, however, is not a sudden denial of trade but a failure of it to grow over a long term, because it is precisely the steady and rapid growth over the long peace of 1815 to 1914 that has led people to attribute to foreign trade great powers for good. Its power for good might have been larger than 6 per cent even in the long run if by chance the people enriched by the extension of foreign trade, such as coal owners and cotton manufacturers, saved or invested more than the people impoverished by the trade, such as timber owners and silk manufacturers. But there is no persuasive evidence that the chances especially favoured foreign trade. Britain was left with its 6 per cent – no trivial sum, to be sure, but measured against the whole rise in output per worker of roughly 80 per cent from 1855 to 1913 it is only one thirteenth of the story.

The move to free trade

The dominant event in Britain's trade in the first half of the century is the abandonment of protection, especially during the years 1841 to 1881. The event is important in itself for political history, and illustrates the limits of foreign trade as an element in economic history.

During the forty years from Peel's to Gladstone's second ministry, the commercial policy of the United Kingdom moved decisively from fettered to free trade. National income rose decisively as well; the income of labour with it. It was no surprise to free traders, of course, that the removal of a pernicious tax on enterprise, most particularly on the enterprise of industrial labourers and capitalists, brought with it greater wealth for all. They were even willing to concede that only a portion of the greater wealth, though a substantial portion, was attributable to free trade. After all, it was not the promise of material well-being alone that buoyed their spirits in the struggle against protection. Their spiritual leader, Cobden, saw far beyond cheaper corn and better markets for British cotton textiles; he saw, indeed, 'in the Free Trade principle that which shall act on the moral world as the principle of gravitation in the universe – drawing men together, thrusting aside the antagonism of race and creed, and language, and uniting us in the bonds of eternal peace' (Hirst 1903: 229). Such cosmopolitan visions dimmed in later controversy, for, unlike the material promise, they had all too plainly not been fulfilled. Later critics of free trade, such as the 'fair trade' historian, William Cunningham, could in the 1900s emphasise the more selfish motivation for free trade, namely, the fixing of Britain's monopoly of manufactures on the rest of the world for a few more decades than its natural term (Cunningham 1910–11). Free traders could (and did) respond that great benefit accrued to Britain's trading partners as well. And in their more pragmatic moods the free traders were willing to make the selfish argument. In his testimony to the Select Committee on Import Duties in 1840, J. D. Hume argued that discouraging foreigners from supplying Britain with agricultural products encouraged them to turn instead to manufacturing. In a passage that foreshadows the gloom of many Englishmen half a century later, when the German and American threat had become plain, he argues that by protecting agriculture 'we place ourselves at the risk of being surpassed by the manufactures of other countries; and. . . I can hardly doubt that (when that day arrives) the prosperity of this country will recede faster than it has gone forward' (Parliamentary Papers, 1840, Q 1198, p. 206). But whether they believed free trade was merely a selfish policy or not, or as appropriate to the twentieth century as to the nineteenth, free trader and fair trader alike agreed that in the middle of the nineteenth century it could be justified if need be on selfish grounds alone: it had produced then, they believed, substantial material benefits for the nation.

Free trade had ideological and political effects, of course, and it would be idle to deny that these in turn may have had large effects on the economy: the constitution, for example, might not have survived the European revolutions of 1848 without the repeal of the Corn Laws in 1846. As we shall see presently, however, the direct economic effects have been exaggerated. Historians have naturally, if not always correctly, assumed that it matters economically how a great issue of economic policy such as this is resolved, the more so as the historical study of the issue has been left largely to political rather than economic historians. The history of economics itself has lent credence to this view of the importance of British commercial policy: since the inception of the discipline its best minds (many of them British) have put commercial policy at the centre of their thinking. The most impressive intellectual tools developed by Smith, Ricardo, Mill and Marshall were developed precisely for the examination of the effect of international trade and of government policy towards that trade on national income, and their practical motive was in large part the early encouragement and late defence of Britain's policy of free trade. The sheer weight of the intellectual achievement would incline an economist, like the historians, towards attributing great significance to free trade in the nineteenth century.

The first step in assessing the economic effects of the change in British commercial policy is to discover what it was and how it changed (Williams 1972).

The free trade movement began in earnest in the 1840s, the most dramatic event in its beginnings (although, despite its symbolic importance, not by itself constituting free trade) being the repeal of the Corn Laws on 26 June 1846. The 1840s are no exception to the historiographic rule that it is always possible to smooth the discontinuities of events by examining their preparations in the past. One can date the beginning of the ideological preparation, of course, at the appearance of *The Wealth of Nations* and the administrative preparation in the 1780s, with some tentative simplifications of a complex tariff inherited from an age in which as it has been put 'the British parliament seems rarely to rise to the dignity of a general proposition'. The Napoleonic Wars interrupted many trends in the British economy, among them these stirrings of a rational tariff policy. Every commodity or transaction within reach of the government was taxed and retaxed to fight the French, from dogs and attorneys to incomes and imports. One major tax alone, that on incomes – 'the oppressive and inquisitorial tax' as contemporaries knew it – was repealed with the peace, reducing the government to a policy of continuing other war taxes to meet payments on the national debt (over half of the budget down to the 1850s) and irreducible expenditures on the civil service. In 1820, Sydney Smith could write, after five years of peace, that 'the dying Englishman, pouring his medicine, which has paid 7 per cent, into a spoon that has paid 15 per cent, flings himself back upon his chintz bed which has paid 22 per cent, and expires in the arms of an apothecary who has paid a license of a hundred pounds for the privilege of putting him to death' (Smith, 1820).

What few changes were made during the next twenty years in the role of customs revenues in this mélange of taxes were accomplished largely by Huskisson's budgets of 1824 and 1825: obsolete duties were repealed on imports of manufactured commodities such as cotton textiles and iron (for which Britain had in any case a crushing comparative advantage), some duties on raw materials were reduced, many export bounties were abolished, and most prohibitions, except those on certain agricultural products, were abolished as well. The goal was rationalisation more than reduction – who, after all, could quarrel with a programme of removing contradictory or inoperative duties? – and even this modest programme was far from complete in 1840 (Clapham 1910). The Select Committee on Import Duties (filled with free traders, who had of late become a formidable political force) reported that, in 1839, 17 of 721 articles in the tariff schedule produced 94.5 per cent of the tariff revenue (Parliamentary Papers, 1840, p. 102). This was a Benthamite calculation: the tariff revenue, it argued, could be collected more efficiently even without a fundamental change in commercial policy. By 1840 the hard political decision to move to lower rather than merely simpler duties – involving as it did the reimposition of the income tax, the removal of duties discriminating in favour of the colonies, and, hardest of all, the abandonment of protection to agriculture – had yet to be made. Even with these rationalisations the tariff on the eve of the move to free trade was complex. It contained prohibitions on imports of live or dead meat, duties on 'slave-grown' sugar two or more times higher than those on sugar from British colonies, drawbacks on timber for use in the mines of Cornwall or in churches, 80-odd different specifications of skins, from badger to weasel, with associated duties, export duties on coal and wool, and over 2000 import duties on items ranging from agates to zebra wood.

Despite the bewildering detail, however, the thrust of the tariff is relatively clear. Its protective effect was felt primarily in land-intensive products, these being in any case the dominant products of importation: late in the nineteenth century, under a regime of free trade and of increasing foreign competition in manufactures, nearly four fifths by value of British net imports were land-intensive raw materials and food. In other words, the categories of the simple theory of trade – importables, exportables, and non-traded goods – correspond well in Victorian Britain with agriculture (including some mining), manufacturing, and the residual sector, services. The Navigation Acts (repealed in 1849) protected shipping services, to be sure, but it is doubtful whether the protection was by this time important for the industry, particularly for its more modern branches. A few manufacturing industries, notably silk manufacturing, received substantial protection in the tariff, but, for most, protection would have been superfluous. Indeed, by 1840 the effective rate of protection for factors of production specialised in manufacturing was slightly negative: as free traders pointed out, Britain's exports of manufactures contained raw materials made more expensive by tariffs, whether for revenue on warm-climate raw materials such as raw cotton, for the good of the empire and its land owners on cold-climate materials such as Canadian timber, or for the protection of British rents on metals such as copper and tin ore. The British tariff in the early 1840s, then, raised the price of land-intensive raw materials and food relative to manufactures and services. A tariff designed by committees of landlords in Parliament and imposed on the imports of a nation that required from the rest of the world little but raw materials and food could hardly be expected to achieve any other result (Fairlie 1965 and 1969).

The tariff in the early 1840s, furthermore, bulked large in British economic and political life: it was high and imports were substantial in relation to national income and the revenues from taxing them were a significant fraction of the revenues of the central government. The height of the tariff and the changes in its height may be measured by the ratio of tariff revenues to the value of imports, as in the first row of table 3.3. The rest of the table tells another story, of why and how free trade occurred: the fall in the tax requirements of the government (from 0.09 to 0.06 of income) and the rise in the ratio of imports to income (from 0.12 to 0.30), itself only partly due to falling tariffs, made it easy to charge low taxes on the larger imports. But the main point here is to have a measure of the

Table 3.3. *Tax rates and the ratio of imports to national income, UK 1841 and 1881*

	1841	1881
Rate of import duties	0.27	0.06
Ratio of imports to national income	0.12	0.30
Ratio of all tax revenues to income	0.09	0.06

Source: McCloskey (1979). The rate of import duties in 1841 is calculated using the shares of various products in total imports of 1881. This manoeuvre reduces the bias due to faster growth in the physical volume of low-duty imports (raw cotton especially).

decline in the tariff, namely, from 27 per cent of the value of imports in 1841 to only 6 per cent in 1881.

The first effect is obvious, in view of the weight of the protection to land-intensive goods that the early tariff gave: by abandoning high tariffs British landlords lost income relative to their countrymen. Political argument at that time took it as axiomatic that what landlords lost the workers would gain, because protection of British corn producers was a tax on the mainstay of the workers' diet. In the event the real wages of workers did rise sharply after the 1840s, but real rents of landlords did not fall. Neither event is strictly relevant, for the historical experiment was not a controlled experiment in which all factors except tariffs were held constant. It is doubtful that a controlled experiment would have produced the required symmetry between the incomes of landlord and of worker, because they were not in fact symmetrically located in the British economy. Landlords were located, of course, in agriculture. But workers were located everywhere: in the very agriculture made worse off by the fall of protection, in the manufacturing made better off, and what is most important in the vast sector of goods and (especially) services that did not cross Britain's borders on their way from producer to consumer. Rich countries in the nineteenth century and after spent roughly half of their income on such intrinsically domestic things as houses, police, beer, servants, schools, roads, railways, canals, and so forth. Workers were not committed to one, vulnerable sector. The consequence is that changes in the tariff could affect workers as a group mainly by way of the effect on the size of national income, not on its distribution among sectors. Most of the distributional consequence of the fall of protection was to shift income from wealthy landlords committed to agriculture to wealthy capitalists committed to manufacturing, and even this was no dramatic amount.

The second effect of the fall in tariffs from 27 to 6 per cent of the value of imports is the effect on the size of national income, and is less obvious. Even its direction is in doubt, although free traders past and present have had no doubts whatever. Surely a man is made worse off if he artificially restricts his dealings with the rest of the world. So too, they argued for the nation. British landlords may be made better off by a tariff on corn, but because the nation as a whole must be worse off with less access to corn the worsening of the rest of the nation is necessarily larger. The argument implies that every extension of British trade, and therefore every reduction in tariffs, was good for Britain (Habakkuk 1940). The argument is flawed. If Britain bulked large in the world's work, as it most certainly did in 1841, then it would be in Britain's interest to somewhat restrict its trade, just as a monopolist will do. In such a case the move to free trade would sacrifice the advantages of monopoly. The case fits the facts: Britain was the world's largest consumer of raw cotton and producer of finished cloth; it was a larger if not the largest consumer of wheat and producer of machinery. Britain had a unique position of monopoly at mid-century, which by abandoning protection it magnanimously scorned to exploit. Paradoxically, it was only late in the century when the monopoly was gone forever that protection recovered its earlier political appeal. In the time of greatest enthusiasm for free trade the usual argument is probably the reverse of the truth: if anything, the move towards free trade in the 1840s and 1850s hurt Britain.

The hurt was not large. At the extreme Britain's monopoly was so powerful that the tariff of 1841 pushed the world price of British exports relative to British imports up by the full extent of the tariff. That is, a tariff of 21 per cent on the free trade price of wheat could at the most lower the world price of wheat by 21 per cent (21 per cent is the difference between the actual tariffs in 1841 and 1881), which is to say it could at most raise the relative price of British exports by 21 per cent. To abandon such an advantageous tariff in favour of free trade would reduce Britain's terms of trade by 21 per cent. By a familiar line of reasoning, then, the hurt would be at most this reduction multiplied by the share of imports in national income, which was 30 per cent at most. The hurt was at most, then, 21 per cent multiplied by 30 per cent, or about 6 per cent. Such a small gift to the rest of the world could easily be offset by the positive effects of free trade such as the reaping of economies of scale in export industries or employment of pools of unemployed labour or a raise in the savings rate consequent on redistribution. That none of these left clear evidence in the historical record is merely testimony to the small size, whether positive or negative, of the effects of free trade on income (cf. Church 1975a: 59–65). The conclusion must be that accumulation and productivity at home, not free trade, were the key to mid-Victorian prosperity.

Exports as an engine of decline

If we do not believe that Britain's rise to workshop of the world before 1870 depended on foreign trade then it is less easy to believe that Britain's relative decline after 1870 depended on foreign trade. Yet the belief is widespread, as we have seen. The rate of growth of industrial production and of income in Britain declined at about the same time that the growth of exports declined; Britain's growth on all scores was slower than that of her 'rivals' (as Germany and the United States came increasingly to be called). These two observations have led many to suggest that the one decline in exports *caused* the other decline in income and industry. In the 1890s especially the editorial pages and parliamentary debates spoke of 'defeat' in a German commercial 'invasion', or of the 'conquest' by Americans of another 'outpost' of British exports (Hoffman 1933). The military metaphor has proven irresistible to later students of the matter, the more so as the less colourful testimony of the statistics of foreign trade seems to agree. Suggestive though it is, that growth at home followed exports abroad does not mean that exports caused growth (nor, as we shall see in the next section, that growth caused exports). The brute fact is not enough. The interpretation of the fact depends on whether or not the British economy at its successive peaks of boom and bust in the late nineteenth century was fully employed. In a fully employed economy an increase in demand for, say, exported cloth does increase the output of cloth, but only by reducing the output of some other, domestic commodity. In the quaint language of economics, in such an economy there is no such thing as a free lunch. An increase in demand for exports can cause little increase in total output, merely a reallocation of resources and a restructuring of output. Under such a constraint, as we have seen repeatedly, events in the international sector can have little influence on the size of national income. The present case is no exception. If the late Victorian economy was fully employed it is no trick at all to show that the 'defeat' at the hands of Germans and Americans in export markets was a trivial cause of slower British growth (cf. McCloskey 1970–71).

If the economy was not fully employed, however, an increase in export demand would have increased the nation's income not only directly, by setting men and machines to work in making ships and coal and machinery for export, but also indirectly, by setting men and machines to work in making steel for the shipyards and pit props for the collieries and machine tools for the machine shops, as well as food, housing, transport, and so forth for the men now earning and spending incomes. Buoyant export demand gave the economy a free lunch; sagging export demand took it away. The assumption of less than full employment is well-suited to the understanding of an economy coming out of bust and moving into a boom, for it is plain in such a case that new workers are indeed being drawn out of involuntary idleness as the economy expands (cf. ch. 2). It is at least doubtful, however, whether the assumption is suited to understanding growth between peaks of the cycle of boom and bust (Matthews 1954a: 79). Doubts on this score have not deterred students of the late Victorian economy, especially economists (Rostow 1948; Coppock 1961), from trying it on. Meyer (1955), for example, noted the sequence of the deceleration of exports and of industrial production, and asked whether maintaining the mid-Victorian growth rate of exports would have maintained the growth rate of industry in late Victorian Britain. Generalising the notion that ships for exports require steel, which requires coal, which requires pit props, and so forth in a gradually diminishing ripple throughout the economy, Meyer constructed a so-called 'input–output table' from the First (1907) British Census of Production in order to measure what the indirect effects would have been of greater exports. He found them to be large. But the conclusion is unacceptable, on several minor technical matters, which need not detain us, and on one major substantive matter. The substantive matter is that the Meyer exercise, like others less explicit in their assumptions, assumes without evidence that the economy was not fully employed. As McCloskey argued (1970) the evidence suggests otherwise; there were simply no large reserves of unemployed resources that could have been set to work if export demand had been larger. The limits on the late Victorian economy, in other words, were limits of supply.

The argument linking export deceleration with late Victorian decline has not depended exclusively on the existence of unemployed resources. It has also been argued that sluggish markets for exports reduced the scope for investment in export industries at home and drove British savings (already low by international standards) overseas, to Indian railways or Brazilian plantations. The private return from such reallocation of resources, it is said, was satisfactory, but the social return was not (D. J. Coppock 1956: 2). Even if this last is true, however, it does not follow that the effects of misallocating savings were large. In the article critical of Meyer, McCloskey examined as well these alternative links in the chain from exports to economic growth in Britain and found them weak. His arguments have been criticised by Kennedy (1974), who contends that McCloskey underestimated the effects of reallocating savings and the labour force in response to more buoyant export demand, and by Crafts (1979), who contends that he underestimated the effect on capital formation of bringing savings home. Nonetheless, it seems clear at present that a simple connection of exports to income is untenable, and that, in short, 'it is implausible...to draw the lines of causation in late Victorian England from export demand to the output of the economy' (McCloskey 1970: 459).

Foreign trade as evidence of decline

Foreign trade, then, does not appear to have been an engine of growth and decline. It is nonetheless an important fact about the British economy, a large sector among a few illustrating the economy's strengths and weaknesses in plain form. The illustrative role of foreign trade in writings on British history is largest at the end of the nineteenth century, when its share in national income was largest.

In every year after 1822 the value of Britain's commodity imports exceeded the value of commodity exports. Both contemporaries and historians became aware that the growing deficit in commodity trade was more than covered by receipts from the international sale of shipping, commercial, and financial services, and by the interest and dividends from foreign assets (see figure 3.1). In fact there was a substantial overall surplus from these receipts to finance foreign lending. Many, however, have seen the slow growth of commodity exports and the rapid growth of imports as evidence of a competitive failure in Britain. Many studies of British industries have focused on the emergence of a foreign challenge in the late nineteenth century and the inability to maintain competitive positions in export markets. Mathias (1969: 315–16) summarised the prevailing view:

The conclusion to be drawn from Britain's accounts with the rest of the world in 1913 is to see to what a great extent the economy was being protected, or cushioned from the failure of exports to pay for imports, by the £4,000 million of capital invested abroad... Even quite a marked degree of failure in the competitive standards of some British export industries might be tolerated without much strain, as long as the £200 million came in interest each year.

Although it is artificial to ignore in this way the spectacular successes in exporting services (the deficit of £130 million on British commodity trade in 1913, for example, was more than made up by a £190 million surplus on service trade), the fixation on commodity trade and its failures is usual. The impression of weakness in Britain's export performance and by inference its industrial performance is enhanced by the market and commodity structure of British exports. Britain's exports throughout the nineteenth century, as we have noted, were heavily concentrated in a few basic industries that had been at the forefront of the industrial revolution. Exports remained concentrated in these industries up to the war, with textiles, iron and steel, and coal – the 'old' industries – contributing two thirds of export earnings. To look at it another way, these few exporting industries were heavily oriented toward export markets. The dependence of export earnings on a few industries whose technology had been set during the industrial revolution and whose prosperity was dependent on export markets has been seen as a weakness in the British economy of the early twentieth century (Aldcroft 1965). 'Over-commitment', it is said, produced a vulnerability to change in international conditions, for newly industrialising countries were protecting and attempting to stimulate domestically these very industries. Their predominance in Britain made adjustment of the economy toward the newer light engineering industries, emerging around 1900 as technological leaders, more difficult.

The British economy, in other words, appears to have maintained its traditional industries instead of taking advantage of the new technologies. When tariffs and domestic industrialisation severely curtailed sales to traditional markets in Europe and the United States, new export markets were found elsewhere. In the 1850s customers in Western and Central Europe and the United States had purchased over 40 per cent of Britain's exports. In 1870 these customers still took nearly 40 per cent of British exports, but by 1910 the proportion had declined to well under 30 per cent. In contrast, British exports found customers in Empire markets and in areas of Latin America and Asia where less formal but still important ties bound primary producing areas to Britain. The British specialisation in less sophisticated markets worried observers. Nor were foreign markets the only problem. By the early twentieth century, foreign manufactured goods were becoming increasingly evident in Britain. Shipbuilders and other users of steel were buying from German firms. American engineering products were finding British markets. Surely something had gone wrong. Many began to believe that the British entrepreneur had failed, or that the policy of free trade was a mistake.

The exploration of the belief in British failure is the task of chapter 1. Here the point is that these conclusions do not necessarily follow from the observed patterns of trade. It seems more likely, in fact, that the primary cause of the late nineteenth century trade pattern was the emergence of the new staple exporters in Asia and the Americas. Falling transportation costs and the expansion of production in these areas drastically transformed the supply of primary products to Europe, and European trade patterns adjusted. These growing staple producing areas drew large amounts of British capital, which, in turn, generated the large inflow of interest and dividends to Britain; and the export of staple products required British shipping, financial and commercial services.

In this and in similar cases, then, conclusions about economic performance cannot be easily drawn from patterns of trade. Trade arises from comparative advantage, not absolute advantage. That is, Britain exported the things it could produce cheaply relative to the other things it could produce – cheap coal, cotton goods, insurance, shipping relative to food, timber, and in the end steel – not necessarily the things that it could produce with less labour or capital than could other nations. So efficient was British agriculture, for example, that Britain could have produced food using less resources than were used to produce it in Argentina or Illinois. But it would have been foolish to do so in 1900, as Britain's continued adherence to free trade then recognised. A better use for British resources was the making of machinery and insurance policies. The 'failure' of Britain to export food and the 'decline' in the size of agriculture (cf. Olson and Harris 1959; and chapter 8) and the 'invasion' of British markets by imports was no sign of technological inferiority in agriculture. So too elsewhere in the economy.

It is worthwhile to underline the conclusion. The pattern of British trade in the late nineteenth century reflected more the world that Britain dealt with than any peculiar new development in the British economic character. The increase in the supply of food and raw materials came from distant, often frontier, areas. By mid-century the innovations in steam power and metallurgy were applied to transportation, and the new railroads and steam-ships dramatically lowered transportation costs over the next half century. As transportation costs fell, a given Liverpool price meant a higher local price in many remote areas of the world. Now the production of staple foodstuffs and raw materials became profitable in areas that had previously been unattractive (Harley 1979; but see Olson 1974). The spread of specialised agriculture and raw material production into distant areas involved the movement of people and the construction of transportation and distribution networks. Because the investment required to build railroads and cities to serve such frontiers as the plains of North and South America far exceeded the resources available there most of the capital was drawn from older areas. British investors found the securities issued by overseas railroads and governments attractive investments and bought them in large amounts. Nearly 70 per cent of the foreign securities issued in London in the late nineteenth century were to finance railroads and other forms of overhead capital (see chapter 4). The staple production for markets in the industrialised regions of Europe and North America increased the demand for various mercantile and financial services. The staple products had to be marketed, financed, insured and transported. British firms already had experience in these fields and the large investments of British capital in the development of the exporting regions further directed this demand toward British firms. Because British-owned ships made up about half of the world's merchant marine the increase in demand for shipping also generated business for British firms.

The commodity composition and the markets of British exports and the bilateral payments patterns at the end of the nineteenth century also reflected the impact of the development of new areas of staple supply. Britain's surplus of imports from Europe and America and relatively large exports to the staple exporting areas – including, importantly, India – had their counterpart in the import surpluses that Europe incurred with all the primary exporters and the United States with the tropics (Saul 1960: chs. III, IV; Hilgerdt 1942). The pattern of multilateral trade balances around 1910 is presented in figure 2.2.

Britain's deficits with the industrial economies and surpluses with the primary producing economies were part of a world settlement pattern. Other industrial

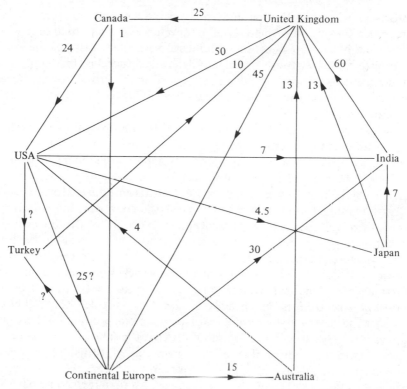

3.2 World pattern of settlements 1910 (£m)
Note: The arrows point to the country of each pair having a surplus with the other,
indicating therefore the direction of the flow of settlement. Thus the United Kingdom
had a surplus of £60m in trade and payments with India.
Source: Saul (1960: 58).

economies balanced deficits with the primary producing areas by running
surpluses with Britain. Interpretation of this pattern is not obvious for it could
have emerged and been maintained in more than one way. Those who see
weakness in the British economy see the trade pattern emerging because British
firms had lost the ability to compete in the markets of developed countries. Ties
of formal and informal empire, it is said, allowed increasingly non-competitive
British firms to sell in primary producing countries. Imperialism supported the
sale of non-competitive exports.

Saul (1960: 62) and Hilgerdt (1942 and 1943) in their studies of world trade
see the pattern quite differently. '[The] world-wide interconnecting network of
trade [emerged] in the last three decades of the nineteenth century mainly from
the rapid growth of primary producing countries and the demand for their

products arising in Europe and America.' As imports of primary products increased Europe and America had to develop exports to finance new imports. Since the means for effecting multilateral settlement existed, these countries exploited comparative advantage multilaterally rather than bilaterally. Germany and America's competitive advantage lay not in the products demanded by the primary producers, but in the products of new industries in demand in developed economies.

British exports remained the products of the old industries of the Industrial Revolution and sold outside the industrial nations while Germany and America gained markets in new industrial products and exported increasing amounts to industrial markets. This pattern appears to have emerged from three characteristics of the late nineteenth century. First, tariffs on industrial products inhibited British manufacturing exports to the industrial countries; but with British free trade there was no symmetrical disincentive on exports to Britain. Second, many of the areas of primary production had expanded with the aid of British capital and commercial expertise. The import trades of these areas were, thus, orientated towards Britain. Third, when British industries were compared with their German and American counterparts it was clear that Britain's competitive position was strongest in certain old industries – textiles, shipbuilding, heavy engineering, and even some branches of ferrous metal production. This advantage appears to have been based on the skills that the labour force had developed over a century of industrial experience. Even though British firms appeared old fashioned in their use of skilled labour and comparative shunning of new machine processes, they produced at a lower cost than they could have achieved with more mechanised methods, or than was achieved elsewhere. In newer branches of industry Britain did not enjoy the advantage of existing skills. Here mechanised production was the rule in Britain, as elsewhere, and Britain had no advantage (Harley 1974). In short, because it industrialised first Britain's comparative advantage lay in the old industries while its rivals' comparative advantage lay in the newer industries. And notice again that this finding about comparative advantage provides no insight into the relative technological or economic efficiency of production in the various countries. Investigation of that issue requires detailed investigation of the technological choices that the industries faced (see chapter 5). The multilateral settlement pattern, then, reflected the process of economic expansion outside Europe and the accident of precedence in industrial growth.

Britain's concentration on exporting products of the old industries to primary producing countries appears to have been part of the working of the international economy. But were there not costs of 'over-commitment'? The concentration in a few industries was the legacy of the lead that Britain had achieved in the industrial revolution. Britain's technological precocity allowed her industries to supply a substantial portion of world industrial demand in historical circumstances where that demand was highly concentrated in a few commodities.

With the benefit of hindsight we can see that twentieth century Britain has paid a considerable price for the industrial concentration that led to the large exports of a few commodities to relatively few markets by the eve of the First World War. Unemployment in the inter-war economy was concentrated in these old industries, because labour that had been drawn to these industries in the pre-war period could not be moved costlessly to other employments. The loss to the economy was enormous. This does not, however, imply that the industrial structure prior to the war was necessarily wrong. Even if we leave aside the issue of the management of the international value of the British pound in the inter-war period – perhaps no small leaving aside – it is not clear that hindsight is appropriate for historical judgement. To be sure, adjustment would have had to occur even without the trauma of the war and the associated disruption of an international system in which Britain was so much involved; but it would have been a slower adjustment. The British economy was beginning to adjust long before the war. Traditional industries were becoming less important as a proportion of national income and of foreign earnings. It is of course unfortunate that much of the shift went into international services that depended on a stable international economic environment, shaken by the war and its aftermath. And it is an irony of history that the interests of these service industries heavily influenced the suicidal exchange rate policy of the inter-war years.

Perhaps an appropriate question to ask is: Would an omniscient, but not prescient, planner have made a different choice than the British economy actually made through the workings of atomistic markets? That question surely does not demand an affirmative answer. Britain's international specialisation conformed to her comparative advantage: there were gains from trade that would have been lost by some alternative structure. The newer industries that expanded relatively slowly in Britain were the wave of the future and were industries where technological change was developing most rapidly. But that does not imply that the economy should have shifted to its future structure more rapidly. The concentration of export markets and the concentration in industries certainly increased the risk to the economy – as the inter-war period dramatically revealed – and a cautious planner might have chosen to forego present gains from trade to reduce this risk. But it certainly turns most of the historical literature on its head to suggest that the structure of the British economy before the First World War was inappropriate, not because of excess caution being exhibited through the market decisions, but rather paucity of caution.

4

Foreign investment and empire 1860–1914

M. EDELSTEIN

Great Britain's immense capital export is among the most important historical phenomena of the period between 1860 and 1914. Rising in the 1850s and 1860s, the flow of net foreign investment averaged about a third of the nation's annual accumulations from 1870 to 1914. As a result of these annual flows, the stock of net overseas assets grew from around 8 per cent of the stock of wealth owned by Britons at home and abroad in the mid 1850s to around 17 per cent in 1870 and then to around 33 per cent in 1913. Never before or since has one nation committed so much of its national income and savings to capital formation abroad.

To some observers the immense capital export went abroad because of the high profitability of railroad and other social overhead investments in the emerging primary product economies of North America, South America, and Australasia. Others have argued that the capital export was a result of weaknesses in the domestic British economy. According to this view, Britons continued to save despite slowing British investment demand and the funds moved abroad by default.

If there is controversy about the reasons for the immense capital export, there is also controversy concerning its effects. On the positive side, it is often argued that the capital exports paid a higher private rate of return than domestic investment and, given a secularly low unemployment rate, it thus augmented British incomes more strongly than alternative domestic investments. Furthermore, by helping to lower the costs of overseas transport and extending the margin of cultivation and mineral extraction into hitherto inaccessible but highly productive soils and deposits, British capital exports helped to lower the cost of British imports of food and raw materials. Sceptics, however, have argued that the capital export may have had a number of pernicious effects. First, some have argued that, in fact, the realised return from investment abroad was lower than at home due to widespread defaults by spendthrift overseas governments and railway executives. Second, it is sometimes argued that the distribution of British incomes was more sharply skewed by directing British savings abroad. Had these funds remained at home they would have helped to augment the stock of domestic housing and other urban social overhead projects which would have more widely benefited the British populace than the uses to which the overseas profits were employed. Finally, modern studies of technical progress have found that an important source of productivity growth stems from the accumulated experience of production, often termed 'learning-by-doing'. If, as seems to be the case, British capital exports tended to increase the demand for the products of the older export industries, it might be argued that to some degree the newer segments of the British capital goods industry were inadvertently starved of demand during their infant and later learning years, with consequent effects on the growth rate of British per capita incomes.

The period from 1860 to 1914 is also notable for the continued expansion of the British empire and of British political influence in the independent nations of the underdeveloped world. Expansion of the British Empire in the seventeenth and eighteenth centuries had often involved competition with Holland, France, Portugal, and Spain. During the first three quarters of the nineteenth century, British expansion was largely a quiet, uncompetitive affair. In the last quarter of the nineteenth century expansion again took place within what can only be termed an international scramble. Britain's rivals were Belgium, France, Germany, Italy, Japan, Portugal, Russia, Spain, and the United States; most of these nations were either among the most advanced industrial economies of the day or were making strong, government-supported efforts to move in that direction. Also unique to the expansion of the late nineteenth century was the fact that the newly acquired territories were not open, sparsely settled ranges in the temperate zones of the world, but areas either so densely populated or ecologically inhospitable that they did not permit extensive agricultural settlement by Europeans. By contrast to the diminished political autonomy involved in the late nineteenth century extensions of empire in Africa and Asia, from the mid nineteenth century onward the older white-settler colonies gradually acquired more and more autonomy, formalised in the grant of Dominion status.

The maintenance and expansion of the empire presents a number of important issues. For example, did the pace and character of the domestic British economy influence the continued expansion of the formal empire during these years? Did Britain have a substantial 'informal' empire, regions of the independent underdeveloped world where British political and economic influence was strong? The difficulty, in fact, is that there are too many important questions to give each of them their due. Thus, in the section on the economics of empire which closes this chapter, the problem which receives most attention is whether the British Empire represented a net gain or loss to the domestic economy, rather than these wider questions; but they must not be forgotten just because they are difficult to answer.

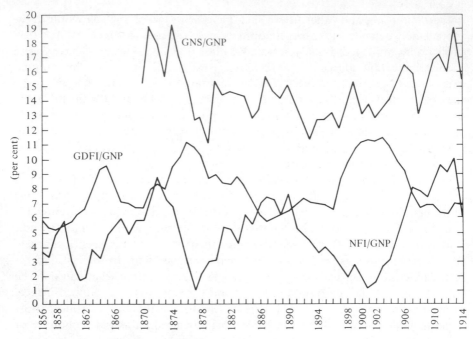

4.1   UK rates of saving and investment 1856–1914
For definitions see Table 4.1, p. 77

The pattern of foreign investment

Net long-term lending by Great Britain is thought to have made its first significant and sustained appearance in the 1820s (Cottrell 1975). In the seventeenth and eighteenth centuries joint-stock trading and colonising companies, interloping merchants, and the individual owners of West and East Indian plantations gathered a certain amount of long-term funds for ships, warehouses, plantations, and slaves. Wealthy Britons may also have held a certain amount of interest bearing debt of various European governments. But these outflows of long-term capital were roughly balanced or possibly surpassed by inflows of Dutch and other foreign funds.

Net foreign investment averaged a little less than 2 per cent of the gross national product from 1811 to 1850, but in the 1850s the rate rose to 3.3 per cent and in the 1860s rose again to 4.0 per cent (Feinstein, 1978). From 1870 to 1914, the average rate was 5.2 per cent. Clearly, there was a major shift in the nature of British capital accumulation in the third quarter of the nineteenth century.

A second feature of British overseas investment in the late nineteenth and early twentieth centuries was its volatility. As figure 4.1 illustrates, this volatility was set in a repeating pattern of long cycles lasting between 16 and 24 years. From troughs of 1.6 per cent of GNP in 1861, 0.9 per cent in 1877, and 1.1 per cent in 1901, the rate of overseas investment went to peaks of 8.8 per cent in 1872, 7.7 per cent in 1890 and 10.1 per cent in 1913. Up to the early 1870s, the broad fluctuations in the rate of overseas investment roughly paralleled the fluctuations in the rate of domestic investment, but thereafter the long swings in overseas and home investment moved inversely.

Overseas investment is called 'portfolio investment' when the assets purchased are either the debentures of governments or the equity and debentures of private enterprises in which Britons own less than 30 per cent of the equity interest. When Britons own more than 30 per cent of the equity interest in an overseas private enterprise, their holdings of the latter's equity and debentures are termed direct investments. Before the nineteenth century and after 1945 most overseas investment took the form of direct investment in overseas structures, land, plant, equipment, and inventories by British businesses primarily engaged in Britain. Between those dates the bulk of British overseas investment took the form of British purchases of portfolio capital (Cottrell 1975; Stone 1977: 696). Furthermore, when Britons made direct investments equity ownership was held by a large number of private individuals rather than large British businesses. Why was British overseas investment in the nineteenth and early twentieth centuries predominantly portfolio and, when it was direct, with British ownership so widely dispersed? The explanation probably lies in the nature and size of the real capital which was purchased with British funds.

Between 1865 and 1914 almost 70 per cent of British new portfolio investment went into social overhead capital (railways, docks, tramways, telegraphs and telephones, gas and electric works, etc.) and 12 per cent went into extractive industries (agriculture and mining) (Simon 1967). Very little, 4 per cent, went into manufacturing. Social overhead capital is lumpy; that is the initial size necessary to give service, let alone to make a profit, is very large relative to the resources of either wealthy individuals or businesses. Consequently, it has rarely been constructed with the personal resources of a few individuals or businesses. The typical borrower for social overhead capital projects in modern times has been either a government or a large joint stock company. Indeed, the institutions of joint stock organisation and public issue of securities were created in the early seventeenth century, at least in part, as a private solution to the problem of the size and risk of social overhead projects and the resources of individual wealth holders. (See vol. I, ch. 12.) In the mid nineteenth century, the principal overseas borrowers for social overhead capital projects were either governments or mixed government–private enterprises (Simon 1967). During the second half of the nineteenth century, however, the trend was toward placements in wholly private, limited liability companies, probably reaching over 50 per cent of social overhead borrowings by 1914. Although the lumps of real investment in the extractive industries are much smaller than social overhead capital, their risks are much larger. Issuing portfolio capital in small denominations represented an efficient method for the original owners and new investors to diversify these high risks.

During the period 1865–1914, 34 per cent of the total new overseas portfolio capital issued in Britain went to North America, 17 per cent to South America, 14 per cent to Asia, 13 per cent to Europe, 11 per cent to Australasia, and 11 per cent to Africa (Simon 1967). Of the total of overseas portfolio assets accumulated in 1913 computed at par (face) value (Feis, 1930: 23), the largest national or colonial receivers were the United States (20.0 per cent), Canada and Newfoundland (13.7 per cent), India and Ceylon (10.0 per cent), South Africa (9.8 per cent), Australia (9.4 per cent), Argentina (8.5 per cent), and Brazil (3.9 per cent). The bulk (68 per cent) of the new trans-European investment went to regions of recent settlement, regions with a disproportionate demand for infrastructure and social overhead capital (Simon 1967).

Except for the United States, British investment in particular countries or colonies between 1865 and 1914 tended to be concentrated in short periods of time. Thus, the greater part of British investment in Australia occurred in the 1880s and early 1890s, in Canada after 1900, in South Africa in the early 1900s, and in Europe in the early 1870s and just before the First World War. Hall (1963) attributed this spurt-like involvement of British capital to the flexibility of British investors who shifted their horizons in the wake of the appearance of new opportunities. Unquestionably, British investors were quite flexible in this respect, but the nature of the opportunities was also important. To some extent the 'one-shot' pattern of British overseas investment reflected the lumpiness of the social overhead needs of the regions of recent settlement, their initially limited savings resources, and their immature capital markets. In a small country recently settled, a large backlog of lumpy social overhead capital projects might have to accumulate before the return was sufficiently great to draw attention to the need for the special funding arrangements just mentioned. Going overseas for some of the entrepreneurship and capital might then be thought of as the cheapest means of arranging for these lumpy projects, and this would lead to a spurt of foreign investment. Later economic development either did not generate as many lumpy social overhead projects or local savings and capital markets were now able to handle the lumps that did appear.

The US import of British capital was also variable but it was continuous. Given the size and pace of the aggregate movements in the US economy and its expansion into unsettled territory until the end of the nineteenth century, the continuous flow of British capital is not surprising. The major use of British funds was either for lumpy social overhead capital projects in the newly settled regions or the purchase of new issues of the older US regions, thereby allowing Americans to purchase the frontier issues.

The causes of foreign investment

In the late nineteenth and early twentieth centuries, there were roughly two views about why overseas investment had surged to such heights. One stream of thought relied upon classical economic thought and saw the money flowing abroad because the rate of return on European capital had finally reached diminishing returns. By the late nineteenth century many observers were aware that technical change might limit or prevent a fall in rates of return, but the idea hung on that at some point there would be more natural resource and industrial projects abroad with high returns than at home and the resulting differential in marginal returns would cause an outflow of capital. The essential ingredient of this view is that capital moved abroad because of a difference in rates of return. However, there was some dispute as to whether the funds were pushed out by fading domestic returns or pulled out by eruptively high overseas returns.

The second stream of thought is best represented by J. A. Hobson's work (1902). Hobson held that because too little of the national income was allocated to wage earners who did most of the nation's consumption and too much income was allocated to property owners who did most of the nation's saving, there was a strong tendency for a prosperous Britain to generate too little consumption and too much savings. The crucial assumption was that property owners saved irrespective of the rates of return they received. Given this invariance to rates of return and a tendency to generate too much savings, funds were inevitably pushed abroad searching for any use. Thus Hobson saw the rise in the rate of net overseas investment as an indication of inadequate domestic aggregate demand; this stemmed directly from an inadequate aggregate demand for consumption goods and indirectly from the fall in demand for capital which would have been used to produce these goods.

In sum, the literature suggests that there were two possible reasons for funds being pushed out of Britain: fading domestic returns and surplus savings, and a single reason for funds being pulled from abroad, eruptively high overseas returns.

As already noted, the rate of net foreign investment first jumped to significant levels in the 1850s and 1860s. It would appear that during this first period overseas flows were pulled abroad by eruptively high overseas returns rather than pushed by fading domestic returns or an excess of British savings, invariant to rates of return.

First of all, there were a large number of regions abroad undergoing economic growth with high demands for social overhead capital, relatively small local savings pools, and immature capital market facilities for bringing these pools and the lumpy social overhead projects together. In Australia the gold discoveries and subsequent broader economic developments provided a strong field for British capital exports. After the Mutiny of 1857, the British Raj wished to extend the Indian railway system in order to move troops and emergency foodstuffs. Indian government guarantees of dividend and interest payments on railway equity and debenture securities were offered to draw British funds. With American cotton exports disrupted by the Civil War, railway lines to the cotton producing regions of India briefly became a lucrative venture. According to Habakkuk (1940) some 40 per cent of the 1850–75 surge in overseas investment went to the British Empire. Europe also offered an excellent field for railway portfolio investments, but perhaps the strongest field for overseas railway investment was the United States. With nearly half the world's track mileage during this period, the US system tripled in size in the 1850s and then doubled in the 1860s. Great Britain's railway system was also expanding in the 1850s and 1860s, doubling the trackage of the British railway network. There is some evidence that the 1850–69 expansion was into lines generating less profit than the earlier railway investments of the 1840s (Pollins 1957–58) but industry-wide averages of the return on real and financial railway capital show no sign of any downward movement (Broadbridge 1970, Hawke 1970). Thus it seems likely that if the surge of foreign investment in the 1850s and 1860s was motivated by a disequilibriating gap between overseas and home returns, the gap was created by newly high returns abroad rather than fading returns at home.

A second piece of evidence supporting the pull hypothesis of overseas investment in the 1850s and 1860s is the simultaneous movement of home and overseas investment spending. Indeed, it would appear that the joint expansion of home and overseas investment through the early 1870s raised the savings rate, instead of a rise in the savings rate leading to an expansion of home and overseas investment.

A final reason why the expansion of overseas investment from the early 1850s to the early 1870s may be attributed to pull factors is the similar pattern of behaviour across the Channel. In France these decades are considered among the strongest growth years of the nineteenth century and in France as well as Great Britain the proportion of French income devoted to foreign investment jumped significantly. Like the British overseas investment, the principal use of the French capital export was railway and other social overhead projects. Unlike the British, however, the major receivers were European and Middle Eastern.

Having risen in the 1850s and 1860s, the ratio of net foreign investment to GNP rose still higher after 1870, to an average of around 5.0 per cent, 1870–1914. As table 4.1 and figure 4.1 make obvious, British foreign investment was highly variable during these years. There were two surges in British overseas lending, one which began in the the early 1880s and peaked in 1891, and another which began in the early 1900s and peaked in 1913. Again the principal use of these funds was railway and other social overhead capital. Geographically, borrowers were the regions of recent settlement, the United States, Canada, Australia, New Zealand, and Argentina. As earlier, the proportion going to the empire was

Table 4.1. *UK rates of saving and investment 1855–1914*

Period	GNA/Y	GDFI/Y	II/Y	NFI/Y	GPS/Y	GS/Y	E/Y	P_h/Y	P_0/Y	Year	W_0/W
1856–64	—	0.06	—	0.03	—	—	0.48	0.49	0.03	1860	0.12
1860–69	—	0.07	—	0.04	—	—	0.47	0.50	0.03		
1865–74	—	0.08	—	0.06	—	—	0.47	0.50	0.03	1870	0.18
1870–79	0.16	0.09	0.01	0.05	0.15	0.01	0.47	0.48	0.05		
1875–84	0.14	0.09	0.01	0.04	0.13	0.01	0.49	0.46	0.05	1880	0.22
1880–89	0.14	0.07	0.01	0.06	0.14	0.01	0.49	0.45	0.06		
1885–94	0.14	0.07	0.01	0.06	0.13	0.01	0.50	0.43	0.07	1890	0.29
1890–99	0.13	0.08	0.01	0.04	0.12	0.01	0.51	0.42	0.07		
1895–1904	0.13	0.10	0.01	0.02	0.13	0.00	0.51	0.43	0.06	1900	0.28
1900–09	0.14	0.10	0.00	0.04	0.14	0.00	0.51	0.42	0.07		
1905–14	0.16	0.07	0.01	0.08	0.15	0.01	0.50	0.42	0.08	1910	0.33

Abbreviations: Y = gross domestic income + net property income from abroad; GNA = gross national savings = gross national investment; $GDFI$ = gross domestic fixed investment; II = change in inventories; NFI = net foreign investment; GPS = gross private savings ($= GNA - GS$); GS = government savings; E = income from employment; P_0 = net property income from abroad; P_h = income from home property ($= Y - E - P_0$); W_0 = the net accumulation of overseas assets and bullion; W = the gross reproducible domestic capital stock + the net accumulation of overseas assets and bullion (W_0). All data are derived from Feinstein (1972) except GS. GS is indirectly estimated from Feinstein's government capital formation figures (T 85–6) and data on government financial liabilities and assets found in Mitchell & Deane (1962), *Burdett's Official Intelligence* and *The Stock Exchange Official Intelligence*.

Table 4.2. *Realised rates of return to home and overseas railway securities, geometric means 1870–1913* (%)

Region	Equity	Debentures
United Kingdom	4.33	3.74
Eastern Europe	2.58	5.33
Western Europe	6.31	5.28
India	4.97	3.65
United States	8.41	6.03
Latin America	8.43	5.33

Source: Edelstein (1976)

steady at about 40 per cent. What balance of push and pull forces was responsible for the massive capital outflow of these years?

First of all, it must be asked whether overseas portfolio returns were greater than those available at home and, if so, when. If the capital market is reasonably competitive, differences among expected rates of return from one investment to another should not appear unless there are differences in the market's evaluation of their relative riskiness. Thus, the only way one can examine whether there were differences in portfolio rates of return is to tabulate the historical record of capital gains and losses, dividends, and interest payments, and compute indices of realised returns. A recent study examined a sample of 566 home and overseas, first and second class, equity, preference, and debenture securities (Edelstein 1976). The sample included issues from every sector of the capital market except overseas mining and foreign governments. Four questions need to be asked of this evidence. First, were overseas rates of return higher than those at home, both on comparable securities and in the aggregate? Second, did the difference between overseas and home returns show a tendency to widen either in the long term or during particular periods? Third, were the differences due to risk differentials or other phenomena? Fourth, does the pattern over time of overseas and home returns suggest that the gap was created by eruptively high returns abroad or fading returns at home?

On comparable types of assets, overseas portfolio investments yielded a higher return than domestic portfolio investments. The most important sector involved in overseas investment was the railway industry (table 4.2). Except in the case of Eastern European railway equity which attracted new British capital only in the early 1870s, overseas railways paid a higher realised return than domestic railway issues. This pattern also held in every other category of portfolio investment where comparison is possible: governments, municipals, other social overhead investments, and banking. When the entire sample of 566 securities including assets issued by domestic manufacturing and commercial enterprises

Table 4.3. *Realised rates of return, aggregate indices, selected subperiods 1870–1913. Geometric means (%)*

	1870–1913	1870–1876	1877–1886	1887–1896	1897–1909	1910–1913
(A) Domestic						
(1) Equity	6.37	11.94	7.19	8.93	0.92	6.64
(2) Preference	4.84	9.08	5.70	6.10	1.85	3.25
(3) Debentures	3.21	4.36	4.12	4.92	1.40	1.84
(4) Total	4.60	7.62	5.37	6.42	1.35	3.60
(B) Non-domestic						
(1) Equity	8.28	7.34	13.27	5.34	9.54	1.37
(2) Debentures	4.92	6.29	6.40	5.16	3.82	1.90
(3) Total	5.72	6.60	8.06	5.23	5.20	1.79
(C) Non-domestic minus domestic						
(1) Equity	1.91	−4.60	6.08	−3.59	8.62	−5.27
(2) Debentures	1.71	1.93	2.28	0.24	2.42	0.06
(3) Total	1.12	−1.02	2.69	−1.19	3.85	−1.81
(D) Market	4.90	7.72	6.51	5.92	2.97	2.84

Source: Edelstein (1976)

is aggregated into weighted home and overseas return indices, overseas place-ments still offered a superior return to home issues (table 4.3, column 1). On average, 1870–1913, overseas first and second class investments yielded a return of 5.72 per cent per annum while home first and second class investments offered a return of 4.60 per cent. When evidence on returns to overseas mining (Frankel 1967) and foreign government debentures (Cairncross 1953) is taken into consideration, it appears that the average gap was probably somewhat larger.

We can measure risk firstly by examining the amount of variation around the mean return on home or foreign assets to see whether the variation around the mean for foreign assets was much higher, making the return on those assets less certain. It was not; on the contrary, the variation was equal for both types of assets. In addition, the return on foreign assets was less closely correlated with the rate of return on all assets than was the return on home assets. Overseas returns, in other words, were slightly less affected than home returns by the unavoidable risks of major economic disruptions and political events (Edelstein 1976). In short, whatever measure of relative risk is used, it does not appear that foreign assets were significantly more risky than home assets.

What accounts for the gap in risk-adjusted returns? The most plausible hypothesis is that overseas regions tended to generate greater amounts of profitable innovations and new market opportunities which periodically led to higher returns abroad than at home.

Contemporary observers of the British economy were concerned to know whether the absolute level of British rates of return was declining. If one wants to know why capital flowed overseas, the more appropriate question is whether the gap between home and overseas returns was steady, increasing, or had some other pattern. The evidence of the first and second class securities is that the trend of *both* home and overseas returns was downwards from 1870 to 1913. However, a far more prominent feature was an inverse long swing in which, first, home returns dominated overseas returns, then overseas returns dominated home returns, then home returns again dominated overseas returns, and so on. These alternating periods of home and overseas dominance have the following approximate dating:

1870–76	Home (weak)
1877–86	Overseas
1887–96	Home
1897–1909	Overseas
1910–13	Home

In the long view, it would appear that realised rates of return tended to anticipate their respective periods of home and overseas investment given in figure 4.1. This was probably because early information of new opportunities resulted in substantial capital gains to the existing financial capital which, in turn, stimulated the demand for real capital and the issue of new long-term securities. Table 4.3 gives the aggregate indices of home and overseas returns during the alternating periods of home and overseas dominance.

Throughout these years, aggregate overseas returns dominated their periods of ascendance more strongly than domestic returns dominated theirs, thus yielding the 1870–1913 average edge of overseas returns. One period of overseas dominance, 1897–1909, was the strongest and longest of any home or overseas dominated period, 1870–1913. There appear to be two reasons for the unusual dominance of overseas returns in 1897–1909. Overseas, the returns on Latin American and United States railway, social overhead, and banking securities were particularly strong. More important, nearly all sectors of the domestic portfolio manifested very low returns. In the previous period of overseas dominance, 1877–1886, returns to home equity in textiles, drink, mechanical equipment, chemicals and communications held up quite well. Returns to mechanical equipment and textiles were probably responding to some extent to the direct and indirect effects of the period's large overseas investments while the remaining groupings represented relatively new and highly profitable industries that continued to yield high returns despite the general focus of investment on overseas projects. In the 1897–1909 period of overseas dominance, no listed domestic industry showed very healthy returns, and in fact home railways, canals, docks, tramways, and omnibuses yielded negative real returns.

In sum, it appears that there was a significant difference between overseas and home rates of return in the years 1870–1913 based on a longer and stronger dominance of overseas returns during their years of dominance than home returns manifested in their periods of ascendance. Throughout most of the period, overseas returns seem to be the strongest disequilibriating element but, in the years 1897–1909, fading domestic returns must be judged as a very important contributor as well. Thus, to the extent that British investors based their decisions to lend abroad on rates of return, these data provide an ample motive for overseas capital investment.

The mere fact that overseas returns exceeded home returns at various points in the period from 1870 to 1913 does not mean that Hobson's push forces were not also present. It could be that there was a glut of private savings from British households and corporations but that it was not large enough to satisfy all foreign investment demand and thus reduce overseas returns to the level of home returns. What evidence is there that the forces of return, income, and wealth tended to deliver too much savings at the start of periods of overseas investment? One method of examining this question is to ask whether estimates of the likely amount of British savings for the years 1870–1913 predict more British savings at foreign investment upturns than actually took place. In a recent investigation of British savings it was shown that estimates of the likely amount of savings (based on relationships of savings to income, interest rates etc.) were much higher than the actual amount of investment in two periods, 1877–79 and 1902–04 (Edelstein 1977). An examination of figure 4.1 reveals that both periods are the first years of a strong foreign investment boom and last of a home investment boom, so the clear implication is that, at least in its initial stages, a foreign investment boom was partly the result of a tendency for Great Britain to generate too much savings during the peaks of home booms. This is exactly Hobson's point, although not necessarily for the reasons Hobson proposed.

Although these data on relative rates of return and aggregate British savings are suggestive, it might be argued that each overseas region contained peculiarities in both its offerings of securities to Britain and the reasons Britons bought them. Fortunately, several regions have been studied in ways which involve a fair test of the push vs. pull issue. Two studies of investment in the United States show that the flow of British funds to the US was dominated by the push of domestic British forces (Williamson 1964; Edelstein 1974). This domination was stronger in the early years of the 1870–1913 period than it was towards the end. A relative dearth of both domestic and other overseas portfolio assets with the high return/medium risk characteristics of US assets and a heightened desire for relatively risky portfolio assets as British national wealth increased seem to have been the most important reasons for the early domination of push forces. Ford argues, by contrast, that Argentina received funds because the country offered high profits within a number of excellent overseas opportunities which, he assumed, pulled funds from Britain (Ford 1971).

It would therefore appear that the massive capital outflow from 1870 to 1913 was determined by both pull and push forces with perhaps the latter somewhat more powerful. There may also have been legal and institutional factors which tended to push capital abroad. Many observers felt that London, as the central capital market of the nation, tended to ignore domestic industry and favour overseas enterprise and governments (Kindleberger 1964; Landes 1969). It seems curious that a central capital market which was so flexible with respect to overseas regions could fail to see new industries and opportunities for profitable intermediation close to home. It is therefore sensible to ask whether in fact domestic industry had a strong unsatisfied demand for funds from London? Probably it did not. First, in the mid nineteenth century, the older industries of Britain had strong internal sources of funding and easy access to local, provincial financing. When firms in these older lines began to enlarge in the late nineteenth century, they found it fairly easy to find funds, either by marketing new equity and bonds in London or by selling older equity and bonds held in the provinces to Londoners and taking up the new equity and bonds locally (B. Thomas 1973). Second, many of the newer industries, such as brewing, bicycles, telegraphs, and telephones, had relatively easy access to either local or London funding (Aldcroft 1968b). Third, direct testing for the extent of bias in the pricing of capital market assets suggests that if there was a small bias it was trivial and did not always operate in favour of overseas assets (Edelstein 1971; McCloskey 1970).

Nevertheless, Britain did not have an institution which is widely considered quite important to the rapid advance of the US and German economies in this period. This was the large investment bank, capable of nursing several large new industrial firms from cradle to adulthood, complete with short-and long-term financing, engineering and accounting advice, and entrepreneurship. Kennedy (1975) suggests that the non-appearance of this institution in Britain may have inhibited the scale and growth of both new and old British industries and thus affected quantity of overseas investment. But the problems of British industry were different from those of German or American industry, where the banks were certainly useful. Davis (1966) found that British industry showed little tendency to change its location or sectoral distribution, nor did it seem to show significant economies of scale. He thus argued that the existing British constellation of short- and long-term financial services was quite adequate and that investment banks would not have been very profitable. In addition, investment banking was a well-known European institutional innovation by the mid nineteenth century, continental investment banks were quite willing to set up branches or new banks in other countries (Cameron 1961), and Kennedy found several unsuccessful British attempts to start investment banks in the 1860s and 1870s. This suggests that there was no demand in Britain for such banks.

Another aspect of the institutional framework for investment was the set of regulations on the purchase of assets by trustees (Keynes 1924). Most trusts gave specific directions on what investments should be purchased. In 1886 the *Economist* noted that municipal stocks, Colonial bonds, English railway deben-ture and guaranteed stock, Indian guaranteed railway equity, and even the better American railway bonds and equity were the securities in highest demand for these purposes. If, however, there were no specific instructions in the Trust, the Trustee was limited by Statute. Up to 1889 the list consisted of Consols, Bank of England and East India stock, and mortgages of freehold and copyhold estates in England and Wales. The list was enlarged by the Trustee Acts of 1889 and 1893 to include the stocks of English corporations and guaranteed Indian railways, the debentures of British and guaranteed Indian railways, and a number of other securities. The Colonial Stock Act of 1900 extended the list to registered and inscribed stocks of colonial governments. However, as Cairncross (1953) notes, the list was rather long to support a claim of special bias. Furthermore, the securities which were added to the list in the 1900 Act were already favourites for the vast majority of accounts where there were specific directions. Again, if these regulations did produce a bias, it was certainly very small (McCloskey 1970).

The consequences of foreign investment

What were the consequences of the massive capital outflow? Economic theory does not suggest that overseas investment by private investors will necessarily lead to increases in the welfare of the investing nation (Pearce and Rowan 1966). Even if the private realised rate of return is greater abroad taking into account defaults and bankruptcies, there are several factors which may make the social rate of return differ from the private rate of return. First, the overseas investment is likely to have effects on the terms of trade. Second, the outflow of capital may affect the rates of return on the existing stocks of both domestic and overseas-held wealth. Third, the overseas investment may change the distribution of income in ways considered bad even if it increases income as a whole. Fourth, the foreign investment may affect the pace of technical change either through effects on the amount of learning-by-doing or because investment in formal education is reduced.

At one time it was argued that one advantage of home over overseas portfolio investment was that if there was default or bankruptcy, then the domestically located machinery, etc., would remain in the UK (Keynes 1924). The argument, however, has a number of ambiguities. The ultimate receivers of a bankrupt overseas firm might be British citizens. Alternatively, consider a domestic firm which entered a new home market, found the profit too small, and ended in bankruptcy. Is this firm's specialised capital equipment convertible to other uses? Rather than undertake an examination of each case of default and bankruptcy, it seems sensible simply to ask whether the loss from overseas default and bankruptcy was so much higher than the loss at home that it outweighed the differential in rates of return.

Something like a billion pounds were lost through domestic company bankruptcy, 1870–1913 (Edelstein 1976). Domestic portfolio capital fell from around 67 per cent of UK-held long-term negotiable capital in 1870 to 55 per cent in 1913. Assuming the average was 61 per cent, net losses from overseas investment would have to be £640 million to have overseas and domestic portfolio holdings equally risky. What is the evidence on the extent of overseas default and bankruptcy?

The gross nominal value of defaulted government issues in the 1870s was around £60 million (Cairncross 1953), but at least 50 per cent of this was recovered. From 1880 to 1913 the worst overseas government defaults occurred during the early 1890s when various Argentine government bodies defaulted on £40 million of debentures, but most of this amount was recovered by the mid 1900s. Thus £50 million appears to be a plausible upper-bound estimate of the net losses from overseas government defaults, 1870–1913. Some £450 million were lost on overseas companies if it is assumed that the overseas rate of net insolvency was the same as that at home. Combined with the £50 million of government defaults, the total lost overseas appears to be around £500 million, substantially short of the £640 million amount which would make the risks of overseas and domestic portfolio capital equivalent. Now, it is likely that the rate of net insolvency of overseas companies was somewhat higher than that at home because the overseas company portfolio contained more firms in risky extractive industries, but this rate would have had to be much higher before the losses from overseas and home default and bankruptcy would have become equal. In sum, the differential between overseas and domestic private rates of return seems to have been substantially unaffected by home and overseas financial failure. Let us now consider the various factors involved in the balance of the social rate of return, the most important factor being the terms of trade.

From 1870 to 1913 the terms of trade, the ratio of British export to net retained import prices, gently rose by about 0.1 per cent per annum (Imlah 1958). The sources of this change are several, but few would question the importance of social overhead and extractive capital formation abroad. In places like Australia, Argentina, Brazil, Canada, and Mexico where the alternatives of water and road transport were missing in many regions, the railway made a significant contribution to reducing the cost of transport from the interior regions to the coast. In the United States the gains were relatively smaller due to the excellent alternative of river and canal transport but were still substantial. Not only was the cost of transport reduced by this investment, but a substantial amount of hitherto inaccessible but highly productive soils and mineral resources became the cheapest sources of the world's agricultural and mineral products.

It is difficult to judge how much of the change in the British terms of trade was due to the capital exports for such projects. Technical change in agriculture and mining was partly responsible. Furthermore, in the absence of capital inflows from Britain the social overhead and extractive industry capital stock of the US, Australia, Canada, etc., would not have been smaller by the size of the actual British capital export. The capital import into these countries occurred because local savings supplies were relatively small and local capital markets were relatively immature. Borrowing from Britain represented a cheaper solution than relying on domestic resources, but not the only solution. While British funds to the smaller economies were often a high percentage of total local saving for a short period, they were never the only source of local savings. In the absence of British funds, local financial and real rates of return, for example on the profitable Latin American and United States railways, would have been somewhat higher, encouraging more local savings and financial intermediation services. Nevertheless, in some of the smaller economies overseas, such as Canada and Argentina, British funds mattered a great deal; if British capital had remained at home, their development would have been slower and later, which would have affected the speed at which the British terms of trade fell. It is difficult to calculate how much of the movement in the terms of trade was due to this irreducible contribution of British capital export; but certainly a broad swath of British society benefited from this relationship in the form of cheap grains, meat, and industrial products dependent on overseas raw materials. (See also ch. 5).

Another effect of a pattern of capital export which is geographically specialised on a particular region is that it may depress returns on British wealth which has previously been accumulated in that region, assuming all else held constant. The spurt-like character of British investment in most regions of the globes tended to minimise this problem, even if the evidence of declining returns in Table 4.3 suggests that it could not be totally avoided. Now, it is perfectly clear that a similar pattern of incremental investment pursued at home might, all else held constant, lower rates of return on the existing stock of domestic capital. However, there is one critical difference. When rates of return fall as a result of an incremental investment, it may in turn lead to a fall in the share of national income accruing to capital and a rise in labour's share. If the incremental investment and consequent fall in returns takes place abroad, overseas labour benefits; if it occurs at home, domestic labour benefits! To complicate matters further, suppose that in the absence of incremental British capital exports, other foreigners replaced British investors or overseas locals saved more, thereby driving down the overseas rate of return. In this case, existing British investments abroad would decline in value. If returns on the incremental investment were greater abroad than at home, Britain as a nation might lose more by not adding to their overseas holdings than by adding to them.

All these hypotheses are quite legitimately open to both theoretical and factual challenge. For example, it is quite likely that investment in the undeveloped regions of recent settlement proceeded for a long time before returns diminished (setting aside the problem of all else, particularly technology, not remaining constant). However, both home and overseas returns did fall, so the substantive issue is whether the good effects on the terms of trade exceeded the ill effects of a declining return abroad, when there is the possibility that other foreign overseas investment or savings might have expanded somewhat in the absence of British capital exports. There is also the problem that in reality 'all else', particularly technology, did not remain constant. However, because of the size of the persistent, risk-adjusted gap between overseas and home returns (Edelstein 1976) and the fact that except in Canada, Argentina, and a few of the smaller colonies, British contributions were small relative to local savings (Green and Urquhart 1976), it is likely that the good effects on the terms of trade outweighed the effect of diminishing returns. If this is so, the social rate of return to overseas investment would still be larger than the private return.

The allocation of British savings between home and overseas outlets was largely a private affair in the nineteenth and early twentieth centuries, each investor balancing ambitions of return and risk. The capital market did not evaluate the social benefits of a project; indeed, due to information costs and other phenomena, the capital market does not perfectly evaluate private returns. For example, housing typically pays a low return spread over a long period. If investors tend to be risk averse and myopic, the private rate of return on housing will be lower than the social return and in consequence private markets will not build enough housing. If foreign investment had been restricted, and if, as suggested earlier, British property owners had continued to save, the fall in the rate of return would have lowered the rate of British total investment but there would still have been more domestic investment than there was. It is, however, difficult to know what form that increased domestic investment would have taken; it might have increased the amount of housing, or of education. Britons may have undervalued education, particularly technical education, and this may ultimately have retarded technological change in British industries. It is an open question, however, whether the social gains in the form of more housing or education would have counterbalanced the effects which overseas investment had on the terms of trade and on the purchasing power of labour over food and other imported necessities. Thus, it is still difficult to estimate the social rate of return to foreign investment, not least because so much of that investment was bound up in an important fact of British social, political and economic life, the existence of the empire.

The growth of the British empire

The expansion of British investment abroad from 1860 to 1914 was paralleled by expansions of trade, migration, culture, and political sovereignty. Five million of the earth's 51 million square kilometres of land came under the rule of the British Isles in those years. By 1914, with nearly a quarter of the earth's population and land mass, the British empire was one of the largest empires the world had ever known. Some of the nineteenth century empire began from entirely new acquisitions, but most of the new empire was the result of extensions into territory near to older holdings in Australia, Canada, India, South Africa, and West Africa. The amounts of new territory taken in each half of the hundred years between 1815 and 1914 were roughly equal. Many historians have given the last quarter of the nineteenth century the title, 'the age of high imperialism'; this overemphasises the extent of the territory acquired in that period. If there is a case to be made for singling out the period from the early 1880s to the early 1900s, that case must be that the acquisitions of these years were motivated by factors which were substantially different from those operating in the earlier part of the century (Wehler 1970; Hopkins 1973; Fieldhouse 1973).

The following factors are thought by some historians to have changed the nature of imperialism in the fourth quarter of the nineteenth century: the altered balance of European power following the Franco–Prussian War of 1870; the higher tariff levels emerging in the rapidly industrialising nations such as France, Germany, and the USA after the mid 1870s; the possible slowing of investment opportunities at home and the fear of reductions in opportunities in other industrial and independent nations; the problems of integrating a newly emergent and vocal urban working class into national political life; and finally the faltering political economies of the independent African regions which were involved in important trading relations with coastal European trading settlements. There is, however, a compelling argument that the economic value of the potential colony, the strength of its political structures, the readiness of local rulers to collaborate with British commercial or strategic purposes, the ability of the local society to undergo economic change with external involvement, and the extent to which domestic British and international politics allowed Britain a free hand, had all operated in the earlier extension of empire rule in the nineteenth century. (Gallagher and Robinson 1953; Louis 1976). Similarly at various times in the nineteenth century, Britain brought its political power to bear on a number of independent nations. This is often termed 'informal' imperialism, although a good deal of controversy surrounds just where such power was employed, how often, and to what end (Gallagher and Robinson 1953; Platt 1973; Fieldhouse 1973; Louis 1976).

There are two aspects of these extensions of British political power which are of interest to British economic historians. First, there is the question of what role economic forces at home and abroad played in the extension of formal and informal empire. Second, there is the question of the economic benefits and costs of formal and informal empire. To some degree these two questions are separable; what caused extension of empire might have nothing to do with the consequences. For example, one motive of Britain's informal imperialism in China was the high profit expectations of Lancashire and overseas British merchants who saw the potential of the immense Chinese market; it is doubtful, however, whether the excess of benefits over costs ever approached these expectations. Conversely there were several territories which were acquired for substantially non-economic reasons but which yielded a large economic reward. Since these questions are to some degree separable the remainder of this chapter is concerned with the realised return to formal and informal empire; the motives for imperialism have been widely discussed.

The gains from the empire

By what standard should the gains from formal and informal empire be measured? One might, for example, sum up the net amounts of profits and wages shipped home, the net transfers of government monies, and divide this sum by the total of public and private capital placed abroad. The result would be the 'social' return from possessing, for example, India at a particular moment in time or over a specified period. The same sum of net private and public transfers home might be divided by British GNP, thereby making it possible to compare the possession of India with that of other British assets. However, either method implicitly assumes that, in the absence of British imperialism, there would have been no economic entity called India from which Britons might have derived an economic return. Britain did very well in its economic relations with the United States without much, if any, employment of formal or 'informal' imperialism after 1815. To some undefined degree, the same pattern of settlement and economic opportunities would have occurred in Australia, Canada, and some other parts of the British Empire, even if Britain had not ruled them.

To determine what the gains are from empire or imperialism, one must first define the 'non-empire' or 'non-imperialist' economy with which the 'empire' or 'imperialist' economy is to be compared. To an important degree, Lenin (1915) avoided this issue by arguing that imperialism was a stage of capitalism, thus making possible the interpretation that the world of the late nineteenth century could not present examples of 'non-imperialist' economic and political relations. It seems likely, however, that Lenin would not have characterised Britain's actual relations with Germany, for example, as imperialist. There was a sufficient balance of power between Britain and Germany to prevent any abuse of political sovereignty or interregional economic exploitation whether through a negotiated treaty or any other economic relationship. This reasoning suggests a second way of measuring the gains from imperialism.

If the state of political and economic relations between Britain and Germany (or France or the US) is an example of 'non-imperialist' economic and political relations, then the gains to Britain from ruling India (for example) can be measured as the amount by which Britain benefited from its economic relationship with India minus the benefits she would have gained if Britain had not ruled India but merely traded with India as she did with Germany, France, or the US. To be specific, as a direct consequence of the British rule in India, all Indian railway equipment in the nineteenth century had to be purchased from Britain. The gain or loss from this exertion of political power was not the profit from all British equipment sales, only that portion specifically due to the Raj purchase requirement or any other colonial policy affecting trade. Some railway equipment might have come from British factories even without the regulation. However, like the first standard of 'non-imperialism' this one also has a hidden and somewhat artificial assumption. That assumption is that roughly the same economic opportunities would have been available in the colonised regions without British formal and informal imperialism. This counterfactual is artificial because if Britain had not meandered and fought its way into its nineteenth century empire, it is likely that there would have been fewer regions of the globe involved in the world economy; also other European powers might have filled the vacuum, and then imposed extra costs on Britain.

In the following discussion of the gains from empire, two standards of 'non-imperialism' will be employed. They will be termed, respectively, the 'marginal non-imperialist' standard, and the 'strong non-imperialist' standard. The 'marginal non-imperialist' standard assumes that the empire had the actual economic development that it underwent in the nineteenth and early twentieth centuries, but that at the moment of measurement of the gains it acquired the political independence and power of the USA, Germany, or France in its economic and political relations with Britain. This standard underestimates the gains from empire because it overestimates the degree of economic development which would have taken place if there had never been a British Empire; it does give the benefit of not relinquishing control of the territories at that particular moment. The 'strong non-imperialist' standard will assume that the countries of the empire were independent from British rule throughout modern economic history with consequent effects on their involvement in the world economy and their political power vis-à-vis Britain.

The gains from trade with the empire

In matters of international trade, political sovereignty over the empire gave Great Britain two powerful policy levers: colonial tariffs, and the regulations guiding the purchase of supplies for colonial government and mixed government–private enterprise projects. Both presented opportunities to favour domestic producers. Were they employed and with what gain or loss to Great Britain?

If we use the 'marginal non-imperialist' standard it is immediately evident that Britain gained from her empire. Tariff levels imposed by France, Germany or the United States were substantially higher than those of the colonies, even the white-settler colonies which were increasing the degree of their political autonomy across this period, and imposing protective tariffs against heated opposition in the British Parliament.

However, if one wishes to demonstrate the full power of domestic British interests the Indian case is revealing (Harnetty 1972). The British Indian government was short of funds due to expenditures connected with the Indian Mutiny of 1857, and wished to enlarge its tax base. The proposed method was to increase tariffs by a small amount. The duty would cover all imports, including cotton yarn and cloth. Lancashire cotton interests mobilised to put pressure on London to defeat the Indian government's proposal. The threat to their interests was clear; an infant Indian cotton textile industry of perhaps a half-dozen firms had recently appeared. Although Manchester interests were quite prepared to allow the proposed tariff to remain on other imports, they felt an exception should be made for British yarn and cloth. In the event, despite pleas from the Indian government, Manchester interests were successful and the British Raj had to finance the deficit by issuing debentures.

The trade flows in railway equipment are another example of the supposed gains from imperialism. Nearly all the equipment of the Indian railways was ordered from Great Britain in the nineteenth century. Legally, there was no choice because the British Indian government stipulated this pattern of purchase. But, given that many of the entrepreneurs guiding the construction and maintenance of the Indian railway system were Scots who wanted Scottish and English materials, the near-zero tariffs were probably more important than the stipulation. The pattern of Canadian railway purchases was also overwhelmingly British until the appearance of their first tariffs (Saul 1960). At this point, as in a number of other industrial branches, a substantial resident Canadian industry appeared. The Indian railway system was larger than the Canadian until just before the First World War, and, secondly, Indian and British entrepreneurship, engineering, and capital were not lacking in the late nineteenth and early twentieth centuries as evidenced by the Indian cotton textile, jute, and iron industries. It must, therefore, be concluded that here also free trade rather than direct regulation was the source of Britain's advantage.

In exploring the size of this advantage in general, let us make the assumption that the relatively low tariff of the white-settler colonies was due to British rule. There is good reason to doubt the full force of this assumption; colonial parliamentary debate suggests that British politics and policies were not often involved directly in their tariff decisions. Still, the tariff levels of these white-settler colonies certainly give political expression to closer economic links between the manufacturing metropolitan country and the primary product economies overseas than was the case for countries outside the empire. Third, it will initially be assumed that the supply of British output is quite elastic, so that the actual level of British output was determined by demand forces. Obviously, these two assumptions are questionable. For that reason the numbers which follow are to be taken as conjectures of direction and order, not precise magnitudes.

Assume that the colonial tariff rate was zero, while the 'non-imperial' rate was 20 per cent in 1870 and 40 per cent in 1913. These latter rates are close to the average tariff imposed by the United States at these two dates (Davis et al. 1969). British commodity and services exports were 30.3 per cent and 33.0 per cent of GNP at these two dates. The shares of commodity exports to the colonies in total British exports were 26 per cent. c. 1870 and 36 per cent c. 1913. Assuming that the colonies bought the same shares of invisible service exports (an underestimate in all likelihood), colonial purchases of commodity and service exports represented 7.9 per cent (i.e. 26 per cent of 30.3 per cent) of GNP in 1870 and 11.9 per cent of GNP in 1913. What percentage of GNP would have been lost if Britain had faced 'non-imperialist' tariff levels in its colonies. Assuming that Canada, India, etc., had exactly the same level of economic development as actually prevailed at these dates, the only hypothesised difference is the tariff-raising power they would have had if they became as independent as, for example, the US.

Wright's studies (1971, 1974) of nineteenth century cotton markets suggests that the price elasticity of British demand for colonial products was probably below unity, say 0.75, and that the price elasticity of colonial demand for British goods was somewhat above unity, say 1.5. If we assume first that the home and colonial marginal propensities to import were equal to 0.2, secondly that (as noted above) Britain's supply curves were highly elastic, and thirdly that the imposed tariff levels would have been 20 per cent and 40 per cent higher than the existing tariff levels of 1870 and 1913 respectively, then we can calculate the gain to Great Britain from the actual state of near-free trade with the colonies. On the basis of these assumptions, it was 1.1 per cent of GNP in 1870 and 3.3 per cent of GNP in 1913.[1] However, enhanced political autonomy for the white-settler colonies (Canada, Australia, New Zealand, and South Africa) meant that the gap between their tariffs and the 'non-imperial' tariff was smaller than 40 per cent in 1913. About 45 per cent of Britain's colonial exports in 1913 went to the Dominions; if it is assumed that their average tariff was 20 per cent (an overestimate) then the gain to Great Britain from 'freer' trade with the Dominions and other possessions becomes 2.6 per cent of GNP in 1913.

If we now use the 'strong non-imperialist standard' it must be argued that if the empire territories had remained independent of empire rule, they would not have participated in the international economy to the same extent. This hypothesis is most obvious in the case of India where the British Raj probably brought a more peaceful, unified, and commercially-oriented political economy than would have been the case in its absence (Morris 1963; Mukerjee 1972). As a guess, let us assume that Britain's trade with India and the other, non-Dominion regions would have been 25 per cent of its existing level in 1870 and 1913 if there had never been British rule. (West African purchases of British goods quadrupled between 1870 and 1913 at the same time that British rule spread from a few enclaves to significant territorial sovereignty.)

To what degree would the economic development of the white-settler areas have been similarly inhibited by the absence of British rule? The US experience might be thought instructive because the US was also founded by British migrants who had a common core of political, cultural and economic institutions. Still, the US industrialised much earlier than the white-settler colonies of the nineteenth century, and had earlier and much stronger income and population growth. One alternative standard might be the pattern of growth and development in Argentina. Although the political and cultural traditions of Argentina are different from those of the British white-settler colonies, Argentina entered the international economy at about the same time as the future Dominions and had a very similar pattern of economic development. Argentina grew through

---

[1] Let E_{cc} and E_{bb} = the price elasticities of colonial demand for British products and of British demand for colonial products; C_c and C_b = the marginal propensities to import of the colonies and Britain; qX = the share of British exports to the colonies in British *GNP*; dt = the change in tariffs; and dW = the percentage change in British *GNP* due to the tariff change. From Pearce, $dW = qX(E_{cc} + C_c)/(E_{cc} + C_c + E_{bb}))dt$.

Table 4.4. *Some conjectures on the gains from imperialism in 1870 and 1913* (% *of GNP*)

	Standard of 'Non-Imperialism'			
	'Marginal': same level of Economic Development: US, German, French standard of international economic policy		'Strong': Independent nineteenth century political and economic development	
	1870	1913	1870	1913
Exports of commodities and services	1.1%	2.6%	3.6%	5.4%
Overseas investment	—	—	0.3%	0.5%
Net government transfers	−0.1%	0.1%	−0.1%	0.1%
Total	1.0%	2.5%	3.8%	6.0%

Source: See text

extensive development of land and mineral resources, using largely British funds to build its railway and other social overhead capital. Argentina's consumption of British exports per capita was about 70 per cent of the average for the white-settler colonies, so we can assume that British investment in those colonies would have been 70 per cent of its actual level if the colonies had been independent.

Summing the 75 per cent reduction to British exports to the non-Dominion colonies and the 30 per cent reduction to British exports in the Dominion regions (weighted by their respective shares in British colonial exports), British colonial exports in 1870 and 1913 would have been 45 per cent of their actual levels under this 'strong non-imperialist' standard of the gains from Empire. Since British exports of goods and services to the Empire were approximately 7.9 per cent and 11.9 per cent of GNP in 1870 and 1913, the 'strong' gain from empire was 3.6 per cent (i.e. 45 per cent of 7.9 per cent) of GNP in 1870 and 5.4 per cent of GNP in 1913 (table 4.4).[2]

[2] Since the shares of white-settler and non-white-settler colonies in British exports to the colonies were approximately 0.45 and 0.55, respectively, the percentage reduction in British exports to both types of colonies would be $= 1 - (0.45)(0.3) - (0.55)(0.75) = 0.4525$.

The gains from investment in the empire

It is doubtful whether the amount of investment in the colonies or its aggregate return would have differed very much from the actual amounts in 1870 and 1913 if we assume that the British colonies were as fully integrated into the world economy and as independent as the US, France, and Germany (the 'marginal non-imperialist' standard). In 1870 the government of the United States regularly gave land grants to help attract domestic and overseas investors to the equity and debenture issues of US private railway companies; the same policy was pursued in Canada, India, and Argentina. British investors who were interested in buying German securities backed by the net income from railway traffic would probably have had to purchase government debentures; British investors interested in the railway lines of New Zealand and Australia had to do the same. It is therefore likely that under the 'marginal non-imperialist' standard the hypothesised independent colonial governments would have subsidised railway investment in much the same way. On the other hand, it is unlikely that investment by locals or foreigners was deterred by empire rule from purchasing portfolio investments. The early history of US direct investment abroad suggests a pattern of relatively free entry into British possessions (Wilkins 1970).

However, if the 'strong non-imperialist' standard is assumed, there would have been less investment income from empire, though not from the white-settler colonies. Returns on colonial governments and colonial railway investments were normally between those on equivalent home and foreign issues (Cairncross 1953; Edelstein 1976). The strong inference is that colonial status lowered whatever risk there was in foreign investment and that investors were therefore willing to accept a slightly lower return. In some colonies, particularly the newer ones, British rule and law directly reduced the potential losses from default and bankruptcy. In others, risk and uncertainty were reduced by the justice which was expected from colonists of British extraction. It therefore seems reasonable to assume that British investment per head in Canada, Australia, New Zealand, and South Africa would have been closer to the Argentine figure if there had been no Empire rule in the nineteenth and twentieth centuries. The required rate of return, however, would probably have been higher to compensate for the greater risk of foreign political pressures and court systems. British investment per head in Argentina was approximately 70 per cent of what it was in Canada, Australia, New Zealand, and South Africa, but the realised rate of return on Argentine (and US) securities was about a third higher than on the Dominion securities. Thus, it seems likely that whatever income would have been lost from a drop in the quantity of investment under these rough assumptions would have been made up in a higher rate of return.

India and the remainder of the non-Dominion Empire are quite different.

Plausible analogies to India without empire rule in the nineteenth century might be the experience of China, Turkey and Japan. Clearly, there was some amount of 'informal' imperialism in these regions affecting their openness to foreigners (McLean 1976; Nathan 1972; Esherick 1972). It is therefore quite generous to assume that the non-white-settler colonies would have had investments of 20 per cent of their actual £140 and £480 million levels in 1870 and 1913. The realized rate of return was approximately 4 per cent on colonial investments, 1870–1913, but in order to draw funds into these hypothesised independent regions, the required rate of return would probably have had at least to double. If we reduce the non-Dominion Colonial investments by 80 per cent and assume an 8 per cent return, the gain to Great Britain from Empire investments based on a 'strong non-imperialist' standard was 0.3 per cent of GNP in 1870 and 0.5 per cent of GNP in 1913 (table 4.4).[3]

Net government transfers to and from the empire

Until fairly recently, little was known about the public finance of colonial and independent nations in the nineteenth and early twentieth centuries (Davis and Huttenback 1977). It is still the case that the public accounts of the various governing bodies of the Empire and elsewhere are not available in standardised form. Nevertheless, it is clear that London governments wanted the colonial governments to finance themselves as far as possible. Most colonies came close to this in normal times, and needed London funding principally when there was a major military campaign or famine conditions. India, however, went further. Not only was India self-supporting in defence but Indian troops and funds were regularly used for Empire military actions in Africa and Asia. According to Mukerjee (1972), some £0.4 million in 1870 and, employing his methods, £4 million in 1913 were transferred to Britain for (a) unjustified debt service for wars which an independent India would not have undertaken, (b) current military expenditures for campaigns in Africa and Asia, and (c) civil charges for empire operations outside India. These Indian transfers, however, must be matched against the current grants paid by the London government in aid of colonial local revenues and special military actions. According to Feinstein (1972), these averaged perhaps £1 million c. 1870 and £2 million c. 1913. Judging by the experience of other developed economies of the period, Britain might have spent more on defence in the absence of empire (Davis and Huttenback 1977), but it is doubtful whether there would have been any direct net transfers abroad. For

---

[3] The stock of British portfolio capital in non-Dominion colonies was £140 million in 1870 (Hall 1963) and £480 million in 1913 (Saul 1960). British GNP was £1081 million in 1870 and £2532 in 1913 (Feinstein 1972). The percentage change in British GNP from the assumed lowered rate of investment in non-Dominion colonial areas in 1870 would thus be

$$((0.04)(140) - (0.08)(0.2)(140))/1081 - 0.003$$

and similarly for 1913.

both standards of 'non-imperialism', it thus seems fair to regard the balance of the Indian transfers on the one hand and the London government grants-in-aid on the other as a close approximation to the direct annual gains of government from Empire ownership. In 1870 the gain was negative, approximately £0.6 million, or 0.1 per cent, of GNP. In 1913, however, the gain was positive at around £2 million or 0.1 per cent of GNP (table 4.4).

Summary of the economics of empire

These rough calculations suggest three important features of the economics of empire. First, the empire meant more for the economic well-being of Great Britain in 1913 than it did in 1870 on both the trade and investment account. In trade, this trend was largely due to the increased proportion of British commodity and service exports which were marketed in the empire. In investment, the proportion going to empire remained fairly constant between 1860 and 1913. Increased income from investments in empire regions was the result of whatever factors annually increased the proportion of total British wealth held outside the British Isles.

Second, if we employ the 'marginal non-imperialism' standard the gains to Britain from her empire do not appear to have been very large. The ability to manipulate the international trade, investment and fiscal policies of the developed colonial economies yielded perhaps 1 per cent of GNP in 1870 and 2 per cent in 1913. Furthermore, this calculation assumed that the relatively low tariffs of the white-settler colonies were due to British rule. Colonial parliamentary debates suggest that this assumption must be modified. If, for example, it is totally dropped, the gains from the 'marginal' standard are halved. Needless to say, the fact that the nation as a whole did not gain much according to this standard does not mean that certain sectors of the British economy did not benefit from freer trade with the Empire. The cotton trades, shipping, overseas insurance and banking, and railway equipment manufacturers are good examples but they are not alone. In other words, private rates of return may have been higher than the social rate of return.

Third, Britain probably received a significant return if we use the 'strong non-imperialism' standard. This is best viewed as an estimate of the return on the role which Empire played in enlarging the extent of the nineteenth century world economy. Furthermore, because the gains from 'informal' empire have been largely ignored, it is likely that the gains from imperialism in table 4.4 are somewhat understated. Argentina, which was used as an example of a 'non-imperialist' economy was certainly subject to the pressures of Britain and other imperial powers at various points in the nineteenth and early twentieth centuries.

However, the size of the gains reported in table 4.4 must be examined in the light of our earlier assumption that supply curves were elastic and hence British output was set by the level of demand. To assume elastic supply curves means that if there had been no empire the domestic labour and capital resources employed in empire-induced activities would have either never participated in the economy or, through lower population growth rates, never come into existence. Alternatively, it might be assumed that some portion of the labour and capital involved in empire-induced activities would have been employed in other economic activities, albeit less productive. Unfortunately, it is quite difficult to measure accurately how much of the labour and capital resources involved in empire-induced activities would have been employed elsewhere in the economy. It is possible, however, to specify a range of possibilities. If, on the one hand, all factors of production were employed elsewhere and the only change was a drop in their rate of return by one percentage point, after 44 years without the empire-induced growth British GNP would have been lower by around 1 per cent. If, on the other hand, it is assumed that the resources involved in the empire-induced economic activity had remained unused (or never come into existence) and the pace of technical change is proportionately lowered as well, British GNP would have been lower by somewhat more than 5 per cent after 44 years.

How can we tell whether this range of proportions is large or small? One way is to compare the gains from empire with the gains from various forms of technical progress. Hawke's study of the diffusion of the railway in Great Britain indicates that in 1860, after 35 years of the railway, GNP was at most 10 per cent higher than it would have been without the railway (Hawke 1970). Since it is likely that the railway was the most important single technological innovation of the nineteenth century, the empire does not appear to have been as important as is sometimes thought. Still, the empire made a significant contribution to the growth in the income and output of Great Britain in the nineteenth and early twentieth centuries. Chapter 1 suggested that between 1870 and 1914 the forces of innovation and economies of scale were exerting a diminishing effect on growth. By contrast, the contribution of the empire was increasing.

Suggestions for further reading

Further study of the economics of overseas investment in the nineteenth and early twentieth centuries should begin with Cottrell's fine survey (1975). On the pace, geographic distribution, and industrial employment of Britain's overseas investments, the premier study is by Simon (1967). The economics of overseas investment, with special emphasis on long swing behaviour, is the focus of an excellent collection of articles edited by Hall (1968); these readings should be supplemented by Abramovitz' (1968) study. Fieldhouse's (1967) compilation is a good source for nineteenth century views. On the costs and benefits of overseas investment, theoretical background can be supplied by Pearce and Rowan (1966), Brown (1974) and Fieldhouse (1967). A judicious account of the historical experience may be found in Cairncross' study (1953). Brown (1974), Fieldhouse (1967, 1973), and Boulding and Mukerjee (1972) are also very useful on the historical experience of the costs and benefits of overseas investment, as well as on the costs and benefits of empire.

5

The entrepreneur and technological change

L. G. SANDBERG

Whenever the performance of a group, organisation or country falls short of widely held expectations, the leaders of that group, organisation or country are likely to be branded as incompetent, venal or both. By the same token, success will result in high praise and widespread admiration for the leaders. Sometimes such condemnation or adulation is warranted: often it is not. Circumstances may well be more important than any contribution made by leaders. Pointing out such circumstances, however, is not always a rewarding task. Those who note that failure or decline was beyond the power of any leader to prevent are 'apologists', while those who credit success to fortunate circumstances are likely to be considered 'small-minded' or 'petty'. This proclivity to condemn or praise certainly includes the economic arena, and does not only concern government economic policy. Business leaders, managers and 'entrepreneurs' are also fair game. (In this chapter, 'entrepreneur' refers to anyone who has responsibility for a firm's decisions concerning choices of technology, rates of investment and scrapping, research expenditures, etc. This group includes individual owner-managers, hired managers and individual or groups of corporate officials.)

It should not be surprising, therefore, that Britain's relative economic decline in the period before the First World War (see chapter 1), elicited a storm of criticism of the British entrepreneur. Journalists, sociologists and economic historians, both at the time and subsequently, have devoted great effort to describing and explaining the shortcomings of those economic weaklings. If only business leadership had been competent, it is argued, the British economy would have fared much better. A fine example of this attitude is the assertion of Burnham and Hoskins in *Iron and Steel in Britain, 1870–1930*: 'If a business deteriorates, it is of no use blaming anyone except those at the top' (1943: 271).

Much of this criticism, naturally enough, consists of unflattering comparisons with the competition, principally America and Germany. Entrepreneurs there are generally praised for their aggressive and innovative behaviour. It is noteworthy, however, that even American and German sectors and regions judged to have performed badly (i.e. where output grew slowly or declined) are also alleged to have been the victims of poor leadership. In the case of the troubled American railroads, for example, a study of management recruitment and practices concludes that they 'clung to ossified and outmoded managerial practices after the industry reached maturity [circa 1900]' (Morris 1973: 317). This judgement, incidentally, compares unfavourably with that of a companion study of British railway management. The latter notes that 'after 1890 there was a slight increase in inter-company movement [of executives], probably a reflection of a growing interest in new ideas in management' (Gourvish 1973: 298–9). Similarly, the previously lionised New England cotton textile managers were roundly condemned when they succumbed to Southern competition after the First World War, and the American coal mining industry, a world-wide example of efficiency before the First World War, was found seriously wanting in managerial performance by the Coal Commission of the 1920s (McCloskey & Sandberg 1971: 90). Finally, a study of the apparently retarded introduction of the diesel engine in America concludes that 'entrepreneurial shortcomings are the most apparent cause of the diesel's early failure in America'. Blame for this particular failure is awarded jointly to the American and German participants (Lytle 1968: 143).

The problem of 'technological backwardness'

By far the most common charge raised against allegedly sub-standard entrepreneurs, British, American or whatever, is some version of 'technological backwardness'; that is, a failure to encourage, appreciate and take rapid advantage of advances in technology. The worst offence of this kind is to have installed economically obsolete equipment in new plants. Other common charges include continuing to operate obsolete equipment after it should have been junked and ignoring new, presumably profitable, opportunities that arose from the advance of technology.

The principle reason for the prevalence of this particular charge is the observation that firms, national industries and even whole national economies that are declining, absolutely or relatively, will almost always have a less modern stock of equipment than will firms, national industries or national economies that are growing rapidly. This is true virtually regardless of the reason for the decline. It is, of course, certainly true if the decline is in fact the result of a failure to keep up with the advance of technology. It will also be true, however, if some industry in a given country (e.g. British cotton textiles) is declining because technological advance has shifted international comparative advantage in that industry to some other country (e.g. Japan). (See ch. 13.) In an extreme case, the British industry may not adopt the new technology at all, either because the old technology is better given Britain's factor endowments, or because Japan's new comparative advantage is so great that Britain is better off abandoning the industry. An apparent technological lag is also likely to emerge in a declining industry even if the decline itself has nothing whatever to do with technological change.

Before discussing the possible economic impact of 'technological backwardness', some preliminary observations are needed. First of all, it must be stressed that it is by no means always harmful to a nation for some branches of its industry to decline or even vanish. This is obvious if the product itself has become obsolete (e.g. covered wagons), but it may also be true if the local industry is destroyed by foreign competition. The theory of comparative advantage makes it clear that all countries gain simultaneously by concentrating on the production of those goods and services where they have the lowest relative costs. Such specialisation is the basis of international trade. Comparative advantage, however, is not a static relationship. As technical change occurs and as a country accumulates relatively large stocks of physical and human capital (the education, experience and skills of its work force), its comparative advantage changes from one set of economic activities to another. Thus, Britain had a comparative advantage in the production of cotton textiles before the First World War, but has it no longer. Today she has a comparative advantage in more capital-intensive – where the capital is both human and physical – manufacturing and service industries than textiles.

Generally speaking, a country is well advised to let its economy adjust to the dictates of comparative advantage. Failure to do so is likely to result in ever larger sections of the economy requiring ever larger subsidies and tariffs, thus becoming an ever heavier burden on the rest of the economy. Government policies to ease the pain of such adjustments, but not to prevent them, may however be justified.

The managers of an industry, such as British cotton textiles, that is in inevitable decline face a difficult task. They have to junk technically well functioning equipment and dismiss workers whose skills and experience have now become worthless – effectively leaving them as middle-aged or elderly unskilled workers. To invest in new, modern equipment would not, however, be a sound strategy. While it would no doubt keep the industry operating, though at a loss, somewhat longer than otherwise, the economy as a whole would be the poorer for it.

Another point is that installing the most modern technology available is not always a sound policy. The very latest in equipment frequently is plagued by 'bugs', and time and experience (not necessarily yours) is needed before it becomes profitable to operate. An example of such a case in Britain in this period is the experience of G. Z. de Ferranti. The financial troubles experienced by his ambitious electrical enterprises stemmed to a large extent from his insistence on operating at the very frontier of technology (Byatt 1968: 248–9).

The case of de Ferranti raises the more general question of the criteria by which the behaviour of industrial entrepreneurs are to be judged. It seems likely that de Ferranti's pioneering work, even including his mistakes, was socially, although not privately, profitable; the knowledge his work created was a valuable public good. He and his financial backers paid for its production but most of the benefits accrued to others throughout the world. Unintentionally de Ferranti and his backers became public benefactors.

Although there are those who argue that entrepreneurs should be judged on the basis of their total contribution to society, this is not a sound criterion. Entrepreneurs cannot reasonably be expected to take benefits and costs affecting others into account. That is properly the function of government.

What criteria, then, should be used to evaluate managerial performance? The most reasonable criterion, at least as a first approximation, is the management's success in maximising the present value of their enterprise; that is, the discounted value of expected future profits. An inevitable difficulty is that such a measure cannot rely exclusively on hindsight, and a judgement must sometimes be made as to whether an entrepreneur should reasonably have been able to foresee later developments in technology or market conditions.

What are the principal economic consequences for the firm and, more importantly, for the national industry and the whole economy, when entrepreneurs fail to meet this standard of competence? By definition, a managerial error, such as investing in the wrong technology or failing to junk obsolete equipment or failing to take advantage of a profitable investment opportunity, is only a failure if it reduces the present value of the expected flow of future profits of the firm. Thus, managerial mistakes must reduce profit levels below what they would otherwise have been. What happens beyond that point, however, depends greatly on the market structure in which the firm is operating.

If the firm is part of a competitive industry, as was the case with most British firms between 1860 and 1914, then the principal question is how the other firms in the industry act. If a given error is limited to a single firm, then for all practical purposes the consequences would also be limited to that firm. The firm would simply operate at sub-normal profits, or at a loss, until the mistake was corrected. Bankruptcy, of course, might intervene, in which case the new owners would be able to rectify the error (e.g. throw out obsolete equipment). The loss of production in an industry resulting from mistakes by one firm, or even a limited number of firms, could easily be offset by new entry or increased production by other firms.

If, however, all the firms in the industry made the same mistake, then the situation would be quite different. The efficiency loss caused by the collective error would now be much larger – roughly by a multiple of the number of firms involved. On the other hand, the cost of these errors might be shifted away from the owners of the firms. In the absence of foreign competition, in fact, each firm might even be as well, or conceivably even better, off with *everybody* making the mistake rather than with *nobody* making it. The loss caused by inefficiency would then be borne by someone else; the consumers of the industry's output and the suppliers of raw materials are the most likely candidates for the role of victim.

Some degree of foreign competition is, however, the rule rather than the exception. If it can be assumed that the foreign producers made the right decisions while all the local producers made the wrong decision, then international competition would force at least part of the inefficiency loss back onto the local producers and probably onto local owners of specialised factors of production (including workers owning skill and experience) used in the industry. The output of the local industry would naturally be lower than would otherwise have been the case. If this forces a reduction in the *absolute* size of the local industry, unnecessary readjustment costs would also be imposed on the participants in the industry.

This scenario, however, seems unlikely. If one or two local firms made the right technological decision, even if by pure dumb luck, their business should prosper and their profits should grow. This, in turn, should cause the other local firms to reconsider, and, if possible, rectify their mistake.

A historical example of such market pressure has been found by a recent student of the pre-First World War British bicycle industry. Commenting on the rapid adoption of new technology in the industry he notes: 'If such a training [an engineering apprenticeship] instilled conservative instincts in its recipients [the bicycle industry entrepreneurs], it was countered by the competitive system which enforced a progressive code of conduct' (Harrison 1969: 302).

This analysis has to be modified somewhat for industries that involve rent-yielding natural resources. These are industries such as coal mining when the value of the coal exceeds the costs of extraction. Firms with superior natural resources can survive some managerial failure by absorbing the losses out of their rental income. In addition, the market signals coming from competitors who have made the right decision will be obscured for two reasons. First, the usefulness of a technological innovation is likely to vary between firms depending on the precise nature of the natural resource being worked; some coal deposits are more suited to mechanical cutting than are others. Second, the increased profits reaped from a proper technological choice can easily be obscured by the presence, or absence, of pure economic rents. This is especially the case if the adoption of new technology has only prevented the total abandonment of relatively low quality resources.

The likelihood of large loss through managerial error increases in the absence of free competition. The fewer the number of firms in the industry, the less effective are the self-corrective forces of the market. The worst case is clearly a single firm monopoly, regardless of the sources of the monopoly, whether that source is economies of scale, cartel organisation or patents. Whatever the props of a monopoly, it has monopoly rents to waste and at least no domestic competitors to worry about. Equally important, the smaller the number of independent decision makers, the more likely it is that no one will stumble on the right choice, thereby setting a successful example for others to emulate. Inefficiency may, however, create a profitable take-over opportunity for alert outsiders; stubbornly inefficient owners are likely to be bought out by more rational entrepreneurs.

A further point is that managerial incompetence cannot make all sectors of a country's economy internationally uncompetitive simultaneously, or at least not for very long. International trade in goods and services is controlled by comparative, not absolute, advantage. Thus, sectors with *relatively* little loss from managerial incompetence may well have their international competitiveness *enhanced*.

Even if it is possible to navigate these theoretical shoals and arrive at an acceptable estimate of the cost to the British economy resulting from entrepreneurial errors, a final problem remains. To test the key hypothesis of the 'entrepreneurial failure' school: 'that Britain's relatively poor economic performance (1870–1914) can be attributed largely to the failure of the British entrepreneur to respond to the challenge of changed conditions' (Aldcroft 1964: 113), it is necessary to establish some standard for the performance of a country's entrepreneurs as a group. Perfect entrepreneurial behaviour is not likely to have been achieved in Germany or America in this same period, or in Britain in earlier periods. Thus a measure of the cost of entrepreneurial mistakes in Britain between 1860 and 1914 only has meaning if it can be compared with similar measures for other periods and countries.

Clearly we do not now have, nor are we likely ever to have, enough information to calculate a final and definitive measure of the role of the British entrepreneur during the 1860–1914 period. Nevertheless we have a good deal of information on entrepreneurial behaviour concerned with technological choice in a number of important industries. Enough information exists, in fact, to permit us to come to a preliminary conclusion on the role of the entrepreneur.

The information available comes from two types of studies. The first type concerns the general economic performance of British firms and industries during the 1860–1914 period. These studies deal with such matters as the rate of growth of output of the firm or industry, their ability to deal with foreign competition, the rate at which they adopted new technology and their rate of productivity growth (either of labour productivity (output per worker) or total factor productivity). Total factor productivity is a much more sophisticated concept (and much more useful to economists) than labour productivity, but it is also more likely to suffer from measurement errors. (See ch. 1.)

The virtually unanimous conclusion reached by the authors of this type of study in cases where the firm or industry has maintained its international competitiveness, has rapidly adopted new technology and has displayed rates of productivity growth similar to German and American competitors, is that the quality of management was good. This is usually an appropriate inference. It is conceivable, however, that there were aspects of the situation which gave a special, unnoticed, advantage to the British industry and thus that it should have performed even better than it did.

The reaction when the firm's or industry's performance is disappointing is more varied. On the one hand, there is the reaction typified by Burnham and Hoskin's assertion quoted at the beginning of the chapter. At the other extreme is the reaction of a recent investigator of the Welsh coal mining industry in the period 1850–1914. After noting the relatively slow rate of mechanisation in the industry, he claims that: 'Had cutters and conveyors been more necessary to the industry in South Wales and had they justified their adoption in terms of factor costs then there can be no doubt they would have been adopted sooner' (Walters 1975: 297).

In most cases, however, the response is more muted. It usually consists of an impressionistic list of extenuating circumstances for the disappointing performance, followed by the conclusion that the leadership of the firm or industry cannot, nevertheless, entirely be excused from blame. Since none of these various conclusions are proven they cannot be accepted; for all we know, there may or may not have been an element of entrepreneurial failure present.

The other type of study tries explicitly to determine how appropriate was some technological or investment choice made by British, and sometimes American, entrepreneurs. The questions which are asked are, for example: given the economic environment in which it operated was it profitable for the British cotton industry to install machine type X rather than type Y, was it profitable for the British chemical industry to keep operating its Z process equipment for making alkali products after, say, 1890; did British ship owners replace sailing ships by steam ships in a way compatible with profit maximisation? The choice of exactly which such questions should be subjected to quantitative analysis has, in effect, largely been made by the proponents of the 'entrepreneurial failure' hypothesis. It is usually a set of decisions that they have branded as examples of entrepreneurial incompetence that has been chosen for study.

If the choices facing the decision makers at the time are correctly specified and the appropriate data (factor prices, interest rates and the characteristics of the technical alternatives) are obtained, such an analysis will allow us to determine whether or not the decision which was made was economically sound. It may also permit a quantitative estimate of the loss resulting from possible mistakes.

Following a brief discussion of the role of technical training, the rest of this chapter will summarise the evidence currently available on the behaviour of British entrepreneurs relative to technological change in a number of industries between 1860 and 1914. The survey is not complete in its coverage, either in terms of industries discussed or including every scrap of evidence available on the industries which are mentioned. An attempt has, however, been made to be exhaustive with regard to studies of the second type just described, except that agriculture is treated in chapter 8.

Technical training and productivity growth

It is often alleged that part of Britain's productivity growth lag after 1870 (see chapter 1), stemmed from inadequate levels of technical training. The alleged low British level of such training is contrasted with reports of higher levels in other countries, especially Germany. Although it was largely governmental authorities in these other countries who provided this technical training, the ultimate blame for Britain's supposed failure is normally laid on the private sector. The claim is that prejudices against employing technically trained workers prevented the emergence of a demand for technical training financed by the government (Landes 1969: 344–6).

This contention raises theoretical considerations similar to those associated with 'technological backwardness'. Given competitive labour and product markets and assuming that technical training really is very valuable, then, if only a few firms make the right choice and hire technically trained workers, the profits of these firms will increase sharply. This will provide a signal for others to follow and firms who hold out will be placed at a disadvantage. Thus since at least some firms hired technically trained workers and since the British economy was highly competitive, it is difficult to believe that an irrational opposition to technical training could have been a major hindrance to economic growth.

In fact, however, closer examination of the facts indicates that the principal difference between Britain and Germany was the nature, not necessarily the extent, of technical training. In Germany it consisted largely of formal, full time class work, while in Britain it consisted of apprenticeship training supplemented by part time, especially night classes. Several possible reasons, other than irrationality, can be suggested for this difference. Most important, Britain had a larger corps of experienced and skilled industrial workers and more large-scale enterprises. These conditions made apprenticeship training more feasible in Britain. It might even be said that Germany, being less able to provide apprenticeship training, was forced to adopt more formal, group oriented methods of instruction. Certainly the expense, particularly in terms of forgone earnings and production, is greater with full time class work than with apprenticeship training combined with night classes (Floud 1976a: 9–11).

Survey of industries

The iron and steel industry

The large-scale production and widespread use of first iron and then steel was a major aspect of industrialisation and industrial growth during the nineteenth century. Britain led the way in both production and consumption. As late as 1880, Britain produced twice as much pig iron as Germany and more than the United States; her per capita consumption was three times as high as in those countries. After 1880, however, there was little growth in Britain and rapid advance elsewhere. Before the First World War, Germany produced twice as much and the United States over three times as much pig iron as Britain and both had distinctly higher levels of per capita consumption.

British pig iron production, in fact, did not exceed its 1882 level until 1896 and only exceeded it by 20 per cent in 1913. Figures on steel production were somewhat more encouraging. Steel production in Britain grew almost as rapidly as in the United States until 1890. After that year, the growth rate dropped to approximately 3 per cent per annum.

Britain's share of world production and world exports fell sharply. In 1875–79, Britain produced 46.0 per cent of the world's pig iron and 35.9 per cent of the world's steel. By 1910–13, these shares had been reduced to 13.9 per cent and 10.3 per cent. The virtual stagnation of her exports meant that Britain's share of world iron and steel exports declined rapidly. Although Britain exported almost five times as much tonnage as Germany in 1880, Germany had pushed ahead before the First World War. In addition, Britain had by then become the world's largest importer of iron and steel (Payne 1968: 72, 78, 85).

These developments were viewed with considerable alarm by contemporary observers. Iron and steel was an important industry. Its gross output (less coal and imported ore) amounted to 11.6 per cent of Britain's GNP in 1871 and 10.3 per cent in 1881, but only 5.8 per cent in 1901 and 6.4 per cent in 1907. In 1880, iron and steel ranked second to cotton textiles among British industries, but by 1907 it had fallen to eighth place (Deane & Cole 1962: 226–7).

As these events unfolded, the British iron and steel industry was subjected to increasingly shrill, sometimes even hysterical, criticism. Admonitions came from the whole spectrum of audible opinion – from journalists to academic economists. The latter, in a relatively moderate vein, noted that while Britain's share of the industry was bound to shrink, it was not bound to shrink so much. More aggressive and innovative leadership could certainly have prevented the relative decline from being so precipitous. The critical view of the industry's leadership before and after the First World War was confirmed in scholarly circles by two major studies of the industry (Burn 1940 and Burnham & Hoskins 1943). Both of these works, but especially the latter, were highly critical of the management of British iron and steel.

These critics present a long bill of particulars against the industry. Consistently heading the list is the British industry's unquestioned lag in adopting the basic (as opposed to acidic) process of steel making and the slow development (presumably related to this) of the phosphoric ores found in Lincolnshire and Northamptonshire. Among other popular allegations are a failure properly to integrate production, neglect of possible fuel economies, neglect of electrical metallurgy and neglect of continuous rolling (Levine 1967: 39–42).

Only very recently, principally in the work of McCloskey (1973), has a serious effort been made to evaluate these alleged entrepreneurial failures. This work consists of a detailed and quantified analysis of the alleged 'failure' rapidly to expand basic steel production together with studies of productivity growth rates and levels in various branches of the British and American iron and steel industries.

As to the alleged neglect of the phosphoric ores, McCloskey is able to show that the users of pig iron (principally steel producers) were paying the same price for pig iron made of this ore as for similar pig iron made from other ores. Thus the product was correctly valued in the market. Secondly, he shows that there were no larger but unexploited potential profits available to investors in that branch of the industry than elsewhere. Thus there were apparently no irrational prejudices against the ores or against investing in their exploitation (*ibid*: 57–67).

McCloskey rejects the charge of general irrational neglect of the basic open hearth process on other grounds. He notes that the spread of open-hearth basic steel making was very rapid in Britain after 1900, the year that saw the commercial introduction of the Talbot tilting furnace. This furnace was designed to deal with the problem of slag accumulation which was particularly serious for the open hearth process, and especially bad in Britain where scrap, which generates no slag, was relatively expensive and therefore little used. Thus the Talbot furnace was particularly well suited to the production of basic open hearth steel in Britain and its more rapid adoption in Britain than in Germany is consistent with rational behaviour by steel entrepreneurs in both countries (*ibid.*: 68–72).

The results of calculations of factor productivity change do not, at least at first glance, seem as favourable to the British cause. British productivity in pig iron production and in Bessemer steel rails grew rapidly until shortly after 1880 and then stagnated, in the case of pig iron all the way into the 1930s. The results for open hearth steel ship plates, a major product in this period, seem more promising. They indicate a substantial rate of productivity growth until the middle of the first decade of this country.

In America, on the other hand, productivity growth continued, at least in pig iron and open hearth steel, after it had stopped in Britain. Furthermore, the study undermines the explanation which is sometimes offered; that the British steel industry's productivity lagged behind that of her competitors as a result of an ageing stock of captial. This ageing, in turn, resulted from the relatively slow growth of British demand (Temin 1966). While such a relationship between growth of demand, age of equipment and rate of productivity change can exist, it was simply not very important in this particular case.

The data on productivity growth is put into quite a different light, however, by two further considerations. First, if the halt in productivity improvement was the result of entrepreneurial failure, it seems strange that the collapse should have occured twenty years earlier in some branches of the industry than in other. More important, not until shortly before the First World War did American total factor productivity reach British levels. In other words, more rapid productivity growth in America before that point only reduced the existing British lead. This observation is consistent with the hypothesis that British entrepreneurs were usually quick in adopting the new technology available up to the 1880s (1905 for open hearth steel), and that productivity growth ceased at that point because the possibilities of available technology had been exhausted in Britain. Thus, British entrepreneurial behaviour after the 1880s appears to be poor only because it had been so good previously. To compound the irony, the Americans now look good because they previously were laggards. These findings tempt one to propose an 'entrepreneurial failure' explanation for the American industry's 'productivity failure' before the First World War (McCloskey 1973: chs. 6 & 7).

Still, it is disturbing that American productivity continued to grow well past British levels. This development raises questions about British interwar entrepreneurship (without proving that it was poor), and throws a shadow backwards onto the Edwardian period. British steel managers may well have encountered productivity ceilings in some sectors in the 1880s, but they also seem to have been slow off the mark when new opportunities for productivity improvement became available once more. The fact that the Americans did not catch up until shortly before the First World War, furthermore, does not guarantee that new opportunities had not opened up somewhat earlier. The Americans give no evidence of ever having hit a ceiling, implying that they were somewhat below it even as they passed their immobile British rivals.

The engineering and electrical goods industries

The engineering and electrical goods industries are of prime importance to any modern, industrialised economy. In Britain, the various branches of the engineering industry jointly passed cotton textiles to become Britain's largest manufacturing industry in terms of value added before 1900. The electrical products industry, entirely dependent on a newer technology, was much smaller but it also was growing very rapidly.

The experiences of the various and diverse branches and firms of these industries during the pre-First World War period have recently been much studied. This work has concentrated on matters such as the rate of growth of total output per worker, the rate of adoption of new technology, the degree of competitiveness with foreign rivals and with profitability. Quantitative studies of particular technological choices or the rate of total factor productivity growth have not appeared.

The major, overall result of this work is that the performance of the branches and firms varied tremendously. Thus, among the older established engineering trades, textile machinery building in particular, and especially spinning equipment, fared very well indeed. The producers of steam engines and turbines and heavy machine tools also enjoyed a considerable degree of success. Lower grades, however, are given to the producers of railway locomotives and rolling stock and to some types of machine tools (Saul 1968: 191–209). The traditional clock making industry met virtually total disaster (Church 1975b). Among the new trades, similar diversity is to be found. Sewing machine and bicycle producers are usually given high marks, while makers of motor cars and agricultural equipment were less successful. In the production of engines, gas and semi-diesels did well while the use and manufacture of the regular diesel engine made relatively little progress (Saul 1968: 209–26).

On a more general plane, there is disagreement as to whether the widespread adoption of American production techniques by the British engineering industry in the 1890s involved the elimination of an existing, uneconomic technological lag. On the one hand, it is sometimes argued that these methods were superior well before this time but that the British industry only adopted them when large-scale American exports penetrated the British market. The alternative hypothesis is that the techniques were in fact not superior earlier. The influx of American products occurred more or less immediately once American technology became economically superior – and it was then rapidly adopted in Britain. The advantage in this contest seems to lie with the latter position (Floud 1974).

In the case of the electrical goods industry, there is first the problem of the relatively slow adoption of electrification in British industry. While the question of possible irrationality has not been definitely settled, it is clear that British manufacturing was relatively heavily concentrated in fields such as textiles, where there was little or no advantage in electrical driving. It is also clear that the electrification that did occur in Britain was, as rational calculation would dictate, concentrated in industries such as engineering and shipbuilding where its advantage was greatest (Byatt 1968: 243). As to the various branches of electrical goods manufacturing, once again there was a great diversity in performance. The most successful branch of the industry in Britain was electrical cables and related telegraphic equipment. Electrical machine building and, especially, light bulb manufacturing, performed less well (*ibid.*: 258–66).

The standard conclusion drawn from this variation in performance among branches of these industries in Britain is that the successful branches are evidence of good entrepreneurship and the weaker ones are examples of poor entrepreneurship. The suggestion is thus that any theory of consistently poor British entrepreneurial behaviour has been disproved, but that poor entrepreneurship did exert some drag on the performance of the economy. Are such conclusions justified?

If it is *assumed* that the single, or at least the dominant, determinant of success or failure by a branch of the engineering industry in some country is the quality of entrepreneurship, then the relative quality of entrepreneurship between countries in engineering can be determined by counting successes and failures in each country. In fact, however, it is clear that other variables, such as the nature of demand and the supply of experienced and skilled labour, also play important roles in the performance of branches of the industry in various countries. Empirical support for a belief that entrepreneurship is not everything is readily available. One example is the experience of the two divisions of Siemens Brothers (the English subsidiary of a Germany company). Their dynamo factory did very poorly (in fact it was 'the most unprofitable factory in the industry' – despite 'close control' from Berlin) as did this whole British branch of manufacturing. The cable division, on the other hand, shared in the general prosperity of British cable manufacturing (*ibid.*: 255–6, 262–3). Another example can be found in the history of British clock manufacturing. As this branch was forced to the wall, principally by Swiss competition, a number of British clock manufacturers, including the largest firm, shifted successfully to other branches of metal working (Church 1975b: 628–9).

This type of evidence, in fact, is compatible with the opposite belief, namely that the supply of managerial talent is infinitely elastic. Since this assumption means that managers of constant (and presumably good) quality will always be available, other factors must determine the success of a firm, branch or industry. Abundant evidence is available, however, indicating that entrepreneurial skill makes a great difference to the performance of different firms engaged in the same line of business. It is reasonable to believe that some variation in entrepreneurial talent also exists, and makes a difference to performance, among branches of industries and even in whole industries. Furthermore, if factors other than entrepreneurship affect the overall success of a branch of industry, then the most favoured branches and industries will also tend to attract the best entrepreneurs. The ability to recognise opportunity is certainly part of good entrepreneurship. This tendency, of course, will reinforce the other factors and will increase international specialisation between branches of a given industry and between industries.

Thus, the varying degrees of success of different branches of the British engineering and electrical goods industries are compatible with the belief that these British industries had both good and bad entrepreneurs. It is not possible, however, to conclude that British management in this industry was better or worse than in other countries simply by counting the number of successful branches in each country. The same factors that affect the likelihood of success between various branches of the engineering industry within a country may also affect the likelihood of success in the industry in general. It may have required greater ability to achieve a given degree of success in the British engineering industry than, let us say, in the German one. This would also imply that a smaller percentage of Britain's supply of skilled entrepreneurs would be attracted to the engineering industry.

The chemical industry

The role played by scientific research and innovation in the chemical industry has frequently caused it to be viewed as more important than is indicated by its share of national value added or industrial employment. Indeed, the production of sulphuric acid has, on occasion, been used as an index of a country's level of industrialisation.

Thus it is not surprising that the performance of the British chemical industry was viewed with great concern in late-Victorian and Edwardian Britain. By some standards, at least, the industry performed quite well. In fact, in terms of employment, the industry grew faster between 1881 and 1911 than any other industrial group in Britain, with the single exception of the public utilities. By the latter year, the industry employed 2.7 per cent of the manufacturing labour force. Four years earlier the chemical industry had contributed 3 per cent of Britain's total net industrial output (Richardson 1968: 279–80).

Clearly any failure in terms of output growth was a relative one. The problem was that the chemical industry was growing even faster, and reaching higher absolute levels of output, in Germany and the United States. In 1913, Britain produced an estimated 11 per cent of world chemical output while Germany and the United States accounted for 24 per cent and 34 per cent respectively (*ibid.*: 278).

What is more striking, however, is the degree to which there was national specialisation among various types of chemical products. Germany, for example, was totally dominant in dyes, drugs and photographic chemicals and the United States led the way in electrochemicals. Britain did well in soap (the province of one of the period's truly great entrepreneurs in industrial organisation and retailing: William Lever of Lever Bros. and Unilever), paints, coal tar intermediates and explosives (*ibid.*: 280).

Despite British success in some fields, the slower overall rate of growth, and the total failure in other fields, particularly dyestuffs, resulted at the time, and ever since, in a flood of criticism of the industry's performance. The principal specific charges are usually: first, the prolonged retention of the Leblanc process in alkali production, despite the superiority of the Solvay process; second, the retention of the lead-chamber process rather than the adoption of the contact process in sulphuric acid production; third, the failure of British research and development (R & D) to keep up with Germany in dyes and drugs. The last of these charges is part of a more general claim that the British industry underemployed scientists and underinvested in research.

The first two of these allegations have been subjected to careful quantitative analysis. The question posed was: At what point in time should the old processes (Leblanc and lead-chamber) have been abandoned by profit maximising entrepreneurs? The most likely answers are in 1897 for the Leblanc process and not before 1914 for the lead-chamber process.

Before 1897 the British Leblanc producers had merged in 1890 to form United Alkali Producers (UAP). In Britain, their chief competition came from Brunner Mond, who held the Solvay patent rights for Britain until they expired in 1886. Despite the profitable example of Solvay production by that firm, and the expiration of the patent, UAP retained its Leblanc capacity in soda ash until 1902 and did not abandon its other Leblanc alkali lines until the First World War. The estimated profit lost to UAP resulting from this retention of economically obsolete equipment, discounted back to 1890, ranges between £1.9 million at 3 per cent interest and £0.9 million at 6 per cent. The sensitivity of these calculations to interest rates is apparent from the result that at 8 per cent the loss would have been zero (Lindert & Trace 1971a, b).

It does seem that UAP made a technological error in keeping its obsolete Leblanc process equipment working some years too long. However, given the modest size of the loss, the error could hardly have been a major blow to the nation; less than £2 million does not seem a very large loss to stem from an error which is usually described as one of the worst examples of 'entrepreneurial failure' in Britain before 1914. It is also interesting to note that UAP had a considerable amount of market power. While other Solvay firms, even in Britain, set an example of greater profitability, UAP was not under nearly as much pressure to do things right as is a firm operating in a competitive environment.

The problem of judging Britain's alleged failure to invest sufficiently in chemical R & D in general, and in the dye field in particular, has not yet been satisfactorily solved. In principle, underemployment of chemists and under-investment in R & D means that the employment of chemists and investment in R & D should yield unusually high returns. Those firms who invested relatively most in such activities should have tended to be the most profitable. This may indeed have been the case, but no convincing evidence on the subject is available.

A somewhat different perspective on Germany's success in dyes and drugs results from looking at the high degree of product specialisation in the industry as a whole. Dyes and drugs were highly research intensive and Germany had, thanks to its educational system, a relatively large supply of scientists and research oriented University chemistry departments. Combining this with the generally admitted shortcomings of the British patent system (there was no effective requirement that foreign patent holders either themselves utilise or license their inventions in Britain), the Germans may well have had a relative advantage in this sector. In a complex technology, furthermore, once someone gets ahead, they usually get increasingly hard to catch. British chemical firms may have been wise, thereby displaying good entrepreneurship, to stay out of Germany's chemical specialties. In fact, the generally praised American industry produced even less in the way of dyes than did the British.

The cotton textile industry

It should hardly be necessary to remind the reader of the importance to the British economy of the cotton textile industry, from the start of the industrial revolution to the disastrous collapse of the industry during the interwar period. Not until the end of the nineteenth century was the industry replaced (by the combined engineering trades) as the leading British industry in terms of value added. In exports, the record is even more impressive. Having constituted an amazing 50 per cent by value of all British exports in 1830, the industry's share slowly declined, but still amounted to 24.1 per cent in 1913. Although the growth rate of the industry was slower after the middle of the century than before, its consumption of raw cotton doubled between 1860, or 1870 for that matter, and the all time record year of 1913 (Sandberg 1974: ch. 1).

Given the industry's admirable record in terms of output and exports right up to the First World War, it is not surprising that contemporary criticism of the industry's management was limited to social, not economic, questions. The rapid decline of the industry during the interwar period, however, resulted not only in criticism of the industry's management at that time, but also produced a very critical reassessment of entrepreneurial behaviour during the period before the First World War. As far as scholarly opinion was concerned, the poor performance of the pre-First World War cotton textile industry became an accepted fact with the publication in 1933 of *Increasing Return* by G. T. Jones. Jones calculated what he called a 'real cost' index (the exact inverse of a total factor productivity index) for the Lancashire cotton industry which showed no improvement whatsoever in the industry's efficiency between 1885 and 1910. Indeed, he found a slight *decline* in efficiency between 1900 and 1910 (Jones 1933: 117, 274).

The key specific charges which were levied against the pre-First World War British cotton managers were that they were unduly slow in adopting the ring spindle in spinning and virtually ignored the automatic loom in weaving. The principle advantage of the ring spindle over the older competing technology, the mule spindle, was that it could be operated by unskilled (largely female) labour, while the mule required the services of skilled (largely male) operatives. Thus the ring spindle saved on labour costs. The principal disadvantage of the ring was that, to make a given fineness (or 'count' – the count is the number of 840 yard hanks per pound of yarn) of yarn, it required a longer staple and usually more expensive cotton than did the mule. This did not matter for low count yarn because even short staple cotton was long enough for low count rings. At higher counts and qualities, however, there was a raw material cost differential between the two technologies.

In the United States, except at extremely high counts (above 100), the labour saving of the ring more than compensated for the extra cotton cost. In Britain, the relatively very large supply of skilled mule spinners considerably reduced the labour cost saving available from the ring. As a result, the ring was superior for counts up to about 40 while the mule was superior for counts above 40. The situation in France and Germany appears to have been similar to that in Britain. An examination of actual behaviour confirms that cotton entrepreneurs were responding rationally to this situation in all four countries. Except for a very few, extremely high count, installations American entrepreneurs installed only rings in new plants, while British, French and German entrepreneurs installed mules for counts above a point somewhere around 40, and rings for counts below that point (Sandberg 1974: ch. 2). A related problem concerns the rate of replacement of technically well-functioning British low count mules with rings. The economics of replacement are obviously different from those of choosing a technique for a totally new installation. In the latter case, the technology with the lowest total cost is superior. In the former case, the old, existing technology should only be replaced if the *total* cost of the new technique is less than the *variable* cost of the old technique. On a set of what appear to be reasonable assumptions concerning the costs of replacing mules with rings in existing plants, it seems that British managers behaved rationally in this regard also. As would be expected, the rate of replacement of mules with rings was more rapid in America than in Britain (*ibid.*: ch. 3).

The principal advantage of the automatic loom was that it enabled each operator to tend more looms, thereby reducing the labour costs per unit of output. The principal drawback was that they were much more expensive than plain looms, thereby raising the capital costs per unit of output. An analysis of conditions in the United States and in Britain indicates that the likely saving in labour costs outweighed the increase in capital costs in the United States, but not in Britain. Thus, American entrepreneurs should have installed automatic looms in new weaving sheds while British entrepreneurs should have avoided the automatic loom entirely. In fact, of course, that is overwhelmingly what they each did. The argument that automatic looms were not installed in Britain because they were incompatible with existing weaving sheds is not applicable to this period. Automatic looms were not installed for good reasons, even in new sheds (*ibid.*: ch. 4). Furthermore, these calculations of the profitability of the automatic loom in Britain are based on conditions before the First World War. The situation was much worse after the war. A massive installation of automatic looms would have greatly increased the losses experienced by the industry during the interwar period. The inevitable and painful dismantling of the British cotton textile industry would have been no less inevitable and even more painful.

While the British cotton entrepreneurs apparently responded properly to these innovations in spinning and weaving, there is no doubt that their world-wide introduction hurt Britain's relative position in the industry. That is always the case with innovations that are more suited to conditions abroad than at home. The ring spindle, in particular, seriously reduced the value of Britain's large stock of human capital which was embodied in her corps of skilled mule spinners.

Nevertheless, it does seem strange that the efficiency of the Lancashire cotton textile industry, as reported by Jones, should actually have declined between 1900 and 1910, particularly since the period witnessed a substantial increase in labour productivity in the industry. An investigation of the Jones index, however, reveals that these peculiar results depend on some highly questionable procedures and data. Most important, Jones' method of joining two series of cotton cloth prices in 1899 is unacceptable. Substituting a more reasonable technique eliminates the peculiar drop in efficiency claimed for the post 1900 period. Instead, a more reasonable recalculation of the index results in a continuation after 1900 of the modest rate of efficiency growth that Jones himself reported for the 1885–1900 period. While this rate is not as rapid as that estimated for Massachusetts, the two can be reconciled without reliance on 'entrepreneurial failure' in Britain (Sandberg 1974: ch. 5).

The coal mining industry

The coal mining industry was a giant in the British economy during the 1860–1914 period. The value of its output was equal to about 3 per cent of GNP in 1860 and 7 per cent in 1913. Employment rose from 350 000 in 1870 to 940 000 in 1907. These data give a picture, not only of a large industry, but of one that is experiencing rapid growth. This is confirmed by the increase in tons of coal produced from 83 million in 1860 to 287 million in 1913. Exports rose over the same interval from seven million tons to seventy-three million tons (Taylor 1968; Deane & Cole 1962: ch. 6; Mitchell & Jones 1971: ch. IV).

Despite these impressive figures, concern about the health of the industry was frequently expressed at the time, and the performance of the industry during the period has been the object of a great deal of retrospective criticism. To some extent, this criticism stems from the even more rapid growth of the industry in Germany and America. Even more disturbing, however, was the decline in labour productivity recorded by the industry starting in the 1880s. British output per man year increased from 270 tons in 1874–78 to 319 tons in 1879–83 and 1884–88 and then declined to 257 tons in 1908–13. In the other European countries, output per man peaked later and had only stagnated, or declined very slightly, by 1908–13. These developments left labour productivity in Britain in 1908–13 at the same level as that in Germany and somewhat above the French and Belgian levels. In America, however, there was continuous advance in labour productivity, leaving the American level well above that in Britain and the other countries (Taylor 1968: 46).

Various factors may have contributed to the sharp drop in British labour productivity. It is reported that the hours of work declined, absenteeism increased and the average quality of the rapidly expanding labour force declined. It is noted second that the coal was subjected to better preparation at the pit head, thus improving the quality of the product. Perhaps most important of all, the quality of the remaining untapped coal deposits was deteriorating; Britain had, with perfect rationality, mined her most accessible coal first. Germany's later start somewhat delayed the point of increasing costs due to thinner, more fractured and deeper seams, while America was still opening up new, high quality coal fields. Finally, it has been frequently stressed that the British industry was much slower to mechanise, particularly with mechanical coal cutters, than was the American industry. The two interrelated questions about the quality of British coal mining management that emerge from these observations are: one, whether the lag in mechanisation behind America was a sign of technological backwardness; two, whether Britain's lower, and declining, level of labour productivity can be explained without recourse to 'entrepreneurial failure'.

The direct quantitative analysis of the first of these questions is made extremely difficult by the varying geological conditions between, and within, the various coalfields. As a result, most of the discussion of the problem is of a qualitative and impressionistic nature. For example, the leading historian of the British coal mining industry argues that the fact that some British coal fields installed coal cutters faster than some others is, in itself, a reflection on the management of the laggards. At the same time, however, he reports that the leading fields had a relatively large number of narrow seams, the kind which benefited the most from mechanical cutters (Taylor 1961: 60–1). Such evidence says nothing at all about the appropriateness of the overall rate of introduction of coal cutters. It does imply, however, that the British coal managers were rational enough to introduce mechanical cutting first into those mines where it did the most good.

In another study, the same author raises another type of argument. Although he cannot show that the British coal mine operators were unwise in not installing more coal cutters, he nevertheless wonders about their motives: 'Insofar as unwillingness to persevere with the coal-cutter was symptomatic, not of a rational assessment of its potentialities, but of the operation of the conservative tendencies in the industry, its consequences could be far reaching' (Taylor 1968:

59–60). This is pure speculation. The author cannot show that there was anything wrong with the behaviour of the coal managers. He grants that they 'may well' have made 'the right choice', but he then adds that *if* they did it for the wrong reason then that is a bad sign. While in a sense this is true, such hypothesising proves nothing.

One further attempt has been made to reconcile the difference in labour productivity in the British and American coal mining industries. This study begins by noting that in 1907 the British industry used about the same number of horsepower per worker as the American industry did in 1909. This implies that the much greater depths of the British mines had increased capital per worker to levels similar to those in America even without mechanical coal cutters. Since American wages were much higher than British wages, this, in turn, implies that Britain was substituting capital for inferior natural resources. Using estimates of the response (elasticity) of output per worker to seam thickness and depth, the study makes a reasonable case that the difference in natural resource quality explains the difference in levels of output per worker (McCloskey 1971a: 289–95).

The mercantile marine

One of the most important and successful sectors of the British economy between 1860 and 1914 was the mercantile marine. Throughout that period approximately one third of total world tonnage was of UK registration. This fraction, in fact, considerably understates Britain's share of world shipping capacity. British ships were much more modern than world average. Almost 4 per cent of the UK fleet was sold abroad each year. Thus, for example, in 1914 85 per cent of all UK registered ships had been built since 1895 (Aldcroft 1968a: 326–7).

Given this performance, it is not surprising that the management of the British merchant marine has been virtually exempt from the kind of criticism levelled against other British entrepreneurs. The reason for including the sector in this chapter is thus simply that a quantitative study has been made of the most important technological decision facing all shipping entrepreneurs during this period, the shift from sail to steam. This shift occurred gradually, starting with the construction of the *Claremont* in 1807 and it was not yet complete at the end of our period. It began with routes where frequent refuelling stops could be made, then continued to routes requiring longer and longer open water crossings. On each route, passengers and perishable goods were the first to be carried by steam and durable bulk cargoes were the last.

The explanation for this process lies in the continuous improvement in the fuel economy of marine steam engines. As fuel consumption per mile fell, fuel costs declined; more important, a smaller part of the ship's cargo space was taken up by fuel supplies. Thus it became economical to travel greater and greater distances without refuelling. To the extent that bunker coal was in any case obtained from Britain, it became economically feasible to use steam ships further and further away from Britain. Thus it is that the grain trade between Australia and Britain around the Cape was the last bastion of the sailing ship. The quantitative study made of this process concludes that the actual timing of these shifts agrees well with the predictions of a decision model using the relative costs of steam and sail. Shipping entrepreneurs apparently responded with alacrity to the changing relative profitability of sail versus steam on various routes (Harley 1971). A more recent but similar study of the adaptation of motor ships by the British mercantile fleet after the First World War does, however, detect an uneconomic lag. The authors of this study blame this lost opportunity on a prejudice in favour of coal and on the excessive claims of the British steam turbine producers (Henning & Trace 1975: 385).

Conclusion

This industrial summary is incomplete. It does not contain everything we know about British entrepreneurship and technical change between 1860 and 1914, much less everything we might like to know. Still, what is known on the subject is far from trivial and, generally speaking, it is unfavourable to the hypothesis of 'entrepreneurial failure'. While some examples of 'technological backwardness' and other types of failure have been found, and more undoubtedly remain to be found, it is not established that the failure rate was any higher than in other countries, including the United States and Germany, during the same period or than in Britain during earlier periods. Much less has it been shown that the British 'entrepreneurial failures' in this period exceeded those in Germany and America by so much that they can materially have contributed to Britain's relative economic decline.

What is perhaps most damaging to the 'entrepreneurial failure' hypothesis is the fact that a large percentage of the serious alleged specific mistakes invariably listed by supporters of the hypothesis (the failure to adopt ring spinning, automatic weaving, basic steel making, Solvay processing of alkalis and mechanical coal cutting) have been carefully studied and the resulting failure yield is very modest indeed. To re-establish the hypothesis, it must be argued that the failures were of a more subtle and insidious kind.

Thus, to the question: 'Did "entrepreneurial failure," and especially "technological backwardness", play a significant role in Britain's relative economic decline?' the answer must be: 'Probably not.'

Suggestions for further reading

The case for 'entrepreneurial failure' in Britain is made by Aldcroft (1964), Landes (1969) and Levine (1967). A set of industry studies that can best be described as neutral on this issue are found in Aldcroft (1968b). Generally sceptical industry case studies are included in McCloskey (1971b). British iron and steel and cotton textile entrepreneurs, respectively, are exonerated in McCloskey (1973) and Sandberg (1974). A more general defense of the British entrepreneur is presented in McCloskey and Sandberg (1971).

6

Income and demand 1860–1914

B. E. SUPPLE

The central concern of this chapter is with variations in the level and pattern of consumer demand in the late nineteenth and early twentieth centuries. At the same time, however, it will be necessary to consider the changes in income which, together with changes in relative prices and consumer tastes, shaped the alterations in demand. It will also be relevant to discuss some of the effects of those shifts on the production of goods and services. To examine the relationship between income, demand, and economic activity is, of course, to examine an essentially circular process: changes in demand obviously affect output, but changes in supply (through their influence on prices and incomes) also affect demand. However, almost any aspect of economic analysis involves some arbitrary starting-point. And it is not illogical to take as given, at least in the first instance, the observed changes in income in the period 1860–1914, going on to explore their character and their consequences in terms of demand, and the consequences of the changes in demand in terms of economic structures.

Income and its distribution

Income growth

Changes in total income are potentially important determinants of demand in a variety of ways. Thus, the level of incomes, for individuals and for the community as a whole, obviously affects the absolute amounts of goods and services demanded. As incomes grow, so does total expenditure. On the other hand, there is some debate about the *proportionate* relationship between income and consumption. Thus, since the 'propensity to consume' (the proportion of total income spent on goods and services) appears to be smaller for the rich than the poor, it has sometimes been assumed that as people or communities grow wealthier, their propensities to consume will fall. More than this, changes in the level of income might be expected to affect its allocation between different *categories* of goods and services. This is because there are differences in the 'income elasticities of demand' – i.e. the extent to which a proportionate change in income is associated with a proportionate change in the demand for a particular item. Naturally, income elasticity varies from commodity to

Table 6.1. *Average annual income, United Kingdom 1860–1913*

		1860–64	1870–74	1895–99	1910–13
(a)	Net national income, 1913–14 prices (£mn)	646	896	1834	2230
(b)	Net national income per capita, 1913–14 prices (£)	22.1	28.1	45.9	49.2
(c)	Gross national product, current prices (£mn)	759	1081	1145	2184
(d)	Gross national product, 1900 factor cost (£mn)	n.a	1098	1786	2269
(e)	Gross national product, per capita, 1900 factor cost (£)	n.a.	34.4	44.6	50.1

Sources:
(a) Calculated by applying population data to per capita data in Deane & Cole (1962: 329–30)
(b) Deane & Cole (1962: 329–30)
(c) Feinstein (1972: T 4–5)
(d) Feinstein (1972: T 14–15)
(e) Calculated from Feinstein (1972: T 14–15 and T 120–1)

commodity, as well as from person to person in the case of any specific type of purchase. In general, however, as people grow richer, they might be expected to spend proportionately more on 'luxuries' and proportionately less on 'necessities'. By the same token, any change in the distribution of income between groups with different propensities to consume or income elasticities of demand will affect the level and pattern of consumption.

All this suggests that if we wish to use income as the starting-point for a discussion of changes in consumer expenditure, it will be necessary to take note of changes in the allocation as well as the overall level of income.

National income or product can be measured 'gross' (i.e. including the resources needed to replace the capital used up in the process of production) or 'net'. Whichever way it is measured, it includes property income from abroad – which in this period rose from just under 3 per cent to just over 8 per cent of gross national product. As Table 6.1 indicates, the money value of GNP rose fairly substantially over the period as a whole: from some £760 million in the early 1860s to about £2200 million on the eve of the First World War – equivalent to an annual average growth rate of 2.1 per cent. (These data are based upon factor incomes – wages, salaries, profits, rents, interest. Measures of GNP derived from expenditure data show somewhat different levels, but a similar trend.) However, the measurement of national income in terms of prevailing prices can be misleading, since it takes no account of price changes.

In fact, for much of the period 1860–1913 prices were falling, with a decisive upward trend occurring only in the last fifteen years or so. When allowance is made for price trends, 'real' national income is seen to have grown at about 2.5 per cent annually (faster in the late nineteenth century, at 3 per cent, than in the early twentieth, at about 1.3 per cent).

These figures refer to total national income and imply that in aggregate terms demand might have risen by at least 2.5 per cent per annum. But they tell us little about welfare and are a very imperfect guide to potential expenditure. On the first score we also need to know the numbers (and changes in the numbers) of people among whom income was distributed. In fact, the UK population rose from 29 to 45 million in 1860–1913. The growth of per capita real income was, therefore, less than that of total income: about 2.1 per cent per annum in the late nineteenth century and less than 0.5 per cent from 1895 to 1913 (an overall growth rate of 1.6 per cent throughout these years). Modest as such numbers might seem, they were not insignificant by historic standards, and since they represented the cumulative trend of more than fifty years, they indicate an important growth in average incomes – a picture which is confirmed by data on real wages, which rose by almost 1.5 per cent per annum in the late nineteenth century, although they stagnated in the years after 1900 (Mitchell & Deane 1962: 343–5).

Although these increases in total and average income provide the basic context for any consideration of changes in consumer demand, it is also necessary to consider the possibility that changes in the relative allocation of that income between different groups produced alterations in the pattern of demand.

Income distribution

One of the most obvious forms of income redistribution normally associated with economic growth is that between rural and urban communities – engendered by the relative, and often absolute, decline of the agricultural sector. In the UK during the period 1860–1914 this process was expedited by the inflow of huge supplies of cheap foods from recently developed overseas areas (see ch. 3). As a result of this, and of associated alterations in demand, the proportion of the labour force engaged in agriculture, horticulture and forestry fell from 18.5 per cent in 1861 to 8.7 per cent in 1901, while farm wages and farmers' incomes declined from an annual average of £112 million (almost 15 per cent of GNP) in 1860–64 to £83 million (just over 7 per cent of GNP) in 1895–99 (Feinstein 1972: T 4, T 60). Concomitantly, there was an increase in the size and significance of the urban population and its income.

In principle, such shifts affect the pattern of demand. Farming communities are generally considered to spend a smaller proportion of their incomes; city dwellers buy virtually all their own food, whereas agricultural labourers at this time grew about one twelfth of their needs (Hunt 1973: 85); more generally, urban consumers characteristically exemplify – by virtue of the social impact as well as the economic opportunities and needs of city life – a more diversified and commercialised pattern of expenditure. They spend more on accommodation, distribution, transport, public utilities, entertainment, leisure, personal and professional services. Their distinctive expenditures derive in part from distinctive tastes and social attitudes; in part from the economies of scale which can be generated in the provision of goods and services to urban areas (food was actually cheaper in town than in the countryside); and in part from the fact that city life is more costly because housing is more expensive, journeys to work longer, the problems of overcrowding greater, the atmosphere dirtier. Over the long run, therefore, urban, industrial societies will differ in their consumption levels and patterns from rural, agricultural societies. At the same time, however, it is not easy to isolate the effects of the change in residence from those of rising incomes. For urban societies, being a product of economic growth, are also generally wealthier. In Britain in the late nineteenth century, for example, when an agricultural labourer moved to the city his income might rise by between one third and 100 per cent (Bowley 1937: 50; Hunt 1973: 92–3). As a result, his new patterns of demand were based upon new wealth as well as on the new opportunities, pressures and tastes of city life. Given this, and the fact that the UK was already fairly well industrialised by the 1860s, it is unlikely that the rural–urban redistribution of the late nineteenth century was itself a significant determinant of evolving consumer demand, although it was undoubtedly involved in the 'modernisation' of patterns of consumption.

A second type of income redistribution which needs to be considered is that between social classes or occupational groups. This was also inextricably associated with changes in the level of purchasing power, since class differences were in large part *based* upon income differences. But, given the cultural and social complexities involved, it is at least worth considering whether groups with overlapping incomes had contrasting expenditure patterns. The question arises because of the coincidence of an increase in wages, on the one hand, and the growth of a 'lower middle class' of clerks, schoolteachers, shopkeepers, technicians, etc., on the other: the proportion of 'white collar workers' in the labour force rose from about 3 per cent in 1861 to some 7 per cent in 1911 (Crossick 1976b: 19); salaries grew as a proportion of total incomes from 6.5 per cent in the 1860s to 10.8 per cent on the eve of the First World War (Feinstein 1968: 119). One measure of the number and incomes of those of modest means who were not wage-earners is provided by data on 'intermediate incomes' under £160 (the lower limit for income tax liability for most of the period). As table 6.2 shows, they rose from 11.5 per cent of total incomes in 1880 to 17 per cent in 1913.

These trends are relevant here because of the presumed tendency of the lower middle class to use their immediate social superiors as reference groups in making decisions about expenditures on such things as housing, domestic service,

Table 6.2. *Changes in the distribution of the national income, 1880–1913*

	1880					1913				
	Number of incomes		Average income	Total income		Number of incomes		Average income	Total income	
	No. (000)	%	£	Amount (£m)	%	No. (000)	%	£	Amount (£m)	%
Wages	12 300	83.3	37.8	465	41.5	15 200	73.4	50.7	770	35.5
Intermediate incomes (under £160)	1 850	12.5	70.3	130	11.5	4 310	20.8	84.7	365	17
Incomes assessed to tax over £160, excluding wage earners	620	4.2	854.8	530	47	1 190	5.8	865.5	1030	47.5
Total	14 770	100.0	76.2	1125	100.0	20 700	100.0	104.6	2165	100.0

Source: Bowley (1920: 16)

holidays, education, clothing, insurance, alcohol. Thus there were significant examples of white collar workers spending more on, say, housing than artisans with similar incomes – although this was partly attributable to greater security and prospects of employment (Crossick 1976b: 34–5). Nevertheless, in terms of the national pattern of demand, it seems highly unlikely that such social nuances were very important: by far the greatest effects must have come from the higher incomes of the newly important income groups. Admittedly, as table 6.2 shows, the average non-wage income of less than £160 came nearer to average wages between 1880 and 1913, thus presumably extending the possibility of overlap. But in terms of changes in the period, even if the entire increase in the proportion of total income earned by the 'intermediate' category (5.5 per cent) had gone into the hands of families with the same incomes as, but different tastes to, wage-earners, it seems unlikely that the resulting change in consumption would have made very much difference to overall demand. For example, suppose that *all* non-wage-earners (intermediate and tax-payers alike) spent 10 per cent of their incomes on services not purchased by wage-earners. In 1880 those services would have attracted 5.85 per cent (i.e. 10 per cent of the 58.5 per cent of income received by non-wage-earners) of total incomes. But in 1913 they would have attracted only a further 0.6 per cent (10 per cent of the extra 6.0 per cent of total incomes going to non-wage-earners) – although the absolute amounts, of course, might well have been quite large.

The final, and most important, consideration concerning changes in the allocation of income relates to redistribution as it is normally understood: between relatively wealthy and relatively poor families. In this respect, however, we encounter a conceptual problem which has dogged all our discussion so far – namely, the simultaneous occurrence of different types of changes affecting incomes (and therefore demand). In this instance, as table 6.2 suggests, we observe four developments: a growth in the total number of income recipients; changes in the distribution of the workforce between different occupations and income levels; a general increase in incomes (i.e. all major categories of income grew on a per capita basis – albeit by different amounts); and what might be termed 'pure' redistribution. Indeed, when we look at the size distribution of incomes we are reminded even more forcibly than earlier that redistribution in its conventional sense was of little importance to the topic under consideration, precisely because redistribution was accompanied by, and indistinguishable from, changes in population, in national income, and in economic structure.

Although the gross categories of table 6.2 are not suitable for any sophisticated measures of redistribution, they do indicate the varied senses in which income change took place. This can be exemplified by calculating (as in table 6.3) the percentage growth in the number of incomes, in average incomes, and in total incomes in each category.

From tables 6.2 and 6.3, it will be seen that average wages increased by more

Table 6.3. *Growth of incomes 1880–1913 (per cent)*

	Number of incomes	Average incomes	Total incomes
Wages	24	34	66
Intermediate incomes	133	20	181
Taxable incomes	92	1	94

Source: calculated from table 6.2

than other incomes. However, because the number of wage earners increased by significantly less than the number of other income recipients, the total wage bill only grew by two thirds, as against a much higher growth for other categories. A corollary of this was that the apparently slow growth of average non-wage incomes was mainly based on the fact that the number of recipients grew fairly rapidly. In other words, new 'entrants' to each category came in at the lower end of the income scales, and thereby held down the relevant averages. In this respect Bowley (1920: 16–17) estimated that whereas in 1880 the proportion of people earning over £160 was 4.2 per cent, in 1913 the top 4.2 per cent of income recipients received over £225 – an increase of 30 per cent.

Whether the purely redistributive aspects of these various changes – compounded of differential increases in, and reallocation of, numbers and incomes – were significant for consumption is not easy to determine. If we examine the conventional measure of income redistribution (the proportions of total incomes received by specified percentages of income earners) then the available estimates are not very helpful because the categories are excessively large, each embracing a very wide range of income and concealing substantial changes in numbers. But recalculation suggests that at the extremes there may have been very little important redistribution (compare Soltow 1968). Thus, Bowley's estimate for the top 4.2 per cent, just quoted, shows only a slight decline: from 47 per cent to 44.5 per cent of total income. Assuming for this argument that wage earners represent the other end of the income scale, then in 1880 the bottom 12.3 million (i.e. all wage earners) accounted for 83.3 per cent of income recipients and only 41.5 per cent of total incomes. It is impossible to calculate the exact proportion of total income earned by the corresponding 83.3 per cent of income recipients in 1913 because the 'upwards drift' of income recipients left only 73.4 per cent in the wage-earning group, and we do not know how well or badly the 'next' 9.9 per cent were paid. But assuming that they fell somewhere between the average of wage earners (£50.7 p.a.) and of intermediate income earners (£84.7 p.a.) – and the latter is almost certainly too high – then the income of the 'bottom' 83.3 per cent of people in 1913 would have been between 40 and 43.6 per cent of total income – as against 41.5 per cent in 1880. In neither case would this have amounted to a very large change.

It seems, therefore, that there was no very substantial redistribution of income in the late nineteenth and early twentieth centuries. Indeed, the striking feature was the persistence and extremity of income inequality. The large numbers of very poor, even after four or five decades of increasing real wages, were disturbingly visible to contemporaries – of whom Charles Booth and Seebohm Rowntree are only the best known. On the other hand, the relatively small number of very rich absorbed hugely disproportionate amounts of income: Bowley (1920: 22) estimated that in 1910 just over 1 per cent of the people received 30 per cent of the national income and L. G. C. Money (1906: 41–2) estimated that in 1904 one ninth received one half.

Broadly speaking, then, there was no change in income distribution which was sufficiently large to affect the pattern of demand during this period. On the other hand, as will be seen, the extent of the inequality which existed *did* have important consequences for consumption patterns at any one time. But in any case there were two developments worth emphasising before we turn to questions of demand. The first was the increase in the average and total incomes of all relevant categories. Even if this increase was 'shared with remarkable equality among the various economic classes' (Bowley 1920: 26–7), the mere fact of its occurrence carried at least the potential for far-reaching changes in the pattern of goods and services consumed. Secondly, however, it does seem possible that *within* the large categories there was some 'upwards drift' – i.e. a tendency for there to be more people in higher- and less in lower-paid occupations. This was obviously the case with wage-earners: in the last 40 years of the nineteenth century real wages rose by about 75 per cent, but almost one third of this increase was accounted for by the changing composition of the work force in favour of better-paid jobs (Wood 1909: 138). And between 1880 and 1910 half of the increase in money wages was accounted for by changes in the distribution of labour between relatively poorly- and relatively better-paid jobs (Bowley 1937: appendix B). Nevertheless, the fact remains that it was income growth, rather than income redistribution, which lay at the base of the important changes in demand during this period.

Levels and patterns of demand

Consumers' expenditure

Although a comprehensive explanation of changes in the level and pattern of demand would have to take account of relative prices and consumer tastes, it is here assumed that the principal determinants of long-run changes in consumption have been shifts in incomes of the sort described in the previous section.

Table 6.4. *Consumers' and public authorities' expenditures as a proportion of UK gross national product 1870–1913 (per cent)*

	(A) Consumers	(B) Public authorities	(C) (A)+(B)
1870–79	87.8	4.8	92.6
1880–89	87.8	5.8	93.6
1890–99	87.9	6.3	94.2
1900–09	85.5	8.6	94.1
1904–13	84.5	8.0	92.5

Source: Feinstein (1972: T 8)

The growth in total incomes which took place in the period was, of course, associated with a large increase in consumers' expenditure. More or less reliable data are available only from the 1870s and show an increase in *total* consumption of about 87 per cent in money terms and 91 per cent in real terms between 1870–74 and 1910–13 (Feinstein 1972: T8, T14). Allowing for the contemporary growth of population, there was an expansion of some 33 per cent in real per capita consumption during the same period – reflecting an increase from about £33 per head (in 1913 prices) in 1870–74 to £41.4 in 1895–99 and to £44 in 1910–13 (Feinstein 1972: T42). These were fairly impressive achievements, although the indication of extreme income inequality, of continuing widespread and degrading poverty, and of an arrest of the upward trend of real wages from 1900, must cloud any very optimistic picture of the beneficial effects of this growth. At the same time, given the relative stability of income distribution, there is no reason to believe that large numbers of the very poor did not share in some of the fruits of the growth in incomes and consumption.

While the increase in expenditure was only to be expected in the light of the increase in income, a more striking aspect of the behaviour of aggregate demand was the relative stability of the proportion of income actually devoted to current consumption (i.e. the propensity to consume). As table 6.4 shows, when measured over periods sufficiently long to average-out annual or cyclical variations, private consumption remained at roughly 88 per cent of GNP throughout the late nineteenth century, dipping only very slightly in the decade before 1914. Earlier estimates (reproduced in Deane & Cole 1962: 332–3) for a longer period show somewhat different levels but basically the same trend: stability, at about 84 per cent of GNP, for the last 40 years of the century, followed by a lower level, about 80 per cent after 1899.

Superficially, this long-run stability during a period of rising incomes may appear surprising in view of the fact that cross-sectional studies – i.e. comparisons of different income groups at the same point in time – bear out the 'common sense' view that those with larger incomes spend a smaller and save a greater proportion of their incomes than those with lesser incomes. It might be expected, therefore, that as a community grows wealthier it would increase its consumption by less than its income – i.e. that its propensity to consume would decline.

That this is not so, at least in the early stages of economic growth, is indicated by comparative data (Kuznets 1962: 23). The tendency to stability in the propensity to consume can be explained in terms of the consumer's concept of a 'permanent' or 'life-cycle' income – i.e. by the assumption that consumers make decisions about expenditure which average-out the effects of 'transitory' changes in income stemming from random events, windfalls, the effect of business cycles, etc. On this assumption there could be a long-run tendency for the proportion of income spent on current consumption by different households to converge.

An alternative, and perhaps more interesting, explanation of the fact that as a population grows richer those with greater incomes do not behave as the corresponding income recipients did at the previous stage, is based on more explicit social–psychological forces. This approach attributes a vital role to *relative* income, to an individual's standing in the scale of income distribution and to the 'social' reasons for consumption, that is to the culturally and socially determined drive towards emulation and esteem via expenditure (Duesenberry 1949: ch. III). If households decide about their level of current consumption with reference to other (and particularly slightly wealthier) groups, and if their attitudes are therefore heavily determined by what other people spend their money on and by the flow of information and persuasion about consumption, then levels of consumption would be explained in terms of income distribution and the social and cultural setting of consumption. People would reduce their propensity to consume only when they grew *relatively* as well as absolutely richer. And from these viewpoints it is significant that there was, apparently, so little change in the distribution of income in the late nineteenth and early twentieth centuries and that in this period we can also discern powerful trends working to sustain consumption levels: the increasing urbanisation of consumers, the growth of advertising and of mass communication, the extension of literacy and of the awareness of social class. These things, and the drive to emulation which went with them, were important not merely to the moderately affluent who aspired to the standards of the established middle classes, but to the relatively wealthy themselves. In 1875, for example, W. R. Greg complained that the increased cost of middle-class living, with its demands for labour-intensive services was 'only half the story' of material pressures on the middle class:

owing to the increasing wealth of the wealthy, and the increasing numbers who every year step into the wealthier class, the *style of living* as well as the cost of necessaries and comforts of which 'living' consists, has advanced in an extraordinary ratio; and however frugal, however unostentatious, however rational we may be, however resolute to live

Table 6.5. *Proportionate flow of goods and services to consumers (per cent)*

	Food	Drink	Other goods	Rent	Other services
1880–89	33.6	13.2	23.8	10.4	19.0
1890–99	31.4	12.8	23.6	10.8	21.4
1900–09	31.6	10.8	25.0	11.5	21.1

Source: Jefferys & Walters (1955: 20)

as we think we ought, and not as others do around us, it is...simply *impossible* not to be influenced by their example and to fall into their ways, unless we are content either to live in remote districts or in an isolated fashion. The result is that we need many things that our fathers did not, and that for each of these many things we must pay more. Even where prices are lower, quantities are increased [quoted in Banks 1954: 67].

Finally, the facts of inequality of income distribution are obviously relevant to the propensity to consume at another level: the large numbers of the very poor, saving nothing or only negligible amounts, still had so many unsatisfied needs that any feasible increases in their incomes over a generation or two were very unlikely to increase savings by a significant amount. Altogether, then, it is hardly surprising that the higher incomes generated by economic growth did not lead to any very great change in the proportionate expenditure on current goods and services.

Patterns of demand: food and drink

Although the growth of incomes did not produce any very radical changes in the proportion devoted to total current consumption, it might be expected that substantial increases in purchasing power would have changed the ways in which expenditure was allocated *between* different categories of goods and services – that as people became richer they spent their new incomes in different ways from their old. How far were there different income elasticities of demand for the principal items of consumption? This is an important question because of the frequent assumption that economic growth is associated with significant changes in economic structure which are partly caused by shifts in the sectorial composition of demand. As table 6.5 suggests, however, the composition of demand (in terms of the large aggregates of food and drink, other manufactured goods, and services), shows surprisingly little change, at least towards the end of this period, although the absence of good data for the pre-1880 decades presumably masks the full extent of change.

Once again there is a contrast between cross-sectional and time-series data. Taking expenditure on food as our first example, virtually all studies of household budgets in the period 1860–1914 substantiate the central proposition of 'Engel's Law' – the view, first put forward in a systematic manner by Ernst Engel in the mid nineteenth century, that the greater the family income the smaller the percentage devoted to food. Broadly speaking, British wage-earning families spent between roughly one half and two thirds of their income on food – about twice as much as the better-off members of the middle class, with, of course, gradations between. And the inverse relations between income and proportionate food expenditures also applied within social groupings, although more distinctly in the case of the moderately well-off. Thus, estimates during the 1870s showed middle-class expenditures on food declining from about 50 per cent of incomes for those with £150 p.a. to some 30 per cent for those with between £400 and £500, to 20 per cent for the really wealthy (Banks 1954: 59ff; Rousiers 1896: 29). In the case of wage-earners, although the better-off spent a smaller proportion of their outlay on food than the poorer, there was a much greater convergence of proportionate expenditures by different groups – partly because most wage-earners were in any case fairly poor, and partly because higher family incomes were often derived from a greater number of young, and hungry, workers in the household.

As with the overall propensity to consume, however, differences in food consumption between different income categories tell us little about changes in demand as per capita national income rose. As table 6.5 shows, as aggregate and per capita incomes grew there was only a negligible decline in the proportionate significance of food expenditures; they remained at roughly one third of total private consumption, and therefore at about one quarter of GNP. (The low level of these proportions is, incidentally, striking testimony to the inequality of income distribution, given the fact that food was almost twice as important in the household budgets of the very numerous poor and wage earners.) Indeed, when account is taken of the possibility that the estimates may exaggerate the extent of food consumption in the 1880s (Feinstein 1972: 15) and of the substantial relative as well as absolute fall in food prices in the late nineteenth century (a cost-of-living enquiry estimated that they fell by about 30 per cent compared with other items in urban, working-class living costs: Parliamentary Papers Cd. 2337 1904: 31), it seems very unlikely that there was *any* tendency for the expenditure on food to fall on account of a rise of incomes. Indeed, if relative prices had remained constant the proportionate expenditure on food would probably have risen. And it is presumably significant that the tendency of the share of food in total consumption to fall levelled-off just as relative food prices ceased to fall in the early twentieth century.

The buoyancy of food expenditures in this period is hardly surprising. The extent of poverty and undernourishment meant that many – perhaps most – families had a long way to go before they would adequately satisfy their basic needs for food. Moreover, although incomes were rising, so was the proportion

Table 6.6. *Estimated weekly per capita consumption of various foods 1860–1913*

		1860	1880	1909–13
Wheat	(lb)	6.20	6.60	6.40
Cheese	(lb)	0.12	0.16	0.14
Potatoes	(lb)	6.8	5.7	4.0
Meat and bacon	(lb)	1.8	1.8	2.5
Milk	(pints)	1.75	2.2	3.2
Butter	(lb)	0.17	0.25	0.3
Tea	(lb)	0.05	0.09	0.13
Sugar	(lb)	0.66	1.21	1.40

Source: Mackenzie (1921: 224)

of adults in the population. Assuming that adults consume more food than young children, the need for food rose, with the changing age composition of the population, at a faster rate than the number of people. Thus, whereas between 1861 and 1911 the population grew by 63 per cent, if we 'translate' the absolute numbers into 'adult equivalents' by counting a school-age child as 0.6 and an infant as 0.3 of an adult (Allen and Bowley 1935: 21), the growth was 70 per cent – i.e. the food needs were greater than implied by the simple growth of numbers.

Yet quite apart from biological reasons for food consumption, there were more general pressures towards a varied and higher quality diet. These might be more explicitly exemplified among the middle classes (Banks 1954: 55ff; Burnett 1968: ch. 9), but they were also widely diffused, and amply demonstrated the extent to which the demand for food was shaped by social and cultural as well as biological factors. Indeed, it is quite misleading to envisage 'food' as a homogenous commodity. Extra income was used not so much to buy more of exactly the same thing, as to increase variety and enhance the level of diet, and to take advantage of higher degrees of fabrication, packaging and convenience in supply.

As far as the choice of commodities was concerned, there was a marked tendency towards greater consumption of animal products as well as more 'exotic' imports, and a lesser emphasis on grains and more traditional foods. Thus, the per capita demand for cheese was broadly unchanged and that for breadstuffs and potatoes (in spite of a dramatic fall in their prices) was also stable or even declining. On the other hand, changes in incomes and tastes now allowed a growing consumption not only of sugar and tea, which benefited from falling prices, but also of meat, milk and butter, the relative prices of which fell only moderately. These contrasting trends are illustrated in the estimates in table 6.6. By 1900, meat, poultry, and eggs accounted for a third, dairy products for about 17 per cent, and bread and cereals for only some 13 per cent of national expenditure on food (Prest 1954: 74). Nor were these proportions greatly influenced by the inequality of income distribution: data on working-class food consumption exemplify a strikingly similar pattern. Thus, a Board of Trade survey of 1944 urban, working-class families in 1904 showed an overall proportionate expenditure of 33 per cent on meat, poultry, and eggs; some 18 per cent on cheese, milk, and butter; and 18 per cent on bread and cereals (Parliamentary Papers Cd. 2337 1904: 5). Even within the wage-earning category, only the expenditure on bread and cereals (at almost one quarter of the total) was significantly different for the poorest group.

It would, therefore, be difficult to deny that the increased incomes of the period were used to improve the quality and variety of the nation's diet – including the diet of the poor. Yet it must also be emphasised that the pattern of working-class food expenditure just mentioned related to very low levels of income. Hence a comparison of available data (Oddy 1970: 321–2) indicates that, among the poorer of the wage earners, there continued to be a low intake of proteins: an unduly high proportion (about 60 per cent) of total calorie intake was in fact derived from a stodgy, carbohydrate diet of bread, flour and potatoes – although it may be that an excessive concentration on household surveys and commercial data underestimates the ingenuity and complexity of working-class cooking and food provision (Roberts 1977). Nevertheless nutritional standards were indisputably low throughout the late nineteenth century – and beyond. They were, presumably, largely a matter of income. But they also derived in part from prejudice, tradition, and taste: there was only a very slow acceptance of fruit, vegetables and milk as items of mass consumption; while an aversion to the blandness of much food led to a relatively expensive preoccupation with palatability in the form of heavy expenditure on sugar, confectionery, jam, pickles, etc. Related to this, and to the increasing urbanisation of Britain, was a trend towards the greater use of commercially prepared and fabricated foods: in addition to confectionery, jams, and pickles, there was a disproportionate expansion in the demand for cakes, biscuits, tinned foods, cooked meats, etc. Broadly speaking, such a development, as with the trend away from a simple reliance on breadstuffs, can be seen as an increase in the quality and variety of diet, particularly among the poor. But such items also reflected the addition of a cheap and sometimes spuriously 'luxurious' element to a low level diet. It is significant that, together with bread and cereals, such items as sugar, jam, treacle, syrup, cocoa and tea were proportionately more important in the expenditure of the poorer than of the better-off working-class households (Parliamentary Papers Cd. 2337 1904: 5).

Looked at more generally, such changes in the pattern of food consumption reflect not merely a mélange of changes in income, tastes, and habits, but also direct responses to alterations in supply conditions. Industrial and technological developments in the late nineteenth century facilitated the supply of a wider and cheaper range of foods and drinks – particularly where the raw material input (cereals, sugar, cocoa, fruits, etc.) fell in price. Hence the expansion of the food industries (Burnett 1968: 137ff) reflected a basic increase in supply associated with an extension of commercial specialisation in areas of activity formerly confined to the home or even, given the cost of raw materials and fuels, not undertaken at all in the houses of the poor. (Comparable developments were exemplified in the rise at this time of the fish-and-chip shop.) At the same time, the new potentialities of large-scale marketing were associated with changes in distribution and in distribution methods. Fabricated foods naturally lent themselves to the sort of branding and advertising which had already begun to characterise the sale of some quality foodstuffs. In this way a genuine mass market for cheap biscuits, teas, pickles, margarine, sugar, chocolate and confectionery, preserves, etc. was developed, analogous to the mass market for soup, toiletries, clothes and furnishing. The increased emphasis on marketing and sales was also associated with the transformation of retailing – based on the growth of urban incomes, on organisational and food-processing innovation, and on developments in the field of lighting, plate-glass and window display. One important result of all this was the emergence of the multiple grocery business: by 1914 the Home and Colonial Tea Company, the Maypole Dairy Company, and Lipton Ltd each had over 500 branches (although two butchery chains each had in excess of 1000 branches: Jefferys 1954: pp. 24–6). By 1915 the combined business of private multiples and the Cooperative stores accounted for almost 20 per cent of total retail sales (Jefferys 1954: 19, 28).

One category of direct consumption – alcoholic drink – had long since been handled by specialist processors and distributors (for a detailed discussion of changes in the consumption of alcohol see Dingle 1972 and Wilson 1940). At the outset of the period it already formed a very important part of national, and especially working-class, expenditure – comprising over 12 per cent of the total throughout the late nineteenth century. Indeed, the absorption of the income of the poor by drink was a frequent subject of comment by social investigators as well as moralists. Peak consumption came in 1875–76, with an annual per capita average (for *all* the population) of 34 gallons of beer and 1.5 gallons of spirits. A decline in the late 1870s established a somewhat lower level (28–30 gallons of beer) until the end of the century, when the fall was recommenced. In budgetary terms drink took 15 per cent of consumers' expenditure in 1876, about 12 to 13 per cent in the 1880s and 1890s, and 9 per cent on the eve of the First World War. The relation between these trends and movements in income is interesting but obscure. Thus, in 1870–76, when real wages rose by more than 15 per cent, the consumption of beer also shot up – by about 20 per cent. This has been attributed to the combination of an abrupt increase in money wages and 'consumption patterns which were both narrow and convention-alised' – i.e. to a short-run reinforcement of traditional expenditure patterns. By the same token, the subsequent decline and stability has been attributed to the fact that real wages increased more slowly and through a general price fall which, together with a steadily augmenting range of consumer choice, meant that the purchase of beer was not so tempting a use of greater effective purchasing power (Dingle 1972: 615). Certainly, generally increasing living standards might have been expected to reduce the relative significance of expenditure on alcohol; if the high consumption was a function of poverty, then rising incomes and an improving environment and range of consumer choice would reduce the need for this form of self-administered thereapy. However, some of the restraint on drink can no doubt be attributed to social pressures and the intense propaganda of the temperance movement.

Patterns of demand: manufactures and services

We have already noted the apparent relative stability of the pattern of demand in terms of the expenditure on manufactured goods and services: between the 1880s and 1900–09 the former rose from 23.8 per cent to 25 per cent, and the latter from 29.4 per cent to 32.6 per cent, of the total flow of goods and services to consumers (Jefferys & Walters 1955: 20). Such a pattern of demand indicates a fairly high degree of economic 'maturity' and even wealth. However, before the data are discussed in more detail, two points need emphasising. First, more or less adequate statistics exist only since the 1880s, when structural changes in demand may already have been well under way. The same source suggests that in the early 1870s services were only about 24 per cent of consumers' expenditure (Jefferys & Walters 1955: 27). This implies a more substantial growth in the importance of the tertiary sector in the last three decades of the century. Second, while the national data point to a fairly 'mature' pattern of demand, with a relatively low expenditure on food and basic necessities, and a relatively high expenditure on services, that is partly a reflection of the skewed distribution of income. For the majority of people poverty entailed a significantly higher proportionate expenditure on food and rent – some 60 to 70 per cent seems to have been normal for wage earners (Parliamentary Papers Cd 1761 1903: appendix v; Cd 8980 1918: 7). On the other hand, the fact that a small proportion of consumers commanded a large share of the national income naturally increased the significance of the purchase of services in terms of domestic help, professional service, recreation and leisure activities, insurance, etc. Hence, 'national' data by no means reflect the situation for very large groups of consumers.

Nevertheless, the fact remains that per capita national income rose by about 30 per cent in the 30 years or so after 1880, with apparently relatively little change in the pattern of demand – nationally or even within social groups – considered in terms of large aggregates. It remains to be considered whether, as was the case with expenditure on food, there were important changes within these rather broad categories.

As far as commodities were concerned, the analogy with food holds in the sense that the bulk of consumer expenditures were for 'basic' goods – notably clothing, fuel, and light, which in 1900 accounted for about 13.4 per cent of total consumer expenditure, or over half of expenditures on non-food commodities (Prest 1954: 175). These items also, and naturally, figured prominently in the budgets of the relatively poor: official surveys suggest that in the 1890s and early 1900s the percentage of expenditure devoted to them was about 20 or 25 per cent (Parliamentary Papers Cd. 1761 1903: 235; Cd. 2337 1904: 32) – although a subsequent survey for 1914 implied a somewhat lower figure of less than 17 per cent (Parliamentary Papers Cd. 8980 1918: 7).

Thus, given the continued importance of the conventional categories of manufactured goods, the growth of total and average income did not produce any far-reaching changes in the basic structure of demand. Certainly, there could have been no large shift towards the range of 'new' commodities associated with the 'high mass consumption' of the twentieth century; it has been estimated that as late as the first decade of this century just over 50 per cent of purchases of goods and services went on perishable commodities, 9.5 per cent on semi-durables, and only 4.9 per cent on durables, including furniture and furnishings (Jefferys & Walters 1955: 21).

It may well be that all this is an indication not merely of the pattern of income distribution but also of the conventionality of British consumption, and consumer tastes, which is sometimes offered as a partial explanation of the presumed lack of innovatory drive in British industry. Yet before we come to any firm conclusions about the conservatism of consumers, we should remember that the growth in incomes was sufficiently great to establish a market, larger in absolute terms even if still small as a proportion of total consumption, for goods which were either new or the demand for which had previously been so limited as to place them in the category of rare luxuries. Examples of the possibility of standardised production based on a small proportion of a large aggregate income, are: bicycles, sewing machines, newspapers, clocks and watches, wallpaper, pianos, window glass, etc. In addition, although households (particularly poor households) apparently tended to allocate increased income to more or less the same categories of non-food expenditure, they did so by channelling more purchasing power to higher quality or more 'modern' versions of traditional purchases: new instead of second-hand clothing, leather footwear, gas instead of candles, coal instead of wood, commercial instead of home-made soap, improved types of linoleum floor-covering, arm chairs instead of kitchen chairs. In other words, as happened with food, there was a tendency to 'enhance' apparently traditional living standards, in terms of the quality of the product and the degree of its fabrication – an enhancement which might not be revealed by measures of monetary expenditures. As a result, changes in demand (interrelated with changes in supply) by no means precluded the emergence of a mass, standardised market for conventional goods – either because of distinct improvements in quality and range (clothing, footwear, soap, linoleum) or because of the use of substitutes for conventional products (proprietary toiletries and drugs instead of simpler household remedies and nostrums, cigarettes instead of pipe tobacco, etc.).

As already indicated, there is some ambiguity about the trend in the expenditure on services during the late nineteenth century. Nevertheless, all the evidence suggests that it was fairly high – say, between one quarter and one third of total outlay – and the indications are that there was a fairly rapid increase in its proportionate importance in the 1870s and a somewhat slower increase in the 1880s and 1890s. The shift in the balance of expenditure which was based on private choice was also bolstered by the political mechanism: government expenditure on social, economic and environmental purposes rose from about 3 per cent of GNP in 1890 to 6.7 per cent in 1910 (Peacock & Wiseman 1961: 86) – although much of the finance of these expenditures has already been accounted for in household budgets through the payment of rates and in direct taxes. In summary, then, although the increase in the proportion of expenditure allocated to services did not rise in any startling fashion in the period 1860–1914, it was the fastest growing category of demand and resulted in a fairly important marginal shift of consumption patterns.

Such a trend towards an increase in the importance of expenditures on services is a familiar feature of long-run economic growth. This is partly because, as incomes grow, consumer demand can move on from purchases in the 'primary' and 'secondary' sectors (food and manufactured commodities) to the 'tertiary' sector – education, health, amusement, leisure, professional services etc. – i.e. to the purchase of more 'luxurious' items or items which could now be purchased in specialised, commercialised forms, rather than obtained in the house or from unspecialised producers. At the same time growth brings changes on the side of supply: technological and organisational changes are more likely to reduce the price of manufactured goods than of many labour-intensive services (such as the cost of domestic servants or education), with the result that the latter absorb more of total outlay because of the shift in relative prices. This influence was compounded in the late nineteenth century by a powerful if transitory shift in the relative price of food. As already noted, this fell by about 30 per cent in the last three decades of the century, thus enabling basic needs to be met for less expenditure than might otherwise have been the case, and allowing proportionately more to be spent on services.

It was not merely the process of economic growth which was at work in this area. For the pattern of demand in which services figured so prominently was also maintained by extreme income inequality. In 1900–04, for example, the proportion of all consumer expenditure spent on domestic service was almost 4 per cent (Prest 1954: 118, 175) – and the proportion of the labour force so engaged was about 16 per cent in 1871 and was still over 14 per cent in 1901

Table 6.7. *Services as a proportion of the total flow of goods and services to consumers in the United Kingdom (per cent)*

	Rent and rates	Other services	All services
1880–89	10.4	19.0	29.4
1890–99	10.8	21.4	32.2
1900–09	11.5	21.1	32.6

Source: Jefferys & Walters (1955: 20)

(Mitchell & Deane 1962: 60). Certainly, the rich must have accounted for a substantial part of the growing expenditure on leisure, travel, private transport, education, medicine, and the like. On the other hand, the relatively poor were far from negligible consumers of services. Quite apart from the necessary expenditure on rent, urban wage earners spent significant amounts on transport, education and medicine: in 1914 about 2 per cent of their expenditure was on fares and over 5 per cent, even for the unskilled, on insurance and sickness clubs (Parliamentary Papers Cd. 8980 1918: 7). Earlier, Charles Booth's survey indicated that in the late 1880s, among all but the very poorest, 2 per cent or more of their income went on education and medicine and over 3 per cent on insurance (Booth 1892: 138), while around the turn of the century, among wage earners in York, insurance and sickness clubs absorbed 3.9 per cent (Rowntree 1922: 289).

Strictly speaking, insurance is a form of savings. But from the present viewpoint the extended habit of life and sickness insurance among wage earners in the late nineteenth century can be seen as part of a new, if limited, pattern of expenditure on services which included not merely such prudential provision but also an increasing attention to entertainment, gambling, holidays, and leisure activity generally. The rise of cheap holidays, the flowering of the music hall, the growth of amateur sport and the development of professional football all exemplify this. Yet there is also a sense in which the measurement of this trend in terms of adjustments of monetary demand is misleading. Its social and even economic significance in this period was undoubtedly great. But it was also to be measured in terms of an increase in available leisure. Indeed, the sharp reduction in the length of the working week in the early 1870s (Bienefeld 1972: ch. 4), and the appearance of the $5\frac{1}{2}$ day week, which made the 'mass consumption' of professional football a possibility, indicate that there was more to real income and expenditure than money alone. The supply of and expenditure on leisure was also an integral part of the changing and maturing economy.

In the last resort, however, each of these activities was one among a proliferating variety of services which were increasingly consumed as national and average incomes grew. Indeed, the only really substantial expenditure on services was on rent and rates – which accounted for about one third and changed very little from the 1880s (table 6.7). Of this total, rates accounted for about one fifth or a little more until the end of the century, rising to just over one quarter on the eve of the First World War (Jefferys & Walters 1955: 32). In fact, local authority expenditure as a whole – excluding such transfer payments as poor relief and loan charges, but including services such as transport and public utilities for which a charge was made, as well as health, educational and environmental services – rose from the equivalent of about 1.8 per cent of personal consumption expenditure in 1872–75 to 4.5 per cent in 1910–14 (Mitchell & Deane 1962: 414–18; Feinstein 1972: T8).

The increase in the expenditure on rent had different implications from that on rates, for whereas the latter was almost entirely an augmentation of consumption, the former was in large part an indication of the increased cost of the same level of accommodation. Thus a contemporary statistician estimated that about half the increase in average working-class rents in the second half of the nineteenth century was attributable to the increased *price* rather than 'consumption' of housing (Wood 1909: 136). To this extent, therefore, the increased expenditure on accommodation was an index of the increased costs of living, consequent upon urbanisation and housing shortages (the same could be said for much of the increase in the expenditure on local transport). What is in any case significant is that the importance of rent in the average household budget barely kept pace with the increase in income. Consumers either did not want, or were not able, to increase the proportion of their incomes allocated to housing.

With respect to the rest of expenditure on services, we are dealing, as already implied, with a diverse and small-scale pattern. Domestic service (at roughly 4 per cent) and transport (which rose to the same level by the 1900s) were the two most important categories. By 1900–04, when reasonably accurate and detailed measures are available, these two stood at 3.8 per cent and 3.7 per cent of consumer expenditure; medical, funeral and life assurance was some 3.1 per cent; education, charities and religion 1.7 per cent; and entertainment and betting 1.5 per cent. Such quantities preclude the possibility of there having been massive changes in the late nineteenth century. But given the substantial growth in total expenditure, of which they were a proportion, they reflect absolute levels of demand which were economically significant.

Consumer demand and structural change

The diffused character of the growth of demand for services is consistent with the general implications of changing expenditures for economic structures in this period – namely, the absence of any really dramatic shift in economic activity which can be directly attributed to alterations in demand. As Table 6.8 suggests,

Table 6.8. *Sectoral distribution of economic activity, Great Britain 1861–1901 (per cent)*

(A) National income

	Agriculture, forestry, fishing	Manufacturing, mining, building	Trade transport	Domestic and personal service	Housing	Overseas income	All other
1861	17.8	36.5	19.6	5.2	7.5	3.0	10.4
1871	14.2	38.1	22.0	5.0	7.6	4.3	8.9
1901	6.4	40.2	23.3	4.8	8.2	6.5	10.7

(B) Labour force

	Agriculture, forestry, fishing	Manufacturing, mining, building	Trade transport	Domestic and personal service	Public, professional & all other services
1861	18.7	43.6	16.6	14.3	6.9
1871	15.1	43.1	19.6	15.3	6.9
1901	8.7	46.3	21.4	14.1	9.6

Source: Deane & Cole (1962: 142, 166)

the most striking aspect of structural change was the diminished importance of agriculture – and this was attributable not to any diminution in the demand for food, but to increased competition from imports. Moreover, the growing importance of the service sector (53 per cent of the national income and 45 per cent of the labour force in 1901) was also based on more varied forces than a growth in British incomes and demand. Part of it was derived from the specialised provision of services (retailing, transport, commerce) which were not directly purchased by consumers, but which were incidental to the supply of physical commodities. This aspect of structural change therefore reflected a more efficient way of supplying goods to a mass market rather than response to a new type of demand. In addition, part of the structural change towards the tertiary sector was based on overseas rather than British demand – on the boom in 'invisible earnings' from the supply of financial, insurance, commercial and shipping services to the international economy (net income from the sale of services rose from some £50 million in 1861 to just over £100 million around 1900 and well over £150 million in 1910–13: Mitchell & Deane 1962: 334).

In fact, Britain's changing position in the international economy was a potent force transmuting the economic effects of changes in demand. Given the importance of commodity exports to British output, for example, their slow growth in the late nineteenth century, together with the very rapid expansion of the export of services, may have been at least as important as any variation in domestic demand as far as structural changes and economic growth were concerned. In addition, given the importance of imports, the growth in domestic incomes was not all available for 'home-based' output: a large part was absorbed in the purchase of consumer goods from overseas – although the fact that import costs fell much faster than the average price level in the late nineteenth century (40 per cent as against less than 15 per cent: Feinstein 1972: T132) meant that the total expenditure on imports rose by less than GNP. The most resounding effect of this development was felt in the case of food and agriculture: in the last 30 years of the century the wholesale price of food and milk fell by about one third but the value of their imports rose by almost as much. On the one hand, largely because of the shift towards cheaper supplies of bulk foods from overseas, much of British agriculture was depressed and its factor incomes fell by about one sixth between 1860–64 and 1895–99 (Feinstein 1972: T60). On the other hand, precisely because of the cheapness of imports, consumers were able to buy more food with a less than proportionate increase in expenditure. This, in turn, meant that they could spend a greater proportion of their incomes than otherwise might have been possible on domestic goods and services. This presumably facilitated or accelerated structural change as far as manufactures and services were concerned. Although it is impossible to isolate and measure this effect, a very rough indication is provided by an estimate of the hypothetical 'savings' on the UK import bill generated by the price decline:

if the average annual food imports of 1895–99 had been purchased at the prices prevailing in 1870–75, they would have cost (other things being equal) 60 per cent more – or an 'extra' food bill of about £125 million, as against an increase in consumers' expenditure on services of some £230 million (Jefferys & Walters 1955: 27).

A less beneficial consequence of the attractiveness of imports was the increase in expenditure on manufactured goods. Accounting for only 18 per cent of total imports in 1870–74, they rose to 27 per cent in 1895–99 (calculated from Parliamentary Papers Cd 1761 1903: 5–6). This was partly because the dramatic fall in the price of food and raw materials meant that less had to be spent on them than might otherwise have been the case. But it is worth emphasising that, at a time when the GNP rose by about 45 per cent, total expenditure on imported manufactures doubled. To this extent they must have represented something of a 'leakage' of purchasing power which could otherwise have gone to stimulate British manufacturing industry. Certainly, what appeared as the heightened competitiveness of foreign industry and the threat of cheap imports were part of a general contemporary anxiety about the performance of the British economy, the apparent deceleration of its industrial sector, and its lack of structural and organisational flexibility.

There are some reasons to doubt whether the performance of the economy warranted this anxiety; but whatever its validity, the fact remains that structural changes in this period were less far-reaching than is sometimes imagined. As so often happens in economic history, the search for a major discontinuity arrives at a more mundane reality: the enlargement of traditional flows, the cumulation of marginal changes. In the late nineteenth century the effects of evolving demand were to be seen less in dramatic changes of level and pattern than in a prolonged, incremental extension of markets and in adaptations in the type and variety of traditional goods and services. Even though the enhancement of income and the parallel extension of demand provide an important context for an understanding of the evolution of the late Victorian and Edwardian economy, the observed changes in economic structure and activity are also attributable to influences much broader than changes in demand. As so often happens in economic history, nothing is simple and, in terms of the groundswell of the community's material existence, few changes are sufficiently spectacular to blot out the influence of the customary, the commonplace, and the ordinary.

7

The labour supply and the labour market 1860–1914

D. E. BAINES

Introduction

This chapter examines population changes, the growth and distribution of the labour force and the operation of the labour market. The chapter has two main aims: first, to explain the causes and consequences of economic behaviour in the period as far as that behaviour was concerned with the way people made a living; second, to try to explain the changes in social attitudes and behaviour which affected economic behaviour. Even the simplest economic decision like taking a job is taken within a set of social and psychological constraints. For example, the position of women in the economic hierarchy was largely determined in the period by the conventional distinction between a woman's job and a man's job. The position of women in the labour market can only be understood if the social context is understood as well.

The first part of the chapter considers the causes and effects of population growth because population growth was the primary determinant of the size and age-structure of the labour force and because births, deaths and migration affected behaviour in so many ways. Because population growth varied from region to region (and also over time) it will be necessary to examine the relative importance of natural increase and migration and to try to determine how far they were affected by economic change. We also need to consider the factors determining the *demand* for labour in different industries and how far the demand affected the numbers who came forward for work. The second part of the chapter will examine the changing fortunes of various groups (e.g. skilled, casual workers, women) within the labour market (or more correctly labour markets) and how far the rewards were distributed between them. It will try to assess the importance of technical change and the operation of the trade cycle on earnings and differentials. The effect on the labour market of institutions like apprenticeship and, most important, trade unions in a period of technical and economic change will be considered. Finally, the chapter will look at changes in the quality of labour, such as increasing literacy.

Table 7.1. *Natural and actual increase in population, Great Britain 1861–1911* (*millions of persons and % of previous census*)

	Total population	Increase since previous census	Natural increase since previous census	Net emigration since previous census
1861	23.13	— —	— —	— —
1871	26.07	2.94 (12.7)	3.14 (13.6)	0.20 (0.8)
1881	29.71	3.64 (14.0)	3.90 (14.9)	0.26 (1.0)
1891	33.03	3.32 (11.2)	4.14 (13.9)	0.82 (2.7)
1901	37.00	3.97 (12.0)	4.09 (12.4)	0.12 (0.4)
1911	40.83	3.83 (10.4)	4.59 (12.4)	0.76 (2.0)

Sources: Parliamentary Papers (1948–49); Mitchell & Deane (1962); Glass (1940)

Population growth: the fall in mortality

Population growth (table 7.1) occurs because of a fall in deaths, a rise in births or in-migration. In this period the death rate fell, from 22.6 per thousand of the population in 1861–65 to 14.3 per thousand in 1911–15. The fall in this *crude* death rate was the consequence of changes in age-specific mortality and changes in age-distribution. (Age-specific mortality relates the number of deaths in a given age-group to the number of people in that age-group, while the age-distribution of the population gives the proportion which each age-group forms of the total population.) Virtually all the mortality fall occurred in the age groups 3–34 and was a consequence of a fall in the incidence of infectious disease (Logan 1950, McKeown 1976). When allowance is made for the changing age structure of the population, infectious disease can be shown to have accounted for about 60 per cent of all deaths in 1848–54, but for only 50 per cent in 1901. 92 per cent of all the fall in mortality was due to the fall in infectious disease and of this the fall in respiratory tuberculosis contributed 33 per cent, scarlet fever and diphtheria 12 per cent, cholera and dysentery 12 per cent, typhoid and typhus 17 per cent and smallpox 5 per cent (deaths from influenza, pneumonia and bronchitis rose) (McKeown 1976: 54–64). Nineteenth century diagnosis left much to be desired and the relation between the autonomous virulence of disease, the carrying vectors (like lice) if any, and the environment is complex but it is still possible to isolate the probable causes of the fall in mortality. Specific improvements in medicine can have affected only smallpox. Public health improvements can only have affected the water-borne diseases (typhoid and cholera). The fall in scarlet fever is inexplicable except as an autonomous fall in the virulence of the disease. This leaves tuberculosis and typhus and several lesser infectious diseases. The former were not difficult to diagnose and there is no evidence that they were less virulent. It follows that over half of the total fall in mortality in the period must have been caused by improvements in the standard of living – in particular the consumption of more and better food.

Infant mortality

Infant mortality (the death-rate of children under one year old), did not show a consistent fall until the early twentieth century. It fell slightly in the late 1870s and 1880s then rose again to its 1860s level of 150–5 per 1000 live births in the 1890s. From then it fell rapidly to about 100 per 1000 by the First World War. The turning point is concealed by the exceptionally hot summers of the late 1890s but it must have been somewhere between 1895 and 1905. A plausible explanation is that a strong falling trend in the late nineteenth century was concealed by increasing births in relatively high risk environments. A high risk environment did not necessarily mean a poor household, for infant mortality was much lower among agricultural labourers than among textile workers or miners (Stevenson 1920). But in urban environments infant mortality was closely related to overcrowding. The fall in infant mortality over the whole period was less than that for young adults because the survival of infants depended not only on environmental changes and public health improvements, but also on changes in personal attitudes to the care of children, something that came only with increased education and was probably related to the fall in working-class fertility in the early twentieth century. It is also possible that the fall in fertility affected infant mortality *directly* since the average age of mother at birth fell and the number of children born high in the birth order fell also (i.e. as family size fell there were fewer fifth or sixth children). European experience provides some evidence for this view: infant mortality began to fall in many countries about twenty years after the initial fall in fertility irrespective of social and economic conditions.

The fall in young adult mortality had two main effects. It increased the mean life expectation of new entrants to the labour force by one year in each decade from the 1870s. More important, it increased the total number of years lived by married women in the fecund age-groups. This should have led to an acceleration of population growth, but this did not occur because fertility fell.

The fall in fertility

Table 7.2 shows the extent of the decline in fertility. The early rise in the series can be disregarded because it is a consequence of improving birth registration, which was properly enforced only after 1874. We can say that fertility fell continuously from the 1870s from a level that had probably not changed much for at least twenty years. The main series fall in parallel which enables us to eliminate several possible causes of falling fertility. It was not caused by a retreat

Table 7.2. *Fertility 1850–52 to 1910–12*

Annual averages of 3 years	Live births per 1000 women, 15–49	Legitimate live births per 1000 married women, 15–44*	Estimated GRR England and Wales
1850–52	131.7	284.2	2.195
1860–62	134.2	281.7	2.256
1870–72	139.2	292.5	2.349
1880–82	134.2	286.0	2.279
1890–92	117.9	263.8	2.041
1900–02	104.4	235.5	1.725
1910–12	88.5	197.4	1.444

Source: adapted from Glass (1940)
* Married women 45–9 cannot be distinguished in the 1881–1901 censuses

from marriage (a constant 84–7 per cent of women always married). Nor was it a consequence of a fall in illegitimate births which were never more than 5 per cent of all births and fell in concert. Changes in age structure were more important. The average age of married women was rising, a tendency that would reduce the birth *rate* per 1000 married women. It is possible to eliminate the effects of changing age structure by the device of calculating the gross reproduction rate – the mean number of female children the average newly-born girl will bear during her lifetime assuming that age-specific fertility remains unchanged. The gross reproduction rate (GRR) fell faster than total fertility after 1890. Hence the fertility of older women fell faster than that of younger women. The conclusion must be that fertility fell because married couples had fewer children. Small families were not achieved by postponing the birth of the first child but by restricting births once a desired family size was reached, and the desired family size was itself falling.

The reasons for the fall in fertility are difficult to explain. Easier access to contraceptives is not a sufficient explanation, since most couples continued to use the 'safe period' or coitus interruptus – methods of birth control known and used for centuries. The most common explanation for the fall in fertility is that it was related to the shift from a partly rural to a mainly urban society. Parents in towns were offered an increasing range of consumer products which were in a sense substitutes for an additional child, while at the same time the towns offered fewer job opportunities for children than rural areas. J. A. Banks (1954) argued that the (upper) middle class began to control family size because of a threat to their conventional standard of living. The costs of 'gentility' rose, in particular the wages of good servants who enabled the mistress to keep out of the kitchen and the costs of starting children in the professions. At the same time the 'Great Depression' of the late nineteenth century threatened middle-class incomes. The upshot was a wholesale reappraisal of the desirability of very large families. Banks' explanation relates explicitly to the British middle class, but other writers have extended it to explain the whole of the decline in fertility, even in other countries, as an effect of the growth of cities and middle class occupations. In this view, the spread of family limitation from the middle classes is caused by the demonstration effect; as the working classes saw the beneficial effects for the middle classes of falling fertility so they emulated them.

But did middle class fertility fall first? Comparing marriages contracted in 1851–60 and those contracted in 1881–86, completed family size fell by 33 per cent for families headed by professionals and higher administrators and by 21 per cent, 20 per cent and 15 per cent for those headed by skilled, semi-skilled and unskilled workers. But no group – not even miners (10 per cent) and agricultural labourers (15 per cent) – failed to experience a fall in each successive decade. The evidence points to a simultaneous fall in fertility from a variety of different levels determined by region and occupation. The fall was fastest for those groups whose families were initially smallest, so that the differences in family size between classes and occupations widened.

This was probably the general European experience. When fertility fell in Germany it fell almost simultaneously in rural and urban areas (Knodel 1974). It fell in many less developed European countries before it fell in Britain; Britain was remarkable because fertility fell so *late* in the industrialisation process. Today, every country that is 50 per cent urban or has less than 45 per cent of the labour force in primary production has undergone a substantial fall in fertility (Coale 1969); Britain met these criteria in 1850. Obviously, we need not expect a universal explanation but the experience of other countries shows that the diffusion process needs further examination. The role of towns may merely have been as communication centres which spread the experience of existing pockets of low fertility, at a time when falling child mortality was increasing the number of child survivors in the family.

The effects of demographic change

The mortality and fertility changes discussed above had important economic and social consequences. One consequence was the effect on age distribution. In a closed population (that is one with no migration), demographic changes are brought about by the effect of current mortality and fertility on the age structure produced by previous fertility and mortality. Figure 7.1 is a representation of the British age structure in the period 1851–1951, and shows that the shape of the pyramid began to change between 1891 and 1911. In 1851 and 1871 life expectancy was low and fertility high; this had been so for many years. The population was therefore young because of the high wastage at each age. It was rather like that of many present-day underdeveloped countries, but with lower

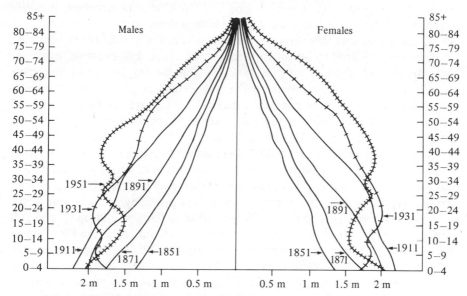

7.1   Great Britain: age structure 1851–1951
Source: Mitchell & Deane (1962).

fertility and higher mortality. Falling fertility reduced the proportionate contribution of the younger age groups and in time created the characteristic
age-structure of a modern industrial society, where each age group is little
smaller than the one beneath it except at the highest ages. This age distribution
was created by fertility. This is because births can only occur at one age. A
shortfall of births will mean a shortfall of *x* year-olds in *x* years' time. In figure
7.1, for example, the effects of the lost births of the First World War stand out
very clearly in the Censuses of 1931 and 1951. Mortality changes on the other
hand rarely affect a single age group and are therefore rarely able to affect its
relative size.

Total population in the period 1860–1914 continued to grow but at a
decreasing rate (1.20 per cent per annum in 1861–70 falling to 0.99 per cent in
1901–10). Yet this growth remained fast by European standards; it was faster
than the rate of population growth in France, Belgium and Switzerland
throughout, faster than that of Italy until just before the war and faster than that
of Germany until the 1890s (Glass & Grebenik 1965). The continued rapid
growth in the face of a massive fall in fertility (GRR fell 39 per cent) was a
consequence of the large numbers in the younger age groups at the beginning
of the period and the rapid fall in their mortality, which compensated for the
fall in family size in the short run. The scope for improving young adult mortality

was much higher in 1860 than it became in 1914. Consequently the full effects of the fall in fertility on the rate of growth were deferred.

One effect was that there were more entrants to the labour force annually, which probably helped technical and structural change. For example, Birmingham was revitalised from the mid 1880s as new factory industries like cycle manufacture were superimposed on the old metal trades economy. The new factory labour force did not come from the old workshop labour force but from their children, who had been brought up in an environment of skilled hand work but owed no allegiance to it (Allen 1929).

A second effect of the fall in fertility was that the proportion of the population in the 15–64 age groups rose relative to the proportion of young and old people outside those age groups. This reduction in 'dependency' would tend to lead to an increase in national income per head, assuming that labour force participation remained constant. (Participation is discussed below.) The full effect of the fall in fertility on dependency was not felt until after the First World War, but by 1931 only 32 per cent of males were in the dependent age groups compared with 41 per cent in 1861 and 37 per cent in 1911. Subsequently, the fall in the numbers of children has been increasingly offset by the increased life expectancy of old people, so that this effect of falling fertility on national income was at its greatest between the wars. On the other hand, in the inter-war period the 15–64 age group was itself ageing; more were aged over 35 than under whereas up to 1911 the proportion under 35 had remained constant.

A third long-run effect of the fall in fertility was on education. Before the First World War a relatively small working population had to pay to educate the very large and growing number of children, although the proportion of the population under 15 fell after 1891. After the war not only did the proportion of children continue to fall, but each year saw a smaller *number* of children entering the schools with great benefit to the quantity and quality of education, irrespective of institutional changes (Lowndes 1937).

Falling family size from the 1870s was also beginning, fourth, to increase the standard of living of some families in the labour market. Casual labourers, for example, could not earn enough to keep a family at the standard determined by social investigators (Booth 1892, Rowntree 1901), partly because their families were too large and partly because the large families produced yet more entrants to the overcrowded casual labour market. The fertility of the better-off fell faster. In the Edwardian period, therefore, variation in family size was a major factor in the noticeable difference in the standard of living between white collar or skilled workers and the unskilled, a fact which may help to explain some of the social unrest of the period. Within each class, however, the fall in fertility was beginning to reduce the variance in average family size. This tended to increase the number of families who had a disposable income in excess of the cost of daily necessities and in consequence increased the market for other consumer goods.

Finally, it is important to remember the demographic effects of heavy net emigration (its causes are discussed below). There were two important net outward flows in the period, one in the 1880s and the other in the 1900s (table 7.1). Assuming (realistically) that two thirds of the emigrants were aged 15–34, then the emigration of the 1880s produced a shortfall of about 550000 young adults by 1891 and the emigration of the 1900s a shortfall of about 500000 by 1911. Of these about 60 per cent were men, so that the direct effect of migration was to reduce the growth in the active male population from 17 per cent to 13 per cent in the 1880s and from 15 per cent to 13 per cent in the 1900s. This was one cause of the large number of women remaining unmarried in the period. The emigration of young adults did not cause the population to age in the long run. For example, had the 1880s emigrants stayed they would have borne about 700000 additional children; about 550000 of their *dependants* would have been alive in the 1900s. Emigration may have had other effects, for example if emigrants were on balance more enterprising than non-emigrants. We do not, however, know what the emigrants would have achieved had they remained, and considered as numbers of people rather than individuals they may not have been missed.

Labour force participation

This section examines the factors which governed the number of people who offered themselves for work at different times. Unfortunately the extent of labour force participation is difficult to measure, because the data reflect the way the labour market operated in the nineteenth century. The classification 'occupied' in the census was very ambiguous and frequently included the unemployed. This merely reflected reality; a man could do no work for a week yet spend that week at the dock gate, or at the railway yard waiting for a carter's load. Casual or intermittent employment was a normal feature of many occupations. In the present century fixed (weekly) hours of work have replaced casual work for most adults – a consequence of the development of collective bargaining and of unemployment insurance. This has created a much clearer distinction between employment and unemployment. Before the First World War unemployment rates are available only for trade unions, which were only 22 per cent of the male labour force as late as 1911.

Figure 7.2 must be viewed in the light of the preceding remarks. It demonstrates that nearly all men worked as long as they were physically able, even if the only employment they could find was part time; without pensions they could not 'retire' and leave the labour force. Able-bodied paupers and those living on friendly society sickness benefit, however, would be returned in the census as 'employed' in their previous occupation. Figure 7.2 also shows that the majority of single women and widows worked as long as they were physically able to do so. Married women did not work very much; the great growth in participation

152

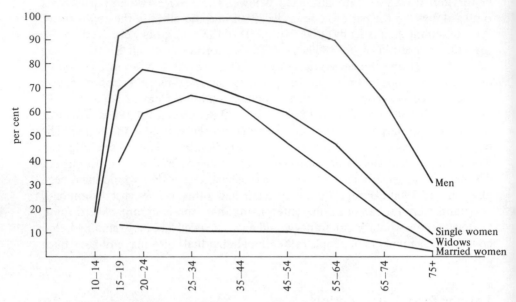

7.2   Participation rates 1911 (England and Wales)
Source: Calculated from the Census of Population 1911.

of married women since the Second World War has occurred because families
are much smaller and completed earlier and because life expectancy has risen.
In 1911, few married women were free to take jobs even had the jobs been offered.

Female participation as a whole fell markedly. If age and marital condition
are taken into account, and the 1911 census categories used, the proportion of
women employed was 8 per cent smaller in 1911 than in 1881, whereas the male
proportion was about the same. To carry this exercise further back is hazardous
becuse there are serious discrepancies between the 1871 and 1881 occupational
classifications, but the evidence suggests that female participation was even
higher in 1861. There are three main reasons for the marked fall: compulsory
education, which removed slightly more girls from the labour force than boys,
because fewer girls were at school when it began; the development of mining
and heavy industrial districts with no occupation for women other than
marriage; the fall in opportunities for employment in rural areas. The last is a
major reason for the low participation of older single women and widows (shown
in figure 7.2) who were disproportionately represented in rural areas. More
generally, Richards (1974) has suggested that the industrial revolution began a
long-run downward trend in women's paid employment which has been reversed
only in this century.

The fall in the relative importance of agriculture, the growth of the mining districts and most important the introduction of compulsory education account for the persistent fall in juvenile participation. In the 1861 census 36.9 per cent of boys aged 10–15 and 20.2 per cent of girls stated an occupation. By 1911 this had fallen to 18.3 per cent and 10.4 per cent.

The industrial distribution of the labour force

Few tasks in economic history have been as onerous and time consuming as the analysis of the nineteenth century occupational censuses. The Victorian concept of occupation which was embodied in the census was that occupation was as much a mark of social status as a description of a man's employment. This meant that *industries* were not distinguished, and many of the occupations stated were common between different industries. Nevertheless the main trends are not in doubt and are presented in figure 7.3.

Figure 7.3 shows that the relative importance of agriculture continued to fall – from 22 per cent of the occupied population in 1851 to only 8 per cent in 1911. Manufacturing employment grew by 3 000 000 in these years but that growth was at a much slower rate than in the first half of the century, and its relative importance remained about the same. Employment in services showed the most spectacular rise, particularly in trade and transport which absorbed 1 500 000 and 1 000 000 more male workers between 1851 and 1911, as would be expected in a mature industrial economy. Moreover, domestic service and services like laundry work remained of massive importance and in 1911 still employed more people than building and mining combined.

The modest rate of expansion of the manufacturing labour force was associated with high and rising productivity. By contrast many of the expanding services like domestic work or corner shopkeeping had very low productivity, which 'explains' their rapid rise in employment, as demand for these services increased with rising population but output per head did not. This suggests that productivity growth was a more important cause of economic growth overall than structural changes in the proportions of the labour force engaged in different types of economic activity. Insofar as a calculation of this kind is possible, this is the opinion of commentators (e.g. Ashworth 1965). These trends in productivity help explain the very wide variations in earnings between industries. Figure 7.3 also shows the failure of employment in building to grow in the 1880s and its fall in the 1900s, the decades of heavy emigration. On the other hand the 1880s and 1900s were decades of great growth in mining employment with the rise in coal exports. International factors therefore had opposite effects on the demand for labour in the two industries.

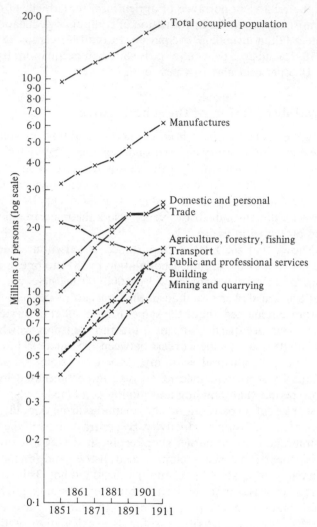

7.3 Estimated industrial distribution of the British labour force 1851–1911
Source: Deane & Cole (1962: 143).

Regional variations in employment

Structural changes in the economy were associated with large changes in the geographical distribution of occupations; the growth of commercial services, for example, was concentrated in certain urban areas, and that of heavy industry was on the coal fields. The main changes in the occupational structure of thirteen wage regions are summarised in table 7.3. In the table, occupations that

Table 7.3. *Growth/fall in major occupational groups, 1851–1911 (000s) (< 5000 ignored)*

Region	Agric. earnings 1867–70 p.w.	Agric. earnings 1907 p.w.	Population 1851 (000s)	Population 1911 (000s)	Net migration 000s	(1) Metals	(2) Domestic service	(3) Silk, straw, hats, stockings	(4) Mines, quarry-ing	(5) Shops, tailors, carpenters	(6) Cars, cycles, electric	(7) Commerce	(8) Agri-culture
London and Home Counties	16s 6d	18s 7d	3544	8935	+928	+100	+289	-30	—	+55	+62	+297	-43
South-West	12s 5d	16s 10d	2223	2691	-1053	+24	+47	-16	-17	-13	+5	+33	-128
Rural South-East	14s 5d	16s 5d	2794	4261	-902	+37	+148	-30	—	+23	+13	+53	-173
South Wales	12s 8d	18s 2d	596	1781	+219	+43	+34	—	+171	+4	—	+24	-21
Rural Wales	13s	17s 8d	689	751	-300	—	+17	—	+12	-14	+6	+6	-47
Midlands	14s 1d	18s 5d	2409	4957	-554	+177	+72	-50	+136	+72	+59	+89	-79
Lincs., East and North Riding	17s 1d	18s 10d	869	1503	-298	+54	+26	—	+10	-6	—	+21	-22
Lancs., Cheshire, W. Riding	17s 1d	19s 7d	3833	8788	+539	+278	+134	-34	+190	+59	+35	+178	-58
Cumbs./Westmorland	18s 6d	19s 2d	254	329	-149	+5	+6	—	+10	—	—	—	-13
Northumberland/Durham	18s 9d	21s 6d	715	2074	+70	+15	+38	—	+157	-13	+6	+13	-32
S. Scotland	15s	19s 4d	273	260	-187	—	—	—	—	—	—	—	-15
C. Scotland	14s 4d	20s 4d	1514	3261	-69	+125	+37	—	+106	+13	+10	+77	-29
N. Scotland	13s 2d	17s 7d	1102	1240	-596	+10	—	—	+9	+7	—	+15	-59
Britain (unweighted mean)	14s 4d	18s 3d	20817	40831	—	+910	+838	-149	+784	+150	+286	+836	-708

Source: based on the work of E. H. Hunt (1973: 127–96)

depended directly on population growth (i.e. teaching and building) are excluded as, for the sake of brevity, are textiles, railways and government services. The contribution of net migration to regional growth is also shown. This could be misleading since the regional boundaries enclose a variety of rural and urban areas. But table 7.4, which is based on registration districts, confirms the regional migration pattern (Cairncross 1953). These changes were associated with wide regional differences in the wages paid for the same job (Lawrence 1899, Hobsbawm 1964b), and usually reflected productivity differences which were the result of external economies in the urban/industrial areas. They were also stimulated by the fact that a rural–urban migrant could expect to benefit from lower urban prices for everything except rent and sometimes from greater employment opportunities for his family.

Internal migration

Out-migration was continuous from all rural areas – suggesting a range of causes. Not everywhere, for example, was badly affected by cheap grain imports after the 1870s. Everywhere was, however, affected by the railway, which created a national market and seriously affected local handicraft industries (columns 3 and 5 of table 7.3). At the same time, the railway spread information about alternative (urban) opportunities. Women were more affected than men and by the measure of net migration they were more mobile; by 1901 the rural areas had a large male surplus, particularly in the age groups 15–25 (Saville 1957). The most important destination of young girls was domestic service, which continued to grow; a common pattern was for a young girl to go to a local farmhouse at about the age of twelve from where she progressed to a town position through a personal contact, arranged perhaps by the farmer's wife. The position of domestic servants in the labour market was quite strong, and their wages rose faster than the national average through most of the period.

The rate of rural out-migration began to slow in the 1880s and fell markedly in the early twentieth century. This was partly the result of the spread of towns into rural areas and partly the revival of agriculture; although it is not clear that *agricultural* labour had been the main source of male out-migrants. There is no simple reason for the decline in rural out-migration. Previous migration had removed the parents of future migrants but not sufficiently to explain the fall in out-migration in the early twentieth century. Rates of migration which take account of the age-structure of the rural population fall as well. It is possible, however, that previous migration had removed the potential migrants from the migration-prone *families* (or villages).

The main migrant destinations were the large towns and for men the heavy industrial/mining areas. London was by far the most important single destination. It had no staple industry but remained the most important centre of consumer

Table 7.4. *Population growth and migration, England and Wales 1841–1911 (000s)*

	Population 1841 (1)	Population 1911 (2)	Natural increase (3)	Migration (net) (4)	(4)÷(3)	(2)÷(1)
Greater London	2262	7315	3802	+1251	31.9%	3.24
8 largest northern towns*	1551	5192	2747	+893	32.5%	3.35
9 colliery districts	1320	5334	3363	+650	19.3%	4.04
Textile towns	1387	3182	1706	+90	5.3%	2.30
Rural districts N.	2426	2875	2093	−1644	−78.6%	1.19
Rural districts S.	3740	4086	3209	−2863	−89.2%	1.10
England & Wales	15914	36070	21336	−1210	−5.7%	2.27

Source: Cairncross (1953)
* Manchester, Liverpool, Birmingham, Leeds, Sheffield, Leicester, Hull, Nottingham

demand and industrial employment. It offered the greatest *range* of opportunities, which is why it had always been the main destination of migrants who continued to move along well-defined paths. Some migrants may have been attracted by the bright lights rather than the higher incomes, but London remained the highest wage region.

Natural increase was, however, the most important cause of urban growth. It accounted for 75 per cent of the growth of London and the eight largest English towns (table 7.4). Even allowing for the effect of migration on urban age-structure, migration accounts for less than 40 per cent of the total population growth. In the colliery districts, natural increase accounted for 84 per cent of all growth or about two thirds allowing for the effect of migration on age-structure. The most important cause of the rapid growth of the coalfields was high (marital) fertility. The textile towns, on the other hand, had low population growth caused by low fertility. This does not imply that fertility varied with current changes in employment opportunities for either men or women, since the low fertility (GRR) of the textile counties and the high fertility of the mining and agricultural counties were features of long standing. Once a fertility pattern was established it tended to persist (Glass 1938).

On the other hand, the slow growth of the rural population was caused by migration and not by a slow rate of natural increase. The population of some areas, notably Wales and the borders, southern Scotland and the Highlands actually fell despite high fertility and low age-specific mortality. Regional population density in 1900 was as varied as it has ever been (Brown 1972). This is hardly surprising, for in the late nineteenth century the main industries were still tied to the coalfields and the continued development of coal increased the degree of localisation still further. We have already seen that rural incomes remained below urban so the effect of migration was to shift population to high wage areas. But many urban jobs, even those which required no training, were unavailable to new arrivals. Migrants often entered a local labour market at the bottom, then built up contacts to obtain more regular, easier and better paying jobs. Average differences in rural/urban wages therefore obscure a complex process.

But did migration work to narrow rural/urban wage differentials or to widen them? Neoclassical economic theory would expect capital to move towards low labour-cost regions and thus to increase demand for labour and its wage in those regions. But rural labour was unlikely to have been relatively as cheap as simple comparisons of wages would suggest, since rural born workers may have been less adaptable and less easily trained than workers born in an industrial environment. However, the movement of agricultural workers to urban occupations probably helped to reduce wage differentials, since if labour had not left the land, agricultural productivity would probably have fallen and with it rural wages. Even today, however, regional income differences seem to have persisted despite government policies designed to eradicate them, and the effects of migration are unclear.

Was labour more mobile in the period before the First World War than subsequently? There were fewer institutional barriers to movement before 1914; there was a free rented housing market, a lower proportion of home ownership and weak trade unions. It is true that information was relatively scarce outside the skilled trades, but even today most workers rely on personal contacts when changing jobs, which partly explains the prevalence of short distance moves – one of Ravenstein's 'Laws of Migration' (1885). The usual method of measuring total migration is to sum the net gains and losses of the various areas. By this measure mobility after the First World War was below mobility in some decades in the late nineteenth century and mobility after the Second World War was substantially less than in all decades 1861–1911. However, this method measures only a fraction of total movement, and it is possible that net migration was a larger proportion of total movement before the First World War than after. A greater proportion was emigration, where first time movements predominated and a greater proportion was rural depopulation. After the War more migration was intra-regional and a larger proportion of the labour force lived in one area and worked in another – which by this measure does not appear as mobility.

Emigration

Emigration from Britain was high and both England and Scotland were leading countries of emigration, though proportionately more emigrants came from Scotland. There is no evidence about returning migrants before 1895 when they made up about one half of outward sailings. The pattern of emigration, with great peaks in the 1880s and 1900s, is, however, confirmed by the net emigration figures (table 7.1), and this discontinuous pattern is common to many European countries. Most work on emigration (eg United Nations 1953, Taylor 1971) has assumed that British and European emigration had similar causes and that emigration was a special case of the general rural-urban movement; its general cause is thought to have been the changes in rural society brought about by contact with urban and industrial influences. Marked fluctuations in emigration occurred because the opportunity to migrate was partly determined by the state of the American economy which was the main destination. This view assumes, correctly, that emigrants had considerable knowledge of overseas conditions provided by newspapers and the letters of previous migrants. Emigration moved along well-established routes which connected particular places in Europe with particular places in the USA and elsewhere.

If British emigrants were mainly of rural origins then emigration should have fallen with industrialisation, but in fact it rose. Were these additional emigrants predominantly rural or people who had experienced the great urban and industrial changes of the period? The most sophisticated analysis is by Brinley Thomas (1972 and 1973), who starts from the idea of an 'Atlantic Economy' – that British and American development was complementary and characterised by alternating decades of investment and migration. When British investment in the USA was rising so was emigration; when it fell, migration fell. British capital exports to America went mainly into railroads and (indirectly) into urban development, while when the capital stayed in Britain it went into house-building. Hence, British investors in one decade provided jobs in the USA and, in the next, jobs that kept potential emigrants in Britain. These potential emigrants, Thomas suggests, were born in rural areas but in the 'building' phase of the cycle deferred emigration and moved to the towns. However, there is no direct evidence to support this thesis. Until the 1890s about 50–60 per cent of emigrants were returned as labourers, but it is impossible to distinguish whether they were rural labourers or had rural origins. The Welton/Cairncross (1953) estimates, however, show net migration to the large towns to have been at high levels in the 1870s and 1890s, and net out-migration from rural areas at high levels in the 1880s and 1900s.

There are several important criticisms of Brinley Thomas's work. In the first place there is no general agreement that the building cycle operated simultaneously throughout the country (Habakkuk 1962b, Saul 1962, Cottrell 1975). Secondly, it is clear that large numbers of emigrants during the emigration peaks were industrial workers (Erickson 1972) but it is unlikely that many were born in rural areas (Baines 1979). Rural emigration (taking account of age distribution) continued to the 1890s at a constant rate irrespective of economic conditions. When emigration was at its height it consisted disproportionately of persons *born* in urban/industrial counties. Moreover, rural counties with high emigration rates also had high levels of internal migration which was therefore not a substitute for emigration but a complement to it.

There is therefore no simple explanation for the overall level and fluctuating pattern of emigration. At least two sets of factors were at work simultaneously. One produced a very high rate of migration out of the rural areas and was part of the classic European 'flight from the land' – although those fleeing were not necessarily farm workers. At least 40 per cent of English and Welsh emigration was of this kind. But at the very minimum another third was of people born and brought up in an urban/industrial environment. Some went because they were technologically unemployed, but the majority because they were prepared to try their luck on both sides of the Atlantic.

The rural labour market

The agricultural labour market was characterised by large and persistent regional differences in wages and real earnings (see chapter 8 and table 7.3). The lowest earnings were in the rural South-East, the South-West and rural Wales, the highest in the North of England, Central and Southern Scotland. In general, earnings were high where industrial and service employment was large, but London and Birmingham had much steeper wage gradients than the northern industrial towns. The different levels of agricultural wages are not correlated very well with out-migration. The South-West, rural Wales and Northern Scotland remained low wage areas despite high out-migration. Southern Scotland, Cumberland and Westmorland had similar out-migration but remained high wage areas. The northern agricultural labourers were almost certainly more mobile than southern. A greater proportion lived in the farmhouse and renegotiated their contracts at an annual Hiring Fair. There is some evidence to suggest that the wage variations may have been partly related to diet, so that low wage areas were caught in a vicious circle of low wages, poor diet and low productivity (Hunt 1967): although this would not explain why differentials were narrowing. Moreover, the evidence of use of allotments which were popular mainly in the low wage counties is contrary to the view that those areas were trapped in a vicious circle of low wages and productivity. They cost considerably more per acre to rent than farms, yet the returns to effort on allotments were usually half as much again as working for a farmer (Mann 1905).

The wages of agricultural labourers increased between 1860 and 1914 but most of the increase was concentrated in two short periods. One, the early twentieth century, saw a rapid change in agricultural fortunes. The other, the early 1870s, coincided exactly with the brief appearance of the only successful agricultural labourers' union before recent times; wages rose about 10 per cent in 1872-74. But it is difficult to see how Arch's union could have achieved this, since it was very vulnerable to lockouts and at its peak it represented not much more than 20 per cent of the labourers. Most important, although it had no membership in the North, wages rose 10 per cent there as well (Dunbabin 1963). A better explanation is that 1850-70 was probably a period of falling labour surplus in agriculture, particularly at harvest time – extra payments for harvest work were rising. The employment of women and boys was falling even before it was controlled by the 1867 Gangs Act and farm servants were becoming difficult to hire. Eventually the force of custom, which tended to keep wage rates stable, had to give way (Jones 1964) and wages rose.

Urban labour

Apprenticeship had been in decline for some time but in the 1860s craftsmen still remained important in parts of the British economy. Many engineers, carpenters, shipbuilders, tailors, bookbinders and printers had served apprenticeships and – except for the application of more power – carried out much the same range of tasks as they had during and before the industrial revolution. They remained the best paid section of the labour force and would do so as long as they could rigorously control recruitment to their trade. In bad times the craftsmen's societies were able to avoid downward pressure on wages by several devices including the payment of out-of-work donations, restriction of overtime and occasionally emigration grants; at that time, for example, no friendly society would offer insurance against unemployment; such insurance could only come from a craftsmen's society. These devices ensured that unemployed craftsmen would not undercut the local price lists which were often of considerable antiquity (Passfield & Webb 1897). The employer accepted these restrictions because they protected his product against under-cutting by cheap labour outside. In the long run, however, technical change made it possible to replace many of the widely trained and experienced craftsmen with a set of process workers, some of them juveniles, each trained to carry out only a single task. The engineers for example could not hold the line against 'illegal men' after about 1885 and from then on fought a constant rearguard action against the erosion of their 'trade practices'; they were also forced to accept piece rates. Craftsmen were usually against piece rates because they were individually negotiated and under-cut the standard time rate embodied in the price lists (each job had a conventional time in which to do it). In flint glass and gun making the craftsmen managed to divorce the high grade trade from the lower quality mechanised section and continued as before. The most important industry to maintain successfully the craftsmen–labourer gulf was building. It is easy to see why; building had the least technical change in the nineteenth century of any major industry and little competition between producing centres.

These examples suggest that the maintenance of craft practices depended partly on the price elasticity of demand and partly upon the degree of competition. But even then the control of entry to the trade was crucial. Ease of entry into the trade destroyed the Birmingham 'Alliances' of the 1890s, agreements between small masters and skilled workers to reduce competition between themselves and maintain the price of small hardware items in the face of pressure from monopsonist middlemen ('factors'). But the factors were in a strong position because they had sole access to credit, and as the alliances checked the downward pressure on prices, journeymen set up as small masters on the margin – which they could do because apprenticeship had gone (Fox 1955).

Table 7.5. *Relative level of real wages* (*1913* = *100*)

Skilled grades	1886		
Bricklayers	80		
Coal getters	63	1886:	1913:
Mule spinners	79	relative wages if the skilled wage = 100	relative wages if the skilled wage = 100
Semi-skilled grades			
Painters	83	92	88
Putters and fillers	72	84	73
Grinders	72	65	71
Unskilled grades			
Building labourers	75	62	66
Coal mining labourers	72	73	66
Women weavers	82	55	53

Source: Rowe (1928: 48–9)

Probably the best example of the way an old industry could expand by subdividing skilled work is the London East End clothing trade. This was in effect a new industry meeting an expanding market for cheap off-the-peg coats and trousers. The bespoke West End trade was little affected until standards of ready to wear clothing were improved after the First World War. The bulk of the labour force were Jewish immigrants, 150 000 of whom settled in Britain between 1881 and 1914 (Lipman 1954). Most of them made for the East End of London which had the greatest concentration of Jewish social and economic institutions. The immigrants all attempted to become proprietors ('sweaters') and were willing to forgo journeymen's incomes to do so. It needed little capital to become a small master beyond the hire of a steam press. It was relatively easy therefore for the wholesalers to force down the contract prices. In addition, the tailors' shops were in direct competition with the Leeds factories. But demand was rising and East End wages for men – between 4d and 9d per hour for an average four and a half day week – were not much less than in the factories. Internal economies of scale must therefore have been low. The serious over-crowding in Whitechapel which was much criticised by contemporaries (see Gartner 1960) was a cost of the external economies created by localisation, the rapid execution of orders and the fickleness of the market (Hall 1962).

Skill differentials

Skill differentials remained very stable during the period in most industries with the important exception of mining, despite many important changes like the decline of apprenticeship and the growth of trade unions (Rowe 1928) (table 7.5). In fact, differentials have only narrowed markedly in three periods in the last hundred years: during the world wars of the twentieth century (Knowles & Robertson 1951) and in the mid 1970s. In all three periods the narrowing of differentials was largely an effect of government policy.

Before 1914 the labourer's position in the market remained weak. His most important protection was the force of custom; the customary wage depended on the subjective standard of living thought appropriate to a local labourer. Except at the peak of a boom the customary wage was above that at which all labourers would find continuous employment. There were also customary wages for unskilled women and juveniles which were much lower than those for men. A man could not normally be offered a boy's wage, but a boy could replace a man at a boy's wage. Sometimes the customary wages had a fixed relation to skilled wages in the same industry – so that a high wage industry had highly paid labourers.

The second reason for the persistence of skill differentials was that the industries with no formal apprenticeship (in particular mining and textiles) became dominated by unions that were as much against narrowing differentials as were the craft unions. Unlike the craft unions, the operatives' unions protected the superior position of the older and more experienced workers by recruiting into the union the unskilled and semi-skilled who worked alongside them. The 'piecers' in cotton spinning and the 'putters' and 'fillers' in mining accepted this because in time they expected to become spinners or hewers themselves. In fact, in coal and cotton the position of the less well off deteriorated relative to the top workers who ran the unions because there were too many new entrants and too high a turnover of less skilled workers. Once the coal and cotton unions represented a larger part of the labour force in their industries there was no need for them to offer concessions to the unskilled as a means of recruiting them. The pattern continued after the First World War. The unions that were expanding into other jobs pressed for flat rate wage increases (which narrow differentials). The cotton and coal unions pressed for percentage increases (Turner 1952, 1962).

Casual labour

The labourers who worked in the unskilled industries were not an undifferentiated proletariat. When Sidney Webb looked at the London docks for the Booth Survey (1892) he distinguished three separate classes of unskilled dock labourers below the skilled stevedores and lightermen. One group were specialists (i.e. at unloading tea) and had regular work. Another group were technically casuals, but never failed to be taken on. A third group were the true casuals who could never rely on regular employment. Weekly earnings for the groups in 1888 were 20–25s; 15–20s; and 12–15s respectively. As many as 15000 of the 22000 in the docks had regular employment. Part of the difference between the groups reflected physical capacity and intelligence and part was the effect of reliance on personal contacts for (good) employment. The fact that many recent migrants had good positions suggests that quality was important. It was impossible for every unskilled worker to find daily work because casual labour was residual employment. In bad years the ranks of the casuals were swollen by those who had lost better jobs. The casual worker rarely had sufficient capital or credit to leave the area where he was known, to find work. This made it very difficult to test the market (Stedman Jones 1971). Hence, only the superior workers of the less skilled benefited much from the 'New Unions' which came onto the scene after 1888 – and some of these workers like the gas workers were not really unskilled. The casual worker was squeezed between the better off above him and the worse off below. He remained an embarrassment to the government and to reformers, some of whom toyed with the idea of sending him to a labour colony at home or abroad (Harris 1972).

Women's employment

When a male unskilled worker obtained a full week's work he earned a wage with which he was conventionally supposed to be able to keep a family. The customary wage for most women was below this and insufficient for subsistence. Women were assumed to be partly kept by husbands or fathers. The effect of this belief and of the conventional distinction between 'men's work' and 'women's work' was to confine women to the lowest paying jobs and to deny them promotion. Most men would not work alongside women at the same jobs because of convention and, more practically, because the women's wage would threaten to undercut the men's. The effect was to prevent women acquiring skills. Even when women carried out the same tasks as men, the men set up the machines and received disproportionately high wages for doing so. Women could assist the male mule spinner but never become spinners themselves. On the rare occasions when men worked alongside women for the same piece rates (e.g. in power loom weaving) they worked for women's rates.

Women were in a similar position in white collar occupations. By 1911 about one third of the two million salaried workers were women who were concentrated in women's jobs like elementary teaching and nursing. The dominant male white collar occupation was that of a commercial clerk, where women did not offer much competition. Either women were not recruited at all, as in the banks, or they worked as auxiliaries (like typists). While male clerks may have felt increasingly insecure the real reason for their fears was the replacement of the small paternalistic 'counting house' by the large bureaucratic office, not the competition of lower paid women workers (Anderson 1976, Lockwood 1958).

The majority of women expected their stay in the labour force to be brief, which affected their desire to acquire skills and to attend union meetings. But women earned less than men in every industry, whether performing skilled or unskilled jobs and whether the industry was unionised or not. This suggests that the women's differential was real and not some other differential in disguise. At least in part there was a distinct women's labour market. But because many women *were* supported by their fathers and husbands they could take more attractive jobs regardless of the wage. Highly skilled trades like corset making, millinery or book binding paid very little more than process work in the metal or food factories. Similarly, artisans' daughters worked in the warehouse rather than on the shop floor even though they could probably have earned more in the factory through their greater dexterity (Black 1915); the 'superior' domestic servants and dressmakers, not factory girls, were thought to make the best war-time munitions workers. Domestic service, however, became less desirable compared with the increasing range of women's occupations, because of its isolation and 'unsocial hours'. As the supply of young country girls fell, domestic service wages (+keep) rose to a higher level than factory wages.

Yet, overall, women's wages were rising faster than men's (Wood 1903). Access to education had increased for girls more than for boys, and the rise of factory and white collar employment was beginning to offer girl school leavers some alternatives even if the actual wage they could command was still very low.

The development of collective bargaining

The greatest institutional change in the period was the growth in the membership and the power of the trade unions. About 12 per cent of male manual workers were members of unions in 1888. Total membership at this time was 750 000. By 1914 about 44 per cent of male manual workers were organised and total membership had risen to more than four million. (At this time male manual workers were about 53 per cent of the occupied population.) (Clegg, Fox & Thompson 1964.) Most of the growth was concentrated in two short periods, 1889–92 when membership doubled, and 1910–14 when it grew by nearly two thirds (figure 7.4). Until 1910 a large part of the growth in membership took place because the industries that were most unionised in 1888 continued to expand. Forty-four per cent of union growth up to 1910 was in coal mining, cotton textiles and ship-building, the major industries with the highest proportion of union members in 1888, and only about one half of this growth was because of an increase in union density in these industries. Similarly, the skilled trades were about 90 per cent unionised by 1892 (Passfield & Webb 1897) and union growth, therefore, depended on the further expansion of skilled occupations. After 1910, however, very substantial gains were made in new industries and occupations.

The discontinuities in union growth were largely the effect of the trade cycle. Before 1890 only craft unions could easily survive a downswing in the cycle. The 1880s depression, for example, destroyed unions of agricultural labourers,

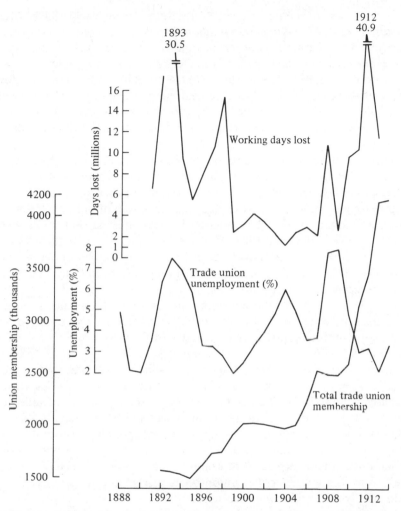

7.4   Trade union membership 1892–1914; days lost in disputes 1891–1913; trade union unemployment 1888–1914
Source: Mitchell & Deane (1962: 64–5, 68, 72).

dockers and miners (Musson 1972, 1974). After 1890, industrial operatives' unions were sufficiently strong to keep their membership, but the general unions were still very vulnerable. The general unions did not try to unionise all the unskilled, but aimed partly at the erection of local job monopolies in unionised industries like docks and gas works, and partly at the grades in the already unionised industries which were unattractive to existing unions (Hobsbawm 1949). Membership of general unions was severely reduced by counter-attacks from the newly formed employers' associations in the early 1890s. After 1910 unemployment fell and the general unions increased their membership markedly. The local job monopolies were amalgamated into large general unions (so that the Tramwaymen became part of the Dockers). The 'all grades' campaign on the railways leading to the foundation of the NUR in 1910, not the London Dock strike of 1889, was in retrospect the beginning of mass unionisation in Britain.

An alternative explanation of union growth is that it depended on structural changes within the movement. This explanation rests on the view that the 'labour aristocracy' developed non-militant craft unions as a reaction to the failure of widespread utopian movements in the 1830s and 1840s (Hobsbawm 1964a, Harrison 1965). The leaders of these unions, the argument runs, ultimately became establishment figures and their gradualist views permeated the movement. Eighteen eighty nine was a watershed when the militant political 'New Unions' rejected gradualism. But the evidence does not suggest that unions were less militant between 1850 and 1889. Strikes were common even in the skilled trades; and some skilled unions actively helped the 'New' unions in plants where the skilled had negotiating rights in order to protect their interests. In any case, the interpretation rests on an artificial distinction between skilled and unskilled unions, which neglects the enormous importance of the miners and textile workers. The 'watershed' of 1889 is equally misleading, since union growth was essentially continuous although punctuated by the trade cycle (Cole 1937, Lovell 1977).

It must also be remembered that membership of trade unions was geographically concentrated, partly because the most unionised industries were highly localised but also because union membership in the less organised industries was higher when in proximity to highly organised industries. Isolated factories in country districts often had no union except possibly for craftsmen. The propensity to join a union was frequently related to the locality rather than conditions at the workplace. For example, the railway office clerks were among the first to join a white collar union because so many of them lived alongside industrial workers who were unionised.

Large-scale collective bargaining most frequently developed as the result of conflict. When the union organised enough employees it became the *de facto* bargaining agent and the employer had no option but to bargain with it. At this stage the employer in a unionised plant would benefit from an extension of collective bargaining to the whole trade. Hence, the big trials of strength were often followed by industry-wide agreements, for example in cotton in 1893, boots and shoes in 1895 and in engineering in 1897–98. But industry-wide agreements were still not general as late as 1914; the shipping companies and the railways were still successfully fighting them, and the miners achieved one only in 1912 (by Act of Parliament), although in this case the delay was partly the result of the inability of the miners themselves to create a national union. Furthermore, national wage bargaining, when it came, did not necessarily mean uniform scales outside the exceptionally localised industries such as textiles. There was great diversity in productivity, market power and union power within industries. The dominant union institution remained the local branch and the unions themselves were in many cases merely weak federations.

Wage flexibility

The market power of the unions can best be judged from the degree that earnings fluctuated over the cycle, in particular the incidence of falls in money earnings. Phelps Brown & Browne (1968) found that annual money wage earnings were quite sticky downwards, falling in only eight years between 1860 and 1914. (They fell in twelve years of the Feinstein (1972) index.) But even allowing for data problems it is clear that these overall averages conceal large variations. Earnings fell in engineering in six years and in cotton in three when average money earnings for the whole country were static or rising; in mining, wages fell in 14 years out of 34 between 1880 and 1913 whilst general earnings only fell in four of them. Moreover, the amplitude of variations was high: the mean deviation of average annual earnings from trend (nine year moving averages) was about ± 5 per cent – not much less than the deviation in GNP (see chapter 2). Yet, in the worst year of the 1929–32 depression (1932) when GNP was $5\frac{1}{2}$ per cent below the trend, annual earnings were only 2 per cent below.

The greatest variations in earnings were in the export industries. Earnings in the South Wales and North-East coalfields, for example, were much more varied than earnings in the inland fields. The coalfields developed in great booms when the selling price of coal was high. Wage rates rose in order to attract migrants because the industry was labour intensive, and since the new pits opened in the boom were remote from existing villages an extra premium had to be paid to attract the more mobile single men. Once the boom broke, output did not fall with prices, because new pits were still coming into production. Wages were at least two thirds of total costs so the collapse of selling prices led to massive downward pressure on wage rates at least until the 1890s. This pressure was made worse by the presence of many 'foreigners' on the coalfields, the low productivity of many of the new pits, and the propensity of the iron works to sell coal if the iron trade was depressed. The ensuing lockouts were always won by the owners and usually ended with the collapse of the district union that the boom had brought into being (Youngson Brown 1953, Morris & Williams 1958). The unions lost because there was little alternative employment or if there was the miners did not have the skill for it; outside the pit the well-paid skilled miner would be a labourer.

After several disastrous attempts to resist wage cuts in the early 1870s, the miners agreed in some fields to fix (district) wages to a sliding scale depending on the selling price of coal. This was an expression of defeat. The sliding scales rarely provided a floor to wages and when the demand for labour was high prevented wages rising as fast as they might otherwise have done. They did, however, save the costs of strikes and lockouts. The miners had also attempted to enforce short-time working in various coalfields where the market was more localised, but even then competition at the margin, the difficulty of maintaining discipline between pits, the inability to control the entry of new miners and the existence of large stocks of coal had stopped prices rising. Moreover, as the scale of mines increased and overheads rose the owners acquired an interest in high output. Sliding scales had become general in the piece work industries (cotton, boots and shoes) by the 1890s and also in the North-East iron trade (Phelps Brown 1959, Porter 1970); these outlasted the sliding scales in mining which (outside South Wales) were beginning to disappear by the late 1880s. The miners came to believe they could resist wage cuts and in 1893 after 300 000 had been locked out in the inland coalfields were able to do so. But it is not obvious that 1893 was the beginning of real strength in the mining unions. Wages became subject to conciliation and it is doubtful if the wage agreements after 1893 were much different from those the sliding scales would have allowed. Earnings continued to fluctuate but the industry did not suffer a collapse like that of 1893 onwards until after the war when conditions were very different. Earnings rose as fast in the North-East iron industry where sliding scales continued until after the First World War as in coal.

In any case wage drift was still possible with or without sliding scales. The cotton spinners had regressive piece rates after the Brooklands agreement of 1893. In the early twentieth century there was a general speed up of the mules, the effect of which was to increase breakages which were paid for by the spinner. Similarly in coal, the hewer had, in effect, to negotiate his own bonus for working a difficult seam. When costs rose (e.g. when the eight hour day increased costs by 5 per cent a man-shift) the owners recouped their losses by systematically reducing the extra payments for difficult work. The rate of pay for working in 'abnormal places' led to the Cambrian Strike of 1910 and eventually to the successful national strike for a legal minimum wage (Jevons 1915). But over the period 1893–1913 mining earnings increased faster than the standard negotiated rates (Rowe 1923) which shows how powerful the miners could be within individual pits.

Trade unions and wages

The conclusions of the most exhaustive study of the relation of trade union activity to changes in money earnings severely circumscribe the role of the unions (Phelps Brown & Browne 1968). It argues that unit wage costs were determined by productivity. Money wages could, therefore, only rise relative to productivity if the selling price could be increased, if the return on capital was allowed to fall or if the capital–output ratio fell. In the five countries studied by Phelps Brown and Browne (1968) the capital–output ratio remained constant for long periods and there was no tendency for the rate of profit to fall. It follows that unit wage costs only rose when prices could be raised (i.e. when the market was 'soft'). In Britain, before the First World War, which was an open economy with no cartels, 'soft' markets were only brought about by exceptional international trading conditions. Unless productivity rose, most unions could only bargain to increase costs to the consumer or to increase their share of total output. When the market was hard they could only do the latter. Within these limits, actual wage rises depended on the vigour with which the claims were pressed. This analysis explains the supposed stability of the share of wages in the national income 1860–1914. There seems little doubt that the powerful unions only increased their share of income at the expense of the non-unionised and of members of other unions. Moreover, wage earnings overall were not affected by changes in the supply of labour. The exceptionally rapid growth of the labour force in the 1890s for example does not seem to have affected wage rates or the share paid to labour. However, it does not follow that the economy could absorb as much labour as was offered at a going wage. The large number of women and boys in the labour market may be a function of the demand for labour rather than the supply, and the national averages conceal great regional and industrial variations.

Many contemporaries untrammelled by national income estimates were in no doubt that unions raised wages (see Pollard 1965). In a whole range of industries wage rises were concentrated in a few years and were contemporary with union growth. By 1890 the unionised industries   with the major exception of boots and shoes – had high wages. The difficulty is separating cause and effect. Potential members believed that a union would raise their wages and they were quick to join or create a union at the first sign of success. But the correlation between total union membership and change in total earnings is not very strong (Phelps Brown & Browne 1968). Exceptional wage increases in 1899 and falls in 1908 and 1909 were not associated with changes in total union membership (figure 7.4). Moreover, the huge membership increase of 1911 was not associated with large wage increases unless they were delayed until 1912 when wages rose exceptionally fast.

Wages were not the same throughout each industry. There was a tendency for all wages within an industry to follow union wages but there were many cases where only the unionised section benefited: in North-East shipping for example. It is possible of course that interplant differences reflected differential productivity. But it is possible to find examples in mining that suggest that wage variations were a consequence of union activity. Physical labour productivity was declining (Taylor 1961) and there was little mechanisation. Earnings in each coalfield depended on the need to attract additional labour, the output and the actual wage rates negotiated by the unions. Cannock Chase and Leicester output expanded rapidly but wages rose only slowly. Cumberland and Somerset output grew only slowly but wages rose fast (Rowe 1923).

It is also likely that the impact effect of new unions was very important. Why, for example, did the London dockers obtain 6d per hour and a minimum four hour day? 1889 was the most prosperous year for a long time but not prosperous enough for full employment in the docks. The union provided (at the peak of the trade cycle) an escape from customary wage scales.

Change in the work situation

The unions were also able to use non-cooperation with management as a bargaining weapon. For example, there are two explanations for the failure of real income to rise in the so-called 'Edwardian Period'. The first and most important is that the marginal productivity of capital in industry fell as a consequence of investment in machinery which was not improving as rapidly as earlier in the century. The second is that the labour force resisted productivity changes, drove up time rates and generally worked less efficiently. Craftsmen attempted to counter the introduction of piece work by restrictive practices which insisted on excessive manning levels. Many industries adapted the 'stint' or 'ca'canny' which in effect determined maximum output irrespective of technical change. This was partly a response to the increasing scale of business and a general reduction in personal contact – which was not improved by clumsy attempts to introduce 'scientific management' (Phelps Brown and Browne 1968).

It is also likely that union militancy increased at this time. This is not the place to discuss the relationship (if any) between the Irish, the Suffragettes and the Unions in 1910–14 but it was about that time when many of the older leaders were replaced. It was pointed out by the militants that all the major stoppages in mining before 1910 had been lockouts (i.e. were defensive actions). They were led by men steeped in the chapel and usually the Liberal party. In one coalfield after another the old generation of leaders were replaced by younger militants (Moore 1974, Evans 1961).

Hours of work are usually assumed to be part of the wages bargain. They altered infrequently but not so discontinuously as to require a special explanation. It was simply that the benefits to the employer of maintaining hours were greater than those to employees from reducing them. The employer preferred longer hours to spread overheads, while leisure preference varied between employees. Therefore it was easier to satisfy both sides with changes in wages (Bienefeld 1972). Hours of work were inversely correlated with income throughout the period, and in many industries before the development of collective bargaining.

Shorter hours were not associated with falling productivity – at least before the twentieth century when they may have led to a 5 per cent fall in output – but according to Phelps Brown this was little compared with the effect of restrictive practices. By 1905 average hours were fifty four in industry and substantially less than in Western Europe where the standard of living was lower.

Changes in the quality of labour

It is very difficult to quantify the changes within individuals which made them more efficient workers, but it is clear that the average skilled (and particularly, unskilled) workers in 1914 was individually better equipped than his grandfather had been in 1860. One major difference was the incidence of education. The worker was unlikely to have had a much better technical education because before the early twentieth century full-time technical education rarely reached the labour force. Elementary schools offered no practical subjects and secondary schools were often against them. Most of the developments in further education were aimed at professional examinations for white collar workers or were non-vocational. It was only after 1880 that evening classes began seriously to teach technical subjects. By 1911, 12 per cent of the 15–24 age group were enrolled, of which a third were doing professional and vocational courses and a quarter maths and science (Cotgrove 1958). Most managers in industry remained opposed to technical education and in consequence their foremen and supervisors were almost entirely self taught – as were the managers themselves (Aldcroft 1975).

The main improvement was in general education. In 1900, for example, only 3 per cent signed the marriage register with a mark compared with 30 per cent in 1860. We can assume, therefore, that nearly all the *new entrants* to the labour force were literate by this time. School attendance rose in the same period from 1.2 million to 4.7 million, that is from 39 per cent to 118 per cent of the 5–9 age group. The greatest relative improvement in literacy, however, was not among industrial workers but among women. Most of the industrial North and particularly Scotland had high literacy for men in 1860. The difficulty is that neither the ability to sign a name nor attendance at school – which was frequently very irregular – is sufficient evidence that the reading ability and comprehension of the labour force was significantly increasing. The greatest contribution of the massive school building programme (3.7 million new places 1870–95) could have been to impart discipline (Altick 1957, Stone 1969). There is, however, ample indirect evidence to show that standards were rising. For example, sales of periodicals rose markedly. Another way of assessing qualitative improvements is to look at alcohol consumption. This fell from a peak in the mid 1870s of about thirty-four gallons *per capita* per year (men, women and children). Convictions for drunkenness peaked a bit later but were falling everywhere, except in South Wales, by the 1890s (Wilson 1940, Dingle 1972). They were concentrated in industrial areas and when wages were high. This sort of evidence raises many problems but at the least it suggests that the industrial labour force was becoming more sober.

8

Agricultural decline 1860-1914

C. Ó GRÁDA

The share of agriculture in the gross national product of Great Britain dropped from about twenty per cent in 1860 to less than seven per cent in 1913 (Feinstein 1972: T4, T60), as the absolute level of agricultural output, measured in real terms, failed to register any sustained increase. This need not signify 'decline' in any pejorative sense, since the change could have resulted simply from greater specialisation in international trade. Indeed, though Britain had long been an importer of some foodstuffs, such as cheese from Holland and live cattle and grain from Ireland, her dependence on food imports grew rapidly after mid-century. The opening up of the vast American prairies for grain production, the improvements in long-distance transport technology both on land and on sea, and the massive increase in the output of dairy products in parts of the European Continent, were important developments for the British economy. Moreover, the substantial rise in imports during these years – a fourfold increase in wheat, a fivefold increase in butter imports, for example – was accompanied by a sharp drop in the relative price of foodstuffs.

Nevertheless, the period is often regarded as one of agricultural 'decline' in a less trivial sense. As R. E. Prothero (Lord Ernle) wrote in 1912, 'Since 1862 the tide of agricultural prosperity ceased to flow: after 1874 it turned, and rapidly ebbed' (Ernle 1912: 377). Since he wrote, the widening gap between agricultural and non-agricultural incomes has been a recurring theme. A relative fall in landlord incomes at the time is understandable, since (following Ricardo) rent levels might be expected to bear the main brunt of free trade; however, similar trends in farmers' and farm workers' incomes, if they are substantiated, need to be explained. The alleged failure of British agriculture to respond to the challenge of foreign competition and the opportunities presented by the shifting patterns of consumer demand is the explanation most often given.

Despite auspicious beginnings, it would seem that 'high farming' along lines advocated by publicity-seekers such as Alderman Mechi or journalists like James Caird was not enough (see volume 1, chapter 10). As Kindleberger (1964: 243) has put it, 'it was left for Denmark, the Netherlands and New Zealand to provide the bacon, eggs, ham and cheese in which the British worker and middle class member chose to take such a large proportion of their increased productivity. These countries did transform under the pressure of British demand. The question is why it was they and not the more strategically placed British agriculture?' By and large, the farmer and the landlord have been given low marks for adaptability and initiative in the mid- and late-Victorian era.

Income and productivity

But did rural incomes really fall behind? A variety of evidence, ranging from cartoons in Punch to doleful data on bankrupt farmers, would suggest a decline even in absolute terms from the early 1870s down to the end of the century. A recent survey, which relies heavily on such information, dwells at length on the 'deteriorating economic and social position' of the landed proprietors, and the 'falling' income of farmers, while conceding that labourers did not fare so badly (Perry 1974: 91, 92, 126). For the 1880s and the 1890s the evidence presented to the Royal Commission on the Depressed Condition of Agricultural Interests (1880–82) and the Royal Commission on the Agricultural Depression (1894–97) is almost uniformly pessimistic (Fletcher 1961a). Reliable accounts of the overall movement in incomes, needed to clinch the issue, are scarce, however, and not easy to construct. Table 8.1 attempts merely to provide a very approximate guide to the course of incomes adjusted for the change in the cost of living between 1861 and 1911. Since per capita real income equals

$$\frac{(\text{output}) \times (\text{agricultural price index})}{(\text{numbers employed in agriculture})} \times (\text{consumer price index})$$

calculation of the standard-of-living index in column 5 of table 8.1 is straightforward.

The figures imply that 1870/72–1880/82 and 1890/92–1900/02 were the most depressed decades as regards incomes. This is in line with more impressionistic accounts. Besides, the former period includes 1878–81, years of dismally bad harvests and low prices, and the latter those years when agricultural prices reached their nadir. But table 8.1 also suggests that mean income rose by over a third during the half-century (from 100 to 136), and by about a tenth during 1870/72–1900/02. It is true that average real income is a somewhat elusive average, which is bound to conceal interesting variations across regions and classes. Regional differences, which have received increasing attention in recent years from historians, are briefly discussed on pp. 192–4 below. Meanwhile estimates of factor shares in agriculture in table 8.1, combined with census information on occupational structure, permit some broad generalisations on the incomes from the land of farmers, farm workers and landed proprietors over the five decades. This tripartite division, though hardly relevant for the whole of Great Britain, offers a useful means of presenting data. For example, the number of farmers in Great Britain decreased from 312000 in 1861 to 280000

Table 8.1. *The trend in agricultural output and incomes 1860–1914*

Period	Agricultural output (1)	Agricultural prices (2)	Cost of living (3)	Population working in agriculture (4)	Average real income from agriculture (5)	Class shares (%)		
						Landlords (6)	Labourers (7)	Farmers (8)
1860/62	100.3	118.3	112	100	100	22	43	35
1870/72	104.9	120	115.3	88.9	115.9	23	43	34
1880/82	99.7	107	106	78.9	120.4	27	51	22
1890/92	105.6	90	91.7	75.0	130.4	23	49	28
1900/02	97.4	86	90	69.2	127.0	19	49	32
1910/12	103.0	98.3	97.3	72.2	136.0	18	47	35

Sources: Output, Feinstein (1972: T 118); prices, Mitchell & Deane (1962: 472–3, 343–5); labour force, Orwin & Whetham (1964: 342), with the following adjustment: 50000 was added to Orwin and Whetham's total for 1861 to allow for seasonal labour inputs, declining by 10000 each decade; class shares from Bellerby (1968: 268), Feinstein (1972: T 60). Average real income from agriculture for 1860/62 was set equal to 100.

in 1911 (Orwin and Whetham 1971: 342); table 8.1, then, assumes that farmers' incomes rose on average by

$$\frac{(1911 \text{ output}) \times (\text{farmers' share})}{(1861 \text{ output}) \times (\text{farmers' share})} \div \frac{(\text{number of farmers in } 1911)}{(\text{number of farmers in } 1861)}$$

i.e. $\dfrac{(103.0)(35)}{(100.3)(35)} \div \dfrac{280\,000}{312\,000} = \dfrac{1.03}{0.90} = 1.14$

or by 14 per cent. By the same token, since the number of landed proprietors hardly changed, their average income from the land fell by about thirty per cent between 1880/82 and 1900/02, while the huge decline in the agricultural proletariat – from over 1.4 million in 1861 to 0.9–1.0 million in 1911 – ensured those remaining on the land an average increase in incomes of over one half.

The growth of average real incomes in agriculture did not match the growth of average incomes in other sectors (chapters 1 and 6). However, a relative decline in per capita average income does not necessarily imply that resources were misallocated to agriculture; efficiency requires, in economic theory, the equalisation between sectors of the economy of marginal returns, not of average returns which are measured by average real incomes. In addition, table 8.1 suggests that there was a sharp rise in output per worker, which is often taken as a sign of increased efficiency. Labour productivity alone, however, may be a misleading guide to economic performance; the movement in total factor productivity, if it can be measured, provides a better guide of overall 'progress' or 'decline'. Total factor productivity may be defined as a ratio of output to inputs, the latter weighted by their respective shares of output. As explained in chapter 1, its measurement is fraught with difficulties, both conceptual and practical. However, an increase in its size over time may be interpreted, though loosely, as a move towards greater efficency in resource use, provided all inputs are included and properly weighted and measured. Accurate measurement is often impossible, but the direction of the bias may be controlled.

In the present context, since agriculture is on trial for sluggish response, the input measures should, if anything, favour the null hypothesis of 'not guilty'. For this reason the indices have not been adjusted to allow for improvement in quality. The results, which are presented in table 8.2, suggest an annual productivity growth rate of 0.3 per cent between 1871 and 1911. While a positive growth rate may seem reassuring, in fact 0.3 per cent is far from impressive. For instance, productivity growth rates up to 1 per cent have been reported for Japanese and American agriculture in the pre First World War period (Kelley & Williamson 1974: 164–96; Kendrick 1961: 362–4). The British data are admittedly less precise, but refinement would probably reduce estimated British

Table 8.2. *Total factor productivity change in British agriculture 1871–1911*

Period	Inputs			Factor shares (%)			Output	Total factor productivity (1870/72 = 100)
	Land (1)	Labour (2)	Capital (3)	Land (4)	Labour (5)	Capital (6)	(7)	(8)
1870/72	100	100	100	23	63	13	104.9	100
1880/82	100	87.7	101.4	27	59	14	99.7	102.3
1890/92	100	84.3	114.9	23	64	13	105.6	109.6
1900/02	100	77.9	114.9	19	69	12	97.4	106.9
1910/12	100	81.2	108.3	18	69	12	103.0	112.9

Sources: Labour (col. 2), as in table 8.1; capital (col. 3), Bellerby and Boreham (1953), adjusted for use by Statist–Sauerbeck overall index in Mitchell and Deane (1962: 474–5); factor shares, Bellerby (1968: 264). For the share of labour (col. 5), the share of 'wages' and 'farmers' and relatives' incentive income' were added together

productivity growth. In addition the estimate for agriculture is also considerably below that for the economy as a whole over the period (see table 1.6). The result might thus be taken as evidence that this was indeed a period of 'decline' in British agriculture. But it does not explain the decline. There are a number of possible explanations, to which we now turn.

The farmer: supply responsiveness

As regards supply responsiveness, it is possible, in the first place, that British agriculture was hoarding resources in 1871–1911 which would have been more productive in other sectors of the economy. The argument that farmers and landed proprietors might forgo income in order to remain within agriculture at a time of adversity is an old one (Bellerby 1956). Alternatively, agriculturalists may have generated a low output simply because they switched inadequately into those farm commodities yielding the best returns at any one time.

British farmers, landlords, and labourers have all been blamed, though not with equal conviction, for British agriculture's allegedly weak performance. Taking the farmer first, the case for sluggish response, for the presumed 'appalling obstinacy of the British farmer', has yet to be cogently made. Admittedly, examples of behaviour which at first sight imply low allocative ability are numerous. R. H. Rew guessed that the refusal of livestock farmers to use the newly-developed weighbridge cost them as much as £7 million in 1888 alone, but this is an extreme case (Perry 1974: 64): £7 million was six per cent of agricultural output in that dismal year. In the same vein, *The Daily News* complained in 1879 that 'as to the ability of the English farmer to take out of

Table 8.3. *Gross agricultural output of Great Britain 1870–76 and 1904–10*

	1870–76		1904–10	
	£m	(%)	£m	(%)
Crops	80.9	(41.4)	44.2	(28.5)
Animal products	114.3	(58.6)	111.0	(71.5)
Total	195.2	(100.0)	155.2	(100.0)
Some individual items:				
Wheat	26.6	(13.6)	8.4	(5.4)
All grains	49.8	(25.5)	20.1	(13.0)
Beef	34.8	(17.8)	29.4	(18.9)
Milk	27.0	(13.8)	36.5	(23.5)

Source: Ojala (1952: 210–11); Ojala's calculations for the United Kingdom have been adjusted by using (with slight corrections) the estimates for Ireland presented in *Irish Agricultural Output 1908* (Dublin, 1912) and Solow (1971: 17)

the hand of foreigners the trade in butter, no one doubts that they might have kept in the country most part of the £10 000 000 which was paid for imported butter in 1878'. Other more mundane examples illustrate the alleged delay in switching resources to 'safer and more promising openings' such as horticulture and dairying, in using the advantages of agricultural co-operation in production and marketing, and in applying cost-saving process innovations.

The list of seeming error and inertia is impressive. Nevertheless, to argue by example is a gambit to be indulged in only as a last resort – particularly since the documentation is not all negative, and some of it is open to different interpretations. Presumably farmer intelligence was distributed among the farm population around some average, as among the population as a whole: if so, individual examples might come from the upper or lower end of the distribution.

The agricultural and price statistics of the period, supported by background data on technical and institutional factors, permit a different approach. A broader focus raises its own problems, however. How slow is sluggish? 'The British farmer,' we are told, 'does not act precipitatedly, but gradually alters his method over long periods of time' (Wrightson 1890: 281). Yes, but where is the dividing line between caution, impetuosity, and sheer pigheadedness? A comparative approach to the problem at hand, drawing on evidence from other countries, may help. But before turning to direct measures of supply response, let us examine briefly the change in the composition of agricultural output over the period.

Table 8.3 presents a picture of substantial shift in the composition of output between the 1870s and the 1900s. Most notable are the decline in the relative importance of grain and the increase in milk production. Moreover, the figures conceal further shifts within these sectors. Thus during the period both oats and barley acreage overtook that under wheat, while within dairying butter and cheese gave way more and more to the production of liquid milk.

The fall in the acreage under grain, which probably began before 1860, is perhaps the best known aspect of British agricultural transformation during this period. In retrospect the development within dairying, though less emphasised by economic historians, seems equally radical. It too took place against a background of increasing intrusion from foreign producers, from Continental Europe at first and from New Zealand after 1880. At a rough guess, between the 1860s and the First World War British butter and cheese production declined by forty per cent, but liquid milk output more than quadrupled and milk consumption per capita doubled (Taylor 1976). The rise in imports of dairy products shocked jingoistic contemporaries, and the notion grew – and has persisted – that British dairying 'failed' in its struggle (Haggard 1911: 248–76; Kindleberger 1964: 243).

In fact, though, for most British farmers the specialisation in liquid milk production made perfect sense under free trade conditions. Transport costs and the problem of quick spoilage ensured that British producers had a monopoly in the home market, and farmers who were suitably located could make almost twice as much from their liquid milk, sold fresh, as from butter. Not surprisingly it was only in remote areas, removed both from the railway network and centres of consumption, that farmers persisted with cheese and butter production on a large scale. The bulk of British butter and cheese was being produced in the south-west of England and in Wales by 1914. Nearer London and Manchester the proportion of dairy produce being sold in liquid form reached nine tenths, but in Wales only slightly exceeded one half. The regional variation was due to locational constraints, not to differences in commercial acumen. Indeed, in the worst-endowed parts of the periphery, just as in parts of Ireland, not only were farmers in no position to get the high prices for liquid milk; the advantages of the centrifugal separator, available in theory from the early 1880s, eluded them as well (Hall 1913: 325–7).

Detailed studies by agricultural economists over the last two decades or so have confirmed what many had long suspected, that farmers generally tend as a group to respond positively to market forces. The British farmer of the late Victorian and Edwardian years was presumably no exception: at least, that is what table 8.3 suggests. Still, because what is at stake is an inadequate rather than a zero response to prices, a more exact notion of price responsiveness is required. We shall therefore examine the supply elasticity – the response of supply to a change in price – of one category of agricultural output, cereals, in more detail. Cereals, 'the besetting temptation of British agriculture' according to Brodrick (1881: 296), were chosen because they have been the focus of much previous writing and – as we have seen above – contributed significantly to agricultural output. Reliable acreage and price data are available from the early

1870s (J. T. Coppock 1956) and can be used to obtain the supply elasticities shown below for Great Britain over the period 1874–1914:

Crop	Short-run elasticity	Long-run elasticity
Wheat	0.63	1.11
Barley	0.35	0.76
Oats	0.26	1.63

Note: The structure estimated was that used by Fisher and Temin (1970) and by DeCanio (1974: 243–61). Data from Mitchell and Deane (1962: 78–9, 488–9). For a somewhat different approach, though giving similar results, see Olson and Harris (1959). See also Nerlove (1958).

Perhaps in themselves the results are unimpressive. They show, for example, that on average a 1 per cent fall in the price of wheat produced a fall of 0.63 per cent in output in the short run, and of 1.11 per cent in the long run: still, they compare favourably with elasticities calculated for nineteenth century agriculture elsewhere. The same estimation technique gives short-run elasticities of 0.07–0.61 for the same grain crops in neighbouring Ireland over the same period; state-wide estimates in the United States give the ranges of 0.08–0.38 and 0.10–0.28 for wheat and cotton; elasticities of 0.08–0.38 and 0.18–0.69 have been calculated for Hungarian wheat and rye over 1892–1911 (Fisher and Temin, 1970; DeCanio, 1974; Eddie, 1971). It seems unfair then, on this evidence to blame the British farmer for cereal 'over-production'. Indeed, because there were important cost-saving innovations in cereal production during these decades – see pp. 182–6 below – the response of farmers to changes in relative prices (the figures estimated here) must have been less than their response to changes in net revenue per unit output. If, as frequently suggested, cereal farmers were likely to be the least responsive group, that creates a strong presumption that response in other sections within British agriculture was 'adequate' at the time.

The farmer and technical change: the reaping machine

Even if farmers were producing the right crops, it is possible that they were not using the best methods, and in particular the best machinery. The mechanisation of British agriculture began before this period. Mid-century farming manuals, such as Henry Stephens' *Book of the Farm* or J. C. Morton's *Cyclopedia of Agriculture*, contain descriptions of much of the machinery in use thirty or even fifty years later (Thompson 1968: 65–6). However, the post-1860 period saw the widespread diffusion and refinement of a few which showed earlier promise. The failures included the steam plough, the successes the threshing machine, the horse hoe, and the chaff machine (Walton 1973; Collins 1972). In this section, though, we concentrate on the most documented and perhaps most important instance, the reaping machine.

The American reapers exhibited at the Crystal Palace Exhibition of 1851 were a great attraction, but British farmers were slow to adopt the new techniques at harvest time. While mechanisation of reaping in the American mid-west proceeded quite rapidly from the mid 1850s, in Britain the 1850s and 1860s saw only modest diffusion. A recent estimate suggests that almost four fifths of American small grain acreage was being cut mechanically by 1869–70, while the proportion in Great Britain was still less than half in 1874 (David 1969: table 2.4). Was the delay simply another instance of British farmers' lethargy? The timing of the reaper's diffusion is a puzzle which still awaits an agreed explanation. A number of competing hypotheses have been put forward, but none have been generally accepted; the paucity and uncertainty of evidence on the temporal and spatial diffusion of machines and grain acreage, and on the regional differences in the wages of harvest labourers, leaves much room for argument.

It seems unlikely that either the organised hostility of agricultural labourers or the paternalism of farmers, who might have retained labourers when it was no longer strictly economic to do so, were significant factors in preventing diffusion in the second half of the nineteenth century. The most obvious explanation is that the speed of diffusion was a response to the relative costs and prices of the old and the new methods. The reaper was a classic example of labour-saving machinery (Wilson 1864: 149; McConnell 1906: 237), and it has been suggested that the state of the labour market was an important determinant of reaper diffusion. Until mid-century and later the British farm population – with considerable help, it should be added, from Irish seasonal migrants – was adequate to cope with harvest demands at low wages. Given the fixed cost involved in buying a reaper, diffusion was delayed by the relative cheapness of farm labour (Habakkuk 1962a: 199).

However, the price of harvest labour relative to capital is not, by itself, sufficient to explain the speed of diffusion. Another possibility is that the smaller farmer, for whom buying a reaper would have meant incurring a higher fixed cost per acre of grain, might have been less likely to adopt the new technique. This consideration has prompted the use of the concept of 'threshold acreage' (David 1975: 195–217). Income-maximising farmers with an acreage above the threshold would buy a reaper, while others would cling to traditional methods. According to this interpretation the size distribution of farms is a crucial determinant of the spread of mechanisation. Its usefulness as an explanation hinges largely, however, on whether the option of renting a machine, rather than buying outright, existed for the smaller farmer; if it did, then small size should not preclude use of a reaper.

Thirdly, it has been argued that the farming landscape in Britain was an added consideration: smaller fields, the use of open furrows for drainage, and blade-breaking stones, in practice meant an additional fixed cost element in preparing arable land for the reaper: 'Mechanisation of the corn harvest would have been a profitable undertaking on a great part of Britain's cereal acreage even at the beginning of the 1850's supposing only that the more serious among the terrain problems...could have been first removed' (David 1975: 244). In other words, the use of the machine required a complementary third factor – proper terrain – whose improvement was more expensive in Britain than in America.

That does not exhaust the list of possibilities. A fourth was the change in the productivity of reaping machines themselves over time. While harvesting techniques remained constrained by hand-tool methods, the scope for productivity increase was rather limited: as soon as cutting became what Marx called 'the mechanism of an implement' this was no longer so (see volume 1, chapter 10 above). Though the machines on show at the Crystal Palace had tremendous curiosity value, they were unwieldy for British use, liable to break down under British conditions, and difficult to service. They were intended for the American prairies, which were flat, had few hedges and fences and whose crops were much less heavy. But after 1851 refinements continued apace both in Britain and in the United States, as the patent records testify – almost three hundred reaper patents were taken out in Britain alone in 1850–70 – and competition between manufacturers was intense. Fourteen years after the Exhibition an observer could state of earlier superseded models that 'they now rot in corners looking in comparison to modern reapers, like skeletons of the Mammoth and the Mastodon among recent animals'. Moreover, though the reliability and performance of the machines improved, price did not increase between 1851 and 1914.

Which of these interpretations best fit the available evidence? As for the threshold model, there is only limited evidence for a market in reaper hiring and the informal sharing of reapers. Even if reaper hiring existed, the smaller farmer may still have been in less of a position to switch techniques, since there could also have been a threshold – though a lower one – for hiring. More serious, though, for the argument that a threshold was a constraining factor, is the objection that in mid-century most of Britain's small grains were grown on acreages exceeding the average utilisation level of early reaping machines, if not their cutting capacity. The size distribution of farms is fundamental, since we are less interested in the number of farmers adopting the reaper than in the total grain acreage cut by it. David (1969: 30–1) has suggested fifty acres as the average annual use per reaper in 1850–70, so the threshold model's main relevance is limited to grain acreages under fifty, where one would not expect to find a reaper being used. A farmer with more acres, say 70, could be expected to use a combination of a reaper and hand labour.

The threshold model may thus help to explain the diffusion lags in Ross and Cromarty or Inverness, where the average cereal acreage was about seven in the early 1870s; it is certainly of less help in the case of the Midlands or East Anglia, where the average in mid-century probably approached fifty. Indeed, it is arguable that the model's potential coverage extends to only a quarter or even a fifth of Britain's grain acrage at the time, since the vast bulk of the crops were being grown on large farms. For example, average farm size in Hertfordshire in 1870 was eighty-one acres, but eighty-one per cent of the land was on farms exceeding one hundred acres. The average size of those large holdings, in turn, was over 250 acres.

Contemporary cost comparisons of hand and machine methods – of which there are several – must be treated with care. However, a number of them, such as Jacob Wilson's careful and detailed study of the early 1860s, imply that the reaper was then a marginal proposition even in areas where harvest wages were relatively high. According to Wilson's calculations for Midlothian in Scotland the saving per acre on labour was about five shillings. But the average acreage cut in a season by Wilson's sample of 160 machines was less than fifty, and depreciation on a £30–40 machine with a five year life – considered usual at the time – would thus have accounted for about three shillings per acre. Nor does it take into account the extra outgoings on horses and oil associated with the new technique, items which might easily account for a few shillings per acre. Problems of terrain apart, then, Wilson's data are consistent with slow diffusion being the sensible option for Britain (Wilson 1864).

The available figures therefore make the coexistence of hand-tools and machines quite plausible, particularly since the regional variation in harvest earnings was substantial in mid-century. Moreover, literary evidence seems to imply that the reaper came into use first in those areas where harvest earnings were highest, so the Habakkuk hypothesis of the importance of the relative costs of capital and labour to mechanisation has a bearing on the problem. As emigration and urban employment tended to reduce the supply of seasonal workers in the 1860s – parliamentary returns suggest a twenty per cent rise in weekly earnings by task work during the 1860s – reapers became increasingly viable.

Improvements in the machines themselves provided an added spur. The earliest McCormick model was pulled by one horse, which also had to carry the driver, while another worker raked the cut crop from the machine as he walked alongside. The model exhibited in England in 1851 had a second seat, but was still very heavy, and tough on the horses. In the late 1850s 'the attainment of a completely effective reaping machine [was] an object yet to be sought for' (Slight and Scott Burn 1858: 343). Yet within a few years several companies were producing a working model which could be operated by one man, and delivered the cut crop in sheaves. In addition, changing the reaper was to a considerable extent a substitute for changing the landscape. Smaller and lighter machines were developed, which could more easily negotiate the furrows and enclosures which created problems for the earliest reapers. The late 1870s finally witnessed the introduction of a successful reaper-and-binder, the last word within a horse-drawn technology. By the end of the period, the cost of harvesting on all but the most intractable fields was four to six shillings per acre, while hand methods would have cost three to four times that much (Wrightson 1906: 99–106). Labour abundance considerations were no longer relevant, and the vast bulk of the grain was mechanically harvested.

The reaper-and-binder, unlike its predecessors, would have paid even at the wage level of the 1850s. In the event, its arrival on the scene at the onset of the collapse in corn prices was a godsend to hardpressed farmers. It lessened the blow of the price slump, and limited the reduction in corn acreage, making it worthwhile to grow wheat at thirty shillings a quarter, 'though no one will grow rich at the job' (McConnell 1906: 238). In sum, the pace of reaper diffusion is no argument against the British farmer: at an aggregate level, it would seem to have followed economic logic.

The landowners

The distribution of landed property in nineteenth century Britain was notoriously unequal. Using official data, Bateman estimated that less than 1700 'peers' and 'great landowners' owned two fifths of the total area of England and Wales in the 1870s (Brodrick 1881: 152–87). Yet relatively few people within British agricultural thought of a radical redistribution of landed wealth as a formula for agriculture recovery and progress. Such a plan was firmly ruled out by Gladstone at the onset of the depression: almost twenty years later, a disillusioned member of the Royal Commission of 1894–97 found that body's majority report 'vigorous and uncompromising only in its defence of the existing land system' (Gladstone 1879: 106; Channing 1897: ix). There was no revolution in landed property at the time; the proportions of land under tenancy and owner-occupancy hardly changed.

Nevertheless, criticism of landlords after the middle of the century was widespread, though more restrained than in neighbouring Ireland. Landlords were accused, for instance, of giving tenants no security of tenure and, on top of that, of refusing them compensation for unexhausted improvements which they had made. The landlords were also blamed for unreasonably delaying rent reductions, and for refusing tenants permission to convert arable land to pasture, when tillage became unremunerative. In such ways, landlords were thought to be responsible for not helping to give tenants 'a fair field' in their struggle against foreign competition.

While many examples may be found to support these criticisms, their overall importance has almost certainly been exaggerated. Initial landlord reluctance to permit the conversion of tilled fields to grass, and to reduce rent claims was normally short-lived. It would have been too much to hope that landlord expectations about future prices would adjust overnight after decades of relative price buoyancy: indeed, neither landlord nor tenant thought at the outset that the fall in prices would last. But surviving estate accounts suggest that most of the decline in 'rent received' was rather quickly reflected in the 'rent demanded' column (Rhee 1949). Even where cuts were delayed, there was usually a liberal attitude to arrears. While a small minority of landlords in the areas of the Celtic fringe – Wales and Scotland – still evicted for political reasons, such behaviour was atavistic by late nineteenth century British standards; it was almost unheard of for a landlord to evict for the non-payment of rent during a crisis year. The absence of litigation about 'tumbled-down' land, and of convincing statistical evidence, make it unlikely that landlords prevented tenants from adjusting land-use in response to the changes in relative prices.

It is true that conflicting claims about rents, from interested parties, in newspapers and in oral evidence to Royal Commissions, pose a problem of interpretation. What is most significant, though, is the existence 'in nearly every county [of] a competition for farms' as late as the mid 1890s (Parliamentary Papers 1897: xv, 213). Such excess demand implies either very foolhardy tenants or, which seems more likely, attractive rent levels. A pro-tenant Royal Commissioner, in desperation, rationalised that 'with most commodities, the supply tends to equal the demand: but the area of land in Great Britain is limited, and the number of land occupiers being recruited from so many sources is practically unlimited' (Parliamentary Papers 1897: *ibid.*). The dubious economics cannot conceal the apologetic nature of the argument.

In addition, although most tenants in Britain were on yearly tenancies by 1860, there is little evidence that lack of security in practice prevented them from improving their holdings (F. M. L. Thompson 1968: 76–7). This is because they were very rarely ejected and because systems of tenant right, formal and informal, were widespread at the time, and seem to have adjusted as economic conditions dictated. As free agents, tenants with cause for concern at lack of security could have insisted on special terms in their contracts; no evidence has been adduced for such pressure, nor, indeed, for any correlation between 'security' and tenants' outlays on the land. The replies to the questionnaire prepared by Assistant Commissioner Little for the Royal Commission of 1880–82 imply that those farmers in the south of England who complained loudest about insecurity were no more reluctant to spend considerable sums annually on lime and fertiliser than those who had tenant right written into their covenants (Parliamentary Papers 1882: xv, 200–27). The same source suggests that despite legal changes, tenancies typically stayed for several decades within the same family. Finally, there is no sign that the land system materially hindered the development of fruit farming and market gardening at this time, though these involved considerable fixed outlays on the part of the tenant.

The traditional view, long associated in particular with Arthur Young and James Caird, that long leases were essential if tenants were to improve the land, therefore does not fit the facts of nineteenth century British agriculture. Tenancy-at-will provided greater flexibility in the face of fluctuating prices; indeed, the widespread use of long leases would have made adjustment during the depression itself more costly. Whether tenancy-at-will promoted efficiency by keeping tenants on their toes – a point suggested by some economists, notably Nassau Senior – is not clear, since the sanction of eviction was hardly ever applied. Individual proprietors, besides, had nothing to fear from a system such as tenant right in its English form, whereby farmers simply recouped the value of their fixed investment in the land.

In many of its aspects, therefore, landlordism did not act as a brake on agricultural adjustment during this period. The story does not end there, however. It has been suggested that the crisis after the late 1870s was exacerbated by landlord economies in the area of landlord improvement. As a recent writer has plausibly put it, 'Successful adaptation...required from the landowner a certain level of expenditure, both on land and on farm buildings...[since] increased livestock numbers usually implied heavier expenditure on new buildings to house them, especially if the farmer concentrated on stall- or yard-feeding' (Perren 1970: 110, 111). The claim that landlord investment influenced rent buoyancy after 1879 – a minimal claim, since in theory landlords could have bankrupted themselves in marginally improving their rental receipts – may be tested with some statistical evidence presented to the Royal Commission of 1894–97. In the course of their inquiries the Commissioners approached several landed proprietors for information on the finances of their estates during the previous two decades and secured some quite useful data. The data tell a somewhat surprising tale; the evidence of almost forty estates in Britain between 1882 and 1892 shows that the correlation between rent change per acre and improvement outlay per acre, though positive, was statistically insignificant. In other words, investment was hardly related to subsequent changes in rent. It is even possible that the realised rate of return on land investment in agriculture was negative at the time (Ó Gráda 1979). This makes it unlikely that landlords were investing too little. It is conceivable that all or part of the return on the landlords' investments were accruing to the farmers, because landlords were not charging economic rents, but a more plausible interpretation is that proprietors, caught in a futile attempt at bailing out hard-hit tenants, were simply throwing good money after bad. This would be in the spirit of recent allegations about landlord investment behaviour during the decades of 'high farming' and earlier: it has been argued that much of their investment before the depression never paid and resulted in an over-capitalised agriculture (Chambers and Mingay 1966: 175–7).

If landowners are to be criticised for inefficiency, it must therefore be largely because they channelled funds into agriculture which would have yielded a higher return in other sectors of the economy at the time. Since this represented a subsidy to farmers, their action must also have reduced the flight of farmers from the land.

The labourers

Between 1860 and 1914, Britain's farm population dropped by about one quarter, and the number of labourers by one third. The fall was accompanied, as already explained, by an increase in earnings of over a half over these years; it also brought a marked decline in interregional wage variations.

Wage payments to labourers differed greatly between counties in mid-century, as the Scottish agricultural expert James Caird noted on his famous tour (1852: 510–19). Caird was surprised to find regular weekly wages for agricultural workers as low as seven shillings in Wiltshire and Gloucestershire, half what a labourer in Lancashire or the West Riding was paid. To some extent the gap may have been offset by the greater prevalence of task-work in the low wage areas during the summer months, but this is debatable; the semi-official returns collected in 1860 and 1870 suggest a strong positive correlation between regular wages and task-work rates. Caird's wage data imply a coefficient of variation by county of 0.20 for England: a recent study by Hunt implies a coefficient of 0.26 for Great Britain in 1867–70 (Hunt 1973: 64). Caird's explanation for this phenomenon was the low mobility of rural workers, a reason supported by Clapham, though in less prosaic language: 'the men of Surrey may be pictured moving easily over their suburban sands; those of Essex, stuck beyond East London in deep clays or hidden in the folds of their north-western chalk', and so on for Buckinghamshire and Oxfordshire (Clapham 1938: 89–90). Others who took a less idyllic view of social relations in the countryside argued that the ignorance of their labourers left farmers in an enviable monopsony position, which the latter exploited to the full (see e.g. Parliamentary Papers 1893–94: XXXVI, 17).

There is an alternative interpretation for this wage variation, which is that statistics such as Caird's merely reflect productivity differences from county to county. This was sometimes suggested by contemporary observers, in the spirit of 'a Lancashire workman at half-a-crown a day is not dearer than most Welsh labourers at a shilling'. It is difficult to prove, given the variety of work carried out by farm workers. Harvest earnings arguably provide a possible clue, since the scytheman's work was similarly carried out in different areas. Reports that it cost only 7s 6d to mow an acre of wheat in the North Riding in 1860, while it cost 12s in Surrey may seem strong support for the Caird–Clapham view that there were persistent imperfections in the labour market. In fact, the story is less simple since crop yields as a rule were higher in Surrey, and thus demanded more work (David 1970; Hunt 1970). If it is assumed that labour input was proportional to yield per acre – a generous assumption, since one might expect increasing returns to higher yields – then a perfect labour market would imply harvest piece rates varying in line with yields. Thus a crude test of the Caird–Clapham hypothesis might be: did the variability of piece rates exceed

Table 8.4. *The mean cost of reaping grain and mean yield per acre in 1850–51 and 1860–61*

County	Mean cost per acre of mowing grain:	Mean yield (bushels per acre)
(A) 1850–51		
1. Yorks., East Riding	7s 6d	27.36
2. Lincs.	9s 0d	32.85
3. Durham	6s 0d	23.78
4. Warwicks.	9s 6d	26.90
5. Berks.	8s 6d	27.41
6. Wilts.	9s 0d	28.53
7. Gloucs.	9s 6d	27.19
8. Cumberland	7s 6d	25.51
Coefficient of variation	0.138	0.089
(B) 1860–61		
1. Surrey	12s 0d	28.00
2. Kent	10s 0d	29.61
3. Berks.	11s 0d	28.53
4. Lincs.	8s 6d	32.85
5. Notts.	10s 0d	29.27
6. Yorks., North Riding	7s 6d	26.38
Coefficient of variation	0.152	0.068

Sources: The cost data are derived from David (1970: 510); D. H. Morgan (1975): 40); *Return of the Earnings of Agricultural Labourers*, Parliamentary Papers (1861: (L), Obs. 45, 74, 122, 431, 442, 526); Bravendar (1850: 141, 150); Dickinson (1852: 233); Spearing (1860: 43). The yield data are those reported as the 'estimated ordinary average' for wheat in *Agricultural Statistics for Great Britain*, 1894, Parliamentary Papers (1894 (XCIII): 150). The coefficient of variation is the standard deviation divided by the mean

that of grain yields? In the absence of comprehensive county data on the piece rates, the partial data in table 8.4 provide some limited guide. The figures are no doubt imprecise, and harvest earnings contributed only a small part of the annual pay of labourers: still, the hint of market imperfections here is suggestive. But the figures certainly do not confirm the productivity argument as the sole explanation for variations around mid-century.

In emphasising the productivity argument, Wilson Fox argued that the men of the north of England constituted 'a finer race, physically and intellectually, than the Southerner . . . because good feeding for generations has done much for them in body and in brain' (1903: 168–9). There is, indeed, persuasive evidence that labourers in low-wage areas in the south were earning less than the minimum amount needed to keep themselves and their families at full physical efficiency, even as late as the 1910s (Heath 1874: chs. 1 and 2; Rowntree and Kendall 1913). It does not follow, however, that it would have profited farmers to pay such workers more, a point sometimes urged by reformers. The farmers

Table 8.5. *The age structure of agricultural workers*

Year	Percentage of male agricultural workers aged over 45	Percentage of all males over ten years aged over 45
1871	31.7	25.6
1891	30.1	24.2
1911	30.7	28.9

Year	Median age of agricultural workers	Median age of all males over ten in population
1871	28.6	27.6
1891	27.8	27.3
1911	28.8	29.3

Source: *Census Reports* of Great Britain

were probably being maximisers in paying less than a 'living wage' (Pigou 1913), because the effort supplied by labour may have been inelastic with respect to the wage rate. The coefficient of variation of earnings for regions in Great Britain dropped to 0.076 in 1898 and 0.059 in 1907 (Hunt 1973: 64), implying that wages in the initially poorest areas increased more than the average. Still, Caird's distinction between a northern high-wage and a southern low-wage area had some relevance even on the eve of the First World War.

The release of labour into the industrial sector is one of agriculture's contributions to economic development. In nineteenth century Britain, though, the flight from the land gave rise to shrill complaints and polemics from interested parties. It was frequently suggested that agriculture after the depression was the refuge of aged and inferior workmen. The point is familiar in other contexts: those with initiative and drive leave, and the employers must manage with a lazier, older, and duller workforce. Contemporaries such as Rider Haggard saw this trend as one of the reasons for agricultural decline: in more polemical vein, he and others argued that it represented a long-term security risk, since agricultural labourers had traditionally been the best soldiers in the realm. But those labourers who remained on the land must not be blamed for the farmers' and landlords' problems simply on the basis of anecdotal evidence from their bosses. The Census data shown in table 8.5 lend no support, for example, to the view that the labourers were an ageing class over the period. Moreover, if the intellectual capacity of agricultural workers is a relevant input to agriculture – a point frequently suggested in the modern literature (Schultz 1964: 175–206) – then British workers of the 1910s were far better endowed with it than those of half a century earlier. The literacy rate of the agricultural labour force grew from about two thirds in mid-century to well over ninety-five per cent on the eve of the First World War.

Supply and demand factors both contributed to the reduction in the rural proletariat from 1.4 million in 1860 to less than a million in 1914. On the demand side the relative importance of mechanisation and the shift from tillage to pasture are difficult to gauge, because of poor data on machine diffusion and the labour requirements of machines of different vintages. Nevertheless, two labour-saving developments stand out. The reaping machine (volume 1, chapter 10, and pp. 182–6 above) in its reaper-and-binder version saved two to three worker days per acre over traditional methods, meaning several hundred thousand harvest workers at full diffusion. Most immediately affected were Irish and urban seasonal harvesters, but the machine also undoubtedly allowed the farmers to reallocate work and therefore reduce their regular workforce. The threshing machine, which came into its own after mid-century, may have involved even greater savings. While a man with a flail might manage six to nine bushels daily with difficulty, the contemporary threshing machine increased his output four- or fivefold (Collins 1972; Fenton 1976: 79–93). If one assumes that half the grain in Britain was still being threshed manually in 1860, then mechanisation of threshing would account for the loss of winter work for as many as two hundred thousand workers. Thus these two innovations alone could explain one half of the decline in the labour force. This finding emphasises the extraordinary labour intensity of traditional British agriculture and its handtool technology. By comparison the 'tumbling down' of arable land was less important: accepting the rule-of-thumb calculations of contemporaries, the conversion of three million acres between 1880 and 1914 could have meant one hundred thousand less jobs. However, there is no clear correlation in the county data between decline in acreage under grain and decline in the agricultural labour force; fruit growing and dairying, which came to the rescue in some of the arable areas, could be more labour-intensive than grain-growing.

Regional aspects

Agricultural practice and specialisation differed markedly between regions of Great Britain. While comfortable farmers in the Lothians and East Anglia discussed the virtues of steam ploughing, liquid manure, or the cost of labour, one might still find in the Highlands or Western Isles of Scotland 'the smaller and poorer crofters...[with] their families sitting around the fire...a whole winter picking the corn from the straw and chaff', or hacking away at stony soils with *caschroms* (MacDonald 1972: 18). Such practices, even if the objects of outsiders' derision, were a sensible answer – short of emigration – to a miserable land–labour ratio.

Farm output too was subject to marked regional variation. The southern and eastern counties, for example, were the main cereal-producing area throughout the period; the South-West had most orchards; Lancashire and Cheshire specialised most intensely in dairying. Since the price slump after the mid 1870s was confined largely, though by no mean entirely, to grain prices, it is not surprising that a minority of the Royal Commissioners of 1894–97 felt obliged to point out that 'the depression has been and still is far more serious in the southern and eastern counties of the United Kingdom'. One fair indication of spatial spread is the fall in assessments of land value. In ten counties – Berkshire, Cambridge, Essex, Huntingdon, Kent, Norfolk, Northampton, Oxford, Suffolk, Wiltshire – assessments declined by over thirty per cent between 1879/80 and 1894/95, while in Cheshire and in Cornwall the decline was less than ten per cent over the same period (Parliamentary Papers 1897: xv, 10).

When wheat prices fell, farmers in the south and the east reduced their acreage more slowly than elsewhere, and much of the reallocation that did take place was through 'tumbling down', i.e. disinvestment in the land, or through using it for other cereal crops. As a result the ten most depressed counties listed above accounted for thirty-one per cent of the wheat acreage in Great Britain in 1874, and forty per cent in 1913. But one should not conclude that the south-eastern farmer was simply more set in his farming ways than his northern or Scottish counterpart. We must take account of the fact that the stiff clay soils of the main corn counties were costly to switch to other uses, and that lower rainfall in the south-east, while good for grain also limited the growth of grass. Nor was the slower shift out of grain in the south and east due entirely to greater adjustment costs. Since the decline in wheat acreage was accompanied by an increase in the average yield per acre, and by a tendency, though slight, for the dispersion in yields to narrow, it would seem that those counties which reduced acreage most were marginal wheat producers. So even if adjustment costs had been zero it is likely that acreage decline would have been less in the south-east.

Price trends and improving communications also affected the pattern of regional specialisation in livestock. Before steam navigation, most British cattle were brought to market by drovers, but the steamship and railway meant that animals could be sent direct to consumption points, quickly and without loss of condition. The change allowed some areas, previously too isolated, to concentrate on beef fattening (Perren 1978: chapter 2). Fattening gave way to dairying in those areas where the latter was an economic proposition, as in the south of England, though less so in Scotland and Wales (Orwin and Whetham 1971: 137, 358). Pig numbers increased by about fifteen per cent between the late 1860s and the First World War, but the increase was by no means universal. The pig population grew most in dairying and potato- and fruit-growing counties, where feed was relatively cheap and increasing in supply, but decreased markedly in most of Scotland, Wales, and the English Midlands. The result was an increase in the coefficient of variation of pig numbers across counties from 0.98 in 1869/70 to 1.16 in 1909/10 – or from 0.57 to 0.71 for English counties alone. This is best interpreted as a move towards increasing specialisation by British farmers, as local markets merged into one national market.

Adjustment outside the south-east was less traumatic because soils were more adaptable. Indeed, it is likely that some mixed farming and dairying areas gained because of the decline in prices. This is because the relative fall in the cost of grain and other inputs decreased their feeding costs. Free trade and cheaper long-distance transport paradoxically improved their competitive position. Fletcher has argued that in Lancashire, milk producers could buy maize and oilcake for a third less at the end of the century than thirty years earlier, while prices of their output, milk, hardly dropped at all. The same can be said for poultry and pig farmers (Fletcher 1961b).

What of factor movements between regions? The migration of labourers has been examined in chapter 7, so only the migration of farmers is discussed here. The British land tenure system, at least in theory, encouraged an active land market and thereby mobility. A rent-maximising landlord would let to the group of tenants – presumably a shifting group – offering the highest prospective return on his property. In practice this did not generate much farmer mobility, however, particularly between regions. The post-1880 period marked the real beginning in Britain of a long-range migration of farmers within the agricultural sector. This migration was largely from the north and west to the south and east: contemporaries noted especially the influx into Essex and Suffolk from Scotland. The farmers moved largely because they were prepared to accept a lower return on their labour and capital than their southern and eastern counterparts. 'They and their families,' reported Assistant Commissioner Wilson Fox to the Royal Commission of 1894–97, 'work immensely hard. The Scotch women certainly undertake work which no Suffolk woman would dream of doing', while the men 'practically take the position of working foremen or bailiffs, being up in the morning when their men arrive and occupied with work connected with the farm after they leave at night' (Parliamentary Papers 1895: xvi, 67–8).

Free trade: agriculture and the consumer

In 1848, soon after the repeal of the Corn Laws, the free trade campaigner John Bright reminded fellow-members of the House of Commons that 'the industry of this great and growing population has escaped from the pressure of that screw, which, through the medium of the Corn Laws, you had laid upon the necessaries of life' (Bright 1869: 428). Yet the relative prosperity of the 'high farming' decades, and especially the buoyancy of corn prices, has led some to the conclusion that Corn Law repeal was of less economic than political import. Thus Kitson Clark has argued that 'the attack on the Corn Laws should not

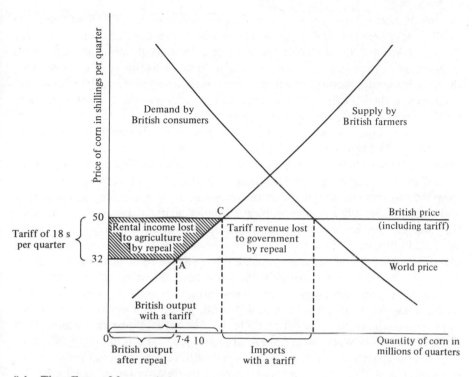

8.1   The effects of free trade in corn

be considered for a moment as a clear demonstration of economic truth, nor even as a passionate statement of economic opinion, but more as an outpouring of social opinion, using a symbol or a myth as a catalyst' (1951: 3). The argument may be true, but the usual evidence for it is inconclusive. It neglects the unprecedented increase in corn imports that took place during the 1850s and the 1860s, a rise which the uncertainties of the 'sliding scale' and the attendant risks for corn exporters before repeal would almost certainly have made impossible. Indeed, in the decade before repeal, imports of corn accounted for only a twelfth of total consumption, while by 1869/71 they were almost half. The assertion that the price of corn would have been the same, repeal or no repeal, is therefore false (Fairlie 1969). The benefit to consumers, it is true, became more visible after 1879, when corn prices began to fall markedly. By 1888/92 domestic production of wheat had fallen to two fifths of consumption requirements: on the eve of the First World War the proportion was slightly over one fifth.

The question is, what were the quantitative effects of free trade in corn? Supply and demand curves offer a method of estimating the static gains and losses to British consumers and producers. The calculation is more limited than that of chapter 3: there the question was the effect on the nation as a whole of free trade in all things; here it is the effect on farmers and corn consumers alone of free trade in corn, and in particular wheat. The corn market before repeal can be represented as the result of a tariff imposed on the world price of corn pushing the British price up, encouraging British farmers to supply more, and (incidentally) encouraging British consumers to demand less. This was the entire point of the tariff: to enrich agriculture at the expense of the rest of the nation.

In figure 8.1 the enrichment of agriculture is the shaded area, rental income lost (by repeal). Point A is the actual domestic output of wheat and its price after repeal. In 1888–92, for example, it was a quantity of 7.4 million quarters (of eight bushels each) selling for about 32 shillings a quarter. Point C cannot be observed from the historical data; it is the counterfactual output and price, i.e. the output and price that would have been observed had a tariff (of 18 shillings) brought the 1888–92 price back up to its pre-repeal level of about 50 shillings a quarter. We could estimate C if we knew the slope of the line from A to C. We do not know it, but we can make a reasonable guess (in the light of the results given above, p. 182) that it was roughly the slope corresponding to unit elasticity, i.e. that the supply curve was roughly a ray through A and the origin, O. In such a case domestic output would, under a tariff, go up in proportion to the rise in price, namely, in the proportion 50 to 32. The actual domestic output of 7.4 million quarters of wheat would therefore have been 7.4 multiplied by 50/32, or 11.6 million quarters. Now it is a simple exercise to find the area of the trapezoid: its height (18 shillings per quarter) multiplied by the average of its lengths (7.4 and 11.6 million quarters), or

$$(18 \text{ shillings per quarter}) \times (\frac{7.4 \times 11.6}{2} \text{ million quarters}) = 171 \text{ million shillings,}$$

or £8.55 millions. This figure is some 5 per cent or so of all agricultural income in 1888–92, or well below 1 per cent of national income. What producers gained, consumers lost, at least approximately – the other large element of the consumers' loss was the government's revenue from the tariff, but presumably a rise in government revenue on this account would have been offset by lower taxes imposed on consumers at some other juncture. In accord with the findings in chapter 3, the transfer to agricultural producers through the tariff seems small. The view that free trade in corn was a symbol rather than a revolution in the economic life of the nation has much to recommend it.

The transfer from consumers to producers was not the only issue in commercial policy, especially in the early years of the twentieth century. The United Kingdom became increasingly dependent on food imports after repeal. While repeal itself and population growth was largely responsible for this, the role of technical developments in transport and storage should not be forgotten. Half the price reduction in American wheat was due to lower freight charges, while new cold storage and refrigeration techniques allowed the importation of frozen meat and

New Zealand butter from the early 1880s on. By 1910–14 consumers relied on imports for the greater part of their bread, butter, cheese, and fruit, as well as for forty per cent of their meat and a third of their eggs. Not surprisingly, agricultural protectionists increasingly returned to home truths in the style of Adam Smith about defence being of more importance than opulence. They warned against the dangers of 'a hostile combination of European nations' starving Great Britain into submission, arguing in effect that the gains from free trade were rapidly diminishing as the probability of open conflict increased. The cost of such an insurance policy of self-sufficiency in grain, however, would have been substantial. And the silliness of such a policy – plain to all except some farm lobbyists – was underlined by a member of parliament who pointed out that self-sufficiency for insurance amounted to assuming that Britain 'was going to be at war with all the nations of the world for ever' (Hansard 1902 (CI): 1160). Government policy was to rely instead on a strong navy to meet any potential blockade, and on the substitution possibilities within the economy itself to increase domestic food-supplies in the short run, if necessary. In the event, this policy was vindicated when war did come in 1914 (Olson 1963).

Conclusion

By 1914, Great Britain relied on imports for more than half its food. Its agricultural labour force, which peaked in 1861 or thereabouts, declined almost continuously after then, as did agriculture's share in GNP. No other country experienced such a transformation during the nineteenth century (chapter 1). The change was naturally not without trauma: for farmers who relied on cereals for most of their income, these were trying decades. For them there was a 'Great Depression' in terms of farm incomes, though for others the picture was much less bleak. Moreover, British agriculture performed badly in the face of foreign competition, judged at least by its very slow total factor productivity growth. We have suggested that slow responses within agriculture itself were less to blame for 'decline', than the gradualness with which the farm population reconciled itself to a reduction in numbers. Between 1860 and 1914 the number of farmers dropped by ten per cent, but all this drop occurred before 1881. Evidently for every farmer who died or moved out of agriculture, there was a son – or a Scotsman – to replace him. Contemporaries argued that many farmers 'were dipped too deep to move', while others remained on in the hope of getting 'a reasonable amount of their capital back' (Bellerby 1956: 65). A more important reason surely is that the psychic income element in British farming was large, and stemmed the outward flow before the First World War. A more substantial fall in the farm population would undoubtedly have meant lower domestic agricultural output, and probably some of the most marginal land going out of cultivation. On the other hand, it would have meant a more efficient use of resources, and therefore a higher productivity growth over the period.

9

Social history 1860-1914

P. THANE

The relationship of economic to social and political change is highly complex. Historians, including those influenced by that perceptive writer Karl Marx, do not conventionally assume that individual thought and action is exclusively influenced by contemporaneous, strictly economic, features of the environment. Economic changes – such as the emergence and decline of occupations – profoundly change individuals' ways of living, acting and thinking; but, plainly, not all individuals respond similarly to similar economic experiences. Agricultural labourers, whose occupational prospects were threatened from the 1870s (chapter 8) initially responded variously: some left the land, some stayed, some protested, some did not. Nor were the responses of landowners uniform. Responses to economic change are various because, important though it is, it does not, at least in the short run, wipe away the inheritance of culture and tradition, of accepted ways of doing things, which may change more slowly. Nor does it eliminate, though it may restrict, the scope of individual choice. An inheritance remains to influence human responses and hence to influence the specific effects of economic change in specific instances.

Bearing this in mind, this chapter will outline the social structure of the society in which the economic changes described in the preceding chapters occurred. It will examine the contributions and responses to change of the major social groups and institutions.

Britain in 1860, although near the height of the mid-Victorian boom, was still a society in which a significant proportion of the population was largely unaffected by industry, still living lives patterned on pre-industrial customs and rhythms of work. There were still significant regional and local differences in social and economic relationships, institutions and traditions. This was so not only within England but among, and within, England, Wales and Scotland. Despite increased geographical mobility, a high proportion of the population lived out most of their lives in one locality, though they might experience a period of mobility to new places between their late teens and mid twenties. Some, but by no means all, of these local differences had diminished by 1914. Between 1860 and 1914 something closer to a single national culture emerged, governed by a state whose actions were more widely pervasive. Much of this change resulted from improved communications (the expansion of transport, the press, the postal system), the further spread of industry and urban service occupations and of towns themselves. These influences drew more individuals away from pre-industrial ways of life.

The steady immigration of the Irish throughout the period and of thousands of Jews from Central Europe from the early 1880s (Lipman 1954) had little effect upon the native population. The incomers were relatively few in number and lived in fairly clearly defined districts mainly in the larger cities.

Urbanisation

In 1851, for the first time, fractionally more than half the population of England and Wales lived in urban districts with populations of 10 000 or more; by 1911 80.1 per cent did so. In 1861 many of these 'urban-dwellers' lived in manufacturing and mining communities still small enough to allow ready access to the countryside (Lampard 1973). However, the population was increasingly concentrated in big cities: 13.91 per cent of the population of England and Wales lived in London in 1861, and 11 per cent in other towns such as Birmingham and Manchester with populations of more than 100 000. By 1891, 14.5 per cent lived in London, 17.3 per cent in other towns of over 100 000. Rapid growth of towns of 20 000–100 000 population brought their percentage of the population to 21.7 per cent. This trend continued to 1914, by which time, for example, one in every five Scots lived in Glasgow.

Between 1861 and 1881, industrial expansion continued to create new concentrations of population, though fewer than before. The only major new developments of this kind were Middlesbrough (mining and engineering) and the Rhondda Valley in South Wales (mining). The other important new towns to emerge were seaside resorts. These reflected the ability and willingness of more individuals to pay for leisure activities, a growing habit of middle-class retirement to the seaside, and, possibly, the longer holidays and weekends of skilled workers, although working-class holiday resorts grew fastest in the 1920s and 1930s. The resorts account for some of the growth of occupations in the service sector. (Ashworth 1954; chapter 7).

The period saw the first serious attempt to plan new centres of industry and working-class residential districts. The ill-effects, especially upon health, of the unplanned near-chaos of earlier Victorian developments were increasingly recognised. Throughout the century spacious suburbs had been laid out for middle-class habitation, often, as at Edgbaston in Birmingham (Cannadine 1977: 462–82), under the determined eye of large landowners, anxious for their land to keep its value. Previous experiments in the planning of new industrial communities had had minimal influence (volume 1, chapter 14). An initial, partial, attempt to plan the growth of Middlesbrough was rapidly overwhelmed by the pace of its growth and it came to resemble the sprawl of much of Manchester or Glasgow.

This failure was followed, however, by successful small-scale planned developments for industrial workers, such as George Cadbury's venture at Bournville, near Birmingham (begun 1895) and W. H. Lever's Port Sunlight (from 1888). Both were built at low density, with gardens, parks and trees. Pressure for other new developments to take this form was inspired by the publication of Ebenezer Howard's *Garden Cities of Tomorrow* (1902). The influential Garden City Association (founded 1899) pressed not simply for improved extensions of existing towns, but for the termination of urban growth. It advocated Howard's ideal that all further industrial expansion should take place in new planned cities, each with populations no greater than c. 32,000.

These efforts coincided with the slowing of the pace of industrial expansion and the only result before 1914 was the foundation of Letchworth Garden City in 1903. However, a more important feature of urban change at this time was the 'suburbanisation' of growing towns. From the 1880s most of the centres of rapid population growth were suburbs, especially those of the biggest city in the world, London (Ashworth 1954: 10–12).

From c. 1870 development of the tram in most large towns and of suburban railways in London enabled the lower-middle class and artisans to emulate the established habit of most of the wealthier middle class of living at a distance from city centre work places, in what they hoped, generally rightly, would be more attractive environments. This process increased the social as well as the geographical distance between those who could afford to move and the poorer workers left behind in city centres (Crossick 1976a: Stedman Jones 1971: 160–78). It may also have created a new source of social tension. Established middle-class suburban dwellers resented intrusion upon their residential enclaves and fought vigorously, though largely unsuccessfully, to prevent the spread to, for example, Hampstead in London or Victoria Park in Manchester of new forms of transport with their cargoes of clerks. Often, when they failed, they fled to still farther flung suburbs (Cannadine 1977c: 466; Thompson 1974: 351–65). By the end of the nineteenth century, suburbs tended, still, to be socially selective, but suburban living was less the preserve of the reasonably wealthy than was the case in 1860.

The idea of a planned 'garden' environment was attractive to many of the middle and lower middle class. Ebenezer Howard's inspiration is most clearly seen in hundreds of English suburbs built since 1900 (Gaskell 1977) as it is in many housing estates built since the 1920s and in the post-1945 New Towns. The government's first significant response to the town planning movement was the Town Planning Act, 1909. This enabled local authorities to insist upon planning of the form and density of new developments (Ashworth 1954). It was the precursor of the more stringent planning regulations developed later in the twentieth century.

The continuing growth of towns created substantial, if often gradual, changes from long-established ways of life, but it did not create a series of communities uniform in social structure, relationships and conditions. These varied with the nature of the local economy. The highly localised nature of much industrial development contributed to these variations. Where most of the population was engaged in the production of cotton textiles, as in much of Lancashire, in coal-mining as in the Rhondda or in ship-building as in parts of the North-East, the local community was more cohesive than in districts, such as East London, where the economy was more heterogeneous. Single-industry communities were dominated by the fortunes of the local industry, by its work rhythms and needs and, often, by the influence of dominant local employers (Joyce 1975). Hence, for example, women could both contribute to the family economy and achieve greater independence in textile Lancashire where there was demand for their labour in factories, but unmarried girls left mining communities in droves, for lack of jobs for them. Voting patterns in Lancashire textile towns in the 1860s were profoundly influenced by the political preferences of powerful employers (Joyce 1975). However, even communities with similar economic structures were not necessarily culturally or politically uniform, though they may have shown some convergence over this period. Joyce contrasts temperate, self-improving, Liberal-voting textile Ashton-under-Lyne in the 1860s, with nearby and considerably more raucous, Tory-voting textile Blackburn. The towns were similar in economic and social structure but were dominated by locally resident employers of rather differing tastes and political inclinations, who influenced these communities as effectively as any rural squire controlled his villagers.

More generally, urban communities differed according to whether or not, for example, they possessed a resident business and professional elite (as, in London, Lewisham did and Poplar did not), a stably-employed factory proletariat (as in much of textile Lancashire), a higher than average concentration of casual labour (such as Liverpool or Bermondsey), or a large proportion of artisans engaged in workshop production (as in Brimingham).

It was a little easier to prevent the creation of problems in newly-expanding urban districts than to cure them in established city centres. Central urban living conditions varied. Most towns throughout the period possessed notorious slum districts of varying size, suffering overcrowding and poorer sanitation than the contemporaneous fall in urban mortality might suggest (chapter 7). Following the example of Birmingham in the 1870s some city councils set out to clear the worst slums and to plan city centre rebuilding. Some provided parks and open spaces, large office blocks and shops. All too often, however, the replanning of city and town centres led to the transfer of overcrowding to adjacent districts. Cleared housing was rarely replaced before the 1890 Housing Act and minimally thereafter (Gauldie 1974: 295–310). Rail and road building contributed to this process. At least 76 000 homes were lost as a result of clearances for urban railway building between 1851 and 1901 (Kellett 1969), most between 1860 and 1880, when railway companies were not obliged to replace cleared housing (Stedman Jones 1971).

Neither local authority nor philanthropic effort succeeded in solving the problems of providing adequate housing for families living in single rooms or parts of rooms, at a rent which the irregularly employed and low paid could afford. The 1890 Housing Act enabled local authorities to use rate income to build houses for rent. A few, notably the London County Council (formed 1888) did so. 5 per cent of London housing was publicly owned by 1914; no other town achieved so much (Wohl 1977: 255–60). The shortage of adequate working-class housing was only substantially reduced by the introduction of government subsidies for local authority housing in 1919.

The fall in capital investment in housebuilding during the 1890s may have slowed the provisions of new housing. It is difficult, however, to see how an entirely private sector housing market could substantially have minimised this problem, in view of the low returns available from housing the poor. Even the '5 per cent philanthropy' companies which attempted, from the 1860s, to provide such housing at an unusually (and hence 'philanthropically') low rate of return, found that only the better and more regularly paid worker could afford the very basic form of tenement accommodation provided (Wohl 1977: 141–78; Tarn 1973.)

The continuing rate of overcrowding and poor sanitation, serious in 1914 and worsened by the wartime building ban, lay behind the post-1916 cry for 'homes fit for heroes' (Gauldie 1974: 307–10). Bad housing and bad health were not the only reasons for rebuilding and planning the centres of established cities. Proud local businessmen erected monuments to their own success, and to eradicate some signs of the social cost of that success. Furthermore, the growth of commerce increased the strain on city streets. Traffic in one street in the City of London was jammed for six hours of the twelve from 8 a.m. to 8 p.m., during at least the one day in 1905 of the Royal Commission on Transport survey (Ashworth 1954: 114). Pollution was uncontrolled. Dirt and dense fog remained central features of popular images of London and the other great cities.

Social stratification

The 're-ordering' of British society, begun before 1860 (volume 1, chapter 14) was completed in this period, although attitudes towards the new order underwent subtle changes between 1860 and 1914. There are two main schools of analysis of social stratification, both appropriate to this period. The first defines each stratum chiefly by its social functions, conventionally giving pre-eminence to function within the productive system, distinguishing primarily among landowners, owners of industrial and commercial capital, small proprietors and the employed. It is assumed that power and status in society derive from position within the productive system. Each of these groups is said to form a 'class'. Classes are not assumed to be totally homogeneous in work experience, political or other ideas, but each is defined by its relationship to other classes. It is assumed that members of each class have more experiences in common with each other than with members of other classes. The extent to which members of a class are conscious of these differences, and of the conflicts that may result, is defined as 'class consciousness', which many may never experience.

The second approach analyses society as a hierarchy of strata determined by 'status'. Status, in turn, is determined by whatever is the criterion of superiority in the society, e.g. descent, power, wealth.

Class

Class was an important reality in this period. Many individuals explicitly defined themselves and others as members of 'classes', rather than of 'ranks' or 'orders', the conventional terminology of the early years of the century (volume 1, chapter 14). Awareness of class and of the activities proper to each class was profound; Henry James observed in the 1870s that 'the essentially hierarchical plan of English society is the great and ever present fact to the mind of a stranger: there is hardly a detail of life that does not in some degree betray it' (Best 1971: 238). Different educational curricula were provided for different classes over differing lengths of time, with the object of training children for their class-specific hereditary roles. The lower the status of a worker's occupation the earlier in life he or she attained maximum life-time earnings. The lawyer received longer training and a longer delay before achieving maximum rewards than the skilled engineer, who, in turn, reached manhood earnings later, after apprenticeship, than the unskilled labourer who might compete on equal terms with adult men by the age of 13 or 14. Style and size of house, even of dress, and individual height and weight varied with class and stratum.

In the 1860s and early 1870s class differences were not widely criticised, in the manner which has become conventional in the twentieth century. Walter Bagehot's influential *The English Constitution* (first edition 1867, second edition 1868) expressed, though sometimes a little too complacently, the widespread acceptance of social inequality in his time. After the challenges of the 1830s and 40s to the emerging shape of the new society, in the 1860s to the mid 1870s the new hierarchy seemed to be peacefully established. This acquiescence even among the less privileged cannot usefully be ascribed, as it frequently is, to 'deference', i.e. the belief that others are socially superior due to their superior skills; it is rather acceptance of the apparently unchangeable that better describes contemporary feelings (Best 1971: 236–7). Yet the extent even of such acceptance, though widespread, should not be exaggerated. Even in the 1860s prominent politicians, such as Palmerston, felt the need to reassure the lower classes that such qualities as hard work would enable them to rise in the social scale, that inequalities were not unchangeable (Best 1971: 233–8). Samuel Smiles' *Self Help*, published in 1859 gave wide currency to a similar message. This hope of social advancement as a result of personal effort was expressed peacefully. It was only from the end of the 1870s that a more aggressive note enters class relationships, stressing the wrongness and unfairness of social inequality. Its clearest expression was in the labour movement, although new tensions were evident, for example, between tenant farmers and landowners. However, before examining attitudes to class, we must attempt to describe class structure quantitatively.

This is difficult due to the variety of dimensions for the definition and measurement of class. Some, such as occupation and income can be quantified to some degree, but these, even taken together, cannot take full account of the subtleties of class. Life styles and subjective attitudes play a significant part in its definition. They are quantifiable only to the extent that, for example, size, style and location of house may reflect class position and may, with difficulty, be measurable. Satisfactory quantification of class structure in the past will require complex multi-factor calculations of a kind which have not yet been achieved. Arguably, however, occupation and income were the major determinants of class and, for the present, these provide the most satisfactory measurements available.

The main sources for information about occupations are the printed decennial census returns between 1851 and 1901. These classified the occupied population only into broad occupational groups, e.g. 'persons engaged in numerous branches of manufacture'. They did not usually distinguish among different strata within these groups. Hence it is difficult, and often impossible where the nature of the occupation stated in the census is unknown or ambiguous, to distinguish skilled from unskilled worker, large from small farmer, or employer from employee, especially in small businesses such as baking or tailoring, where the distinction between employer and artisan was often fluid or indistinct (Armstrong 1972).

It is therefore difficult to obtain from the early printed censuses a clear picture of class structure. The best available estimates (bearing these difficulties in mind) for the beginning of the period are those produced in 1867 by the statistician Dudley Baxter. He attempted to divide the population of Great Britain into classes based on income (derived from tax returns and information about wage rates supplied by employers) and occupations (from the 1861 census) (see table 9.1).

Baxter included in his 'upper and middle classes' (chiefly in 'Class III') all clerks and shop assistants, two thirds of total land occupiers, all foremen and supervisory workers and one third of the police, which suggests something about contemporary perceptions of where the boundary lay between 'middle' and

Table 9.1. *Incomes of Great Britain 1867*

	No. of assessments	% occupied population
Upper and middle classes		
Class I: large incomes		
(1) £5000 & upwards	8100	0.07
(2) £1000–5000	46100	0.4
Class II: middle incomes		
£300–£1000	163900	1.4
Class III: small incomes		
(1) £100–300	947900	8.6
(2) Below income tax – under £100	1159000	10.5
Total	2200000	20.07
Manual labour class: men's average wages:		
Class IV: Higher skilled labour		
and manufacturers: £50–73	1260000	11.4
Class V: Lower skilled labour and		
manufacturers: £35–52	4377000	39.9
Class VI: agriculture and unskilled		
labour: £10 10s to £36	3270000	29.8
Total	8907000	81.2
Grand total	10960000	

Total population of Great Britain 1867 (est.): 24152000
Source: R. D. Baxter, *National Income* (1868: 64)

'working' class. His figures refer only to those returned in the census as employed. They exclude children, the retired and all others not gainfully employed. They do not distinguish among landowners, members of the professions, large and small employers and those living on unearned income from investment. They exclude the great majority of women, who did not work and had little or no independent income. Conventionally, women are assigned to the social class of husband or father, which, for this period, generally conformed with reality.

In order to classify the entire population Baxter estimated that in the upper and middle classes there were three dependants for every two independent incomes; for the 'manual labour class' rather more than one dependant for every one independent earner. He calculated, therefore, a total of 5562000 members of the upper and middle classes, 18590000 of the manual labour class. His figures, however, give a useful indication of the proportion of the population in each stratum.

For the end of the period, a more detailed classification (of the employed population only) by Routh can be given for Great Britain, derived from the 1911 census (table 9.2).

Table 9.2. *Occupations in Great Britain in 1911*

Occupational class	Nos. (thousands)	% occupied population
Higher professional	184	1.03
Lower professional	560	3.00
Employers	763	4.16
Self-employed	469	2.55
Managers and administrators	629	3.43
Clerical workers	887	4.83
Foremen, inspectors and supervisors	236	1.28
	3728	20.34
Skilled manual workers	5608	30.59
Semi-skilled manual workers	7224	39.41
Unskilled manual workers	1767	9.64
	14599	79.65
Total	18327	

Population of Great Britain in 1911: 42861000
Source: Guy Routh, *Occupation and pay in Great Britain 1906–60* (1965: 105)

Routh's boundary between middle and working class is similar to Baxter's. His figures suggest no major changes in the proportions of the population in each of the broad classes over the period. Important changes, suggested by his figures, such as the growth of the lower-middle class, including clerical workers, are discussed below. Those living on unearned income or income from land are excluded from this classification.

The census returns supplement this information with such data as the number and type of domestic servants per household. Since we can assume that households supported as many servants as they could afford, this is a useful indicator of wealth and status. Hence in London in 1901 Hampstead had 81.4 domestic servants per 100 families; Bethnal Green only 5.8. But middle-class Hampstead had fewer male servants (butlers and footmen being the mark of aristocratic style) than upper-class Westminster, Chelsea or Kensington (Thompson 1974: 50–1). Information of this kind gives us a broad picture of class structure.

Status

Awareness of status: 'the subtle distinctions which stem from the values that men set on each other's activities' (Lockwood 1958: 208), the existence of social distinctions more minute than those of class, was a powerful reality at all social levels, but an elusive one. 'The wife of a lighterman felt that she was with her equals when she went out shopping with the wife of a stevedore or the wife of a ship-wright, but never with the wife of a docker or unskilled worker' (Gosling 1927, quoted by Crossick 1976a: 203). This comment on London dockland society before the First World War recaptures contemporary sensitivity to status.

Similarly Hobsbawm (1964a: 210–11) points out that the stevedore, though amongst the most skilled of dock workers, was not readily accepted as an equal by skilled workers in other industries. Unlike a boilermaker or carpenter he did not possess a standard set of qualifications and experiences; he developed his skills on one wharf, whose specific problems and customs were not necessarily easily transferable to another.

Status, then, at least among the working class, could derive from job experience. To some degree this was also the case among other classes – wealth from trade could be regarded as inferior to wealth from land, though closely related conceptions of birth and family connections were highly influential in élite circles.

Emerging new social groups had to carve their own place in the status hierarchy. Among the professions, the growing group of civil engineers considered themselves superior to mechanical engineers. They had however to struggle to be accorded high status. Only the very wealthy, such as Cubitt, the builder of Bloomsbury and Pimlico, and Brassey the railway magnate, penetrated high society. Barristers had higher status than solicitors, doctors than dentists. Even in professional circles high status was not always transferable. R. W. Dale, for example, was an influential non-conformist minister in Birmingham in the 1870s, but meant nothing in the county circles of nearby Warwickshire (Best 1971: 249–50; Hennock 1973: 154–169).

Conceptions of with whom it was proper to associate, and of the proper functions and occupations of specific groups, could influence willingness to adapt to change, e.g. of some landed gentlemen to become directly involved in business, or of skilled working people to associate in social or political activity with the unskilled.

Those who regarded each other as of similar status tended to associate together, increasingly in this period to live in the same part of town, to join the same voluntary associations (churches, sports clubs, friendly societies, gentlemen's clubs). The most sensitive indicator of such social closeness is intermarriage. Marriage registers (which record occupations of spouses) club and church records have been used all too rarely for information about social relationships. They have helped so far to establish the status differences between 'aristocratic' skilled labour and other manual workers in south-east London between the 1850s and 1870s (Crossick 1976a: 206, 210–15) and increasing contact between the two groups in Edinburgh, as the security of certain skilled workers was ended from the 1880s (Gray 1976). Hence perceptions of status might change due to changes in the economic and power positions of specific groups.

Status was also influenced by the elusive but profoundly important notion of 'respectability'. This implied adherence to conceptions of suitable behaviour held widely in all classes. The respect accorded to mannerly conduct, restraint in dress and moderation in all things contributed significantly to the vertical cohesion of society. The landowner, or professional man (either of whom might or might not, according to the prevailing criteria of respectability, be described as a 'gentleman') or artisan who did not so conform, could suffer a corresponding decline in status (Best 1971: 238–62).

Social mobility

It has already been suggested that, even in the 1860s, general acceptance of social inequality was reinforced by the promise of upward mobility as an accessible reward for hard work and respectable behaviour. In 1865 Lord Palmerston informed spectators at the prize-giving of the South London Industrial Exhibition:

It is true that aristocracies of wealth and rank exist in other countries, but, unfortunately, there are almost impassable barriers separating them from the rest of the nation, while no such barriers exist in this country...you must all have seen in your own experience, men starting from the smallest beginnings who have in this very city realised princely fortunes. In the manufacturing districts, examples of this kind are abundant, for no man can go, even for a few days, into those districts without hearing of great wealth, acquired by men who started with little, but by their talents and genius, raised themselves, and their families to opulence. Then again, does the aristocracy of rank in this country consist simply of those who can count in their pedigree generations of noble ancestors? Look at all the great men who have figured in public life...you are all conversant with names renowned in the history of the country who belonged not to noble families, but who founded noble families; springing many of them from the very class which I now have the honour of addressing...Wealth is, to a certain extent, within the reach of all...You may not all become generals or admirals; you may not all become members of the Cabinet; but depend upon it, you will, by systematic industry, raise yourselves in the social system of the country – you will acquire honour and respect for yourselves and your families. You will have, too, the constant satisfaction of feeling that you have materially contributed to the dignity of your country, to its welfare, to its prosperity and greatness, and that you have been worthy of the nation to which you belong [Best 1971: 234–6].

This well-intentioned, if sometimes ambiguous, speech expressed many of the characteristic beliefs and aspirations of the mid-Victorian period. It suggested that upward social mobility was open to those of talent to an extent which subsequent research has shown not entirely to be the case.

Social mobility is an elusive feature of social structure. Its assessment presupposes an understanding of the contemporary hierarchy of prestige and status, which is essential for discerning whether movement was felt by contemporaries to be upwards, downwards or horizontal (Thernstrom 1964; Blumin 1973). It requires examination of individual careers, which are not recorded in the printed censuses. Individual details survive in the manuscript census enumerators' books (available for study up to 1871, at present, for England and Wales) but it is difficult to trace more than a possibly unrepresentative handful over the decennial periods; many individuals would have moved house or district. (But see Thernstrom 1964).

Marriage registers, again, record occupations of parents as well as spouses. Since critical career decisions (e.g. for the son of an artisan to become a clerk) were likely to be made before marriage, these can provide an indicator of inter-generational mobility.

Use of this data suggests that in south-east London between 1851 and 1875 there was a strong tendency for the sons of unskilled labourers to remain labourers; for similar continuity in certain long-established crafts with an especial pride in handing on skills from father to son (such as shipbuilding craftsmen, watermen and lightermen); but more generally for a son's life opportunities to be enhanced directly with the status of the father. Upward mobility from unskilled labouring status was possible but rare (Crossick 1976a: 191–200). The results of a survey of five British towns in 1913 by Bowley & Burnett Hurst confirm these conclusions. Upward or downward social mobility for a woman was overwhelmingly possible only as a result of marriage or the changing fortunes of her father.

For higher social classes, the use of probate records suggests that most millionaires and half-millionaires alive during this period began life substantially wealthy, though as many as 28 per cent of millionaires dying between 1858 and 1869 (i.e. living most of their active lives before our period) can be described as 'self-made'. The proportion thereafter declined, being 12 per cent for those dying between 1910 and 1929. Recruitment to 'half-millionaire' status shows a similar pattern. Mobility into both of these groups is comparable to that in the mythically more mobile USA (Rubinstein 1974).

Few leaders of large, highly capitalised businesses, such as steel making, came from other than the families of employers, owners or managers in the same or related businesses, or from banking, merchant or professional families with close links with the business. From 1865 to 1925 the sons of manual workers supplied only a steady 3–4 per cent of steel employers and managers (Erickson 1959).

Even in smaller and less successful businesses, such as Nottingham hosiery firms, there was similar continuity, although with a larger recruitment of sons of skilled workers (16 per cent in 1877, 6 per cent in 1905) mainly from within the hosiery trade (Erickson 1959).

Within industries requiring little initial capital, especially those with more archaic forms of organisation, such as Lancashire cotton spinning, there was greater scope for upward mobility within the trade, from manual worker to manager or owner, than in modern industries requiring large capital investment.

The rate of mobility appears to have been high in Lancashire cotton spinning, even as late as 1912 (Chapman & Marquis 1912; Waites 1976). More businessmen entered the peerage after 1886, but few were of humble origins and few were not members of landed families or themselves landowners (F. M. L. Thompson 1963: 293–4).

In general, however, a substantial amount of literary evidence suggests that, in a period when upward mobility was achieved more characteristically through work than through formal education, opportunities for movement from clerical to higher management status diminished with the increasing size of firms and the increased scale of clerical recruitment (Crossick 1976b); so did opportunities for movement from skilled worker to small employer in some industries (Waites 1976). The great expansion of the 'white-collar' lower middle class after 1870 (see below) must have been largely due to recruitment of children of working class parents, since there was no other obvious source from which they could have come.

This new lower middle class, however, suffered a real threat of downward mobility to unskilled worker status. In depression periods, such as the mid 1890s, they ran a high risk of unemployment, and their often limited skills narrowed their alternative employment opportunities (Crossick 1976b). In general, however, we have notably little information about downward mobility. The probable general decline from the 1870s in opportunities for upward mobility, which had never been so great as Palmerston implied, coincided with growing resentment about class differences and contributed to some degree to the acute tensions of the Edwardian period (see below).

Age structure

British society was also, in this period, increasingly stratified by age. Changing perceptions of the roles of and activities suitable to different age groups were closely related to economic changes. With the decline, though not yet the eradication, of child labour and the spread of compulsory education, childhood became more clearly demarcated from adolescence and the latter from adulthood. Children of all classes were increasingly expected, as those of the wealthier classes had long been, to follow distinctive daily routines and leisure activities; among other changes, the number of books and periodicals written especially for children increased in this period, as did publications for all age groups.

Children were given increased protection by society. They were progressively excluded from a growing range of occupations, although such prohibitions were not always fully enforced. The spread of compulsory education may have added to the length and rigours of the active day for some poorer children. They might work in shops, street-markets and workshops, or run errands before and/or after school, although such work was prohibited for children under fourteen in 1903.

The 'half-time' system for factory children survived until 1918; in 1906, children of thirteen worked in the jute mills of Dundee from 6 a.m. to 6 p.m., and attendance at school from 7.15 p.m. to 9.15 p.m. on four evenings a week was rigidly enforced (Phelps Brown 1959: 58–9).

Cruelty to children became a crime for the first time in 1889; the Children's Act, 1908, placed delinquent children under the jurisdiction of separate, non-criminal juvenile courts, and permitted the removal of children from the care of cruel or negligent parents (Pinchbeck & Hewitt 1973; Gillis 1975).

From about 1890, increasing numbers of organisations emerged to fill the leisure time of adolescent boys and girls. The Boy Scouts, Boys' Brigade, Girls Friendly Societies and youth clubs were founded to give not merely entertainment but military and moral discipline to an age group who were beginning to be seen as potential threats to social order. (Gillis 1975; Springhall 1972).

Working-class adolescents came to be seen as a distinctive problem group in this period partly because unskilled boy and girl labour grew more rapidly than skilled employment. Apprenticeships became harder to obtain. Adolescents had greater purchasing power and independence at an earlier age than before. This created fears among other classes and among their own parents about the license that might result, and about the longer-term effects of the emergence of a larger unskilled sector of the labour force, unruly due to its lack of prospects for advancement.

As a result parents who could afford both to pay school fees and to forgo their children's earnings, encouraged boys to remain in secondary education in greater numbers to acquire further skills. More generally, unruliness among this age group was made the subject of court proceedings more frequently than before; the problem of 'juvenile delinquency' was born. Fear of the adolescent was apparently declining by 1914, but the community and, reciprocally, working-class adolescents themselves, had come to define those between the ages of fourteen and twenty as a group with different characteristics from adults. Richer students of this age group had long been perceived in this way, although, since they were regarded as potentially responsible members of society, they continued to be allowed a degree of licensed unruliness denied to young labourers (Gillis 1975).

At the other end of the age scale old age began to be defined by the introduction of fixed retirement ages, firstly for civil servants and other government employees, normally at 60 or 65. When state pensions were introduced in 1908 the onset of old age was officially defined for manual workers at seventy. Increasingly in this period the aged were discussed as a group with specific needs, above all for care and for cash incomes, when past regular work. These needs were partially provided for by some liberalisation of the poor law in the 1890s (Crowther 1978) and by the introduction of old age pensions in 1908. This concern was due partly to a slight increase in the proportion of aged in the population, but more to the growing belief on the part of workers and employers that the increasing pace of modern industry was making workers unfit for regular work at earlier ages, and that pressure for increased efficiency made older workers unattractive to employers. The movement of younger workers from the countryside left more of the aged without family support, although in general there is little evidence that economic change, including migration, increased the extent of isolation of old people. As for centuries before, the unsupported old were predominantly those who had never had children or whose children were dead or too poor to support them (Thane 1978b).

The social structure of Wales and Scotland

Wales and Scotland differed sufficiently from England in important respects to merit special mention. Wales, despite almost three and a half centuries of official assimilation to England, was almost wholly in 1860 and to a large extent still in 1914, different from England in essential features of social structure. In 1860, the principality was largely composed of peasant tenant landholders engaged in mixed agriculture mainly for subsistence. They were predominantly Welsh speaking and also, to a very much greater extent than the English, attached to the more democratic forms of nonconformist religion. The latter contributed to a more extensive and less socially stratified enthusiasm for and provision of education among the Welsh and to a preference for radical politics which was demonstrated in the nineteenth century in support for radical Liberalism, in the twentieth century for the Labour party.

The owners of land in Wales were Anglicised, and often English, but poorer, with smaller landholdings, than their English peers. The Welsh economy, however, was transformed after 1860 by the growth of mineral mining, especially for coal, and of the iron and shipbuilding industries. Wales had taken little part in the first stage of British industrialisation. The new developments were concentrated in South Wales, especially in the counties of Glamorgan and Monmouthshire. One result was the near doubling of the Welsh population between 1861 and 1911, largely due to the migration of English, and to a lesser extent Irish, miners. Again, this increase was concentrated in the two industrialising counties, which came increasingly to resemble the great industrial communities of the English north, without, however, entirely losing the Welsh tastes for education and radical politics. The Welsh continued characteristically to produce eminent preachers, journalists, teachers and, in the twentieth century, leaders of the British labour movement.

Non-industrial Wales remained, as before, a society of peasant hill farmers, although it suffered a persistent loss of population. Nevertheless, indeed partly as a result of the industrialisation of South Wales and of increasing contact of the remainder with a previously remote English government, rural Wales became increasingly conscious of, and defensive about, its Welshness. From the late nineteenth century there was a conscious reassertion of Welsh cultural traditions with the revival of such activities as the eisteddfodau and the invention of others, such as druidic ritual (Morgan 1977; Hobsbawm 1968: 252–6).

Scotland had been a dual society for much longer than Wales. The Gaelic speaking, tribal, great landowner dominated, poverty stricken, beautiful Highlands contained a tiny population after the eighteenth-century clearances. Those who remained lived by subsistence farming and/or fishing. From the 1870s new roads and railways made some of this vast area a little less remote from the rest of Britain; in the 1860s it had taken a week to travel from Edinburgh to the island of Skye. Highland Scotland, also, from the 1880s showed signs of emerging cultural nationalism, originating largely among urban teachers and journalists who were émigrés or descendants of émigrés from the Highlands (Dunbabin 1974: 183–4). Lowland Scotland was integrated into the English industrial economy from its earliest stages. Its social structure was similar to that of England, although living standards were generally lower in both towns and countryside than in much of England (Hunt 1973).

The whole of Scotland retained throughout this period separate legal, educational and local administrative institutions, including a Poor Law established on different principles from the English, (Paterson 1976; Treble 1978) and it possessed a different (Calvinist) established church.

How, then, did the major groups within British society change and respond to change?

Landed society

The landed aristocracy in the most industrialised country in the world showed a remarkable talent for survival. Their political and economic influence diminished gradually, but remained, for much of this period, disproportionate to their numbers and to the economic importance of land. It remains a little surprising that 'the last government in the western world to possess all the attributes of aristocracy in working condition' (Tuchman 1966: 3) should have taken office in England in 1895. It contained two Marquesses (including the Prime Minister, Lord Salisbury), two dukes, one earl, one viscount and three barons (most of whose families had served in government for generations), two squires (whose families had represented the same counties in parliament since the sixteenth century), one director of the Bank of England, and one businessman, Joseph Chamberlain. But for Chamberlain, it was a group which could have held office at any time in the preceding two centuries. Although, in some respects, industrialisation and agricultural decline threatened the landed aristocracy, it also offered the shrewder of them new opportunities for making money and wielding influence.

The aristocracy and gentry, of course, predominated among the established hereditary peerage with an automatic right to membership of the House of Lords. In 1911 it had more than 570 hereditary members, and had only just been made to relinquish its veto over legislation. Even among the 246 new peers created between 1886 and 1914, about 50 were from noble families and about half had landed connections, being either younger sons of gentry or sons of entrepreneurial fathers who had marked their success by buying land (F. M. L. Thompson 1963: 294).

The size of the latter group suggests the continuing prestige associated with land ownership. This desire of successful businessmen to buy land cannot generally be explained as a form of diversification of investment, in view of the decline of profits from land after 1870 (chapter 8). The trend for new peers of non-landed origins to buy country estates continued until 1906. Between 1906 and 1914 five sixths of this group failed to do so; the prestige of land ownership seems at last to have faded, largely due to fear of threatened Liberal land taxes (F. M. L. Thompson 1963: 317–26).

The Liberal governments formed in 1906 and 1908, indeed, marked the first major breaks in the landed presence in government. After 1908 the only cabinet member from a substantial landowning family was Winston Churchill. Asquith, a lawyer of middle-class origins, was the first Prime Minister not to own a landed estate.

The House of Commons acquired an increasing proportion of members of business and professional origins; they predominated after 1885. However, landed society retained its influence in rural local government, even after the introduction of elected county councils in 1888. Many of them continued to be chosen as mayors of large and small towns (Cannadine 1977b; Escott 1879).

The continuing importance of the landed aristocracy, and of the surrounding circle of established country gentry, surprised and impressed European observers. Yet English landowners had for generations embraced with enthusiasm the opportunity not only for advanced methods of agricultural production, but for such enterprises as urban development and the exploitation of mineral discoveries. Hence it is not perhaps surprising that they continued to exert influence upon an industrial society with whose economic and political values many of them were quite in tune. Many of them took advantage of new opportunities for wealth-making in a style which justifies Engels' description of them as 'a bourgeois aristocracy'.

Others, however, made major contributions to the infrastructure of the new society and economy in a style more distinctively influenced by traditional aristocratic values. When the Marquesses of Bute poured investment into the building of Cardiff docks (they spent £2½ million by 1882) they made minimal, if any, profit. Their concern appears to have been not so much with short-term profit maximisation as with prestige, status and traditional family responsibility in the enhancement of their land and provision of work for their tenants. This undertaking facilitated coal export from Glamorgan on an unprecedented scale and the rapid expansion of the South Wales coalfield. Such a risky and unprofitable venture was unattractive to conventional entrepreneurs concerned primarily with satisfactory returns, who would in any case have had difficulty in raising the loans necessary for such large-scale investment. The prestige of the Butes, and the security of their considerable landholding could and did attract the necessary loans from banks and insurance companies. By this means middle- and lower-class savings were channelled into investment of considerable value to the economy. This and similarly financed ventures were distinctive and major aristocratic contributions to the new society and economy (Cannadine 1977a: 642–4).

Similar, though less economically vital aristocratic ventures such as the development of prestige middle-class housing estates, which though once again speculative and low-profit, imprinted an expression of landed values upon those towns and parts of towns (such as Bloomsbury in central London) built wholly or partly on great estates (Cannadine 1977c: 463–4).

Such activities brought about a closer community of interests between the more innovative great landowners, financiers and manufacturers, whose business activities were facilitated and whose residential aspirations were fulfilled on the urban estates of Manchester or Birmingham; second, they reinforced existing close links between financiers and landowners (Cannadine 1977a; Rubinstein 1977b).

There were no other sources of conflict between land and either of these other influential groups which might have led either of the latter to wish to dislodge men of landed connection from power. This community of interest on political and economic matters between influential financiers, businessmen and land-owners, whatever cultural differences and snobberies may have divided them in less essential matters, was most clearly expressed by the shift of the most success-ful representatives of all three groups (Rubinstein 1977b: 621) to support of the Conservative party in the 1890s. The composition of the 1906 and 1908 Liberal cabinets reflected this change.

Furthermore, landed circles remained small but were rather less exclusive than their members sometimes liked to suggest; and members of landed society worked hard for their survival. They had time to devote to politics, administration or to the magistracy, which businessmen lacked and which they used well and often with dedication. Their continuing influence was assisted by the fact that the depression in agricultural incomes was not universal (chapter 8). Apart from those landowners who continued to farm their land profitably, owners of land in even partially urban and industrial use continued to prosper as urban land prices rose. The Duke of Westminster had an income of £1000 a *day* in 1914, mainly from his ownership of Pimlico and Belgravia, acquired through judicious marriage. In 1886, the aristocracy and gentry were major landlords in one third of English provincial towns. London was almost exclusively owned by the aristocracy, the Crown and institutions such as Eton College. Not until 1909 were they taxed, and then minimally, on the unearned gains from increasing rents (Cannadine 1977c: 457–82; 1977b).

A section of the landed aristocracy maintained and even increased their family fortunes by forming ever closer connections with finance and industry. By 1896, 167 noblemen (over a quarter of the peerage), held directorships, most of them in more than one company, mostly in the City of London and concerned with commercial rather than industrial enterprise (F. M. L. Thompson 1963: 305–8). A peer lending his prestige to the board of directors was, even by 1875, a necessity for status conscious companies (Best 1971).

From the 1880s, shrewder landowners were spreading their assets through investment, especially overseas. Such manoeuvres were least likely among the more stricken owners of wheat producing land, who had fewest assets. In general, the richer landowners, with incomes above £50000 per annum, appear to have survived the fall in agricultural incomes, indeed to have continued to flourish. Predictably, the squirearchy and minor gentry with incomes of £1000–£10000 p.a., such as the ubiquitous small squirearchy of Wales, fared worst since their resources were too slender for diversification (Cannadine 1977a: 648). This may have resulted in a growing gap between those of the old landed society who adapted to and profited from economic change, and those who did not or could not.

Arguably, the cultural differences between landed society, or at least those of its members who continued to flourish, and that of finance and to a lesser extent of big business diminished at an increasingly rapid pace, especially after 1900 (volume 1, chapter 14). The extent to which distinctive 'landed values', supposed to be those of élitism and amateurism, survived to influence other significant sectors of society, remains debateable, and will be discussed later.

Farmers and rural labourers

Tenant or owner occupying working farmers are less well documented than either large landowners or labourers. The lower rate of mobility of farmers than of farm labourers from the land was partly due to landlord investment behaviour (chapter 8). Also, farmers could be expected to be more reluctant than landless labourers to move, due to their closer material ties to the land. Like French and German peasants in the nineteenth century, they were unwilling to surrender the security of effective hereditary land tenure for an uncertain urban future. They could also supply their basic food needs from the land, although some small farmers, notably in Highland Scotland and Wales survived only at a low level of subsistence.

Few farmers can have had the skills to enable them to hold an urban position of equivalent status and security to their position in rural society. Awareness of the importance of security, and fear of the alternatives, may explain the increasing tension between farmers and large landowners. Tenant farmers in England, Scotland and Wales agitated in the 1880s for greater security of tenure, *de jure* as well as *de facto*. Such pressure later declined, probably due to the willingness, not only of landlords, but of governments, to concede at least some of their wishes. The Agricultural Holdings Act of 1883, for example, prohibited landlords from avoiding payment of compensation for unexhausted improvements of the land; Scottish rent rises were regulated from 1889 and agricultural de-rating was introduced in 1896 (Dunbabin 1974).

The growth of activities such as market gardening and fruit growing (chapter 8) provided new opportunities for small-scale farming, often operating with only family labour.

The large numbers of landless labourers, upon whom most English farming depended, received less protection against the ill effects of agricultural decline. Very many of them responded by flight to the colonies, or to the cities (chapters 7 & 8), causing a shortage of labour in some farming areas (mainly in East Anglia and the South-West), by the end of the century. Having neither hereditary tenure nor ownership of the land, they had less reason than the farmers to stay.

Living conditions, wages, prices and employment opportunities were as variable regionally for rural as for urban workers (chapter 7; Hunt 1973) despite the decline in the range of variation (chapter 8). The greatest depths of poverty, throughout this period, were suffered among agricultural labourers, especially in the South-West (chapter 8; Hunt 1973) and among small farmers in Wales and Scotland. The polemics against, and surveys of, poverty which are a feature of this period, concentrated, with few exceptions, upon its unmistakeable urban manifestations, especially in London. Poverty in the countryside was often hidden, less obvious to the casual, or even careful, glance, than overcrowded city slums. Rural poverty was due, above all, to low wages and seasonal under-employment. It was increased a little by the growing proportion of old people in rural areas. One of the effects of the national decline in adult mortality (chapter 7) was the gradually increased proportion of aged in the population (hence the pressure for old age pensions from the 1870s and their introduction in 1908). The continuous flow of migration of young people from the countryside magnified its effects in rural communities. The 1891 census showed that 7.6 per cent of the population of rural districts were over 65, compared with 3.3 per cent in London, 3.5 per cent in a sample of other large towns and 3.3 per cent in mining districts. Fewer old people were supported by family and friends in rural areas (18 per cent of men, compared with 40.4 per cent, 38.5 per cent and 42 per cent of aged men in metropolitan, urban and mining areas) (Parliamentary Papers 1898, vol. XLV). The relatively higher survival rates of old women over old men minimised the effect of this demographic change upon the rural labour force (chapter 8), but it increased the pressure upon the poor rates. The rural poor had opportunities for supplementing low incomes by poaching, gathering wood for fuel, or exchanging produce of country gardens. Or they might combine seasonal jobs in agriculture with a variety of other occupations, such as the Suffolk labourers who spent winter fishing at sea or in the malt kilns of Burton-on-Trent (Evans 1970; Samuel 1975).

Increasing numbers found survival even by these means impossible, but not all labourers fled willingly from the land. Many stayed and some tried, at least in the short run, to fight for a permanent stake in the land. The first growth of effective agricultural trade unionism in the early 1870s (Dunbabin 1974) pre-dated the onset of agricultural depression. It declined under the impact of depression during the 1880s, reviving mildly, possibly due to the inspiration of urban 'New Unionism', in the late 1880s. It revived permanently in the period of relative labour scarcity in agriculture, and of national increase in trade union membership, after 1906.

More important than trade unionism, in the 1880s, was the demand for smallholdings, to 'give back' the land to the people. The demand for more equal distribution of the land had long played a role in British radical politics, and it remained strong through the 1880s, although temporarily subsumed in the demand for the vote, which was extended to £10 rural householders in 1884.

Redistribution of land in smallholdings had an obvious appeal at a time when the urban labour market could not provide full-time work for all, and land was unprofitable and in some areas going to waste. It appealed to many radicals and reformers and was stimulated by the militant demand for land rights in Wales, Scotland and Ireland in the 1880s (Dunbabin 1974). The demand for secure land tenure had a more immediate apeal to the peasant farmers of the celtic countries than to English farm labourers who had long ceased to be landholders. The importance of fair distribution of the land in British radical thinking may explain the widespread support in the 1880s for Henry George's proposals for taxation of the unearned increment in land value.

Liberal and Labour politicians continued to advocate varieties of land reform (Russell 1973) until 1914, although celtic rural militancy and the demands by rural labourers to revive the long dead English peasantry diminished in the 1890s, as more of them accepted the apparently inevitable and left the land. The only results of their pressure were the minor Allotments Extension Act, 1882, which enabled land owned by village charities to be let for allotments (Ashby 1961), an insignificant extension of this legislation in 1908, and Lloyd George's small tax on the unearned increment in land values introduced in 1909. The large landowners in parliament opposed land redistribution, pointing to the greater efficiency of large-scale farming, compared with European small-scale agriculture. Liberal attachment to land reform may have completed the estrangement of many of them from the Liberal party.

The middle class

The English landed aristocracy and gentry and rural labourers provide useful studies of the adaptation of social groups to economic change, which are well documented. The 'middle class' was less cohesive, and less is known for this period about the distinctive groups of bankers, brewers, shipowners, coalowners and professional people, intellectuals and big and lesser businessmen, metro-politan and provincial élites who comprised it, and whose characteristics were by no means identical. We probably know more about their numbers of domestic servants and horses, draped pianos and stuffed armchairs than about their relations with each other or their networks of personal contacts, formed through schools and universities, clubs and churches. It was a small group, comprising until 1871 c. 17 000 merchants and bankers, about 1700 shipowners, 15 000 doctors, 3500 barristers, and 7000 architects, among others (Hobsbawm 1968: 130).

Among the heterogeneous group of businessmen the most crucial distinction was between the very wealthy, the owners and executive directors of large, highly capitalised successful enterprises – such as steel and ship manufacture – and the rest. This has already been suggested in the discussion of recruitment of leaders of steel and hosiery manufacture. The masters of highly capitalised steel enterprises not only came generally from wealthy backgrounds, but married into wealthy families often of higher status than their own; they increasingly came from, and sent their sons to, élite public schools and to Oxford and Cambridge. They had rarely undergone apprenticeship or technical training.

The Nottingham hosiers married women of similar or lower origins than their own, were rarely educated beyond the age of seventeen and usually at private day schools (more rarely at state schools). Most underwent a period of apprenticeship. The wealthy steelmasters were members of the national élite, the hosiers of only local importance (Erickson 1959).

Economic historians have discussed whether the continuing prominence of landed society contributed to relative 'entrepreneurial decline' in this period, by directing the aspirations of businessmen towards gentlemanly landed status and amateurism, for their children if not for themselves, rather than towards continuing business success and the acquisition of technical expertise (Landes 1969: 334–358; Coleman 1973). The implied contrast is with the USA, where business success and professionalism is assumed to have been considered a desirable end in itself.

The most successful businessmen of this period did, as we have seen, at least until 1906, buy land, and they sent their sons to public schools, which devoted much of their energy to disseminating a sense of the *esprit de corps* of a ruling class (Bamford 1967). These schools, great and small, contributed much to furthering cultural fusion among the business, commercial and landed élites. By

1870 they were free of the obligation to educate the poor, for which many of them had been established, and were exclusively and consciously élite institutions. The effect of these facts upon the behaviour of businessmen is much less clear. Chapter 5 points out that many industries did not fail, but performed satisfactorily. There is no evidence that unsuccessful sons were in closer contact than others with landed values. Nor, as already suggested, was much of landed society itself averse to making money from business or commerce; nor had they despised professionalism as applied to improved agricultural productivity. The public schools, whatever their values, produced generations of successful bankers. An increasing proportion of boys from major public schools chose business careers by 1880, although it is uncertain how this relates to the increasing number of businessmen's sons attending such schools (Reader 1966).

It is possible that the public schools encouraged 'professionalism' less than by some hypothetical comparative standard they might have done, though they may have failed all of their pupils rather considerably by poor teaching (Bamford 1967). This might have been compensated by the post-school apprenticeship required for a few occupations such as engineering. In addition, businessmen could increasingly gain further training at evening classes or at the new provincial universities, although many by 1914 did not. More important is the fact that most business owners and managers were not wealthy steelmasters or shipowners. They could not realistically afford to aspire to landownership, or to élite public schools for their children. Worldly success for most of them could only be achieved through business success. Family connections were often crucial to their making and spending wealth. To explore the world of most businessmen, the total of whose activities affected the performance of the economy, we must look not only at public schools, Oxford and Cambridge, but at the big private schools of the provincial cities such as Manchester Grammar School, and at the lesser schools and the provincial universities which businessmen helped to finance and which their children attended. All too little is known, especially about the schools. Universities such as Birmingham were founded specifically 'to provide a thorough, systematic education in science with a distinctly practical application to the industries of the Midland district' (Sanderson 1972).

The possibility remains that hostility to dedicated professionalism was, and perhaps is, an influence upon British business, and other, behaviour. But the origin of such a belief, if indeed it exists, and its influence upon business behaviour, remains to be satisfactorily revealed.

A little more is known about the connections and social, political and religious activities of businessmen in some parts of the country. They formed local urban élites controlling literary and political clubs, town councils, charities and churches, adorning the redeveloped centres of the cities where they had made their fortunes with town halls, art galleries, libraries and other monuments to their own secure success. They formed self-confident, inter-married, self-contained circles, separate from those of the country gentry and London-based aristocratic élite. They managed the cities, as Chamberlain ran Birmingham in the 1870s, as efficient business enterprises, even taking into municipal ownership such services as gas and water supplies, when they ran inefficiently to the business eye; though they would passionately oppose socialist inspired nationalisation (Briggs 1963; Hennock 1973).

But businessmen did not act identically everywhere. They dominated Birmingham politics, but in Leeds the business and professional élite abandoned the council to small tradesmen between 1872 and 1895 and returned only when their successors' administration proved unsuccessful (Hennock 1973).

The increasing presence of businessmen in politics has been noted. Without differing sufficiently from the landed élite to form a distinctive political party, they created influential pressure groups, for example employers' associations, such as those in engineering and shipbuilding, which were formed in the 1890s. However, it has already been noted that businessmen made a less distinctive contribution to national politics than the conventional picture of Victorian Britain as 'the workshop of the world' might lead us to expect. They also comprised a surprisingly small proportion of great wealth holders. Great landowners were numerically the largest group among millionaires and half-millionaires up to 1900. Only after 1900 were their numbers outstripped by holders of commercial (not manufacturing) wealth. Between 1880 and 1899, 175 landowners were millionaires or half-millionaires at their deaths in respect of their land holding alone (excluding personalty), compared with 89 holders of commercial wealth and 82 manufacturers; between 1900 and 1914 the numbers were 107, 129 and 79 respectively (Rubinstein 1977a: 102–3). The political and social importance of manufacturers was greatest in the centres of industry, in the north, lowland Scotland and the Midlands (Joyce 1975). It was much less in London, which was dominated rather by aristocratic 'society' and the commercial and financial élite of the city of London, whose social and financial interconnections were close and became closer during this period (Rubinstein 1977a; 1977b).

The professionally secretive City financiers have hidden themselves from the historian with remarkable success. Their wealth, influence and prestige have been surprisingly rarely noted despite their undoubted economic importance and success in this period. This must largely be due to the invisibility of their activities. They did not build factories, dig holes in the ground or require large labour forces, nor at any point in the nineteenth century did they march as a distinctive group onto the public political stage. Their styles of life and of work were undeniably gentlemanly, sufficiently inoffensive to aristocratic traditions to enable them to survive with apparently unscathed prestige the substantial foreign, especially German and Jewish, presence in their ranks. The financial world was dominated by products of public schools, by men who owned land but whose international success was in no way diminished by these experiences. It was a closely intermarried world, increasingly dominated by wealthy dynasties.

Their influence and importance should not be underestimated. Not only did they include many of the greatest wealth holders in Britain, but the clear preference of the City of London (Britain's, indeed the world's, greatest stock-market) for channelling investment funds abroad, into government loans or, to a lesser extent, into aristocratic investment rather than into British manufacturing should not be ignored in examining underinvestment in British industry in this period (chapter 3). Manufacturers obtained their funds from local banks and the smaller provincial stock-markets. Few of them appear to have had such close social contacts with London financiers as existed between City men and landed society.

Still less is known about the political influence of the City of London. After 1886 its richer members increasingly congregated in the Conservative party. In view of their economic importance and close links with government finance it would be surprising, though the subject remains unexplored, if they did not play a major role in influencing Britain's lone adherence to free trade in the increasingly protectionist world after 1880.

Arguably in this period Britain had three influential élite groups: landed society, which was increasingly closely allied both socially and financially with London based men of commerce, and, politically and socially the weakest and poorest of the three, the manufacturing élite based in the provinces (Rubinstein 1977a; 1977b).

The growth of business, commerce and the capital market created a new social group, often closely related to the business and banking élite, the 170 000 'rentiers' who, in 1871, lived exclusively upon the income from the profits and savings of the previous generations. Many of them were widows and unmarried daughters who could adequately be provided for by stocks and shares (Hobsbawm 1968: 97). This had some results not always welcome to businessmen. But for the £1000 a year inherited by Beatrice Webb (the granddaughter of a tenant farmer and a Lancashire manufacturer), she and her husband Sidney could not have had the leisure to produce their monumental works of social description and criticism. Fabians, though not Beatrice Webb herself, suffered agonies of conscience about the source of their incomes, but without the stock market much would have been lost to English radicalism and socialism. Another important English socialist, William Morris, was one beneficiary of £900 a year from his father's 'fortunate mining speculation' (Thompson 1977).

Nor, without such security, could England's small intellectual élite have flourished. This impressive group, many of them descended from the Quakers and other reformers of the Clapham sect of the 1830s, were bound together by their philanthropic interests, by a profound and remarkable inherited dedication to reform of social conditions, of the condition of women, of administration and the universities. Trevelyans, Stracheys, Gurneys, Wedgwoods, Darwins, Huxleys and others, the senior branches of some of whose families were successful landlords, bankers or businessman, provided a remarkable succession of academics, home and colonial administrators, and social reformers. Rather ascetic, somewhat philistine, much intermarried, inhabiting book-strewn homes in Bayswater, North Oxford and Cambridge, their wider connections by marriage drew into their circles such notable figures as Charles Booth and Beatrice Webb, but few members of the landed élite. Their most effective influence, apart from the results of some immeasurable intellectual advances, was upon the reforms of the universities and of government administration (both largely achieved in the 1870s) designed to admit those of talent but of insignificant birth (Annan 1955). Their influence and pervasive presence in intellectual and administrative circles was at its peak between 1840 and the late 1880s. In the 1880 and 1890s their descendants, and increasing numbers of younger members of commercial and manufacturing families, removed from the need of the older generations to fight for success and status, their lives cocooned and much sweetened by inherited money, were free to devote themselves to philanthropy or to the aesthetic movements in art and architecture which emerged in those years (Girouard 1977).

Some of the children of these and of business families entered the professions, which, especially the law, had more members in parliament than had either business or finance. Professional men (there were very few women even by 1914) did not have a united political voice. Some were highly critical of the social and economic system and of its costs, and (notably the clergy) formed the active membership of growing charities and pressure groups for social reform; they dominated the influential Charity Organisation Society (founded 1869) (Stedman Jones 1971: 241–61).

This was a period of uneven growth for the professions. Accountancy, civil engineering, surveying and architecture all became firmly established, setting up professional institutes with power to fix standards of entry. In 1841 the census recognised only the old professions, law, medicine, the church. In 1861, in an apparent fit of hedonism, the census added to the professional category not only schoolmasters, professors and civil engineers, but actors, authors, journalists, artists and musicians (none of whom had quite the social status in England of the professions judged more respectable). In 1881, architects, land agents and surveyors were added; accountants not until 1921. The largest and, apart from the new profession of dentistry, the fastest growing profession, schoolteaching, had never, especially at the elementary school level, been considered an élite or influential occupation. Unlike other professions its members were often of lower-class origins, or were women, and for both reasons were unlikely to be

Table 9.3. *Percentage increase or decrease in main professions between censuses*

	Census year		
Profession	1851–61	1881–91	1901–11
Teachers	+32	+15	+9
Surveyors	+63	+18	−21
Solicitors	−14	+18	−8
Physicians and surgeons	−18	+26	+3
Clergy	+9	+12	−1
Civil engineering	+11	+35	−35
Dentists	+34	+39	+63
Barristers	−1	+22	−2
Architects	+29	+14	−17
Accountants	−6	−31	+5

Accountants increased by 58 per cent, 1861–71, and by 18 per cent, 1871–81
Source: W. Reader, *Professional Men* (1966)
The total number of civil servants (all levels) was 31 943 in 1861, 79 241 in 1891 and 172 352 in 1911 (including Post Office staff) (Finer 1927)

accorded high status. The professions in general barely grew as fast as population. Professional fees and salaries did not increase significantly in this period, and they included an insignificant proportion of great wealth-holders, notably fewer than in the early part of the century (Rubinstein 1977a: 122). The fate of some of them, e.g. civil engineers (of whom there were 3329 in 1861, 7124 in 1881 but only 7208, including mining engineers, in 1911, reflects a significant feature of economic change (Hobsbawm 1968: 130).

Entry into the professions from other than reasonably wealthy families was rare. All required a standard of education rarely open to working or most lower-middle-class children. Sidney Webb's progression via scholarships from elementary schools to the higher civil service was exceptional.

The lower middle class

The 'lower middle class' from which Sidney Webb emerged, was largely a new creation of this period, associated with the growth of service occupations. The increasing concentration of capital, on the one hand, diminished the numbers and importance of the classical 'petty bourgeoisie' of independent small employers and merchants. The exceptions to this trend were retail shopkeepers, whose numbers grew at all levels from the large downtown store to the corner shop, due to the growth of more efficient national systems of distribution.

On the other hand, the period saw the still faster growth of the dependent 'white collar' employment of clerks, lower level management, technicians and commercial travellers, primarily for men, but increasingly for women also. The size and composition of these new occupations have been discussed in chapter 6. Their incomes from the 1870s varied from a lower level of £150 per annum, similar to those of many skilled artisans, to the £300 of the well-established clerk.

The insecurity of their occupations may help to explain the surprising cohesiveness of this 'lower middle class', as they saw themselves and were seen by others. There is no obvious reason why small employers and shopkeepers, employed clerks and commercial travellers should have had more in common than, for example, clerks and artisans. Their economic positions, especially those of employers and employed, were different and could conflict. It is questionable whether they can be described as a 'class' rather than as a series of status groups at the lower end of the middle class. Yet evidence from marriage patterns, places of residence and memberships of voluntary associations, suggests higher levels of contact among these groups than between them and others, though the boundaries above and below were not clear cut. Such evidence provides justification for treating them as a separate class.

Members of these occupations appear to have identified closely, though often in vain, with the middle class, in aspirations and ways of life, and to have been more aware of differences from than of similarities to skilled workers. Their aspirations may have led to consumption patterns different from those of the skilled working class, as is suggested by literary evidence (Crossick 1976b), though this is difficult to establish from statistics of consumption (chapter 8). Economic pressures, and their relatively low incomes, distinguished them from the established middle class. They could afford smaller houses, fewer servants or none, and more restricted leisure activities, and had little control over their working lives. The skilled worker had a similar income, but more skill and job control. But they differed in their work experience, in surroundings for office workers which wouldn't dirty a white collar, shorter hours and the status traditionally ascribed to occupations requiring some formal education. The employed lower middle class differed from skilled workers in their unwillingness to unionise; though clerks, in particular, showed an increasing tendency to do so in the 1900s, as they felt the pressure of falling real incomes and the danger of unemployment.

Generally, but not universally, white-collar workers preferred different leisure pursuits, and had different attitudes from skilled workers; they took leisure pursuits *en famille* rather than in sexually segregated pubs and clubs, and aspired to a high level of education for their children, and to intense 'respectability' in dress and behaviour (Crossick 1976b; Gillis 1975: 107–17).

It is possible, though this is still largely unexplored, that this new class reinforced political conservatism, though never with the force of their more numerous German counterparts. Arguably, their very insecurity made them fear and resent increasing political organisation among the working class, especially where this resulted in increased government expenditure from rates and taxes, for education, housing and other welfare benefits for workers. Loss of income through rates and taxation reduced relatively low lower middle class incomes, and they did not benefit proportionately from these measures. Hence their participation in ratepayers' protests, and fears in the Liberal party of the lower middle class flocking to the Conservative party following the post-1906 social reforms (Emy 1973).

Urban workers

The changing work experience of skilled and unskilled workers, the growing numbers of semi-skilled process workers, their patterns of migration, wages and the growth of trade unions have been discussed in chapter 7.

It is generally, and rightly, assumed that standards of living improved during this period for a high proportion of the working class (chapter 6). Yet the poverty surveys, from Booth's in London in the 1880s to Bowley's work in 1913 showed up to 30 per cent of the population, in several areas of the country, at or near the margin of subsistence. It is most unlikely that the proportion was lower in 1860, although there is no statistical evidence for the earlier period. Booth himself was convinced that poverty had diminished by the 1880s (Hennock 1976). The survey results do not suggest that 30 per cent of the British population lived in poverty throughout their lives. Rowntree (whose survey of York in 1901 was statistically sounder than Booth's, though his results were similar) pointed out that families were most prone to severe poverty when they had young children or when the head of the household was aged, than in the period of relative ease before the first child was born, or when the children were old enough to earn. Hence more than 30 per cent of the population (or the 27 per cent Rowntree found in poverty in York) might suffer poverty at some point in their lives; a small number in irregular or low-paid employment might live in permanent poverty.

Both Booth and Rowntree made the further distinction between those suffering primary poverty, so much 'in want' that they could barely afford sufficient food for survival and who could die of diseases associated with malnutrition (8.4 per cent of Booth's London sample), and the larger number (22.3 per cent in London) in secondary poverty, i.e. 'neither ill-nourished nor ill-clad according to any standard that can reasonably be used, [but] their lives are an unending struggle and they lack comfort' (Booth 1892; Hennock 1976).

Knowledge and concern about urban poverty increased throughout the period. Polemic and sympathetic portrayal especially of London's poverty was a growing literary, academic and journalistic *genre* from the 1860s (Stedman Jones 1971). From Booth's survey onwards, it was quantified. Hardly any aspect of working-class life went unexplored by a Royal Commission or Select Committee between 1880 and 1914. Understanding of the complex causes of poverty was certainly greater in 1900 than in 1860, yet the central problems of poverty, the insufficiency of work, inadequate wages and overcrowded slum housing improved little by 1914.

'Unemployment' became, for the first time in the 1880s, a word in common usage, and the problem was analysed with unprecedented precision by William Beveridge, among others (Harris 1977). From 1886, local authorities were enabled to establish public works to provide employment; in 1909 labour exchanges, and in 1911 Unemployment Insurance, were established. Yet the two former could not provide for the excess of unemployed over available work, and Unemployment Insurance was designed only to tide the regularly employed over periods of short-term unemployment (Harris 1972). Due to the absence of unemployment statistics covering unskilled workers it is difficult to quantify to what degree legislation diminished the problem. Public responsibility for housing, education and working conditions and hours was extended. Compensation for accidents at work was introduced in 1897. The popularity among reformers such as Booth of proposals for labour colonies to house the huge surplus labour force (of 345000 in London, he estimated [Brown 1968]) to remove them from the struggle to find work in an overstocked labour market was a measure of the difficulty of finding more plausible solutions within the conventional framework of economic ideas.

New provisions multiplied after the election of the Liberal government in 1906: free school meals for poor children in 1906, medical inspection in schools in 1907, Old Age Pensions in 1908, Health Insurance in 1911, among others (Hay 1975). However, the institution which continued to support, though minimally, most of the poor, the Poor Law, changed little despite the efforts of the Webbs after 1905 to reform it, and the work of the great Royal Commission on the Poor Laws and the Relief of Distress which reported in 1909.

Nevertheless, the period of Liberal government, 1906–14, saw a major extension of State recognition of its responsibility for the poor. To some degree, the state compensated with welfare benefits those whose standard of living was held back by the slowed pace of industrial growth (chapter 1). Resistance to state welfare action, strong to the 1890s, declined thereafter, although it did not disappear. The welfare role of the state, opposed in the 1880s as eroding desirable individual independence among the masses, became accepted as essential to increase British economic and military efficiency and to compromise with the demands of labour for improved conditions (Rose 1972; Fraser 1973; Gilbert 1966; Pelling 1968; Thane 1975, 1978a: Intro.). Such measures as health and unemployment insurance and the introduction of labour exchanges can be interpreted as being to some degree attempts to increase productivity by increasing the health and sense of security of the work force and to maintain social order amongst a materially secure population. Many employers supported them for this reason (Hay 1977).

Table 9.4. *Central government welfare expenditure as percentage total UK government expenditure*

	Education art and science	Old age pensions	Unemployment insurance and employment exchanges	National health insurance
1860	1.83	—	—	—
1885	5.76	—	—	—
1909	12.02	1.45	—	—
1914	10.14	6.50	0.47	3.17

Source: B. Mitchell & P. Deane, *Abstract of British Historical Statistics* (1962)

Table 9.5. *Local authority welfare expenditure as percentage total local authority expenditure, England and Wales*

	Poor relief	Education	Housing	Lunacy	Hospitals
1868	24.50	—	—	—	—
1885	12.59	8.52	0.20	3.33	0.19
1914	7.26	20.48	0.78	2.83	1.54

Source: B. Mitchell & P. Deane (1962)

Both the revolution in ideas and the redistributive nature of these measures can, however, be exaggerated. All of them aimed to help the 'deserving' respectable poor, but at a low level of subsistence; the Poor Law's traditional assumption that an 'undeserving', feckless class existed and should be punished by deterrent treatment continued to thrive. Although 'welfare' accounted, by the end of the period at least, for a substantial part of public expenditure (tables 9.4 and 9.5) its redistributive effect was minimal.

Perhaps 40 per cent of government revenue came from indirect taxes paid by those below the income tax limit (£160 p.a.). Those below this limit contributed substantially to local rates and directly to health and unemployment insurance benefits.

The poor, however, were a minority of the working class. More enjoyed improved living standards and had access to better food, more leisure and a wider range of consumer goods (chapter 8). From 1867, protective legislation was extended to factories outside the cotton industry. The improvement was real, though undramatic and for many workers insecure.

A striking feature of this period of improvement is the increased participation of working people in political institutions. Between 1867 and 1918 all working men over 21 and women householders and wives of householders over 30 obtained the vote in national elections. In 1867 it was granted to urban £10 householders; in 1884 to the counties on the same terms. However, by 1914 40 per cent of men over 21 and all women still had no vote. The men were excluded under the property or residence qualifications or due to failure to register (Blewett 1965).

From 1894, all ratepayers might stand for local office on local councils, boards of guardians or boards of education, and many working people did so. From 1911 they could be paid to serve as members of parliament. Such changes encountered much less opposition from the business, commercial and landed élites, now confident of their supremacy in the new industrial society, than had been faced by the Reform Act of 1832. Trade unions achieved legal recognition in the 1870s (chapter 7). During the 1914–18 war consultation with the unions became part of the normal political process in a way that could not have been foreseen in the 1860s.

From 1892 an independent party of labour was permanently established. Working men trickled into parliament from the 1870s. John Burns, tamed ex-leader of the dock workers, entered the Cabinet in 1906; also in 1906 there were the unprecedented number of 53 labour representatives in parliament. Labour was not, however, a party capable of winning a general election until after the First World War, partly because so many of its potential supporters were excluded from the vote. Most working men before 1914 voted Liberal, the traditional radical party, or more rarely, except in Lancashire (Clarke 1971), Conservative. Yet, that a Labour party could exist at all was unthinkable in 1860.

The chief base of support for the Labour party was not among the poorest, but generally among the more secure workers, those with time to spare from scraping a living. They might well have enjoyed improving living standards, but had other grievances enough to inspire support for a working class party. The emergence of the Labour party derived both from widespread working-class dissatisfaction with social conditions and with the system of political representation, which was not new, and from the capacity to organise successfully on a national scale to express that dissatisfaction, which was new.

To some extent, the growth of the labour movement was fuelled by the realisation that it was impossible any longer, after the depression of the mid 1880s, to rely upon sustained economic growth to improve conditions sufficiently. It was also important that changes in the labour process (chapter 7) contributed to a growing sense of common interest between the two major sections of the working class. There was an important status distinction within the working class which was most acute in the first twenty years of the period. Unionisation grew in the élite trades of the relatively well-paid, secure workers of the 'labour aristocracy' and it achieved greater legal and social acceptance there. Membership of a respectable trade union set them apart from other workers. They developed a distinctive culture based upon trade unions, Friendly societies, Co-ops and working men's clubs, which was reinforced by a high degree of intermarriage (Crossick 1976a: 176–362; Hobsbawm 1964a: 272–317). It was a culture which developed in, and was influenced by, the period of quiescence in class relations of the 1860s and 1870s.

This status division diminished gradually from the 1880s. The security of élite craftsmen and factory workers declined (chapter 7; Samuel 1977) and the number of semi-skilled process workers increased, wearing away the boundary line between the two groups, and increasing the sense of injustice among some of the old élite, diminishing their previous inclination towards political and industrial quiescence. Cultural changes reinforced this process of fusion between skilled workers and the rest, without eroding the barrier between the working and other classes. Compulsory education gradually provided the children of artisans and labourers with a common experience (although the process was not complete until education actually became universal, in the 1890s at the earliest). Few artisans could afford to send their children to the private schools patronised by some of the lower middle class and all of their social superiors. The continued movement to the suburbs of the middle classes and better off workers increased the spatial division among classes, diminishing the long established community restraints and direct contact among classes that in some communities had kept conflict to a minimum (Crossick 1976a: 456–7). The growth of the lower middle class, interposed between the working and middle classes, and very conscious of their superiority to workers, may have exacerbated working-class awareness of class differences and of their own common bond (Gray 1976; Crossick 1976b).

It is arguable that the period after 1880 saw the creation of a new, more homogeneous working-class culture, replacing older localised customs. The local, employer influenced, differences in beliefs, voting patterns and leisure pursuits discernible among economically similar textile communities in Lancashire in the 1860s (Joyce 1975: 546–53) and elsewhere in the mid century gradually diminished under the growing influence of national changes and pressures. Football and the music halls became national working-class leisure pastimes. More workers joined trade unions. The general 'new unions' of the unskilled increasingly emulated older unions in their forms of organisation (Phelps Brown 1959: 224–5). Friendly societies became less significant as providers of welfare and leisure, as state welfare and new leisure pursuits developed. State welfare measures themselves did not acknowledge the conventional status divisions within the working class. If the working class was 'made' (E. P. Thompson 1963) in the 1830s, it can be argued that it was being 'remade' culturally and politically from the 1880s (Stedman Jones 1974), although the process was incomplete by 1914.

All these changes created a tendency towards the formation of a strong, though narrow and distinctly non-revolutionary, working-class consciousness, which only gradually and unevenly took on a political form. Local experiences influenced the speed and form of the spread of the political labour movement. Many were aware of the separateness of their class, and of their relative deprivation compared with others, but only a few believed that substantial change was possible or that the working class had the potential power to effect change.

The growth of a desire for, and recognition of the possibility of, separate labour representation led to dissatisfaction with the Liberal party as the accepted outlet for working-class political aspirations. Tension grew within local Liberal party branches, between middle- and working-class claims to serve on local authorities and in parliament and over policy issues (Crossick 1976a: 457).

This gradual change in political affiliation among working-class activists was due sometimes to ideological change, as with Keir Hardie (Reid 1971), from Liberalism to some variant of the socialist ideas developing in Europe at this time, or it was tactical. Many labour supporters continued to accept some of the central principles held by the Liberal Party – belief in a high degree of free enterprise, in self-help and suspicion of centralised state bureaucracy – but came to believe that the capacity of workers to benefit from the exercise of these principles would be improved by better social conditions. These, a working-class party seemed better capable than the Liberals of achieving.

Theories of socialism – commitment to profound change in the locus of power in the economic and political systems, and in their organisation, the abolition of exploitation and the achievement of maximum self-fulfilment for individuals – were important in Britain after 1880, as they had not been since 1848. They inspired many prominent trade unionists and political leaders. William Morris and Sidney Webb, in their very different ways, were significant British socialist thinkers. But equally influential among very many supporters of the labour movement was a less complicated desire for more moderate change: for working-class parliamentary power and some modification of the economic system, in order to diminish gross inequality; for a society which in fact, rather than just in theory, allowed working people to be self helping and independent.

Even the political group which regarded itself as most committed to revolutionary change, the small Social Democratic Federation (founded, like the Fabian Society, in 1884) hoped to go some way towards its objective by non-violent parliamentary means. Its leaders believed, as Marx had done, that the largest and most united working-class movement in Europe could achieve profound change by constitutional action (Collins 1971).

Hence, when the Labour Party was formed in 1906, its dominant ideology was a moderate socialism which aspired to the peaceful achievement of equality through the legislation of a Labour government.

Industrial conflict

Nevertheless, open conflict did break out from time to time, to a much greater degree from the mid 1870s, when the economy began to fall into recurrent difficulties, than before. Chiefly it took the form of industrial action. The growth of trade unions and the incidence of strikes has been discussed in chapter 7, but strike activity was not the only form of protest. The depressions of the mid 1880s and mid 1890s saw demonstrations of the unemployed in London and the North-East. Conflicts of interest were also expressed in the very formation of the competing organisations of trade unions and employers' federations.

The series of strikes of the 1880s (chapter 7) were followed by a brief period of peace. The years 1893–98 saw another increase in the number of strikes and lock-outs, followed by a more peaceful period between 1899 and 1906. The tensions of the 1890s are probably best explained in terms of both workers' and employers' fears about the economic present and future. Skilled workers feared not only unemployment but new work processes (chapter 7). Employers were unwilling to concede wage increases for fear of further falls in profits and competitiveness. The confident willingness of many of them to allow unions a stronger legal position in the peaceful period of the early 1870s was eroded by the fears engendered by economic depression and growing resistance to social inequality. Society had not proceeded, as had seemed likely in the 1870s, along the path of peaceful removal of inequality. The emergence of the 'New' unions in the 1880s increased employer mistrust of all unions (chapter 7). It must also be remembered that most employers faced a unionised work force for the first time. They took time to learn to deal with them, and their initial reaction was often hostile or fearful.

The decade of the 1890s saw the growth of 'free labour' organisations to supply strike-breaking blackleg labour (Saville 1974). Some employers' organisations attempted to co-ordinate the actions of employers against the unions. Only gradually and incompletely by 1918 did some employers regain their faith in the desirability of strong, moderate trade unionism.

In the 1890s, unions faced not only employer opposition but the progressive narrowing of their freedom of action by the Law Courts. Court decisions, culminating in the Taff Vale decision of 1902, increased the belief of some trade unionists in the need for political power to overrule the courts (Phelps Brown 1959: 190–6).

Understanding of industrial conflict in this period might be improved by quantitative studies of the incidence of collective action, of the kind carried out by C. Tilly and others (Shorter and Tilly 1974; Tilly and Tilly 1975) for France and other European countries in the nineteenth century. No such published studies exist at present for Britain. They could provide useful information about the geographical and occupational incidence of conflict.

Non-quantitative evidence underlines the influence of local experiences upon strike action. Hull, for example, was a fertile breeding ground for conflict. The main sources of employment were the docks, which were controlled by increasingly well-organised employers, hostile to unions and in control of the magistracy and the board of guardians (Saville 1974). In contrast, in parts of London, workers were scattered among a variety of occupations, often small in scale, with employers of variable views, who shared control of the community with professional people or even workers (Ryan 1978) who would not necessarily support employers against labour. In such areas there was less likelihood of outright confrontation.

Similar local differences can be seen in the outburst of strikes between 1906 and 1914. It would be surprising if the general growth of strikes in these years (see figure 7.3) was not associated with the decline in real wages. This decline was greatest *before* 1906, but the Taff Vale decision, which severely impeded strike action, remained in force until reversed by the Liberal Trade Disputes Act, 1906. The growth and militancy of trade unions after 1906 may have been partly a response to the removal of this restriction, which facilitated attempts to recoup earlier losses in real wages. However the extent and nature of the association between this phase of militancy and the fall in living standards has never been systematically established (Hobsbawm 1964a: 126–57). Most of the strikes of this period were for union recognition, an essential preliminary to effective demands for higher wages; most of the remainder directly for higher wages.

Industrial action after 1906 differed from that of previous times not only in extent, but 'in its high level of aggressive, sometimes violent and often unofficial industrial militancy' (Holton 1976: 73). But, once more, there were important local differences. In Hull, dock employers remained notably hostile to unionisation, and there was far more violence than in the Liverpool docks, where employers were conciliatory. The London Transport strike of 1912 followed the concession of higher wages and union bargaining rights to provincial transport workers after shorter and peaceful strikes in 1911. Only in London had transport employers resisted collective bargaining.

Local economic change, for example when leading to the migration of large numbers of new workers to old communities, could alter traditional relationships. The miners of South Wales showed unprecedented militancy in 1910. Their traditional response to falling real wages was to prefer non-violence and class harmony. In 1910 in parts of South Wales, they rioted, attacking the shops of tradesmen who had declared against them. Arguably, the large influx of new workers into the region since the 1890s had disrupted the traditional nonconformist culture and cultural controls, setting a new pattern which re-emerged in 1918 (Holton 1976: 78–88).

It is also important, however, that the South Wales miners were led by a new generation of trade union leaders, more radical than their predecessors. The influence of leaders, or of new theories such as that of syndicalism, are always difficult to assess. Syndicalism was the belief that the state could be overthrown by industrial action, to be replaced by a political system based upon workshop councils. Without doubt, Tom Mann, and other leaders influenced by syndicalism, aimed to encourage militancy. Equally obviously they could not have created a high level of activity had there been no sense of grievance and insecurity to sustain it. They may have opened the eyes of some workers to inequalities and hence increased the length and bitterness of some disputes, yet their influence remains difficult to estimate. Very many strikers experienced no discernible outside influence of this kind. Their actions were directed against local employers who refused to negotiate with the unions and left determined workers no alternative but to strike (Holton 1976). Most of the strikes of this period were for strictly industrial rather than political ends. Workers involved in strikes for higher pay or for union recognition did not necessarily support socialist politics. The coming of war put a temporary end to the strike wave, although it revived strongly in 1918 (Briggs & Saville 1971).

Women

Another important manifestation of conflict in the 1900s was the unusually high level of protest by women. The various forms of demand for equality by a minority of women were neither so widespread nor so violent as among trade unionists or as contemporaneous events in Ireland. The violent nature of the actions of the militant suffragists after 1909 is generally exaggerated. This is partly due to the colourful nature of such incidents as Emily Davison's suicide at the Derby of 1913, but more notably to the shocking and unprecedented fact of women involving themselves in such actions at all. The women posed no immediately serious threat to social order, as the militant workers did, but they were undoubtedly more militant than at any previous time.

The movement for female occupational, political, social and to a much lesser extent sexual emancipation is a persistent theme of this period: from the attempts of J. S. Mill and his supporters to extend the vote to women in 1867, to the activities of the suffragists after 1909. It emerges in the attempts of well-educated women to enter the professions; in middle-class women's demands for, and achievement of, some degree of legal right to their own incomes, of the right to obtain divorces in certain circumstances, and to some control of their own children (McGregor 1957), though in none of these situations were the rights of women equal to those of men by 1914. It appears also in the persistent demands of some women for the vote, rising to a crescendo in the 1900s; and in the equally persistent attempts to unionise working women and to involve them in politics. The growth of women's labour organisations was a feature of the rise of the labour movement. By 1900, the women's Labour League and the Women's Co-operative Guild were energetic campaigners for such social reforms as improved working-class housing, better care for mothers and babies, better health care for all women, and equal divorce rights, as well as for the vote (Llewelyn Davies 1977). There were probably more active and influential women in many spheres, including the writing of outstanding literature, in this period than at any previous time.

Nevertheless, women of all classes had excellent reason for protest. The changing structure of occupations closed some opportunities for working-class women, for example in agriculture. This period also saw the growth of abysmally paid sweated out-work, mainly in the clothing industry, especially in London. This was partially controlled by the Trades Boards Act of 1909, the result of much outcry.

Some improved occupational opportunities opened for working- and lower-middle-class women. In general, prospects improved for unmarried women, in terms of the wider range of jobs available to them. More of them had higher incomes and greater independence at an earlier age than before. Women made up 5 per cent of the clerical labour force in 1891, 11 per cent in 1901. Nevertheless this and similar expanding respectable occupations for women, such as nursing and shop work, offered lower pay and much poorer promotion prospects than equivalent male opportunities and despite these new, if limited, prospects, overwhelmingly the largest female occupation remained domestic service, employing c. 2 million women. This was not only low paid but highly restrictive; a high proportion of servants lived in (Davidoff 1974). Its unpopularity is suggested by the speed with which women left it when the war opened, for the first time, alternative job opportunities on a large scale. Occupations available to working-class women paid on average one third of the average male manual wage.

In contrast even to the limited improvements in the prospects of unmarried women, the lot of married women changed hardly at all. They still conventionally did not work, unless economic necessity forced them to. There were, however, many families poor enough to need the wife's economic contribution, occasionally or permanently, although the numbers are difficult to estimate. Most such wives took part-time work, as sweated out-workers, washerwomen or cleaners, which was rarely recorded in the census; less frequent was work in factories or workshops. When such women did work, the limitations upon their opportunities which were imposed by their family responsibilities exposed them to some of the severest exploitation discernible in this period.

The census of 1911, bearing its limitations in mind, showed 5.4 million women recorded as employed; 11.3 million as unoccupied. A few educated women crept into professions such as medicine or journalism, although not until 1919 were they allowed to enter the Law and the higher civil service.

The limited, ill-paid job – still less career – opportunities for women mattered because of the restrictions imposed upon women's opportunities to choose and to direct their futures or, in some cases, even to live in moderate comfort. Equally important, the surplus of women in the population, and the relatively high risk of widowhood, destroyed the opportunities for many women even to attempt to conform to the contemporary stereotype of the female role by spending their adult lives as wives and mothers. Poorer women without male support were forced to support themselves and their children in remarkably unfavourable conditions. Richer ones faced a bleak lack of alternatives to marriage.

The very large numbers of woman applying for the first civil service 'white-blouse' occupations, opened to them in the 1890s, suggests the size of the reservoir of unsatisfied female demand for alternative opportunities. Improved schooling for middle-class girls resulted from pressure for women's rights and further fuelled the women's movement. However, in the absence of any apparent shortage of labour in most occupations and the outright hostility to competition from female labour articulated by male workers at all levels, there was no strong pressure upon employers to take the unlikely step of employing even educated women in occupations traditionally closed to them.

Among the majority of women who did marry and were not widowed early in life, those in families with incomes above £300 p.a. lived in reasonable comfort and leisure, supported by servants. In the larger number of families with incomes of £100–£300 p.a., marriage was followed by an existence very different from the conventional stereotype of the life of the Victorian lady. Keeping house and caring for children, with few appliances and rarely more than one young servant, was hard and time-consuming (Branca 1975).

Women bore fewer children a little more safely by 1914 than in 1860, though most and most dangerously among the poorest. The nutritional standards of working-class women remained atrocious – below the standards of comparable men – but probably grew no worse (Oren 1974). The general concern about poverty increased awareness of the problems of poorer women, leading some philanthropic women, such as the prison reformer Mary Carpenter to the belief, by the 1870s, that such problems could only be solved when women had the vote and used their political power in the interests of their sisters (Manton 1976).

The vote was more than a symbol of the aims of the women's movement. It was seen by the 1900s, as it has long been seen by working men, as an essential means to the achievement of equality with the privileged and of wider opportunities in a variety of spheres. As more working men received the vote in 1867 and 1884, some educated women were affronted, others were stimulated to action by the examples of male working-class pressure, and of that of women overseas. The number of independent, educated 'new women', from middle- and lower-middle-class origins, working as journalists or teachers, was growing and was largest in London. Many such women were acutely aware of the absurdity of their exclusion from political rights, and provided much of the active core of the suffrage movement. They could not, however, command mass or even majority female support. Many women shared the male view that it was unseemly for women to vote or otherwise to compete with men. Many working-class women had worries enough and little spare time for agitation. Their deprivations were shared equally with their menfolk. Poor men did not have the vote, and there was little for anyone to gain from female competition in an already overstocked manual labour market. Hence the strong trade union opposition to improved job opportunities for those women with husbands to support them. Instead, they argued, men should be better paid to enable them to support their families unaided. There were ardent working-class feminists in the women's labour organisations, especially in areas where women convention-ally worked, such as Lancashire and East London and they had some active male supporters, such as Keir Hardie, but more better off women had the leisure to be single minded in pursuit of equality.

The most prominent, and eventually the most militant of the women's organisations was the Women's Social and Political Union (WSPU), founded in 1909. Its leading figure, Mrs Pankhurst, and her daughters were associated with the Independent Labour Party, and initially became interested in women's suffrage as an essential step towards full democracy, rather than primarily due to a wider interest in women's problems (Rosen 1974; D. R. Morgan 1975). In 1909 the Labour party was the only political party committed to adult franchise for men and women.

One major stumbling block to votes for women, in the eyes of the leaders of the other two parties, was the peculiar form of chivalry which regarded women as above participating in decisions concerning themselves. Equally important were questions as to the political consequences of a considerable extension of the franchise to a very large number of people whose political views were unknown, and as to the basis on which women could be granted the vote. All women could not be enfranchised whilst all men were not, and universal adult franchise was not on the immediate political agenda by 1914. The most widely proposed and increasingly politically acceptable compromise was the enfran-chisement of women on their own and their husband's property qualification, on the basis of the existing franchise legislation. This would have omitted many single women, who were among the most active suffragists. The second parliamentary Bill embodying such a measure failed only narrowly in 1912. The success of the women's movement had been to bring these issues to the forefront of politics by 1912. They had been of no discernible importance in the election of 1906.

The failure of the 1912 Bill increased WSPU militancy. Most of the well-known acts of violence by women and by the authorities belong to the period between 1912 and 1914 (Rosen 1974). The war brought militancy to an end: Mrs Pankhurst and her friends were praised for supporting the war effort. In 1918 adult franchise for men and women was widely supported and, at last, implemented. The vote was granted to all men over 21 and to all ex-servicemen, some of whom were under 21, but only to women over 30 who were householders or wives of householders. Hence the danger of a female majority of the electorate was temporarily averted. Women were not granted votes on the same terms as men until 1928.

Conclusion

By 1914 British society was, as regards culture and the experience of more pervasive state authority, more homogeneous than in 1860, with the exception of nationalist areas of Wales and Scotland. Some of its more severe social problems, of overcrowded polluted towns, unemployment and poverty were just beginning to be tackled seriously. Most of its population experienced rather more comfortable lives than in the past. It remained profoundly unequal, among social strata and among regions, as all societies at all times have been. A major change over the period was that very many subordinate members of society, workers (though not yet the very poor) and women, did not by 1914 so readily accept their subordination as the natural way of things, as most of them had done in 1860. Older forms of cultural control, for example through the influence of local squires and employers, had become less effective, although new controls exercised through state-managed education and welfare were developing to replace them. Differences in access to power had become sources of conflict, and were far from being resolved with the opening of the Great War. The war did not put an end to social conflict though it greatly changed the world in which it was fought.

10

Britain 1900-45: a survey

N. VON TUNZELMANN

The interwar world was one of insecurity: for the individual employee, for the individual firm, for the nation as a whole. Economic life was scarred by industrial turmoil, by waste and decay. Elsewhere, these forces could contribute to the rise of totalitarian regimes, as in Nazi Germany or Soviet Russia. In Britain, extremist ideologies of both left and right pressed their case. Electorally the country remained opposed to interventionism as a matter of dogma; but the economic needs of the moment were so pressing that, almost irrespective of political belief, the state was dragged into a wider-ranging economic commitment. The celebrated Macmillan Committee on Finance and Industry, reporting in June 1931, expressed such a view:

To this trust in the operation of natural causes [i.e. laissez faire] we owe the development of our great political, financial and social institutions and the amazing growth of our industrial activities. But we also owe to it in part many of our deficiencies, such as our industrial instability, our social maladjustments, our slums... In the case of our financial, as in the case of our political and social, institutions we may well have reached the stage when an era of conscious and deliberate management must succeed the era of undirected natural evolution [Parliamentary Papers 1930-31].

For the economic historian, the most profound theme sounded by Britain in the first half of the twentieth century is the rise of the managed economy: parallel in significance to the rise of industrial capitalism in the first volume of this book, and the maturing of industrial society in the earlier chapters of this volume. This chapter will trace out the interactions between economic trends and such advance as there was towards managed capitalism.

Problems of economic management first came to a head in the First World War. Before 1914 the economic role assigned to British governments comprised: (i) social policy and welfare, (ii) finance, and (iii) commercial relations with other countries. They were expected to be heard but not seen in production; even the apparently radical reforms of Asquith's Liberal administration after 1906 merely intensified governmental concern with (i) and (ii). Strident calls in 1914 to confront the war with 'business as usual' were, however, unavailing. Not that there was ever any intention of relying purely on market mechanisms (e.g. the government took over final responsibility for the railways on the declaration of war), but in the course of waging war the government was sucked into direct intervention. Through a 'command spiral' intervention by means of (say) price control in one market eventually dragged the authorities into related markets. At the time of the Armistice they had full control of land and sea transport; in agriculture they determined land utilisation, organised distribution, and fixed prices; both coal and iron mining were completely under their control; while factories and establishments directly managed by government employed over two million people, and not less than two thirds of the industrial workforce were subject to special wartime regulation.

Yet – contrary to the explicit intentions of the War Cabinet and the Ministry of Reconstruction (Johnson 1968) – the controls were frenetically disbanded by Lloyd George's government elected in 1919. A few such as rent control remained, many were undoubtedly irrelevant to peacetime conditions, but no discrimination was exercised over abandoning those that might have helped Lloyd George build his desired land 'fit for heroes to live in' (Tawney 1943). Nonetheless it is conceivable that the experiences of the war ultimately acted to encourage government involvement in economic life, especially in the 1930s (Milward 1970 sets out this debate). Above all, the level of government spending per head in constant prices was 80 to 100 per cent higher in the 1920s than in the years from 1900 to 1913, even after such war-related expenditures as war and widows' pensions are allowed for (Peacock & Wiseman 1961).

Quite apart from the destruction entailed in the fighting, the First World War created severe dislocation in both short and long term. Still, as a number of economic and social historians have recently emphasised, it is misleading to depict the British economy between the wars in unremittingly gloomy tones. Slump followed slump, yet the domestic economy did not stagnate entirely. After a short 'breathing space' in the immediate wake of the Armistice there came a spectacular re-stocking boom – a scramble for goods and working capital to replace materials exhausted by the war effort. The boom lasted from the spring of 1919 to that of 1920, before giving way to a deep and sustained slump as Britain was finally compelled to come to terms with the losses and dislocation arising out of the war.

The remaining years of the 1920s were ones of weak and unsteady boom, punctuated by events such as the General Strike in 1926. From the middle of 1929 the economy experienced severe and protracted depression: three years of mounting unemployment and declining activity before the first stirrings of revival in August 1932. Recovery from the Great Slump continued without a break until the final quarter of 1937; whereupon a twelve-month dip was succeeded by the last twelve months of peace. The course of boom and slump broadly followed that of the industrial world as a whole, though with very different amplitudes from peak to peak and peak to trough. The boom of the late 1920s for instance was much more restrained than in other industrialised countries (except Japan), and the ensuing downswing – partly in consequence – was also less violent.

For the first quarter of the twentieth century the growth rate of the British economy was abysmally low. From 1899 to 1924 the growth of net national product was barely 0.5 per cent per year, measured in constant prices. To a great degree the performance of the later years of this period is dominated by the upheavals arising out of the First World War, but slow growth is also evident in the first decade of the century – the years denoted as the 'Edwardian climacteric' by one economic historian (McCloskey 1970). Once the immediate after-effects of the Great War had been swallowed up in the 1921–23 slump, the growth of incomes recovered. Even though the 1929 peak was quite a modest one, net national product at 1938 factor cost had been growing at an average of 2.5 per cent a year since the preceding peak in 1924. Over the next ten years it was to grow at 2 per cent annually, despite the calamities of slump on the scale to be surveyed in the next chapter. Figures of 2 to $2\frac{1}{2}$ per cent typify the Britain of the mid and later Victorian period. Indeed, it is possible that, averaging again over upswing and downswing, the British economy has been growing at this pace since the early Industrial Revolution period; always excepting the 1899–1924 break. It is almost as if the range of 2 to $2\frac{1}{2}$ per cent per annum had been meted out to the British economy by divine grace – or, in the eyes of many critics, by divine retribution.

In another dimension, some writers have sought to redeem the interwar economy by comparisons with the growth rates of other industrial countries over the same years. For many of them the data are much less reliable, though, than for the UK. Even were this no problem the fundamental usefulness of comparisons with other countries – or for that matter with other periods in British history – when so many factors must be supposed to vary, remains in question.

Rather than airily treating interwar growth as satisfactory, therefore, this chapter will analyse it component by component. The ideal would be to measure the attainment by comparison with full potential – especially the potential that might have been reached by more enlightened economic management. In this way, the traditional background of interwar waste and decay is brought to the forefront. Economic historians are beginning to approach this ideal (see chapter 14); the limited advance undertaken in this chapter is to relate levels of demand to the potentials of supply.

Supply factors

Labour supply

Consider first supply, and first of all the supply of labour. Four major determinants of the supply of labour to manufacturing in interwar Britain must be considered: (i) the growth of population and changes in its age-structure; (ii) its participation-rate (the proportion of the population who are part of the labour force); (iii) the amount of labour engaged in occupations other than manufacturing; (iv) migration. If the supply of labour was limited by changes in any one of these determinants, then this could have led to a reduction in the natural rate of growth; in fact, none constrained growth.

(i) Population growth rates fell to less than half those which had been experienced in the 1860–1914 period. The loss of lives in the First World War bears some part of the responsibility; three quarters of a million British and Irish were 'left hanging on the wire'; one hundred and sixty thousand perished in the influenza epidemic of late 1918. Demographically speaking, however, the short-run effects of war made little difference to the long-run trends (Winter 1977). The decline of death rates achieved in the late nineteenth and early twentieth centuries flattened out, but birth rates continued to drop in the interwar years, apart from a brief burst, when servicemen returned from the trenches, in 1919–20 (see chapter 7 for a fuller analysis). Seen over the very long term, these patterns might be interpreted as the final stages of the 'demographic transition', i.e. the phase in which birth rates fall to approximate equality with death rates, the latter having been reduced by modern medical knowledge and widespread public health measures. On the other hand, one cannot rule out the possibility that economic factors such as high unemployment speeded up this phase of the transition in Britain.

The results of these demographic changes in the age-structure of the population merit special attention. W. B. Reddaway's book, *The Economics of a Declining Population* (1938) epitomised contemporary attitudes; there is no evidence that population did actually decline in any year from 1919 to 1940, yet at the time Reddaway wrote the number of school-age children (i.e. 5 to 14 years) was smaller than the number of young workers (i.e. 15 to 24 years), whilst the latter in turn were smaller than the number of potential parents (25 to 34 years of age). In the early part of our period, these factors had produced a bulge in the proportion of population of working age, thus exacerbating unemployment. One of the consequences of this bulge was a rise in the marriage rate, which itself led to a high rate of family formation – even though the falling birth rates meant that the size of the average family fell sharply. It has, for instance, been estimated that between 1911 and 1939 the number of families in Great Britain rose some 40 per cent, although total population rose only 14 per cent (Abrams 1945). Trends in family formation affected demand, especially for housing. In general, the British were getting older – the whole of the increase in population between 1911 and 1938 lay in the over-45 age-group, as those under 45 years actually fell slightly. Fears of secular stagnation of population were understandably rife in the late 1930s.

(ii) At a conservative estimate, five million people enlisted or were conscripted into the armed services during the Great War at a time when the total male work force numbered about thirteen millions. The home fires could be kept burning only by drafting in hitherto untapped labour resources, amongst whom the most conspicuous were women and girls. This provoked antagonism to 'labour dilution' among some of the organised sections of the labour movement. As the trade unions were hamstrung by a patriotic pledge not to strike, the initiative passed to the individual shop floors and to the shop stewards who ralled them – with enduring effects on British industrial relations.

Despite the enthusiasm for women workers voiced by many employers during the war, most of the female workforce specifically recruited melted away soon after the Armistice, with ex-servicemen given priority for what employment there was. Traditionalist elements in the labour movement gained a further significant victory. In the re-stocking boom of 1919–20 – a boom known in labour history as the 'labour offensive' – the number of hours worked was shortened by about five a week (around 13 per cent) for unionised workers, bringing in the eight-hour day across the board. Moreover, this gain proved a lasting one, except for the coal-miners in the aftermath of their 1926 strike. Dowie (1975) considered this reduction an important factor on the supply side constraining the ability of the British to compete internationally after 1919, by arguing that hourly productivity rose insufficiently to affect this. His analysis neglects, however, the replacement of women and children by the returned servicemen, who may have been more productive. Bienefeld (in a rare application of economic theory to labour history, 1972) has contended that unions in general strongly press for reduced working hours even at the cost of higher wages they might attain because of an overriding dread of unemployment. To shorten hours shares the cake (the available work) around a larger number of union members. Paradoxically the unions can have this policy accepted only in periods of exceptionally full employment, when it is unnecessary. Bienefeld's study, however, ignores productivity changes altogether. Whatever the details, however, it seems likely that for these reasons participation fell after 1918.

(iii) Kaldor (1966) has attempted to show that the availability or scarcity of manpower to manufacturing industry was the strategic variable – in his case, for dictating Britain's relatively slow rate of economic growth after 1945. He saw declining employment in primary production as the key to this labour supply.

Employment in agriculture has been falling in absolute amounts since the middle of the nineteenth century; if wartime influences operating during the 1940s are excluded, this shedding of labour by agriculture has continued unabated up to the 1970s at least. Agriculture released on average some 18 200 men and women a year between 1920 and 1938 (calculated from figures in Chapman & Knight 1953), compared with 7700 annually between the censuses of 1851 and 1911. The reduction in primary production as a whole, including agriculture, has been still more significant since the First World War, mainly because of the troubles of the coal industry – 42 700 fewer employed each year 1920–38 (compared with an annual gain of 7000, 1851–1911).

Kaldor's view that the British economy suffered from premature 'maturity' (1966: 31), in the sense that a labour surplus from primary production had been largely eliminated by the time of the Second World War, therefore appears difficult to accept. If one excludes the immediate post-1918 upheavals, one finds that in relative terms the most pronounced increase in employment was in the tertiary sector – services rose from about 32 per cent of total employment in the early 1920s to 37 per cent by 1939. Some of this increase will have been dead-end jobs as delivery boys and the like, much commented upon by the socially-concerned; as George Orwell (1937) remarked with grim-faced pity of newspaper canvassers, 'Their job seems to me so hopeless, so appalling, that I wondered how anyone could put up with such a thing when prison was a possible alternative.' It seems likely that, through advances such as mechanisation in farming and mining, the primary sector could have churned out whatever labour the manufacturers required, and that the service sector could also have shed labour. This view gains further credence from year-by-year considerations of sectoral employment. Agricultural employment fell much less than total employment in years of depression, i.e. the agricultural labourers held off moving into towns until the prospects for getting a job there were much better. Underemployment was thereby intensified: labour was not in tight supply.

(iv) Migration from rural to urban areas was one flow; another was migration to other countries. The high rates of emigration that had characterised depression conditions in Britain throughout the nineteenth century were less in evidence between the wars; indeed there was a substantial net inflow of migrants into Britain in the 1930s. The 'push' and 'pull' factors operative in the previous century were to some extent reversed. Barriers were raised against immigration into most of the important 'regions of recent settlement'. British foreign investment, once prominent in creating employment opportunities for Britons overseas, fell off in the inter-war years, as shown in table 10.1. The depression was much more severe, relatively speaking, in the recipient primary-producing countries than in Great Britain. Last, there were some 'push' effects directing people towards Britain, e.g. Central European refugees from Hitler.

In sum, notwithstanding the slowing down of population growth and factors which operated to lower its participation in the workforce, the growth of the labour force was no supply constraint on growth. This view is underlined by the phenomenally high unemployment of labour of these years – over one million out of work, even excluding temporary stoppages, in every year from 1921 on.

Internal migration

These conclusions, however, are too aggregative to prove conclusively that manufacturing industry found it easy to come by the labour supply it needed. Such job opportunities as there were in the 1920s and 1930s were overwhelmingly clustered in the south-east and Midlands regions of England; the areas whose fashionable title was 'Inner Britain'. Greater London alone accounted for five sixths of the net increase in the number of factories over the number of factory closures during the recovery from slump between 1932 and 1937, and for one third of all recorded extensions to factories in those years, in spite of having only one fifth of total population. Other conurbations, principally Birmingham, took the bulk of the rest of what was a fairly small net increase. In the north-west and north-east of England and in Scotland more factories closed than opened during the recovery. 'Outer Britain' therefore saw not only higher unemployment rates but, as chapter 11 indicates, much higher proportions of the hard-core, long-term unemployed. This had effects on the labour supply in those regions. The Parliamentary Investigator into the Industrial Conditions in Durham and Tyneside in 1933–34 noted that,

Instances occur of men who have been out of employment for long periods being unable to stand the return to work. They find new conditions obtaining in the shops, they themselves are lacking in confidence and vitality, and as a result they throw up the job, often after only a few hours, although an increase in earnings means everything to them [Parliamentary Papers 1933–34].

Singer (1940) expressed the same point more vividly, when he emphasised that people could not be thought of as deep-frozen, and ready to be served up afresh on the labour market when at long last demand revived.

Why did the demand for labour revive to differing degrees in different areas? The pattern of industrial location is widely agreed to have been the chief determinant. The great export staples such as coal, iron and steel, shipbuilding, and textiles, had underpinned the prosperity of the northern and western regions in which they were most highly concentrated in the nineteenth century, and by so doing enriched the UK as a whole. The vulnerability of a country heavily dependent on exports of a comparatively small range of products was to become apparent only in the present century.

What in turn dictated the fortunes of different industries; was it demand factors, for which suffering industries cannot necessarily be blamed, or was it supply factors, suggesting that those industries could have done more to adapt themselves to changing fortunes? Booth and Glynn (1975), like many other historians, have argued that interwar employment was essentially regional, the product of a maldistribution of industry in relation to the resources available. This is, by implication, an argument of deficiencies in supply; it is important because, if it is true, Keynesian policies of demand management would have done little to cope with unemployment, since regional disparities would not have been alleviated, and might even have been exacerbated. However, Booth and Glynn offer no formal proof of their hypothesis, which is indeed difficult to test. One possible method might be to hypothesise an increase in aggregate demand, and then to assess its effects on the regions, but this would require an elaborate national and regional model.

It will be presumed here that that hypothetical increase in aggregate demand has been assessed so that the question becomes one of the response of the individual regions to it. In the absence of that elaborate model, the question will be approached back to front, by asking what it was that determined the location of existing industries. That is to say, were industries distributed among the regions according to general supply considerations, so as to maximise the benefit of the various advantages possessed by each (especially access to labour and capital resources)? If so, then increases in aggregate demand may have been helpless to secure higher employment in the less well-off areas.

Scrutiny of the 1935 Census of Production fails to support any general theory of industrial location according to regional differences. First, it might be argued that regions should specialise in industries for which the region has *comparatively* high labour productivity (i.e. relative to the same industries operating in other regions – this is the classical or Ricardian theory). Though most regions were indeed specialising in this way, the two most thriving areas – Greater London and the Midlands – conspicuously were not. This suggests that classical specialisation was not the way to success. Alternatively, one might argue that regions should specialise in industries which best suit their relative factor endowments; that is, a region where capital is cheaper relative to the cost of labour than in another region should attract capital-intensive industries, and vice versa (this is the Heckscher–Ohlin theory). There was little evidence in 1935 for such a pattern: by and large the harried districts of 'Outer Britain' had more capital-intensive industries than 'Inner Britain'; though it is customary to think of the former as having high capital costs (see next section) and low labour costs relative to the latter. More generally, it can be observed from the same source that few areas showed the behaviour believed by some historians of concentrating on low-productivity industries, even in 'Outer Britain'.

As a result, none of the orthodox supply-side arguments seem to explain the distribution of industries by region very well. If this is so, then higher levels of demand were unlikely to run up against general barriers of supply (e.g. low-productivity labour) or high capital costs in any important way. This is not to say, of course, that supply factors can be neglected. On the contrary, the very suggestion that at the point of time our snapshot of regional production is taken (1935) resources were not allocated as efficiently among the regions as they might ideally have been can be interpreted as a supply deficiency. Specific factors of supply like the spread of electric power and the improvement of road transport were helping industry to be more mobile, but what was happening was that much of the industry was being helped to migrate to areas of high *demand* (albeit to the suburbia and exurbia of London rather than the city centre).

Demand factors should on these grounds be emphasised at the expense of the supply-side regional characteristics entertained by Booth and Glynn. This is nowhere more evident than in the old export staples. Though Britain's share in world trade in these export staples had been falling before 1914, confidence did not appear shattered on the eve of the First World War, and the war itself (with its needs for munitions, ships, fuel, uniforms and so forth) gave the staples the illusion of life. Profits were easy, employment was bountiful, and expansion without improvement of technique or expansion of foreign markets rendered artificially simple. The collapse of the re-stocking boom in mid-1920 extinguished those hopes. Thereafter decline of the staple exports was erratic but inexorable.

Two aspects of domestic (as distinct from export) demand are worth noting. First, some of the old staples were heavy industries which produced durable capital goods. Any decline in demand for consumer goods had greatly amplified consequences in the short run for these capital-goods industries, since investment in all industries would fall much faster than output (the phenomenon known to the economist as the 'accelerator'). For instance, unemployment rose from 10.4 per cent of the insured British labour force in 1929 to 22.1 per cent in 1932 (see chapter 11). In the shipbuilding industry alone, by contrast, unemployment rose from 21 per cent in 1929 to no less than 62 per cent in 1932; similarly unemployment rates in the pig iron industry rose from 9.5 per cent to 46.7 per cent over the same three years. Second, the jobs arising from the pay packets of those employed in the prospering trades were mainly in the south and east. In consequence the service sector and even the less buoyant industries enjoyed lower unemployment rates in the south (chapter 11).

The natural reaction was for people to move from Outer to Inner Britain in search of jobs – Wales was estimated to be losing 3.3 per cent of its population annually through emigration alone in the mid 1930s. Industrial firms did not move physically to the same degree. According to J. H. Jones (Parliamentary Papers 1939–40) the springs of industrial growth lay in sectors long concentrated in Inner Britain. London had had the lion's share of the market for cables, for example, since the 1830s. Outer Britain actually gained a marginally larger slice of the expanding industries in the interwar period, but this was insufficient to offset the growing industrial inequality caused by the loss of contracting industries. The proportion of net industrial output which was contributed by the areas officially designated as 'old industrial' and 'new industrial' (the latter primarily London and the West Midlands) at censal years was as follows:

	1924	1935
'Old Industrial Areas'	49.6%	37.6%
'New Industrial Areas'	28.7%	37.0%

The familiar division between Inner and Outer Britain dated only from the First World War. Before 1914, the North and Celtic fringe were almost certainly the more prosperous. To take only one extreme example, unemployment in the Welsh town of Merthyr was 1.4 per cent of its labour force in 1913, whilst even at the cyclical peak of 1937 it was as much as 41.6 per cent of the town. The very abruptness of the turn-around between Outer and Inner Britain, coupled with its intensity, helps account for the length of the shadow cast over interwar Britain.

Capital

The study of migration has perforce had to touch upon the migration of capital. Chapter 4 considered the argument that in the late nineteenth century there were limitations on the mobility of capital funds within the country: whether the lines of contact between the capital markets in the south-east and the industrial producers of Outer Britain were adequate. After 1918 the capital market may have been better equipped to supply them with funds, but the needs of the old staples were in some respects less pressing. Even before the onset of the Slump in 1929, the shipbuilding industry was believed to be operating at not more than half its total capacity; cotton likewise at under three quarters of capacity (Balfour Committee 1927–28). In the same manner, the coal industry was said to be capable of raising half as much coal again as it could sell at lucrative prices. As depression struck, demand dropped catastrophically. With their backs to the wall, the staple industries entered into formal arrangements to restrict competition, by international cartels, pools, mergers, or 'gentlemen's agreements'. If they did not collude by themselves, as in the case of coal mining where the competitive blood-lust refused to be easily quelled, Parliament stepped in and tried to do it for them. In several of the decaying export staples, the cartels were notoriously better at gunning down the lame ducks than replacing them with up-to-date equipment (the actions of the National Shipbuilders Securities Ltd in prohibiting modernisation in shipyards at Jarrow on Tyneside led directly to the celebrated Jarrow Crusade of 1936). In general, it may be doubted whether the shutting down of idle plant was taken far enough to reduce the degree of excess capacity in these trades.

On the other hand, there existed a range of industries in the 1920s and 1930s with vastly more attractive market prospects. Some of the classic 'new industries', such as motor vehicles and chemicals, were dominated by large-scale firms that were probably well catered for in their appeal to a wide segment of investors. However, a huge number of small private firms in many industrial spheres only slowly escaped the eighteenth-century kind of dependence on friends and acquaintances for their capital requirements. The Macmillan Committee spoke of a gap (ever since known as the 'Macmillan Gap') in the structure of the organised capital market, with few channels open to the small firm. It was sometimes claimed that firms diversifying into new products in Outer Britain had a particularly difficult time in raising finance, because of the increasing centralisation of banking in London.

At the macroeconomic level, the outcome of alleged defects in the supply of capital and weaknesses in the demand for investment can be observed. It is a

Table 10.1. *Proportions of capital formation to national income, in gross terms, 1900–59, by decade* (%)

	1900–09	1920–29	1930–38	1950–59
Gross capital formation/GNP	13.3	12.0	10.5	18.0
Gross domestic capital formation/GNP	8·9	9.9	11.1	17.4
Gross foreign investment/GNP	4.4	2.1	−0·6	0.6
Residential dwellings/GNP	1.5	2.3	3.4	3.4

Source: Feinstein (1965: 36)

commonplace to argue that Britain's poor growth record since the Second World War owes at least something to its low rate of investment to national income (see chapter 16 for a critique). If so, then the country ought to have been much further restricted (other things being equal) by failing to invest not nearly so large a proportion of its income between the wars, as the summary of Feinstein's data in table 10.1 suggests. The first line of that table shows that gross capital accumulation by British investors, at home and abroad, was proportionately lower in the interwar period than either before the First World War or after the Second World War. The question is whether the supply of savings or the demand for investment was at fault. This may appear at first sight to be an arcane theoretical question, but on the contrary it is crucial to the most important debate in policy-making in the period. On one side stood the 'Treasury View', expressed to the International Labour Organisation in 1927 as follows: 'The decision taken by the government at the end of 1925 to restrict grants for relief schemes was based mainly on the view that, *the supply of capital in this country being limited*, it was undesirable to divert any appreciable proportion of this supply from normal trade channels.' Government expenditure to prime the pump would in this view merely 'crowd out' private investment. The return to modest respectability of the crowding-out hypothesis in the 1970s, in which public expenditure is seen as crowding out investment that would otherwise have been undertaken by private capitalists, e.g. by forcing up interest rates, may yet give the 'Treasury View' a new lease of life in histories of interwar Britain. At the same time the requirements for *complete* crowding-out, such as the Treasury seems to have verged on believing was true for the Britain of the late 1920s and early 1930s, are exceedingly stringent. Above all, they include the assumption of perfect certainty, while the world described in this chapter was one of anything but perfect certainty.

Ranged against the Treasury View was the argument of Keynes' *General*

Theory, although this was not fully articulated until its publication in 1936. 'Keynes's intellectual revolution was to shift economists from thinking normally in terms of a model of reality in which a dog called *savings* wagged his tail labelled *investment* to thinking in terms of a model in which a dog called *investment* wagged his tail labelled *savings*' (J. E. Meade, in M. Keynes 1975: 82). In decisions to invest, the expectations of businessmen were central – the confidence or lack of it they exuded, their uncertainties and their insecurities, in sum their 'animal spirits'.

It is possible to give indirect support to the Keynesian interpretation. Chapter 4 above examined savings behaviour and comes down strongly on the side of an inadequate demand for investment, pointing out that the sudden expansion of government spending in the Boer War went with a rise in rates of investment. There was a significant and negative correlation between annual changes in government expenditure and in private investment between 1898 and 1950, which might suggest some degree of crowding-out; though it could also reflect government responding to shortfalls in private investment. More to the point, there was also a significant and positive correlation between annual changes in government spending and in *all* investment (public and private) over the same years, showing that crowding-out was far short of absolute. Edelstein's equations can be used to show that savings in the interwar period were 12 to 15 per cent lower than in equivalent circumstances before 1914 (Edelstein 1977).

If the deficiency in investment demand can be accepted, it would clarify matters to know its sources. The second line of table 10.1 shows that, in fact, capital formation in domestic activities was greater in the 1920s and 1930s than before 1914. One might explain this by a fortuitous fall in investment abroad, freeing funds for investment at home. This, however, is not enough to prove causation. The City of London strove to recapture its prewar domination of world financial and capital markets partly through the restoration of long-term overseas lending. For reasons developed in chapter 12 its success was incomplete. As will be shown below, the exigencies of protecting Britain's exchange reserves frequently caused the financial authorities to put pressure on investors not to lend abroad – a policy that had some successes to its credit. As table 10.1 indicates, the 1930s actually saw a net inflow of funds into Britain, matching the net inflow of population described earlier.

The investment figures employed so far have been measured in gross terms, that is they include both new capital and replacements. Up to the degree of accuracy of the procedures of estimation, they reflect flows of new plant, equipment, stocks, and similar physical assets. However useful gross capital formation may be as an indication of the alertness of the economy to new investment opportunities, in assessing the productive potential of the older as well as the new spheres of activity, it is desirable to know how far the capital stock of previous generations has been run down. The series on net capital formation thus make allowances for wear and tear, obsolescence, and accidental damage. Comparing gross with net investment brings out the weaknesses of the interwar economy starkly. No less than 80 per cent of the gross fixed capital formation in plant and equipment alone was absorbed by mere replacement (Feinstein 1965: 51). Going beyond plant and equipment to capital formation of all kinds, net capital formation (the non-replacement portion) constituted but 29 per cent of the gross figure. (Since the Second World War about one half of gross investment – i.e. a half of the higher gross estimate given in table 10.1 – has been net investment.) Of this desperately low level of net capital accumulation between the wars, some 70 per cent was in the form of residential dwellings. This percentage captures the reason why economic historians have customarily placed so great an emphasis on housebuilding as a mainspring for interwar economic growth; a point that will be discussed further in chapter 13. If attention at this moment is limited simply to the contribution to capital formation, it may be objected that the large share of dwellings in net capital formation is only to be expected in view of their very long useful lives compared to, say, machinery. The ratio of investment in dwellings to capital formation where both are measured in gross terms is therefore substantially lower – compare the first and fourth lines of table 10.1. If instead, though, we relate the fourth line of that table to the *second* (gross *domestic* capital formation) and pursue it decade by decade, we find that virtually the whole of the increase in gross domestic investment to GNP between the 1900s and the 1930s comes from the increase in the ratio of dwellings to GNP shown in the final line.

The ' Residual'

It follows from the discussion of labour and capital supply that economic historians have been right to look away from the supply of the real factor inputs in explaining British interwar growth rates – from labour because of its ready availability (in aggregate) and from capital because the supply constraints seem weaker than demand constraints. According to Matthews, employment of labour and the productivity of the labour employed both grew at a little over one per cent per annum from 1924 to 1937 (Aldcroft & Fearon 1969: 81). How much of the 1.1 per cent annual increase in labour productivity is the result of having more machinery for each employee to work with, and how much from his having *better* machinery? The question is by now a familiar one. In gross terms, capital per man rose at the rate of 0.2 per cent per annum (net capital per labourer actually fell). If growth can be decomposed in a straightforward way into these components – a proposition that is supported by some economists but strongly rejected by others – then the remaining 'residual' component accounts for some 0.9 percentage points of the annual 2.3 per cent growth rate. If the procedure is accepted, one can try to allocate this rise in overall efficiency ('total factor productivity', i.e. the efficiency of all factor inputs taken conjointly) among the leading causes, the quality of the labour force, economies of scale, and technological changes.

Quality of the labour force. Unemployment meant that the actual labour force could differ in composition from the potential. The unskilled were always most affected by unemployment in both relative and absolute quantities. Yet painstaking craftsmanship on the nineteenth-century pattern was in little demand – partly because many of the crafts had been established in the now decaying staple industries of iron, cotton, and coal. The most active needs of interwar Britain were for intermediate skills of the machine-minding type. Astonishingly, despite the extraordinarily high unemployment in coal mining, people of this kind had to be imported into the mining regions when mechanical coal-cutters were substituted for hand methods (Singer 1940).

Direct government measures to retrain the unemployed for the new challenges were undertaken, but only with a pitifully small budget, and too often in the 'new industrial areas', where trainees were much in demand but by the same token unemployment was relatively small. Indirect measures included technical schooling. The Balfour Committee noted that full-time junior schools providing technical education had only about 12 000 pupils enrolled in 1927, although another 820 000 were taking part-time classes of technical instruction. More generally, between 5 and 15 per cent of the pupils of elementary (primary) schools in most towns in England went on to secondary education – by comparison, the Department of Education estimated that some 75 per cent could have benefited from secondary education.

A more direct estimate of changes in the quality of the interwar labour force is that given by Matthews (Aldcroft & Fearon 1969: 92–5). Here, the growth rates of labour in the various industrial groups are adjusted by differences in earnings among the groupings, as a rough measure of quality differentials. The adjusted growth rates are considerably larger than the unadjusted ones for industrial production generally. The declining labour force in textiles, traditionally employing a high proportion of low-wage female labour, contributed notably to this rise in 'quality'. On the other hand, there was a slight fall in labour quality in services and distribution, reflecting the rush of the unemployed into newspaper canvassing and the like. On the basis of a more detailed sample of manufacturing industries, however, Salter (1966: 128–30) claimed that differences in labour quality failed to explain the differences he observed in productivity achievements among those industries.

Economies of scale. Concentration of resources in the larger industrial firms went ahead erratically during the period. At the time of the Census of Production in 1935, nearly one half of the labour force was to be found in firms employing 500 or more workers. The simplest index of concentration to understand is the share of the hundred largest firms in manufacturing net output. Hannah's figures (1976: 216) show this share rising from about 15 per cent in 1909 to 26 per cent by 1930, then dwindling gradually in the 1930s and 1940s (since the mid 1950s concentration has again proceeded apace). The causes of this pattern are studied at length by Hannah; here the concern is with its consequences, which will be developed further in chapter 13.

The effects of industrial combination on efficiency are an open question. At best, the two were equated, as by the proponents of 'rationalisation'. Obsolete plant could be scrapped and replaced by the advanced; there could be specialisation of functions and unification of management. At worst – as with the National Shipbuilders' Security Ltd – only the negative was accentuated and the positive ignored. On balance, it is difficult to avoid the conclusion that for successful rationalisation, the typical 1930s response of loose, terminable associations fell far short of the minimum necessary degree of reorganisation. Hannah (1974) has put the point in the context of postwar interpretations of the theory of the firm. Diseconomies of managerial scale that arose through growing like Topsy inhibited not the *size* but the *rate of growth* of firms. Mergers taken in comparatively small steps and properly digested by creating rational divisions of authority and patterns of command could be highly successful; otherwise the merger was likely to be unsuccessful. Prais (1976) examined the years since the mid 1930s in detail, and concluded that economies of scale in the conventional sense were unimportant in increasing centralisation, primarily because the share of the hundred largest *plants* (as opposed to *firms*) did not expand appreciably. Differences in marketing arrangements, e.g. transportation and advertising, played a detectable role but probably a supporting one. Financial factors were much the most significant.

Technical progress. Little work has yet been done on process innovation in the first half of this century; for the interwar period attention has been rivetted upon product innovation in the light of changes in industrial structure. Recent re-statements of the view that structural shifts were responsible for the fact that growth rates were not abnormally low between the wars began by compounding these two aspects of innovation. Richardson (1962; reprinted Aldcroft & Richardson, 1969: 225) wrote that, 'An examination of the new industries reveals that these technical advances were too ubiquitous to be ignored and were also, to a large extent, concentrated in the new industries to the exclusion of others.' 'More arithmetic' by Dowie (1968) questioned this hypothesis, and recent opinion, of Richardson as well as Dowie, is that most industries, old and new, shared in the technical advances. It is conceivable, however, that a sharper focus on process innovation would re-establish a crucial role for technical progress in economic growth at this time.

Full treatment of the role of the new industries is reserved for chapter 13, but it is again evident that (as with labour and capital) constraints from the side of the supply of technological changes can hardly have been binding. It is indeed normally assumed, even if exaggeratedly, that entrepreneurs in interwar Britain faced shelves full of up-to-date methods on which they could have drawn if demand conditions had been more favourable.

Aggregate demand

Since the publication of Keynes' *The General Theory of Employment, Interest, and Money* in 1936, it has been conventional to ascribe the weaknesses of the interwar British economy (and those of many other countries) to deficiencies of aggregate demand. The subject is so important that it is given a separate chapter (chapter 14). The findings of that chapter support the interpretation of interwar Britain as an essentially 'Keynesian' economy – i.e. an economy in the grips of chronic unemployment, as envisaged by Keynes – with the reservation that implementation of the policies advocated by Keynes himself in 1929 would only have scratched the surface of the problem (compare also chapter 11).

The distribution of income and wealth

A full analysis of determinants of demand is presented in chapter 14; the present chapter looks further into changes in the distribution of income and wealth in the period as these may have affected the pattern of spending. That is, relative shifts of income towards wages and away from profits would be expected to result in an increase in the share of consumption in incomes, for example. Considering first incomes from employment (Feinstein 1972: table 21) we find that wages constituted much the same share of GNP between the wars as over the years 1870–1914 – about 41 per cent on average. However salaries rose from being about $7\frac{1}{2}$ per cent of GNP in the 1870s to about $18\frac{1}{2}$ per cent in the 1930s; a rise of two and a half times the proportion of GNP. From Keynesian theory one would expect the proportionate shift from wages to salaries to have lowered the aggregate demand for consumer goods, other things being equal. The plausibility of this inference gains ground by further observing that wages were falling as a share of GNP during the years of slow growth from 1899 to 1913, and that their share rose rapidly (to nearly 50 per cent of GNP) during the wartime inflation between 1914 and 1918; whilst salaries showed the opposite tendency. Moreover, historians seem agreed that there was considerable levelling *within* the class of wage incomes as a whole in the course of the First World War, as skill differentials narrowed and some of the worst poverty was alleviated (Bowley 1930; Milward 1970).

That there are no simple conclusions to be drawn is shown by the rising share of salaries being matched by declining shares for income and self-employment and for rent (Feinstein 1972: table 1). Just as wage incomes levelled out in the war so, it appears, did non-wage incomes – for instance much of the landed wealth possessed in Edwardian times by the fictional Forsytes disappeared in or after the war.

The burden of taxation on differing socioeconomic groups was widely discussed in the interwar years. The working classes met a high proportion of the regressive 'indirect' taxes, levied primarily on necessities, whilst the upper income classes paid a relatively high proportion of the direct taxes, levied on land and income. The lower middle class altogether got off lightly (Hicks 1938). Before the First World War, taxation as a whole was actually regressive: the working classes paid more tax than they received in benefits by way of public expenditure (Barna 1945; Clark 1937). Much increased direct taxation during the war and the need to pay extensive unemployment benefits thereafter reversed this between the wars: by 1938 Barna estimated that the pre-tax share of 56 per cent of personal income going to the working classes was raised to about 62 per cent post-tax.

The thesis that resilience and even some increase in real wage earnings for the employed helped limit the severity of the slump in Britain as compared with that in the United States, through effects on demand, has enjoyed some popularity (e.g. Richardson 1967). In his famous sequence of surveys of all the working-class population of York, Rowntree (1901, 1941) found that the proportion of absolute ('primary') poverty caused by low wages fell from 52 per cent of cases in 1899 to just 9 per cent in 1936. At the same time, one must recognise the deprivation arising out of mass unemployment – in Rowntree's surveys unemployment and irregularity of work caused 5 per cent of the primary poverty in 1899 and over 50 per cent in 1936. Nor should the improvement of real wages be overstated – the average growth rate of under 1 per cent per annum for the 1920s and again in the 1930s was less than half as fast as that of real wages in the late nineteenth century, and less than half as fast as that of real output or labour productivity between the wars.

The broad divisions between wages and non-wage incomes, and between the employed and the unemployed, are suggestive but no more. More highly disaggregated figures on income distribution are unfortunately hard to obtain, because the government abandoned the collection of suitable data as part of its economy drive in 1920, and no further official data are available until 1937–38. It seems likely from wage trends and other indications that much of that increase in equality took place in the middle and later 1930s.

On the other hand, and this is particularly important because of its possible impact on savings and investment, while the distribution of wealth is always substantially more unequal than that of income, this was exceptionally true of Britain before the Second World War (Barna 1945).

Table 10.2. *Quinquennial averages of major elements of the balance of payments, in current prices (£ million p.a.)*

	1920–24	1934–38
1. Exports and re-exports	1060	541
2. Imports	−1194	−798
3. Balance of visible trade	−134	−257
4. Net invisible income	312	221
5. Balance on current account	+178	−36
6. Long-term capital movements	−139	−1
7. Additions to official reserves	−13	−32
8. Other equilibrating movements	−26	+70

Source: Ware (1974)

The external sector

In the short run, it was foreign trade that dragged Britain into a slump (Corner 1956). To those in authority after 1918 it was axiomatic that Britain's prosperity before the First World War had been due to its adherence to free trade and the international Gold Standard. Sometimes the two were thought to be interconnected, though there was no necessary reason for them to be so. This prevalent mood of economic internationalism could be justified on several grounds. Regrettably, it ran counter to the dominant spirit elsewhere, a spirit making for protectionism and self-sufficiency in trade. Britain, and 'Outer Britain' especially, had reason to fear these trends.

Britain's international deficiencies in the interwar world can best be emphasised by examining the country's own balance of payments. In table 10.2 are shown annual averages of some strategic aspects of the balance of payments, where the averages are measured in money terms.

The decline in British exports – a compound, naturally, of supply and demand influences – shown in the first line of the table paved the way for a deterioration of the visible balance of trade (line 3), because Britain remained largely dependent on imports for many necessities. Although the prices of imports fell relative to the prices of exports, the gain to Britain was illusory; the income of countries supplying food and raw materials to Britain was seriously reduced, with the result that the volumes of British exports and hence employment in export industries fell very sharply (these volume figures do not appear in table 10.2). In the early 1920s, the negative balance of visible trade was turned into a positive balance of payments on current account (line 5) by returns from overseas investments, insurance and shipping services, etc., even though the waging of war had compelled some sacrifice of these invisible items (see chapter 12). The positive current account balance in turn allowed Britain more often than not to lend long-term development capital funds, especially to the primary-producing countries of the empire (line 6). Already, however, there were years in which Britain's ability to balance its external accounts was sufficiently in doubt as to jeopardise this long-term foreign lending.

By the mid 1930s, invisible earnings were no longer great enough to cover the larger deficit on visible trade. Consequently, the current account deficit had to be offset by running a surplus on capital account. Recall from table 10.1 that, for the decade of the 1930s as a whole, there was a net inflow of foreign investment amounting to 0.6 per cent of current national income. First, long-term foreign lending virtually ceased. Second, the current account deficit was mainly financed by short-term capital imports of various kinds, listed generically under 'other equilibrating movements' in line 8 of table 10.2.

Britain had resorted increasingly to such short-term imports in the 1920s, in order to maintain the volume of its overseas loans, although the dangers of 'borrowing short and lending long' had long been known to bankers. In the inter-war period, moreover, the dangers of borrowing short were increasing, as floods of short-term capital – 'hot money' – fled from country to country in quest of the most advantageous interest rates, capital gains or currency revaluations.

The freedom of action of the British government to deal with these difficulties in the new and unsettled financial world of the post-war years was greatly affected by the decision to return to the Gold Standard at pre-war parity after the First World War. Adherence to the Gold Standard before 1914 was taken to mean not just convertibility of the currency (sterling) into gold, but convertibility at fixed rates of exchange. The policy of thus fixing the exchange rate for sterling, instead of allowing exchange rates to vary, further restricted the opportunities offered to British governments to balance the international accounts and at the same time pursue any active domestic economic policy (e.g. reducing the high levels of unemployment).

Matters were made worse by the return to the Gold Standard in 1925 at a rate of exchange which is agreed to have been overvalued – what Keynes (1925) and Moggridge (1972) called the 'Norman Conquest of $4.86' ($4.86 to the £ was the pre-war parity, restored in 1925). Through cheapening imports for British consumers and rendering British exports more expensive to foreign consumers (measured in foreign currencies) this overvaluation of sterling can hardly have helped Britain to balance its overseas accounts. In practice, it was to feed back on internal imbalances. As Keynes (1925) stated, 'the miners are to be offered the choice between starvation and submission'; their plight was 'the first – but unless we are very lucky – not the last of the economic consequences of Mr. Churchill'. His remarks were borne out with a vengeance in the General Strike of 1926. Parity, as his contemporary and later fellow-economic-advisor G. D. H. Cole pointed out, consumed the unemployed as a kind of human sacrifice. Recently, H. G. Johnson has gone so far as to declare that overvaluation was responsible for the whole of the unemployment, other than frictional unemployment, in the Britain of 1925 to 1929 (M. Keynes 1975). Estimates of the relevant elasticities (see chapter 14) together with comparisons with the later 1930s, make this extreme view untenable, but the precise contribution of the 1925 overvaluation to internal imbalance is an intricate matter (even leaving aside the many statistical problems).

Government policy

The balances of trade and payments imposed severe external constraints on the exercise of monetary policy. Monetary policy in the 1920s meant interest-rate policy. Both the Treasury and the Bank of England were terrified by the menace of inflation during the re-stocking boom of 1919–20, and in this they carried much opinion with them. Keynes, for example, wrote in *The Economic Consequences of the Peace* (1919: 221): 'There is no subtler, no surer means of overturning the existing basis of society than to debauch the currency.'

After some delay, the Bank of England attempted to combat inflation by raising Bank Rate (its rate of rediscount) to 7 per cent in April 1920. Within a very short time, boom gave way to slump. It would be misleading to blame the high unemployment, plummeting prices and money wages, and so forth entirely on the rise in Bank Rate. Nevertheless, the monetary authorities must bear some part of the blame, not so much for the increase to 7 per cent as for keeping it there for over a year despite widespread indications of economic hardship. For keeping the squeeze on too long there were three main reasons: (i) The Bank of England wanted to reassert its control of the money market, a control it had lost through the massive issue of war debt during and after the war; (ii) There was a rise in the rate of discount of the Federal Reserve Bank of New York to the same figure of 7 per cent, to cope with a parallel re-stocking boom in the United States – the Bank of England felt obliged to follow; (iii) High interest rates were the means chosen to revalue sterling in order to return to gold at $4.86 to the £.

Through being required to satisfy both internal and external policy objectives at the same time, 'dear money' became the epitome of financial policy in the 1920s. On the one side, the growing weakness on international account meant that the authorities had to keep interest rates fairly high in order to 'borrow short', so they tended to set them at one half a per cent or thereabouts above those in the source of much of the short-term capital – Wall Street. On the other, to the extent that domestic employment could be promoted by monetary policy, they were pressured to keep interest rates as low as possible. Inevitably, compromises were typical of the late 1920s. Rates of about 5 per cent were neither one thing nor the other. When the policy of 'borrowing short' was seriously threatened by events elsewhere, interest rates could not be pushed up enough to discourage the outflow of these account-balancing short-term funds. The demand for sterling (and therefore the stability of the exchange rate considered so important by contemporaries) then came to depend upon 'moral suasion': inveighing against new issues of foreign securities on the London Stock Exchange. Moral suasion was on occasions surprisingly effective (Atkin 1970; Moggridge 1971) partly because Montagu Norman, Governor of the Bank of England, was able to prevail upon the 'old boy network' of the City of London. Even so, this sporadic dependence on the quality of the wine served at his lunches seems a potentially hazardous way of running a trading economy.

What were the consequences of 'dear money' for investment? Fuller econometric studies may eventually allow more precise reckonings than are yet possible, but even so some powerful evidence can be marshalled. Fear of inflation persuaded the Treasury to 'fund' as much of the war debt as they could, i.e. convert it from the supposedly precarious floating debt (maturing at five years or under) to long-term debt (maturing at 15 years or more), 'whenever reasonable opportunity allowed' (Howson 1975: 37, quoting Sayers 1958). They were all too successful at funding the debt, displacing over £500 millions from the former to the latter category between 1925 and 1931; 'all too successful' because to induce holders of the floating debt to convert their holdings to long-term securities they had to offer more attractive premiums on the long-term securities. Thus they simply pushed up long-term interest rates. It seems likely that this would have had marked effects on the industrial capital market (Howsons 1975: 50–1).

Howson has remarked that these comparatively high rates of interest for industry did not stop the volume of new issues from expanding up to 1928. Granted that, there are three reasons she gives for expecting the flow of funds into productive new investment to have been restricted or distorted at this time: (i) A higher proportion of the new issues of shares in the late 1920s were speculative (e.g. investment trusts and holding companies), offering quick returns and high yields, but often quick collapse; (ii) The over-capitalisation of many businesses in a world of high interest rates meant a particular struggle to meet fixed charges arising out of these past debts, and thus discouragement from new borrowing; (iii) The existence of the 'Macmillan Gap' in especially acute form. Aware of present-day scepticism about the disincentive to investment created by high rates of interest, Howson argues that ease of access to cheap external funds *whenever special strains require them* does encourage a firm to use the resources it generates on its own ('plough-back') on a more generous scale for long-term expansion.

These questions become of particularly great importance when attention is shifted from the 1920s to the 1930s; in the latter period 'cheap money' was spoken of time and again as the cornerstone of the government's policy for recovery from the ravages of the slump. There can be little doubt that the conversion of the 5 per cent War Loan (involving over a quarter of the national debt) to $3\frac{1}{2}$ per cent stock in April 1932 was one of the most effective and positive monetary operations of the period. The Treasury had in fact been wanting to lower interest rates from the mid 1920s on, but was unable to do so while Bank Rate had to be kept up for external stability. The fall in American discount rates after the Wall Street Crash, the final departure from the Gold Standard and consequent devaluation in September 1931, and the use of powerful supporting action permitted the conversion to go ahead without a hitch in the middle of 1932. Bank Rate came down to 2 per cent as part of the conversion programme and stayed down until 1951 (with the exception of a few weeks in 1939).

It should be noted that the scope for 'cheap money' to operate domestically was widened not only by favourable events in the USA but also by the potentially more powerful instruments that Britain now adopted to balance her overseas payments. The devaluation of 1932 began to have an appreciable impact on the trade balance after about twelve months (the so-called J-curve lag; see Howson 1975). Tariff barriers were raised, especially against countries outside the British Empire. Drummond (1974: 286) estimates that the trade-diverting effects of the Ottawa Agreements which consolidated Imperial Preference increased British output by no more than 1 per cent at most. The effects of 'cheap money' merit detailed investigation of its spheres of influence; far more so than can be done here (compare Nevin 1955). In housing, above all, a strong case can be made for its having a quantitatively large impact (chapter 14: equation 3 of the full model). Moreover, as Howson (1975: 108–17) argued, through housing and similar channels 'cheap money' may be seen as sparking off the recovery.

At the same time, it was to be a major new policy implication of Keynes' *General Theory* that monetary policy via interest rates alone was unlikely to be enough. Keynes' own attitude in 1936 was more flexible than the oversimplified interpretation of the Keynesian standpoint current in many political quarters since the Second World War, that monetary policy could have little or no aggregate effect. The twenty-seven Reports of the Committee on Economic Information, 1932–39 – most of which 'bore the impress of Keynes' – consistently emphasised the contribution of cheap money, and regarded the housing boom and the accompanying increase of consumer durables as the most important factor in Britain's recovery (Howson & Winch 1977). The converse emphasis of Keynesianism on fiscal policy was but lightly treated in the *General Theory* itself (Patinkin 1976).

Such fiscal policy as existed in the 1920s went to amplify the country's economic difficulties. Responsibility lay with the Treasury. The Treasury was obsessed with the evils of inflation, and in that light with reducing the national debt, which had grown from about £650 millions in 1913 to some £7500 millions by 1920 (in current prices). Faithfully digested principles of nineteenth-century budgetary principles required them to redeem as much of this debt as was feasible, and that implied running a semi-permanent budget surplus. As the Treasury saw the virtue of stimulating the private sector by lowering taxation, this in turn meant searching for cuts in public expenditure. Public finance generally had deflationary consequences in the years after 1920. Moreover the 'funding complex' described above meant that to industrial investors in the 1930s loans may not necessarily have been so 'cheap' after all. Nor did fiscal policy make up for this aberration in other ways. Some use was made of public works projects designed to alleviate unemployment in the early 1920s, but these too cut against the grain of the Treasury's fear of inflation and instability. Exploiting some wider dissatisfaction, the government tapered off its spending on public works from 1925, and the sums involved were negligible after 1928.

Why should the 'Treasury View' have carried such sway? The Liberal Party had been campaigning vigorously for increased public works to attack unemployment in the elections of 1924 and 1929, and had recruited the persuasive pen of Keynes to argue its case. Yet the elected governments (Conservative in 1925; Labour in 1929; then 'National' in 1931) treated these alternatives with increasing hostility. For a start, economists were polarised in their opinions. An influential school of thought in the London School of Economics held that 'it was useless to allow working-class sentiment to govern monetary policy' (Winch 1969: 159). Skidelsky believes that the cross-currents of economic theorisers were of practical importance only to the extent that they fell on politically receptive ears (M. Keynes 1975). Keynes' pleas for public works (buttressed by deficit budgeting in 1933) were unacceptable because they contravened two political orthodoxies: (i) the principle of economic internationalism – Britain's supposedly central role in the world economy which prevented it from looking after its own interests; (ii) the doctrine of minimal government – the state's economic role was to tailor the best suit of clothes for laissez-faire capitalism. It is in any case likely that the Liberal Party's programmes would have done little more than scratch the surface of the unemployment problem, as chapter 14 suggests.

Winch (1969: ch. 10) argued that it was misleading to see the interwar period as entrenching the managed economy in Britain. Rather, he contended, it was the mixed economy that had triumphed in 1939. If the Macmillan Committee had been correct in forecasting a parting of the ways, then the more conservative of the possible paths forward had been selected. If so, then it was the Second World War and after that reversed this drift. However, Winch's subsequent research (Howson & Winch 1977) has revealed that some of the ingredients had gone into the mix before the outbreak of war. As the mid 1930s boom drew towards its peak late in 1936, the Treasury began to predict unemployment when the housing boom finally ran out of steam. The increasingly powerful voice of Sir Frederick Phillips within the Treasury stated, 'The position is that we are

Table 10.3. *Defence expenditure and the budget surplus, 1934–38* (£ *million*)

Year	Defence expenditure	Government surplus
1934	118.9	+50
1935	140.8	+23
1936	183.0	+14
1937	254.7	−2
1938	473.2	−109

Source: Howson (1975: 122)

budgeting for a deficit, that the pretence of producing a balanced budget is a fiction' (Howson 1975: 123). By the end of 1936 Phillips was recommending the preparation of public-works schemes when the forecast recession started. It was instead rearmament that provided the answer. The figures in table 10.3 demonstrate the correspondence with budgetary practice – it is true that the deficit arose under the pressure of rearmament for war, but opinion in Whitehall had already begun to change in quite fundamental fashion.

As in the First World War, the mobilisation of resources for fighting the Second World War committed the government to a radical departure in its economic function. In both wars inflation acted as the proximate cause of increasing state intervention, and on both occasions inflation was traced to 'cost-push' sources (primarily shortages of imports and shipping space) in the first year or so, then to potentially massive 'demand-pull' factors. Personal incomes, swelled by an insatiable hunger for more employment (new recruits – particularly women – to the labour force, longer hours, and more overtime), exerted multiplier effects upon a contracting supply of consumer goods. By late 1940, Keynes estimated the 'inflationary gap' between the demand for investment (including government expenditure) and the supply of savings (public and private) as £400 millions; others, including the Treasury itself, were to put the figure still higher.

Hitherto financial policy had been guided by the experience of the First World War, with rises in the rates of income tax, taxes on excess wartime profits etc., plus a few innovations of which the most significant was the introduction of purchase tax (1940). *The Times* dismissed these as 'a few more turns of the old familiar screws'. Though Keynes' teachings had been spreading in official circles, the adoption of his perception of war finance awaited Sir Kingsley Wood's budget of 1941 (Keynes' fully worked-out remedies as espoused in *How to Pay for the War* (1940) were even then thought too heretical and only partially adopted). Wood as Chancellor of the Exchequer grasped that the earlier policies could lead only to inflation, and inflation he rejected partly because of its devastating social consequences and partly because it was so ineffective in bringing forth a greater volume of supplies of the kind desired for the war. Hence he linked his taxation proposals (further rises in income tax and additional taxes to be repaid after the war) with subsidies intended to stabilise the cost of living. These subsidies were quite specifically directed at a widely-accepted cost-of-living index. Food prices were controlled by rationing, guaranteed prices, and selective price control; clothing and other items were assisted by the so-called 'Utility' policy. Stabilisation has been called a failure in the light of its fundamental objectives (e.g. by Nash 1951), yet it all but halted the rise in the cost of living (though not of other prices) and through so doing eased the rate of wage inflation (Hancock & Gowing 1949: 152).

Adoption of the stabilisation policy implied the adoption of national income accounting as a crucial policy weapon. Only by this means could the Chancellor gauge the excess of purchasing power that he needed to mop up by forced savings or regulate by controls such as subsidies. Paradoxically, however, the leap towards a recognisably modern programming of finance based on demand management and budgetary arithmetic coincided with the downgrading of financial policy as a whole. The emphasis shifted towards direct regimentation of supply. This shift of balance was signalled on the administrative front by the easing out of the Treasury – the Chancellor himself did not sit in the War Cabinet between May and September of 1940 and between February 1942 and September 1943 – and the concomitant rise to importance of new committees (such as Attlee's Home Policy and Food Policy Committees) and Ministries (e.g. of Labour and Production). The emphasis was transferred to direct mobilisation, especially in areas of most acute shortage such as imports, coal, or skilled engineers. Factory capacity was probably the biggest brake on rapid expansion of the war effort in 1940 and 1941, e.g. in aircraft; shipping the major constraint for most of 1942; but thereafter manpower deficiencies proved the greatest problem (Robinson 1951).

By the autumn of 1941 unemployment was 'frictional' at most (under 200 000). In this kind of environment, policies for holding unemployment after the war down to low levels took root – exemplified not so much in the well-known 1944 White Paper on Employment Policy (which remained obsessed with cyclical fluctuations) as in studies like Beveridge's *Full Employment in a Free Society* (1944). Beveridge had earlier captured public attention by his scheme for social insurance (Beveridge 1942–43). Social reform in such guises as the National Health Service or the 1944 Education Act were to have an enduring effect on postwar Britain (Titmuss 1950). As in the First World War, government expenditure per capita on non-war items rose to a much higher plateau.

Total mobilisation for a war of this scale left the economy in 1945 in a state described by Keynes as 'a financial Dunkirk'. Nowhere was this clearer than in the external account. Britain depended on Canada and the United States, above all the 'Lend-Lease Act' of March 1941. The Americans supplied Britain and the empire with over $30 000 millions of munitions, ships and other goods ostensibly 'for the public good' of Americans; after allowing for some reciprocation by the British, the British owed the Americans around $21 000 millions of which only $650 millions were required to be paid back in settlement (Hancock & Gowing 1949: 547). Yet Britain's balance of payments problem in 1945 was overwhelming. Between September 1939 and June 1945 Britain sold off £1118 millions of its overseas assets (much of it sold at below-market prices to satisfy Americans that Britain was 'scraping the barrel'); reduced gold and dollar reserves by £152 milions even after careful husbanding; and ran up additional external debts of £2879 millions. On the other side of the account, Britain's ability to meet its import bill for food and materials was undermined by the volume of its exports falling to one third of prewar levels in 1944 and rising again to little over 40 per cent of 1938 standards in 1945. Britain's military victory had left it the greatest debtor the world had ever seen (Sayers 1956).

11

Slump and unemployment

S. HOWSON

Unemployment was the most conspicuous economic and social problem in Britain in the interwar years. This chapter will discuss its characteristics; what light modern economic theory can shed upon its causes; how economists and government reacted to it at the time; and the effects of the steps that were taken to deal with it.

The unemployment problem

Despite fears that peace would bring depression and unemployment as it had after the Napoleonic Wars, the interwar unemployment problem did not manifest itself *immediately* after the First World War. The violent but short-lived postwar boom was a period of high employment despite demobilisation of soldiers and munitions workers (partly because many women drawn into the labour force during the war left it soon afterwards), so that 'the great postwar transfer [of persons from war to peace-time employment] was substantially completed by the spring, or at the latest the early summer, of 1920' (Pigou 1947: 33). In the severe slump that followed, however, unemployment reached, according to official figures, a non-strike peak of 18 per cent in December 1921 (and 23.4 per cent during the Coal Strike in May 1921); it was particularly heavy in the export industries (Pigou 1947: 38–9). During the long slow upswing to 1929 unemployment initially fell, but then hovered around 10 per cent as measured by the Ministry of Labour; unemployment was as high as 6.8 per cent of the civilian working population even in the otherwise apparently prosperous years of 1927–29 (figure 11.1). When the worldwide slump hit the British economy at the end of the 1920s, unemployment again soared, reaching in 1932 15.6 to 22.5 per cent depending on the series used. Again the export industries were hardest hit: in 1932 almost half the workers in the iron and steel industries were registered as unemployed, a third in coal mining, and nearly two thirds in shipbuilding (Mitchell & Deane 1962: 67). The economy began to climb out

The author would like to thank B. W. E. Alford, Sir Alec Cairncross, I. M. Drummond, R. Floud and D. E. Moggridge for their helpful criticism, B. Kochin for permission to cite an unpublished paper (Benjamin & Kochin 1976), the Controller of Her Majesty's Stationery Office for permission to cite Public Record Office documents, and the Houblon–Norman Fund for financial support.

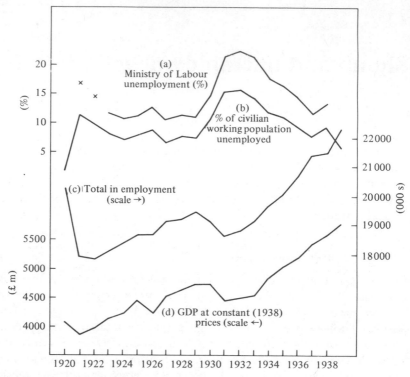

11.1 Unemployment, employment and income 1920–39
Sources: (a) Mitchell & Deane (1962: 67 for 1923–38); Pigou (1947: 221 for 1921–22);
(b) and (c) Feinstein (1972: T 57); (d) Feinstein (1972: T 5).

of the slump in late 1932; but the strong recovery in income and employment
could not reduce the unemployment percentage below 7.8 (of the civilian
working population) or 10.8 (Ministry of Labour figure) (figure 11.1). The brief
recession of 1937–38 temporarily increased unemployment once more.

There are thus two facts in need of explanation: the year-to-year fluctuations
in unemployment, which largely follow the course of the interwar business cycle,
and the persistence of a high level of unemployment throughout the interwar
years.

It is difficult to decide just how high interwar unemployment was, particularly
compared with prewar. The data are by-products of unemployment insurance,
the basic source of information for the interwar years being the Ministry of
Labour's series of persons registered as unemployed at labour exchanges as a
percentage of persons insured under the national unemployment insurance
scheme. The scheme was introduced in Part II of the National Insurance Act

of 1911, extended in 1916 and 1920, and amended by a long series of Acts of Parliament in succeeding years. From 1920 to 1927 it covered all persons over 16 in Great Britain and Northern Ireland except those in agricultural or domestic service, established civil servants, railway officials, the police, and non-manual workers earning more than £250 p.a. In 1927 workers over 64 were excluded; agricultural and domestic workers were included in 1936 and 1938 respectively. In 1930 the 'genuinely seeking work' condition, originally introduced for 'extended benefit' (i.e. benefit not covered by a worker's insurance contributions) in 1921 and applied to all benefit in 1927, was removed, only to be reintroduced in 1931 by the Anomalies Act; in those two years of high unemployment this temporarily boosted the Ministry of Labour's figures for registered unemployment, particularly of married women. This effect cannot be removed from the figures, but a series consistent with respect to the other changes can be constructed. One can also use the 1931 Census of Population data on the occupied population to derive a more comprehensive series covering uninsured workers. This has been done by Feinstein (1972) building on Chapman and Knight (1953); the resulting series is given in figure 11.1 along with a Ministry of Labour series which excludes agricultural and domestic workers throughout. This shows that the Ministry's figures overstate the size of the interwar unemployment problem among the whole population of the United Kingdom.

The prewar unemployment figures relate only to members of certain skilled trades unions receiving unemployment benefit paid by those unions. Comparing these (adjusted to reduce the weight of the engineering and building trades) with Feinstein's interwar series, average unemployment was 4.4 per cent in the last twenty prewar years and 10 per cent in the interwar years (and 1.5 per cent for the first twenty years after the Second World War) (Feinstein 1972: table 57). Feinstein's figures may be too high because the adjustments to the Ministry of Labour figures were based on Census data for a year of very high unemployment (Booth & Glynn 1975: 613–14), the trade union figures are probably too low because they omit underemployment in the form of short-time working (Beveridge 1944: 331–2, 335), but if the trade union figures are adjusted upward to make them comparable to the interwar official figures they yield an average of 5–7 per cent for 1883–1913 compared with 14 per cent for 1921–38 (Beveridge 1944: 72–3) and if Feinstein's figures overstated the interwar percentage by 15–25 per cent their average would still be 7.5–8.5 compared with 4.4. Whatever the deficiencies of the data, unemployment *was* higher in the interwar period.

To consider the causes of the high level of unemployment we must break down the aggregate data. Ministry of Labour statistics reveal two important sets of features: (1) higher rates of unemployment in traditional export industries and in the areas of the British Isles where those industries were concentrated, even in apparently non-export-sensitive industries (e.g. building); (2) a shorter duration of registered unemployment among women, a higher than average percentage of unemployment among older men, and a marked increase in the average duration of unemployment in the 1930s (Mitchell & Deane 1962: 67; Beveridge 1936: 381; 1937a: 6, 7 and 14).

The distribution of unemployment

In his analysis of the official unemployment statistics Beveridge (1930; 1936; 1937a; 1937b; 1944) considered the distribution of unemployment by industry, district, duration, age and sex. He found that the relation between the growth of and unemployment in an industry was not simply one of higher unemployment in the declining or slow-growing industries (1944: 50). It depended on the reaction of the labour force to the changes in the demand for labour. If the redundant labour force of a declining industry did not move to other industries, then the unemployment rate did indeed rise with the decline of the industry (e.g. in coal mining). But a movement from declining industries to more prosperous ones, though it would lower the unemployment rate in the declining industry, might also *raise* the unemployment rate in the more prosperous industry if that industry was not growing fast enough to provide permanent employment for the displaced labour; this seems to have been the case in the service industries and building where employment and unemployment were both higher in 1937 than in 1924. This is one way that depression affected unemployment in non-declining industries; it also affected it by reducing the growth in the demand for these industries' products and hence the growth in their demand for labour. As a result, generally prosperous industries had heavier unemployment if they were located in areas where the declining industries were traditionally important employers. There was a severe regional unemployment problem which was not merely a fall in the overseas demand for the goods produced mainly in certain areas (Northern Britain and Wales) but a stagnation of the whole economies of these regions by a regional multiplier process (Brown 1972: chapter 8; see also Champernowne 1937–38 and 1938–39).

The observed distribution of unemployment among persons shows that while the fall in employment in the slump of 1929–32 hit both sexes and all age groups, recovery did not affect all the unemployed equally: 'the legacy of the Great Depression was a host of long-period unemployed' (Beveridge 1944: 6). The distribution of chronic unemployment was skewed in two ways, by geographical district and by age. In June 1937, the proportion of 'long-term unemployed' (unemployed for twelve months or more) among applicants for benefit and allowances ranged from 7.7 per cent and 9.6 per cent in London and the South-East respectively to 40.3 per cent and 39.3 per cent in the North and Wales (Beveridge 1944: 68). There was a greater proportion of long-term unemployed in the older age groups (while the probability of losing one's job was no higher for an older man than for a younger man the probability of remaining unemployed once out of a job was much higher); but equally marked was the large number of men in the prime of life remaining unemployed for twelve months or more (Beveridge 1937a: 7, 14). (For the effects on the men and their families see Pilgrim Trust 1938.)

Causes of unemployment

These features of interwar unemployment have led many economists to divide unemployment into categories: frictional, structural and cyclical unemployment, voluntary and involuntary unemployment, etc. For example, Beveridge distinguished between 'short-period unemployment due to friction in the labour market and to seasonal fluctuations', 'long-period unemployment due to large and rapid structural changes in industry. . . or to personal infirmities – of age or physical capacity or character', and 'cyclical unemployment in trade depressions' (1937b: 180). Similarly, H. D. Henderson, D. H. Robertson and A. L. Bowley, when preparing an official report in 1935 on 'The Trend of Unemployment' estimated the numbers in the classes of 'normal minimum unemployment', 'cyclical unemployment' and unemployment representing a geographical or occupational maldistribution of labour (Public Record Office Cab. 58/30 E.A.C.(S.C.)22 'The Trend of Unemployment': paras. 15–26). The two tripartite divisions are not identical. Some of Beveridge's 'structural unemployment' would be in the others' 'normal minimum' or 'frictional' unemployment and vice versa; partly because of this fine line between frictional and structural unemployment (both refer to the non-matching, by skill or location, of labour demand and labour supply), dichotomies between demand-deficient and frictional unemployment or between involuntary and voluntary unemployment have also been popular (Pigou 1914; Robertson 1915; Keynes 1936). These two distinctions are not identical; what they share, however, is an attempt to identify unemployment which could not be eliminated by the worker(s) in question agreeing to work for a lower wage (in real terms). Then involuntary unemployment exists 'to the extent that at the current money-wage and with the current price-level, the number of men desiring to work exceeds the number of men for whose labour there is a demand' (Kahn 1976: 21); such a definition covers unemployment caused by the vagaries of the business cycle. More recently, economists have attacked all the classifications, for one or other of two reasons. One school of thought (the 'new microeconomics' of unemployment) argues that all unemployment is frictional and voluntary; the other school believes that all unemployment should be regarded as (to some extent) involuntary.

The 'new microeconomics' began as an attempt to explain why there should always be frictional unemployment even where the labour market is in equilibrium in the sense that the aggregate demand for labour equals the aggregate supply of labour; such an explanation could then be used to explain the observed coexistence of unfilled vacancies and unemployment and the fact that wage rates tend to rise well before full employment is reached. (The classic empirical study of this relationship is that of Phillips 1958.) The explanation given runs roughly as follows. (For more sophisticated accounts see Phelps 1970; Fisher 1976; Brunner & Meltzer 1976, and, for a critique, Hines 1976.) A worker in search of a job always has in principle a choice between taking the first job offered and prolonging his search in the anticipation that he will find a better-paid or otherwise more suitable position. A worker may also decide to leave existing employment in order to invest in search activity. The length of time spent in job search will depend on the individual's resources (defined as his expected lifetime income and therefore dependent on his past investment in acquiring skills as well as current resources in the form of savings or unemployment benefits). Similarly, employers search for suitable employees, choosing at any moment of time between hiring those that are immediately available and waiting to find those who are more qualified or willing to work for a lower wage. The duration of the employer's search will depend on the expected demand for his product as well as on his current resources; he will be prepared to pay a higher price (i.e. higher wages) the higher the expected demand for his product. Therefore, at least part of observed unemployment is, in this sense, voluntary. Further, the labour market can be in equilibrium, in the sense that everyone has voluntarily chosen his current occupation or has chosen not to have an occupation, with (quite possibly substantial) unemployment, due to the existence of voluntary search activity on the part of workers and employers. The amount of voluntary search activity and hence observed unemployment will also increase with a decline in aggregate demand. (An increase in aggregate demand may raise or lower search unemployment, as employers become less choosy, workers more so.)

Although this theory explains some at least of existing unemployment it is difficult to believe that the high unemployment in interwar Britain consisted of voluntary search activity. Many proponents of the theory would agree (Brunner & Meltzer 1976; Fisher 1976). Benjamin and Kochin (1976) have, however, attempted to use the search theory of unemployment to argue that unemployment in at least the 'prosperous' late 1920s and late 1930s was 'the consequence almost solely of the dole'. They test the search theory's prediction that the higher the level of unemployment benefit the higher will be observed unemployment (workers can 'choose' to stay unemployed longer); their comparison of the amount of unemployment with the ratio of unemployment benefits to wages do show the former rising with the latter as well as with the deviation of output below its trend rate of growth. The problem is that this test, using Ministry of Labour data on male, female and juvenile unemployment, does not discriminate between 'search theory' and the proposition that the number of unemployed people registering at labour exchanges tended to rise with the amount of benefits obtainable by so doing. It seems unlikely, for example, that the actual, as opposed to the recorded, amount of unemployment among women in 1930 was increased by the relaxation of benefit conditions in that year's Unemployment Insurance Act.

Let us assume, then, that not all unemployment is voluntary. Can we split up interwar unemployment into different categories, say voluntary and involuntary? The question is a practical as well as a theoretical one, for the appropriate remedies may well depend on the nature of the unemployment. If unemployment is frictional and vouantary the way to reduce it is not necessarily to increase aggregate demand, even though such unemployment increases with a fall in aggregate demand; the remedy might rather lie in improving information as to employment prospects so that workers did not remain unemployed simply because they had over-optimistic expectations of the type of work and the amount of remuneration they could expect to receive by waiting. Insofar as unemployment is due to large structural changes rather than to a temporary fall in aggregate demand (e.g. a permanent shift in the demand curve for Britain's exports), a better remedy might be measures to increase occupational labour mobility. These two policies are not, of course, mutually exclusive; but both analyses suggest that macroeconomic measures to increase aggregate demand are not always required.

The attempts made in the 1930s and 1940s to break down unemployment into different categories usually tried to estimate the lowest levels of unemployment it would be reasonable to anticipate or hope for. For example, Henderson's committee in 1935 estimated 'normal minimum unemployment' (defined as the amount of unemployment which would prevail if all regions in Britain had the same unemployment percentages as the most prosperous areas had had in May 1929, i.e. if all the current unemployment attributable to the phase of the trade cycle and to structural changes were eliminated) as 6 per cent; it went on to forecast that the official unemployment percentage would average $15\frac{1}{2}$–16 over the decade 1936–45 if there were no change in government policy (Public Record Office Cab. 58/30 E.A.C.(S.C.)22 'The Trend of Unemployment': paras, 27–30, 80–5; Howson & Winch 1977: 136–7). In 1942 Keynes revised this estimate to get a 'probable minimum level of unemployment for the postwar period of 5 per cent (Kahn 1976: 29–36). As Kahn has emphasised, Keynes did not in such quantitative work utilise the distinction between involuntary and voluntary unemployment. What he was concerned with was what actual unemployment, voluntary and involuntary, could be reduced to by macroeconomic policy. Subsequent postwar experience has made it clear that it is not just demand-deficient unemployment that can be reduced by an increase in aggregate demand but also frictional and structural unemployment; the higher effective demand means increased incentives for employers in expanding industries to take on less qualified labour or pay higher wages to skilled labour and for potential employers to set up new industries, and thus increased incentives also for workers to move or to acquire new skills in search of new employment in another area or occupation. That is, 'frictions' or hindrances to mobility, even those severe enough to warrant the titles of regional or structural problems, are more easily overcome in times of buoyant or expanding demand. The real problem with macroeconomic unemployment policy is not an irreducible minimum of unemployed but the threat of inflation. As demand expands, prices will rise, and the more immobile are labour and capital, the faster prices for a given increase in output. If employment is sufficiently high or if demand is rising rapidly, there may come a point when increases in demand can only raise prices with little or no increase in output; this point will come sooner the greater the frictions. Thus a 'full employment policy' cannot ignore 'structural' questions of capital and labour mobility. This is not a recent discovery (see Keynes 1937 and Beveridge 1944: 166–75), but it has, not surprisingly, received more attention in recent years than it did in the 1930s. Some economists (e.g. Phelps 1972 and Friedman 1968) have gone further and added the proposition (the 'natural rate hypothesis') that even if a government is prepared to aim for a very high level of employment despite the cost of inflation, it will not in the long run succeed in maintaining that level of employment but only one, the 'natural rate', that is consistent with either a zero or a constant rate of inflation. The recognition that there are limits to a full employment policy has not, however, made it any easier than it was previously to distinguish between demand-deficient (or non-natural) and frictional unemployment (see Thatcher 1976; Hill 1976; and Metcalf & Richardson 1976); the natural rate of unemployment, which depends on the structure of the labour market, is not invariant with respect to the level of aggregate demand if labour mobility depends on aggregate demand.

What then can we say about the causes of unemployment in the interwar period? First of all, it is not satisfactory to regard the high level of unemployment as voluntarily chosen by the workers, possibly as a consequence of the increased scale of unemployment benefits compared with prewar. It would be preferable to regard all the unemployment as involuntary. (And even if one accepts the 'natural rate hypothesis', so that some interwar unemployment was 'natural', there is no need to believe that much or most of the unemployment was natural.) At the same time, not all of the unemployment can simply be called cyclical, even if its treatment as such might well have improved the design of policy (see below); there was a large and permanent decline in the demand for Britain's traditional exports (see chapter 12), which necessitated large structural shifts of labour and capital, if a reasonable level of employment was to be maintained. The fact that the declining industries tended to be located in north Britain and Wales while the industries producing goods for which demand was expanding were located largely in south Britain, compounded the problems of mobility; and the regional multiplier process increased unemployment still further. While we can be sure that Britain's unemployment problem was partly cyclical, partly structural, partly regional, we cannot be certain how much of the unemployment should be attributed to each cause. They reacted on and aggravated each other, and in any case 'the breakdown of any total unemployment into these categories would depend on the level of unemployment itself' (Worswick 1976: 306). Probably the best estimate we have is that of the 1935 Committee on the Trend of Unemployment, namely that at July 1935 240 000–350 000 of the total of approximately 1 900 000 unemployed could reasonably be classed as essentially due to the operation of the trade cycle, 800 000–900 000 as due to the geographical maldistribution of the supply of labour relative to the demand for it, and 760 000 as due to all other causes. The Committee did not regard the boundaries of these categories as rigid, and with respect to the figure of 1 560000–1 660000 non-cyclical unemployed they noted that 'if general economic activity were to continue to be satisfactory, we might expect the unemployment figures to be reduced steadily, if slowly, by the migration of labour to expanding areas. But...we should expect that if the level of unemployment indicated were to be reached, any further recovery would be slow, subject to increasingly strong resistances, more likely to entail an upward movement in prices and wage-rates' (Public Record Office Cab. 58/30 E.A.C.(S.C.)22 'The Trend of Unemployment': para. 52). This seemed to be borne out in the 'boom' conditions of 1936–37 when prices and wages rose quite sharply and unemployment fell to 1 482 000 (Ministry of Labour average for 1937; Feinstein 1972: Table 58). This does not mean, however, that 11 per cent unemployment (as officially measured) was *the* natural rate: if aggregate demand had been higher in earlier years, more people would probably have moved, so recovery might have been able to go further before inflation appeared.

Before turning to the remedies for unemployment proposed in the interwar years, one should note that modern economic theory has also thrown some light on a question often posed in interwar Britain, namely, 'Were real wages too high?' Classical economic theory implied that if involuntary unemployment existed real wages must be too high and that wage reductions would enable employers to hire all the available labour (for a simple statement see Malinvaud 1977). Wages in interwar Britain were perhaps too high in one sense: if they had been lower, British exports might have been more competitive in international markets (see chapter 13). But this does not mean that the remedy for unemployment lay in wage-cutting; this is now generally recognised, but it was not at the time. The classical view is a misapplication of partial equilibrium analysis (applying to a single firm or industry) to the economy as a whole; furthermore, a reduction in wages might well intensify depression, by inducing employers, workers and consumers to expect lower prices in future (Malinvaud 1977: 1–12; Keynes 1936: chapter 19; Patinkin 1951). Wage-cutting was not, however, the only policy suggested at the time.

Unemployment policy

Hancock (1960 and 1962) has usefully surveyed economists' attitudes and government actions with respect to unemployment policy in the 1920s. A prevailing attitude among economists was a tendency to regard the unemployment as a cyclical problem which would in due course disappear as the expected upswing in activity got under way. Awareness among economists that the problem might be more longstanding did not come until the later 1920s (Hancock 1960: 307–8). The policies most commonly recommended before, say, 1927, were, therefore, intended to remove war-induced obstacles to the normal operation of the trade cycle; in this category can be classed proposals for the settlement of war debts and reparations, the removal of tariffs, domestic deflation, and restoration of the prewar gold standard. Some bolder spirits, notably Hawtrey and Keynes, proposed reducing the amplitude of cyclical fluctuations by monetary management (Hawtrey 1919; 1923; Keynes 1923; 1930). Hawtrey's monetary theory of the cycle attributed fluctuations in income and employment to fluctuations in the supply of bank credit, which the central bank could control; Keynes' theory, though not purely monetary, allowed that the monetary authorities by controlling interest rates could regulate investment and hence income and employment. Other economists in the Marshallian tradition regarded monetary factors as merely aggravating forces in the cycle: fluctuations in employment were bound to occur because of 'errors of optimism and pessimism' on the part of businessmen (Pigou) or the uneven nature of technical progress (Robertson), therefore *persistent* unemployment must be due to 'frictions' which resist the normal working of the economic system. The logical thing to do, once aggravating monetary factors had been removed, was to attack these structural problems, and to mitigate the temporary hardship by public works (Pigou 1927; Robertson 1926; 1928). The structural policies could include assistance to the movement of labour from declining industries to expanding ones or overseas; the lowering of wages and/or costs of production and distribution of goods, by wage cuts, wage subsidies, and the 'rationalisation' of industry; and direct measures to promote exports. (For a famous debate (in 1930) over these alternatives see Howson & Winch 1977: 46–72 and 180–243.)

Official reactions to unemployment reflected both budgetary considerations and views similar to (some of) the economists. The first of many conflicts between unemployment policy and financial policy occurred three months after the Armistice. Demobilisation threatened to bring high unemployment, and unemployment threatened to bring labour unrest and possibly revolution. Cabinet conferences in February 1919 on 'Unemployment and the State of Trade' faced a choice between four policies, according to the Minister of Reconstruction:

(1) The orthodox financial (gold standard) policy
(2) The Federation of British Industry (back to 1914) trade policy

(3) The social (better Britain) policy
(4) The Imperial policy.

The first policy meant reduction of government expenditure, debt repayment, dear money, and a determined effort to return to the gold standard at prewar parity; the second involved an immediate end to wartime control of industry and government subsidies to business; the third, government expenditure on health, housing, education, transport, etc.; the fourth, protection and the encouragement of emigration (Public Record Office Cab. 24/75 G.T. 6880 'Interim Note on Rehabilitation of Trade and the Provision of Employment'; see also G.T. 6887, of which an extract appears in Drummond 1972: 155–66). Although the Chancellor of the Exchequer decided to set free the sterling–dollar exchange (which had been pegged at about $4.76 since January 1916) in March 1919, by the end of the year the Treasury and the Bank of England persuaded the Cabinet to adopt the first policy (Johnson 1968: 364–74, 444–51; Howson 1974: 90–8; Howson 1975: 11–17). The immediate consequences were the November 1919 and April 1920 rises in Bank Rate; and thereafter until 1931 the orthodox financial policy was dominant.

The Lloyd George government's further concern with unemployment during the 1920–22 slump manifested itself in a series of Unemployment Insurance Acts relaxing the terms and conditions of unemployment benefit; a public works programme employing about 73 000 in the winter of 1920–21 and the setting up of the Unemployment Grants Committee (in December 1920) to allocate Exchequer funds for the assistance of local authorities' public works projects; some increase in Exchequer assistance to the Juvenile Unemployment Centres established in 1918; the Trade Facilities Act (November 1921) providing for Treasury guarantees for loans toward capital development schemes designed to relieve unemployment up to a maximum of £25 million; the introduction of export credits (Board of Trade guarantees for exporters' bills); and the Empire Settlement Act of 1922 (Gilbert 1970: 69–86; Hancock 1962: 334; Garside 1977: 324–5; Gilbert 1970: 46–8; Drummond 1974: chapter 2). The Cabinet Unemployment Committee, after consulting the Treasury and the City, outlined the rationale for these measures to the Prime Minister in October 1921. The fundamental cause of unemployment was the economic and political problems in Britain's export markets caused by the war, aggravated by high production costs due to high wages in Britain. While 'there [was] no short cut for avoiding the necessary process of adjusting our costs to those of our competitors...and no scheme of relief should hinder this process', unemployment relief was inevitable, exports could be encouraged, and 'means [might] be found by which State assistance could enable works to be undertaken which otherwise would not be done at the present time' (Public Record Office T. 172/1208 Draft Proposals of Commander Hilton Young's Committee submitted to the Prime Minister at Gairloch, 2 October 1921). The Treasury's attitude was uncompromising: since the government was committed to restoration of the gold standard 'the problem...[was] while giving the minimum assistance necessary to prevent starvation to do as little as possible to create permanent unemployment by maintaining uneconomic prices', and this limited the amount of state assistance made available (Public Record Office T.172/1208 'Niemeyer Memorandum on Deflation 1921'; Howson 1975: 27–9).

Thus apart from the gold standard policy which was expected ultimately to improve employment prospects (Sayers 1960; Moggridge 1972: 68–9, 76–7), unemployment policy in the early 1920s was a matter of *ad hoc* emergency measures. The persistence of unemployment *after* the return to gold prompted some new measures. Partly because of the reaction to attempts to cut wages in 1926 (the 'General Strike'), attention now turned to 'structural' remedies, to the rationalisation of the older industries such as the cotton and iron and steel industries, and to the retraining and movement of surplus labour from these industries to expanding ones through the Industrial Transference Board set up in 1928. This was the first step toward a regional policy in Britain (McCrone 1969: 92; on rationalisation see Clay 1957: chapter VIII; and Sayers 1976: chapters 14 and 20G). The Baldwin government abandoned the Trade Facilities Acts in 1926, though continuing the export credits scheme; it also applied some 'safeguarding' duties, i.e. limited tariff protection for a few industries, and continued the wartime McKenna duties on some luxury items such as motor cars; under the Local Government Act of 1929 it introduced 'derating', whereby industries were relieved of three quarters of their rates (property taxes) while the Treasury made up the local authorities' revenues by block grants. At the same time Treasury discouragement of public works expenditure increased; by the end of the decade the Treasury was using Hawtrey's ideas to reject the Liberal party's proposals for an ambitious loan-financed programme of public expenditure and to defend its policy against, *inter alia*, Keynes in the Macmillan Committee. On Hawtrey's theory public works would not increase aggregate employment unless they were financed by credit creation; this implied that public works were at best unnecessary, and otherwise either inflationary or useless (Hawtrey 1925; Hancock 1962: 336–8; Winch 1969: 113–22; Howson & Winch 1977: 17–18, 27). Other Treasury objections – administrative difficulties, the small amount of direct employment on public works projects – pointed to the experience with the schemes of the 1920s. But at bottom the Treasury disliked public works expenditure because it conflicted with other objectives. As well as the general aims of balanced budgets, debt redemption and the maintenance of the gold standard, the Treasury in the later 1920s also wanted to convert a large portion of the war debt (5 per cent War Loan 1929–47) to a lower interest rate, for this would both lower government expenditure (on interest payments) and encourage private investment; borrowing to finance public works schemes would reduce the prospects of such an operation by driving *up* interest rates (Howson 1975: 38–40, 68–74).

In June 1929 the second Labour government took office, pledged to deal with the unemployment problem; within a few months it found itself faced with a rapid increase in unemployment due to the world slump. There was an attempt to intensify existing measures: some encouragement of conventional public works schemes, attempts at export promotion, inquiries into the possibilities of promoting rationalisation in the cotton and iron and steel industries, and relaxation of conditions for unemployment benefit. MacDonald as Prime Minister also set up the Economic Advisory Council which improved the economic information available to the government and gave numerous proposals an airing; these included tariffs which were recommended, for different reasons, by businessmen, the Conservative party, Keynes, and some trade union leaders. But the government could take no new initiatives while Britain remained on the gold standard and Philip Snowden, firmly committed to 'sound finance' and free trade, was Chancellor of the Exchequer. The depression brought declining tax revenues and increased government expenditure, especially on unemployment relief. This meant increased Treasury pressure on the government to keep down expenditure, more government emphasis on rationalisation, and, eventually, once it was believed that an unbalanced budget was contributing to the weakness of the exchange rate, proposals to cut unemployment benefit. The Labour Cabinet split in August 1931 over expenditure cuts which included a 10 per cent cut in the standard rate of unemployment benefit and which were intended to help to save the gold standard by enabling the government to borrow overseas to support the pound. The National government then formed under MacDonald imposed the cuts but failed to save the gold standard (Howson & Winch 1977: 18–25, chapter 3, and 82–95; Howson 1975: 68–78; see also Skidelsky 1967; Marquand 1977: chapters 22–6).

After the fall from gold there were several major changes in economic policy. The Import Duties Act of February 1932 introduced a general 10 per cent tariff on all goods except basic foodstuffs, raw materials and the few goods already subject to duty, and an Import Duties Advisory Committee to recommend higher duties for specific products. The Exchange Equalisation Account was set up in the spring of 1932 to manage the exchange rate. The War Loan conversion operation, announced on 30 June, initiated a sustained policy of cheap money. The Ottawa Imperial Conference of July–August 1932 extended imperial preference. These constituted the National government's 'recovery policy'; the 'economic policy' of reducing government expenditure was thought to back this up by maintaining the 'confidence' necessary for the cheap money to have its intended effect on private investment, and by allowing the possibility of future tax reduction. On this basis the government easily rejected proposals for an expansionary fiscal policy such as that put forward by Keynes in 'The Means to Prosperity' (1933), and gave financial assistance only to projects which were 'revenue producing or... of public import', for example, London underground railway extension and suburban railway electrification (Feiling

1946: 201–4, 235–6, 241; Howson 1975: 90–4; Howson & Winch 1977: 122–3, 128–30).

Unemployment policy was based on the assumption that 'the unemployed really fell into...those persons who could, on a return of industry to normal conditions, be absorbed into trade and industry; and...those persons who, so far as could be foreseen at present, could not be absorbed on any revival of trade that could reasonably be anticipated' (Public Record Office Cab. 27/503 1st meeting of Trade and Employment Panel, 23 November 1932). The recovery policy would sooner or later (more specifically, within three or four years) solve the problem of the cyclical unemployment; with respect to the remaining unemployment the government at first proposed to do little more than to continue to assist in retraining via the Industrial Transference Scheme and to reform unemployment relief. The Unemployment Insurance Act of 1934 created the Unemployment Insurance Statutory Committee which would administer the unemployment insurance scheme and the Unemployment Assistance Board which would provide relief outside the insurance scheme, thus replacing the 'extended' or 'transitional' benefits which had proved so expensive to the Exchequer in the 1920s. Despite the initial stress on economy, unemployment relief did become more generous in the later 1930s (Howson & Winch 1977: 125–7; Gilbert 1970: 178–92).

'Structural' unemployment received more attention as recovery threw regional disparities into sharper relief. The first official reaction to the (officially commissioned) 'Reports of the Investigators into Industrial Conditions in Certain Depressed Areas' (Parliamentary Papers Cmd. 4728, 1933–34) was to propose some extension of industrial transference, the encouragement of work by voluntary organisations to provide smallholdings or other occupation for the unemployed, and a limited amount of public works schemes to improve the infrastructure of the depressed areas. To provide for the last, the Special Areas Act of 1935 appointed two commissioners to administer £2 million to be spent on projects satisfying very strict conditions in four 'Special Areas', South Wales, North-East England, West Cumberland, and Clydeside, excluding the major towns in these areas. Although in 1935 the government '[did] not believe that the introduction of new industries into the depressed areas [was] going to play any very large part in the near future in solving the problem of those areas', and wished to rely on transference of labour, the complaints of the Commissioner for England and Wales led to the subsequent provision of incentives for firms to move into the Special Areas, such as loans, low-rent buildings on trading estates, and tax inducements (Public Record Office Cab. 27/577 Cabinet Committee on the Reports of the Investigators into the Depressed Areas; McCrone 1969: 93–7). The reason was probably summed up by Neville Chamberlain when he told his Treasury officials: 'the Commissioner has made certain proposals and politically it might be helpful to try. If they failed, as I think they would, we should have done little harm, but we should have met the reproach that we neither accept others' suggestions nor produce any of our own' (Public Record Office T.172/1828, Neville Chamberlain to Hopkins, 14 November 1936).

Meanwhile, there had been important developments in economic theory with respect to unemployment, namely Keynes' *General Theory of Employment, Interest and Money* (1936) and the debates it generated. According to the *General Theory*, involuntary unemployment was due to a deficiency of aggregate demand, there was no automatic mechanism to keep aggregate demand at the full employment level, and therefore the state would have to intervene to manage aggregate demand if large-scale involuntary unemployment was to be avoided. Monetary and fiscal policy thus acquired a new role: instead of reducing the amplitude of fluctuations they should eliminate slumps. At the time that the *General Theory* was published, there were widespread fears that recovery would shortly come to an end and give way to renewed slump. Thus Keynes and some other economists attempted to persuade the government to plan to avoid a slump by maintaining its cheap money policy through the boom and postponing public works projects (except those in the depressed areas) to have them ready to start as soon as signs of slump appeared (Keynes 1937; Committee on Economic Information 1937). There was, of course, more support among economists for counter-cyclical public works than for Keynes' monetary policy, since they could be justified on the older theories. There was also support for both strands of policy in the Treasury which was currently preoccupied with the problems of rearmament and the prospect of the end of the rearmament programme coinciding with the end of the housebuilding boom. In consequence, though after considerable delay, the Cabinet agreed to the advance planning of central and local government public works programmes (Howson & Winch 1977: 140–3; see also Howson 1975: 127–30). There was also some attempt to use rearmament more directly to improve employment by placing government contracts in depressed areas (Public Record Office T.172/1828 Government Contracts placed in Special and Depressed Areas by Defence Departments).

Effects of unemployment policies

It is useful to consider the different types of policy separately, beginning with public works. First let us consider how much impact on unemployment the public works schemes of the 1920s and early 1930s *might* have had *if they had been carried out as originally planned*. To do this, let us assume that £1 million government expenditure provided 2500 man-years of direct primary employment plus an equal amount of indirect primary employment on transport and raw materials, and that the employment multiplier relating total employment created to primary employment lay between 1.5 and 2. These are over-optimistic assumptions, for two sets of reasons. First, more realistic estimates of the multiplier would halve the maximum amount of total employment and allow that it would take several years for the full effects to come through (see, for example, Thomas 1975 and chapter 14 below). Secondly, the planned schemes were in fact drastically cut down, to something like £60 million for the Unemployment Grants Committee schemes and £77 million for road works spread over a longer period than initially intended; much of the expenditure would probably have been carried out by local authorities in the normal course of events (Hicks 1938: 194 and 199).Hence the calculations (table 11.1) are *not* estimates of the actual effect of public works policies in the years 1920–32. What they do show, however, is that the maximum potential reduction of unemployment by these schemes was fairly small in relation to actual unemployment. For example, *if* the second Labour government's expanded public works programme had been carried out as planned, *and if* all its potential employment-creating effects had occurred within 12 months, then existing unemployment (3 252 000) would have been reduced by 648 750–865 000. The actual amount of employment created by the public works schemes must have been much smaller. It is also interesting to compare table 11.1 with the similar calculations of Bretherton, Burchardt and Rutherford (1941: 83–93) of the possible effects of rearmament expenditure in 1937–38, namely that if there had not been £120 million loan-financed defence expenditure in 1938 there *might* have been 3 million unemployed rather than the actual 1.8 million. While these exercises are wildly conjectural, one can conclude that the only 'public works' expenditure actually carried out in the interwar period that could have had a significant impact on unemployment was rearmament.

This conclusion can also be reached by looking at some of the components of government expenditure (table 11.2). Both non-defence current expenditure on goods and services and gross domestic fixed capital formation by central and local authorities were always small in comparison with unemployment benefit payments, defence expenditure, and debt interest. The last was larger than the central government's current expenditure on goods and services in all years except 1936–38, when defence expenditure more than doubled. The Treasury's persistent efforts to balance the budget and repay debt show up in current account surpluses in 1920–23 and small deficits in most subsequent years until rearmament put an end to such efforts. Meanwhile the local authorities always produced surpluses on current account, which were usually larger than the central government's deficits; the exceptions were 1926, 1930–31 and 1938. In 1926 unemployment benefit payments rose because of the effects of the strikes, and debt interest payments were at their maximum for the two decades; in 1930–31 the rises in unemployment benefit payments almost exactly matched the increases in the current account deficit, though grants to local authorities and transfer payments also rose and debt payments fell slightly.

Table 11.1. *Possible employment effects of planned public works*

Period	Planned expenditure (£m.)			Planned direct employment, man-years (4) = (3)×2500	Direct and indirect primary employment, man-years (5) = (4)×2	Total primary and secondary employment, man-years (6) = (5)×(1.5 or 2)
	Unemployment Grants Committee schemes (1)	Road works (2)	(3) = (1)+(2)			
Dec. 1920–Mar. 1922	26.6	13.6	40.1	100 250	200 500	300 750–400 100
Mar. 1922–June 1923	15.9	10.8	26.7	66 750	133 500	200 250–267 000
July 1923–June 1924	24.2	5.1	29.3	73 250	146 500	219 750–293 000
July 1924–June 1925	20.6	4.7	25.3	63 250	126 500	189 750–253 000
July 1925–June 1926	17.6	3.7	21.3	53 250	106 500	159 750–213 000
July 1926–June 1927	0.8	3.7	4.5	11 250	22 500	33 750– 45 000
July 1927–June 1928	0.3	2.7	4.0	10 000	20 000	30 000– 40 000
July 1928–June 1929	6.2	2.9	9.1	22 750	45 500	68 250– 91 000
June 1929–Aug. 1930	43.5	12.9	56.4	141 000	282 000	423 000–564 000
Aug. 1930–Dec. 1931	35.2	51.3	86.5	216 250	432 500	648 000–865 000
Dec. 1931–June 1932	0.2	2.3	2.5	62 500	125 000	187 500–250 000
	191.1	113.6	304.7			

Source: ((1) and (2)) Hicks (1938: 194, 199)

Table 11.2. *Government expenditure, UK 1920–38 (£m)*

	1920	1921	1922	1923	1924	1925	1926	1927	1928	1929	1930	1931	1932	1933	1934	1935	1936	1937	1938
Central government																			
Current expenditure on goods and services	277	259	214	181	180	186	187	185	181	182	180	181	177	176	184	209	252	322	439
of which:																			
military and civil defence	186	166	121	104	104	111	116	114	111	110	107	106	102	102	110	130	172	242	353
national insurance benefits	15	71	64	56	59	65	80	78	88	98	130	154	125	108	108	110	105	107	122
debt interest	320	303	307	315	315	313	328	303	312	316	304	283	279	243	226	227	223	228	232
Total expenditure	949	962	851	767	751	772	800	769	785	818	859	884	818	822	813	851	885	960	1110
Current balance	+54	+10	+24	+38	-10	-14	-53	-11	-4	-33	-68	-82	-29	-28	-13	-48	-50	-66	-152
Local authorities current balance	+22	+30	+39	+38	+32	+30	+27	+44	+47	+45	+53	+54	+52	+53	+53	+59	+66	+66	+65
GDFCF of combined public authorities	104	159	121	88	93	123	137	143	125	121	127	132	107	84	89	108	132	166	188

Source: Feinstein (1972: 12, 33, 13, 36)

Fiscal measures that were intended to improve the unemployment situation indirectly (e.g. the Trade Facilities Acts) appear to have had little impact, at least in the 1920s. Certainly the sums involved were generally small, and the schemes often had other defects; derating, for instance, reduced the overhead costs of all industries wherever located, while lowering the incomes of local authorities in depressed areas more than those in prosperous areas (Hicks 1938: 66, 71–5, 80–1, 164–5). On the revenue side tax receipts rose markedly in 1920, reflecting a sharp rise in taxes on expenditure, and in 1932, thanks to increases in both income and expenditure taxes, and thus tended to aggravate the cycle rather than act as a stabilising influence (Feinstein 1972: table 12).

Monetary policy probably had more impact on unemployment, as well as on the timing and amplitude of cyclical fluctuations. The postwar boom soon ended when over-optimistic expectations of future demand were recognised as such; the initiation of the dear money policy in late 1919–early 1920, while not responsible for the collapse, contributed greatly to the severity and duration of the ensuing slump. Interest rates were kept high, the money supply was reduced, and the policy of debt repayment (by means of a budget surplus) and refunding (replacement of maturing short-term debt by long-term bonds) was pursued with particular vigour in this period (Howson 1975: 23–9; Pigou 1947: chapter V). Financial policy, which was consistently deflationary, also restricted the performance of the economy during the slow upswing to 1929. The Bank of England raised short-term interest rates in its efforts to restore and maintain the gold standard at prewar parity; the Treasury helped to keep long-term interest rates up by funding operations. Whatever the (as yet unknown) quantitative impact on investment, income and employment, these measures certainly did not provide incentives for new investment, and could not, therefore, contribute towards readjustment and reorientation of the British economy away from the traditional export industries towards the new domestic-based industries. While the low incomes of the depressed areas reduced the domestic markets for the new industries, the slow growth of employment opportunities elsewhere reduced the incentives for labour to move from the depressed areas. But the policies of the 1920s were not designed with such considerations in mind (Moggridge 1972: chs. 4 and 6; Howson 1975: ch. 3; Sayers 1967: 61–3; chapter 12 below).

The 1930s 'recovery policy', with its different aims, had rather more favourable effects on employment. The management of sterling allowed the authorities not to regard the balance of payments as a constraint, while the cheap money policy, which produced a marked reduction in mortgage rates and conditions as well as lower costs of industrial borrowing, was a major factor in setting off the housing boom, which underpinned the domestically-based recovery (Nevin 1955: chs. VI–VIII; Howson 1975: ch. 5; Howson 1976). The recovery was also strong because of the rise in real incomes (for those in work) due to the improvement in the terms of trade in the slump, and the reduction in imports due to depreciation and the tariff (which also helped to encourage investment in the iron and steel industry, particularly after 1934) (chapter 12 below; Richardson 1967: ch. 10; Landes 1969: 475).

Finally, there were the more direct efforts to reduce unemployment in the depressed areas: migration policy, industrial transference and the special areas legislation. (On export promotion, see chapter 12.) The gathering world depression put an early end to migration policy; it had never been as popular with the Dominions as with some members of the government. Nonetheless, under the Empire Settlement Act 332000 persons received assistance between 1922 and 1929 and 13400 in 1930–31, while 58000 people travelled to Canada on a subsidised £10 fare; these are large figures compared with total emigration from Britain in those years (885000) but one cannot go on to conclude that the Act made a *major* contribution to the reduction of British unemployment, particularly when many of those assisted would probably have left anyway (and some came back) (Drummond 1972: 81–7; Drummond 1974: ch. 3). Essentially similar problems arose with the Industrial Transference Scheme. Some 70000 persons transferred from the depressed areas in the first two years of the scheme but the numbers fell off sharply during the depression, picking up again in the later years of the recovery. Some of those transferred might well have moved in the absence of the scheme, and the total was in fact small relative to total migration from depressed to prosperous areas, which increased substantially in recovery. The scheme, and internal migration generally, amply illustrate the point that mobility of labour is much higher in conditions of high aggregate demand. Further, the effects on the depressed areas may have been unfavourable, if only by reducing Treasury contributions to local authorities' revenues; the scheme certainly became unpopular and resulted in the emphasis of postwar regional policy on 'taking work to the workers' (McCrone 1969: 98–9; Hancock 1962: 338–41; Brown 1972: 281–4; Makower, Marschak and Robinson 1939). The Special Areas Acts, at least the second one, did, if nothing else, demonstrate the feasibility of attracting new firms, albeit small ones, to depressed areas by tax and other incentives; but rearmament probably had more impact on unemployment in the depressed areas by reviving demand for the products of the old, heavy industries as well as for the new (Brown 1972: 284–5; McCrone 1969: 99–102).

Conclusions

Such unemployment policy as there was in the interwar period was more successful when it included or coincided with measures to maintain aggregate demand – even if it cannot be said that all unemployment was simply due to deficient aggregate demand. It has been argued above that there is no single explanation of Britain's interwar unemployment problem. Part if not most of the unemployment in slumps was a cyclical phenomenon; part of the high unemployment in 'booms' was the manifestation of a regional problem, at whose roots lay a structural problem whose causes remain to be discussed. This chapter has concentrated on unemployment and the policies that directly affected it, largely ignoring both the state of British industry and the state of the balance of payments, though these probably have greater claims to be *the* causes of unemployment. These important topics are treated in the next two chapters.

12

Britain and the World Economy 1900-45

I. DRUMMOND

Between the death of Queen Victoria and the end of the Second World War, the international economy was transformed. In 1901, the British economy was at the centre of world trade and payments. London provided finance to the overseas world. British exports, though increasingly obliged to compete with other countries' goods, were dominant in some markets and important in most. Trade was impeded by tariffs, but otherwise almost unregulated. The pound was of unquestioned strength. All currencies were freely convertible into one another, and most were freely convertible into gold. That is, the holder of a pound note could freely buy any other money, and he could also buy gold at a fixed price. By 1939 Britain's trading position was far less secure. Though some currencies were still said to have a definite value in terms of gold, in few countries could ordinary people buy or sell gold at a fixed price, and in many countries, especially in continental Europe and in Latin America, governments had introduced rigorous controls over the buying and selling of foreign moneys. Tariffs were much higher, and many governments also regulated their imports directly. In world finance, Britain's role had become much less central, and the United States had emerged as the colossus of the future. During the Second World War, some of these changes were extended, and others were generalised, so that the world of 1945 was a world of controls over trade and foreign exchange, where international flows of goods and finance counted for much less than in 1929 or 1913 or 1901. By 1945, furthermore, there was real and justified doubt about Britain's ability to pay her own way.

In an effort to explain how and why Britain's position changed so dramatically, this chapter traces the development of UK trade and payments between 1900 and 1945. To avoid ambiguity and save space, much of the discussion is organised around the schematic balance of international assets and liabilities that appears in table 12.1. The table contains definitions that are not fully repeated in the text, and is a key to terms used later in the chapter.

From the end of the Napoleonic Wars until 1930, Britain regularly lent overseas, increasing her external wealth (NW) from the proceeds of her current-account surplus (export earnings minus import payments) (Imlah 1958;

Table 12.1. *An outline balance of international assets and liabilities*

A	Assets (UK claims on the rest of the world) A = LA + IA	L	Liabilities (overseas claims on UK economy) L = LL + IL
LA	Liquid assets (assets which are quickly convertible into other moneys with little or no loss, plus UK holdings of foreign moneys) LA = AR + OB + R + E	LL	Liquid liabilities (those which can quickly become a demand for gold and/or foreign money which the UK authorities must meet) LL = AP + SB
AR	Accounts receivable (amounts owing) from overseas buyers of UK goods and services	AP	Accounts payable (amounts owing) to overseas suppliers for sale of goods and services to UK
OB	Overseas bills (short-term obligations of overseas firms) held by UK residents – largely banks and other companies	SB	Sterling balances (principally overseas deposits in UK banks and overseas holdings of short-term sterling obligations especially those of the UK Government)
R	Official UK reserves of gold and foreign exchange (gold plus foreign money, such as US dollars)		
E	Private holdings of gold and foreign exchange in UK	SB/P	held by overseas commercial banks, businesses, persons
IA	Illiquid assets (UK assets which are convertible into foreign money only slowly and/or at considerable sacrifice) IA = B + ODI	SB/G	held by overseas monetary authorities – central banks, governments, currency boards.
B	Long-term obligations that overseas companies and governments have issued to UK persons and companies and to the UK government (including evidence of debt, such as company debentures and overseas government stock, and evidences of ownership, such as ordinary and preference shares) B = B/P + B/G	IL	Illiquid liabilities (UK liabilities which are not quickly convertible into an overseas demand for gold and/or foreign money) IL = IL/P + IL/G + EDI
		IL/P	Obligations of UK companies and persons
B/P	Issued by overseas companies	IL/G	Obligations of UK government
B/G	Issued by overseas governments	EDI	External direct investments (buildings, machinery, other goods, land, natural resources) located in UK but owned by overseas firms and persons
ODI	Overseas direct investments (buildings, machinery, other goods, land, natural resources) located overseas but owned by UK firms and persons	NW	Net worth (or wealth) of UK vis-à-vis overseas NW = A – L

NOTE: NW is net claims of the UK on the rest of the world. It can grow in two ways: from a current-account surplus in Britain's balance of payments, and from increases in the values of past overseas acquisitions, relative to old overseas obligations. If NW grows but L does not, extra A = extra NW. But A and L may grow together, as when the nation borrows abroad to finance extra A. Hence a growth in assets does not necessarily mean that NW must be growing.

and chapter 4 above). In addition, because the overseas world was willing to increase its holdings of sterling (Britain's SB), the UK could expand her overseas assets even more. Many overseas banks, businessmen, and governments held sterling. Not until the early 1930s did Britain's monetary authorities – the Treasury and the Bank of England – gather information regularly on these balances, but it has recently been estimated (Lindert 1969: table 2) that in 1913 they were in excess of £93 million. The principal creditors, so far as these can be identified, were the government of India (£28 million) and the government and official banks of Japan (£39 million). Since before 1900, London's sterling balances had grown more rapidly than official gold reserves (R), which were £35 million in 1913. For our period there are no usable data on liquid assets but before 1913 these were assumed to be far larger than sterling balances (Sayers 1976: vol. III, 4–30).

When a country's exchange rate is fixed, and when one money is freely convertible into another, the nation's monetary authorities must so arrange things that the demand for foreign money equals the supply at or very close to the fixed exchange rate. So as to match supplies and demands of foreign money, the authorities hold gold and foreign exchange reserves (R). They also manage, or try to manage, other liquid assets (LA) and obligations (LL). For instance, if a country attracts an inflow of foreign funds, this can be used to pay for imports, or for an increase in assets overseas (IA) that would otherwise require a reduction in official reserves (R). Before 1914 the UK monetary authority was the Bank of England, a private corporation that operated in remarkable independence of government. Though the Bank was not nationalised until 1946, its independence could not survive the outbreak of war in 1914. Even in the 1920s it had to share some responsibility with the Treasury, whose authority became paramount after 1931. Naturally the authorities always know what reserves (R) they have, and how freely they can use them. But they are always much concerned with liquid assets and liabilities. To manage these they can use some mixture of pressure, political argument, and direct control. Or they can rely on the price mechanism, raising interest rates so as to attract funds to London and lowering them to repel funds.

Before 1914 London's overseas lending was normally immense (see chapters 2 and 4 above). It was significant, also, during the First World War (1914–18) and in the 1920s, while even in the 1930s Britain's new overseas direct investment (ODI) was far from insignificant. Further, the London financial system provided a large amount of finance (included in liquid assets (LA)) for world trade. But because sterling could all too easily be turned into gold or other currencies, neither the London market nor the UK authorities could automatically extend credit whenever the world or the UK economy wanted to borrow more. There was always some risk that Britain's financial system might accidentally create more sterling than the world wanted to hold. Before 1939 nothing in the financial system prevented such a situation, which would exert pressure on the reserves

(R). But so long as Britain's trading position was strong, as it was before 1914, new foreign lending was quite likely to generate extra exports, thereby creating a larger current-account surplus. Further, by stimulating world economic activity it might make the world want to hold larger sterling balances (SB), as these were useful for financing world trade, much of which was invoiced and paid in sterling. The larger the UK economy relative to the world economy, and the more competitive UK industry, the more likely were these happy adjustments. Perhaps for these reasons, such 'overlending' does not seem to have been a problem before 1914. In the 1920s and 1930s it was a much more serious problem, and one which greatly worried the authorities.

Fortunately, before 1914 there was no question about the stability of the pound. The gold standard, by itself, did not do the trick. What mattered was the general confidence that exchange rates would not change, and that currencies would remain freely exchangeable for one another and for gold. This faith did not survive the First World War. In the 1920s, the gold standard, though painfully reconstructed, did not last long enough or look secure enough for confidence to be re-established. In the 1930s there was general uncertainty about exchange rates, exchangeability of moneys, and the trade flows that in part depended on these monetary arrangements.

Before 1914

Until the 1940s no one regularly measured all the items in the balance of payments, and very few people talked about it, but before 1914 well-informed people knew that illiquid assets (IA) were growing rapidly and were already very large, producing large annual flows of property income – that is, interest and profits – from abroad. Feinstein (1972: 204–5) estimates that in 1913 net worth (NW) was £4180 million, and he reports (T 15) that property income from abroad was £224 million, having doubled since 1900. Total export earnings were then £1042 million, and imports cost £807 million, leaving £235 million to be added to net worth (NW) in that year alone.

The economy was adjusted to these large and growing receipts of property income from overseas. To a large extent it received them as commodities – especially food and raw materials, which made up more than 60 per cent of all imports. Excess receipts were annually returned to the rest of the world through new overseas direct investment (ODI) and through the London financial market, which was largely oriented to the provision of long-term loans. If the current account had not produced a regular surplus, the financial system could not have become, or remained, so oriented to overseas lending. Because assets rose regularly, the UK economy received an ever-growing flow of property income, and this was an essential supplement to the current earnings from shipping, financial services such as insurance, and the export of goods.

After considerable disquiet in the later years of the nineteenth century, by 1913

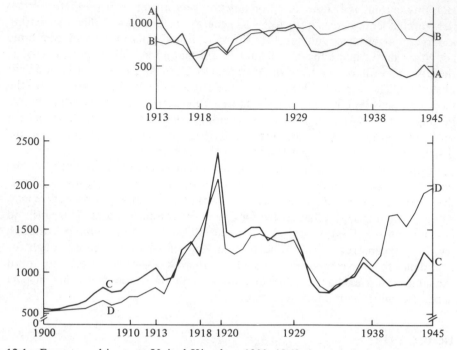

12.1   Exports and imports United Kingdom 1900–45 (£m)
(A) exports of goods and services at 1938 market prices, from Feinstein 1972: T 5, column 5; (B) imports of goods and services at 1938 market prices, from Feinstein 1972: T 5, column 7; (C) total current-account receipts, from Feinstein 1972: T 15, column 8; (D) total current-account payments, from Feinstein 1972: T 15, column 15.

Britain's politicians and publicists had regained their confidence about the future of the nation's export trade. Indeed, the volume of that trade had expanded by 72 per cent between 1900 and 1913. Nevertheless, there were grounds for unease. In 1913, Britain supplied 30 per cent of world trade in manufactures; in 1899, she had supplied 33 per cent (Key Statistics: Table N). In many overseas markets American, Belgian, and German competition was ever more noticeable (Saul 1960: pt. II). In Britain's own market, foreign manufactures continued to make the inroads that had begun well before 1900. Throughout the period 1900–13, some 25 per cent of Britain's imports were manufactures, though in 1913 only one quarter of these were finished, while the rest were meant for further processing. This competition would not go away. The prudent observer might expect it to increase.

   Though immensely varied, Britain's export trade still rested very heavily on a few relatively simple and traditional products, such as cotton (24 per cent of export earnings), coal (10 per cent), woollens (6 per cent), and iron and steel

(11 per cent). Machinery, chemicals, and ships produced another 14 per cent of the total, but the chemical exports consisted largely of older products produced with older technology, while in such new industries as electrical goods, vehicles, and aircraft, exports were still insignificant, earning only 2.2 per cent of export receipts in 1913.

Similarly, though British goods went almost everywhere the trade was noticeably dependent on a few areas. By 1913, the United States market had largely been lost. It took only 5 per cent of Britain's exports. But India took 13 per cent, and the smaller overseas 'countries of new settlement' – Canada, Argentina, South Africa, Australia, and New Zealand – took nearly one quarter.

What would happen if overseas tariffs rose higher? Such industrial protectionism, already rampant in Canada and Australia, could become more virulent or more widespread. Britain's economy would then have to adjust, and in so specialised a trading economy that adjustment could not but be painful, especially for coal and cottons. On the other hand, there was no obvious reason why that adjustment would necessarily be impossible, or extremely prolonged. Britain already exported the products of many relatively new consumer goods industries – bicycles, shoes, soap, chocolate, biscuits, not to mention the Christmas crackers about which George Bernard Shaw was so rude (Shaw 1930). In some heavy industries, such as armaments and explosives, she had enjoyed a similar success with new products, often borrowing technology from overseas. If the economy could retain something of the flexibility that had characterised it in the Victorian age, there was no obvious reason why such success should not be repeated many times over. Admittedly, one small island could not expect indefinitely to supply so large a proportion of the manufactures that a growing world economy would require (Kindleberger 1964: 268ff). But Britain could not be said to have 'failed' merely because that proportion would almost certainly fall. With sufficient ingenuity and keen pricing, even protectionism might be overcome: protectionist Europe still took 35 per cent of Britain's exports, and Canada and Australia, the protectionist Dominions, took another 11 per cent. But it should already have been apparent that Britain's export economy could not long continue on the old lines that had been laid down in the first Industrial Revolution.

In 1913, 73 per cent of Britain's imports were food and raw materials, while another 2 per cent consisted of fuels, chiefly petroleum. With the spread of motor transport Britain would import more oil. With population growth she would import more food, and, with economic growth, more raw materials, though if anything happened to her old export trades she would buy much less raw cotton, wool, and iron ore. By 1913, after 67 years of free trade and 300 years of overseas economic development, Britain's economy had adjusted itself to plentiful supplies of these basic necessities, supplied at prices that were often falling. If the supplies should be interrupted or if import prices should rise substantially relative to export prices, life could quickly become very unpleasant indeed. Furthermore, property income paid for 28 per cent of all imports. Without that overseas income, the balance of payments would be under immense strain.

In the 1920s, people looked back on the years before 1914 as the era of the gold standard, and they tended to see this system as a sort of ideal. It appeared that by raising or lowering interest rates in London the Bank of England had usually been able to reverse any undesired change in its gold reserves (R). It did not have to wait until longer-term changes in commodity prices, incomes, or employment could expel gold or bring it back (see chapter 3 for some of these longer-term mechanisms). But why was the Bank so successful? After all, interest rates in other countries often moved synchronously with London's.

If all countries had been fighting over a constant quantity of gold, the 'ideal' system might have broken down quickly. Fortunately, thanks to discoveries in the Klondike and South Africa, from the 1880s to 1914 the world's supply of gold was growing quite rapidly. The Bank could easily capture some of the newly-mined gold without having to draw gold from other central banks. This would happen in part because a rise in London interest rates would tend to reduce London's short-term lending for the finance of overseas trade (OB), and increase her borrowings from overseas (SB). Even if other countries followed London's lead on rates, this initial adjustment must generally have attracted the small quantity of gold that the Bank wanted to add to its reserves, which never changed very much. Further, though London's sterling balances were large relative to the reserves many balances were immobilised by political circumstances, and would not be withdrawn at times inconvenient to the Bank, or possibly at all. For instance, since 1899 the Government of India had been building up sterling balances so as to manage the rupee–sterling exchange rate. These balances might be depleted from time to time, but they would not be deliberately transferred to Paris, Berlin, or New York. Nor would the balances that belonged to the monetary authorities and commercial banks that operated all over the empire and the Far East. If such funds and balances were depleted, the transfer would almost certainly be to the account of a UK resident, because of the trade, financial, and governmental connections between the overseas territories and Great Britain. Gold would seldom be demanded. Japan, too, held large sterling balances, in large part because her own currency-law required her to do so. Further, she was allied to Britain, and her authorities were responsive to Bank pressure (Lindert 1969: 32). As for private sterling balances (SB/P), because Britain stood at the centre of world trade and finance the rest of the world wanted to hold large amounts of these, regardless of interest rates elsewhere.

In the 1920s, or before 1914, the working of the gold standard system was not well understood, even in the relatively simple terms that we have used. There was a tendency to believe that by raising its lending rate the Bank could always attract the gold it wanted, and to forget, or ignore, the supplementary measures and the co-operation with other central banks that had sometimes been necessary (Sayers 1976: 54–60). There was also, perhaps, a tendency to overlook the fundamental fact: the pound was strong and easy to manage because the UK balance of payments was so healthy.

The impact of the First World War

For Britain's delicately balanced financial system, continental war meant trouble. Europe took 35 per cent of Britain's exports, and supplied 40 per cent of her imports. Much of Europe's trade was financed in London. When war broke out, therefore, a substantial part of Britain's liquid assets (LA) became at least temporarily illiquid, and perhaps worthless. Though until 1 April 1919 the paper pound was theoretically convertible into gold, to protect the reserves the authorities made it difficult to obtain gold for export. India and the Dominions looked to London for war finance. So did Britain's continental allies. The UK government, therefore, lent large sums to the Empire, and much larger sums to the Continent, especially France, Russia and Italy. By 1919 these war loans totalled £2062 millions (Moulton & Pasvolsky 1926: 23). Outside Europe, however, Britain could not earn enough to pay for imports. Though the exchange rate first rose above the pre-war par of $4.86 to £1, it soon floated downward. The government borrowed about £207 million in New York, and arranged for the sale of some £261 million worth of dollar illiquid assets (IA). The proceeds were used to pay for imports of American goods, thereby supporting the pound at $4.76. From the Canadian government and banks, too, special credits were obtained. In 1917, when the USA at last entered the war, the United States Government began to supply goods without demanding immediate payment. An inter-governmental war debt of £1122 million, or just under $5500 million, thus soon accumulated.

These painful financial developments should not blind us to the remarkable underlying strength of Britain's position. Only in 1918 did she have a current-account deficit of any size. In 1914–15 and in 1917 she had surpluses. If all currencies had remained exchangeable for one another and if all the war-debt contracts had been honoured, the new superstructure of debt would not have mattered. Britain would have collected with one hand and paid out with the other. Her net worth (NW) had been depleted, but not by much – indeed, by less than the export surplus of a single pre-war year. Most of the assets of 1913 had survived, and in the 1920s these provided an income that helped to keep Britain's current account in surplus.

In 1918–19 Britain's trade did well out of the post-war boom that was generated by the world-wide effort to rebuild stocks. Nevertheless, the longer-run prospects were less favourable than in 1913. The continental market, of immense importance to Britain, appeared to be shattered. In heavy industry such as iron and shipbuilding the war had induced capital investment that would produce over-capacity; this would lead to vigorous price-cutting or to combination to restrain competition and share orders internationally. In Europe, the new countries created by the Treaty of Versailles, such as Hungary and Poland, would certainly be protectionist. In Europe, Asia, and elsewhere, tariffs were not likely to fall to pre-war levels, if only because governments would need extra revenue from their customs duties. Further, governments would be inclined to protect their war-expanded industries.

The Indian prognosis was especially grim. In 1913 the subcontinent had taken more than 13 per cent of Britain's exports, and the cotton trade, in particular, depended heavily on this market. Imperial policy had long insisted on low tariffs and on countervailing domestic excises on the products of Indian cotton mills, but during the war tariff rates doubled, and excises were soon ended. The domestic textile industry had already seized its opportunity, and so had the iron industry, where the first modern steel mills had been laid down. By 1919, the Imperial authorities had announced that they would not normally oppose protective tariffs at the Indian frontier (see Drummond 1972: chapter 4). In India, political action would increasingly be directed at Britain's exports in general, and at Lancashire cottons in particular.

As for the coal trade, which produced 10 per cent of Britain's export earnings, the prospects were unattractive. Especially in shipping, petroleum was beginning to replace coal. Britain herself was spending more on oil imports, which rose from 1.4 per cent of the total in 1913 to 4.8 per cent in 1918. In a few of her markets, hydro-electricity would shortly displace coal to some extent. In Bolshevik Russia coal imports, like other imports, would be proscribed or closely controlled.

Reconstruction in the 1920s

Partly because import prices fell relative to export prices, in the event things went a great deal better than might have been expected. The export surplus reappeared in 1920. Except for a small deficit during the troubles of 1926, it remained until 1931. In the boom of 1919–20 export volumes rose gratifyingly, and after slumping in 1921 they climbed once more, while import volumes rose rather less. Again Britain could add to her assets and net worth. Though the authorities worried about the volume of external lending, the London financial market revived. Empire borrowers, in particular, came to London, but so did European governments, which were often borrowing with encouragement from the League of Nations or for international reconstruction. In 1923, Britain arranged for the gradual repayment of her American war-debt, and Germany's regular reparations payments soon began. Though the Bolsheviks had defaulted, the other continental debtors were paying something, helping to service Britain's debt to the USA. Britain's industry, especially in oil, chemicals, rayon, soap-making, and mining, was investing abroad much more energetically than before the war, accumulating the overseas direct investments that were later so important and so valuable.

For decades some American corporations had been at work in Britain, just as some British firms were at work in the USA. In the 1920s external direct investment (EDI) became more noticeable on the UK scene, most obviously in the car industry. As for finance, the New York market had become a more attractive place to raise long-term loans and hold short-term balances of funds. Before 1914, the American financial system had already become a lender to the rest of the world. Its role expanded in the 1920s, when it appeared as a financial competitor with London. Further, with the relative growth of American commercial and financial power the world became more willing to hold dollar balances, both absolutely and relative to its demand for sterling balances in London.

In spring 1919 the UK authorities had allowed the pound to float. But the Treasury and the Bank always intended to return to the gold standard, at the 1914 exchange rate with the dollar (Moggridge 1969: 12ff). To this end, the authorities soon began to pursue contractionary monetary policies, keeping domestic credit scarcer and domestic interest rates higher than would otherwise have been required (Howson 1975: 9–54; Sayers 1976: 110–52 and chapter 25). Because the pound was a floating currency until 1925 Britain's reserves were safe, since a payments deficit would cause a fall in the exchange rate rather than having to be paid from reserves. But the authorities wanted sterling to rise relative to the dollar. Hence they had to manage credit policy with an eye to overseas interest rates, lest sterling balances leave London. Relatively high interest rates, furthermore, could attract new though volatile balances permitting a more rapid growth in total assets or forcing up the exchange rate. These obligations, however, would be convertible into gold, on demand once the country returned to the gold standard.

Having adopted the gold standard once more in spring 1925, the authorities were obliged to protect the reserves both through their own efforts and through co-operation with other central banks (Sayers 1976: 211–35, 297–313, 331–59). Their task was made more difficult by the changes in the world economy since 1913. Their leverage over sterling balances had been weakened because London was less central to world trade and finance. Because in the world economy Britain counted for somewhat less, foreigners were less willing to hold sterling relative to other moneys, especially American dollars. Hence sterling balances were more volatile – more likely to move abroad when interest rates rose in New York or in continental centres, relative to London's rates.

The behaviour of foreign governments made the system still harder to work. In 1913 there were government-owned sterling balances and some of these were large. In the 1920s such balances reappeared, with encouragement from international conferences. The French holding of sterling balances became immensely large, until, in 1927, France began a deliberate conversion of sterling into gold. Though it now had a large and growing export surplus, the United States remained resolutely a high-tariff country. Only American lending prevented a worldwide shortage of dollars. Nevertheless, what gold was produced flowed inexorably to Paris and New York. In neither centre were the authorities usually willing to let the gold push up the supply of money or domestic credit. In other words, France and the United States accumulated new gold and then sterilised it.

Further, Britain herself was borrowing short and lending long. In 1925–29, illiquid assets (IA) rose by £445 million, while the current-account surplus was £250 million (*Bank of England Quarterly Bulletin*, March 1974, table B). The difference was covered by an increase in sterling balances – that is by borrowing from abroad. But in December 1929 these were already considerably larger than £275 million (Parliamentary Papers 1930–31: 301), while the reserves were only £146 million. It was increasingly hard to retain sterling balances in London, and increasingly important to do so.

The development of world trade and tariffs made the task of the authorities more difficult, and the life of UK manufacturers more unpleasant. The war seemed to have made American goods more competitive. Already, in the Far East, Japanese competition was perceptible. In Central Europe and Latin America, German competition reappeared more quickly than had been foreseen. Some of these changes reflect a change in Britain's comparative advantage (see above, chapter 3). For textiles this was almost certainly the case. But matters were not helped by the continued movement toward protectionism in overseas markets. For some industries it was this, not structural change, which mattered.

Whatever their competitive position, all manufacturing industry would have been better off if the world economy had been more active, and more open to Britain's products. The UK wanted a gold standard, indeed, largely to encourage world revival and open markets by making trade more secure and predictable. Most observers now doubt whether the gold standard really did have this effect. Indeed, if expensive credit and an expensive pound impeded Britain's production, home investment, and exports while encouraging imports, then Britain's monetary policy bears some of the blame for the troubles not just of the old industries, such as textiles and coal, but of the new, such as cars and rayon. This is a set of relationships that neither historians nor economists have yet been able to disentangle. No doubt the gold standard, through its impact on the profitability of coal exports, helped to bring on the General Strike of 1926. No doubt it raised unemployment, and lowered profits for many firms. But the world economy turned downward in 1929, and in many of Britain's important overseas markets, such as Australia, the slump began at least a year earlier. Further, it is widely suspected that the productivity of Britain's workers, though rising more rapidly than before 1914, was rising less rapidly than the productivity of America's. If so, and if productivity growth is an independent cause of economic performance and not just a reflection of it, many British firms would presumably have faced awkward American competition even if the pound had been pegged in 1925 at $4.40 instead of $4.86. Further, in most of the empire markets which were so important to Britain the locally issued currencies were already, in effect, pegged to sterling and not to the dollar or to gold. Against competition from producers within such countries as India or Australia, Britain would not have improved her position by making her own pound cheaper relative to the dollar or the mark. Monetary and exchange policies were certainly inconvenient, but no conceivable policy could have obviated all Britain's industrial difficulties in the 1920s, because these stemmed so largely from the nation's own industrial past and from overseas developments that Britain could neither prevent nor control.

In the circumstances, it is not surprising that Britain herself took some halting steps toward tariff-protection. Free trade, of course, had never been inconsistent with customs duties on certain products, such as wine and coffee, where it was thought there could be no protective effect. Even for these old-established 'revenue duties', however, the situation could be complicated. The sugar duty, for instance, gave incidental protection to Britain's producers of sugar-beet, and the wine-duty protected beer, except insofar as domestic excise taxes offset the protective effect. In 1920 and thereafter, Parliament produced new duties for certain chemicals and other 'key industries'. There was also provision for 'safeguarding' industry, but these new duties were few. In 1923–24 the electorate was thought to have pronounced in favour of old-style free trade. Nevertheless, the McKenna Duties, imposed in 1915 to save shipping space and foreign exchange, were retained until 1924 and re-imposed in 1925. They covered cars and parts, musical instruments, and a few other consumer goods. Behind their shelter developed Britain's car industry, and a few other industries, such as the piano industry (Ehrlich 1976: 176–93), grew or revived. Also, the duties helped to attract external direct investment (EDI) to the UK, as foreign firms jumped the tariffs by constructing factories in Britain.

The government also tried to develop empire markets for UK exports, but its efforts were ineffectual, and the overall impact was derisively small (Hancock 1942; Drummond 1972: ch. 2). Only in a few small and commercially insignificant colonies could Britain simply impose preferential tariffs or purchasing policies. India's authorities would grant no tariff-preferences, and in purchasing government stores they began to favour India's own producers. The Dominions controlled their own tariffs. In most of tropical Africa and in the former German colonies that Britain and the Dominions held as mandated territories under the supervision of the League of Nations, international treaties precluded any preferential system. Britain, therefore, could act only by offering concessions or gifts that would induce the Dominions and India to do the same. In 1919 she reduced her tariffs on those empire goods which already paid the old revenue duties or the new McKenna Duties. In 1920–25, successive UK governments made other tariff and non-tariff concessions (Drummond 1972: ch. 2; 1974: chs. 2, 3). Gradually the empire became a more important source of Britain's imports. For a few products, such as motor cars and dried fruits, the preferential tariffs are the explanation. In general, however, the cause was the expansion of productive capacity in the empire. The statistics are also affected by the increase in the relative size of the empire in 1918–23 as former German colonies became mandates, and as the Irish Free State emerged from inside the United Kingdom. Regrettably, Britain's concessions did not warm the hearts of Indian civil servants or Dominion politicians. All the 'white Dominions' had long offered tariff-concessions on UK goods, but in the 1920s their value was eroded by changes in tariff-arrangements, and by increases in basic rates. Whatever the value of these preferences, in empire markets British goods were losing ground to foreign. In 1913, Britain had supplied more than 40 per cent of the Empire's commodity imports, but through the 1920s this percentage fell gradually but perceptibly.

Contraction and breakdown 1929–31

As the world moved into depression in 1929–30, Britain's exports naturally contracted and her current-account balance diminished, but as her overseas lending continued her illiquid assets (IA) continued to increase, and net worth (NW) went up with the continuing current-account surplus. Until 1931, reserves (R) changed little. However, everything then went wrong at once. First, as Central Europe lapsed into financial chaos there was doubt about the safety of Britain's liquid assets (LA), many of which were owing from that region. Second, as overseas banks and governments sank deeper into difficulties some paid gold to London to service their obligations but others drew down their London sterling balances (SB) so as to maintain payments to the American economy, which had ceased to lend the dollars that in the 1920s had financed Germany's reparations and America's own export surplus. Third, in 1931, for the first time since 1918, Britain herself had a large current-account deficit. Fourth, as monetary disorder spread, some private holders of private sterling balances (SB/P) seem to have fled from the pound into safer moneys – chiefly the franc and the dollar. Fifth, in all probability importers and exporters began to time their payments in the expectation that the pound would fall. As fear increased in the summer of 1931, the situation worsened, and by August external funds could not be drawn to London or held there. Thanks to the co-operation between central banks that had developed during the 1920s (Clarke 1967), the

Bank of England was able to get some short-term credits. Of these, and emergency government borrowing, some £82 million was spent. But this was not enough. During 1931, the overseas world reduced its holdings of sterling (SB − LA − R) by £293 million. In September 1931 the authorities were forced to abandon their commitment to sell gold at a fixed price. In the London gold market one could still buy gold with paper pound notes. But the price fluctuated, being determined by the dollar–pound exchange rate and by the price at which the American and French authorities were prepared to sell gold. The paper pound was now a floating currency. It promptly depreciated relative to the dollar, the franc, and the other gold currencies.

Trade developments during the depression 1931–39

One aspect of the 1929–31 slump, and of the monetary disturbances that accompanied it, was a widespread retreat into autarky. The United Kingdom soon confronted a world in which tariffs were markedly higher than in the 1920s. Behind these tariffs, such important markets as India, Australia, and Argentina tended to increase domestic production at the expense of imports. In some markets, such as Japan and Australasia, this process was accelerated because local currencies had depreciated relative to sterling. Many primary-producing countries in Europe and overseas had been prostrated by the collapse in the prices of their exports. Even in the 1920s, many such countries had balanced their international accounts only by borrowing in Britain, the more prosperous countries of Western Europe, and the United States. After 1929 such loans were few, though Britain did her best to finance the empire. In central and eastern Europe and in Latin America, governments responded by introducing exchange controls. That is, they regulated the buying and selling of foreign money, usually collecting all export-receipts and rationing the funds among would-be importers, travellers, and payers of interest and dividends. In 1931, Germany, whose international accounts had been balanced only by credits from American lenders, showed the way. Exchange control rapidly became a most pernicious form of protectionism. The details were immensely varied and constantly changing. The effect, however, was clear: the controls impeded Britain's exports, and made it harder for her citizens to collect the interest and dividends that were due them from the rest of the world.

Though recovery began in 1931–33, matters became little better. Until the outbreak of war in 1939, Britain and the empire resisted exchange controls almost completely. In France, the USA, and the smaller democracies of north-western Europe, such controls were relatively weak, or fleeting, or altogether unknown. But recovery was slow, and it did not end balance-of-payments problems. Behind her fence of exchange controls, Germany was busily reflating her economy, absorbing the unemployed through a dramatic programme of government expenditure both civil and military. In smaller and weaker economies, exchange controls appeared the only way to manage the exchanges. Further, though some countries reduced their tariffs from the hysterical peaks to which greed and fear had pushed them in 1930–32, the world remained more protectionist than it had been before 1929. In the winter of 1931–32 Britain herself abandoned her traditional policy of free trade. Thereafter, her rates of duty tended to rise, though in the later 1930s UK officials began to question the efficacy of such a policy. Further, in Britain, France, and certain other countries governments introduced a new protective device – import quotas. Britain used them chiefly to protect her cotton trade and her meat producers. France used them to support the franc by restraining imports. The USA used them as part of a general scheme to protect her farmers.

For Britain, an autarkic world was a trying one. The UK economy was adjusted to the expectation that surpluses could be earned in some directions and spent to cover deficits in others – in other words, to a multilateral system of payments. (See chapters 3 and 4.) Extreme protectionism, exchange controls, and the bilateral balancing of international accounts that so often accompanied such controls, all spelt trouble for Britain's export trade. These troubles were added to the general contraction of export demand that followed from the collapse and slow recovery of world output and employment.

In a world slump, Britain's export trade could not be expected to prosper, and the UK could not herself reflate the world economy, even if her government had wanted to try. But by clever negotiation and judicious bargaining, Britain might make foreign controls less obstructive, foreign tariffs less protective, and the empire markets more receptive. With such ends in view, Britain's statesmen and officials spent much time on commercial negotiation – with empire countries, at the 1932 Ottawa Conference and thereafter; with South American and Scandinavian states, in 1933–34 and thereafter; with the United States, in 1936–38. These and other efforts were not without value, either for exports or for the collection of interest and dividends from overseas. But their effect was small. Certainly they did not revive the export trade, which did not recover, either in volume or in value, to the level of 1929. By 1938, furthermore, Britain supplied slightly less of a shrunken world trade in manufactures, and substantially less of total empire imports, than in 1929.

In the 1930s the UK current account was decidedly unhealthy. During the First World War, the current-account deficit had been only £56 million, a trivial sum relative to overseas assets or current production. From 1920 to 1930, Britain cumulated a surplus of £1156 million on current account. But from 1931 to 1938 there were deficits in every year except 1935, and the cumulative current-account deficit was £375 million. This deficit combined with defaults and with the decline in the values of many overseas assets to make important inroads on net worth (NW).

This dreary performance is especially striking when we recall that Britain herself had become a protectionist country. One would suppose that protection must have insulated the UK economy from the outside world to some extent. In the revival of 1933 to 1937, UK imports certainly rose less, relative to the growth of domestic output, than they had done in the revival of 1925 to 1929. But the effect, though positive, was not enough.

Perhaps exchange rates deserve some of the blame. Though the pound depreciated and fluctuated in 1931–33, from early 1934 to mid-1938 it hovered around the $5.00 mark. If a $4.86 pound was an inconvenience in the late 1920s, a $5.00 pound may have been a hindrance in the middle 1930s, even though the moneys of the European gold bloc did rise relative to sterling. Further, in the currency realignments of 1930–32 and 1937–37, several currencies – for example, the Australian and New Zealand pounds, eventually the franc, and, in effect, the mark – were devalued relative to sterling, though others, such as the Indian rupee and the South African pound, were not. The gold standard had been abandoned, but the set of exchange rates could still affect Britain's industrial economy and her exporting and import-competing industries.

Nevertheless, an important culprit was the property account. In 1938, Britain's gross and net receipts of property income from overseas were much the same as in 1913, and very much smaller than in 1929. If overseas property income had flowed into Britain in the 1930s as in the late 1920s, between 1930 and 1938 Britain would have netted an extra £647 million – nearly twice the cumulative deficit on current account during these years.

In so great a depression, property income was bound to behave inconveniently. Many overseas borrowers defaulted for a time, or for good. Where old loans were still being serviced, they were often allowed to run out, and overseas borrowers were often unwilling or unable to borrow anew for developmental purposes. Indeed, the UK authorities tried to control their approach to the London market. After 1931, interest rates fell sharply; therefore Britain suffered whenever her old debtors replaced old obligations with new ones that bore the new and lower rates of interest. Many overseas direct investments (ODI) became unprofitable, or much less profitable. In 1913, Britain's property income was more than enough to pay the cost of all her food imports. By 1938, though food was cheaper than in 1913, the food bill had risen from £217 million to £294 million, but overseas property income was then only £204 million.

Export volumes fell, and recovered only in part. So did export prices. In 1937 export volume was still only 77 per cent of the 1929 figure, and only 67 per cent of 1913. For employment, it was volume that mattered. Before 1913, a few great staples had dominated Britain's exports. Even in 1929 the old staple trades produced 42 per cent of export receipts and the new industries, such as vehicles, only 8.2 per cent. In the slump, the old staple exports collapsed and did not recover. However, the machinery industry and the newer industries did rather better not only at home but abroad. Their export values rose substantially from 1931–32 to 1937, by which time they contributed 21 per cent of export values, while the old staples yielded a mere 37 per cent.

Of all Britain's traditional markets, only Africa had much to offer in the 1930s. Thanks to the rise in the relative price of gold, South Africa boomed after 1931, and her purchases from Britain rose impressively. By 1938 Africa was taking 13.2 per cent of Britain's exports. The USA took only 4.3 per cent, and Canada 5 per cent. Though eager to industrialise, the South African government made haste slowly, and as its general tariffs were relatively modest the narrowness of preferential concessions did not matter very much. Further, there were close ties between the South African mining industry and the City of London. These may have helped to ensure that import orders went to Britain, not the USA.

In the early 1930s it was widely believed that only a recovery in prices could help Britain to export more. The primary-producing countries had trouble paying interest on their external debts, which bulked large in Britain's overseas assets (IA). They were buying less, and borrowing less, because they had become poorer, and their impoverishment reflected the fall in the prices of the things they had to sell. Higher prices would help them to service their overseas debts, and would produce more prosperity overseas, increasing the flow of orders both governmental and private (Lewis 1949: 147–8, 153–5, 196; Kindleberger 1973: 291–308).

No one doubts that the troubles of the primary producers were important for many of Britain's export industries. But for the old staples, such as cotton or coal, they cannot have mattered much. Overseas prosperity might simply have increased the demand for Japanese cottons, or German and American exports of machinery and consumer goods. Further, to a large extent Britain gained on the swings what she lost on the roundabouts. Because she imported food and raw materials, she could, and did, gain massively from the fall in her import prices. Her domestic economy recovered largely because of a growth in domestic demand, not overseas demand. In this domestic recovery cheaper food and raw materials were important; the new industries grew, and housing estates mushroomed, partly because the typical household had more real income left over to spend on such things.

Some of Britain's own protectionist innovations had the effect of lowering prices for the rest of the world. As tariffs and quotas were introduced for wheat, meat, and dairy products, the UK market was constricted and UK production was stimulated, so that overseas suppliers had to compete for the remaining trade. But many other forces, especially in the early 1930s, tended to increase production relative to demand, and to discourage the holding of stocks. It was not the underdeveloped countries, inside or outside the empire, who were the victims. Rather, the principal sufferers were Australians, New Zealanders, Argentinians, some Europeans, and perhaps North Americans. These were the countries which exported the products where the agrarian protectionism of the UK was making itself felt. Neville Chamberlain, the Chancellor of the Exchequer from autumn 1931 to mid-1937, worried about low prices, and specialised in agricultural protectionism. He would have been shocked to learn that his cherished protectionist devices were price-lowering.

In so far as Britain's preferential system, elaborated at the 1932 Ottawa Conference, stimulated empire production of tropical products relative to world demand, the system itself was price-lowering even when not linked to the protection of Britain's own producers. Further, overseas sugar producers must have suffered from Britain's efforts to stimulate beet-sugar production at home. But, for empire sugar producers at least, this harm was offset partly and perhaps entirely by a variety of special preferential concessions. It is also hard to believe that such effects were important, relative to the other price-depressing forces of the 1930s.

Does the rather flabby export record, and the weak current account, reflect some sort of fundamental failure? Probably not. We have already seen that the change in interest and profit receipts is more than enough to account for the weakness in overseas receipts. For more than a century, Britain had financed a large and growing proportion of its imports by spending the profits and interest from abroad. When these returns fell, the economy could not quickly forgo the imports, or replace them. After a slow start, Britain did not do badly in exporting the products of her newer industries, even under the difficult conditions of the 1930s. To these industries the system of imperial preferences developed at the Ottawa Conference in 1932 may have given a little help. But, for Britain, empire markets could never suffice, whether British goods paid lower duties or not; the Dominions and India were determined to industrialise, while even in the 1930s more than 30 per cent of Britain's exports went to Europe.

By 1938 Britain had somewhat disengaged herself from Europe and the United States while involving herself more closely with the overseas countries of new settlement, to many of which she gave preferential tariff-concessions. In 1938, 31 per cent of UK imports came from Europe, as against 41 per cent in 1913, and 13 per cent from the USA, which had supplied 18 per cent in 1913. The empire provided about 22 per cent of Britain's imports in 1913, and 36 per cent in 1938. The principal foodstuffs accounted for 32 per cent of all imports. Industrial raw materials absorbed more than 22 per cent, and petroleum, 5 per cent. Finished manufactures still made up only 7 per cent, as against 6 per cent in 1913. Few of these manufactures came from the poorer parts of the empire, or from Japan. No one seems to have imagined that empire suppliers could sell many manufactures in Britain. Indeed, at the Ottawa Conference, tariff discussions proceeded on the assumption that UK production would always be cheaper than empire production, and at least as high in quality. Yet Canadian-assembled motor cars had already developed a certain market in the UK.

Further, by 1939, Japanese and Indian cottons had begun to arrive, while Hong Kong and Singapore were sending some clothes and rubber goods. The 'third world' had begun to industrialise; the patterns of the 1960s and 1970s were beginning to emerge.

The floating pound 1931–39

So far as sterling was concerned, the troubles of the summer of 1931 passed with remarkable speed once Britain had left gold. The pound, unlike the mark and many other currencies, remained freely convertible into gold and other moneys, but no longer at a fixed price. At first the exchanges fell sharply. In the winter of 1931–32 the low point was in December, when sterling touched $3.24. Thereafter funds flowed back to London. By the spring of 1932 the UK authorities, worried lest the pound rise too high, devised the Exchange Equalisation Account, which was to manage the floating pound by dealing in the markets for gold, sterling, and foreign moneys. Overtly, it was to smooth day-to-day fluctuations in exchange rates. Covertly, it was to keep sterling at a suitable price. From time to time the authorities changed their ideas about what this suitable price might be. In 1932–33 they were obliged to acquiesce in considerable fluctuations, which took sterling down to $3.145 in November 1932 and up to $5.00 at the end of 1933. Thereafter, though the current account remained weak, until the spring of 1938 there were large inflows of funds to London. Thus sterling balances increased, and to prevent the pound from rising unduly the Account bought large quantities of foreign money, converting these into gold. In effect the repayment of old loans (IA) was roughly covering the current-account deficit and the continuing flow of new overseas direct investment (ODI); extra sterling balances provided the finance for the extra reserves which rose from 34.7 thousand ounces of gold in early 1932 to 119.4 thousand in early 1938.

Throughout the western world, interest rates were remarkably low for most of the 1930s. In London, for instance, the shortest-term government obligations paid very much less than 1 per cent. Thus there was little room for interest rates to attract or repel sterling balances. Since before the Ottawa Conference the UK had been committed to a regime of low interest rates and easy credit for legitimate commercial purposes. The commitment was reaffirmed at the World Monetary and Economic Conference of 1933, and repeated in parliament. What then determined the inflow and outflow of sterling balances? One influence was the policies of the overseas monetary authorities, who had pegged their currencies to sterling in 1931–33. Thus the policies of the South African Reserve Bank and the Australian Commonwealth Bank could, and sometimes did, produce noticeable changes in the balances. Much more important, however, were political fears and expectations about exchange rates. For instance, when the franc was expected to fall in summer 1936, enormous sums were transferred from Paris to London. Late in 1938, when the franc appeared more secure, these sums flowed back across the Channel.

In spring 1938, with the darkening of the European scene, political uncertainty began to work against sterling itself. London's sterling balances having risen from £411 million in December 1931 to £808 million in December 1937 then fell steadily and dramatically, touching £542 million in June 1939 (Parliamentary papers, 1950–51). Knowing that the American government would be annoyed if the pound fell, the UK authorities spent reserves, first to support sterling and then to slow its decline. Of the £808 million reserves in December 1937, £268 million was spent in 1938, and another £73 million in the first six months of 1939. By summer 1939, the UK authorities were worried not just by the prospect of war but by a more technical matter: they feared their reserves (R) had already become too low relative to the sterling balances (SB) which were still freely convertible into other moneys. On 25 August 1939 they let the pound float, and when war broke out they fixed the exchange rate at $4.03.

In a general way, the Bank and the Treasury never stopped hoping that the gold standard would come again. But in 1932 they decided that Britain should not peg the pound to anything, except in the context of a most unlikely general reconstruction of the world monetary scene. In 1933–36 their resolve was strengthened by the antics of President Roosevelt, who liked to play with the gold-value of the dollar, and by the importunities of the French, who believed that if only Britain would return to gold France need not leave it. In September 1936, when the French finally admitted that they would have to reduce the gold-value of the franc, the Chancellor agreed to issue a consoling declaration that paralleled similar French and American statements. These 'Tripartite Declarations' committed the three governments to consult about exchange rate changes, and not to retaliate against one another. They were honoured in the breach, especially by the French, but they did provide a framework within which the three central banks could co-operate in the foreign exchange markets. Further, they led the Americans to promise that they would let the French and the British central banks buy gold from the US authorities whenever they had accumulated dollars. In the course of the discussions which had preceded the Declarations, the Americans and the French pressed long and hard for a 'stabilised' pound. Chamberlain resisted their pressure on principle, not simply because both foreign governments wanted a relatively expensive pound. The UK authorities were not willing to make any commitments which might force them to manage domestic monetary policy with an eye to the exchange rate. They had learned the lesson of the 1920s.

The Second World War 1939–45

In 1939 Britain possessed a weak current account, at least £4910 million of net worth (NW) (Feinstein 1972: 205), falling reserves (R), and a distressing quantity of obligations in the form of sterling balances (SB). Reserves were much larger than in 1914, but other liquid assets (LA) were almost certainly smaller. The country could not hope to finance its allies as it had done in the First World War. Nor could its wartime exports pay for all its needs. Further, the UK could incur no new dollar debts to the USA, since Congress had proscribed all loans to defaulters. (Since 1933, Britain had not been paying interest on the war debts she had incurred in 1915–18.) Until the USA began to provide lend-lease aid in March 1941, Britain had to draw heavily on her reserves, reducing the total from £305 million in mid-1939 to less than £70 million early in 1941. By this time Britain had begun to sell some dollar illiquid assets (IA) often on unfavourable terms, and often under pressure from the American authorities.

Without lend-lease aid, Britain could not have maintained so ample and energetic a war effort. Sayers (1956) rightly reminds us that American help, though not unstinting, was extraordinarily ample and generous. But because the American authorities distrusted Britain, they hoped that when war ended the UK would find herself so dependent on American help and good will that the USA could enforce her own policies for postwar reconstruction. Ever since 1932 American officials and ministers had suspected Britain of manipulating the exchanges in her own favour, and of scheming to exclude American goods from the markets of Britain and the empire. They wanted to prevent such manipulations and schemings. Hence they were most reluctant to let Britain retain any sizeable reserves, in spite of Britain's ever-growing obligations to the sterling area in the form of sterling balances.

Most parts of the empire were inside the sterling area, though Canada was not. Soon after the outbreak of war, Britain and the sterling area were fenced about with the exchange controls that had been avoided before 1939. Even then, British officials were timid about such controls, and reluctant to impose them. But wartime pressures obliged them to act, and to make the controls ever more stringent. As Britain's imports were carefully controlled and as her export capacity fell spectacularly, the exchange rate was of little significance to trade. As the empire countries supplied Britain with goods and services, they repaid old long-term obligations (B) and accumulated new sterling balances (SB) which were unspendable under wartime conditions. These rose by £2879 million from 1939 to 1946. Meanwhile, reserves (R) fell by £152 million. Canada gave Britain $1000 million, and provided another $700 million as an interest-free loan. Nevertheless, Britain's illiquid external assets (IA) were reduced by £118 million, and total external disinvestment was £4198 million, allowing for extra SB and the fall in R (Sayers 1956: chs. VIII to XIII and table 14, p. 503). By 1946, Britain's overseas wealth had fallen disastrously, and with the lost illiquid external assets (IA) had gone much of the property income from them on which Britain had so long relied. Also, though the war itself generated only £650 million in new British government debts to other countries (IL/G) the country could not begin her postwar reconstruction without large additional loans (IL/G) – $3750 million from the USA, $1250 million from Canada, and £80 million in gold from South Africa. Further, in 1948–53, Britain received many thousands of millions of dollars in Marshall Plan aid. Without such loans and gifts, reconstruction would have been even more painful, and the postwar export drive even more desperate.

The new sterling balances were a real threat. A fence of exchange controls would prevent them from immediately exerting pressure on the reserves while giving Britain a protected empire market more secure than any the preferential tariff system could have provided. But Britain's own reserves, in gold and dollars, now served the sterling area as a whole. Further, Britain could not force governments to hold sterling balances indefinitely. Sooner or later it would have to allow conversion into goods, gold, or dollars.

The war had made for rapid progress in new industries and new products, if in nothing else. In developing the sterling-area market, and in re-entering the markets for manufactures in North America and Europe, Britain's industry showed how much it had recently learned. The new skills, and the new protected market, helped to cushion Britain's descent into a new and crueller world, where current production must pay for current imports and where foreigners must be convinced that sterling is worth holding. Perhaps, indeed, the cushion was too soft, and lasted too long. Even in the 1970s, it seems, the lessons may not have been learned.

13

New industries for old? British industry between the wars

B. W. E. ALFORD

Economic historians are sharply divided in their opinions on the performance of British industry between the wars, and are likely to remain so until a great deal more is known about the development of individual industries and firms during these years. It is the incongruity of such features as high unemployment and decaying centres of production together with the new-found freedoms and pleasures of motor cars, talkie films, and rayon underwear, which calls for explanation beyond the level of characterising the period as an economic watershed. Not surprisingly, attempts to provide such an explanation often contain more than an echo of the fierce political disputes of the 1920s and 1930s. The sharpest division is between those economic historians who see high unemployment and the collapse of the staple trades as convincing proof of the slide into the last stages of British industrial capitalism, and those who see these old industries as giving way to an entirely new breed which not only provided the means of recovery in the 1930s, but which also ensured the longer-term viability of the economy. There are, of course, variations on these themes, but, apart from them, there is another fairly distinct approach, which is not so much a compromise as an attempted synthesis of the others. It emphasises the qualitative changes which were producing a world recognisably more like our own than that of the late Victorian and Edwardian ages. Unemployment there was, and low industrial growth there might have been, but the basis of a new economic order was being laid: the interwar years were witnessing the emergence of a mass consumer society, albeit from very humble origins. These differing views provide the framework for the following discussion which will concentrate mainly on manufacturing industry.

The staple industries

Central to any analysis of industrial development over this period are the staple industries – coal, iron and steel, cotton and woollen textiles, major branches of engineering including, most particularly, shipbuilding. They had been fundamental to Britain's economic development up to 1914; the other major industrialised nations had not been similarly dependent. The end came in the immediate post First World War years when these industries fell into deep depression. In the early 1930s conditions worsened and signs of return to vigour did not appear until the very end of the period; even then, only steel was strongly affected, and there was an artificiality about the industry's recovery, as it was largely a response to re-armament within the secure environment of trade protection.

Most analyses of these events turn on three basic economic relationships, though the significance attached to each varies considerably. First, British industry was clearly suffering from changes in world supply conditions. This is most noticeable in the expansion of the Indian and Far Eastern textile industries during and after the First World War: but it was generally true of staple goods production and was associated with an eruption of tariff protection which closed previously available markets. Secondly, the nature of technology and innovation in industry was becoming increasingly concentrated on devising new and more complicated ways of putting together raw materials (often of quite new kinds) to produce new sorts of capital and consumer goods. The overall result was for net value-added in manufacture to form an increasing proportion of the final value of finished goods; in turn this meant that suppliers of raw materials – most especially of traditional kinds – found it difficult, to the point of being impossible, to achieve rises in their incomes commensurate with those of producers of manufactures. This was exacerbated by growing world production of basic commodities. This problem also affected suppliers of foodstuffs, since rising levels of industrial income resulted in a falling income elasticity of demand for food from industrial sectors. The second-round effects of this – that is the effects on demand from primary producers for manufactured goods had particularly serious consequences for British staple goods industries, since approximately 40 per cent of British manufactured exports in 1913 had gone to markets which depended significantly for their income on the supply of raw materials and foodstuffs to the industrial world. This helps to explain why the level of Britain's trade fell over the 1920s against a rising volume for the world as a whole. Thirdly, these difficulties were intensified by the availability of new substitute goods and materials.

Thus the staple industries were being squeezed from both the supply and demand sides and, in the most general terms, it would be possible to represent this by demand and supply curves moving in appropriate directions, showing falling quantities being supplied at falling prices. This implies a very simple model which divides the international economy into primary producers and suppliers of industrial goods, with the UK economy concentrated on the production of particular types of manufactured goods and a major primary commodity, namely, coal. The world does not, however, divide conveniently in this way, to say nothing of the whole range of constraints which arise from direct government intervention in the flow of goods and services. Nevertheless, this analysis does suggest that the solution to the problems facing the staples would have to lie mainly on the supply side, since the greater part of the fall in demand for their goods was permanent.

This view would have to be modified to the extent that the return to the gold exchange standard in 1925, at the prewar parity of $4.86 to £1, is judged to have weakened the export price-competitiveness of British goods. Was the pound over-valued in relation to the dollar and other major currencies by about 10 per cent as is sometimes argued? Even if it was, would it have been possible to devalue? In fact, the manner in which the other major countries returned to gold makes it appear unlikely that they would have allowed the British to devalue sterling by adopting a lower parity (Sayers 1960). Nevertheless, it is still valuable to attempt to answer the question: 'What would have been the effects of a lower parity *ceteris paribus*?', since to do so is one way of estimating the basic competitive efficiency of British industry. Some rough calculations have been made by Moggridge which suggest that for 1928 ('as a typical post-1925 year') a 10 per cent lower rate would have produced an overall balance of payments improvement of £70m which would have been sufficient, for example, to reduce unemployment by 729 000 and still leave a margin of £25m. which could have been used to finance other objectives (Moggridge 1972: 98–112, 245–50). The assumptions on which this calculation is made, however, are open to serious question; it fails for example to take into account the weight of evidence indicating that, effectively, British goods were not wanted at any price; in other words, shifts in demand curves would have swamped probable movements along demand curves through lower supply prices (see Balfour Committee 1925; Sandberg 1974). Moggridge also fails to recognise that, because of the high proportion of British trade which went to countries whose currencies were tied closely to sterling, a much larger devaluation than 10 per cent would probably have been necessary to achieve these effects on the balance of payments.

Returning to the staple industries, one which has recently been closely investigated is cotton textiles (Sandberg 1974), particularly in relation to the question of whether the apparent failure to introduce the most advanced technology over the late nineteenth and early twentieth centuries represented entrepreneurial failure (see chapter 5). Sandberg estimated the costs of and returns to alternative investments in new techniques and concluded that manufacturers were behaving rationally in not adopting the most up-to-date machinery. Most commentators have broadly accepted his judgement, though there have been qualifications about the assumptions involved and the total reliance on data relating to the industry as a whole as against individual firms. Nevertheless, what establishes the main thesis is Sandberg's analysis of the declining comparative advantage of the industry in the international market; this is based on the traditional theory of international trade combined with careful appraisal of the statistics of overseas markets and production. Study of the other staple industries might reveal a similar decline in comparative advantage.

Table 13.1. *Britain's output of iron and steel as a percentage of that of Germany and France (by volume)*

	Pig iron and ferro alloys			Steel ingots and castings		
	1913	1927/28	1936/37	1913	1927/28	1936/37
Germany	85	50	53	55	51	65
France	114	74	115	111	100	173

Source: Svennilson (1954: 134)

In examining the problems of the staples, it is particularly important not to concentrate on the interwar years in isolation from the previous period. For example, the iron and steel industry appears to have improved its position markedly in relation to its counterparts in France and Germany between the mid 1920s and the mid 1930s but, as table 13.1 shows, this performance was not so impressive when it is viewed against comparative positions in 1913. Furthermore, these figures take no account of the sharp relative decline in the British position which had already occurred over the quarter century before the First World War. There is, also, the question of the extent to which the upswing of the 1930s resulted from tariff protection. In 1935, for example, *The Economist* gleefully reported what it saw as Lord Nuffield's conversion to free trade: after some years of campaigning for protection for British cars, Nuffield was now complaining about the high price he was having to pay for protected domestic steel.

Another way of judging industrial performance is to examine productivity changes. In all industries, such measures are notoriously difficult to calculate; accordingly, they have to be used with great care, particularly when comparisons between industries are attempted. To make matters more difficult, in this period there is a shortage of basic data. Nevertheless, a major study of labour productivity by Rostas (1943; 1948) revealed differences in productivity between British and foreign industries of such an order as to be unattributable to statistical error. For 1936 he found that in relation to the corresponding British industries, physical productivity per man in German coalmines and coke ovens was 50 per cent higher, in cotton spinning, rayon and silk between 20 per cent and 25 per cent higher, and in blast furnaces, steel smelting and rolling between 10 per cent and 20 per cent higher. Comparative figures for the USA were even more striking: productivity was substantially higher in all US industries and enormously higher in some, with a maximum difference of 200 per cent for blast furnaces. Alternative, though similar estimates by Clark (1951: 246–315) show little correlation between size of firm or industry and productivity, a finding which has been confirmed by a very recent investigation into concentration in UK industry (Hannah and Kay: 1977). Hence it seems unlikely that Britain was

Table 13.2. *United Kingdom: rates of change of output, employment, capital stock, output per employee, capital per employee, and 'total factor' productivity, 1924–29, 1929–37 and 1924–37 (per cent per annum) – manufacturing industries*

	Output			Employment			Capital stock			Output per employee			Capital per employee			Residual		
	1924–29	1929–37	1924–37	1924–29	1929–37	1924–37	1924–29	1929–37	1924–37	1924–29	1929–37	1924–37	1924–29	1929–37	1924–37	1924–29	1929–37	1924–37
Building materials	5.2	4.4	4.7	2.6	2.2	2.4	-0.2	0.5	-0.4	2.6	2.2	2.3	-2.7	-2.7	-2.7	3.5	3.0	3.2
Chemicals	2.4	3.6	3.1	1.8	1.1	1.4	1.4	1.5	1.5	0.7	2.5	1.8	-0.4	0.4	0.1	0.8	2.3	1.7
Ferrous metal manufacture	0.7	4.4	3.0	-0.1	1.3	0.8	-0.1	0.6	0.4	0.8	3.1	2.2	0.0	-0.7	-0.4	0.8	3.3	2.3
Non-ferrous metal manufacture	3.6	5.7	4.9	1.1	3.1	2.4	0.4	1.7	1.2	2.5	2.6	2.5	-0.7	-1.5	-1.2	2.7	3.0	2.9
Shipbuilding	1.9	0.9	1.2	-2.6	-0.6	-1.4	-0.3	-1.3	-0.9	4.5	1.5	2.6	2.3	-0.7	0.5	3.8	1.7	2.5
Mechanical engineering	3.9	0.7	1.9	1.4	2.2	1.9	-0.1	0.4	0.2	2.5	-1.5	0.0	-1.5	-1.8	-1.7	2.9	-1.0	0.5
Electrical engineering	4.0	7.8	6.3	4.8	6.1	5.6	2.1	1.7	1.9	-0.8	1.7	0.7	-2.7	-4.4	-3.8	0.0	3.0	1.8
Vehicles	5.6	6.6	6.2	3.3	2.6	2.9	2.5	4.4	3.7	2.3	3.9	3.3	-0.8	1.8	0.8	2.6	3.4	3.1
Precision instruments	5.2	2.4	3.5	2.5	-1.1	0.3	—	—	—	2.7	3.5	3.2	—	—	—	—	—	—
Metal goods, n.e.s.	4.7	4.9	4.8	2.1	3.0	2.7	—	—	—	2.6	1.8	2.1	—	—	—	—	—	—

Other manufactures	5.9	5.1	5.4	3.3	0.7	1.7	0.8	0.9	0.9	2.6	4.3	3.7	−2.5	0.2	−0.9	3.4	4.3	4.0
Cotton	—	—	—	−1.0	−3.0	−2.2	−0.2	−4.0	−2.6	—	—	—	0.8	−1.1	−0.4	—	—	—
Woollen and worsted	—	—	—	−2.4	−0.5	−1.2	−0.4	−0.4	−0.4	—	—	—	2.0	0.1	0.8	—	—	—
Rayon and silk	—	—	—	11.7	1.0	5.0	11.3	5.1	7.4	—	—	—	−0.4	4.1	2.5	—	—	—
Other textiles	—	—	—	0.9	0.2	0.5	−0.5	−0.6	−0.6	—	—	—	−1.4	−0.8	−1.1	—	—	—
Textile finishing	—	—	—	−0.1	−1.7	−1.1	−0.5	−0.9	−0.8	—	—	—	−0.4	0.8	0.3	—	—	—
Textiles	−0.9	3.1	1.6	−0.2	−1.2	−0.8	0.1	−1.6	−0.9	−0.7	4.3	2.4	0.3	−0.4	−0.1	−0.8	4.4	2.4
Leather	−1.1	3.7	1.8	−0.6	1.3	0.6	2.3	1.6	1.9	−0.5	2.4	1.2	2.9	0.3	1.3	−1.4	2.3	0.9
Clothing	2.7	1.7	2.1	0.5	0.4	0.5	2.6	1.4	1.9	2.2	1.3	1.7	2.1	1.0	1.4	1.6	1.0	1.2
Food	3.5	4.2	3.9	1.2	2.2	1.8	0.2	0.6	0.4	2.2	2.0	2.1	−1.1	−1.5	−1.3	2.6	2.5	2.5
Drink	0.0	1.1	0.7	0.6	1.0	0.8	0.5	0.3	0.4	−0.6	0.1	−0.2	0.0	−0.7	−0.4	−0.5	0.3	0.0
Tobacco	5.4	2.3	3.5	2.5	−0.5	0.6	2.5	1.4	1.8	3.0	2.8	2.9	0.1	1.9	1.2	3.0	2.2	2.5
Paper and printing	2.9	2.6	2.7	2.4	1.4	1.8	2.0	1.8	1.9	0.6	1.2	1.0	−0.3	0.3	0.1	0.7	1.1	0.9
Timber and furniture	7.4	3.2	4.8	2.9	1.3	1.9	1.5	2.1	1.9	4.5	1.9	2.9	−2.0	−0.5	−1.0	—	—	—
(Construction)	(7.4)	(2.9)	(4.6)	(3.6)	(2.8)	(3.1)				(3.9)	(0.0)	(1.5)				(4.5)	(0.2)	(1.8)
Manufacturing	2.8	3.5	3.3	1.2	1.2	1.2	0.6	0.4	0.5	1.6	2.4	2.1	−0.6	−0.8	−0.7	1.8	2.6	2.3

Source: Dowie (1968)

suffering from unavoidable disadvantages through the limitations of the domestic market. Furthermore, these comparisons of productivity per head for a particular year, crude though they are, give perspective to estimates of productivity *change* over the period as a whole. Thus, while output per employee and total factor productivity each show varying rates of growth for the staple industries (see table 13.2), the cumulative effects of these were still far from enough to close the large gaps which existed between British and best foreign performance.

A complicating factor arises from the high incidence of unemployment in the basic industries and the consequent 'shake out' effects of these on productivity. Marginal units went out of production and this caused average levels of productivity to rise independently of any changes in technology or organisation in those which remained. While such reductions in labour were desirable in respect of longer-term efficiency, this still left major problems of achieving higher levels of productivity within the firms that remained, a process which almost certainly required further reductions in labour forces.

More generally, the difficulty of interpreting productivity measures at the industry-wide level is shown by the considerable variations over all manufacturing industry. Productivity gains were recorded by industries where employment was rising, in others where it was falling, and in yet others where it was stable. It is impossible, moreover, to make sense of these figures by using a 'new/old' division of industries, since neither 'new' or 'old' industries behaved in a uniform manner (Dowie 1968).

Finally, it is necessary to consider whether there was a relationship between the length and depth of the depression experienced by the staple industries and possible cycles in domestic and international economic activity. For all the intellectual effort and enterprise which has been put into cyclical theory by economists of different generations, it has had little success when applied to the real world. Economic activity fluctuates; the problem is that it does not do so with anything approaching predictable regularity: 'random shocks' play a big part in most trade cycle analyses, and random shocks are part of the very stuff of historical reality (see chapter 2). Perhaps somewhat ironically, when viewed with the advantage of hindsight, it was the international nature of certain aspects of depression in the interwar years which stimulated a sharp upswing in trade cycle theorising. However, Kindleberger (1973), surveying much earlier work in this area, has made out a strong case for the importance of structural and institutional weaknesses in the international economy – particularly in respect of shifts in the supply and demand of primary products and the unwillingness of the USA to take over Britain's traditional creditor role – in the unusual impact of external factors on domestic economies; by so doing, he has effectively ruled out an explanation in terms of possible conjunctions of regular international and domestic trade cycles. Moreover Svennilson (1954) produced an impressive amount of evidence on various sectors of the major European economies which gives powerful support to the view that sees industrial problems of this period – especially in relation to the staples – as being fundamentally structural in nature; a view which is indirectly borne out by the manner of the secular shift to higher rates of economic growth among the industrialised nations after the Second World War.

Growth in the 1930s

What was happening in other sectors of industry? Perhaps the most convenient way to approach this question is to examine the school of thought which focusses its analysis on the 1930s as a decade of economic recovery. This idea was first put forward by Kahn (1946: 105–24) but it was taken up in full-blooded fashion by Richardson (1967) and it has attracted other adherents. Richardson begins by arguing that no one economic theory provides an adequate explanation of economic development over the 1930s, on the convincing grounds that the assumptions and definitions involved simply don't match the evidence from the real world. In particular, he stresses the wide variation in behaviour between sectors of industry, which cut across any kind of analysis in terms of regular cyclical behaviour. Accordingly, he adopts a somewhat eclectic theoretical approach.

First, the so-called 'over-commitment' of resources to declining, or slow-growth, sectors of industry is analysed. It is seen as a cumulative process at work since the end of the nineteenth century, one long recognised by commentators who have stressed the structural basis of Britain's industrial problems. The second, and distinctive, element of the analysis is its claim that there was a significant structural change in British industry over the 1930s, which accounted for economic recovery and which was the outcome of a fortuitous (i.e. non-regular) conjunction of demand and supply factors. On the demand side, the depression led to a rise in real incomes for those remaining in employment – especially in the middle income ranges – because prices fell while money incomes remained stationary or fell only slightly. This is alleged to have resulted in a changing composition of demand towards a new range of consumer goods. Coincidentally on the supply side, so the argument goes, a group of industries – the so-called new industries including chemicals, electrical engineering, vehicles, precision instruments, artificial fibres – were beginning to harvest the fruits of technological change and together they formed an interdependent development block in the economy, which responded strongly to the new current of demand which was being generated. Hence the recovery.

Richardson stresses the empirical side of the analysis and presents a range of data to support his thesis. Nevertheless, to establish his mechanism convincingly requires more than the presentation of percentage swings in aggregate figures for production, capital formation and consumer expenditure, on which he mainly relies. More directly, a number of careful investigations of the same data sources have fundamentally undermined his analysis. Dowie's (1968) careful examination of productivity changes reveals nothing unique about the productivity performance of the so-called new industries. More recently Buxton (1975) has examined data on capital formation and levels of employment and output. So far as capital is concerned his analysis elaborates the view (Alford 1972: 19–29) that figures for levels and distribution of capital stock between manufacturing industries at the end of the period simply do not support the hypothesis of substantial structural changes towards 'new' (capital-intensive) industries over the previous decade, and this is reinforced by figures for employment and output. Moreover, the output of these industries is shown to have been too small to have acted as the central driving force of the alleged shift to a higher growth plane over the 1930s. As will be seen, overall levels of capital formation in manufacturing industry were low during this period.

A more ambitious test of the development block thesis has been attempted by von Tunzelmann (1977) by using the techniques of input–output analysis (Shackle 1973: 11–13). Given the nature of available data the results are bound to be rough and ready, but they suggest strongly that the level of interdependence between 'new' industries during the early 1930s was far too low for them to have made up a distinct development block; indeed, in a number of cases the interdependence of 'new' and 'old' is shown to have been substantially greater – an obvious example being the motor car and steel industries. In addition, this group of industries could hardly have operated as the triggering mechanism for recovery by virtue of rising demand for their products. By taking the motor industry – the favourite example of the recovery school – it can be shown that in terms of value, there was a very sharp *fall* in demand for cars from 1929 to 1932, and demand had only just topped the 1925 level by 1937; even then, it did not match the upswing in total manufactured production. Those who have stressed the impact of rising demand for cars have measured it in terms of volume and have not, therefore, made allowance for smaller cars at cheaper prices. Of course, there are a number of statistical problems involved in either of these measures – particularly concerning corrections for changes in prices and quality – but the *magnitude* of the fall in the value of cars purchased is independently significant.

The recovery thesis links the 'new' industries to the well-known expansion of building, particularly of domestic homes, during the early 1930s, though building is usually assigned a secondary role. However, if we imagined that the gross output of building had remained stationary between 1930 and 1935 then, *ceteris paribus*, the gross output of the five major 'new' industries would have been reduced by only £2.1m. (von Tunzelmann 1977). Building, moreover, was not especially important in terms of its independent contribution to output. It certainly accounted for a very high percentage of capital formation – though in significant measure this was a reflection of low investment in other sectors – but in output terms the industry's contribution averaged 5 per cent of the total for the economy over the interwar years as compared with 28 per cent for manufacturing industry. Nevertheless, this is not to deny that the pattern of building development had some important, though non-quantifiable, effects on industrial performance; this will be considered later.

More generally, the recovery thesis is based on false premises.

The figures show that overall growth in domestic product in the 1920s and 1930s was broadly similar. There are, however, sectoral differences between the two decades... growth over the thirties was maintained by an acceleration in growth in the manufacturing and distribution sectors which offset decelerations elsewhere. But at the same time this switch must not be allowed to obscure the fact that there were *relative* changes within the total: agriculture, for example, failed to maintain its high rate of growth of the twenties, and distribution and manufacturing, although improving their performances, were by no means the leading sectors overall [Alford 1972: 20].

Furthermore, the division of industry between 'old' and 'new' is conceptually, let alone statistically, unacceptable:

In a number of cases 'new' industries grew out of 'old' industries and were, in effect, the tangible results of efforts at modernisation; one of the best examples of this is provided by the silk and rayon industry...this artificial distinction results in large part from defining industries simply in terms of technical innovation, and ignoring such aspects as organization and management. There is, too, as Dowie points out, the danger of defining 'new' in terms of expanding, and by this means establishing what it is wished to prove by tautological definition [Alford 1972: 21].

Discussion of statistical evidence of this kind may, however, obscure important qualitative changes which, if they occurred, might have affected growth in the long run. Such changes are difficult to measure, not least because of the lack of useful economic theory, which might allow us to assess the possible effects and indications of structural imbalances in the economy. However, it is still worth examining individual industries and firms in more detail, in a further attempt to see how far their performance reflected structural deficiencies or merely lack of demand.

Change in particular industries

During the period from 1900 to 1939, British industry as a whole was expanding and matching new patterns of consumption, which were reflected in changing patterns of social behaviour. In this process the First World War had a profound influence, even if many of the promises of new social welfare, made by Lloyd George and other leading politicians, were cynically dishonoured by the same men once peace was restored. Yet it is exceedingly difficult to determine the effects of the war on industry. Such factors as the introduction of standardisation and mass production in important sectors of engineering, and the extensive employment of women in skilled and semi-skilled jobs, have to be weighed against the distorting, and in some cases, retarding effects of war requirements on long-term development. Over-expansion and over-capitalisation in the staples were obviously large items on the debit side, while the desire to return to the conditions of what was seen as the prewar golden age – which was largely a kingdom of the mind – worked to shut out whatever thoughts there might have been of dealing radically with what were becoming long-term weaknesses in British industry. When, eventually, some attempt was made to meet these difficulties, it was left to a motley band of bankers, financiers, and industrialists marching under the banner of 'rationalisation', a new orthodoxy which at least had the virtue of flexibility in that it could mean all things to all men.

In judging the performance of industry use has already been made of comparative data, and since British firms were operating within an international market this seems the most appropriate yardstick to adopt, making due allowance, of course, for such factors as trade restrictions. Comparisons of productivity, for example, have revealed the staple industries in an unfavourable light, but when the full spectrum of manufacturing is considered the picture appears more satisfactory. Kahn (1946) produced figures showing the burgeoning in the inter-war years of sectors of industry producing new goods. Moreover, the performance of some of these in terms of physical productivity was equal to or better than their German counterparts, though still substantially below their American ones. However, the problems of comparison are particularly acute here because of such wide variations in the type and quality of goods concerned. It is necessary, therefore, to examine the level of performance of these other industries more closely.

First of all it is important to get output levels into perspective. In the case of the motor industry, for example, the number of passenger cars per 1000 inhabitants in the UK in 1938 was 39 as compared with 194 in the USA, and the UK did not match the 1938 USA level until 1967/68. Moreover, while Britain overtook France as the main European producer in 1932, France still had a higher per capita consumption in 1938 (42 per 1000). Germany's consumption was significantly lower (21 per 1000) but the striking thing is the rate at which it increased over the 1930s. UK consumption of electricity for domestic purposes was substantially higher than for other major European countries – for example, it was over three times that of France in per capita terms in 1938. By contrast, however, UK consumption of electricity per units of industrial production (which reflected total use and not efficiency of use) was relatively low in 1938 – only the Netherlands, Czechoslovakia and Denmark were lower, and the UK was two thirds the German level.

In the chemical industry, Britain's position had been a laggard one since the late nineteenth century. Arising from worrying problems in relation to the supply of strategic materials during the war and, subsequently, from government involvement, there was a major reorganisation of the industry leading to the formation of ICI in 1926 (Reader 1970), and this helped to improve Britain's international showing. Chemicals embodied, in effect, a number of industries and this makes comparisons hazardous. Britain's output of synthetic dyestuffs by volume increased from 3 per cent to 12 per cent of world production between 1913 and 1924, and output for the industry as a whole grew at 3.1 per cent per year between 1924 and 1937. Yet the industry's overall international performance was less impressive. As a percentage of world production, by value, Britain's share fell from 11 per cent in 1913 to 9 per cent in 1938. This cannot easily be regarded as the result of infant industries growing up in other countries, since Britain's own position is generally regarded as having been fairly infantile in 1913.

In synthetic fibres Britain had led the world in the development of rayon in the 1920s through the major company of Courtaulds. Inevitably this lead was bound to disappear with the establishment of new producers, especially in the USA, Japan and Germany. Nevertheless, Coleman shows how a growing measure of inefficiency, resulting from bad management in Courtaulds, which still accounted for almost 60 per cent of UK rayon output, added significantly to the decline in the industry's international position in the 1930s. Of even greater importance, Coleman observes that despite its laggard performance in the 1930s, Courtauld's output per man year was still double that for UK industry as a whole between 1925 and 1938, which reflects badly upon UK industry (Coleman 1969: 171–428).

What was happening to levels of production was, in part, determined by levels of capital investment. Table 13.2 shows the rate of growth of capital per employee to have been generally low for all industries and it was *negative*, in fact, for approximately half the industries listed. This could well reflect relatively high ratios of capital per employee at the beginning of the period. If it does, then it would be reasonable to expect output per man to have grown correspondingly rapidly, subsequently, because of a more efficient use of capital; this might have come from capturing economies of scale. Significantly, this rise in output per man did not occur in mechanical engineering, electrical engineering, drink, paper and printing; and only in vehicles, precision instruments, and 'other manufactures' did the growth rate of output per employee rise above 3 per cent per annum.

The low rate of growth of capital stock in manufacturing is also clear from table 13.2. These calculations represent the accumulation of *net* capital investment; gross investment is in some ways a more appropriate measure since replacement capital usually embodies a fair amount of innovation. Even for gross investment, however, the record is poor, particularly for the 1930s (chapter 10; Feinstein 1965: 34–51). There are enormous difficulties in arriving at reasonable estimates and those which are available are recognised as being subject to significant degrees of error. Nevertheless, the effect of these factors would have to be very substantial and in the same direction in order to undermine our broad conclusion as to the low investment performance of manufacturing; this, in turn, means that there was a slow rate of technical innovation.

It is possible that industry should not be blamed for this deficiency. One possible cause is the alleged lack of co-operation between industry and finance, to which the Macmillan Committee (Parliamentary Papers 1930–31) drew attention. The Committee argued that there was a lack of funds for capital investment by medium-sized firms – those left in the 'Macmillan gap' because of a lack of interest in them by city financiers. Such evidence as is available, however, does not reveal finance as the major guilty party. Quite apart from the activities of the Bank of England and some commercial banks, which will be discussed shortly, institutions in the capital market were reorganising themselves in response to the collapse of overseas business, so that traditional agencies such as acceptance houses were turning their attention to domestic industry as were the rapidly growing insurance companies and investment trusts. Moreover, the success of the new issues market, when it was used, does not indicate a shortage of 'speculative' capital. For all this, in the light of post Second World War developments in this area it would appear that there was a shortage of financial expertise in the company sector, and firms might have co-operated more with financial institutions to develop such expertise in their joint best interests.

Organisation of production and technical change will be considered in a little more detail shortly, but even at the industry-wide level there are some indications of backwardness in Britain compared with foreign industries. Two examples are worthy of particular note here: cars and electrical applicances. 'In 1939 the six leading British producers, making roughly 350 000 private cars, turned out more than forty different engine types and an even greater number of chassis and body models, which was considerably more than the number offered by the three leading producers in the United States making perhaps 3 500 000 cars' (Kahn 1946: 112–13). German car production was rising more sharply than British in the 1930s and was being developed on the basis of large volume and low cost (Overy 1975), and this was obviously of more than short-term significance. In the electrical goods field, imports of mass-produced (mainly American) radios, vacuum cleaners, batteries, etc., flooded on to the British Market, rising in value from £670 000 in 1907 to £2.6m. in 1924 and £6.3m. in 1930 (Kahn 1946: 113–20). They were simply cheaper than corresponding British goods. After 1932, however, a tariff cut back imports and by 1935 they had been reduced to £3m., which was still significantly higher than imports of other types of electrical goods. Moreover, although there was growth in domestic production behind the tariff, the degree of market penetration achieved by 1939 was quite low even by the standards of the early 1950s.

Discussion of productivity cannot be satisfactory, even at this fairly general level, without some related consideration of the labour supply. This subject is discussed more fully in chapter 11 but certain aspects of it are of particular relevance here. According to some commentators, for example, labour supply is not judged to have been a constraint on the restructuring of industry in this period: first, the rate of growth of the labour force rose; second, there were exceptionally high levels of unemployment; third, in so far as it was necessary to transfer labour from lower to higher growth sectors, the need was mainly for unskilled and semi-skilled workers so that there were no problems of training. Such suggestions are attractive to economists trying to build models of the period, since if they are correct then the supply of labour can be taken to be completely elastic over wide ranges of output; the problem lies, however, in the assumption that an abundant stock of labour implies a corresponding degree of mobility.

A number of studies have shown how voluntary labour mobility during this period was induced by comparative levels of unemployment and distance, whereas the attraction of higher wages was relatively unimportant (Makower, Marschak and Robinson 1939). Moreover, the numbers involved were proportionately very small, even allowing for the problems of measurement (chapter 7); much of the mobility was intra-regional and reflected changes in residence and not changes of occupation. There were attempts to promote movement of workers through industrial transference schemes, first introduced in 1928, but the results achieved by these and by certain provisions of the Special Areas policy (1934) were very small (Dennison 1939). All the time, moreover, mobility was becoming more difficult because of the opening up of new factories in London, the South-East, and the Midlands, areas away from the major centres of the declining sectors of the staple industries. The popular explanation for this shift – and one particularly favoured by the Barlow Commission (Parliamentary Papers 1939–40) – has been in terms of the alleged cost-advantages to consumer-goods manufacturers in being located near large markets. More recent evidence on individual cases would suggest, however, that the first Commissioner for the Special Areas was near the mark when he stated: 'much of the growth of Great London is not based on strictly economic factors; psychology plays an important part in the matter'; as another writer has put it (Hall 1962: 121–71), it was often a case of '*J'y suis, j'y augmente*', and this can be taken to include elements of pure chance. Nevertheless, once the movement started in a particular sector of industry it tended to generate growth in a whole range of ancillary and cognate industries and trades. Because of this concentration in particular areas the regenerative potential of more diversified industrial activity was limited and the plight of the depressed areas intensified.

If industry refused to go to labour, why did labour not move to industry? There were a number of reasons. The way in which the labour force expanded, both in overall size and as a proportion of the total population, resulted in a rise in its average age; this naturally tended to retard mobility, especially among the oldest age groups which were those experiencing the highest levels of unemployment. The decline in the staple industries made substantial numbers of skilled craftsmen permanently redundant and such men did not then – any more than similar men do now – move easily into semi- or un-skilled jobs even for higher wages; pride in skills and antipathy towards production-line factory work were major obstacles to flexibility. Another reason was union practice on wage differentials and manning levels. Although the bargaining position of unions weakened between the wars, most obviously because of high unemployment, there is no evidence of substantial undermining of these practices. Indeed, a worrying development, in terms of efficient production, was the manner in which traditional patterns of union organisation – including a multiplicity of unions within a given industry – were reproduced in expanding sectors such as motor vehicles and electrical engineering; the effects on productivity are, however, difficult to determine.

Beyond these immediate reasons, there were certain obstacles which deterred some workers from shifting jobs if to do so involved geographical mobility. One consequence of the highly localised nature of much of nineteenth-century industrial development was the associated growth of a complex pattern of social overhead capital. Thus, the dismal features of northern towns such as Stockton-on-Tees were vividly described by Priestley (1934: 342): 'The real town is finished. It is like a theatre that is kept open merely for the sale of drinks in the bars and chocolates in the corridors'; yet these towns still provided essential services and provided some meaning to life for whole communities. While it would have made economic – let alone social – nonsense to have written off such places, if labour was to move out of them then alternative services had to be provided elsewhere; this was something which only central government could have done, whether directly or through the agency of local authorities. But for the greater part government either lacked the political will for this or was determined to pursue other goals, in particular sound finance through strict limitation of public expenditure. Whatever the government might have believed, such policies did not get to the root of industrial problems.

Housing is a particularly important example. A large number of new houses were built between the wars – just over four million – and there was a particularly sharp boom in the early 1930s. But the effects of this activity on the industrial labour force were complex. State assistance to housing, whether through local authorities or through subsidies to private builders, made provision for the lower middle class and better-off working class; unsubsidised private building, which averaged 71 per cent of the number of houses built in the 1930s, was almost entirely for the middle-class market; rent control on certain types of homes, mainly council homes, operated as a disguised subsidy to labour inertia; the addition to housing stock during this period fell well short of what was required when account is taken of the number of houses which could be classed as uninhabitable and of the rise in the number of families; there was little attempt to plan building development, and the distribution of middle-class housing, especially, laid the basis for costly urban problems in the future, while working-class housing was provided somewhat haphazardly since it was dependent on local politics and local resources (Ashworth 1954: 191–237). In certain respects Britain became better housed over this period, but the manner of this improvement probably hindered rather than helped the longer-term development of the economy.

Changes in the structure of industry

What changes in industrial structure did occur, in spite of these obstacles? A number of studies of industrial structure were made in the 1930s (Clark 1951) but much more comprehensive work has been done since then. On the basis of the 1935 Census of Production, Leak and Maizels (1945) examined sizes and types of firms, the relative importance of subsidiary firms, connections between industries, and degrees of concentration by trade and product. The main measures used were gross and net output and employment and this study provides a very useful, detailed cross-section view of British industry at the mid 1930s. But it is of limited value when comparisons between industries are attempted, and of even more limited use in attempts to examine *changes* in industrial structure. There are well-known weaknesses to prewar censuses of production in terms of definitions and coverage but, beyond this, there are three major problems. First, crude employment figures measure only one aspect of firm size – by themselves they tell us nothing about capitalisation, sales, or profits; while this may not be too much of a handicap when making comparisons within industry, it is a major obstacle to inter-industry analysis. Second, gross and net output figures for industries, firms and, more particularly, employees, can be thoroughly misleading measures unless one has precise information about capitalisation and about the price and market structure within which firms operate; variations in output may, for example, reflect no more than comparative market power and be of no *real* significance in terms of productivity. Third, gross and net output are average figures which tell us nothing about marginal outputs.

A direct analysis of concentration was carried out by Hart and Prais (1956) who focused their enquiry on the changing degree of concentration in the UK over the period 1885–1950. Their measures were based on the capitalisation of a sample of firms quoted on the London stock exchange, and these led to the main conclusion that concentration in UK industry had been increasing up to 1939 and that it had occurred with a high degree of statistical regularity: 'the number of companies which quadruple their size is approximately equal to the number that quarter it...the number that grow sixteenfold is approximately equal to the number that are only a sixteenth of their original size, and so on; further the frequency of these proportionate growths is distributed as the normal curve of error' (Hart and Prais 1956: 171). Their second major conclusion for this period was that 'in studying changes in business concentration over time more attention should be paid to the internal growth of firms than to the possibility of combination among firms' (Hart and Prais 1956: 169).

Hannah and Kay (1977) have cast strong doubt on this analysis even though they are in substantial agreement with it on the *level* of concentration which it indicates. They, too, use the capitalisation of firms at market value as the basis for their measures, though their sample and techniques differ in certain important respects from Hart's and Prais's; this leads them to give much greater weight than the latter to merger as a source of concentration. They show a fall in concentration between 1930 and 1948, though it was probably of a lower order than the figures indicate because of the relative growth of small firms, which are not entirely captured in their sample. Following from this, their final conclusion offers little support to those who see continually increasing concentration as the natural condition of modern mixed economies.

Finally Prais (1976) suggests that mergers were not a major cause of the growth in concentration; in line with the earlier study by Hart and Prais (1956) he stresses instead the varying rates of growth of firms which will, on the basis of statistical assumptions, be likely to lead to concentration. Thus, the causes of increased concentration remain a matter of dispute.

Analysis of concentration certainly provides no support, however, for the hypothesis of there being a close positive correlation between scale and productivity. Indeed, the available evidence casts doubt on the validity of Verdoorn's Law which alleges that there is a correlation between the rate of growth of output and the rate of growth of productivity, which in turn is dependent on economies of scale and learning by doing (Dowie 1968: 71–2). Dowie's results, point, instead, to the need to examine the quality of changes which occurred at the level of individual firms, independently of size, if a clear understanding of the process of structural change is to be achieved.

The need for reorganisation was most obvious in the staple industries, and a leading candidate was the coal industry. The saga of events through which the miners led the country to the General Strike of 1926 is well known; for all the industrial trauma this caused – no doubt, in part because of it – the problems of the industry remained obdurately unresolved. By the end of the 1920s 'ration-alisation' had become the accepted panacea for its ills, though while this was understood to involve reorganisation and the closure of some pits, there was no generally agreed basis on how it should be administered. Confusion was compounded in the Coal Mines Act of 1930 (Kirby 1973a and b), so, although by the end of the 1930s a considerable amount of concentration had been achieved, surplus capacity and uneconomic pits remained; defensive controls and output sharing were preferred to more thoroughgoing reorganisation, by owners and miners alike.

In many ways cotton was in more desperate straits than coal. By the end of the 1920s it was coming to be accepted that the industry had suffered a permanent decline, but it was more difficult to get agreement on how to adjust to that decline. In this case rationalisation was initiated by the Bank of England through its involvement in the promotion of the Lancashire Cotton Corporation in 1929–30 – a mammoth corporate oddity whose main *raison d'être* was to provide emergency relief to certain clearing banks which had over-extended themselves in lending to cotton firms. In the course of this and other forays into the industrial field the Bank established two agencies through which it could in future operate in matters of this kind: the Securities Management Trust (1929) and the Bankers' Industrial Development Co. (1930) (Sayers 1976: 314–30). However, cotton's problems did not end with the Corporation. Any sensible long-term solution required a central agency with the ability to write off past financial mistakes in accordance with a carefully worked out overall plan. For example, if rationalisation had been based on a financial yardstick, then a number of firms should have been closed down which were, in fact, technically the most up-to-date, simply by virtue of their earlier financial profligacy in respect of re-equipping. Unfortunately, much more needs to be known about individual companies before any thorough analysis can be made, but sufficient is known to make it certain that the best of all possible worlds was not achieved. The Bank did its bit – not least in order to forestall demands for more radical political action in this and other industries – and the government did its bit through the Import Duties Advisory Committee (Lucas 1937: 146–73). In return for trade protection the government extracted undertakings from industries that certain measures of reorganisation would be undertaken. For its part the cotton industry agreed to reduce the number of spindles in operation; this was reinforced by further legislation in 1936. Substantial reductions were made, but even so in 1939 only 75 per cent of spinning capacity and 68 per cent of weaving capacity was employed (Kirby 1974).

Similar problems were faced by the steel industry, though here the long-term prospects were necessarily brighter, if Britain had any future as an industrial power. The Bank of England was very active in attempting to restructure the industry, not least because Montagu Norman, the Governor, felt he had a mission to lead the industry out of its difficulties. The Bank became involved in major schemes affecting Armstrongs, Beardmore, Richard Thomas, and others. The guiding principle in this activity, however, seems to have been the need to achieve financial reconstruction, while investigations into commercial and managerial matters were accorded distinctly secondary importance. Correspondingly, reconstruction schemes initiated within the industry tended to suffer from a surfeit of financial advice (often conflicting) with, once again, insufficient attention being paid to longer-term commercial realities. Indeed, a lot of thought seems to have been given to safeguarding certain industrial dynasties from heavy financial losses. In addition, the steel industry became particularly sensitive politically in the 1930s, as witnessed by the pressures imposed on Richard Thomas & Co. to site its new strip mill at Ebbw Vale. Nevertheless, protection enabled the industry to soft-pedal on reorganisation and associated technical change.

Other government and private schemes were applied in other industries such as shipping, but with limited success (Lucas 1937; Pollard 1962: 110–25). Sayers has summed up the involvement of the Bank and other City agencies as follows:

it looked as though the City might be on the brink of a new era in the finance of British industry. In the event these agencies proved not to be agents of rationalization through a great array of industries; their principal task was rather to oversee the unwindings of commitments into which the Bank had already ventured, or into which it was about to be drawn by political pressures [1976: 547].

Underlying particular problems was a much more complex general issue: the relationship between industry and the state. By the very nature of industrial change, and most especially as a consequence of the development of technology, some increase in concentration of production was essential in whole areas of industrial activity; in Britain, as in other non-totalitarian countries, this amounted to a need for some form of managed, or regulated, capitalism. But by virtue of Britain's early start and the long span and relatively slow pace of her industrialisation, the required changes, in political and social institutions which had become so entrenched over the years, as well as in the structure and processes of industry itself, were particularly difficult to achieve, and were still a long way from resolution by the end of the period. Moreover, it would be simplistic in the extreme to conceive of the causes of or solutions to these problems in terms of the quality of industrial entrepreneurship.

Outside the staple industries there was quite a lot of intra-firm innovation in organisation, mainly through mergers; and there was certainly a great deal written about British management methods, frequently comparing them unsatisfactorily with practices in Germany and the USA. But while much was written and concentration grew apace (particularly in the 1920s), it is far less clear what was actually done within new corporate creations to raise their performance in terms of profitability and longer-term growth and productive efficiency. As has been observed, studies for this period show no close relationship between changes in scale and productivity, and evidence available in detailed business histories should warn against optimism in this regard. ICI was probably the outstanding merger of those years and its creation involved substantial changes in organisation and management (Reader 1975); these changes are regarded by some as symptomatic of changes in British companies generally, even if other large firms probably did not match ICI (Hannah 1974). But examination of ICI's record counsels caution. Between 1927 and 1930 the company made investments totalling £20m. in a fertiliser plant at Billingham – equivalent to nearly one third of total fixed capital formation in manufacturing industry in 1930 – and it had to be written off as a gigantic failure. Throughout the 1930s the firm's return on total capital employed averaged no more than 7 per cent, though to some extent this is a measure of achievement in other divisions of the company since they had to carry the crippling burden of the Billingham fiasco. Nevertheless, ICI can still be considered to have been slow in developing new discoveries which its scientists had made in the field of plastics. Whether this should be charged to the tyrannical domination of Lord McGowan or to the vested interests of different product divisions which reflected the original constituent companies, either way ICI can hardly be extolled as a highly successful trail blazer to up-to-date management.

Major shortcomings in organisation and management have been revealed in other leading companies such as Courtaulds and the Imperial Tobacco Company (Coleman 1969; Alford 1973); and a survey of the motor industry (Maxcy and Silberston 1959) provides substantial evidence of management deficiencies, which probably owe something to the fact that manufacturers were able to sell 97 per cent of their output in protected markets. Against these cases contrary ones can be cited; for example, substantial improvements were made in Pilkingtons and Boots (Barker 1976; Chapman 1976). Furthermore, there were other leading companies – including Tube Investments, Tootal Broadbent, Hawker Siddeley, GKN, EMI – about which little is yet known; and the economy still depended heavily on medium- and small-sized firms which were growing relatively in importance over the 1930s, but whose detailed development remains largely uncharted. Besides, what is known of a whole range of new technical departures during this period suggests that there must have been some related measure of advances in business organisation and methods (Sayers 1950), a view which is in line with one recent general survey of the available evidence in this field (Hannah 1975).

Yet serious doubts remain. To whatever degree one stresses merger activity as a force for progress, it has to be recognised that a significant number of mergers were defensive acts in the face of shrinking markets or intensifying competition, and new company names were banners under which loose federations of firms, tied together by financial holding arrangements, operated with a fair measure of individual independence. Where a merger was more thoroughgoing – as with ICI for example – the form adopted was often based on the original constituent companies so that sectional, or divisional, interests could work against efforts to produce an overall company strategy. Indeed, a recent study of organisation and management in British manufacturing industry over the post Second World War period indirectly reveals much about the interwar years (Channon 1973). Even allowing for possible retarding effects resulting from the war – and in many cases it would seem that the war had the reverse effect of shaking up management – British companies had already fallen well behind the general level of American industry by 1939 (Chandler 1962). Further, although comparison with France and Germany is extremely difficult, it is striking that recent studies show how much more rapidly companies in these countries adopted modern methods than did their counterparts in Britain (Dyas and Thanheiser 1976); for whatever reasons the entrenched nature of traditional practices in Britain has remained deep (Caves 1968). Some stimulus to changes must have been provided by the American firms which expanded their activities in Britain in the 1920s but, with the major exception of motor vehicles, the degree of market penetration they achieved was limited. This could well have been a consequence of the debilitating effects of the American depression on the parent companies; it could, too, be partly explained by the limited nature of the British market.

Regardless of types or sizes of companies there are two areas of business activity which warrant special mention: marketing and labour relations. Marketing, in modern terms, involves deciding marketing objectives in relation to a firm's products and then integrating research, production, advertising, selling and distribution into a policy and programme designed to secure these objectives. Failure to see the interdependence of these activities can easily lead economic historians to misinterpret developments in this broad area in the interwar years, especially in respect of the extensive use of new forms of advertising and selling, which made household names of a number of goods. The most advanced practitioners of these arts between the wars were probably tobacco manufacturers; yet they had little or no understanding of the basic concepts of marketing: advertising was regarded as a means of popularising what was produced, not as a means of exploiting what had been discovered about consumers' tastes and wants. With cigarettes this limitation did not curb expansion because the nature of technical changes had automatically produced a standardised product for a large potential market, but with motor cars, for example, marketing problems were far more crucial and complex. Manufacturers certainly made efforts to popularise motoring and motor cars through advertising, and the need to provide reliable agencies for servicing and spares was understood by the late 1920s, but they did not see far beyond this. Nuffield progressed far in the 1920s by vigorous salesmanship but in the early 1930s his company floundered for want of a clear marketing strategy, a condition from which it never fully recovered (Maxcy and Silberston 1959). Similar examples could be cited from studies of other industries showing how Britain was falling behind America in the development of marketing, particularly of mass-produced consumer goods (Chandler 1962). While a considerable part of the explanation for this might be found in differences in the character of demand within the domestic markets,

British firms were losing out unduly if they were to sustain their competitive position in a whole range of goods which were becoming part of the stock in trade of every advanced industrial economy operating in international markets.

Second, there is the sphere of labour relations. Anyone with even the slightest interest in Britain's economy since the Second World War can hardly fail to recognise this as a major, if not the single most important, factor in industrial performance – or in the lack of it. It is equally obvious that the underlying causes of problems in labour relations have developed over a long period and the interwar years are a period of particular relevance in this process. On the one hand, there were disastrously bad labour relations in the staple industries, which became the focal point of national political conflict. On the other hand, there were industries which were expanding but in which there was generally little concern to achieve innovations in labour relations; provided there were no problems of labour supply and wage rates could be kept at reasonable levels (which was not very difficult against a background of falling prices and high unemployment) employers were well content. Paradoxically, these quite different conditions produced similar results. The bitterness of disputes in the staple industries served to harden the attitudes of organised labour even though its bargaining position was currently weak. In other sectors of industry old methods were propagated for want of alternatives. Yet over a wide range of industry substantial changes were needed in union structure, manning levels, demarcations and differentials, if higher levels of labour productivity were to be achieved.

By pinpointing weaknesses and shortcomings in company organisation it is easy to slip into an explanation of them in terms of individual entrepreneurial failure. In certain respects this might be justified but, as the example of the staple industries shows, in the main it would be far too simplistic. We have concentrated on manufacturing but this sector was interrelated with others – in particular finance, distribution, transport – in ways which limited and in part determined its own actions. Moreover, within manufacturing there was another stratum of interdependence between industries. Operating at both levels were major institutional factors; though, in this chapter, particular attention has been drawn only to organised labour and to the operation of government. Other constraints were probably important, such as broader social and cultural factors as they affected, for example, the pattern of education and the provision of industrial training. Moreover, modern business history provides a great deal of evidence on the impossibility of assigning *individual* responsibility for the performance of large, complex companies, which were becoming an increasingly dominant feature of the economy during this period. Thus the problems to which attention has been drawn have to be seen in this broader context. Lastly, if the problems facing British industry required centralised solutions, then the role of the individual entrepreneur is correspondingly devalued.

Demand for manufactured goods

The concern of this chapter has been the organisation and development of manufacturing industry; this has led to a concentration on supply factors. It is necessary, therefore, to conclude this survey by commenting briefly on the nature of demand. One way of approaching this subject is provided by the analysis in chapter 14, where it is assumed that the interwar economy was essentially Keynesian so that the high level of unemployment represented (to a large degree) a shortfall of effective demand, with consequent effects on the growth of income. In these terms, the obvious weakness lay in government policy, which was founded on a preference for monetary stability through orthodox sound finance and the conversion of the public debt. Thus, Chamberlain could appear on cinema screens in 1934 and 1935 in buoyant mood, claiming success for the government having produced 'healthy' budget surpluses which, according to him, had won the admiration of the world. There seems little doubt, by contrast, that deficit financing would have provided some degree of stimulus to the economy, though it is questionable whether this could have been done in a way which would have restored something approaching full employment in a manner which would, in turn, have generated a high level of long-term growth. Even Keynes accepted the need to combine fiscal and monetary policies with some measures of positive direction by central government in industrial and other fields, though he was somewhat ambiguous about the extent of such action. The question here, however, is whether the government's preferred policy acted as a serious constraint on industry; was industry, so to speak, operating at the limit of the market?

It is difficult to see how this can have been so for the staple industries in the early 1920s, in the light of their startling mismanagement in the immediate postwar boom. High profits were not used to finance adjustments to match a changed and changing demand for their goods, but were deployed as if the pre-1890 – rather, even, than the pre-1914 – world had returned. In any case, their major problems involved contraction and reorganisation. For other sectors of industry prospects were plainly different, but while demand may have been a constraint it was not so much the volume as the nature of demand which was deficient.

In the nineteenth century, the introduction of capital-intensive (and relatively mass) production methods in the USA cannot be explained entirely in terms of relative factor prices: the nature of market demand, turning on the level and distribution of income, and the nature of consumers' tastes, were very powerful factors. In Britain, by contrast, emphasis on specialist, quality markets was a pronounced feature of new consumer goods production and distribution. This demand pattern reflected a markedly uneven distribution of income which was also reflected in a plentiful supply of capital at low rates of interest, with large quantities of it fuelling the prodigious foreign investment boom of the Edwardian period. To the extent that capital was gaining at the expense of labour the market for mass-produced consumer goods was limited. This feature could well have helped to establish and entrench patterns of production which proved somewhat inflexible once markets expanded after the First World War.

Throughout the interwar years, however, a number of factors exogenous to industrial expansion were operating to raise average real incomes; for certain sections of the population the rises were quite sharp. There was some redistribution of income away from profits to wages and salaries. The obverse to the decline of the staples was the income effect of the fall in the import prices of food and raw materials. This was a compensation for falling export volumes, but it also represented a redistribution from the unemployed to the employed with some corresponding effect on the marginal propensity to consume. Finally, there was a fall in average family size which, combined with an inverse relationship between income and family size, widened the band of middle-income groups.

Although these changes took place, real wages rose by only 18 per cent between 1920 and 1938, which is not particularly impressive. It seems unlikely that growth of this kind, even when combined with possible changes in tastes and in propensities to consume, could have wholly overcome the effects on demand of traditional patterns of income distribution. These could well have been stumbling blocks to vigorous economic growth.

Conclusion

Attempts to distinguish between demand and supply factors in industrial development are necessarily somewhat artificial, but they do help to clarify the strength of different elements in the process. This chapter has concentrated on supply factors – particularly in relation to structural change – because of the obvious strength of evidence in this direction. Nevertheless, the available evidence is still such that the analysis has been concerned mainly with a critical appraisal of performance rather than with an attempt to offer a firm set of conclusions. It is, however difficult to resist making the judgement that, because of unwillingness or inability to get to grips with fundamental problems, British industry was developing in a way in which consumers' expectations would increasingly outrun industry's performance. Failure to match expectations with performance was probably a growing feature of the British nation generally.

14

Aggregate demand in the United Kingdom 1918-45

T. THOMAS

The period 1918–45 is important to economists for two reasons. The spectre of the unemployment of the interwar period stands as a warning of the consequences of misguided domestic and international economic policy, and the period also saw the publication of J. M. Keynes' *The General Theory of Employment, Interest and Money*, a book which was the foundation of modern macroeconomics. The innovation in economic theory, of course, was not independent of the state of the British economy. As Joan Robinson has written: 'Keynes' *General Theory* smashed up the glass house of static theory in order to be able to discuss a real problem – the causes of unemployment' (Robinson 1956: v). This chapter uses an explicitly Keynesian framework to analyse the British economy plagued by that problem.

Aggregate demand and the economic loss from the depression

Figure 14.1 shows the course of GNP and employment between 1920 and 1938. According to Feinstein (1972: T 57), 2.0 per cent of the working population were unemployed in 1920 while 9.3 per cent were unemployed in 1938. Because of the growth in the labour force, 1938 appears to be a peak year for employment in the interwar period. The years between 1920 and 1938 were obviously years of less than full employment; in the years 1931 and 1932 more than 15 per cent of the working population were unemployed (and more than 20 per cent of insured employees were out of work) (Feinstein 1972: T 57 and 58). The economic loss of this unemployment is studied below. Since so many people were unemployed, it is reasonable to believe that output in the interwar period was less than it would have been if all those people, and the capital with which they would combine in production, had been working. But how much less? What is needed is a series for full or potential output that may be compared with actual output; the difference is the loss due to unemployment. It is the loss which Keynesian policies, intended to stimulate aggregate demand, were designed to reduce or eliminate.

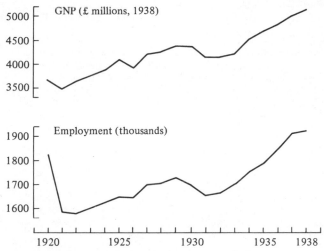

14.1   GNP and employment during the interwar period
Source: Feinstein (1972).

GNP lost 1921–38

One method of obtaining a series on full, or potential, GNP is the peak-to-peak method. By this method the peaks in the actual GNP series are connected by trend lines and potential GNP in any non-peak year is an interpolated figure (Brown 1956: 857). The gap between the trend lines and the actual GNP series gives the GNP lost. Unfortunately, in the interwar UK economy peaks in economic activity are only peaks because the other years are so much lower. The relative peaks in 1929 and 1937 were associated with unemployment near the 10 per cent mark (Feinstein 1972: T 58).

An alternative method of obtaining the potential output series is to multiply a series on full employment in the labour force by an estimate of output per man. This shifts the problem back one step as a series for full employment of labour must be obtained. An upper limit to the series would imply employment for everyone in the labour force or zero unemployment. This is unattainable, for reasons which are discussed in chapter 11, and something less than zero unemployment has to be taken as the feasible rate of employment at any one time.

In a discussion of policy goals in the 1920s Moggridge lists the employment target of 95.3 per cent (1972: 98). Lloyd George (1929: 53), to cite one example, suggested public works spending to bring unemployment down to 'the normal prewar percentage of unemployment' of 4.7 per cent. Howson points out that the goals changed in the 1920s: the 1935 target, set in 1932, was a lowering of unemployment to its 1927 level (Howson 1975: 142), which was 1 373 000 men

Table 14.1. *GNP lost by unemployment 1921–38 (GNP £m. 1938 prices/man;
GNP lost: £m., 1938 prices)*

	GNP per employee	GNP lost (4.7)	GNP lost (full)
1921	195.3	247.3	432.0
1922	203.9	199.6	389.2
1923	208.7	134.1	327.0
1924	211.9	100.5	297.5
1925	221.6	135.6	345.5
1926	211.8	170.0	372.6
1927	220.8	90.3	303.2
1928	223.6	125.5	343.4
1929	225.9	116.7	339.5
1930	229.9	314.7	546.9
1931	222.5	494.4	723.6
1932	221.5	522.5	753.1
1933	221.0	451.4	682.2
1934	229.9	358.9	599.8
1935	234.7	324.0	572.0
1936	234.3	241.3	492.0
1937	235.2	161.9	417.7
1938	241.7	255.1	523.0
Total		4443.8	8460.0

Source: Calculated from Feinstein (1972: tables 5 and 57)

or 7.4 per cent. Because the target was set in a year with over three million men unemployed, pessimism may have prompted the choice of a very modest 'full employment' goal. Use of a series based on 7.4 per cent unemployment would probably give an underestimate of lost GNP.

Lloyd George's suggestion of 4.7 per cent unemployment and zero unemployment were used in table 14.1 together with a series on output per man to derive two series of GNP lost. Average GNP in 1938 prices was £4278 million between 1921 and 1938, so total GNP lost was somewhere between one and two years' production. However, the estimate of lost GNP based on 4.7 per cent unemployment is probably conservative, for two reasons. First, there is no reason why 95.3 per cent should be the upper limit to employment: for the years 1911 to 1913 employment averaged 97.2 per cent (Feinstein 1972: T 57). Secondly, as Howson (1975: 58) points out, the series for output per man does not include any productivity growth that might be associated with higher output and fuller employment. That is, if output had been higher, such factors as economies of scale might have increased output per man, so full employment output would have been higher than shown in the table.

The series of GNP divided by employment provides a rough indication of the course of productivity during the interwar period. Although the series does not indicate the contribution made by non-labour inputs and measures labour in man-years instead of man-hours, it does display the cyclical behaviour of productivity implied by Howson. The big drop in length of the working week occurred in 1919–20, and the standard hours of work were relatively constant between 1920 and 1940 (Sayers 1967: 138); so the use of man-years does not introduce a large bias in the productivity calculation.

Modern Keynesian theory would suggest that deficit spending, not budget balancing, was the appropriate policy to reduce unemployment during the interwar period. It is relatively easy to arrive at a qualitative judgement of the impact of fiscal policy between the wars. Between 1927 and 1938 the budget had an average surplus of £6.6 million, and only in 1937 was there exact balance. Alford (1972: 66) suggests that an informed guess would reckon the interwar budgets as 'fairly neutral' although he qualified this by adding that 'in the conditions of the period this is as good as saying that the overall effect was contractionary'. Obviously some adjustment is needed to transform an actual neutral budget to a hypothetical contractionary one. As Alford writes: 'it would be necessary to do a sophisticated econometric analysis of government income and expenditure before it would be possible to make any judgements on the overall, net effect of budgetary policy' (Alford 1972: 66). The results presented here depend upon such an analysis, which is described in detail at the end of the chapter.

Attempts to derive a single quantitative measure of the impact of fiscal policy have led to many alternative adjustments to the actual government budget. The most popular measure is probably the full employment surplus used first by E. C. Brown (1956) in his analysis of the US fiscal policy in the 1930s. In order to see how expansionary or contractionary fiscal policy was it is necessary to adjust the observed budget deficit or surplus because 'actual budget results reflect not only what fiscal policy is doing to the economy, but also what the economy is doing to the budget through its effects on tax revenues and unemployment benefit payments' (Lewis 1968: 6). Calculating the Full Employment Surplus involves imagining what government receipts and expenditure would have been at full employment. The FES is then the difference between the hypothetical receipts and hypothetical expenditure.

Tables 14.2 and 14.3 give the data used to derive the FES under the two assumptions of the rate of unemployment associated with full employment. The most obvious point in these tables is the positive sign and the large size of the full employment surplus. This means that the policy of the government – whether they knew it or not – was strongly contractionary, and became more so as the slump worsened. In three years the actual budget was in deficit. In only one year, and then only under a conservative estimate of full employment, is the full employment surplus negative. For example, the actual 1931 budget showed a deficit of £28.6 million, thus apparently stimulating the economy, while the full

Table 14.2. *Derivation of full employment surplus (£ million (1938))*

	INTX	+	TAX	−	GRNT	=	Budget	+	Actual budget	=	FES
1927	27.2		6.3		−41.5		75.0		38.6		113.6
1928	30.8		7.4		−47.5		85.7		35.1		120.8
1929	30.4		7.6		−47.1		85.1		11.8		96.9
1930	49.0		14.1		−76.7		139.8		−14.8		125.0
1931	64.8		20.0		−105.0		189.8		−28.6		161.2
1932	67.5		20.8		−113.4		201.7		24.4		226.1
1933	61.1		19.9		−104.3		185.3		26.9		212.2
1934	53.7		18.7		−92.3		164.7		43.4		208.1
1935	51.2		18.4		−87.0		156.6		11.8		168.4
1936	44.1		16.8		−74.4		135.3		17.0		152.3
1937	37.4		14.7		−60.7		122.8		0		112.8
1938	46.9		17.6		−74.2		138.7		−87.0		51.7

Source: See sources for table 14.3

Table 14.3. *Derivation of full employment surplus (£ million (1938))*

	(1) Indirect taxes	(2) Direct taxes	(3) Government grants to the private sector	(4) Change in government surplus (1)+(2)−(3)	(5) Actual government surplus	(6) Full employment surplus (4)+(5) (FES)
	Increase or decrease as employment at 95.3% is achieved					
1927	7.8	1.9	−12.4	22.1	38.6	60.7
1928	11.0	2.7	−17.3	31.0	35.1	66.1
1929	10.2	2.6	−16.2	29.0	11.8	40.8
1930	27.9	7.9	−44.2	80.0	−14.8	65.2
1931	45.3	13.5	−71.7	130.5	128.6	101.9
1932	49.7	14.0	−78.7	142.4	24.4	166.8
1933	43.6	13.0	−69.0	125.6	26.6	152.5
1934	34.9	11.2	−55.2	101.3	43.4	144.7
1935	31.2	10.6	−49.8	91.6	11.8	103.4
1936	23.0	8.7	−36.5	68.2	17.0	85.2
1937	14.8	6.4	−23.5	44.7	0	44.7
1938	22.8	8.8	−36.2	67.8	−87.0	−19.2

Source: Col. 5: Feinstein (1972: 14); cols. 1, 2, 3: Calculated with the interwar econometric model described later in this chapter, by increasing GNP by the amount of 'GNP lost' in actuality by comparison with only 4.7 per cent unemployment

Table 14.4. *Effects of the Lloyd George public works programme*

Year	(1) Actual unemployment ('000)	(2) Reduction in unemployment from the programme ('000)	(3) Change in national income from the £100m. increase in government spending (£m.)
1929	1503	268	97.2
1930	2379	300	108.3
1931	3252	329	119.0
1932	3400	346	125.0
1933	3087	359	129.7

employment surplus was between £101.9 million and £161.2 million. The average size of the actual budget surplus or deficit from 1927–38 was +£6.6 million, while the average full employment surplus was £84.4 million or £145.8 million depending on the assumed level of full employment GNP. Of special interest is the fact that the full employment surplus was large, positive and increasing for 1930 and 1931, years when the actual budget was negative.

Public works and the interwar economy

The government's object throughout this period was to balance the budget. The calculation of the full employment surplus indicates that in reality this object led to highly deflationary results. The government should, therefore, have unbalanced the budget, running a budget deficit, in order to help the economy move to full employment.

The public works programme suggested by Lloyd George and supported by Keynes and Henderson which would have expanded government spending is thus looked upon as a missed opportunity. If only the Lloyd George proposals had been carried out – or so the story goes – the economic history of the interwar period would have been less bleak.

It is usually supposed that the Lloyd George public works proposal would have increased government spending by £100 million per year for five years. Table 14.4 shows how such an increase would have affected employment and GNP.

Comparing the change in employment (col. 2) with the actual level of unemployment (col. 1) for the years 1929 to 1933, one sees that the Lloyd George proposals would not have solved the unemployment problem. If the underlying calculations are accepted, the implication is that additional government spending had rather small multiplier effects on national income: £100 million spent in 1933 would have led to an increase in income of only £129.7 million, even taking into account the delayed effects of similar spending in earlier years.

If the proposals of Lloyd George were inadequate, it may seem that all that was needed was an increase in the size of the programme. The openness of the British economy to the world, however, would have prevented this. Since every £100 million increase in GNP would have increased imports by £20.8 milion, a bolstered public works programme would have led to problems with the balance of payments. Although the calculations assume that prices are not affected by the level of output, a massive increase of spending and output would probably have increased prices and worsened the deterioration of the trade balance (Shapiro 1976; and ch. 12).

The trade account, moreover, would not have been the only component of the balance of payments to suffer. Given the conventional wisdom during the interwar period of balancing budgets, capital would probably have fled Britain if the government had introduced a public works scheme.

Only by closing the economy – as Germany did during the 1930s – could Britain have introduced a successful programme of deficit spending. As Arndt (1944: 134) pointed out, the balance of payments difficulties associated with such a programme 'would have meant the transformation of the British economy into a largely State-controlled, if not planned, economic system'. Certainly this would have been a far cry from simple Keynesian expansionary policy.

A Keynesian model

The numerical results which have been presented in this chapter – for example the full employment surplus and the effect of the Lloyd George programme – depend upon a model of the operation of the British economy between the wars. The model is based upon the theory stated by Keynes and refined by other economists. Like other models which have been developed, it assumes the existence of consistent relationships between major variables in the economy – output, employment, consumption and others – and estimates the numerical nature of those relationships by the use of the tools of econometrics. Once these estimates have been made, it is possible to use the model to see how imaginary or hypothetical changes in some of the variables (such as an increase in government spending on public works) would be likely to affect other variables (such as output or employment).

A simple aggregate model

Economic models vary greatly in sophistication, and in particular in the number of variables which they consider. Figure 14.2 presents the simplest Keynesian view of the aggregate economy, the 45° diagram or Keynesian cross, described in many textbooks of economics.

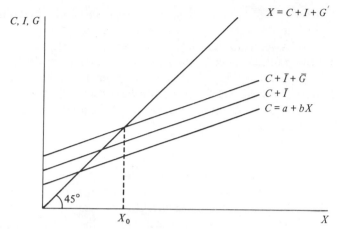

14.2   Keynesian aggregate demand model

The figure corresponds to the simple system of equations:

$$X = C + I + G$$
$$C = C(X)$$
$$I = \bar{I}$$
$$G = \bar{G}$$

where X is the aggregate output or income, C is consumption, I is investment and G is government spending. Consumption in this model is a function of income, while investment and government spending are fixed. The line $C + I + G$ is often called the aggregate demand schedule and the 45° line is occasionally called the aggregate supply schedule. Where aggregate demand crosses the 45° line one finds the equilibrium output – X_0 in figure 14.2.

At this point the demands of consumers for a certain amount of consumption C_0, of investors for an amount of investment I_0, and of government for an amount of spending G_0 are added up to obtain aggregate demand y_0. To call the 45° line aggregate supply means that there are no supply constraints that prevent actual output from equalling demand. This does not mean, however, that aggregate demand pushes the economy to a full employment level of output; one of Keynes's main contributions was the demonstration that aggregate demand might be insufficient to bring the economy to the full employment level of output. This argument stood in contrast to the pre-Keynesian view that there were automatic forces in the economy that would lead to full employment. Keynes showed that without these automatic forces it was still possible to reach full employment; a conscious policy could be followed to increase C, I, G or some combination of all three. It is easy to show with figure 14.2 that an increase in G will increase the equilibrium level of output. Notice, for example, what happens to output

(X) in moving from $C+\bar{I}$ to $C+\bar{I}+\bar{G}$; output rises, and could be consciously driven in this way (adding further $\bar{G}$s) towards full employment.

An increase of G by some amount £m., moreover will cause X to increase by more than £m.; the 'multiplier' gives the ratio of the change in X to the change in G. In the simple model of figure 14.1 the multiplier depends on the slope of the consumption function. Although the idea of the consumption function is very general – C depends on X – the consumption function used in figure 14.2 has a specific linear form, namely:

$$C = a + bX$$

The coefficient b is called the marginal propensity to consume and shows the change in consumption given a change in income. (Because of the simple nature of the model, X represents output and income. Other models distinguish between output and personal disposable income, with the latter determining consumption.)

The greater the coefficient b (which is assumed to lie between 0 and 1), the greater will be the effect on X of any change in G. That is, a given upward movement in the line $C+\bar{I}+\bar{G}$ will result in a greater shift in the point of intersection with the 45° line, the steeper is the slope of the $C+\bar{I}+\bar{G}$ line. In the very simple model the multiplier turns out to be equal to $1/(1-b)$. With more detailed models the simple formula must be modified, though it continues to be true that the multiplier will be greater as spending becomes more sensitive to changes in output and income, i.e. as the slope of $C+\bar{I}+\bar{G}$ increases.

During the interwar period Keynesian policies of attempting to control aggregate demand were not tried, and the economy stayed at less than full employment. One of the defects of the model of figure 14.1 is that there is no explicit link between output and employment. The cost, in terms of lost output, of having high levels of unemployment is not readily apparent.

Extending the simple aggregate model

In the equations associated with the model of figure 14.2 only the consumption function would be estimated (normally by the use of a regression equation). Investment and government spending are fixed, so they are not influenced by the movements of other variables in the model, and do not need to be estimated. (The level at which these variables are fixed depends on forces or decisions outside the model.)

From the estimated consumption function one can obtain values for the marginal propensity to consume and, after some elementary manipulation, the multiplier. These values are important in assessing the possible effects of changes in the fixed level of investment or of government spending. Estimates for the multiplier will be given below, and those estimates were used to assess the potential of the Lloyd George programme of public works.

Simplicity in a model can be a virtue, although a model that is too simple can ignore much that is important in the real world. One flaw in the model of figure 14.2 is the lack of an explicit link between output and employment. There are other flaws. Investment is fixed in figure 14.2 at $\bar{I}$ irrespective of the level of output. There is no labour market in the model; nor are there any prices. There is also no scope for monetary policy. Changes in interest rates or changes in the stock of money cannot affect output or employment.

The simple model can be extended in two steps to provide a testable model that overcomes many of the flaws listed above. The first step extends the algebraic model to eight equations (Evans 1969: 346–61):

$$X = C + I + G$$
$$C = C(X)$$
$$I = I(X, i)$$
$$X = X(N, K, t) \quad \text{or} \quad N = N(X, K, t)$$
$$\Delta X / \Delta N = w/P \quad \text{or} \quad P = w/(\Delta X/\Delta N)$$
$$w = \bar{w} \quad \text{or} \quad w = w(p, UNN)$$
$$M_s = M_d = kpX - \lambda pi$$
$$UNN = L - N$$

where i is the interest rate, K is the capital stock, t is technical progress, N is employment, Δ is the first difference operator (ΔX equals the difference between X this period and X last period), $\Delta X/\Delta N$ is the marginal product of labour, w is the money wage rate, P is the price level, UNN is unemployment, M_s is money supply, M_d is money demand, k and λ are constants in the money demand equation, L is the labour force. This model is the backbone of many intermediate macro texts; even the huge macroeconometric models used by some universities or government departments bear a strong family resemblance to this model.

The second step towards a testable model includes disaggregating some variables, adding some new variables and introducing time lags to provide a dynamic structure for the model. Many of the changes made to the intermediate model follow from post-Keynesian research in macroeconomics.

Consumption in the testable model is a function of disposable income, not simple GNP. The components of aggregate investment have been found to be influenced by different variables or to follow different paths over the business cycle. Imports and exports, and government taxes and subsidies are important variables that should be included in the model (Evans 1969: 494–503).

A full model of the United Kingdom 1921–38

This section presents an estimated version of a macroeconometric model of the UK during the interwar period. The full model and notation will be given followed by a brief presentation of the estimates of important propensities and elasticities that are implicit. It is an extension of the basic aggregate model we have just described, and has been estimated using the technique of ordinary least squares. Because of one year lags in the model and because the national accounts data were not available for the years before 1920, the model starts with 1921.

The estimated model

(1) C $= 276.903 + 0.443Y + 0.467C_{-1}$
               (2.467) (7.004) (5.470)

      $\bar{R}^2$ $= 0.9890$

      DW $= 1.5103$

(2) IP $= -42.343 + 0.052X + 0.282(PCB/P)_{-1}$
             (-0.898) (2.769) (3.854)

      $\bar{R}^2$ $= 0.8985$

      DW $= 1.6509$

(3) IHP $= 96.005 - 14.482ILT + 0.684IHP_{-1}$
             (1.816) (-1.462) (4.116)

      $\bar{R}^2$ $= 0.8658$

      DW $= 1.6079$

(4) $INVD = -82.058 + 0.125X + 11.884TIME - 111.823DUM32$
              (-3.347) (2.056) (3.851) (-3.308)

      $\bar{R}^2$ $= 0.4717$

      DW $= 2.1867$

(5) NW $= 6005.820 + 2.765X - 83.43TIME + 428.83DUM32$
             (5.228) (8.052) (-2.116) (4.283)

      $\bar{R}^2$ $= 0.9558$

      DW $= 1.8694$

(6) $WS/P = 321.559 + 0.369X - 191.95PFI + 0.333(WS/P)_{-1}$
             (1.492) (4.512) (-3.226)

      $\bar{R}^2$ $= 0.9740$

      DW $= 1.6893$

(7) FI $= 386.066 + 0.208X - 260.530(PFI/P)_{-1} - 156.444DUM32$
             (2.186) (7.130) (-3.333) (4.325)

      $\bar{R}^2$ $= 0.8439$

      DW $= 1.3283$

(8) FE $= 11.547 + 387.413WRLD + 382.325(PFI/P)_{-1}$
             (0.065) (2.020) (4.157)

      $\bar{R}^2$ $= 0.6694$

      DW $= 1.3065$

            (Equation estimated for 1925–38)

(9) $PCB = -380.7777 + 0.197(P \cdot X) + 0.192 \triangle (P \cdot X)$
         (2.128)   (4.948)   (4.812)
    $\bar{R}^2 = 0.7529$
    DW $= 1.6122$

(10) $ILT = 1.993 + 0.141 ITR + 0.435 ILT_{-1} - 0.325 DUM32$
         (4.546) (2.797)   (4.785) (-1.704)
    $\bar{R}^2 = 0.9526$
    DW $= 1.5848$

(11) $RI = 36.304 + 0.036(P \cdot X) + 85.55 ILT + 0.819 RI_{-1}$
        (0.340)   (2.061)   (3.952)   (9.170)
    $\bar{R}^2 = 0.9103$
    DW $= 1.7458$

(12) $INTX = 90.867 + 0.090 X + 90.842 DUM32$
         (1.528)   (6.101) (6.801)
    $\bar{R}^2 = 0.9414$
    DW $= 1.4824$

(13) $TAX = 0.07(P \cdot Y')$ 1921–1929
          $0.08(P \cdot Y')$ 1930–1938

(14) $GRNT = 123.261 + 0.051 UNN$
          (5.789)   (5.303)
    $\bar{R}^2 = 0.6147$
    DW $= 0.1650$

Identities

(15) $X = C + IP + IHP + IHG + INVD + G + FE$
        $- FI - INTX + SUBS + NPIFA + Z$
(16) $P \cdot Y = WS + PB + RI + GRNT - TAX - NTA$
(17) $WS = WR \cdot NW$
(18) $UNN = L - NW$
(19) $P = WS/(WS/P)$

Where

C   is consumption £m. (1938)
DUM32   is dummy variable 1932–38 $= 1$
FE   is exports £m. (1938)
FI   is imports £m. (1938)
G   is government purchases of goods and services (excluding housing)
             £m. (1938)

GRNT	is grants to the private sector £m. (current)
IHG	is government residential investment £m. (1938)
IHP	is private residential investment £m. (1938)
ILT	is long-term (3% consols) interest rate (%)
INTX	is indirect tax £m. (1938)
INVD	is change in stocks £m. (1938)
IP	is domestic fixed capital formation (excluding dwellings) £m. (1938)
ITR	is treasury bill rate (%)
L	is labour force (thousands)
NPIFA	is net property income from abroad £m. (1938)
NTA	is personal sector net transfers and taxes paid abroad £m. (current)
NW	is wage and salary workers (thousands)
P	is implicit GNP deflator (1938 = 1.00)
PB	is income from self-employment £m. (current)
PCB	is corporate profits £m. (current)
PFI	is import price deflator (1938 = 1.00)
RI	is rent, dividends and net interest £m. (current)
SUBS	is subsidies £m. (1938)
TAX	is personal taxes £m. (current)
TIME	is time trend
UNN	is unemployment (thousands)
WR	is annual earnings per worker £ (current)
WRLD	is index of world imports (1938 = 1.0)
WS	is wages, salaries and supplements £m. (current)
WS/P	is real wages, salaries and supplements £m. (1938)
X	is GNP £m. (1938)
Y	is personal disposable income £m. (1938)
Y'	is personal income £m. (1938)
Z	is residual error £m. (1938)

Numbers in parentheses are *t*-statistics; $\triangle$ represents a first difference and $_{-1}$ a one period lag.

From the structural equations presented – equations 1 to 14 – it is possible to extract a number of important propensities and elasticities. The consumption function is of the permanent income or habit persistence variety and gives a short-run marginal propensity to consume of 0.433 and a long-run mpc of 0.831. The marginal propensity to import is 0.208, and the import demand price elasticity, allowing for the one year lag, is −0.42. The export price demand elasticity, again incorporating a one year lag, is −0.53. The average tax rate was 7 per cent from 1921 to 1929 and 8 per cent from 1930 to 1938; the tax equation is the only structural equation that was not estimated by ordinary least squares. For a complete discussion of the model see Thomas (1976).

Some remarks on the full interwar model

The first obvious weakness in the model is the absence of any equations explaining international capital flows. As chapter 12 points out, the numerical values for the capital flows will probably never be precisely known. In contrast, the data on the interwar national accounts are quite good. By estimating relationships between real flows one might be able to gain some insight into the nature of the financial flows.

Although the new economic history is primarily neoclassical (Temin 1973: 8), the model in this chapter is a strict Keynesian model, with emphasis on income effects instead of price effects or financial variable effects. The model corresponds to what Branson (1972: 95–7), appropriately enough, calls 'the simple depression model'. Two monetarists have also labelled the interwar period as 'strongly Keynesian' (Barrett and Walters 1966: 403).

A recent econometric study by M. H. Pesaran (1974: 164), however, concluded 'that as long as we are faced with small samples and higher collinear data, as is the case in most empirical work in economics, the possibility of effectively discriminating among rival models will be rather limited'. Because of this difficulty in discriminating among models, it is best to consider the use of the strict Keynesian model as an assumption that is made to facilitate the analysis.

As in any study in the new economic history the results presented in this chapter depend on the underlying model. The use of an explicit model is one of the hallmarks – and one of the primary virtues – of the new economic history.

Uses of the full model

Estimation of the multiplier

In the simple model of figure 14.2 a £1 change in G produces a $£1/(1-b)$ change in X. The larger the multiplier the greater the effect of an exogenous change in aggregate demand, so the size of the multiplier provides some useful information about the actual or potential working of the economy.

As macro models become more complicated the formula for the multiplier also becomes more complicated. Eventually, a simple formula must be replaced by different techniques – computer simulations – to derive the multiplier. Before using computer simulations to derive dynamic multipliers, it is possible to extend the simple formula to:

$$\Delta X/\Delta G = 1/\{1 - mpc(Y/X) - mpi + mpf\}$$

where mpc, mpi and mpf are the marginal propensities to consume, invest and import, respectively. $\Delta Y/\Delta X$ is the change in personal disposable income given a change in GNP. Using the short-run mpc from the model and assuming $\Delta Y/\Delta X$ equals 0.90, one obtains a rough multiplier of 1.3.

After Kahn's (1931) celebrated article on the multiplier and especially after the *General Theory* there were a number of estimates made of the multiplier. Kahn (1931) considered 1.88 the most realistic figure but presented a range of 1.56 to 1.94. Keynes (1936) gave a number of estimates; it is probably fair to say that he expected it to be in the 2 to 3 range. Colin Clark (1938) suggested a sharp jump in the multiplier during the 1930s with a value of 2.07 for 1929–33 and 3.22 for 1934–37. Richard Stone (1938–39) derived a multiplier of 2.1 after estimating a consumption function from time series data, but conceded that the neglected import leakage would lower the figure. Kaldor (1944) took the multiplier in 1938 as approximately two. None of these estimates distinguished between the short-run and the long-run multiplier.

With an estimated econometric model it is possible to derive dynamic multipliers. First, the historical data are placed back into the estimated model and a 'control solution' is obtained. Then one of the exogenous variables is changed by some known amount and a new solution is obtained. The difference between the new and control solutions is attributed to the change in the exogenous variable.

In the model of this chapter, the exogenous variable G was changed by £1 million. The first period change in the model was £0.98 million and the twelfth period change – the 'long-run' for this model – was £1.44 million. Rounding, one may say that the short-run multiplier is unity and the long-run multiplier is 1.5. Compared to previous estimates of the multiplier, the estimates derived from the model of this chapter are much lower. The interwar economy was not affected by exogenous shocks to the extent previously thought.

15

Social history 1900–45

ASA BRIGGS

Evidence and attitudes

It is easier to identify the main themes of social change in Britain between 1900 and 1945, relating them to or distinguishing them from those of the nineteenth century, than it is to measure social trends, to date social processes, and to weigh the relative influence of the different social forces involved. This is not merely because the statistics are patchy and incomplete in their coverage (Halsey 1972; Mitchell & Deane 1962; Cole and Cole 1937; Cole 1956; Carr-Saunders et al. 1958; Moser 1958; Marsh 1958), because changing social vantage points between 1900 and 1945 have provided and still provide a shifting sense of social landscape, or because the relative influence of social forces changes from one period to another; it is because in a pluralistic and stratified society there are bound to be divergent perceptions of social change at any particular point in time (Briggs 1972; Rex 1961; Lockwood 1966; Lawton 1968; Bulmer 1975). Throughout the whole period, there were two main divergences of perception. The first related to policy: 'the structure of society did not encourage those who influenced social policy (beginning with the Poor Law) to understand the lives of those for whom the services were intended' (Titmuss 1958: 19–20). The second related to location: the division between village and city (with a variety of towns between) did not encourage common ways of thinking and feeling, although the division was becoming far less sharp during the 1930s, when the cult of the countryside was at the height of its influence, than it had been in the first decade of the century (Thomas 1939; Gardiner 1944; Baker 1953; Frankenburg 1966; Moser and Scott 1961).

However patchy and incomplete the statistics (official and unofficial) may be, they are fuller than for most previous periods, and however separated the vantage points – 1901, the year of Queen Victoria's death, for example, or 1914, the year of the outbreak of the First World War, 1926, the year of the general strike, and 1945, the year of Second World War victory and a huge Labour Party majority – many features of the social landscape and the social calendar remained the same. As Mark Abrams wrote in 1945, 'A citizen from our own day moving in [the] world of the few years before 1914 would have found in every context almost everything which has come to be regarded as distinctive of the culture of the inter-war years' (Abrams 1945).

Even the balance of social forces was steadier than it has been since the mid 1950s. Thus, although the number of trade unionists had risen from 1 500 000 in 1902 to 2 682 000 in 1914, 4 164 000 in 1926 and 6 671 000 in 1945, TUC membership as a proportion of total union membership had risen over these years only from 74.5 per cent to 84.7 per cent, while the proportion of union membership affiliated to the Labour Party actually fell from 42.1 per cent in 1902 to 31.9 per cent in 1945. As late as 1959, E. H. Phelps Brown could write that 'the system of British industrial relations remains today in its essentials as it was before the First World War' (Phelps Brown 1959). The same might be said of basic aspects of the British system of politics and parliamentary government, although the Press and politicians frequently made the most of the differences; 'Humanity is like the sea', said Lloyd George in 1910, 'it is never quite free from movement, but there are periods of comparative calm and others of turbulence and violent disturbance' (Phelps Brown 1959: 1; see also Laski 1938; Beer 1965; Ginsberg 1959; Guttsman 1963): other politicians, particularly Labour politicians, talked of a 'march'. If so, it was a long march. More than half (53 per cent) of the members of the House of Commons in 1945 had passed their thirtieth birthday by 1914; their formative years were Edwardian years (Laver 1955: 1; Read 1972).

The 'fundamental conception, or directing idea' in sociology may be that of 'social structure' (Bottomore 1962), but the social historian, like an anthropologist, is concerned not only with changing social structures but with individual and group experience and how it is perceived at the time and in retrospect. He must take account, therefore, of generational contrasts and changing values, of habits, routines, disturbances and innovations, of what have been called 'unpremeditated textures of experience' (Hoggart 1963). These must be related to the organising pulls of social, religious or political commitment. He must treat 'class', in particular, in terms of social relationships, processes and the consciousness (or unconsciousness) of them, not just as a label to attach to particular groups of persons, the social statisticians' classes I to V. Equally important, he must take account also of other elements in social psychology – grievance and resentment, expectation and aspiration, nostalgia and myth (Runciman 1966).

For these reasons, social surveys, to which increasing care and attention were being paid at the beginning of the century, have to be supplemented by other evidence. In this connection, Seebohm Rowntree's *Poverty: A Study of Town Life* (1901), an extremely influential book of the new century, is as interesting for the light which it throws on Rowntree's intense but cautious philanthropy as it is for its detailed statistical evidence about primary and secondary poverty in York or the theory, backed by statistics, of the poverty cycle (Briggs 1961a; Simey 1960; Mencher 1967; Townsend 1962; Kincaid 1973).

The achievement of the statistical movement of the Edwardian years, which led to the uncovering of facts not only about the incidence of poverty but the distribution of wealth (L. G. C. Money 1906), needs to be related in all its stages to the growth of popular communications – both to the nature of 'the media' and the limits to their exposure of the contrasts of contemporary society (Scott-James 1913; Jones 1920; Pound and Harmsworth 1959). The story is not a simple one: Balfour boasted of never reading a newspaper and Baldwin's appeal survived the attacks of the great newspaper proprietors. The perception of 'the masses' as a target to be aimed at as well as a topic to be explored was sharpened during these years, and it affected the retailing of ideas as much as the retailing of products. Yet it was only one perception.

For long, direct evidence about reactions 'from below' has been limited and historians have had to check or qualify statements 'from above' by comments from 'outsiders'. Among these a 1913 comment by the United States Ambassador Page stands out:

To an American democrat the sad thing (in England) is the servile class. Before the law, the chimney sweep and the peer have exactly the same standing. They have worked that out with absolute justice. The serving class is what we should call abject. It does not occur to them that they might ever become – or that their descendants might ever become – ladies or gentlemen [Brand 1950].

Page was referring not to the working class but to the 'serving class', which included over two and a half million people in 1911; recently its 'downstairs' voice has been heard more strongly than it was at the time (Powell 1968; Dawes 1973) and in general a bigger number and wider range of working-class voices (some of them the voices of historians) now provide historical evidence about a far bigger group.

Much recent writing on social history, indeed, particularly 'history from below', pivots on oral reminiscence: the inarticulate becomes more articulate. Thus Paul Thompson has set out on the basis of a sample of 500 interviews of men and women, all born by 1906 and the earliest in 1872, to recover 'actual' Edwardian experience: for example, how 'the poor' heard 'the voice of the relieving officer' or how they survived his refusals (Thompson 1975). Visual evidence from photographs and films (including evidence about styles and fashions) is also being increasingly collected and studied (Bentley 1974; Whybrow and Waterhouse 1976; Clapinson 1978; Mander and Mitchenson 1978; Rotha 1960). The photographic material is sometimes wider in range than the oral.

Consensus and conflict: the two world wars

The obligations of the social historian necessarily lead him into the exploration not only of continuities and discontinuities in social life but of consensus and conflict in social attitudes and behaviour. The two world wars of the twentieth century were great divides in individual and family experience (Fussell 1975; Marwick 1965; Longmate 1971; Briggs 1975), but social conflict was most apparent in the four years before the First World War and in the eight years between the end of that war and the general strike of 1926, years when resentment seemed to be hardening into intransigence. When G. R. Askwith, Chief Industrial Commissioner, visited Hull during a fiery dock strike in 1911 he was told by a local Councillor, who had been in Paris during the Commune, that 'he had never seen anything like this' (Askwith 1920). 'Among the advanced people', wrote Basil Thompson, Director of Intelligence in the Home Office in 1918, 'there appears to be a quiet certainty that revolution is coming' (Public Record Office Cab 24/71, 2 Dec. 1918; Parliamentary Papers Cmd. 8668, 1917–18).

The Second World War, particularly after 1940, stands out by contrast as a time of consensus. In consequence, large-scale social changes took place – both through social policy and through what Arthur Marwick calls 'unguided' private and public activities – at a far more rapid pace than had been deemed feasible during the 1920s and 1930s. In March 1939 the Ministry of Health had asked the India Office for the loan of an official used to dealing with large crowds: he would be able to help, it was hoped, with 'the masses' who might retreat in panic from a bombed metropolis. Instead by the autumn of 1940 practical relief was being provided on the spot for all the victims of 'the Blitz'. The concept of 'universality', so central to post-1945 'welfare state' policies, sprang to life out of the hectic experiences of the Dunkirk summer and the 'solidarity' of a nation in danger. And as the war went on, the projects proliferated. The Prime Minister might devote most of his energies to winning the war: large numbers of civilians and soldiers thought that winning the war was a necessary prelude to social reconstruction (Titmuss 1950; Marwick 1964 and 1968a; Calder 1969; Addison 1975).

Civilians and soldiers had not worked together so easily during the First World War. Yet there had been an emphasis on 'reconstruction' then also. The Ministry of Reconstruction, set up in 1918, dealt in detail with a complex agenda; it was concerned with such items as the 'deficiency and inefficiency of our present medical services, especially for maternity and infant welfare', the advancement of science, public housing policy, industrial relations and education (Johnson 1968). 'The nation was in a molten condition', Lloyd George told his first Reconstruction Committee, 'it was malleable now and would continue to be so for a short time after the War, but not for long' (Johnson 1968: 38).

He was right, for the hopes of large-scale reconstruction, like those of continuing economic controls, after the war were soon dashed (Tawney 1943; Abrams 1963; Milward 1970; Lowe 1978). Nonetheless, it was on the basis of the experience of both wars that Andrzejewski evolved his (too precise) theory of 'the military participation ratio', demonstrating that there was a direct connection between the extent to which war involved the total population and the extent of social change. As he suggested, the greater the participation of low-income and low-status groups in the war effort, the greater would be the social claims made on the state then and later (Andrzejewski 1954; Bowley 1930; Masterman 1909 and 1922).

The extent to which the two wars modified the directions in which nineteenth-century British society was moving has been sharply debated (Milward 1970; Marwick 1968a and b): Indeed, the debate is at least as sharp as that about the economy. Increasing attention has also been paid recently to the social effects of an earlier war, the Boer War, which linked nineteenth and twentieth centuries. The Boer War did not change directions, but it focused attention on particular and urgent social issues, notably 'deterioration' and deprivation (as measured, for example, in malnutrition) and 'efficiency' (White 1901; Searle 1971; Emy 1973; Morris 1974; Nowell-Smith 1964; Van Wyk Smith 1978). In the light of three wars, the view has been abandoned that – through their direct and indirect cost – wars are simply 'destructive'. So, too, has the view that they represent only 'discontinuity' (Waller 1940). The most pithy generalisation is that of A. J. P. Taylor, who claims that during the First World War 'the history of the English State and of the English people merged for the first time' (Taylor 1965: 2 and 400).

Change and diversity

The main long-term general themes in twentieth-century British social history lead through the two wars. They include increased material well-being; the development of new communications complexes based on new technologies; decreasing family size; a change in the social position of women; extended provision of education; the growth of social services and shifts in their orientation; the advocacy of and eventual implementation of large-scale projects in public housing; consequent expansion in the powers of the state; expanded urbanism; movements in the division of labour; changes in the organisation of the work place; and an increase in leisure. Yet, with or without referring to a 'logic of industrialisation' common to other countries besides Britain (Kerr et al. 1960; Goldthorpe 1966; Bell 1974; Touraine 1974; Giddens 1973), it is not easy to relate all these different themes to each other or to see their connection to other themes like 'secularisation' (B. Wilson 1966; Edwards 1969), crime (Mannheim 1940; Cadbury 1938; Radzinowicz 1966), or the move from 'local' initiative to national integration (Read 1964; Martin 1958; Minihan 1977). Nor is it easy to relate any of them to the wide spectrum of individual and group experience.

There are also built-in divergencies of interpretation, in relation to all these themes, many of them reflected in the use of comprehensive, but controversial key phrases like 'the silent revolution' as applied to education, 'the welfare state' as applied to social policy, or 'the mass society' as applied to 'culture' 'Lowndes 1937; Titmuss 1950; Briggs 1961c; Carr 1951, Shils 1962; Giner 1976; Swingewood 1977; Williams 1961 and 1976). There are difficulties, too, which arise out of inherited local and regional differences in British society. These differences include not only wages, occupations and conditions of work and provision of social amenities, including houses and hospitals, but are reflected also in the language, the distribution of religious groups, and, not least, in demography.

The local and regional inheritance changed substantially between 1900 and 1945, but the inequalities, social and environmental, persisted. During the twenty years between the Census of 1921 and the outbreak of the Second World War, when 86 per cent of British population growth was concentrated in the Midlands and the South-East, there were abnormally high death rates in the West Riding, Lancashire and Cheshire, Northumberland and Durham, and South Wales (the last two of which actually lost population, the latter by more than 8 per cent). During the most economically depressed years, 1929–37, the registered unemployment rate (never less than 10.4 per cent (1928) for the country as a whole) was twice as high in Wales and the industrial North as in the Midlands and the South-East. In 1936 only 6 per cent of the population of Deptford was unemployed, while the figure for Rhondda was 63.1 per cent (Pilgrim Trust 1938).

However difficult it may be to relate the different twentieth-century social themes to each other, there is no difficulty in showing how major variations in life chances were related to social differentials. The variations started with the chance of life itself. Titmuss, using 1930–32 statistics of infant mortality, drew the important conclusion in 1943 that where a region or district was economically depressed, social class differences within that region or district were greatly accentuated. Nationally, infant mortality increased with descent in the social scale, but there were remarkable regional differences. While mortality in Class V (unskilled workers) exceeded that of Class I ('middle and upper class') in the South-East by 63 per cent, in Lancashire and Cheshire the comparable figure was 198 per cent (Titmuss 1943).

By 1943 when Titmuss published these figures, social and economic differentials had been narrowed by the demands of war. Rationing was a leveller at least in relation to minimum needs, and what rationing symbolised – 'fair shares for all' – became a political election slogan of 1945 (Meade and Stone 1944; Lydall 1959; Atkinson 1973). Meanwhile, the destruction of war, more threatening to the future position of Britain in the international economy than to the strength of the war effort itself (Milward 1970: 44–52; McCurrach 1948), checked the improvement of material well-being, an improvement which had continued since 1900, though not evenly and for all.

By 1943 the proportion of personal income devoted to consumer goods had fallen from 87 per cent to 66 per cent. Many items of consumers' expenditure –

including drink, tobacco and entertainment – had had their prices deliberately raised by indirect taxation to raise revenue for the war effort, and though a significant share of that revenue was used for subsidies to keep down the price of national essentials, there was enough 'belt-tightening' to justify the general use of the term 'austerity'. And because of the effects of the war on Britain's position in the international economy – and the need for the immense post-war export drive – 'the age of austerity' continued into the period of planned social change after 1945 (Sissons and French 1964). More emphasis was placed throughout the whole period from 1939 to 1951 on the extent to which social change could be politically, fiscally, and administratively effected than on social change as the product of market forces. Indeed, it is only since the 1950s that the social history of the century has been scrutinised to take full account of the intricate interplay between market forces and social policy.

Material well-being

The concept of a 'second industrial revolution', centred on new industries employing new materials and creating new products (synthetic textiles, plastics, steel alloys and non-ferrous metals, scientific instruments, motor vehicles and aircraft and processed foods) and depending on a new form of power (electricity) became commonplace during the 1930s, although all the facts relating to the 'revolution' were seldom put together (Allen 1935; Plummer 1937; Kahn 1946; Sharlin 1963; Hennessey 1972). The 'revolution' involved shifts in location and manpower and the application of technical skills to the home as well as to the workplace (Sayers 1950).

The local and regional differences in British society in part reflected these economic changes. Many of the areas of the country where the great industries of the first industrial revolution had been created became the 'depressed areas' of the interwar years. Whole communities languished, although there was often a strong community sense; and the derelict physical environment, already ransacked during the earlier periods of growth, was further blighted (Priestley 1934; Orwell 1937; Hannington 1936; Wilkinson 1939; Hilton 1944; Beales & Lambert 1934). By contrast, in those areas of the country where the 'new' industries emerged – near Coventry and Birmingham, and in parts of London – there was a superficial glitter: new houses and new public houses, new shops, palatial new cinemas, new garages and new by-passes. Inside people's homes everywhere the 'revolution' progressed fast – electric lighting, fires and ovens; bakelite and chromium fittings; canned foods (sales of 'tinned fruit' rose by a half between 1920 and 1938); more casual clothes. The reaction against the blackened stove, the cluttered parlour and the wilting aspidistra was often sharp. Yet homes looked at least as different as communities, and there were significant variations – essentially class variations, but with variations within each class –

even in the same social community (Hoggart 1957; Lewis and Maude 1949).

Retailing, which linked factory, warehouse and home, itself underwent substantial changes between 1900 and 1939, sometimes exaggeratedly described as a 'retailing revolution' (Mathias 1967; Jefferys 1950; Pasdermadjian 1954; Briggs 1956; Cole 1947). On the eve of the Second World War, single unit retailers still accounted for 88 per cent (657 000) of the number of retail establishments, but they were dealing in only 66 per cent of the total trade. 66 000 multiple shops, some of the most successful of which had grown with the century, accounted for 18.5 per cent of the trade, and 24 000 retail co-operative societies, links between nineteenth and twentieth centuries, disposed of 10 per cent of the trade. There were 425 department stores in the big cities, centres of shopping expeditions from miles around, and in almost every sizeable town there were Woolworths and Marks and Spencer stores. A Woolworths store, indeed, along with 'a group of three or four banks, insurance companies, a hospital, secondary grammar schools and two or more cinemas' was often taken as being 'indicative of full urban status' (Smailes 1953). Between March 1927 and March 1939 the number of Marks and Spencer stores increased from 126 to 234 (Rees 1966).

Marks and Spencer spent little on advertising and developed its own branded goods. Yet retailing in general depended on increasingly heavy expenditure on local and national advertising. The volume of advertising increased substantially until it reached 2 per cent of the national income in 1938 (Hindley & Hindley 1972; Hall 1921; Turner 1952; Whitehead 1964), but there was more hunch than market research behind the expansion of consumer markets (Adler 1956). Moreover, that expansion, unlike the expansion in the United States, was not hitched to the development of radio. The numbers of British wireless licences increased from 2 269 644 in 1927, the year of the foundation of the British Broadcasting Corporation, a new public corporation which was the product of distinctive British social forces, to 8 968 388 in 1939 and 9 710 230 in 1945 (Briggs 1961b and 1965; Clayre 1973), but the programming policies of the Corporation with their emphasis on giving the people (treated as 'listeners' not as customers) not 'what they wanted', but what they might come to want, were in sharp contrast with most philosophies of retailing. The latter at their most articulate involved turning the luxuries of today into the necessities of tomorrow so that all might share them.

In fact, however, the nearer 'the classes' were drawn together by 'the objective facts of income, style of life and housing' – and they were still far apart during the 1930s – the more were middle-class people 'liable to pull them apart, by exaggerating the differences subjectively regarded' (Willmott & Young 1960). The status differences of the 1930s received at least as much attention as the class differences.

Newspapers, unlike radio, depended on advertising, and the average working-class family was reading twice as many newspapers and periodicals in 1937–38 as compared with 1913/14 (Abrams 1945). In general, sharp distinctions between 'popular' and 'quality' newspapers were not blurred between 1900 and 1945, although for a time (1908–22) Lord Northcliffe, the pioneer of the popular *Daily Mail* (from 1896) also owned *The Times* (Pound & Harmsworth 1959; Williams 1961 and 1968; Manvell 1961). Another new form of entertainment, the cinema, grew rapidly: 3500 cinemas were already open by 1914, and by 1939 there were 4800, selling a million tickets each week (Political and Economic Planning 1952; Browning and Sorrell 1954). As food was rationed, petrol cut and newsprint supplies restricted between 1939 and 1945, admissions increased by a half. Broadcasting, too, was at the height of its influence during the Second World War (Briggs 1970), with the world's first regular television service having been introduced for a small London audience in 1936, but suspended when war broke out.

Consumers' expenditures at constant prices rose by more than 20 per cent between 1900 and 1945, greater than real income per head because of a decline in the rate of savings, but at a lower rate than in many other industrialised countries. Real income per head fell during the Edwardian years, reached a postwar peak in 1919/20, fell from 1920 to 1922, rose slightly during the middle 1920s, reached the 1919 level in 1928, and rose again during the 1930s. At the outset of the depression the 'average workman' in London in 1929 could buy a third more consumer goods in return for a day's labour than at the time of Charles Booth's late nineteenth-century survey, even though he was working an hour less, and in 1936 the standard of living of the average workman in York was said by Rowntree to be about 30 per cent higher than it had been at the time of his first survey (Rowntree 1941; Llewellyn Smith 1930–35; Bowley & Hogg 1925; Parliamentary Papers 1942–43).

The distribution of consumer expenditure changed also, although the share of food remained fairly constant from 1903 (28.1 per cent) to 1913 (28.3 per cent) to 1938 (29 per cent) and 1945 (29.3 per cent) (Braithwaite & Dobbs 1932; Stone 1954). The *per capita* consumption of alcoholic drink fell sharply – a trend which impressed not only the Quaker Rowntree but most foreign visitors to London and the great cities – and the share of consumers' expenditures devoted to it was more than halved (1900: 20.8 per cent; 1939: 7.6 per cent; 1945: 8.9 per cent). The share of furniture, electrical goods and other consumer durables doubled between 1900 and 1937, and motor cars, which were a luxury in 1900, were commonplace by the 1920s. The number of licences for private cars rose from 314 769 in 1922 to 1 042 238 in 1930 and 1 834 248 in 1937. The millionth Morris car left the Cowley works on 22 May 1939, four months before the outbreak of the Second World War (Andrews and Brunner 1955).

The social consequences of the development of the motor car have been carefully studied (Richardson 1977; Perkin 1976). It was not a 'mass phenomenon' as it was in the United States, but by the late 1930s, 1 300 000 people derived their livelihood from the manufacture, operation, sale and servicing of motor cars. By then, average prices had fallen from 684 (in 1920) to 210, but the six large producers of private cars offered them to a stratified public in forty different models; 24 of the 40 models sold less than five thousand. The new 'car culture' (like the telephone culture) carried with it all the badges of status.

C. F. G. Masterman, who described cars as 'wandering machines racing with incredible velocity and no apparent aim' down the country lanes of Britain, had forecast that the day would come when 'every man of a certain income has possessed a motor car' and the expenditure would be accepted as 'normal' (Masterman 1909: 28). Although Masterman did not believe that life would be 'happier' or 'richer' for such an acceptance, the motorists of the 1920s and 1930s had few doubts. The Motor Show, a middle-class occasion, had an attendance of 275 000 in 1927; numbers fell to 188 000 in 1932, but rose again during the 1930s. And as the numbers of cars increased, it was not only 'country lanes' which were affected but central city areas. There were many complaints of congestion, 'Safety-first campaigns' started in 1928, and the gradual introduction of new street signs and 'furniture' – in 1934 'roundabouts' and 'Belisha beacons' – changed the face of the environment more even than telephone poles and wires. The battles about taxation on cars revealed the presence of a powerful new interest in British life (Plowden 1971).

Demography and wealth

While much motor car advertising related to 'family cars', it was often argued during the 1920s that 'babies' and 'baby Austins' (after the first 'baby car', the Austin 7, introduced in 1924) were in competition with each other (Graves and Hodge 1940). Decreasing family size was a feature of the whole period from 1900, although the decline was halted during the 1940s. The average number of children born to couples married in mid-Victorian England had been between 5.5 and 6.1; for those married between 1925 and 1928 it was 2.2. There were variations of family size according to social class – with a persistent tendency for families of non-manual workers to be smaller than those of manual workers. The social class differences in fertility were diminishing, however, after 1931 (Cox 1970).

The dominant factor determining the decrease, according to J. A. Banks and others, was the desire to maintain material standards of comfort (Banks 1954), and calculations about how to maintain – or to improve it – were made at the time and have subsequently been checked. It was contraception, however, which provided the means, and in this connection there were important changes in attitudes. Already by 1913 the Malthusian League, founded in 1877, was noting that birth control was becoming acceptable: 'when one remembers the fierce opposition from almost every class which used to be encountered fifteen or twenty years ago, and even more recently, the change in public opinion seems nothing short of miraculous...Our doctrines will soon be openly professed by the community at large' (The Family Planning Association was founded under a different name in 1930) (Fryer 1965; Ledbetter 1976).

There were, however, many critics of the social consequences of the decline in family size. 'Small families are apt to mean a far less rich and interesting family life than larger ones... Is it not far better to have families with many children each with their own gifts and interests and individual characters?' (Hubback 1945). The same critics were concerned about 'a declining natural population' and were proposing policies (family allowances, maternity benefits, for instance) to seek to reverse the decline (Reddaway 1939; Parliamentary Papers 1948–49; Rathbone 1924). One cause for concern was the increase in the proportion of 'over-65s' in the total population; they represented 5 per cent of the population in 1901, 7 per cent in 1931 and and 12 per cent in 1951. Old-age pensions, hedged round with moralistic limitations, had been introduced in 1908, but during the 1930s 'the elderly were forming a continually larger proportion of those forced to apply for public charity' (Gilbert 1970), a way of putting it which raised sharp opposition even at that time.

Demographic factors were thus recognised during the 1930s and 1940s to be influencing the shape of society. It was less often recognised, however, and this was a link with the rise in material well-being, that since the number of people in the 'working age group had risen as a proportion of the total population – from 0.60 to 0.68 from 1891 to 1947 – national income per head was greater – other things being equal – than if the nineteenth century age distribution had been maintained'. The Royal Commission on Population, reporting in 1949, maintained that 'this change in age balance' had been 'an appreciable factor in the rise of the standard of life over the last seventy years' (Parliamentary Papers 1948–49: 112).

The position of women

A change in the social position of women affected both material well-being and the dynamics of family life. In 1900 one quarter of the country's married women were in childbirth every year; thirty years later the fraction had halved to an eighth. With smaller families women found it easier to go out to work, although it is impossible fully to test the further hypothesis that a growing desire to be 'emancipated' led them out of the family and into work (Laski 1964; Myrdal & Klein 1956; Dahlstrom 1967).

There were already far more work choices available for women during the Edwardian period when the Suffragettes were struggling for the vote, than there had been in the Victorian period. By 1911, there were already three women teaching to every man, and during the previous decade the proportion of female clerks had risen from 18 to 32 per cent of that occupation. On the other hand, although the size of the female labour force increased from 4 731 000 in 1901 to 5 699 000 in 1921, to 6 265 000 in 1931 and to 6 961 000 in 1951, there was very little change in the proportion of women at work. This proportion rose only from 29.1 per cent in 1901 to 29.5 per cent in 1921 – in spite of the increased range of jobs for women in the First World War – to 29.8 per cent in 1931 and to 30.8 per cent in 1951.

Nonetheless, women's perception of their own role – and their husband's perception of it also – changed significantly. Charlotte Perkins Gilman, described in 1911 our 'androcentric culture': 'in large generalisation, the women of the world cook and wash, sweep and dust, sew and mend for the men'. 'We are so accustomed to this relation', she went on, 'have held it for so long to be the "natural" relation, that it is difficult to show it to be distinctly unnatural and injurious' (Gilman 1911). The extent to which the First World War changed such perception of what was 'natural' has been debated. Yet Mrs Pankhurst could already write in 1914 after the outbreak of war – and before women began to be mobilised in large numbers for war work – that 'our battles are practically over' (Pankhurst 1914). 'The House of Commons yesterday recognised the services of women to the State by approving by 341 votes to 62 woman suffrage', a diarist wrote in 1917. 'The War could not have been carried on without them' (McDonagh 1935). The further extension, in 1928, of the vote to women over 21 – the so-called 'Flapper Vote' – aroused little excitement except in the *Daily Mail*.

During the Second World War the position of women changed even more drastically than during the First, and at last the 'androcentric culture' began to erode (Calder 1969). 'Women of Britain, come into the factories', one war poster read. It was not only to the factories that they went: conscription was first applied to women in December 1941 and in 1943 was extended to women up to the age of 50. Women served on the land – through the Women's Land Army – and in the Forces. By 1945 there were over 300 000 of them in a war-time Civil Service which had expanded from 375 000 to 670 000.

Education

The development of education influenced the position of women and was one of the campaigns in which women had often been actively involved. It was, indeed, one of the major sustaining themes of the period, whether considered in terms of 'socialisation', the identification and development of individual potential or the diffusion of skills. Interest in educational development was fitful, however, and reached its peak before the passing of landmark legislation – in 1902, 1918 and 1944. Religion was less of a dividing issue after the fierce denominational struggles surrounding the Act of 1902. These struggles, like the free-trade resistance to Chamberlainite protectionism the following year, brought nineteenth-century themes to a climax rather than set the themes for the new century.

In 1900, full-time school attendance often stopped at 12, when children were permitted to work half-time, but the statutory age was raised to 14 in 1921 and 15 in 1947. The number of children from 12 to 14 who were at school increased, therefore, from 41.5 per cent of the age group in 1901 to 74.5 per cent in 1930 and of children aged 15 to 18 from 0.3 per cent to 6.6 per cent. The range of schools provided increased in parallel following the Education Act of 1902 which led to the further development of the secondary school sector (although technical education tended to be neglected). There were important changes, too, during the 1920s – 'reform by reorganisation' not by statute (Lowndes 1937; Simon 1974; Banks 1955; Hadow Committee 1926; Gosden & Gosden 1976; Argles 1964). Thereafter, the theory of an educational 'ladder', which had been propounded in the nineteenth century, became a key to twentieth-century policy (Glass 1959).

The scholarship examination had its origins in a 1907 decision to make secondary schools offer a quarter of the places free to pupils recruited from public elementary schools, and by 1938 53 per cent of the pupils in grammar schools, the most favoured secondary schools within the framework, had free places. One in twelve children attended such schools. It has been argued that they played a vital part not only in the peace-time history of the country, but in the war effort between 1939 and 1945. As Trevelyan wrote: 'The flyers of the R.A.F. are not and could not be the product of rural simplicity. If we win this War, it will have been won in the primary and secondary schools' (Trevelyan 1952: Vol. IV, 125).

One of the main features of the educational system, if it could be called a system, was that it was managed (with preponderant financial support from the State) by the local authorities; whatever its merits this mode of management made for continuing local and regional disparities in the quality, quantity and range of educational provision (Vaizey and Sheehan 1968). There was also throughout the period a private educational sector, strengthened by prestigious institutions, and increasingly attacked from the left, but the number of private schools continued to fall.

The proportion of children from secondary schools going on to further full-time post-secondary education varied considerably from one part of the country to another, although the national proportions did not change dramatically throughout the period. The number of university students, which was only 20 000 at the beginning of the century had more than doubled (42 000) by 1924–25, but thereafter there was little change until after the end of the Second World War. The figure for 1938/39 was 50 000. There were then said to be 63 000 teachers in training (as against 5 000 in 1900/01) and 6000 students in 'further education'.

Given such a segmented system, there was room for diversity of attitudes, even of goals, within it. The country was no more moving towards 'mass education' than towards 'mass motoring'. R. H. Tawney might argue that 'educational problems cannot be considered in isolation from the aspirations of the great bodies of men and women for whose sake alone it is that educational problems are worth considering at all' (Tawney 1914). Yet the aspirations were more blurred than he suggested, and there was more popular interest in housing and health than in education.

As far as 'socialisation' was concerned, the formal responsibilities of the family in relation to education diminished as the school became a compulsory institution, an institution concerned for the whole of the period with the maintenance of order as well as with the promotion of mobility and change. Yet 'chalk and talk' were by no means the only factors 'socialising' the child. Increased attention was being paid by psychologists to the separate identity of each child, and this influenced ideas of child rearing, the role and procedures of the law in relation to juvenile delinquency and the development of youth clubs. Meanwhile, cinemas catered for children, there was an extension of sports facilities and of scrutiny and guiding, and those children's 'sub-cultures' which owed little to the new media still flourished.

Schooling was only one influence on social mobility, also, even though its relative importance grew as compared with other influences (Turner 1961; Halsey 1964). The theory of the 'ladder' did not encourage large-scale mobility, but it allowed 'freedom of opportunity' to selected individuals to climb the 'stairway to the higher storeys of the social structure' (Glass 1959; Percy 1958). Other factors which need to be taken into account in assessing mobility include the ratio of 'higher' to 'lower jobs' in the occupational structure, the number of jobs available, trade union rules affecting entry, the degree to which occupations called for specific motivation or skills or more diffuse criteria of ability, and the distribution of 'innate' ability, information and influence (Lockwood 1962: 509–21). In all these respects, the twentieth-century social scene was different from the nineteenth. Insofar as there was a sense, in 1939, that Britain had become a far more mobile society than it had appeared to be in 1913, it rested mainly on a view of the educational advance of what came to be called a 'meritocracy'. This meritocracy was active in professional groups and increasingly active in management. Yet there were still more 'circles' and grooves than ladders.

Social services

Education could be considered – although it rarely was – as a 'social service', and in the whole field of the social services there was an extension throughout the period of state intervention. 'Ladders' were not needed in this process of extension, however; what was required were supports on the ground. 'Opportunity' figured little either; Winston Churchill in his advocacy of greater resources of social intervention in Edwardian England dwelt not on egalitarian objectives but on the 'awful uncertainty' of workers' lives. 'However willing the working classes may be to remain in passive opposition to the existing social system,' he explained, 'they will not continue to bear, they cannot, the awful uncertainties of their lives. Minimum standards of wages and comfort, insurance in some effective form or another against sickness, unemployment, old age – these are the questions by which parties are going to live in the future' (Wilson Harris 1946: 81).

Churchill and Lloyd George are often thought of as 'pioneers of the Welfare State', during the Edwardian years, and it is true that they both advocated large and expensive schemes of social welfare which involved the development of state machinery. Yet the protracted processes whereby different social services, each with its own history, were 'integrated' – insofar as they were by 1945 – are complex, not simple. They involved politicians, administrators, 'experts' and public opinion, including working-class opinion, and the timetable was at least as complex as the argument as to what should figure on the agenda. The sharp contrast sometimes drawn between the nineteenth and twentieth centuries – the former the age of 'the night watchman state', the latter the age of the developing 'welfare state' – is certainly misleading (Bruce 1973; Fraser 1973; Marshall 1965; Briggs 1961c).

In immediate post-1945 perspectives, the 'welfare state' (an extension of civil and political rights) was a state which endorsed 'social rights' and which concerned itself with 'social contingencies'. Yet before 1945 contingencies counted for more than rights. Only after the process had advanced far was it possible to generalise about its continuities or to reach a degree of consensus on a definition that the welfare state was a state which used organised power to deal with the limitations of the market (below subsistence income; fluctuations of employment; and access to necessary health 'care') as far as the least well-off sections of the population were concerned. It was always possible to justify the use of such organised power for 'conserving' order rather than facilitating change, and, thus, among some of the most active critics of the Liberal politicians returned to power in 1906, there were always some who supported the extension of social services. Likewise at the end of the period, the welfare measures of the Second World War won a broad political assent from individuals with different social philosophies and from quite different social and political groups.

The most important change between 1900 and 1939 was the end of the old poor law, a law which not only carried with it stigmas and in abstract terms divorced social rights from welfare provision, but also in very concrete terms ensured that in every place of any size there was a workhouse, 'the institution' (Webb 1929; Rose 1971 and 1972; Longmate 1974; Gilbert 1970). The Royal

Commission on the Poor Law recommended in 1909 that the poor law should go, but it was not until 1928 that a Local Government Bill was passed which finally destroyed the system. 'At midnight tonight a page of English local history will be turned over', *The Times* wrote on 31 March 1930, a night when the workhouse was finally abolished and 'public assistance' took the place of the poor law. Yet the end of the poor law coincided with growing mass unemployment, and the new system of public assistance (like the system of social insurance which had been introduced as a substitute for poor law reform in 1911) came under immense strain during the 1930s (Harris 1972; Gilbert 1970; Briggs 1971c; International Labour Organisation 1942).

It was not until the Beveridge enquiry, begun in 1941, that efforts were made 'to consider social insurance as a whole, as a contribution to a better new world after the war' (Harris 1977: 387). Beveridge's wife had urged him – though he needed little urging – to plan the future 'as a gradual millennium taking step after step, but not flinching on ultimate goals' and this is what he tried to do. His Report, with its stress on solidarity, had immense appeal in war time. While it was concerned with minima, some social critics saw it, as his wife did, as one step in the 'progress of citizenship', with 'social integration' spreading from 'the sphere of sentiment and patriotism into that of material enjoyment'. 'The diminution of inequality strengthened the demand for its abolition, at least with regard to the essentials of social welfare' (Marshall 1950: 47).

All this was from the vantage point of 1945, a very different vantage point from the divided Edwardian years and the mean 1930s. Part of the mean-ness could be accounted for by the petty-mindedness of bureaucracy; part was due, however, to the parsimony of the Treasury. It should be noted, however, that, despite sometimes fierce 'cuts', as in 1922 and 1931, there had been a substantial and continuing increase in expenditure on the social services since 1900, as figure 15.1 shows (Peacock and Wiseman 1961: 87). It should be noted, too, that although much of the expenditure on the social services during the mid 1930s was devoted to social services for which there had been no public provision in 1900, poor relief expenditure, the classic type of social support spending, actually increased between 1935 and 1936 from £12 million to £51 million. Nonetheless, the lower income groups were still paying more for their own welfare schemes than they were paying in health and unemployment insurance. In 1935, employers' contributions to social security amounted to £59 million and workmen's contributions to £54 million, but workmen were also paying £80 million on voluntary insurances and other self help schemes (excluding building societies).

These were years when traditions of voluntary mutual help on the part of the working class and of public service on the part of the substantial sections of the aristocracy, the gentry and the middle classes had not been broken, and they affected both local and national life. The Prime Minister for a large part of the

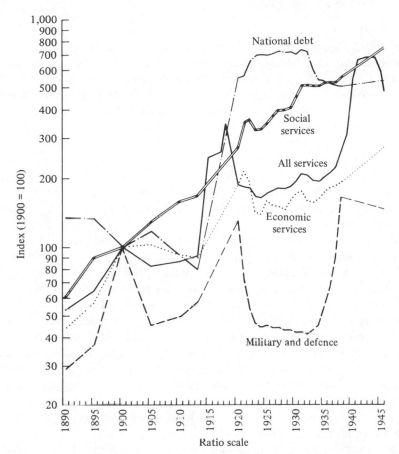

15.1   Indexes of government expenditure and expenditure by function per head of
population at 1900 prices 1900–45
Source: See text.

interwar years, Stanley Baldwin, declared himself proud to be presiding over
such a society, whatever its problems. And he was often able to rely on support
from surprising quarters, both in the aftermath of the general strike and in the
slow climb to 'recovery' during the 1930s. It was a favourite theme of his to
contrast the situation in Britain with the situation in the 'dictatorships' in
continental Europe. The American New Deal – with a completely different
ethos – was very far away.

Housing

One of the signs of concern during the interwar years, however, was the great growth of public housing. In quantitative terms the house building of the interwar years made up for the deficiencies of the decade from 1911 to 1921 and had a marked counter-cyclical effect during the depression. This is merely the shell of the story, however, so far as the social historian is concerned. First, demography came into the picture. With the diminishing size of natural families due to the fall in the birth rate, the number of 'private families' was increasing much faster than the population (Pigou & Clark 1937). This – and population redistribution – led to increasing pressure on housing, and the 'housing problem', which had been clearly identified before 1914, was not 'solved' by 1939. (It was aggravated again, of course, by the termination of house-building during the Second World War.)

Second, changes in demand for housing and in the interpretation of 'housing standards' began to have an effect. The five million houses built between 1911 and 1939 would have been able to house the $3\frac{1}{2}$ million new families, but there was increasing private and public dissatisfaction with 'sub-standard' older housing. In 1911 over 30 per cent of the population had been living in houses with more than three persons per two rooms, and ten years later 14 per cent of the population was living in houses with more than two persons per room. Overcrowding was only one indicator; another was physical deterioration ('slums'), and a third lack of adequate domestic amenities. Only 350 000 of the millions of slum properties in existence in 1911 had been demolished by 1939 – despite 'slum campaigns' – and 4 million people were still living in working-class housing (most of which was not 'modernised') built in the mid-Victorian period or earlier.

Third, the situation would have been far worse had not the state intervened in housing – through various schemes with the local authorities – between 1919 and 1939 (Bowley 1945; Wendt 1962). Of the 12 700 000 dwellings in 1939, 1 350 000 or just over 10 per cent of the total had been built by local authorities during the preceding twenty years and were owned by them. The Housing Act of 1919, prepared for by the Ministry of Reconstruction, was the first of a number of Acts of Parliament; it was as much of a landmark in the history of British social policy as the Education Acts, and although the economics of public housing policy were intricate and subject to regular review in subsequent legislation, the social consequences were immense.

Slum clearance schemes were associated with the transfer of population to new 'housing estates' on the edges of towns or cities or sometimes outside their formal boundaries. The schemes did not get under way until 1934, but between then and 1939 there were 50 000 demolitions a year and 200 000 people were moved. The slums had had a 'classic' way of life – intense, often hectic, noisy, highly personalised: the new 'estates' were sometimes lifeless, dull, silent and anonymous (Roberts 1971). Yet the best of them were superbly conceived and in all of them family amenities were enhanced. Their importance to the social historian of the twentieth century is as great as the importance of the country house to the social historian of the eighteenth century. It was sometimes said that they were turning a proletariat into a *bourgeoisie*, a favourite theme of the period, but from the evidence both of political and social behaviour this was and is an unsatisfactory assessment (Abrams 1945: 54–5).

Fourth, there was a growing private housing sector which did encourage the development of *bourgeois* attitudes – detached or semi-detached. Of the new dwellings built after 1919 the larger share were occupied by owners or mortgagees. Indeed, the rate of local authority housing never caught up with the rate of private building between 1919 and 1939 so that by 1939 more than twice as many private houses as local authority houses had been built. The private building could not have been sustained had it not been for the support of the building societies. Already by 1913 their assets were £65 million and they were advancing £9 million in that year on mortgages. By 1924 the amount outstanding to them on mortgages had risen to £24 million, by 1935 to £530 million and by 1940 to £678 million. The final figure represented advances to 1 503 000 borrowers, one in eight of all British families (Cleary 1965). These borrowers had a stake in private property: they were as much of a new force in social life as the council house tenants.

Both council estate and private developments were at the edge of towns. Inner cities during this period began their process of decay, although in the absence of immigrants there was a less obvious ecology than there was in the cities of the United States (Park 1952). The castles of suburbia were just as prominent on this side of the Atlantic, however, and there were often clashes between owners and tenants (Richards 1946).

Urbanisation

The fact that most of the private housing developments and the local authority housing estates were on the edge of towns and cities or beyond their limits (sometimes swallowing up villages) altered the relationship between home, work and community. The link was transport. Electric traction had established itself before the end of the nineteenth century (Sherrington 1934; Simmons 1962; Bagwell 1974), but the golden age of the tram – the 1920s – was only one decade earlier than the golden age of wireless and lasted for an even shorter time (Klapper 1961). The year of peak mileage was 1924, but more than a quarter of the mileage had passed out of use by 1933. While they lasted, trams were 'gondolas of the people', as Richard Hoggart has called them: the motor car, by contrast, was for the individual and the family. Yet it was the petrol-driven motor bus, which required no fixed tracks, rather than the private car which led to their eclipse, just as it had led very quickly to the eclipse of the horse bus.

In London, the extension of the underground further speeded both eclipses (Barker and Robbins 1976). In 1903, only thirteen licences for 'mechanical stage carriages' were issued by the Commissioners of Police for the Metropolis out of a total of 3423 licences for *all* stage carriages: by 1909 there were 1180 out of 2951, and by 1913 3522 out of 3664. The London Passenger Transport Board, founded twenty years later, dealt with bus, train and rail services. Meanwhile the first Ministry of Transport was created in 1919.

Throughout the period, London was the largest of the country's major 'conurbations', an ugly word coined to describe what many people thought of as an ugly fact – the massing of cities, towns and submerged villages with tracts of derelict land between, and 'ribbon roads' and indeterminate 'rurban' territory – neither urban nor rural – at the edges (Geddes 1915; Fawcett 1919). $4\frac{1}{2}$ million people lived in London in 1901, and more than 20 millions outside it lived in urban areas. During the interwar years approximately half the British people lived in the sixteen major conurbations of more than 250 000 inhabitants, with as many as 40 per cent located in the seven largest – London, Manchester, Birmingham, West Yorkshire, Glasgow, Merseyside and Tyneside. The number of people living in small towns with a population of less than 10 000 fell from 12.4 per cent in 1901 to 8.5 per cent in 1931, and there was even a decline, though far smaller, in the proportion living in towns of 10 000 to 50 000 – from 29.7 per cent to 28.1 per cent.

There were small towns (often rival towns) within the centres of play as well as of work – with spectator sports (professional football was already 'the sport of the people' by 1900 (Walvin 1975), and two new sports, greyhound racing and 'speedway' were introduced during the interwar years); with 'pubs' and clubs, new and old; with a wide range of cultural institutions, including theatres, museums and art galleries. In many of the conurbations there were holiday resorts also – Blackpool, Morecambe, Southport, Whitley Bay – although many of these (like race-courses) were situated further away – Brighton, Scarborough, Rhyl. The first Holiday with Pay Act (1938) gave the Minister of Labour power to help to support voluntary schemes. The total number of holidaymakers away from home in 1937 was about 15 millions, and two years later 11 million were on holiday with pay (Pimlot 1947).

The pattern of English holidays in the 1930s was very different from the pattern of the 1970s. Indeed, both in the choice of places and in the forms of pleasure the main influences still derived from the nineteenth century. Yet there had been signs of decline in both the distinctiveness and vitality of provincial cultures from the 1890s onwards, and the First World War broke many continuities. Some of the new social and cultural forces were national or international – the BBC (despite its efforts to promote 'regional' radio); the cinema (unlike the BBC geared almost exclusively to entertainment); the Press, which became less 'local'; dance music; the arts revival after the Second World War. Dialect was being eroded too, partly as a result of BBC programmes, more as a result of the development of education.

New housing developments, tending to use not local materials but the same standard materials everywhere (transport was a key factor in this connection also), made large areas of the conurbations look alike, although in every conurbation some relief was offered in the shapes and colours of cinemas and the wide variety of 'homes' on offer, each with its own garden, however minute.

This was certainly not a golden age of town planning, although much had been made of town planning as an ideal in the decade before 1914 and there were important new developments pointing to the future during the Second World War. 'Societies that provide good houses for people within reach of their occupation, and who improve dwellings already erected, are doing apostolic work', wrote W. L. George in 1907 (George 1907). Two years later John Burns, the former trade-union organiser, now Liberal Minister responsible for housing and planning described the objects of planning: 'comfort in the house; health in the home; dignity in our streets; space in our roads; and a lessening of the noises, the smoke, the smells, the advertisements, the nuisances that accompany a city that is without a plan because its rulers are governors without ideas and its citizens without hopeful outlook and imagination'. The Housing and Town Planning Act of 1909, however, was scarcely an exciting, nor even a promising, measure. It was permissive not mandatory, and very few schemes based on it were approved before 1914 (Ashworth 1954; Cherry 1972).

Planning powers were extended during the interwar years: there was an important new Act of 1932, for example, which went further than any previous legislation, and London's Green Belt policy was launched in 1935. In general, however, less attention was paid to existing cities than to new 'garden cities'. The first of these, owing its inspiration to Ebenezer Howard, was Letchworth (1903) (Howard 1902; Purdom 1925). Welwyn Garden City followed in 1920 (Osborn 1942; 1969; 1970). With tree-lined streets, low building densities and careful zoning, 'garden cities' or 'garden surburbs' were not a general answer. Much of the rhetoric about them is now dated, however effective it may have been at the time: 'The absence of the permanent smoke-clouds of the large city will mean a purer atmosphere – curtains and clothes will keep clean much longer, and the house-keeper will save money on soap and be relieved of much harassing housework' (Purdom 1925: 17). The smoke continued to pour out of the factory chimneys in the cities, and the soap business (with ancillaries like toothpaste and hair cream) continued to boom. Meanwhile, the Barlow Commission, appointed in July 1937 to consider the distribution of the industrial population, received evidence from the Town Planning Institute. 'Excessively large centres of population deprive the individual of the full and balanced life which is necessary for his health...In the large town he is a nonentity – a cog of such minute size in the great machine that he feels himself unessential to the working of it.'

Such an argument had greater relevance, perhaps, to industrial relations than to industrial location. In any case, the Barlow Commission did not report until 1940, by which time the population of the battered cities had proved that it did not consist only of cogs. Instead of examining the rise of spectator sports in the conurbations, the Barlow Commission bewailed 'the absence of adequate provision for open recreation and games'. Instead of describing the attractions of a home and garden in the suburbs, it complained of the 'social disadvantages' associated with long journeys to work (Parliamentary Papers 1939–40). The whole Report was a striking testimony to the inherent paternalism behind much official thinking during the interwar years (Glass 1955). Yet it was the Barlow Report – plus physical destruction – which encouraged the rash of Second World War plans, among which *The County of London Plan* (1943) and Abercrombie's *The Greater London Plan* (1944) were outstanding. The motto of the latter was 'Give a man and his wife a first-rate house, a community, and occupation of various kinds reasonably near at hand, within a regional framework which enable them to move freely and safely about, to see their friends and enjoy the advantages of London; add to these a wide freedom of choice, and they will not grumble in the years immediately following the war.'

They did grumble, and one of the reasons was that although houses, schools, towns and cities had changed, life in the workplace had changed less. The scale of the largest enterprises grew – in engineering, the motor car industry and chemicals, in particular – but most establishments still employed less than one hundred people. Management techniques altered less than in the United States and in some industrialised countries in Europe (Fox 1966), and owner employers remained a major economic and social group, differentiated by style (some paternalistic, some toughly unyielding) more than by role. They were by no means completely represented in the Federation of British Industry (1915). They were usually sharply distinguished from 'the salariat' which after suffering income cuts and tax increases during the Great Depression (though benefiting from falling prices) was widely hailed as a new 'force' (Durbin 1940: 109ff; Pollard 1962: 287–8; Clark 1937: 41). The public sector had only a small industrial component, and the role of the state remained regulatory (through industrial protection and inspection) rather than controlling. The trade unions, however, wedded though they were to traditional collective bargaining, pressed consistently for more nationalisation, beginning with coal. The old industries – coal, cotton and shipbuilding – were problem industries during the interwar years (Pigou & Clark 1936; Stevenson & Cook 1977), and the unions had their problems too, before, during and after the General Strike (Allen 1960; Pelling 1963: 121–49; Bullock 1960; Cole 1939; Barou 1947). There were over 1000 of them in 1931 (as against 1323 in 1901) although their numbers fell to 781 in 1945.

The financial and moral support that they gave to the Labour Party was one of the main factors in its return to power in 1945, and it is not surprising that one of the first measures which that Government took was to repeal the Trades Disputes Act passed after the General Strike.

This was only one of a number of measures, however, which separate the social history of England after 1945 from that before. In considering the separation, market forces were as significant as legislative measures. The relative affluence of the late 1950s and 1960s – and all that went with it, including television, carried the sense of a greater divide than the Labour Government of 1945 to 1951. The mood of the new age – not quite a new Elizabethan age – was shaped by three 'miraculous' years from 1952 to 1955, years of full employment without inflation. It was only later that the economic and social history of Britain began sharply to diverge.

16

The postwar years 1945-77

The economic history of the postwar period is in some ways easier to write than that of any earlier period. From 1945 onwards there is an abundance of official statistics including estimates of the main economic magnitudes: national income and expenditure, industrial production, employment, the balance of payments, and so on. This does not by any means guarantee their reliability or consistency and substantial revisions may occur many years after the figures are first published (for example, because of reconsideration of the appropriate seasonal adjustments). But it does provide the historian with a better and fuller picture of the way in which the economy worked than ever before; and since similar improvements in official statistics were made in other countries, international comparisons can be drawn with much greater confidence. This allows us to look at the historical record in better perspective and with greater insight.

At the same time the sheer abundance of economic aggregates from official sources is liable to divert attention from other data that may be of at least as great significance. If we are to judge economic performance we need to know what happened on the average or in total. But if we want to know *why* economic performance was good or bad we may have to look at individual instances for a clue and we may find what happened in particular occupations, industries or regions more revealing than what can be gleaned from the aggregates for output, investment, employment, and so on.

Before we turn to the main economic indicators we need a sketch of the sequence of events over the postwar period to provide a background for the trends illustrated in the statistics. It is convenient to divide the period into three: first, the transition from war to peace; then the years of creeping inflation and full employment that followed; and finally the beginnings of more rapid inflation and retreat from full employment after 1967.

The first of these periods can be seen as extending to 1948, when the balance of payments was restored to equilibrium and demobilisation was complete; or to 1949 when the first postwar devaluation occurred; or, conceivably, to 1952 when the war in Korea was at an end. During this period war-time controls were gradually relaxed or abandoned although some continued until well into the 1950s or, like exchange control, were given statutory form. Attention was concentrated on the restoration of stable peace-time conditions. The emphasis was on full employment and external and internal balance. Even in the debate on planning that went on throughout the transition it was stabilisation policy not growth that dominated the discussion. Growth was an objective that came to the fore gradually as the objective of full employment became more secure.

The second period, from 1948–49 to 1967, was one of comparatively limited fluctuations in activity along a path of steady growth: the years of Butskellism (from the names of the Conservative and Labour politicians, R. A. Butler and Hugh Gaitskell) when demand management proceeded from one 'crisis' to the next without anything really untoward judged by the standards of what was to follow. This was a period when the practice of demand management following the ideas of Keynes was developed and refined, and operated primarily through the budget to the accompaniment of growing complaints of 'stop–go'. Short-term objectives associated with this preoccupation with demand (and hence with stability) remained the dominant ones; but aspirations to faster growth took hold as the lag behind other industrial countries became perceptible; these aspirations produced a renewed infatuation with economic planning in the early 1960s. Failure to reconcile the conflicting objectives of the period culminated in devaluation in 1967.

In the third period following devaluation the factors making for instability, not only in Britain but in the world economy as well, gathered force. More and more violent changes took place in prices, in employment, and in the balance of payments. By 1975 prices were rising faster than in any post-war year, unemployment was higher, the deficit in the balance of payments was larger and, for the first time since the war, output was perceptibly lower than in the previous year.

Full employment

The most conspicuous contrast between postwar and prewar Britain was full employment. From 1920 until 1940 unemployment never fell below 1 million; from 1945 until 1975 it never, except for a few weeks, rose above it. The transformation was felt in the home as the fear of unemployment dwindled and family income expanded; it was felt in the standard of living as the extra manpower made its contribution to output; it was felt also at the place of work as scarcity reinforced the bargaining power of labour. Much of what happened over the three postwar decades can be traced back to the dominating influence of a long spell of continuous full employment.

Yet the public was never completely convinced that full employment had come to stay. In consequence, many of the advantages expected from it in the form of better industrial relations were withheld. Manning restrictions and demarcation rules remained in force. Fear of redundancy still acted as a brake on technical change. Nor was the fear altogether without some justification, since full employment did not put an end to redundancy.

Unemployment, moreover, did not remain at the extremely low level to which it fell. In 1944 it was as low as 80 000 (under 0.5 per cent) compared with over two million at the beginning of 1939, and not far short of one million during the Battle of Britain in 1940. At the end of the war there was a temporary rise with demobilisation in 1946 and a much sharper rise to over one million in the fuel crisis of 1947, but in the succeeding ten years unemployment fluctuated around 300 000. It then began to creep up from one cycle to the next. The peak of 400 000 in 1952 was succeeded by one of 500 000 in 1958, another of 600 000 in 1963 and later peaks of 900 000 in 1972 and 1 250 000 in 1976. The postwar 'Norm' of 300 000 was not reached again after 1956 except briefly in 1966. 'Full employment' was re-defined in the light of this upward trend. In 1945 Beveridge defined it in terms of 3 per cent unemployment, and it had come to be thought of as implying about 1.5 per cent in the 1950s. By the 1960s this had become 2 per cent and in the 1970s 3 per cent or more. Full employment was in retreat both in practice and in precept.

It was well understood when the aim of full employment took hold that it carried with it the danger of instability in wages and prices. There was much discussion, long before incomes policy was conceived, of the need to exercise some control over the bargaining power of labour under conditions of full employment and the danger of inflation if that power were exerted to the full. The discussion was not without effect as was evident from the agreement of the trade unions after the devaluation of 1949 not to press wage claims so long as prices rose by no more than 5 per cent. Nevertheless, throughout the period, wages showed the expected tendency to rise progressively, carrying prices up with them.

Even in the 1930s unemployment had not prevented a gradual rise in wages from 1933 onwards. In the three postwar decades the average weekly earnings of men working in manufacturing increased successively by 80 per cent, 74 per cent and 206 per cent. Retail prices over the same three decades increased by 62 per cent, 36 per cent and 128 per cent. It was not full employment alone that gave rise to inflation. But for most of these three decades full employment, together with the high pressure of demand and expansion in the money supply that were its inevitable concomitants, provided the main thrust behind rising prices. As one devil was driven out, another entered.

While full employment retreated from one decade to the next, inflation gathered strength. It is true that in the second postwar decade wages rose a little less sharply than in the first and prices only about half as fast. But this is partly a matter of accident in that the first decade included the price explosion during the Korean war (when retail prices rose by nearly 20 per cent in two years), the devaluation of 1949 and the removal of war-time controls and subsidies. In the second decade on the other hand, world commodity prices were remarkably stable and there was no devaluation of sterling. When devaluation did come, in 1967, it ushered in a period of increasingly rapid inflation both in wages and in prices. This coincided, not with falling unemployment, but with a level that was high by postwar standards.

Why was unemployment so low after the war? (Matthews 1968). How was it that the experience of the interwar years was not repeated? Since all industrial countries shared the same experience it is obvious that no satisfactory answer can be given in terms of economic forces peculiar to one country. A world phenomenon has to be explained by reference to world forces.

Chief among these forces was the postwar investment boom. In all the leading industrial countries there had either been extensive war damage to buildings and plant, or an accumulation of arrears of new construction during the war when defence requirements took priority, or a hangover from the interwar years when the long depression checked new investment and the labour force grew without any corresponding expansion in capacity. The First World War succeeded a period of world-wide prosperity and was accompanied by physical destruction within comparatively limited areas. It was therefore much easier to work off the accumulated arrears after 1918 than after 1945.

Coupled with the effects of the war was the more rapid rate of technical progress which made output per year grow much faster than ever before (probably two to three times as fast in the OECD area as a whole). With full employment this meant both a rise in the initial level of output compared with prewar years and a faster rate of growth. The growth was in real incomes as well as in output and the spending of these higher incomes maintained the pressure on capacity and renewed the need for more investment. Technical progress operated to perpetuate the investment boom and with it full employment, because the rate of capital accumulation out of current savings never overtook the expanding requirements for capital that were generated by increasing prosperity.

This was by no means the whole story; for it might have happened that the way to world prosperity was barred by a lop-sidedness in world economic development, with some countries in chronic deficit on current account, others in chronic surplus, and no mechanism for making the savings of the creditors available to the debtors. Fortunately, soon after the end of the war the United States took responsibility under the Marshall Plan for meeting the external deficits of the capital-hungry industrial countries of Western Europe and subsequently ran a sufficiently large deficit itself to relieve them of any fear of insuperable difficulties in maintaining external balance. Until the 1970s, when the US could no longer ignore the state of its balance of payments, no country felt obliged to modify to any serious extent, much less abandon, its full employment objective because of difficulties in balancing its external accounts.

Other elements in the situation were more peculiar to the United Kingdom. For example, long-term interest rates which had remained around 5 per cent in the early 1920s when prices were falling did not rise above 3 per cent until well after the Second World War although prices were rising. Monetary policy operated as a brake on investment in the first half of the interwar period but was far from a deterrent to investment after the Second World War.

So far, the explanation of full employment has been in terms of the investment boom and the expansion in world economic activity and international trade and capital flows to which it gave rise. But what of conscious policy? Did Keynesian ideas as interpreted by governments play no part? The answer is that although Keynesian ideas, by prolonging the postwar period of cheap money, undoubtedly contributed to the early establishment of full employment, they were rarely put to the test in the 1950s and 1960s. Demand was usually tugging at the leash of fiscal restraint and the efforts of governments were concentrated on keeping inflation in check almost as much as in trying to ensure full employment. 'Fine tuning' was the order of the day: that is, the British government (like many other governments) sought to adjust government revenue and expenditure through the budget so as to maintain a steady pressure of demand on available resources. But the operations of government were based on forecasts that were necessarily imperfect and often mistaken; they did not always have the desired effects, but, more important, these effects were usually quite small and equivalent, in their impact on unemployment, to a change hardly ever in excess of one per cent in a year. In that sense the government never had to handle a situation in which full employment was really in jeopardy. Moreover, throughout the period the central government ran a substantial surplus on current account that until 1973 met most of the borrowing requirements of the nationalised industries. The posture of the government was essentially, therefore, one of holding back demand to prevent excessive pressure on the economy quite as much as of seeking to top up demand to the full employment level. The techniques of demand management were shot through with Keynesian ideas; but demand management itself operated on buoyant market forces and even then only within narrow limits.

Growth

With full employment went growth. This was a reflection that had not occurred to the interwar generation and took some time to be understood in the later 1940s. For the first time figures of national income became available regularly and attention was directed to the growth in production from year to year experienced throughout the world.

Growth is usually measured in terms of economic potential, i.e. the rate at which output would expand if full use were made of available resources. This has the advantage of concentrating attention on the underlying rate of growth as distinct from the actual record of growth which is bound to be affected by fluctuations in the utilisation of resources and indeed is known to fluctuate more widely than the level of employment or the pressure put on available capacity. But the concept of economic potential is by no means unambiguous. It is impossible to make *full* use of all resources simultaneously and continuously or to reconcile whatever passes for full use with other objectives of policy such as internal and external balance. Full use has to be interpreted in terms of some rather arbitrary measure of optimum use – usually the highest level of employment judged to be sustainable – and this may have to be revised from time to time. A further difficulty is that the growth of economic potential is not independent of the actual growth of output since success in achieving steady and continuous growth is likely of itself to make possible the attainment of higher future rates of growth. We cannot assume that the rate achieved between two points in time at which the pressure on resources was equal can safely be interpreted as the underlying rate of growth in some objective sense nor that it constitutes a ceiling whatever the path of growth by which it is approached.

There is nevertheless a striking consistency in the trend rates of growth exhibited over the postwar years by all the leading industrial countries. If we take quinquennial periods between 1950 and 1970 so as to omit the years of recovery immediately after the war and the years of retreat from full employment in the early 1970s, we find comparatively little variation from one period to the next. Everywhere growth was faster than ever before. But in the United Kingdom the acceleration was less dramatic than in other industrial countries. The rate of growth hovered around 2.5–3 per cent while in the EEC the rate was generally between 5 and 6 per cent, i.e. about twice as high.

As earlier chapters have shown, this lag behind continental rates of growth was not new: it went back to the last quarter of the nineteenth century, if not earlier. But in the postwar period it was larger, more sustained and more conspicuous. A margin of, say, 0.5 per cent per annum takes some time to add up to a visible difference; but when there is a margin of 3 per cent per annum between two countries that start level, the faster growing country will have twice the output of the other within 25 years. If faster growth merely reflected a more rapidly rising working population and a correspondingly higher input of resources of all kinds it would not imply superior efficiency or translate itself into a difference in living standards. But in fact employment in Britain rose in each sub-period at roughly the same rate as in the EEC so that the margin of difference is hardly affected if the comparison is made in terms of output per head rather than output as such. The lag in production was also a lag in productivity and this necessarily led to a lag in the standard of living. Where this had been higher in the United Kingdom than in any EEC country except Belgium in 1950 – about twice as high as in Italy and 50 per cent higher than in Germany – it had become much lower than in all of these except Italy in

Table 16.1. *Annual growth rate of real gross domestic product 1950–73 (per cent per annum)*

	1950–55	1955–60	1960–64	1964–69	1969–73
UK	2.9	2.5	3.4	2.5	2.8
France	4.4	4.8	6.0	5.9	6.1
Germany	9.1	6.4	5.1	4.6	4.5
Italy	6.3	5.4	5.5	5.6	4.1
EEC[a]	6.2	5.3	5.4	5.3	5.0
Japan	7.1[c]	9.0	11.7	10.9	9.3[b]
US[b]	4.2	2.4	4.4	4.3	3.4

[a] France, Germany, Italy, Belgium and the Netherlands
[b] GNP
[c] 1952–55

Sources:
    for UK: *Economic Trends*, Annual Supplement (1975)
    for US: *The National Income and Product Accounts of the U.S., 1929–74* (Supplement to the Survey of Current Business)
    for EEC countries 1950–55: *National Accounts of O.E.C.D. Countries*, 1950–61.
    for EEC countries from 1955: D. T. Jones 'Output, Employment and Labour Productivity in Europe since 1955', *N.I.E.S.R. Economic Review*, **77** (Aug. 1976: 80)

1973 and was on one calculation no higher than in Italy (Jones 1976: 84). British levels of output per head (as measured by gross value added – the value of output less the cost of raw materials – per person employed) had fallen well below those in the countries of the Community: in some of the major branches of manufacturing, output per head on the continent was 50 per cent higher than in Britain.

Even so, growth was faster than in any previous period of equal length in British history. Over the 25 years 1948–73 GDP doubled in real terms and the average annual rate of increase was 2.8 per cent. This compares with a growth rate of about 2 per cent in the forty years before the First World War (when the working population was growing at 1 per cent per annum) and a slightly higher rate between 1923 and 1937.

There is also some evidence of an acceleration in the growth of productivity over the postwar period. Table 16.2 shows a faster rise in output per employed person, particularly in manufacturing, at the end of the period than at the beginning, and suggests a closing of the gap between the rates of improvement in Britain and the rest of Western Europe. Other calculations, however, do not sustain this conclusion. In a comparison by NEDO between the United Kingdom and Western Germany using slightly different dates, the contrast in rates of growth over the period 1954–72 remains just as striking but the trends in table 16.2 completely disappear. The NEDO study points to a marked deterioration in productivity growth over the last few years covered in the

Table 16.2. *Employment and output per person employed in the UK, USA, and EEC, 1955–73 (average annual rates of increase)*

	1955–60	1960–64	1964–69	1969–73
	Total employment			
UK	0.7	0.9	0.0	0.1
USA	1.1	1.4	2.4	1.9
EEC	0.8	0.3	0.0	0.3
	Manufacturing employment			
UK	0.6	0.1	−0.2	−1.6
USA	−0.1	0.7	3.2	−0.1
EEC	2.2	1.7	0.5	0.7
	Output in manufacturing per person employed			
UK	2.2	3.2	3.4	4.5
USA	2.0	4.8	3.1	3.3
EEC	4.6	4.8	5.9	4.6
	GDP per person employed[a]			
UK	1.8	2.2	2.5	2.8
USA	1.1	3.0	2.2	1.5
EEC	4.5	5.1	5.3	4.6

Sources: D. T. Jones, loc. cit., pp. 76–82; *The National Income and Product Accounts of the United States, 1929–74*
[a] GNP for USA

comparison while the National Institute arrives at exactly the opposite conclusion.

Careful examination of the figures, taking account of the effects of the very severe winter in early 1963 in depressing output and the opposite effects of a boom in 1973 in inflating output, makes it reasonable to conclude that there was an undoubted upward trend in the 1950s and 1960s. There may have been a similar upward trend in the EEC as well. From the mid 1960s onwards it is more difficult to take account of changes in capacity utilisation, which can exercise a critical influence on the usual measures of productivity. There was not only heavier unemployment but probably also more unused manufacturing capacity in 1972 than in 1968. In addition, employment in manufacturing was falling steeply, except in 1969–70, and by 1975 it was 12 per cent lower than in 1965. Under these exceptional conditions not only is measurement difficult but the significance of any slight change in trend is ambiguous since it might be associated with a contraction of the manufacturing sector in relation to the economy as a whole (Bacon & Eltis 1976). There are quite strong grounds for associating a steep upward trend in output with faster growth in productivity (Kaldor 1966); and the expansion in manufacturing output was much less between 1968 and 1972 than in any of the other periods in table 16.3.

Table 16.3. *Rates of growth in labour productivity and total productivity in manufacturing in the United Kingdom and Western Germany 1954–72*

| | Labour productivity | | Total productivity | | | | Percentage increase in manufacturing output in |
| | | | Underlying | | Achieved | | |
	UK	WG	UK	WG	UK	WG	UK
1954–59	2.2	3.6	1.5	2.5	0.8	2.1	13.6
1959–63	2.0	4.3	1.5	2.6	0.9	2.0	12.4
1963–68	4.2	5.8	1.8	2.5	2.7	3.4	22.8
1968–72	3.1	4.5	1.1	2.7	0.6	3.0	6.9
1954–72	2.9	4.6	1.5	2.6	1.3	2.7	67.7

Source: *The U.K. and West German Manufacturing Industry 1954–72* (ed. M. Panic, NEDO Monograph 5, 1976)

Growth: sources and constraints

The sources of growth include some that are measurable and some that are not. We can measure the growth in employment, the transfer of workers to industries and occupations where productivity is higher, the contribution made by a higher stock of capital, and other changes in inputs. But the enlargement and redeployment of resources accounts only for a fraction – sometimes quite a small fraction – of the observed increase in output compared with increases in their productivity in existing uses. In the study by E. F. Denison of the sources of growth in the United Kingdom between 1950 and 1962, for example, additional inputs of labour and capital accounted for 36 per cent of the average annual rate of growth in national imcome, improved education and better allocation of resources for 18 per cent, while the remaining 46 per cent – nearly half – although attributed almost entirely to economies of scale and advances in knowledge, is better regarded as a residual still to be explained (Denison 1968: 235). Indeed one can go further. Not only does the residual embrace all the influences on growth that one cannot measure with any claim to precision, from technical change and expanding markets on the one hand to restrictive practices, managerial incompetence, fluctuations in demand, and so on, on the other. The measurable influences, such as increased employment, may be brought into play by one or other of those wrapped up in the residual, such as expanding markets, so that their independent contribution to the process of growth is exaggerated by a calculation that treats them as exogenous.

Taking a very long view, the main sources of increasing income per head are likely to be: improvements in technique, including the technique of organisation and management; wider markets and the economies of scale which they permit;

and capital accumulation. Each of these brings the other two into operation so that all three tend to work in the same direction. Improvements in technique make a country more competitive and strengthen its position in foreign markets; raise output and income in the domestic market and so allow increasing returns to operate; and, as a rule, call for additional capital investment embodying the new techniques. Wider markets in the same way encourage technical innovation both because of the larger scale of operation that they permit and because an expanding volume of sales provides an environment favourable to experiment and rapid technical change. Wider markets also interact with capital investment since the bigger the volume of sales the greater the need for additional physical capacity; at the same time, the higher the rate of capital accumulation the bigger the output that can be sustained and the wider in due course the market can become.

Do these three factors provide any clue to the slower rate of growth in the United Kingdom? At first sight it might seem that they do. Investment, for example, has been a lower proportion of GDP in the United Kingdom than in the other countries of Western Europe. From 17 per cent of GDP in the early 1950s it rose to 22 per cent in the mid 1960s and was still at that level in the early 1970s. But in France and Germany the percentage in the 1960s averaged 24 per cent and 26 per cent respectively and in Japan it was as high as 34 per cent. If we take investment in manufacturing industry alone and confine ourselves to the 1960s the percentage of GDP was again lower than in other Western European countries. Allowing for all the difficulties of making accurate comparisons, it would appear that manufacturing investment absorbed less than 4 per cent of GDP in the United Kingdom, above 5 per cent in Germany, over 6 per cent in France and about 9 per cent in Japan. Only the United States shows a lower percentage than the United Kingdom.

But what significance should be attached to this comparison? Where output is growing faster, it is only to be expected that investment will share in the faster growth just as personal consumption, government expenditure and other elements in the national income share in it. Investment will also tend to absorb a higher share of output where the faster growth of output makes it imperative to expand capacity more rapidly. It is easy to show that if capital and output grow at an equal rate everywhere and if the ratio between the two is also the same in every country the share of GDP absorbed by investment will exactly reflect differences in the rate of growth from country to country. But this tells us nothing about the underlying cause of growth. It could be investment that was driving up output or output that was driving up investment. Without more evidence the behaviour of investment seems more likely to be symptomatic than causal.

When we compare the rate of investment with the rate of expansion in output the 'social yield' on new investment appears to have been remarkably low in

Britain. For the years 1963–72 the crude incremental capital–output ratio works out at 1.5 for Germany and 3.4 for the United Kingdom (National Economic Development Office 1975: 3n). For manufacturing industry alone the ratio for the period 1963–73 was 2.5 and 7.2 (Confederation of British Industry 1976: 25). Employment changed only imperceptibly over that period in both countries and the industrial structure was similar in each of them. It is not unreasonable to conclude that capital (as well as labour) was used to better purpose in Germany since Britain required more than twice as much investment to match a given increase in output. There is much other evidence to the same effect.

The constituents of investment, of which housing is the largest, make very different contributions to growth. This year's new houses may be very much like last year's while this year's new machinery may be much superior so that equal increments, even when measured gross (and still more when measured net of depreciation) have quite different impacts on the growth of GNP. In the years before the First World War house-building was at a low ebb because of heavy emigration and uncertainties over taxation of land values. Industrial investment was by no means so depressed; and a low level of total investment in such circumstances in comparison with, say, the United States would be no indication of a corresponding failure on the part of industry to instal new equipment, especially when the labour force needing equipment was expanding faster in the United States and many of the more important improvements could be made in the UK in the normal course of replacement of obsolete equipment (chapter 1).

The rate of capital accumulation, even if it approximates closely to the rate of growth of income so that the capital–output ratio remains steady, is not a very useful guide to the sources of growth. Instead of using investment to explain the behaviour of income it is usually necessary to start from the other end and explain investment after observing how income and output are growing. For example, in a comparison of the age of US and UK machinery R. W. Bacon and W. A. Eltis conclude that the higher level of productivity in the US cannot be attributed to more modern or technically superior plant. They suggest as alternative explanations more skilful management and lower manning ratios (Bacon & Eltis 1974). The more the figures are studied the greater the tendency to treat investment as one medium – but by no means the only one – through which other factors operate on growth.

The first of these other factors is technical change. If we look back over the past two centuries there is not much doubt that this has dominated economic growth, that it has accelerated over the past generation or two, and that we need look no further for an explanation of the simultaneous acceleration in economic growth throughout the world. But does this help us in finding reasons for the divergence between British and foreign rates of growth? Again the answer would appear to be, no.

If the lag in growth reflected a lag in the use of the most modern equipment this might be expected to show up in a demonstrable sluggishness in British industry in the adoption of important new techniques. But research by the National Institute of Economic and Social Research, covering some of the major innovations of the postwar period from float glass to jet engines, does not bear this out and suggests that the British record was about average in comparison with other countries (Nabseth & Ray 1974). However, it can be argued that major innovations, offering a decisive commercial advantage over existing processes and products and sufficiently in the public eye to make these advantages apparent, are not a conclusive test. There may have been greater sluggishness in those less conspicuous advances in technique that, although less striking individually, form the main stream of technical progress and call for greater managerial alertness and a favourable economic environment. But there is no easy way of demonstrating that this was or was not so.

When we turn to the influence of wider markets there is a greater abundance of statistical evidence but it is not easy to interpret. The domestic market grew as productivity grew and the one fed on the other. As productivity improved, output and incomes expanded; the growth of GNP in turn widened the market and exercised the beneficent influence on productivity on which Adam Smith insisted when he developed the argument that division of labour is limited by the size of the market. It is an argument that has since been taken further by Allyn Young (1929) and more recently by Lord Kaldor (1966).

We need not stop to enquire whether the link between the widening of the domestic market and higher productivity lies in economies of scale and is confined to manufacturing, as Lord Kaldor argues, or whether it has more to do with the encouragement that a rapidly expanding market gives to advances in technique by providing more scope for them and reducing the uncertainty that might otherwise delay their adoption. There seems little doubt that it was easier to introduce new products and processes in France and Germany than in the United Kingdom because the pay-off was faster: this is not only in keeping with common sense but is also the testimony of multi-national firms operating in Britain and on the continent. Similarly, in a rapidly growing market more of the equipment in use is of the latest vintage and this raises output per head in relation to the average in more static markets (Pratten 1976).

The significance of wider markets is reinforced in an open economy with an expanding volume of trade. The liberalisation of trade in the 1950s and the establishment of the Common Market involved a progressive opening of the markets of the member countries of the EEC to one another. This brought about an enormous expansion in trade, particularly in manufactures, with greater opportunities of specialisation within particular industries and corresponding gains in productivity. Britain on the other hand was supplying markets outside Europe that were less dynamic and that were less inclined than before the war to offer preferential advantages to British suppliers. This meant that exporters from the UK supplied a diminishing share of markets for manufactures that were less buoyant than those of the EEC. Exporters were therefore obliged to establish themselves in European markets which they had previously neglected and change the balance of their exports until Western Europe, which bought only half as much from Britain as the countries of the sterling area in the early 1950s, was buying as much by 1965 and a good deal more by 1970.

The contrast between the United Kingdom and the countries of the EEC in respect of market influences on growth is sometimes put in rather different terms. Growth, it is argued, was export-led on the continent while this was conspicuously not so in Britain. Alternatively, it is pointed out that British policy was dominated by stop–go: periodic 'stops' imposed by the government, usually because of external deficits, followed by brief spells of rapid expansion or 'go' that were too short to allow industry to move into higher gear. Both explanations lay emphasis on the constraints imposed by a weak balance of payments; but while the first stresses the feed-back of expanding exports on the rest of the economy, the second puts in the forefront the adverse effects of fluctuations in demand and puts the blame for those fluctuations on the government.

We shall deal with these views below when we come to look at the evolution of the balance of payments and Britain's trading position. It is conceivable but not very likely that the countries of the EEC owe their faster growth to uniformly greater skill in demand management or to some happy stroke of luck that enabled them to translate constant undervaluation of all their currencies *via* buoyant exports into faster growth in productivity. It is possible, that is, to lay emphasis exclusively on demand influences to the exclusion of influence on the side of supply. But most observers of British industry would find it somewhat paradoxical to explain its loss of competitiveness in terms of the buoyancy of demand or particular components of demand without regard to independent influences affecting costs: restrictive practices, managerial failings, an environment unfavourable to business pursuits and all-out competition, and the widespread desire for a quiet life.

These are not things that one can easily quantify; and most efforts at quantification select inappropriate variables such as the frequency of strikes or the total burden of taxation. The essential issue is whether the costs and benefits of innovation (which is indispensable to steady growth) are the same in the United Kingdom as elsewhere. No one doubts that it was easier for countries defeated or occupied in war-time to accept the need for all that went with rapid growth, including sustained, uncomplaining effort and the maximum use of new techniques. Equally, once those countries set out along a steeper growth trend it was easier for them to keep going since an expanding market then smoothed the path of the innovator. But the advantages were not all on one side since Britain, with her industrial potential largely intact, could establish herself quickly and firmly in foreign markets, and by 1948 British exports had grown in four years from one third of the 1939 level to nearly 50 per cent above this level. By 1950 Britain's share of world trade in manufactures was over 25 per cent higher than in 1929 and nearly as high as America's. But there is no evidence that the export-led growth of those years was faster than the (consumer-led) growth that followed. Between 1946 and 1950 output per man-year rose by less than 10 per cent, i.e. by about 2–2.5 per cent per annum, and by 1950 was not much above the prewar level. As in other countries, the rate of growth established in the early postwar years tended to perpetuate itself whatever the vagaries of demand management and the balance of payments. For reasons that are more social and political than economic and lie deep in the outlook, spirit and institutions of the British people the response to full employment was more sluggish and less dramatic in the United Kingdom than on the continent.

We may take, by way of example, four phenomena characteristic of the UK economy since the war.

(1) First of all, the low level of investment. As we have seen, investment, whether in total or in manufacturing alone, was low in relation to GNP. But it was not low in relation to the achieved rate of growth. In fact, capital investment in manufacturing grew faster than manufacturing output over the period after 1955 for which figures of the capital stock are available. What was different in Britain was what happened to output per unit of new investment. If new investment was low it was because the return both in additional output and in financial yield was inadequate. This leaves open the question whether this poor return was attributable chiefly to the failings of management or of labour: for example, to wrong investment decisions or to over-manning and restrictive labour practices.

There is little doubt that there were failings on both sides. It is, however, more difficult to rank managements on a country by country basis than to demonstrate the conspicuous prevalence of restrictive practices. It is also easier for managements to find an alibi. The evidence suggests that when British managements sought to raise productivity by the use of modern methods and equipment, they found themselves obliged to accept conditions as to manning, operation, or pay that cancelled out much of the advantage of making changes and were not insisted upon by the employees of their competitors abroad. Managements also had to devote much more time to dealing with labour disputes and to contend with a heavy weight of government regulation that absorbed scarce managerial time and deflected effort from innovatory tasks of prior importance to economic growth.

(2) Next, bad industrial relations. Foreign observers are apt to emphasise the contrast between working relations in Britain and in other countries such as Germany, Scandinavia or Japan and the class differences in British industry

which in their view interfere with harmony between employers and employed. There is perhaps more questioning of managerial prerogatives, and less sense of identity of interest inside a large British factory than in some of those on the Continent. There is undoubtedly a greater multiplicity of unions and more scope for wrangling between unions (e.g. over demarcation or promotion) with a corresponding diversion of the energies of the management to problems not of its own making. If this makes for slower growth and not just lower productivity, it is because change always adds additional strain and where relations are bad there is likely to be more shrinking from the upsets of change whatever the long-term benefits to be earned.

(3) A third circumstance is the aversion of the élite in Britain from business, and particularly from production and marketing: financial and legal aspects of business have more attraction. The public attitude to business success and the profits that go with it is, to say the least, luke-warm. Prominent business men have been heard to maintain that 'business is no longer a respectable occupation in Britain'. The engineering industries which account for nearly half British exports and recruit a large slice of the top talent of other industrial countries have a much weaker attraction for intelligent young men in the United Kingdom. If those who have to plan and carry out economic change in industry enjoy little prestige and include few of the ablest (in point of intelligence) of their generation it is hardly surprising if the rate of change is somewhat slower.

(4) Finally, the sluggishness of British exports. Whether international markets were in a state of boom or slump made remarkably little difference to British exports. In a year like 1958 when world trade in manufactures actually contracted, the British share, instead of continuing to fall, more or less stood still. In 1975 when world trade fell more heavily than in any post-war year the British share rose quite sharply. Similarly, while continental countries found that deflationary pressure on their home market rapidly swung their balance of payments round from deficit to surplus they observed with astonishment that deflationary pressure appeared to have little or no effect on British exports. This inelasticity is open to different explanations, but it is difficult not to regard it as a symptom of the general sluggishness of the economy and to suspect that it answers to some deadening of the response to ordinary economic incentives.

Balance of payments

The coincidence between a low rate of growth and the recurrence of balance of payments deficits in post-war Britain makes it natural to infer some causal relationship between the two. But as to the direction of the causal connection there is no agreement. The same forces that produce a slow growth in productivity might be expected to show up in a corresponding sluggishness in exports and a weakening in the competitive position of British producers in their own market. In that event the line of causation would run from slow growth to external deficits. On the other hand, if balance of payments difficulties deter a government from allowing the economy to expand or induce it to bring expansion to a premature stop the causation can run the other way. A more obvious explanation of the succession of external deficits is that they reflected excess demand at home and were the product of loose budgetary and monetary control, combined with an over-valued currency.

In their anxiety to achieve higher rates of growth, ministers were nearly always prepared to expand demand more rapidly and more continuously than was desirable and felt themselves thwarted in their praiseworthy objectives by the perversity of the balance of payments. Attlee was by no means the only Prime Minister to feel some bewilderment that when trade was brisk at home sterling should be weak abroad. British industrialists spent much of the early sixties denouncing 'stop–go' policies which were designed to check a sudden deterioration in the balance of payments brought about by an upswing in domestic demand. In voicing their opposition to such policies they appeared at times to be contending that an unconstrained expansion in demand was the surest foundation for faster growth when it might with at least equal justification be regarded as a safe prescription for more rapid inflation. On this interpretation, much in vogue at the official level, deficits in the British balance of payments provided a safety valve for excess demand and were to be heeded as a warning of the inflation that would follow if the excess persisted.

It is true that the course of expansion in output over the postwar years was punctuated at intervals by a stop, imposed by governments, which arrested the growth of industrial production for a period of about two years and sometimes longer and was usually precipitated by balance of payments difficulties. This happened in 1950–52, 1955–56, 1960–62 and 1965–66. But there were other occasions when industrial depression coincided with a surplus in the balance of payments on current account, as in 1957–58 and 1970–71, and on the latter occasion at least there was no external threat to expansion. Where there was such a threat and the government took restrictive action, did the resulting fluctuation do continuing injury to economic growth? And was there a clear loss of production in relation to the sustainable level consistent with other objectives?

These are not easy questions to answer. Nor is it easy to disentangle the effects of stop–go from other issues relating to the competitiveness of the British economy at the going rate of exchange.

It helps to put stop–go in perspective if the fluctuations in the British economy are seen alongside fluctuations elsewhere. The evidence suggests that in point of amplitude and frequency they were no worse. Other European countries had similar fluctuations with or without exchange crises (National Economic

Development Office 1976: T. Wilson 1966). If there was a waste of resources it never reached the point at which unemployment touched 3 per cent until 1971, so that if 3 per cent is taken as the measure of what was sustainable, output was uniformly above the level this would imply. But the example of Germany and France where unemployment, in the 1960s at least, was less than in Britain suggests that this may be too exacting a standard. The economy may well have been run on too narrow a margin of spare capacity and the effort to maintain unemployment at a level below 2 per cent may have been bound to bring on inflation. Even if this were so, a rather higher level of output might have been maintained with 2 per cent unemployment had it been possible to secure a steadier rate of expansion.

This implies that the fluctuations that occurred did do some continuing injury to economic growth. But if we press the question why this should be so the answer is not very clear. If we think of growth as resulting primarily from the commercial exploitation of new techniques there is no very obvious reason why the ups and downs of business, within comparatively narrow limits and with a general expectation that expansion will in due course be resumed, should do more than delay for a year or two the introduction of these techniques. It is only if interruption means the loss of chances that will never recur or if some other, quite different, explanation of growth is accepted that stop–go can do more than temporary harm to industrial productivity.

Judgement on the effects of stop–go is tied up with judgement on its causes. Those who regarded it as the major reason for Britain's poor rate of economic growth were inclined to attribute the balance of payments difficulties precipitating it to an over-valued rate of exchange. This provided them with an easy prescription for faster growth since devaluation (or alternatively a floating rate of exchange) would remove the obstacle by bringing the balance of payments into equilibrium or surplus.

It is hardly possible to believe that the pound was continuously over-valued from 1949 to 1967 and there is in fact no logical reason why periodic deficits in the balance of payments should be treated as an infallible sign of over-valuation. In the 1950s the current account was in surplus in every year but two (1951 and 1955) and exports grew in value at least as fast as imports. It was only in the 1960s that deficits became the rule rather than the exception: apart from small surpluses in 1961–63 and in 1966 there was no year free of deficit in the 1960s until 1969. The balance of visible trade showed the same trend: by 1967 the excess of imports was over £500m. where in 1959 it had been just over £100m.

These trends do not by themselves establish the over-valuation of the pound in the 1960s or its absence in the 1950s. It is, for example, remarkable that British exports grew in volume year by year with only minor inflections more symptomatic of world prosperity than of British competitiveness and along a curve that rose with the same sluggishness as British production. The more telling indications of over-valuation lay in the various measures of exchange control or trade protection by which the government sought to preserve external balance.

The balance of payments includes a great deal more than commodity imports and exports and any view as to the overvaluation of the exchange rate has to take account of these other components. Invisible earnings, for example, were already more than half as large as the visible items in the 1950s and by the 1970s were nearer to two thirds. There was a surplus on invisibles from 1948 onwards which was as high as £450m. by 1952 but fell in the later 1950s, continued to fall in the 1960s and was under £200m. in 1964–66. The trend was thus broadly similar to the trend in the commodity balance. After devaluation in 1967 the trend swung round even more strikingly than the trend in the visible balance and more enduringly, bringing a surplus of £250m. in 1967 up to nearly £1500m. in 1973. *Prima facie*, therefore, the movement of invisibles would appear to support the view that the pound was over-valued in the mid 1960s and that invisibles respond positively to changes in the exchange rate.

It was sometimes argued that the balance on invisibles could be improved by administrative action and efforts were made to encourage the remission of profits from abroad, limit expenditure abroad by tourists, and so on. There was also much discussion of the heavy burden of defence obligations and of military expenditure abroad: this came to about £270m. a year (net) in the mid 1960s. But the total economies in foreign exchange resulting from administrative measures were probably quite small, although not negligible in relation to current deficits of £200–300m., and tended to diminish as time went on.

The adverse trend in the current account was liable to communicate itself to the capital account, especially in view of the large accumulation of sterling balances that could be drawn down if the pound seemed in imminent danger of devaluation. These balances, amounting for much of the period to £4000–5000m., were much larger than the reserves and far in excess of annual surpluses or deficits on current account. If a succession of deficits alarmed even a few holders of these balances the parity might prove very difficult to sustain; but, at the same time, if it were changed, other holders might decide to get out of sterling before it slid down further and so start off a vicious circle of depreciation, rising import prices, general inflation and further depreciation.

Balance of payments difficulties were by no means peculiar to Britain. France, for example, was in constant balance of payments difficulties in the 1950s and even Japan did not begin to enjoy current account surpluses until well into the 1960s. What does distinguish British trade is the steady decline in Britain's share of world exports of manufactures (table 16.4). This goes back well into the nineteenth century. But the rate of decline has been much faster since the war as the expansion of world trade accelerated while British exports rose comparatively slowly.

It is this declining share that lends attraction to the idea of export-led growth

Table 16.4. *UK exports 1899–1975*

	UK share in world exports of manufactures (%)	Volume of UK exports (1958 = 100)
1899	34.0	33
1913	30.9	91
1929	22.9	74
1937	21.3	59
1950	25.3	91
1960	16.5	109
1970	10.8	170
1975	9.3	221

Source: The figures in col. 1 for 1899–1950 are calculated from A. Maizels, *Industrial Growth and World Trade*, CUP and NIESR (1963). Those for later years are from the NIESR *Economic Review*. The two series are broadly comparable: for example, the percentage given by the NIESR *Economic Review*, for 1957 is 17.8 while Maizels' figures yield 18.0.

The figures in col. 2 for 1899–1960 are from *Key Economic Statistics 1900–1966* (London and Cambridge Economic Service).

which coloured thinking in Britain for much of the period. The countries gaining share were those that grew fastest, especially Japan, while those losing share were the slow-growing countries like Britain and the United States. But the link between exports and growth is not self-evident. If the failure of exports to grow faster precipitates balance of payments difficulties we are back in the argument outlined above. Such difficulties may not arise: the common experience is that imports keep in step with the growth of national income and if exports do so too there need be no upset in the trade balance. Indeed, if British exports had kept pace with the growth of world trade there would have been a colossal surplus by 1975 unless the faster growth of exports had somehow stimulated a corresponding acceleration in the growth of output, income and in due course, imports. But under conditions of more or less continuous full employment why should the substitution of more exports for some other element in output have such favourable repercussions on productivity? There might have been some modest impetus to faster growth if the export sector were peculiarly subject to increasing returns; but even so, in the absence of some more powerful influence on productivity, it would have required only a very slightly less rapid fall in the share of world trade in manufactures to bring the British current account into satisfactory surplus in, say, the mid 1960s. If exports can be said to have lagged, the lag was not very large and was not obviously decisive. On the contrary, it seems much more in keeping with the evidence to regard exports as held back by the same forces and to roughly the same extent as output itself.

Table 16.5. *National income and the trade balance in the UK 1938–75*

	GDP at factor cost[a] (£m.)	Exports (f.o.b.) (£m.)	Ratio of exports to GDP (%)	Imports (f.o.b.) (£m.)	Ratio of imports to GDP (%)	Trade balance (£m.)	Terms of trade (1970 = 100)
1938	4 983	533	10.7	835	16.7	−302	98
1950	11 360	2261	19.9	2 312	20.4	−51	83
1955	16 875	3 073	18.2	3 386	20.1	−313	82
1960	22 640	3 737	16.5	4 138	18.3	−406	93
1965	31 235	4 848	15.5	5 071	16.2	−223	98
1970	43 250	7 907	10.3	7 932	18.3	−12	100
1975	91 550	18 768	20.5	21 972	24.0	−3204	81

Source: *Economic Trends* Annual Supplement (1975); *National Income and Expenditure*, various issues
[a] Expenditure basis

The position over the postwar period is summarised in table 16.5 which shows that there was a gradual decline in the relative importance of foreign trade in the total economy on both sides of the account between 1950 and 1965 and a more substantial and rapid expansion between 1965 and 1975. This picture to some extent reflects the devaluations of 1949 and 1967, both of which jerked up international prices in relation to domestic prices. The very high level of imports in 1975 corresponds to the jump in oil prices at the end of 1973 and the rise in primary product prices over the quinquennium. This involved a swing in the terms of trade of nearly 20 per cent between 1970 and 1975 so that although the volume of exports grew nearly as much as the volume of imports, export and import values diverged and a very large trade deficit emerged. A swing in the opposite direction in the 1950s, when the terms of trade improved by 12 per cent, made it possible for the *volume* of imports to keep pace with GDP although the value was showing a relative contraction.

It is worth examining the trends in table 16.5 in a longer-term perspective. In the immediate postwar period the government set as an objective the attainment of a volume of exports 75 per cent greater than in 1938 and this was achieved in 1950 when imports still fell 15 per cent short of the 1938 volume. Many of the war-time controls remaining in operation in 1950 were essentially directed towards economy in imports, especially imports from dollar sources. Even after the controls began to be dismantled the contrast between imports and exports remained: it was not until 1955 that the prewar volume of imports was recovered.

Moreover, estimates of the volume of exports are based on deflated values rather than on the amount of work done on the goods exported. In prewar years a large proportion of exports consisted of textiles and clothing with a high import content while in postwar years exports of manufactures were more heavily weighted by metal and engineering products in which the import content was low. Textiles and clothing for example accounted for over half British exports of manufactures in 1899, and a little under half in 1913. By 1937 the proportion had fallen to 34 per cent, by 1950 to 22 per cent and by 1957 to 12 per cent (Maizels 1963: 482). Thus the increase in British resources occupied in the manufacture of exports was rather higher than the increase measured in terms of volume. By the same token the expansion in the volume of imports *for consumption* was also under-stated in the figures for total imports. Broadly speaking, however, the postwar period started off with an adjustment between exports and imports that was very large, that was partly undone in the years before 1967, and that recommenced after 1967.

Too little importance has in the past been attached to the impact on the British economy of the large swings in the terms of trade that have occurred over the past sixty years. After the First World War the early years of peace saw a remarkable swing in favour of the United Kingdom that eased the transition but at a high cost in unemployment in the export industries. In the slump after 1929 a further swing again eased the problem of recovery after an initial rise in unemployment concentrated on the export industries. The situation in those years stands in marked contrast to the situation in the mid 1970s when the swing went the other way in a world depression. After the Second World War a double adjustment had to be made to adverse terms of trade on the one hand and the loss of foreign investment income on the other. The terms of trade when balance was restored in 1948–50 were some 13 per cent worse than in 1936–38; while net investment income, which had paid for nearly 50 per cent of British imports before the First World War and about 25 per cent before the second, covered only 15 per cent in 1948–50. Equilibrium in the balance of payments in the 1950s was preserved by a steady swing in favour of the United Kingdom and it was partly because this swing was arrested in the 1960s that devaluation proved necessary. It took until the early 1960s for the terms of trade to regain the favourable prewar rate and by the mid 1970s they had returned to the lowest levels of the early 1950s.

Inflation

From the peak in 1920 after the First World War consumer prices had fallen 30 per cent by the outbreak of war in 1939. They had already begun to rise gradually in the last six years of peace and in the six years of war they made up the whole of the fall since 1920. It took nineteen years after the Second World War for prices to double – an average annual rate of 3.7 per cent. Between 1964 and 1972 this rate accelerated to 5.4 per cent and over the next three years to 15.8 per cent. By 1975 the value of money to the consumer was not much more than one fifth of what it had been thirty years previously.

Inflation is a normal concomitant of war and the Second World War was no exception. Prices were jerked up sharply because of shop shortages and higher import costs; and in spite of rationing, price control and other devices designed to keep the rise within limits, retail prices went on rising throughout the war. The rate of increase, however, fell off, a rise in the first three years of war by nearly a third being followed by one of only 10 per cent in the next three. Meanwhile wage-rates had risen by 50 per cent, again with a marked flattening out in the later war years. In a broad sense, and allowing for the defects of the indices, wages and prices had kept in step.

In the early postwar years, excess demand continued to be held in check by the war-time controls which deflected spending from scarce foodstuffs and materials (as well as from imported or exportable goods) to purposes that could be gratified at less cost in resources. Some of these controls were intensified: bread, which had never been rationed in war-time, was put on the ration in 1946 and potatoes, of which the same was true, in 1947. Other controls, such as the rationing of meat, were prolonged until well into the 1950s. Consumers and business firms had accumulated vast liquid assets in the course of the war and their freedom to draw on these was limited indirectly by controls at the points of scarcity, not by any blocking of accounts or incentives to delay expenditure. The position was well summed up in the phrase 'suppressed inflation'. But what was suppressed was demand. The pressure from the side of costs was allowed to come through into prices except where the government used price control or subsidies (and in doing so added further to excess demand). Cost pressure was not associated with efforts to push up real wages: it originated largely in the rise in commodity prices in international markets as the postwar boom got under way.

As supplies improved and exports expanded the need for war-time controls gradually eased. It was less necessary to limit demand in specific directions but just as necessary to limit demand in total. Inflation continued but since it was less 'suppressed' it was less open to explanation in terms of excess demand plus controls. Prices had risen 10 per cent between 1945 and 1947. They rose by a further 10 per cent between 1947 and 1949. At that stage the rise seemed to be moderating. But in September 1949 devaluation introduced fresh inflationary impulses and in June 1950 the outbreak of the Korean War produced a price explosion on world commodity markets. Prices rose by nearly 20 per cent in two years.

For the next twenty years prices continued to rise at a rate not very different from that in most other countries, i.e. about 2 to 3 per cent per annum. Inflation was a world-wide phenomenon and proceeded at a fairly stable rate. It was variously explained in terms of an expanding money supply, heavy government spending, trade union pressure for higher wages and the contagious effects of rising prices in other countries communicated through a fixed exchange rate. The first two explanations (discussed below) attributed inflation to demand factors, implying that if demand grew less strongly inflation would moderate. The second two explanations laid emphasis on the behaviour of costs and on factors not responsive to the pressure of domestic demand.

There has never been any doubt that inflation is closely linked to monetary influences or that heavy government spending is liable to be financed out of additions to the money supply. The dispute between monetarists and non-monetarists that developed in the 1960s related to the causal sequence and was essentially between those who regarded wage-bargaining as governed by the behaviour of the money supply and those who thought that the money supply danced to the tune of wage-bargaining. It is easy to show in a general way (and not only for the United Kingdom since the same issue arises in other countries) that since the war the money supply has expanded faster than real national income and it is natural to expect the excess creation of money to be translated sooner or later into a fall in its value. But if money incomes are rising for other reasons the creation of additional money plays an accommodating role and the source of inflation lies in those 'other reasons'.

From the point of view of government policy the crucial question was whether there was some fairly determinate relationship between the demand for labour and its price in terms of current money wages. If there were such a relationship the government could operate on it through demand management and it would hardly matter whether in the process it made use of budgetary or monetary weapons. If on the other hand there was a substantial element of indeterminacy it might be possible for the government to exert direct influence on wages without having to create additional unemployment. It was this reflection, reinforced by recognition that, in the absence of excess demand, if wage-rates could be stabilised, prices could sooner or later be brought into line, that prompted governments to devise various forms of incomes policy. Sometimes these were voluntary, sometimes they were backed by legislation. But the distinction between the two was more apparent than real since in the face of strike action the government had no obvious sanction more powerful than public opinion that was capable of use without the support of public opinion.

Incomes policy of a sort was first used after the devaluation of 1949. It then amounted to a wage freeze which held for about a year but proved unsustainable for a longer period in the face of higher import prices and the anomalies resulting from factory settlements involving wage drift through changes in piece rates. Between October 1949 and October 1950 hourly wage-rates rose by only 1.3 per cent but in the following year, with retail prices climbing by 12 per cent, men's hourly wages and hourly earnings both shot up by 10 per cent. While it is possible that the policy might have proved more successful if there had been no Korean War to produce inflation on an international scale subsequent experience confirmed the general conclusion that a wage freeze tends to have a limited life.

In July 1961 incomes policy of a different sort was introduced as part of the package of that year. The Chancellor (Mr Selwyn Lloyd) called for a 'pause' in the wage round and announced his intention of applying it to workers in the public sector. The policy won no support from the TUC and foundered before the end of the year on an award increasing wages in the electrical supply industry. The average increase in hourly earnings for men over the year from October 1961 was, however, limited to 4 per cent.

The next effort to introduce an incomes policy came in 1965 and was continued in various forms until 1969. There was no conspicuous slowing down in wage increases in 1965–66, the rise in hourly earnings for men averaging nearly 10 per cent in the year to April 1966. But when a wage freeze was introduced in July 1966 as part of another deflationary package, wages remained remarkably stable: hourly earnings were virtually unchanged between June 1966 and March 1967. Again, however, the freeze was succeeded by a period of rapidly rising wage-rates. The increase in hourly earnings over the year from April 1967 averaged just under 8 per cent – well above the norm set by the government. From the end of 1969 when the government's weakness vis-à-vis the trade unions had been plainly demonstrated by its retreat on the policy announced in 'In Place of Strife' the increase accelerated: in 1970 and again in 1971 the rise in weekly rates exceeded 12 per cent and in 1972 it reached 16 per cent before moderating slightly in 1973. Then came a dramatic rise in world commodity prices and the price of oil in 1973 and with it a sharp increase in prices in Britain. Wage-rates accelerated once more to a 26 per cent increase in 1974 and again in 1975.

Inflation in the 1970s was of a different order from anything experienced in Britain this century except in 1916–20 and 1950–51. All of the suggested causes were present – rapid expansion of the money supply, high government spending, large increases in money wages and rising import prices. All of these were also present in 1950–51. What is most striking about the two major bursts of inflation since the war is the behaviour of the last of these influences. Import prices rose by over 50 per cent in the two years 1949–51 and doubled in the two years 1972–74. On the other hand, for most of the long interval between these dates import prices were remarkably stable. Earlier, they had risen by nearly 50 per cent between 1945 and 1948 without much apparent effect on retail prices, presumably because of the use of heavy government subsidies on food. They fell quite steeply between 1951–53 then changed very little for the next fourteen years until the devaluation of 1967 while other prices moved steadily upwards. Retail prices, for example, rose by more than 50 per cent in those fourteen years. After devaluation the order was reversed: import prices outran the rest, trebling in seven years while retail prices little more than doubled.

Table 16.6. *Components of inflation in the UK 1969–76*

	Increase from year to year in consumer prices (%)	Contributions to this increase of:		
		Import prices (%)	Wages (%)	All other (including taxes) (%)
1969–70	5.92	1.60	5.05	−0.73
1970–71	8.18	1.34	4.99	1.85
1971–72	6.71	0.55	5.20	0.96
1972–73	8.58	4.88	6.00	−2.30
1973–74	16.11	11.42	9.69	−5.00
1974–75	23.09	6.78	14.08	2.23
1975–76	16.25	5.83	9.45	0.97

Source: Based on table 5.3 in the Cambridge *Economic Policy Review* for March 1977

If we leave aside for present purposes monetary influences, the natural interpretation to put on these facts is that while import prices played little or no part in the comparatively slow inflation of the 1950s and 1960s – and left the Chancellors of those days with a simpler task – no other factor was of equal importance in the two spells of high inflation. Economists have analysed the direct contributions of import prices, wages and other factors to inflation over the period 1969–76 and one such analysis is shown in table 16.6.

The contribution of import prices was erratic in comparison with that of rising wages but *in relation to the acceleration in inflation* it was clearly the dominant element, all the more if the movement in wages was itself to some extent a lagged response to the rise in prices. Moreover, calculations of this kind usually make little or no provision for any overflow from higher import prices on to the price of competitive materials or finished goods produced domestically. In an open economy this overflow may be at least as important as the direct effect of higher prices for imported goods.

This analysis is purely statistical and does not imply that each element contributed *causally* to the rise in prices in the proportions shown. It would be consistent with the figures, for example, to suggest that the acceleration in wage increases was to some extent a lagged response to the rise in prices. The rise in import prices, measured in sterling, can in the same way be attributed, in part at least, to the depreciation of sterling brought about by inflation instead of being depicted (as in table 16.6) as one of the major contributory causes of inflation. It is also conceivable that monetary influences not shown in table 16.6 at all dominated the whole process. Nevertheless it would be fair to deduce from the table and other evidence that while the influence of import prices was relatively small and erratic in the first three years shown, the increase in 1973–74 was the outstanding factor behind the acceleration in inflation in those years, just as it was the outstanding factor in 1950–51. This is true even if import prices are measured in foreign currencies so as to eliminate the effect of a fall in the exchange rate. Indeed, table 16.6 understates the importance of rising import prices because it takes no account of repercussions, first on the price of competitive materials or finished goods processed domestically and later on wage settlements once the full effects of this overflow on to domestic prices have been felt in a higher cost of living.

The labour market

Full employment up to the 1970s exceeded even the standard proposed by Lord Beveridge in 1944 for ensuring at least as many jobs as men. Whereas Beveridge spoke of 3 per cent, unemployment was uniformly below this level for twenty-five years, in recession as well as in boom, apart from two episodes in 1947 and 1963 when exceptionally severe weather and (in 1947) a fuel crisis caused a brief surge in the figures to an abnormal level. By any ordinary standards the labour market remained extremely tight throughout.

There was moreover a slower secular expansion in labour supply than there had been before the war and, still more, before 1914. In the 1950s for example, the working population of the UK grew in ten years by some 1.55 million or 6.5 per cent. Even this exaggerates the rate of expansion, for if one takes male workers alone the increase in the 1950s was no more than 3.5 per cent. This directs attention to one of the major changes in the labour market that full employment encouraged: the rising proportion of women workers, especially married women. More job opportunities drew more women workers into the labour market. They also brought more immigrants from abroad and induced some older workers to postpone retirement.

In 1931 the Census figures for Great Britain showed exactly 10 per cent of the married women in jobs or looking for jobs. By 1951 the proportion was 21.7 per cent and by 1971, 42.2 per cent. Had the 1931 ratio applied in 1971 there would have been 4 million fewer women available for paid work out of a total female working population of just over 9 million. This change was the more important because of the much higher proportion in 1971 of women who were married. Of every eight women workers in 1971 five were married compared with not much over one in seven in 1931. The ratio of women to men workers rose simultaneously from 42 to 58 per cent and nearly three quarters of the addition to the working population over those 35 years were women workers (Department of Employment and Productivity: 109). Some at least of this addition was the direct result of full employment which cannot therefore be defined exclusively in terms of the absence of unemployment.

The change was accelerated by the war but continued in peace-time. By 1950 a stationary working population of males was within sight and it was reached by 1965. Between these dates only 900 000 men were added to the working population compared with 1.6 million women. Moreover after 1965 while the male working population fell, the female working population continued to increase. Department of Employment estimates of the working population put the increase in women between 1965 and 1975 at 1 million, and the decrease in men at 700 000.

Women provided the most important element of elasticity in the working population in the short run as well as in the long. In every recession women workers who lost their jobs tended to take their names off the register and the fluctuations in employment were usually about twice as large as the fluctuations in unemployment. In a bad year like 1958, for example, there were some 65 000 fewer women in the working population than a year previously in spite of a normal year-to-year increase of 100 000. But female unemployment was only about 25 000 higher in spite of a reduction in the number of women in jobs of 90 000. Relatively to trend some 165 000 women withdrew from the labour force, while only 25 000 registered themselves as unemployed. For men the corresponding figures, with an upward trend in numbers of 60 000 per annum, were approximately 125 000 and 95 000 and these figures relate to a working population twice as large. The comparison shows the bigger impact of a recession on female employment and the lesser tendency for the loss of employment to be reflected in registered female unemployment. It also shows a rise in unemployment of 120 000 compared with twice as large a drop in employment (90 000 women and 160 000 men, or 250 000 in all). This ratio appears to have been the normal one in the 1950s and 1960s.

The trend over the postwar period was towards earlier retirement in spite of full employment so that this offered no additional elasticity except in the short run: when the shortage of labour became acute in time of boom there seems to have been some willingness to delay retirement. In the 1890s nearly two men out of three over the age of 65 were still at work. By 1931 the proportion was about one in two. Since 1951 when it was 31 per cent the fall has slowed down a little in spite of the increasing average age of pensioners over 65 and between 1961 and 1971 the fall was from 24 to 19 per cent. For women workers over 60 the proportion, after a steep fall over the first half of the century, has been quite sharply on the increase.

The effects of immigration and emigration on the labour force are less well documented. The Census for 1961 established that in the previous decade civilian emigration had been almost matched by immigration and in the following decade it was slightly in excess. This was the outcome of large flows in both directions; United Kingdom residents moved out at a rate that reached a net annual total of about 150 000 in the late 1960s. while immigrants from the so-called 'New Commonwealth' and Pakistan moved in at a net annual rate of about 50 000 with some falling-off in the 1970s. By 1975 there were estimated to be 1.8 million immigrants from the New Commonwealth and Pakistan in the United Kingdom, mainly in the south and midland parts of the country. In addition, Irish immigrants, who constituted the largest foreign-born element in the population, continued to arrive at a net rate of about 10 000 per annum. These population movements helped to relieve the shortage of workers in some of the less agreeable but low-paid jobs but intensified the shortage of skilled and highly qualified workers.

Labour shortages were not spread uniformly over the economy. Since the total supply of labour was so inelastic an expansion in employment at one point tended to require contraction elsewhere, and the shortages were concentrated at the points of expansion. Some of the sluggishness of the economy was due to the combination of inelasticity in labour supply and immobility between industries, occupations and regions. The faster the contracting industries released labour, the easier it was for the expanding industries to build up their labour force. It was only later, when unemployment became much heavier in the 1970s and industry was increasingly reluctant to take on more labour as the cost of dispensing with it increased that the processes of expansion and contraction ceased to be closely linked.

The structural adjustments taking place over the postwar period are illustrated in table 16.7. Services, the construction industry, the distributive trades and manufacturing industry, apart from textiles and clothing, were all absorbing additional man-power between 1951 and 1966. Well over half their requirements for men were met (numerically at least) by a simultaneous run-down in agriculture, mining and textiles, and not much more than a third by an increase in total labour supply. In the case of women nearly the whole of the requirements of the expanding sectors of the economy came (again numerically) from additions to the labour supply, textiles and clothing being practically the only industries to reduce their employment of women.

Table 16.7 does not, of course, show the *total* transfer between industries, more narrowly defined. For example, 100 000 men left the shipbuilding industry (included with the expanding metal and engineering industries) and 200 000 left railway employment (included under 'transport and distribution'). Within each industry, as within each sector, there was a further transfer from contracting to expanding enterprises. But the general picture is not likely to be much altered. Nearly everywhere, more women were needed and more women entered employment. Large sectors of male employment were in course of contraction and the labour they released went a long way to meeting the needs of expanding sectors.

It is unfortunately not possible to analyse shortages by occupation in the same way as by industry. The shortages were always most acute for skilled labour. This was even more true in the days when unemployment was far higher and

Table 16.7. *Changes in the distribution of employment by sector, Great Britain 1951–66*

	Males		Females	
	Net increase	Net decrease	Net increase	Net decrease
Services	490	—	1045	—
Construction	432	—	60	—
Metal and engineering industries	387	—	250	—
Gas, water and electricity	32	—	22	—
Transport and distribution	—	91	551	—
Textiles and clothing	—	167	—	278
Mining and quarrying	—	286	4	—
Agriculture, forestry fishing	—	363	—	—
Other manufacturing industries and 'inadequately described'	—	40	121	—
Total	1534	947	2053	278

Source: *British Labour Statistics: Historical Abstract 1886–1968*, table 108

one effect of full employment might be assumed to be an increase in the demand for unskilled labour greater than the increase in the demand for skilled. On the other hand there was probably a greater relative inflow into the labour market of unskilled workers, including those from abroad and a greater proportionate outflow of skilled workers as emigrants. Whatever the historical change, shortages of skilled labour were a chronic drag on rapid expansion even in conditions of industrial depression. But the differential in the remuneration of skilled workers compared with unskilled workers after widening in the early postwar period had narrowed again by 1975, especially on an after-tax basis.

Regional mobility was promoted by differences in unemployment levels and was probably higher than in earlier periods. Unemployment was usually lowest in the South-East, including London, where it did not rise above 1.6 per cent until after 1970; it was also low in East Anglia, the South-West, the Midlands and Yorkshire; it was highest in the North and North-West, Wales, Scotland and Northern Ireland. In the latter regions unemployment in a boom year like 1965 varied between 1.5 per cent in the North-West and 2.8 per cent in Scotland, with Northern Ireland much higher at 5.9 per cent. In the more prosperous regions in the same year it went as low as 0.6 per cent in the West Midlands and as high as 1.5 per cent in the South-West. By the autumn of 1975 every region was up to 3 per cent but in none of the low unemployment regions was it over 5 per cent and in none of the high unemployment regions was it less. By that time the highest rates were 6 per cent in the North and 7.9 per cent in Northern Ireland. Although the relative position of different regions varied from one year to another there was remarkably little change in the order throughout the whole post-war period.

The role of government

By the end of the war the government had come to dominate the economy as never before, absorbing half the national output and regulating production and consumption by a complex system of controls, from consumer rationing to allocation of materials and direction of labour. There was much debate about the future role of government and with a Labour Government enjoying a Parliamentary majority for the first time the possibility of comprehensive planning of the economy in peace-time was widely discussed. There were many who assumed that what had been appropriate in war-time would be equally appropriate in the very different circumstances of peace-time. There was no revulsion from extensive government control such as was felt in many continental countries where it was associated not with socialism but with national socialism. Above all there was a general haziness as to what constituted planning and what degree of freedom for the consumer, the worker and the businessman was compatible with it.

In practice the government maintained direct control at those points in the economy where demand and supply were badly out of balance so that immediate de-control would have resulted in sharp increases in price. In particular it continued to ration foreign exchange rather than rely on a major devaluation of sterling: to control capital investment through building and machinery licensing, steel allocations and other devices rather than through high interest rates and credit restriction: and to limit the demand for key foodstuffs and materials by various forms of consumer rationing. But the controls were never co-ordinated by reference to some pre-arranged 'plan' (if only because the supply position was changing too fast to adhere to any such plan); the tightness of the controls was relaxed as supplies expanded; and no attempt was made to direct labour (although there was statutory authority to do so) or exercise compulsion over consumers or producers except through systems of allocation and rationing. As more men were demobilised and absorbed into employment and world markets became more active and accessible, the shortages and bottlenecks in supply gave way progressively and controls were abandoned in a series of 'bonfires' because they had ceased to be effective or necessary.

Many of the controls derived from a fundamental shortage of foreign exchange. When the war ended, exports had fallen to one third of their prewar volume and there was simply no way of bringing them back into equilibrium with imports at a tolerable level of employment in less than two years. The cessation of lend-lease, coupled with the enormous liquid liabilities to foreigners in the form of sterling balances accumulated during the war, made it imperative to borrow abroad to cover the inevitable deficits over those years. The sums made available in the Loan Agreements with the USA and Canada, $3.75 thousand million and $1.25 thousand million respectively, were no more than sufficient to meet the current account deficit forecast for 1946 and 1947; and as it happened the forecast proved to be remarkably accurate. But in order to limit the deficit to what was foreseen it was necessary to maintain drastic restrictions on imports, ration imported goods, and put pressure on exporters to give preference to export orders. It was not until 1948 when exports had expanded more than fourfold while imports were held below their prewar level that the current account came back into balance. Another year passed before the rate of exchange was allowed to play its part in the process of adjustment.

It is true that the move in September 1949 from $4.03 to the pound sterling to $2.80 was not part of a deliberate strategy but was far more the consequence of market pressure in the autumn of 1949, brought about by a short-lived recession in the United States. Nevertheless it was in keeping with the general tendency to let market forces take over from controls once the controls had outlived their usefulness. The devaluation was fundamentally a recognition that the time had come to let adjustments in exchange rates contribute to the elimination of the so-called dollar shortage rather than attempt to provide a fresh stimulus to sterling exports. Nearly all the other major currencies moved with sterling so that what was involved was not so much a devaluation of sterling as a revaluation of the dollar. An incentive was created throughout the world to redirect exports to dollar markets and switch purchases to non-dollar sources and so help to end the imbalance in the world economy by making soft currencies harder and hard currencies softer.

The devaluation of 1949 did not spell the end of import restriction, the establishment of convertibility of currencies or the disappearance of balance of payments constraints. It is possible that in the absence of the Korean war, which started nine months after devaluation, faster progress would have been made. But the violent rise in import prices in 1950–51 renewed the anxieties that devaluation might have allayed and the apparatus of control was not dismantled.

Not all shortages had their origin in limitations on supplies from abroad. There was, for example, a continuing shortage of coal until well into the 1950s. The vulnerability of the economy to this key material was brought home by the fuel crisis of 1947 when severe weather conditions coincided with a rundown in stocks over the winter of 1946–47 to an extremely low level. That supplies might run out had been foreseen during the previous autumn but no action was taken to provide for the emergency until it arrived. The government then adopted extraordinary measures including the shutting down of factories in order to build up stocks at the power stations. It was estimated at the time that the crisis involved the loss of $200 million (not far short of 20 per cent) in exports. But in spite of the vital importance of coal supplies it proved impossible to regain the prewar level of output. Even in 1950, three years after the crisis, coal output had increased less than 10 per cent and it was still being rationed as late as 1958. In the end it was not coal but oil that came to the rescue, supplying the whole of the expansion in demand for primary fuel from the 1950s onwards and displacing coal more and more in the 1960s and early 1970s.

As the controls were relaxed, government influence on the economy was exerted in different ways. The vogue for planning returned periodically but there was an increasing tendency to talk of economic management rather than planning. Economic management embraced demand management (which was primarily short term and directed towards greater economic stability), a range of policies intended to influence supply and the various measures that come under the general heading of the welfare state.

The prime instruments of economic management were fiscal and monetary. The budget had grown enormously in money terms but much less in relation to GNP. In 1937 expenditure on goods and services by the central government and local authorities amounted to about 11 per cent of GNP at market prices and total public expenditure including transfers and subsidies to about 21 per cent. Ten years later in 1947 these proportions had become 16 per cent and 32.5 per cent. Ten years later still, in 1957, public expenditure on goods and services remained at 16 per cent but total public expenditure had fallen back to 28 per cent. Thus, although the government gave up many of its controls and no longer dominated the economy as in war-time, when it employed half the manpower, it exerted a weight on the economy in its taxing and spending that was about half as large again as it had been in the years immediately before the war. The only really big item of expenditure that failed to keep pace with the growth of GNP was debt interest: thanks to low war-time and postwar rates of interest and the steady drip of inflation, the interest burden, in spite of six years of war, grew only threefold between 1937 and 1957 while GNP in money terms grew fourfold. This was a very different outcome from the twenty years after 1913 when debt interest grew from £19 million to £281 million while the money value of GNP no more than doubled.

Fiscal policy, while retaining its wider and more long-term economic and social objectives, was used in successive budgets to control the pressure of demand by varying the level of taxation or public expenditure. Since public expenditure took much longer to respond to governmental efforts to limit or accelerate the rate at which it was growing it was natural to depend more heavily on changes in taxation through the budget. But this in turn had its disadvantages since the government could hardly expect to be able to refrain from making adjustments from one annual budget to the next. The use of monetary policy was therefore revived, chiefly as in the past with an eye to its effects on the balance of payments but increasingly to supplement the domestic effects of budgetary changes. Later the government sought freedom to make tax changes at more frequent intervals through the use of 'regulators'. The most notable attempt of this kind was the introduction in 1961 of power to vary indirect taxes up or down by 5 or 10 per cent. The Finance Act conveying this power was no sooner on the statute book than the government had resort to the regulator in order to deal with an exchange crisis in July, thereby laying itself open to the criticism that it should have proposed to raise taxes in the Finance Bill itself. The regulator was subsequently used on a number of other occasions between annual budgets (e.g. July 1966, November 1968 and December 1976).

A second regulator giving the government power to vary national insurance contributions was introduced at the same time but never used. It excited adverse comment from numerous critics who believed (often for no intelligible reason) that what British industry needed was a permanent poll-tax to make labour more expensive to employers. Whatever the case for such a tax it had no bearing on the form of regulator best calculated to allow the government to offset cyclical pressures.

Demand management was not in practice confined to annual budgets supplemented by monetary policy. It tended to operate through packages of measures hurriedly put together in a succession of crises, most of which originated in pressure on the foreign exchange reserves. These packages, although differing in detail, followed a certain pattern. There was usually a tax component: an increase in some indirect tax or taxes – on tobacco, beer or petrol, for example, or purchase tax on a range of consumer goods. Hire purchase restrictions were imposed or tightened in order to limit consumer credit and purchase of consumer durables. Some fresh restriction was placed on foreign investment. The banks were asked to limit credit, usually to the accompaniment of a letter from the Governor and a rise in Bank Rate.

The purpose of these measures was partly to check over-heating of the economy, partly to improve the balance of payments, including the capital balance, and partly to impress foreign opinion and provide a background for borrowing operations from foreign central banks or the IMF. Such borrowing operations were a frequent constituent of the total package.

The recurrence of crises and the introduction of one package after another could not be regarded as evidence of skilful management and were the subject of much criticism of government policy. Indeed it was difficult to see what the government's aim was since in the interests of stabilisation it seemed to be de-stabilising the economy (Worswick 1971; Caves 1971). Some of the criticism of stop–go was based on the rather naive assumption that demand management could disregard the balance of payments and concentrate exclusively on stabilising domestic demand (Hansen 1969). Other critics argued (mistakenly) that there was no appreciation that employment lagged behind output, so that action was taken at the wrong time. Many economists still maintain (on rather doubtful evidence) that the government took deflationary action only when the economy was moving down. If anything, the government leant over too far in allowing demand to expand without weighing up sufficiently carefully in advance what level of demand could be sustained on a continuing footing. It tended to set about expanding up to or beyond the limits of domestic capacity as soon as the last 'stop' had brought some temporary relief to the pressure on the balance of payments. Except possibly in 1962 and 1968 no government was willing to hold back expansion so as to secure consistency between its external and domestic targets. It was just not possible to balance the external account at the level of domestic demand that the government (with popular backing) conceived of as full employment.

One reason why governments repeatedly aimed at unsustainable levels of demand was the unevenness of the resulting pressure between one region and another. Unemployment in Scotland in the 1950s and 1960s, for example, remained obstinately at twice the national level so that it tended to shoot up to 5 per cent when the national average was comfortably below three and the level in the South-East was just over two. This as much as any concern for more 'balanced' development drove governments in the 1960s to look for new instruments of regional policy. They found nothing that did the trick half as successfully as North Sea oil. But the use of investment grants, free depreciation, the Regional Employment Premium and other devices had a cumulative effect which is hard to measure but was far from negligible (Moore & Rhodes 1973, 1974).

For most of the period monetary policy played a subsidiary part. In the years before 1951 Bank Rate remained at 2 per cent as it had done since 1932: the supply of money had a purely accommodating role. The banks were asked to be selective in their lending policies but were otherwise free to meet the demands made on them and had no lack of funds for the purpose. Long rates of interest had already begun to creep up from 1946–47 as it became clear that inflation was continuing unchecked. After 1951 the use of Bank Rate was revived, at first very tentatively – the Treasury Bill rate did not reach 3 per cent until 1955 – but then with increasing vigour. In 1955 for the first time the Chancellor emphasised in his Budget his reliance on monetary measures to keep the economy in balance. But if he was counting on restriction of bank credit there was little sign of it until much firmer pressure was applied in July and the banks were specifically asked to reduce the level of their advances by 10 per cent. In this they were successful: as a consequence, industrial production ceased to rise and the balance of payments moved into surplus the following year. This was the first major credit squeeze of the postwar years and it was followed by lesser squeezes in later crises, e.g. in 1961 and 1966.

In the period between the two devaluations of 1949 and 1967 the government took only a desultory interest in the money supply – indeed, there were no comprehensive statistics for the money supply until the 1960s – and concentrated mainly on bank advances as a means of influencing domestic activity and short-term rates of interest as a means of operating on the balance of payments. There was some tendency to rely on monetary policy on the restrictive tack and to make use of the budget when the time came to expand.

Income tax, for example, was increased (by 6d in the £) first by the Labour Government in 1951 in its last budget before the Conservative Government took office and next in 1964 in its first budget when the Conservative Government left office; but in all other postwar years up to the second devaluation any change in income tax – and there were very few – was downwards. On the other hand, increases in bank rate took place with increasing frequency whenever restrictive measures were introduced: in 1952, in 1955 and 1956, in the run on sterling in September 1957, in 1960 and again in 1961, in 1964 and 1966, before and after devaluation in 1967, in 1969, and in most years from 1972 onwards. This use of bank rate was accompanied by a steady upward drift from never more than $4\frac{1}{2}$ per cent up to 1956 to rates fluctuating between 4 and 7 per cent up to the second devaluation, and to rates that remained persistently about 7 per cent thereafter (except for a short time in 1971–72) and were hardly ever below 10 per cent in the four years between mid-1973 and mid-1977.

This combination of rising interest rates and increasing fiscal ease had its critics, particularly amongst those who were anxious to see investment increase at the expense of consumption. Credit restriction and high short-term rates depressed both the gilt-edged market and the new issue market and increased the difficulty of financing business investment while tax concessions were more likely to favour consumer spending. This criticism rests on the view that higher investment was the key to improved economic performance – a view open to dispute for reasons given above. It is not self-evident that business investment could have responded readily to lower interest rates under conditions of full employment, especially when the real rate of interest, allowing for the upward trend in prices and the treatment of debenture interest as a business cost, was usually very low. On the other hand, had the government's fiscal stance been more restrictive, the initial effect would have been to reduce employment as well as consumption and any shift of resources into investment or exports might have been very gradual unless other instruments of policy such as a change in the exchange rate had been brought to bear.

Here, rather than in any inherent characteristics of the monetary and fiscal components of policy, lay the weakness of demand management of the postwar type. It was easy enough to vary aggregate demand but more difficult to bring about a change in the relative size of the main components of the aggregate, especially exports and investment (and still more difficult, by the manipulation of demand, to change the productivity or efficiency of available resources once they were fully employed). Yet exports and investment were traditionally the key variables in employment policy and, for many economists, in growth policy as well.

Although monetary considerations came increasingly to the forefront in the later 1960s, the authorities concentrated mainly on short rates of interest because of their influence on the balance of payments and on restriction of credit as a means of influencing domestic activity. Long rates tended to be held as stable as possible for the sake of encouraging sales of gilt-edged securities. Up to 1967 there were only two years – 1956 and 1960 – in which the return on $2\frac{1}{2}$ per cent Consols changed by over $\frac{1}{2}$ per cent and in neither year was the rise greater than $\frac{3}{5}$ per cent. But the trend was strongly upwards. By 1967 the rate, which had stood at 2.60 per cent in 1946 – lower than in any interwar year – had reached 6.69 per cent. Seven years later, at the end of 1974, it touched a peak of over 17 per cent, justifying those who had predicted that the yield and the price would ultimately intersect.

Three major changes were involved in the steep rise after 1967. First of all, inflation began to speed up. This transformed the prospects for holders of gilt-edged who had no longer to adjust their expectations to a mere 2–3 per cent annual depreciation of the currency but were compelled to think in term of much larger and much less predictable changes. The long rate had already moved up sharply in 1968 partly in response to devaluation and the inflation this produced but partly also because of the sharp rise in the Euro-dollar rate brought about by America's efforts to improve her capital balance. This was one of the few occasions before 1972 on which the authorities readily accepted as a matter of policy a large upward adjustment in long-term rates. Secondly, the budget entered a period of heavy long-term deficit. The public sector financial deficit, which had fluctuated around £500 million in the late 1950s, between £500 million and £1000 million for most of the 1960s, and had actually been replaced by a surplus in 1969–70, swung from a surplus of £700 million in 1970 to a deficit of £8300 million in 1975 and showed little sign of returning to the level of the previous decade. Finally the current balance of payments simultaneously moved from a surplus of £1000 million in 1971 to a deficit of £3500 million in 1974, and persisted in deficit for two more years at a very high rate.

These three factors interacted in various ways and it is possible to put different interpretations on the causal sequence between them. All three had unfavourable implications for long-term rates of interest. All of them affected the money supply so that it was natural to view their interconnection in terms of monetary factors and to look to the monetary authorities for a remedy. But monetary policy was still largely ancillary to fiscal policy, and the setting of targets for the growth of the money supply, beginning in 1976, acted as an injunction to the Chancellor in the framing of his budgetary policy rather than to the monetary authorities, who could exert a powerful *independent* influence on the money supply only if they were willing to submit financial markets to dangerous stresses.

The use of bank rate and the movement of short term rates of interest was intimately linked with exchange rate policy. For most of the period the rate was fixed. It remained at $4.03 to the pound sterling from the outbreak of war until the first devaluation in September 1949 and at $2.80 from then until the second devaluation in November 1967. The interval between the two devaluations was the longest period of fixed sterling exchange rates this century. After 1967 the rate was at first fixed at $2.40 to the pound sterling but moved up to $2.60 under the Smithsonian agreement in December 1971. For a few brief months in 1972 the pound was brought within the arrangements linking the currencies of members of the EEC but from June 1972 it was allowed to float at rates that fell progressively in relation to the Smithsonian parities.

When the first devaluation took place direct controls were still in use and transfers out of sterling were subject to strict official regulation. These controls provided the means by which imports were kept within the limits of what could be afforded and movements of funds could be held in check. As controls were abandoned (exchange control apart), balance rested increasingly on demand management unsupported by the strongly directional measures previously in use. From 1952 demand management was the principal means of operating on the level of imports and (indirectly) on exports and it is rather surprising that so blunt a weapon came near to maintaining external balance over the next fifteen years with comparatively small fluctuations in output and employment. In view of the even more limited weapons available for keeping domestic costs in line with costs abroad it is even more surprising that this near-balance was maintained without a change in parity. No doubt the boom in other countries made it possible to move back into balance by lagging behind the rest of the industrial world from time to time and allowing the level of unemployment and interest rates to creep up from one cycle to the next. But how far the upward creep was an act of policy rather than an almost inescapable response in an inflationary world is by no means clear.

In the early 1950s the government was undecided about its exchange rate policy. The pound was not at that time a convertible currency and did not become one until the end of 1958. After a brief period of convertibility for current (but not capital) transactions in 1947 in conformity with the Loan Agreement with the United States, exchange control over current transactions was re-imposed. In the crisis of 1951–52 when the swing in the terms of trade against the sterling area gave rise to a heavy deficit and a drain on the reserves, a plan was devised for making the pound convertible to dollar area residents at a floating rate of exchange and freezing a large part of sterling balances in the hands of other holders. (The plan was labelled Operation Robot after the three men who put it forward: Sir Leslie Rowan, Sir George Bolton (then in the Bank of England) and Sir 'Otto' Clarke (like Sir Leslie Rowan a Treasury official).) This plan was never publicly announced and was ultimately rejected but other proposals for floating rates continued to be discussed. In 1955, after the authorities had announced their intention to support the market in transferable sterling, and so make the pound in practice convertible at a rate close to the official rate, there was talk of a flexible rate that would be allowed to move within generous limits on either side of a fixed parity. But this, too, came to nothing and the authorities dismissed the idea of a floating pound for over a decade. It was not until June 1972 that a fixed parity was abandoned and floating began.

The move to convertibility and the withdrawal of direct controls both increased the vulnerability of the exchange rate to sudden pressure while at the same time the great expansion in privately-held liquid funds all over the world (for example, with the development of the Euro-dollar market) increased the chances of such pressure. Efforts to control the movement of short-term capital were not very successful, particularly where such movements reflected distrust in the ability of the authorities to maintain the existing rate of exchange. Apart from the large holdings of sterling balances in the hands of foreign monetary authorities or held by private businesses to meet commercial requirements, there was always a vast amount of trade credit which it was impossible to police and which might through 'leads and lags' (i.e. by advancing or delaying payment in another currency) cause funds to shift from one centre to another. Short-term interest rates might help to moderate movements of funds so long as confidence in the currency was not in question. But this implied that rates would have to be kept above the level in other financial centres. This was the penalty of having run up large liquid obligations to foreign holders of sterling. Monetary policy had to be consistent with the maintenance of the interest differential in relation to other currencies; and if these currencies seemed likely to be more stable in value than sterling the differential might have to be embarrassingly high.

Supply management

In 1945 the concept of demand management hardly existed. The instinct of the public, of politicians and even of business men was to think in terms of government action on supply rather than demand. One example of this was the programme of nationalisation embarked upon by the incoming Labour Government in 1945. In 1939 the government had run the Post Office, the naval dockyards, and a few undertakings in public ownership like the Carlisle pubs. The local authorities played a much bigger part in the industrial and commercial life of the country through their operation of various public utilities: gas, water, electricity, the London Underground, buses, tramways etc. By 1950 all this was changed. Public corporations had been set up to run the coal and steel industries, electricity generation and distribution, the gas industry, the railways and road haulage and air-line services. The Bank of England had been nationalised. The nationalised industries were employing one worker in fifteen and their capital expenditure amounted to one sixth of total gross investment.

Twenty-five years later most of these changes still stood but only minor additions had been made to the list of nationalised industries. Road haulage was denationalised almost at once and became one of the fastest growing sections of the economy. The steel industry was restored to private ownership but remained subject to public control and was eventually re-nationalised. The list of candidates for nationalisation shrank at one point to water undertakings and then expanded again to include docks, the aircraft industry and shipbuilding. The clearing banks and insurance companies, once prominent candidates, did not re-appear again until 1976.

It is difficult to see what difference nationalisation made to faster growth or fairer distribution of income or any of the other major objectives of policy. It may have given the government greater control over the economy but it is the export industries not the nationalised industries that have the better title to be regarded as 'the commanding heights of the economy'. Over the postwar period nationalisation came to be assigned a more technical and less political role and began to take second place to other conceptions of how the private sector should be controlled.

One such conception was national economic planning. Britain learned most of what needs to be known about planning as a systematic way of handling risks in the pursuit of competing objectives in the Second World War – and promptly forgot. Planning came to be equated with control, consistency and certainty, with disregard for market forces and, above all, with the preparation of a plan almost for its own sake; as if the essence of planning were not risk-taking and constant re-planning. Those who took part in the controversy about planning after the war were rarely those who had experience of it and the whole controversy had itself been forgotten by the time a second effort to plan the economy was made in 1964–65. A National Plan was produced, abandoned forthwith and again forgotten. It professed to be based on the maintenance of the current sterling parity at a time when it was not very clear how this was consistent with the assumed rate of growth. In other respects, too, the projections to which it devoted much technical skill seemed divorced from any statement of the policies that might give substance to the projections. No plan can ever be better than the policies underlying it: no policies, no plan. Later attempts to prepare a national plan were less ambitious but had equally little effect.

Another conception was the 're-structuring' of industry. In the first twenty years after the war the prevailing philosophy was hostile to monopoly in any shape other than nationalisation. A Monopolies Commission was set up in 1948 and further legislation was directed at restrictive business practices in 1956 and resale price maintenance in 1963. Mergers were also made subject to approval by the Monopolies Commission in legislation which however was only rarely brought into operation. After 1964 there was a marked change of policy. The government set out to encourage the formation of larger business units and created the Industrial Reconstruction Corporation to promote amalgamations intended to improve industrial efficiency. The change of policy brought about a large-scale amalgamation movement in which the IRC played only a limited part and for a few years industrial concentration increased rapidly.

This set off yet another conception of industrial policy. It was seen that a comparatively small number of firms now dominated manufacturing industry: by 1970 the 100 largest firms held perhaps 40 per cent of the assets of British industry compared with under 20 per cent before the First World War (Prais 1976). The government was therefore urged to acquire ownership of some of these large firms and induce the others to enter into planning agreements so as to allow joint planning on a sectoral basis. At the same time the government found itself running several large firms (including British Leyland) in different industries because of the financial difficulties encountered by these firms – a situation not unlike that in which the Bank of England, almost by accident, had come to have a large stake in the British steel industry in the 1930s.

Extension of area of government

Although the horizon of government economic policy remained predominantly short term, the government machine was geared to preoccupations of a very different kind. Each department had to work out policies intended to endure over a much longer run, whether for health, education, defence, social welfare, or any other objective. These policies involved a strong tendency for government expenditure to grow and a parallel tendency for personal remuneration to consist of a slowly expanding cash income after tax and a more rapidly expanding income provided by the government in the form of pension rights, welfare services, etc.

Between 1950 and 1975 public expenditure (including the capital expenditure of the nationalised industries) grew from about £5000 million to over £50000 million and the ratio of public expenditure (on this definition) to GDP from about 45 per cent to about 60 per cent. This was not, however, a steady and continuous increase. In the 1950s public expenditure increased less rapidly than GDP and the ratio between the two was below 42 per cent in 1955 before climbing back in the 1960s to 45 per cent in 1965 and reaching 50 per cent by 1970.

This measure of public expenditure is not a particularly satisfactory one nor

Table 16.8. *Current public expenditure on goods and services: ratio to GDP at factor cost*

	Ratio at current prices (%)	Ratio at constant (1970) prices (%)
1952	21.4	28.9
1958	18.5	23.5
1970	21.0	21.0
1975	25.0	23.2

Source: *Economic Trends*, Annual Supplement (1975)

is it the one in general use by other countries. It is not customary, for example, to lump together three distinct categories of public expenditure: capital expenditure on commercial assets such as those owned and operated by the nationalised industries; payments that supplement the real income of the beneficiaries by transferring to them money paid in taxes or social service contributions by other people; and expenditures on goods and services involving the direct absorption of man-power and other resources in the provision of public services such as defence, health and education.

When people talk of the public sector of the economy it is usually the last category of expenditure that they have principally in mind. The first category is akin to ordinary business investment and since 1976 it has been excluded from the official total for public expenditure except to the extent that it is financed directly with government money. The changes in definition introduced in 1976 lowered the ratio of public expenditure to GDP at factor cost for 1975–76 from about 60 per cent to 52 per cent.

The transfer payments included in the second category, such as pensions, unemployment benefit, and debt interest, add to the size of the budget but not to any great extent to public employment since the expenditure usually takes the form of purchases from the private sector to meet private requirements.

Of public expenditure on goods and services part goes on fixed assets such as housing. The rest is current expenditure and has generally been a little above 40 per cent of total public expenditure as defined above, and around 20 per cent of GDP. Measured at current prices this component of public expenditure expanded at about the same rate as GDP in the 1950s and 1960s with some decline in the proportion in the 1950s and a rise in the 1960s (see table 16.8). The sharp increase in the early 1970s was associated mainly with the relative price effect, i.e. with the tendency for the costs of goods and services brought by the government to rise more rapidly, for technical reasons, than the costs of other goods and services. The more rapid rise in costs reflects the assumption that the productivity of doctors, teachers, soldiers and others in the public service is constant and that gains in efficiency cannot be set against an increase in their incomes.

This implies that if we leave aside the nationalised industries and transfer payments there was no increase in the relative size of the public sector in the twenty years after the Korean war. The point can be made even more emphatically if expenditures are deflated so as to eliminate the underlying tendency for public expenditure on goods and services to increase in relation to GDP at current prices because of the relative price effect. Measured at constant prices the current expenditure on goods and services of public authorities fell in relation to GDP over the early postwar years because of retrenchment on defence expenditure, expanded again with the Korean War to a peak of 28.9 per cent in 1952 and then fell, quite steeply in the 1950s and more slowly thereafter. It was down to 21.0 per cent in 1970 when it started climbing again. By 1975 it was back to about the same level as in 1958.

So far as this major component is concerned, therefore, the principal reasons for rising public expenditure lay in growing affluence (as measured by GDP) and the relative price effect. But there were, of course, large changes within the total. Defence expenditure, which accounted for half in 1952, was less than a quarter by 1975; on the other hand, the National Health service and education had expanded from 29 per cent to 44 per cent. The strong pressure for these and other social services to grow implied that aggregate expenditure would begin to increase as soon as the rundown in defence expenditure came to an end.

If one turns to transfer payments, the largest single item – social security benefits including pensions – showed a corresponding tendency to outrun GDP. Taking the same period as before, i.e. 1952–75, this item increased from 5.4 per cent of GDP in 1952 to 8.6 per cent in 1970 and just over 9 per cent in 1975. Total expenditure of all kinds on health, education and social security benefits grew from 13 per cent of GDP to 23 per cent over the same period. While these were among the most rapidly growing items there were others, such as housing and subsidies, that grew nearly as fast or even faster. But the general conclusion stands: the growth of public expenditure was concentrated on non-commercial services, pensions, housing and all that we associate with the welfare state. Economies on defence expenditure provided a partial offset and the main reason why the total showed a net increase over the period out of proportion to the rise in GDP was the faster rise in costs in the public sector and the rapid growth in pensions and other social security benefits.

This meant that the big expansion of the public sector that took place during and immediately after the war was not prolonged over a longer period. The weight of the budget on the economy did increase and the government made that weight felt in relation to all its longer-term objectives: income distribution, social welfare, regional balance, industrial organisation and so on. But that is a story for which there is no room here.

Conclusion

Postwar Britain is a mature industrial economy sustained by a wide range of skills and a complex infrastructure that is renewed from generation to generation by heavy capital investment. Production is organised in comparatively large business units, including multi-national concerns and public corporations, adapted to the generation and absorption of rapid technical change and under the surveillance of correspondingly large departments of state.

Much of the discussion of economic development in earlier chapters has little application to such an economy. The fears excited in the first half of the nineteenth century by rapid population growth now seem far away. Deaths exceed births and emigration continues to outstrip immigration. The working population is more or less stationary. The food supply is ample. Domestic agriculture produces nearly half the total with a tiny and dwindling labour force.

Yet there are many themes from earlier times that keep recurring. This is particularly true of Britain's dealings with foreign countries. Let us take three examples: the role of exports, swings in the terms of trade and capital flows.

Economists continue to discuss the place of exports in relation both to cyclical fluctuations and to economic growth. Exports have always been a comparatively volatile element in demand and are plainly one of the least controllable. It is arguable that exports, more than any other constituent of total demand, have set the pace for expansion and contraction in more recent cycles as in the past. This helps to explain why the balance of payments continues to figure so prominently in discussion of stabilisation policy. Similarly, expanding export markets may have a special importance in stimulating industrial growth, whatever the century under discussion. The idea of export-led growth may now have a more sophisticated basis than in the seventeenth and eighteenth centuries: but it would have found an echo among the mercantilists of those days.

Swings in the terms of trade are also still with us and are if anything more pronounced. These swings, particularly the larger swings in international commodity prices, had a major influence on world economic development in the nineteenth century when they were closely linked both to the long waves of inflation and deflation throughout the century and to the flow of capital from the centre to the periphery. Experience in Britain since the Second World War shows their continuing importance: many of the dilemmas of policy in the early postwar years and again in the 1970s can only be fully understood in the light of the sharp swings in the terms of trade against the United Kingdom.

Capital flows to and from the United Kingdom have also continued to remain a subject of controversy. The great outpourings of long-term capital of the period before 1914 were not repeated between the wars but foreign lending was still on a scale that many observers (including Keynes) thought excessive. After the Second World War controls over capital movements were preserved and tightened from time to time. But they have proved to be quite compatible with continued long-term investment out of reinvested foreign earnings or from funds borrowed abroad; and they have also been largely ineffective in preventing the movement of short-term funds on a sufficient scale to compel changes in exchange rates and interest rates. Thus it remains an issue how the balance of payments on capital account should be controlled and how far control can be effective if applied only to foreign lending and investment.

Economic growth is another subject where old controversies have revived. There have always been those who looked to demand factors and those who looked to supply factors for an explanation of the rate of growth. On the whole, pamphleteers since the mid nineteenth century have put their money on supply factors and have produced a familiar catalogue of the causes (or at least the symptoms) of industrial decline in Britain: neglect of business and technological education; lack of able entrepreneurs; inattention to export marketing; acceptance of restrictive practices and demarcation rules; unnecessarily high manning ratios; fragmentation of trade unions; class division within the factory; and so on. But there is also a long tradition, going back to Adam Smith, that takes the need for demand pressure and an expanding market as its starting-point. This tradition found expression in the campaign to join the EEC for the sake of access to a wider market on the one hand and the attacks on stop–go on the other, although there was little else in common between the two movements. The doctrine of export-led growth and Lord Kaldor's thesis of the central importance of a competitive and expanding manufacturing sector are more sophisticated and theoretical expressions of this tradition.

As earlier chapters show, there is nothing particularly new in the lag in productivity in postwar Britain behind other countries; it continues a divergence going back for over a century. It is difficult, therefore, to accept an explanation couched primarily in terms of market behaviour that is comparatively recent, and more natural to lay stress on weaknesses of structure known to be of long standing. What is new is the ability to make statistical comparisons in aggregative terms through the use of national accounts, the perspective that this gives to judgement of economic performance, and the urge of governments to achieve faster growth without any general agreement on how it is to be done.

The tendency for history to repeat itself is nowhere more evident than in two of the major controversies revived by a high rate of inflation. First there is the re-emergence of the quantity theory of money which was for so long the cornerstone of monetary theory and which Keynes found blocking the way to a more realistic analysis in terms of output and employment. Also re-emerging is the much-derided 'Treasury doctrine' of the 1920s which implied that public works were a waste of time because any money borrowed by the government to finance them would be at the expense of loan-expenditure in some other direction. In the literature of the 1970s this now features as 'crowding out'. Keynes demonstrated that generalisations that apply to a world of full employment do not apply in a world of large-scale unemployment. But in a world that is neither one nor the other the operation of monetary and financial influences conforms to neither type of generalisation. Increasing the money supply when prices and activity are both falling works differently from increasing the money supply when prices are rising and activity falls short of full employment.

A second example is the argument over import restriction and protection that broke out in the mid 1970s. The free trade argument of the nineteenth century has long been made subject to important reservations. Just as the contention that the domestic economy is not self-regulating opens the door to increasing government intervention so also does the proposition that the external accounts are not automatically self-balancing. An external deficit may not be cured but aggravated by depreciation of the currency if this has little immediate effect on the commercial balance but a very marked immediate effect on domestic prices, on wages and so on competitiveness. It may be more effective to restrict imports and hold the rate once this begins to reduce the pressure on the exchanges. Similarly, there has always been a case for combining expansion to a higher level of output and employment with measures of protection that hold back imports to their current level. These and other arguments were the common currency of debate in the 1930s and were reinforced by other arguments for import restriction based on war-time experience in the years immediately after the war. The arguments do not necessarily have the same force as they once did because there are now other ways of handling external deficits. But whether or not they are right, the arguments are not novel.

Earlier chapters have traced the emergence of a commanding industrial leadership and its gradual disappearance as other countries industrialised. There has been no decline in any absolute sense but only in comparison with thriving competitors, some of them far more handicapped than Britain by the ravages of war. Where once it occupied a dominant position as a great empire, the workshop and financial centre of the world, the United Kingdom is now a small fragment of the world economy, vulnerable to changes in conditions abroad and to decisions in which it may have no, or a negligible, part. It has geared itself more closely to Europe through membership of the Common Market and loosened its ties with the Commonwealth, giving up the preferential access to Commonwealth markets it enjoyed for so long. It has ceased to be one of the great creditor nations by piling up heavy debts in recurring bouts of foreign borrowing but has remained a net creditor in receipt of more investment income from abroad than it pays in interest to foreigners. Even in 1976 foreign assets still exceeded foreign liabilities. In spite of two world wars the country had grown richer: especially the mass of urban manual workers with whom bargaining power in industry and political power at the polls increasingly rests. But it was a country more conscious than for a generation of acute and apparently insoluble economic problems: troubled by the consistent lag behind other countries in economic growth, lacking in pride and self-confidence and given to moods of frustration, despair and at times desperation.

Further reading

A survey of the postwar period as a whole is J. F. Wright, *Britain in the Age of Economic Management: An Economic History since 1939* (Oxford 1979).

For the period up to 1960 the best detailed account of developments is contained in the two volumes edited by G. D. N. Worswick and P. H. Ady, *The British Economy 1945–50* (OUP, 1952) and *The British Economy in the 1950's* (OUP, 1962). These include full bibliographies. The standard work on the evolution of central economic policy over this period is J. C. R. Dow's *The Management of the British Economy 1945–60* (CUP, 1964). For useful international comparisons reference should be made to A. Maddison, *Economic Growth in the West* (Twentieth Century Fund, New York, 1964). The memoranda submitted to the (Radcliffe) *Committee on the Working of the Monetary System* (1959) are also important as contemporary assessments of various aspects of policy.

The most thorough examination, by a group of distinguished American economists, of the problems of the British economy, as seen in the middle sixties is R. E. Caves (ed.), *Britain's Economic Prospects* (Brookings Institution and Allen and Unwin, 1968) which should be read in conjunction with its sequel, A. Cairncross (ed.), *Britain's Economic Prospects Reconsidered* (Allen and Unwin, 1971). Also useful as an indication of how things were seen in the 1960s is W. Beckerman (ed.), *Britain in 1975* (CUP, 1965).

For the period since 1960 see *British Economic Policy 1960–74* (ed. F. Blackaby) (NIESR, 1978); there are many other studies of policy during this period, including the following:

W. Beckerman (ed.), *The Labour Government's Economic Record 1964–70* (Duckworth 1972). Essays by a group of economists, some of them given to special pleading, on different aspects of policy in the middle and late 1960s.

C. D. Cohen, *Britain's Economic Policy 1960–69* (Butterworth's 1971). A useful survey, modelled on Dow, but less successful.

F. W. Paish, *How the economy works* (Macmillan 1970). Eight essays mainly on monetary policy and incomes policy.

M. Stewart, *The Jekyll and Hyde Years: Politics and Economic Policy since 1964* (J. M. Dent, 1977). Includes a succinct explanation, from the standpoint of a neo-Keynesian, of the main controversies over economic policy from 1964 onwards.

All of these deal primarily with macroeconomic policy and are not designed to be used as economic histories of the period. There are plenty of studies of inflation, incomes policy, and monetary, fiscal and financial affairs but very few of changes in industrial and commercial structure, the growth of international trade, the trends observable in the labour market, and other microeconomic developments.

On monetary and financial developments the most useful books for the later period are: D. R. Croome and H. G. Johnson (eds.). *Money in Britain 1959–69* (OUP, 1970).

J. E. Wadsworth (ed.), *The Banks and the Monetary System in the U.K. 1959–71.* Reprints of articles from the Midland Bank Review.

On Industry the reader may consult:

G. C. Allen, *British Industries and their Organisation* (2nd edn, Longmans, 1959).

G. C. Allen, *The Structure of Industry in Britain* (3rd edn, Longmans, 1970).

D. L. Burn (ed.), *The Structure of British Industry* (2 vols., CUP, 1958).

S. J. Prais, *The Evolution of Giant Firms in Britain* (CUP, 1976).

There is no satisfactory study of British trade in the postwar period. A running commentary on economic developments and a number of useful articles on specialised aspects of the British economy over the period will be found in the National Institute *Economic Review* (from 1959 onwards) and in the Bank of England *Quarterly Review* (from 1960 onwards).

Bibliography

Place of publication is London unless otherwise stated.

Abramovitz, M. 1968. The passing of the Kuznets cycle. *Economica*, **35**, 349–67.
Abrams, M. A. 1945. *The Condition of the British People 1911–45.*
Abrams, P. 1963. The failure of social reform, 1918–20. *Past and Present*, **24**, 43–64.
Addison, P. 1975. *The Road to 1945: British Politics and the 2nd World War.*
Adelman, I. 1960. Business cycles endogenous or stochastic. *Economic Journal*, **70**, 783–96.
Adler, M. K. 1956. *Modern Market Research. A guide for business executives.*
Aldcroft, D. H. 1964. The entrepreneur and the British economy, 1870–1914. *Econ. Hist. Rev. 2nd Ser.* **17**, 113–34.
    1968a. The mercantile marine. In *The Development of British Industry and Foreign Competition 1875–1914*, ed. D. H. Aldcroft, pp. 326–63.
    ed. 1968b. *The Development of British Industry and Foreign Competition 1875–1914.*
    1974. McCloskey on Victorian growth: a comment. *Econ. Hist. Rev. 2nd Ser.* **27**, 271–4.
    1975. Investment in and utilisation of manpower: Great Britain and her rivals, 1870–1914. In *Great Britain and her world, 1750–1914*, ed. B. M. Ratcliffe, pp. 287–307.
Aldcroft, D. H. & Fearon, P. eds. 1969. *Economic growth in Twentieth Century Britain.*
    eds. 1972. *British Economic Fluctuations 1790–1939*
Aldcroft, D. H. & Richardson, H. W. 1969. *The British Economy, 1870–1939.*
Alford, B. W. E. 1972. *Depression and Recovery? British Economic Growth 1918–39.*
    1973. *W. D. & H. O. Wills and The Development of The U.K. Tobacco Industry, 1786–1965.*
Allen, G. C. 1929. *The Industrial Development of Birmingham and the Black Country, 1860–1927.*
    1935. *British Industries and their Organisation.*
Allen, R. G. D. & Bowley, A. L. 1935. *Family Expenditure: A Study of its Variation.*
Allen, V. L. 1960. The Re-organisation of the Trade Union Congress, 1918–27. *British Journal of Sociology*, **11**, 24–43.
Altick, R. D. 1957. *The English Common Reader. A Social History of the Mass Reading Public 1800–1900.* Chicago.
Anderson, G. 1976. *Victorian Clerks.* Manchester.
Andrews, P. W. S. & Brunner, E. 1955. *The Life of Lord Nuffield; a study in enterprise and benevolence.* Oxford.
Andrzejewski, S. 1954. *Military Organisation and Society.*
Annan, N. 1955. The intellectual aristocracy. In *Studies in Social History: A Tribute to G. M. Trevelyan*, ed. J. H. Plumb, pp. 241–87.
Argles, O. M. V. 1964. *South Kensington to Robbins: English Technical and Scientific Education since 1851.*
Armstrong, W. A. 1972. The use of information about occupation. In *Nineteenth Century Society*, ed. E. A. Wrigley, pp. 191–310. Cambridge.

417

Arndt, H. W. 1944. *The Economic Lessons of the Nineteen-Thirties.*

Ashby, M. K. 1961. *Joseph Ashby of Tysoe, 1859–1919; a Study of English Village Life.* Cambridge.

Ashworth, W. 1954. *The Genesis of Modern British Town planning: A Study in Economic and Social History of the Nineteenth and Twentieth Centuries.*

1960. *An Economic History of England, 1870–1939.*

1965. Changes in the industrial structure: 1870–1914. *Yorkshire Bulletin of Economic and Social Research,* **17**, 61–74.

Askwith, G. R. 1920. *Industrial Problems and Disputes.*

Atkin, J. 1970. Official regulation of British overseas investment, 1914–31. *Econ. Hist. Rev. 2nd Ser.* **23**, 324–35.

Atkinson, A. B. ed. 1973. *Wealth, Income and Inequality: selected readings.* Harmondsworth.

Bacon, R. W. & Eltis, W. 1974. *The Age of US and UK Machinery.* National Economic Development Office Monograph 3.

1976. *Britain's Economic Problem: Too Few Producers.*

Bagehot, Walter, 1867. *The English Constitution.*

Bagwell, P. S. 1974. *The Transport Revolution from 1770.*

Baines, D. E. 1981. *Emigration and Internal Migration in Late Nineteenth-Century England and Wales.*

Baker, W. P. 1953. *The English Village.*

Balfour Committee. 1925. *Survey of Overseas Markets.*

1927–28. *Factors in Industrial and Commercial Efficiency.*

Bamford, T. W. 1967. *Rise of the Public Schools; a Study of Boys' Public Boarding Schools in England and Wales from 1837 to the Present Day.*

Bank of England Quarterly Bulletin.

Banks, J. A. 1954. *Prosperity and Parenthood; A Study of Family Planning among the Victorian Middle Classes.*

Banks, O. 1955. *Parity and Prestige in English Secondary Education.*

Barker, T. C. 1976. A family firm becomes a public company; changes at Pilkington Brothers Limited in the interwar years. In *Management Strategy and Business Development,* ed. L. Hannah, pp. 85–94.

Barker, T. C. & Robbins, M. 1976. *A History of London Transport. Volume 2: The 20th Century to 1970.*

Barna, T. 1945. *Redistribution of Incomes through Public Finance in 1937.* Oxford.

Barou, N. I. 1947. *British Trade Unions.*

Barrett, C. R. & Walters, A. A. 1966. The stability of Keynesian and monetary multipliers in the United Kingdom. *Review of Economics and Statistics,* **48**, 395–405.

Baster, A. S. J. 1933. A note on the colonial stock acts and dominion borrowing. *Economic History,* **2**, 602–8.

Baxter, R. D. 1968. *National Income. The United Kingdom.*

Beach, W. E. 1935. *British International Gold Movements and Banking Policy, 1881–1913.* Cambridge, Mass.

Beales, H. L. & Lambert, R. S. eds. 1934. *Memoirs of the Unemployed.*

Beer, S. H. 1965. *Modern British Politics; a study of parties and pressure groups.*

Bell, D. 1974. *The Coming of Post-Industrial Society: a venture in social forecasting.*

Bellerby, J. R. 1956. *Agriculture and Industry Relative Income.*

1968. Distribution of farm income in the United Kingdom, 1867–1938. In *Essays in Agrarian History*, ed. W. A. Minchinton, Vol. 2, pp. 261–79. Newton Abbot.

Bellerby, J. R. & Boreham, A. J. 1953. Farmer occupiers' capital in the United Kingdom before 1939. *The Farm Economist*, **7(b)**, 257–63.

Benjamin, D. K. & Kochin, L. A. 1976. Searching for an explanation of unemployment in interwar Britain. University of Washington, August 1976 (mimeo).

Bentley, N. 1974. *Edwardian Album.*

Best. G. 1971. *Mid-Victorian Britain, 1851–75.*

Beveridge, W. H. 1930. *Unemployment; A Problem of Industry (1909 and 1930).*

1936. An analysis of unemployment. *Economica N.S.*, **3**, 357–86.

1937a. An analysis of unemployment II. *Economica N.S.*, **4**, 1–17.

1937b. An analysis of unemployment III. *Economica N.S.*, **4**, 168–83.

1942–4. *Social Insurance and Allied Services Report* (Cmd. 6404).

1944. *Full Employment in a Free Society.*

Bienefeld, M. A. 1972. *Working Hours in British Industry: An Economic History.*

Black, C. ed. 1915. *Married Women's Work.*

Blewett, N. 1965. The franchise in the United Kingdom 1885–1918. *Past and Present*, **32**, 27–56.

Bloomfield, A. I. 1968. *Patterns of Fluctuation in International Investment Before 1914.* Princeton.

Blumin, S. 1973. The historical study of vertical mobility. In *Applied Historical Studies*, ed. M. Drake, pp. 233–50.

Booth, A. E. & Glynn, S. 1975. Unemployment in the interwar period: a multiple problem. *Journal of Contemporary History*, **10**, 611–36.

Booth, C. 1892. *Life and Labour of the People in London*, vol. 1.

Bottomore, T. B. 1962. *Sociology, A Guide to Problems and Literature.*

Boulding, K. E. & Mukerjee, T. eds. 1972. *Economic Imperialism.* Ann Arbor.

Bowley, A. L. 1920. *The Change in the Distribution of the National Income, 1880–1913.* Oxford.

1930. *Some Economic Consequences of the Great War.*

1937. *Wages and Income in the United Kingdom since 1860.* Cambridge.

Bowley, A. L. & Hogg, M. H. 1925. *Has Poverty Diminished?*

Bowley, M. 1945. *Housing and the State, 1919–44.*

Braithwaite, D. C. & Dobbs, S. P. 1932. *The Distribution of Consumable Goods.*

Branca, P. 1975. *Silent Sisterhood: Middle Class Women in the Victorian Home.*

Brand, E. C. F. 1950. Democracy in Great Britain. *Pacific Historical Review*, **19**, 113–16.

Branson, W. H. 1972. *Macroeconomic Theory and Policy.* New York.

Bravendar, J. 1850. Farming of Gloucestershire. *Journal of the Royal Agricultural Society of England*, **11**, 116–77.

Bretherton, R. F., Burchardt, F. A. & Rutherford, R. S. G. 1941. *Public Investment and the Trade Cycle in Great Britain.* Oxford.

Briggs, A. 1956. *Friends of the People.*

1961a. *Social Thought and Social Action: A Study of the Work of Seebohm Rowntree, 1871–1954.*

1961b. *The History of Broadcasting in the United Kingdom, Vol. 1: The Birth of Broadcasting.*

1961c. The Welfare State in Historical Perspective. *Archives Européennes de Sociologie*, **2**, 221–58.

420

1963. *Victorian Cities*.

1965. *The History of Broadcasting in the United Kingdom, Vol. 2: The Golden Age of Broadcasting*.

1970. *The History of Broadcasting in the United Kingdom, Vol. 3: The War of Words*.

1972. The history of changing approaches to social welfare. In *Comparative Development in Social Welfare*, ed. E. W. Martin, pp. 9–24.

Briggs, A. & Saville, J. eds. 1971. *Essays in Labour History 1886–1923*

Briggs, S. 1975. *Keep Smiling Through*.

Bright, John, 1869. *Speeches on Questions of Public Policy by the Right Honourable John Bright, M.P.*, ed. J. E. Thorold Rogers.

Broadbridge, S. 1970. *Studies in Railway Expansion and the Capital Market in England, 1825–1973*.

Brodrick, G. C. 1881. *English Land and English Landlords*.

Brown, A. J. 1972. *The Framework of Regional Economics in the United Kingdom*.

Brown, E. C. 1956. Fiscal policy in the thirties: a reappraisal. *American Economic Review*, **46**, 857–79.

Brown, J. 1968. Charles Booth & labour colonies, 1889–1905. *Econ. Hist. Rev. 2nd Ser.*, **21**, 349–60.

Brown, M. B. 1974. *The Economics of Imperialism*. Harmondsworth.

Browning, H. E. & Sorrell, A. A. 1954. Cinemas and cinema-going in Great Britain. *Journal of the Royal Statistical Society*, **117**, 133–65.

Bruce, M. Ed. 1973. *The Rise of the Welfare State; English Social Policy, 1601–1971*.

Brunner, K. & Meltzer, A. H. 1976. *The Phillips Curve and Labor Markets*. Amsterdam.

Bullock, A. 1960. *Life and Times of Ernest Bevin*, Vol. 1.

Bulmer, M. ed. 1975. *Working-Class Images of Society*.

Bureau of the Census, 1976. *The Statistical History of the United States*. New York.

Burn, D. 1940. *The Economic History of Steelmaking, 1867–1939: A Study in Competition*. Cambridge.

Burnett, J. 1968. *Plenty and Want: A Social History of Diet in England from 1815 to the Present Day*. Harmondsworth.

Burnham, T. & Hoskins, G. 1943. *Iron and Steel in Britain, 1870–1930*.

Buxton, N. K. 1975. The role of the 'new' industries in Britain during the 1930s: a reinterpretation. *Business History Review*, **49**, 205–22.

Byatt, I. C. R. 1968. 'Electrical products'. In *The Development of British Industry and Foreign Competition, 1875–1914*, ed. D. H. Aldcroft, pp. 238–73.

Cadbury, G. S. 1938. *Young Offenders, yesterday and to-day*.

Caird, J. 1852. *English Agriculture in 1850–51*.

Cairncross, A. K. 1953. *Home and Foreign Investment, 1870–1913*. Cambridge.

1961. International trade and economic development. *Economica N.S.*, **28**, 235–51.

Calder, A. 1969. *The People's War; Britain 1939–45*.

Cameron, R. 1961. *France and the Economic Development of Europe*. Princeton.

Cannadine, D. 1977a. Aristocratic indebtedness in the nineteenth century: the case re-opened. *Econ. Hist. Rev. 2nd Ser.*, **30**, 624–50.

1977b. Lords and landlords. *New Society*, **40**, No. 757, 7–9.

1977c. Victorian cities: how different? *Social History*, **4**, 457–82.

Carr, E. H. 1951. *The New Society*.

Carr-Saunders, A. M., Caradog Jones, D. & Moser, C. A. 1958. *A Survey of Social*

Conditions in England and Wales. Oxford.

Caves, R. E. 1971. Second thoughts on Britain's economic prospects. In *Britain's Economic Prospects Reconsidered*, ed. A. Cairncross, pp. 204–17.

Caves, R. E. et al. 1968. *Britain's Economic Prospects*.

Caves, R. E., North, D. & Price, J. eds. 1979. Forthcoming Conference volume on trade and economic growth in the nineteenth century.

Chambers, J. D. & Mingay, G. E. 1966. *The Agricultural Revolution: 1750–1880*.

Champernowne, D. G. 1937–38. The uneven distribution of unemployment in the United Kingdom, 1929–1936. I. *Review of Economic Studies*, **5**, 93–106.

1938–39. The uneven distribution of unemployment in the United Kingdom, 1929–1936, II. *Review of Economic Studies*, **6**, 111–24.

1973. *The Distribution of Income between Persons*. Cambridge.

Chandler, A. D. 1962. *Strategy and Structure: Chapters in the History of Industrial Enterprise*. Cambridge, Mass.

Channing, F. A. 1897. *The Truth about Agricultural Depression*.

Channon, D. F. 1973. *The Strategy and Structure of British Enterprise*. Boston.

Chapman, A. L. & Knight, R. 1953. *Wages and Salaries in the United Kingdom, 1920–38*. Cambridge.

Chapman, S. D. 1976. Strategy and structure at Boots the Chemists. In *Management Strategy and Business Development*, ed. L. Hannah, pp. 95–107.

Chapman, S. J. & Marquis, F. J. 1912. The recruiting of the employing classes from the ranks of the wage-carners in the cotton industry. *Journal of the Royal Statistical Society*, **75**, 293–313.

Cherry, G. E. 1972. *Urban Change and Planning; a history of urban development in Britain since 1750*. Henley-on-Thames.

Chester, D. N. ed. 1951. *Lessons of the British War Economy*. Cambridge.

Church, R. A. 1975a. *The Great Victorian Boom, 1850–73*.

1975b. Nineteenth-century clock technology in Britain, the United States, and Switzerland. *Econ. Hist. Rev. 2nd Ser.*, **28**, 616–30.

Clapham, J. H. 1910. The last years of the navigation Acts. *English Historical Review*, **25**, 480–501 & 687–707. Reprinted in *Essays in Economic History*, ed. E. M. Carus-Wilson, Vol. 3, pp. 144–78.

1932. *An Economic History of Modern Britain: Free Trade and Steel 1850–86*, Cambridge, 1963.

1938. *An Economic History of Modern Britain III: Machines and National Rivalries, 1887–1914*. Cambridge, 1963.

Clapinson, M. 1978. *Victorian and Edwardian Oxfordshire from Old Photographs*.

Clark, C. 1937. *National Income and Outlay*.

1938. Determination of the multiplier from national income statistics. *Economic Journal*, **48**, 435–48.

1951. *The Conditions of Economic Progress*.

Clarke, P. 1971. *Lancashire and the New Liberalism*.

Clarke, S. V. O. 1967. *Central Bank Co-operation: 1924–31*. New York.

Clay, H. 1957. *Lord Norman*.

Clayre, A. 1973. *The Impact of Broadcasting*. Salisbury.

Cleary, E. J. 1965. *The Building Society Movement*.

Clegg, H. A., Fox, A. & Thompson, A. F. 1964. *A History of British Trade Unions since 1889*. Oxford.

Coale, A. J. 1969. The decline of fertility in Europe from the French Revolution to the Second World War. In *Fertility and Family Planning: A World View*, eds. S. J. Behrman, L. Corsa & R. Freedman, pp. 3–24. Ann Arbor.

Cole, G. D. H. 1937. Some notes on British trade unionism in the third quarter of the nineteenth century. *International Review of Social History*, **2**, 1–27.

1939. *British Trade Unionism Today*.

1947. *A Century of Cooperation*.

1956. *The Post-war Condition of Britain*.

Cole, G. D. H. & Cole, M. I. 1937. *The Condition of Britain*.

Coleman, D. C. 1969. *Courtaulds: an economic and social history II. Rayon*. Oxford.

1973. Gentlemen and Players. *Econ. Hist. Rev. 2nd Ser.*, **26**, 92–116.

Collins, E. J. T. 1972. The diffusion of the threshing machine in Britain, 1790–1880. *Tools and Tillage*, **2**, 16–33.

Collins, H. 1971. The Marxism of the Social Democratic Federation. In *Essays in Labour History 1886–1923*, ed. A. Briggs & J. Saville, pp. 47–69.

Committee on Economic Information 1937. Twenty-second Report. Economic policy and the maintenance of trade activity. In *The Economic Advisory Council, 1930–39*, eds. S. Howson & D. Winch, pp. 343–53. Cambridge, 1977.

Confederation of British Industry. 1976. *The Road to Recovery*.

Coppock, D. J. 1956. The climacteric of the 1890s: a critical note. *Manchester School of Economic & Social Studies*, **24**, 1–31.

1961. The causes of the great depression, 1873–96. *Manchester School of Economic and Social Studies*, **29**, 205–32.

1972. The causes of business fluctuations. In *British Economic Fluctuations 1790–1939*, eds. D. H. Aldcroft & P. Fearon, pp. 188–219.

Coppock, J. T. 1956. The statistical assessment of British agriculture. *Agricultural History Review*, **4**, 4–21 & 66–79.

Corner, D. C. 1956. Exports and the British trade cycle: 1929. *Manchester School of Economic and Social Studies*, **24**, 124–60.

Cotgrove, S. F. 1958. *Technical Education and Social Change*.

Cottrell, P. L. 1975. *British Overseas Investment in the Nineteenth Century*.

Court, W. H. B. 1965. *British Economic History, 1870–1914; Commentary and Documents*. Cambridge.

Cox, P. R. 1970. *Demography*.

Crafts, N. F. R. 1973. Trade as a handmaiden of growth: An alternative view. *Economic Journal*, **83**, 875–84.

1979. Victorian Britain did fail. *Econ. Hist. Rev. 2nd Ser.*, **32**, 533–7.

Crossick, G. J. 1976a. *Social structure & working-class behaviour: Kentish London 1840–80*. University of London; PhD thesis 1976.

ed. 1976b. *The Lower Middle Class in Britain 1870–1914*.

Crouzet, F. 1958. *L'Economie britannique et le blocus continental, 1806–13*, Paris.

1964. Wars, blockade, and economic change in Europe, 1792–1815. *Journal of Economic History*, **24**, 567–88.

1979. Towards an export economy: British exports during the Industrial Revolution, forthcoming in Caves, North & Price, eds. (1979).

Crowther, M. A. 1978. The later years of the workhouse, 1890–1929. In *The Origins of British Social Policy*, ed. P. Thane, pp. 36–55.

Cunningham, W. 1910–11. Free Trade. In *The Encyclopaedia Britannica 11th ed.*, **11**, pp. 88–92, Cambridge.

Dahlström, E. ed. 1967. *The Changing Roles of Men and Women.*

Dangerfield, G. 1936. *The Strange Death of Liberal England.*

David, P. A. 1969. The Diffusion of Mechanical Reaping: A Quantitative Assessment of British and American Progress before 1875. Unpublished.

1970. Labour productivity in British agriculture, 1850–1914: some quantitative evidence on regional differences. *Econ. Hist. Rev. 2nd Ser.*, **23**, 504–14.

1975. *Technical Choice, Innovation and Economic Growth: Essays on American and British Experience in the Nineteenth Century.*

Davidoff, L. 1974. Mastered for life: servant and wife in Victorian and Edwardian England. *Journal of Social History*, **7**, 406–28.

Davis, L. E. 1966. The capital markets and industrial concentration: The U.S. and the U.K. a comparative study. *Econ. Hist. Rev. 2nd Ser.*, **19**, 255–72.

Davis, L. E., Hughes, J. R. T. & McDougall, D. M. 1969. *American Economic History*, 3rd ed. Homewood.

Davis, L. E. & Huttenback, R. A. 1977. Public expenditure and private profit: budgetary decision in the British empire, 1860–1912. *American Economic Review* **67** *Papers and Proceedings*, 282–7.

Dawes, F. 1973. *Not in Front of the Servants. Domestic Service in England, 1850–1939.*

Deane, P. 1968. New estimates of gross national product for the United Kingdom 1830–1914. *The Review of Income and Wealth*, **14**, 95–112.

Deane, P. & Cole, W. A. 1962. *British Economic Growth, 1688–1959.* Cambridge.

De Canio, S. J. 1974. *Agriculture in the Post-Bellum South.* Cambridge, Mass.

Denison, E. F. 1968. Economic growth. In *Britain's Economic Prospects*, ed. R. E. Caves et al., pp. 231–79.

Dennison, S. R. 1939. *The Location of Industry and The Depressed Areas.*

Department of Employment & Productivity. 1971. *British Labour Statistics: Historical Abstract 1886–1968.*

Dickinson, W. 1852. On the farming of Cumberland. *Journal of the Royal Agricultural Society of England*, **13**, 207–300.

Dingle, A. E. 1972. Drink and working-class living standards in Britain, 1870–1914. *Econ. Hist. Rev. 2nd Ser.*, **25**, 608–22.

Dixon, R. J. & Thirlwall, A. P. 1975. *Regional Growth and Unemployment in the United Kingdom.*

Domar, E. D. 1947. Expansion and Employment. *American Economic Review*, **37**, 34–55.

Dowie, J. A. 1968. Growth in the inter-war period: some more arithmetic. *Econ. Hist. Rev. 2nd Ser.*, **21**, 93–112.

1975. 1919–20 is in need of attention. *Econ. Hist. Rev. 2nd Ser.*, **28**, 429–50.

Drummond, I. M. 1972. *British Economic Policy and the Empire, 1919–39.*

1974. *Imperial Economic Policy, 1917–39.*

Duesenberry, J. S. 1949. *Income, Saving, and the Theory of Consumer Behaviour.* Cambridge, Mass.

Dunbabin, J. P. D. 1963. The 'Revolt of the Field': the agricultural labourers' movement in the 1870s. *Past and Present*, **26**, 68–97.

1974. *Rural Discontent in Nineteenth Century Britain.*

Durbin, E. F. M. 1940. *The Politics of Democratic Socialism; an essay on social policy.*

Dyas, G. P. & Thanheiser, H. J. 1976. *The emerging European enterprise: strategy and structure in French and German industry.*

Eddie, S. M. 1971. Farmers' response to price in large-estate agriculture: Hungary 1870–1913. *Econ. Hist. Rev. 2nd Ser.*, **24**, 571–86.

Edelstein, M. 1971. Rigidity and bias in the British capital market, 1870–1913. In *Essays on a Mature Economy: Britain after 1840*, ed. D. N. McCloskey, pp. 83–106.

1974. The determinants of U.K. investment abroad, 1870–1913: the U.S. case. *Journal of Economic History*, **34**, 980–1007.

1976. Realized rates of return on U.K. home and overseas portfolio investment in the age of high imperialism. *Explorations in Economic History*, **13**, 283–329.

1977. U.K. savings in the age of high imperialism and after. *American Economic Review*, **67**, *Papers and Proceedings*, 288–94.

Edwards, D. L. 1969. *Religion and Change*.

Ehrlich, C. 1976. *The Piano: A History*.

Emy, H. V. 1973. *Liberals, Radicals and Social Politics, 1892–1914*. Cambridge.

Erickson, C. 1959. *British industrialists: steel and hosiery, 1850–1950*. Cambridge.

1972. Who were the English and Scots immigrants to the United States in the late nineteenth century? In *Population and Social Change*, ed. D. V. Glass & R. Revelle, pp. 347–81.

Ernle, Lord. 1912. *English Farming Past and Present*. 1961.

Escott, T. H. S. 1879. *England: Its People, Polity & Pursuits*.

Esherick, J. 1972. Harvard on China: the apologetics of imperialism. *Bulletin of Concerned Asian scholars*, **4**, 9–16.

Evans, E. W. 1961. *The Miners of South Wales*. Cardiff.

Evans, G. E. 1970. *Where Beards Wag All: The Relevance of the Oral Tradition*.

Evans, M. K. 1969. *Macroeconomic Activity*. New York.

Fairlie, S. 1965. The nineteenth-century Corn Law reconsidered. *Econ. Hist. Rev. 2nd Ser.*, **18**, 562–75.

1969. The corn laws and British wheat production, 1829–76. *Econ. Hist. Rev. 2nd Ser.*, **22**, 88–116.

Fawcett, C. B. 1919. *Provinces of England: a study of some geographical aspects of devolution*.

Feiling, K. G. 1946. *The Life of Neville Chamberlain*.

Feinstein, C. H. 1961. Income and investment in the United Kingdom, 1856–1914. *Economic Journal*, **71**, 367–85.

1965. *Domestic Capital Formation in the United Kingdom 1920–38*. Cambridge.

1968. Changes in the distribution of the national income in the United Kingdom since 1860. In *The Distribution of National Income*, eds. J. Marchal & B. Ducros, pp. 115–39.

1972: *National Income, Expenditure and Output of the United Kingdom 1855–1965*. Cambridge.

1978. Capital accumulation and economic growth. In *The Cambridge Economic History of Europe*, eds. P. Mathias & M. M. Postan, Vol. 7, pp. 82–94. Cambridge.

Feis, H. 1930. *Europe, The World's Banker, 1870–1914*. New Haven.

Feller, I. 1966. The Draper loom in New England textiles, 1894–1914. *Journal of Economic History*, **26**, 320–47.

Fenton, A. 1976. *Scottish Country Life*. Edinburgh.

Ferns, H. S. 1953. Britain's informal empire in Argentina, 1806–1914. *Past and Present*, **4**, 60–75.

Fetter, F. W. 1977. Lenin, Keynes and inflation. *Economica N.S.*, **44**, 77–80.
Fieldhouse, D. K. ed. 1967. *The Theory of Capitalist Imperialism*. New York.
1973. *Economics and Empire*, 1830–1914.
Finer, H. 1927. *The British Civil Service*.
Fisher, F. M. & Temin, P. 1970. Regional specialization and the supply of wheat in the United States, 1867–1914. *Review of Economics and Statistics*, **52**, 134–49.
Fisher, M. R. 1976. The new micro-economics of unemployment. In *The Concept and Measurement of Involuntary Unemployment*, ed. G. D. N. Worswick, pp. 35–57.
Fletcher, T. W. 1961a. The great depression of English agriculture, 1873–96. *Econ. Hist. Rev. 2nd Ser.*, **13**, 417–32.
1961b. Lancashire livestock farming during the great depression. *Agricultural History Review*, **9**, 17–42.
Floud, R. 1974. The adolescence of American engineering competition, 1860–1900. *Econ. Hist. Rev. 2nd Ser.*, **27**, 57–71.
1976a. Entrepreneurial failure and technical education in the late nineteenth century. Unpublished manuscript.
1976b. *The British Machine Tool Industry, 1850–1914*. Cambridge.
Ford, A. G. 1962. *The Gold Standard, 1880–1914: Britain and Argentina*. Oxford.
1963. Notes on the role of exports in British economic fluctuations, 1870–1914. *Econ. Hist. Rev. 2nd Ser.*, **16**, 328–37.
1965. Overseas lending and internal fluctuations: 1870–1914. *Yorkshire Bulletin of Economic and Social Research*, **17**, 19–31.
1969. British economic fluctuations, 1870–1914. *The Manchester School of Economic and Social Studies*, **37**, 99–129.
1971. British investment in Argentina and long swings, 1880–1914. *Journal of Economic History*, **31**, 650–63.
Fox, A. 1955. Industrial relations in nineteenth-century Birmingham. *Oxford Economic Papers*, **7**, 57–70.
1966. Managerial ideology and labour relations. *British Journal of Industrial Relations*, **4**, 366–78.
Frankel, S. H. 1967. *Investment and the Return to Equity Capital in the South African Gold Mining Industry, 1887–1965*. Oxford.
Frankenberg, R. 1966. *Communities in Britain; social life in town and country*. Harmondsworth.
Fraser, D. 1973. *The Evolution of the British Welfare State*.
Friedman, M. 1968. The role of monetary policy. *American Economic Review*, **58**, 1–17.
Fryer, P. 1965. *The Birth Controllers*.
Fussell, P. 1975. *The Great War and Modern Memory*.

Gallagher, J. & Robinson, R. 1953. The imperialism of free trade. *Econ. Hist. Rev. 2nd Ser.*, **6**, 1–15.
Gardiner, C. H. 1944. *Your Village and Mine*.
Garside, W. R. 1977. Juvenile unemployment and public policy between the wars. *Econ. Hist. Rev. 2nd Ser.*, **30**, 322–39.
Gartner, L. P. 1960. *The Jewish Immigrant in England, 1870–1914*.
Gaskell, S. M. 1976. 'Housing and the Lower Middle Class 1870–1914'. In *The Lower Middle Class in Britain 1870–1914*, ed. Geoffrey Crossick, pp. 159–83.
Gauldie, E. 1974. *Cruel Habitations: A History of Working Class Housing, 1780–1918*.

426

Geddes, P. 1915. *Cities in Evolution.*

George, W. L. 1907. *Engines of Social Progress.*

Giddens, A. 1973. *The Class Structure of the Advanced Societies.*

Gilbert, B. B. 1966. *The Evolution of National Insurance in Great Britain.*
 1970. *British Social Policy, 1914–39.*

Gillis, J. R. 1975. The evolution of juvenile delinquency in England 1890–1914. *Past and Present*, **67**, 96–126.

Gilman, C. P. 1911. *The Man-Made World.*

Giner, S. 1976. *Mass Society.*

Ginsberg, M. ed. 1959. *Law and Opinion in England in the 20th Century.*

Girouard, M. 1977. *Sweetness & Light: The 'Queen Anne' Movement 1860–1900.* Oxford.

Gladstone, W. E. 1971. *Midlothian Speeches, 1879.* Leicester.

Glass, D. V. 1938. Changes in fertility in England and Wales, 1851 to 1931. In *Political Arithmetic: A Symposium of Population Studies*, ed. L. T. Hogben, pp 161–212.
 1940. *Population Policies and Movements in Europe.* 1967.
 1959. Education. In *Law and Opinion in England in the 20th Century*, ed. M. Ginsberg, pp. 319–46.

Glass, D. V. & Grebenik, E. 1965. World population, 1800–1950. In *The Cambridge Economic History of Europe*, eds. H. J. Habakkuk & M. Postan, Vol. 6, Part I, pp. 56–138. Cambridge.

Glass, R. 1955. Introduction to urban sociology in Great Britain: A trend report. *Current Sociology*, **4**, 5–19.

Goldthorpe, J. H. 1966. Social stratification in industrial society. In *Class, Status and Power*, eds. R. Bendix & S. M. Lipset, pp. 648–59. New York.

Goodhart, C. A. E. 1972. *The Business of Banking, 1891–1914.*

Gosden, P. H. & J. H. 1976. *Education in the Second World War: a study in policy & administration.*

Gosling, H. 1927. *Up and down stream.*

Gould, J. D. 1972. *Economic Growth in History: Survey and Analysis.*

Gourvish, T. R. 1973. A British business elite: The chief executive managers of the railway industry, 1850–1922. *Business History Review*, **47**, 289–316.

Graves, R. & Hodge, A. 1940. *The Long Weekend: A social history of Great Britain, 1918–39.*

Gray, R. Q. 1976. *The Labour Aristocracy in Victorian Edinburgh.* Oxford.

Green, A. & Urquhart, M. C. 1976. Factor and commodity flows in the international economy of 1870–1914: a multi-country view. *Journal of Economic History*, **36**, 217–52.

Guttsman, W. L. 1963. *The British Political Elite.*

Habakkuk, H. J. 1940. Free trade and commercial expansion, 1853–70. In *The Cambridge History of the British Empire*, ed. J. Holland Rose, A. P. Newton & E. A. Benians, Vol. 2, pp. 753–805. Cambridge.
 1962a. *American and British Technology in the Nineteenth Century.* Cambridge.
 1962b. Fluctuations in house building in Britain and the United States in the nineteenth century. *Journal of Economic History*, **22**, 198–230.

Haberler, G. 1959. *International Trade and Economic Development.* Cairo.

Hadow Committee 1926. *Report of the Consultative Committee on the Education of the Adolescent.* Ministry of Education.

Haggard, H. R. 1911. *Rural Denmark and its Lessons.*

Hall, A. D. 1913. *A Pilgrimage of British Farming, 1910–12.*
Hall, A. R. 1963. *The London Capital Market and Australia 1870–1914.* Canberra.
    ed. 1968. *The Export of Capital from Britain 1870–1914.*
Hall, P. G. 1962. *The Industries of London since 1861.*
Hall, S. R. 1921. *The Advertising Handbook.* New York.
Halsey, A. H. 1964. Education and mobility. In *The Frontiers of Sociology*, ed.
    T. R. Fyvel, pp. 1–12.
    1972. Trends in British Society since 1900; a guide to the changing social structure of
    Britain.
Hancock, K. J. 1960. Unemployment and the economists in the 1920s. *Economica*, **37**,
    305–21.
    1962. The reduction of unemployment as a problem of public policy, 1920–29. *Econ.
    Hist. Rev. 2nd Ser.*, **15**, 328–43.
Hancock, W. K. 1942. *Survey of British Commonwealth Aff   Vol. 2; Problems of
    Economic Policy 1918–39, Part I.*
Hancock, W. K. & Gowing, M. M. 1949. *British War Economy.*
Hannah, L. 1974. Managerial Innovation and the rise of the large-scale company in
    interwar Britain. *Econ. Hist. Rev. 2nd Ser.*, **27**, 252–70.
    1976. *The Rise of the Corporate Economy: the British experience.*
Hannah, L. & Kay, J. A. 1977. *Concentration in Modern Industry: Theory, Measurement
    and the U.K. Experience.*
Hannington, W. 1936. *Unemployed Struggles, 1919–36.*
Hansard. Record of British Parliamentary Debates.
Hansen, B. 1969. *Fiscal Policy in Seven Countries, 1955–65.* OECD Paris.
Harley, C. K. 1971. The shift from sailing ships to steam ships, 1850–90. In *Essays on
    a Mature Economy*, ed. D. McCloskey, pp. 215–34. Princeton.
    1974. Skilled labour and the choice of technique in Edwardian industry. *Explorations
    in Economic History*, **11**, 391–414.
    1976. Goschen's conversion of the national debt and the yield on Consols. *Econ. Hist.
    Rev. 2nd Ser.*, **29**, 101–6.
    1979. Transportation, the world wheat trade and the Kuznets cycle, 1850–1913.
    Forthcoming in Caves, North & Price eds. 1979.
Harnetty, P. 1972. *Imperialism and free trade; Lancashire and India in the Mid-Nineteenth
    Century.* Vancouver.
Harris, J. 1972. *Unemployment and Politics.* Oxford.
    1977. *William Beveridge; A Biography.* Oxford.
Harrison, A. E. 1969. The competitiveness of the British cycle industry, 1890–1914. *Econ.
    Hist. Rev. 2nd Ser.*, **22**, 287–303.
Harrison, R. 1965. *Before the Socialists: Studies in Labour and Politics, 1861–81.*
Harrod, R. F. 1939. An essay in dynamic theory. *Economic Journal*, **49**, 14–33.
Hart, P. E. & Prais, S. J. 1956. The analysis of business concentration: A statistical
    approach. *Journal of the Royal Statistical Society Series A*, **119**, 150–81.
Hawke, G. R. 1970. *Railways and Economic Growth in England and Wales, 1840–70.*
    Oxford.
    1975. The United States Tariff and industrial protection in the late nineteenth century.
    Econ. Hist. Rev. 2nd Ser., **28**, 84–99.
Hawtrey, R. G. 1919. *Currency and Credit.*
    1923. *Monetary Reconstruction.*
    1925. Public expenditure and the demand for labour. *Economica*, **5**, 38–48.

Hay, J. R. 1975. *The Origins of the Liberal Welfare Reforms, 1906–14.*

    1977. Employers and social policy in Britain: the evolution of welfare legislation, 1905–14. *Social History*, **4**, 435–55.

Heath, F. G. 1874. *The English Peasantry.*

Hennessey, R. A. S. 1972. *The Electrical Revolution.* Newcastle.

Henning, G. R. & Trace, K. 1975. Britain and the motorship: a case of delayed adoption of new technology? *Journal of Economic History*, **35**, 353–85.

Hennock, E. P. 1973. *Fit & Proper Persons: Ideal and Reality in Nineteenth-Century Urban Government.*

    1976. Poverty and social theory in England; the experience of the eighteen-eighties. *Social History*, **1**, 67–91.

Hicks, J. R. 1950. *A Contribution to the Theory of the Trade Cycle.* Oxford.

Hicks, U. K. 1938. *The Finance of British Government, 1920–36.*

Higonnet, R. P. 1957. Bank deposits in the United Kingdom, 1870–1914. *Quarterly Journal of Economics*, **71**, 329–67.

Hilgerdt, F. 1942. *The Network of Trade.* League of Nations: Economic Intelligence Service. Geneva.

    1943. The case for multilateral trade. *American Economic Review*, **33**, *Papers and Proceedings*, 393–407.

    1945. *Industrialization and Foreign Trade.* League of Nations: Economic, Financial and Transit Department. Geneva.

Hill, M. J. 1976. Can we distinguish voluntary from involuntary unemployment? In *The Concept and Measurement of Involuntary Unemployment*, ed. G. D. N. Worswick, pp. 168–84.

Hilton, J. 1944. *Rich Man, Poor Man.*

Hindley, D. & G. 1972. *Advertising in Victorian England, 1837–1901.*

Hines, A. G. 1976. The 'micro-economic foundations of employment and inflation theory': bad old wine in elegant new bottles. In *The Concept and Measurement of Involuntary Unemployment*, ed. G. D. N. Worswick, pp. 58–79.

Hirst, F. W. ed. 1903. *Free Trade and Other Fundamental Doctrines of the Manchester School.*

Hobsbawm, E. J. 1949. General labour unions in Britain, 1889–1914. *Econ. Hist. Rev. 2nd Ser.*, **1**, 123–42. Reprinted in *Labouring Men*, E. J. Hobsbawm, pp. 179–203.

    1964a. *Labouring Men.*

    1964b. The nineteenth-century London labour market. In *London, Aspects of Change*, ed. R. Glass, pp. 3–28.

    1968. *Industry and Empire.*

Hobson, J. A. 1902. *Imperialism, A Study.*

Hoffman, R. J. S. 1933. *Great Britain and the German Trade Rivalry, 1875–1914.* Philadelphia.

Hoffman, W. G. 1965. *Das Wachstum der deutschen Wirtschaft seit der Mitte des 19 Jahrhunderts.* Berlin.

Hoggart, R. 1957. *The Uses of Literacy: Aspects of Working Class Life, with special reference to publications and entertainment.*

    1963. *Schools of English and Contemporary Society.* Birmingham.

Holton, R. H. 1976. *British Syndicalism, 1900–14, myths and realities.*

Hooker, R. H. 1909. The meat supply of the United Kingdom. *Journal of the Royal Statistical Society*, **72**, 304–76.

Hopkins, A. G. 1973. *An Economic History of West Africa*.

Howard, E. 1902. *Garden Cities of Tomorrow*.

Howson, S. 1974. The origins of dear money, 1919–20. *Econ. Hist. Rev. 2nd Ser.*, **27**, 88–107.

1975. *Domestic Monetary Management in Britain, 1919–38*. Cambridge.

1976. The managed floating pound, 1932–39. *The Banker* **126**, 249–55.

Howson, S. & Winch, D. 1977. *The Economic Advisory Council, 1930–39*. Cambridge.

Hubback, E. M. 1945. *Population Facts and Policies*.

Hunt, E. H. 1967. Labour productivity in English agriculture, 1850–1914. *Econ. Hist. Rev. 2nd Ser.*, **20**, 280–92.

1970. Quantitative and other evidence on labour productivity in agriculture, 1850–1914. *Econ. Hist. Rev. 2nd Ser.*, **23**, 515–19.

1973. *Regional Wage Variations in Britain 1850–1914*. Oxford.

Imlah, J. A. H. 1958. *Economic Elements in the Pax Britannica: Studies in British Foreign Trade in the Nineteenth Century*. Cambridge, Mass.

International Labour Organisation. 1942. *Approaches to Social Security. An International survey*. International Labour Office: Studies & Reports Series M, No. 18. Social Insurance. Geneva.

Irving, R. J. 1976. *The North Eastern Railway Company, 1870–1914*. Leicester.

Jefferys, J. B. 1950. *The Distribution of Consumer Goods. A factual study of methods & costs in the U.K. in 1938*. Cambridge.

1954. *Retail Trading in Britain 1850–1950*. National Institute for Economic and Social Research. Economic and Social Studies 13. Cambridge.

Jefferys, J. B. & Walters, D. 1955. National income and expenditure of the United Kingdom 1870–1952. In *Income and Wealth*, Series 5, ed. S. Kuznets, pp. 1–40. International Association for Research in Income and Wealth.

Jevons, H. S. 1915. *The British Coal Trade*.

Johnson, P. B. 1968. *Land Fit for Heroes: The Planning of British Reconstruction, 1916–19*. Chicago.

Jones, D. T. 1976. Output, employment and labour productivity in Europe since 1955. *National Institute Economic Review*, **77**, 72–85.

Jones, E. L. 1964. The agricultural labour market in England, 1793–1872. *Econ. Hist. Rev. 2nd Ser.*, **17**, 322–38.

Jones, G. T. 1933. *Increasing Return*. Cambridge.

Jones, K. 1920. *Fleet Street and Downing Street*.

Joyce, P. 1975. The factory politics of Lancashire in the later nineteenth century. *Historical Journal*, **18**, 525–53.

Kahn, A. E. 1946. *Great Britain in The World Economy*. New York.

Kahn, R. 1931. The relation of home investment to unemployment. *Economic Journal*, **41**, 173–98.

1976. Unemployment as seen by the Keynesians. In *The Concept and Measurement of Involuntary Unemployment*, ed. G. D. N. Worswick, pp. 19–34.

Kaldor, N. 1944. The quantitative aspects of the full employment problem in Britain. In *Full Employment in a Free Society*, ed. W. H. Beveridge, Appendix C.

1966. *Causes of the Slow Rate of Economic growth of the United Kingdom: an inaugural lecture*. Cambridge.

Kellett, J. R. 1969. *The Impact of Railways on Victorian Cities.*

Kelley, A. C. & Williamson, J. G. 1974. *Lessons from Japanese Development.* Chicago.

Kendrick J. W. 1961. *Productivity Trends in the United States.* Princeton.

Kennedy, W. P. 1974. Foreign investment, trade, and growth in the United Kingdom, 1870–1913. *Explorations in Economic History*, **11**, 415–43.

    1975. Institutional Response to Economic Growth: Capital Markets in Britain to 1914. Unpublished manuscript.

Kerr, C., Dunlop, J. T., Harbison, F. H. & Myers, C. A. 1960. *Industrialism and Industrial Man.* Cambridge, Mass.

Key Statistics. 1965. *The British Economy. Key Statistics 1900–64.* London School of Economics and Political Science. London and Cambridge Economic Service.

Keynes, J. M. 1919. *The Economic Consequences of the Peace.*

    1923. *A Tract on Monetary Reform. The Collected Writings of John Maynard Keynes*, Vol. 4. 1971.

    1924. Foreign investment and the national advantage. *The Nation and the Athenaeum*, **35**, 584–7.

    1925. *The Economic Consequences of Mr Churchill.*

    1930. *A Treatise on Money. The Collected Writings of John Maynard Keynes*, Vols. 5 and 6. 1971.

    1933. The means to prosperity. Reprinted in *The Collected Writings of John Maynard Keynes*, vol. 9. *Essays in Persuasion*, ed. D. E. Moggridge, pp. 335–66. 1971.

    1936. *The General Theory of Employment, Interest and Money.*

    1937. How to avoid a slump. *The Times*, 12–14 January.

    1940. *How to Pay for the War: A Radical Plan for the Chancellor of the Exchequer.*

Keynes, M. ed. 1975. *Essays on John Maynard Keynes.* Cambridge.

Kincaid, J. C. 1973. *Poverty and Equality in Britain: a study of social security & taxation.* Harmondsworth.

Kindleberger, C. P. 1961. Foreign trade and economic growth: lessons from Britain and France, 1850–1913. *Econ. Hist. Rev. 2nd Ser.*, **14**, 289–305.

    1964. *Economic Growth in France and Britain.* Cambridge, Mass.

    1973. *The World in Depression 1929–39.*

Kirby, M. W. 1973a. The control of competition in the British coal mining industry in the thirties. *Econ. Hist. Rev. 2nd Ser.*, **26**, 273–84.

    1973b. Government intervention in industrial organization: coal mining in the nineteen thirties. *Business History*, **15**, 160–73.

    1974. The Lancashire cotton industry in the interwar years: A study in organisational change. *Business History*, **16**, 145–59.

Kitson Clark, G. 1951. The repeal of the corn laws and the politics of the forties. *Econ. Hist. Rev. 2nd Ser.*, **4**, 1–13.

Klapper, C. F. 1961. *The Golden Age of Tramways.*

Knodel, J. E. 1974. *The Decline of Fertility in Germany 1871–1939.* Princeton.

Knowles, K. G. J. C. & Robertson, D. J. 1951. Differences between the wages of skilled and unskilled workers 1880–1950. *Bulletin of the Oxford University Institute of Statistics*, **13**, 109–27.

Kravis, I. B. 1970. Trade as a handmaiden of growth, similarities between the nineteenth and twentieth centuries. *Economic Journal*, **80**, 850–72.

    1973. A reply to Mr Craft's note. *Economic Journal*, **83**, 885–9.

Kuznets, S. 1961. Quantitative aspects of the economic growth of nations VI. Long-term trends in capital formation proportions. *Economic Development and Cultural Change*, Vol. IX, Part 4, Part II, 3–124.

1962. Quantitative aspects of the economic growth of nations VII. The share and structure of consumption. *Economic Development and Cultural Change*, vol. X, Part 2, Part II.

Lampard, E. 1973. The urbanising world. In *The Victorian City: images and realities*, eds. H. J. Dyos & M. Wolff, vol. 1, pp. 3–57.

Landes, D. 1969. *The Unbound Prometheus*. Cambridge.

Langer, W. L. 1935. *The Diplomacy of Imperialism, 1890–1902*. New York.

Laski, H. J. 1938. *Parliamentary Government in England; a commentary*.

Laski, M. 1964. Domestic life. In *Edwardian England, 1901–14*, ed. S. Nowell-Smith, pp. 139–212.

Laver, J. 1955. Introduction. In *The Age of Extravagance*, eds. M. E. Edes & D. Fraser, pp. 1–9,

Lawrence, F. W. 1899. *Local Variations in Wages*. Studies in Economics and Political Science No. 6.

Lawton, D. 1968. *Social Class, Language and Education*.

Leak, H. & Maizels, A. 1945. The structure of British industry. *Journal of the Royal Statistical Society*, **108**, 142–99.

Ledbetter, R. 1976. *A History of the Malthusian League*. Columbus, Ohio.

Leijonhufvud, A. 1968. *On Keynesian Economics and the Economics of Keynes: a study in monetary theory*.

Lenin, V. I. 1915. *Imperialism, The Highest Stage of Capitalism*. Moscow, 1947.

Levine, A. 1967. *Industrial Retardation in Britain, 1880–1914*. New York.

Lewis, R. & Maude, A. 1949. *The English Middle Classes*.

Lewis, W. A. 1949. *Economic Survey 1919–39*.

   1978. *Growth and Fluctuations, 1870–1913*.

Lewis, W. ed. 1968. *Budget Concepts for Economic Analysis*. Washington.

Lindert, P. H. 1969. *Key Currencies and Gold 1900–13*. Princeton.

Lindert, P. & Trace, K. 1971a. Discussion. In *Essays on a Mature Economy*, ed. D. McCloskey, pp. 280–2. Princeton.

   1971b. Yardsticks for Victorian entrepreneurs. In *Essays on a Mature Economy*, ed. D. McCloskey, pp. 239–74. Princeton.

Lipman, V. D. 1954. *Social History of the Jews in England 1850–1950*.

Llewelyn Davies, M. ed. 1977. *Life as we have known it: by co-operative working women.*

Llewellyn Smith, H. *et al.* 1930–5. *The New Survey of London Life and Labour*.

Lloyd George, D. 1929. *We can conquer unemployment*. The Liberal Party.

Lockwood, D. 1958. *The Blackcoated Worker*.

   1962. Social mobility. In *Society*, eds. A. T. Welford, M. Argyle, D. V. Glass & J. N. Morris, pp. 515–26.

   1966. Sources of variation in working class images of society. *Sociological Review N.S.*, **14**, 249–67.

Logan, W. P. D. 1950. Mortality in England and Wales from 1848 to 1947. *Population Studies*, **4**, 132–78.

Longmate, N. R. 1971. *How We Lived Then: A history of everyday life during the Second World War*.

   1974. *The Workhouse*.

Louis, W. R. ed. 1976. *Imperialism: The Robinson and Gallagher Controversy.* New York.

Lovell, J. 1977. *British Trade Unions 1875–1933.*

Lowe, R. 1978. The erosion of state intervention in England 1917–24. *Econ. Hist. Rev. 2nd Ser.*, **31**, 270–86.

Lowndes, G. A. N. 1937. *The Silent Social Revolution.* Cambridge, 1969.

Lucas, A. F. 1937. *Industrial Reconstruction and The Control of Competition.*

Lydall, H. F. 1959. The long-term trend in the size distribution of income. *Journal of the Royal Statistical Society Series A*, **122**, 1–37.

Lytle, R. 1968. The introduction of diesel power in the United States, 1897–1912. *Business History Review*, **42**, 115–48.

McClelland, P. D. 1975. *Causal Explanation and Model Building in History, Economics and the New Economic History.* Ithaca.

McCloskey, D. N. 1970. Did Victorian Britain fail? *Econ. Hist. Rev. 2nd Ser.*, **23**, 446–59.

1970–71. Britain's loss from foreign industrialization: a provisional estimate. *Explorations in Economic History*, **8**, 141–52.

1971a. International differences in productivity? In *Essays on a Mature Economy*, ed. D. McCloskey, pp. 285–304. Princeton.

ed. 1971b. *Essays on a Mature Economy: Britain After 1840.* Princeton.

1973. *Economic Maturity and Entrepreneurial Decline: British Iron and Steel, 1870–1913.* Cambridge. Mass.

1974. Victorian growth: A rejoinder. *Econ. Hist. Rev. 2nd Ser.*, **27**, 275–7.

1979. Magnanimous Albion: free trade and British national income, 1841–81. Forthcoming in Caves, North & Price, eds. 1979.

McCloskey, D. N. & Sandberg, L. 1971. From damnation to redemption: judgements on the late Victorian entrepreneur. *Explorations in Economic History*, **9**, 89–108

McCloskey, D. N. & Zecher, J. R. 1976. How the gold standard worked 1880–1913. In *The Monetary Approach to the Balance of Payments*, eds. J. A. Frenkel & H. G. Johnson, pp. 357–85.

McConnell, P. 1906. *The Diary of a Working Farmer.*

McCrone, G. 1969. *Regional Policy in Britain.*

McCurrach, D. F. 1948. Britain's U.S. Dollar Problems, 1934–45. *Economic Journal*, **58**, 356–72.

McDonagh, M. 1935. *In London during the Great War. The diary of a journalist.* Entry for 29 March 1917.

MacDonald, W. 1872. On the agriculture of Inverness-shire. *Transactions of the Royal Highland and Agricultural Society of Scotland*, 4th series, **4**, 1–65.

McGregor, O. R. 1957. *Divorce in England.*

Mackenzie, W. A. 1921. Changes in the standard of living in the United Kingdom, 1860–1914. *Economica*, **1**, 211–30.

McKeown, T. 1976. *The Modern Rise of Population.*

McLean, D. 1976. Finance and 'informal empire' before the first world war. *Econ. Hist. Rev. 2nd Ser.*, **29**, 291–305.

Maddison, A. 1964. *Economic Growth in the West.* New York.

Maizels, A. 1963. *Industrial Growth and World Trade.* Cambridge. And his 'Corrections' 1969.

Makower, H., Marschak, J. & Robinson, H. W. 1939. Studies in mobility of labour: analysis for Great Britain, Part I. *Oxford Economic Papers.* **2**, 70–97.

Malinvaud, E. 1977. *The Theory of Unemployment Reconsidered.* Oxford.

Mander, R. & Mitchenson, J. 1978. *Victorian and Edwardian Entertainment from Old Photographs.*

Mann, P. H. 1905. Life in an agricultural village in England. *Sociological Papers 1904,* 161–93.

Mannheim. H. 1950: *Social Aspects of Crime in England between the Wars.*

Manton, J. 1976. *Mary Carpenter.*

Manvell, R. 1966. *This Age of Communication: press, books, films, radio, T.V.*

Marquand, D. 1977. *Ramsay MacDonald.*

Marsh, D. C. 1958. *The Changing Social Structure of England and Wales, 1871–1961.*

Marshall, T. H. 1950. *Citizenship and Social Class, and other essays.* Cambridge.

1965. *Social Policy.*

Martin, E. W. 1958. *Where London Ends.*

Marwick, A. 1964. Middle opinion in the thirties: planning, progress and political 'agreement'. *English Historical Review,* **79,** 285–98.

1965. *The Deluge. British Society & the First World War.*

1968a. *Britain in the Century of Total War... War, peace & social change, 1900–67.*

1968b. The impact of the First World War on British society. *Journal of Contemporary History,* **3,** 51–63

Masterman, C. F. G. 1909. *The Condition of England.* 1911 edn.

1922. *England after War. A Study.*

Mathias, P. 1967. *Retailing Revolution.*

1969. *The First Industrial Nation: An Economic History of Britain, 1700–1914.*

Matthews, R. C. O. 1954a. *A Study in Trade-Cycle History: Economic Fluctuations in Great Britain, 1833–1842.* Cambridge.

1954b. The trade cycle in Britain, 1790-1850. *Oxford Economic Papers,* **6,** 1–32.

1959. *The Trade Cycle.* Cambridge.

1968. Why has Britain had full employment since the War? *Economic Journal,* **78,** 555–69.

Maxcy, G. & Silberston, A. 1959. *The Motor Industry.*

Meade, J. E. & Stone, J. R. N. 1944. *National Income and Expenditure.*

Meier, G. M. & Baldwin, R. E. 1957. *Economic Development: Theory, History, Policy.* New York.

Mencher, S. 1967. The problem of measuring poverty. *British Journal of Sociology,* **18,** 1–12.

Metcalf, D. & Richardson, R. 1976. Unemployment in London. In *The Concept and Measurement of Involuntary Unemployment,* ed. G. D. N. Worswick, pp. 203–20.

Meyer, J. R. 1955. An output–input approach to evaluating British industrial production in the late nineteenth century. *Explorations in Entrepreneurial History,* **8.** Also in *The Economics of Slavery and other Studies in Econometric History,* eds. A. H. Conrad & J. R. Meyer, pp. 183–220. Chicago.

Milward, A. S. 1970. *The Economic Effects of the two World Wars on Britain.*

Minihan, J. 1977. *The Nationalization of Culture: the development of state subsidies to the arts in Great Britain.*

Mitchell, B. R. 1976. *European Historical Statistics 1750–1970.* New York.

Mitchell, B. R. & Deane, P. 1962. *Abstract of British Historical Statistics.* Cambridge.

Mitchell, B. R. & Jones, H. G. 1971. *Second Abstract of British Historical Statistics.* Cambridge.

Moggridge, D. E. 1969. *The Return to Gold, 1925: the Formulation of Economic Policy and its Critics.* Cambridge.

1971. British controls on long term capital movements, 1924–31. In *Essays on a mature economy: Britain after 1840*, ed. D. N. McCloskey, pp. 113–42.

1972. *British Monetary Policy 1924–31*. Cambridge.

Money, L. G. C. 1906. *Riches and Poverty*.

Moore, B. C. & Rhodes, J. 1973. Evaluating the effects of British regional economic policy. *Economic Journal*, **83**, 87–110.

1974. Regional policy and the Scottish economy. *Scottish Journal of Political Economy*, **21**, 215–35.

Moore, R. 1974. *Pitmen, Preachers and Politics*.

Morgan, D. H. 1975. The place of harvesters in nineteenth-century village life. In *Village Life and Labour*, ed. R. Samuel, pp. 27–72.

Morgan, D. R. 1975. *Suffragists & Liberals: the Politics of Woman Suffrage in England*. Oxford.

Morgan, P. 1977. From a death to a view: the hunt for the Welsh past in the romantic era. Unpublished paper, Past and Present Conference. Mimeo.

Morgenstern, O. 1959. *International Financial Transactions and Business Cycles*. Princeton.

Morris, A. J. A. ed. 1974. *Edwardian Radicalism, 1900–14*.

Morris, J. H. & Williams, L. S. 1958. *The South Wales Coal Industry 1841–75*. Cardiff.

Morris, M. D. 1963. Towards a reinterpretation of nineteenth century Indian economic history. *Journal of Economic History*, **23**, 606–18.

Morris, S. 1973. Stalled professionalism: The recruitment of railway officials in the United States, 1887–1940. *Business History Review*, **47**, 317–34.

Moser, C. A. 1958. *Survey Methods in Social Investigation*.

Moser, C. A. & Scott, W. 1961. *British Towns. A Statistical Study of their Social and Economic Differences*.

Moulton, H. G. & Pasvolsky, L. 1926. *World War Debt Settlements*. New York.

Mukerjee, T. 1972. Theory of economic drain: impact of British rule on the Indian economy, 1840–1900. In *Economic Imperialism*, eds. K. E. Boulding & T. Mukerjee, pp. 195–212. Ann Arbor.

Musson, A. E. 1972. *British Trade Unions 1800–75*.

1974. *Trade Union & Social History*.

Myrdal, A. & Klein, V. 1956. *Women's Two Roles, home and work*.

Nabseth, L. & Ray, G. F. eds. 1974. *The Diffusion of New Industrial Processes*.

Nash, E. F. 1951. Wartime control of food and agricultural prices. In Chester 1951, 200–38.

Nathan, A. J. 1972. Imperialism's effects on China. *Bulletin of Concerned Asian Scholars*, **4**, 3–8.

National Economic Development Office. 1975. *Finance for Investment*.

1976. *Cyclical Fluctuations in the United Kingdom Economy*. Discussion Paper No. 3.

Nerlove, M. 1958. *The Dynamics of Supply: Estimation of Farmers' Response to Price*. Baltimore.

Nevin, E. T. 1955. *The Mechanism of Cheap Money: A Study of British Monetary Policy 1931–39*. Cardiff.

Nowell-Smith, S. ed. 1964. *Edwardian England, 1901–14*.

O'Brien, P. & Keyder, C. 1978. *Economic Growth in Britain and France, 1780–1914: Two Paths to the Twentieth Century*.

Ó Gráda, C. 1979. The landlord and agricultural transformation, 1870–1900: a comment on Richard Perren's hypothesis. *Agricultural History Review*, **27**, 40–2.

Oddy, D. J. 1970. Working-class diets in late nineteenth-century Britain. *Econ. Hist. Rev. 2nd Ser.*, **23**, 314–23.

Ojala, E. M. 1952. *Agriculture and Economic Progress*. Oxford.

Olson, M. 1963. *The Economics of the Wartime Shortage. A History of British food supplies in the Napoleonic Wars and in World Wars I and II*. Durham, N.C.

  1974. The United Kingdom and the world market in wheat and other primary products, 1870–1914. *Explorations in Economic History*, **11**, 325–55.

Olson, M. & Harris, C. C. 1959. Free trade in 'corn': a statistical study of the prices and production of wheat in Great Britain from 1873 to 1914. *Quarterly Journal of Economics*, **73**, 145–68.

Oren, L. 1974. The welfare of women in laboring families: England 1860–1950. In *Clio's Consciousness raised; new perspectives on the history of women*, eds. M. Hartman & L. Banner, pp. 226–44. New York.

Orwell, G. 1937. *The Road to Wigan Pier*.

Orwin, C. S. & Whetham, E. H. 1964. *History of British Agriculture 1846–1914*.

Osborn, F. J. 1942. *New Towns after the War*.

  1969. *Green Belt Cities*.

  1970. *Genesis of Welwyn Garden City: Some Jubilee Memories*. Town and Country Planning Association.

Overy, R. J. 1975. Cars, roads and economic recovery in Germany, 1932–38. *Econ. Hist. Rev. 2nd Ser.*, **28**, 466–83.

Palgrave, R. H. 1903. *Bank Rate and the Money Market*.

Pankhurst, E. 1914. *My Own Story*.

Park, R. E. 1952. *Human Communities: the city and human ecology*. Glencoe, Illinois.

Parker, W. N. 1971. From old to new to old in economic history. *Journal of Economic History*, **31**, 3–14.

Parliamentary Papers 1840, V, 99. Paper 601. *Select Committee on Import Duties*. Report: Evidence.

  1861. L, 583. Paper 14. *Return of the Earnings of Agricultural Labourers*.

  1882. XV, 1. C.3375. *Royal Commission on Agriculture. Report by Mr Little: Appendix E.*

  1893–94. XXXVI, 1. C.6894–xiv. *Royal Commission on Labour. The Agricultural Labourer.*

  1894. XCIII, 105. C.7316. *Board of Agriculture (Produce Statistics)*.

  1895. XVI, 311. C.7755. *Royal Commission on Agriculture. Report by Mr Wilson Fox.*

  1897. XV, 1. C.8540. *Royal Commission on Agriculture: Final Report.*

  1898. XLV, 465. C.8911. *Minutes of evidence of the Departmental Committee on old age pensions.*

  1903. LXVII, 253. Cd. 1761. *Memoranda, Statistical Tables, and Charts Prepared in the Board of Trade with Reference to Various Matters Bearing on British and Foreign Trade and Industrial Conditions.*

  1904. LXXXIV, 1. Cd. 2337. *2nd Series of Memoranda, Statistical Tables, and Charts, Prepared in the Board of Trade with Reference to Various Matters Bearing on British and Foreign Trade and Industrial Conditions.*

  1914–16. LXXVI, 1. Cd. 7636. *Statistical Abstract of the United Kingdom for 1914.*

  1917–18. XV, 83. Cd. 8668. *Commission of Enquiry into Industrial Unrest.*

436

1918. VII., 825. Cd. 8980. *Report of the Committee Appointed to Inquire into and Report upon (i) the Actual Increase since June 1914. in the Cost of Living to the Working Classes and (ii) any Counterbalancing Factors (Apart from Increase of Wages) which may have Arisen under War Conditions.*

1930–31. XIII, 219. Cmd. 3897. *Committee on Finance and Industry ('Macmillan Report').*

1933–34. XIII, 313. Cmd. 4728. *Reports of Investigations into the Industrial Conditions in Certain Depressed Areas.*

1939–40. IV, 263. Cmd. 6153. *Report of the Royal Commission on the Distribution of the Industrial Population.*

1942–43 VI, 119. Cmd. 6404. *Social Insurance and Allied Services.*

1948–49. XIX, 635. Cmd. 7695. *Royal Commission on Population.*

1950–51. XXI, 849. Cmd. 8354. *Reserves and Liabilities 1931 to 1945.*

Pasdermadjian, H. 1954. *The Department Store; its origins, evolution and economics.*

Passfield, Lord & Webb, B. 1897. *Industrial Democracy.* 1920.

1929. *English Poor Law History.* Part II. Vol. 2.

Paterson, A. 1976. The poor law in nineteenth-century Scotland. In *The New Poor Law in the nineteenth century,* ed. D. Fraser, pp. 171–93.

Patinkin, D. 1951. *Money. Interest and Prices.* 2nd edition. New York.

1976. *Keynes' Monetary Thought: A Study of its Development.* Durham N.C.

Payne, P. L. 1968. Iron and steel manufactures. In *The Development of British Industry and Foreign Competition, 1875–1914,* ed. D. H. Aldcroft, pp. 71–99.

Peacock, A. T. & Wiseman, J. 1961. *The Growth of Public Expenditure in the United Kingdom.* Princeton and NBER.

Pearce, I. F. 1970. *International Trade.*

Pearce, I. F. & Rowan, D. C. 1966. A framework for research into the real effects of international capital movements. In *International Investment: Selected Readings,* ed. J. H. Dunning, pp. 163–97. Harmondsworth, 1972.

Pelling, H. M. 1963. *A History of British Trade Unionism.*

1968. *Popular Politics and Society in late-Victorian Britain.*

Percy, Lord, 1958. *Some Memories.*

Perkin, H. 1976. *The Age of the Automobile.*

Perren, R. 1970. The landlord and agricultural transformation 1870–1900. *Agricultural History Review,* **18**, 36–51.

1978.*The Meat Trade in Britain, 1840–1914.*

Perry, P. J. 1974. *British Farming in the Great Depression 1870–1914.* Newton Abbot.

Pesaran, M. H. 1974. On the general problem of model selection. *Review of Economic Studies,* **41**, 153–71.

Pesmazoglu, J. S. 1948–49. Some international aspects of British cyclical fluctuations, 1870–1913. *Review of Economic Studies,* **16**, 117–43.

1951. A note on the cyclical fluctuations of British home investment, 1870–1913. *Oxford Economic Papers,* **3**, 61.

Pethick-Lawrence, F. W. 1899. *Local Variations in Wages.*

Phelps, E. S. 1972. *Inflation Policy and Unemployment Theory.*

Phelps, E. S. et al. 1970. *Microeconomic Foundations of Employment and Inflation Theory.* New York.

Phelps Brown, E. H. 1959. *The Growth of British Industrial Relations.*

Phelps Brown, E. H. & Browne, M. H. 1968. *A Century of Pay.*

Phillips, A. W. 1958. The relation between unemployment and the rate of change of money wage rates in the United Kingdom, 1861–1957. *Economica N.S.*, **25**, 283–99.
Pigou, A. C. 1913. A minimum wage for agriculture. In *Essays in Applied Economics*, ed. A. C. Pigou, pp. 41–58. 1923.
    1914. *Unemployment*.
    1927. *Industrial Fluctuations*.
    1947. *Aspects of British Economic History 1918–25*.
Pigou, A. C. & Clark, C. 1936. The economic position of Great Britain (1935). *Memorandum No. 60. Royal Economic Society*, 1–43.
Pilgrim Trust. 1938. *Men Without Work*. A report made to the Pilgrim Trust. Cambridge.
Pimlott, J. A. R. 1947. *The Englishman's Holiday, a Social History*.
Pinchbeck, I. & Hewitt, M. 1973. *Children in English Society*. Vol. 2.
Platt, D. C. M. 1973. The national economy and British imperial expansion before 1914. *Journal of Imperial and Commonwealth History*, **2**, 3–14.
Plowden, W. 1971. *The Motor-Car and Politics, 1896–1970*.
Plummer, A. 1937. *New British Industries in the Twentieth Century*.
Political and Economic Planning. 1952. *The British Film Industry*.
Pollard, S. 1962. *The Development of the British Economy 1914–50*.
    1965. Trade unions and the labour market, 1870–1914. *Yorkshire Bulletin of Economic and Social Research*, **17**, 98–112.
Pollard, S. & Crossley, D. W. 1968. *The Wealth of Britain*.
Pollins, H. 1957–58. Railway contractors and the finance of railway development in Britain. *Journal of Transport History*, **3**, 41–51 & 103–10.
Porter, J. H. 1970. Wage bargaining under conciliation agreements, 1860–1914. *Econ. Hist. Rev. 2nd Ser.*, **23**, 460–75.
Postan, M. M. 1935. Recent trends in the accumulation of capital. *Econ. Hist. Rev. 2nd Ser.*, **6**, 1–12.
Pound, R. & Harmsworth, A. G. A. 1959. *Northcliffe*.
Powell, M. 1968. *Below Stairs*.
Prais, S. J. 1976. *The Evolution of Giant Firms in Britain: A Study of Concentration in Manufacturing Industry in Britain, 1909–70*. Cambridge.
Pratten, C. F. 1976. *Labour Productivity Differentials within International Companies.* Cambridge.
Prest, A. R. assisted by Adams, A. A. 1954. *Consumers' Expenditure in the United Kingdom, 1900–19*. Cambridge.
Priestley, J. B. 1934. *English Journey*.
Purdom, C. B. 1925. *The Building of Satellite Towns*.

Radzinowicz, L. 1966. *Ideology and Crime*.
Rathbone, E. F. 1924. *The Disinherited Family*.
Ravenstein, E. G. 1885. The laws of migration. *Journal of the Royal Statistical Society*, **48**, Part II, 167–227.
Read, D. 1964. *The English Provinces, c. 1760–1960. A study in influence*.
    1972. *Edwardian England, 1901–15: Society and Politics*.
Reader, W. 1966. *Professional Men*.
    1970, 1975. *Imperial Chemical Industries: A History*, 2 vols.
Records and Statistics. 1953. *The Economist*, **13**, No. 328, p. 438.
Reddaway, W. B. 1938. *The Economics of a Declining Population*.

Rees, G. 1966. *St Michael: A History of Marks and Spencer.*

Reid, F. 1971. Keir Hardie's conversion to socialism. In *Essays in Labour History 1886–1923*, ed. A. Briggs & J. Saville, pp. 17–46.

Rex, J. A. 1961. *Key Problems of Sociological Theory.*

Rhee, H. A. 1949. *The Rent of Agricultural Land in England and Wales, 1870–1946.* Oxford.

Richards, E. 1974. Women in the British economy since about 1700: an interpretation. *History*, **59**, 337–57.

Richards, J. M. 1946. *The Castles on the Ground.*

Richardson, H. W. 1962. The basis of economic recovery in the nineteen-thirties: a review and a new interpretation. *Econ. Hist. Rev. 2nd Ser.*, **15**, 344–63.

1965, Overcommitment in Britain before 1930. *Oxford Economic Papers N.S.*, *17*, 237–62.

1967. *Economic Recovery in Britain, 1932–9.*

1968. Chemicals. In *The Development of British Industry and Foreign Competition 1875–1914*, ed. D. H. Aldcroft, pp. 274–306.

1972. British emigration and overseas investment, 1870–1914. *Econ. Hist. Rev. 2nd Ser.*, **25**, 99–113.

Richardson, K. 1977. *The British Motor Industry, 1896–1939.*

Roberts, E. 1977. Working-class standards of living in Barrow and Lancaster, 1890–1914. *Econ. Hist. Rev. 2nd Ser.*, **30**, 306–21.

Roberts, R. 1971. *The Classic Slum; Salford life in the first quarter of the century.* Manchester.

Robertson, D. H. 1915. *A Study of Industrial Fluctuation.*

1926. *Banking Policy and the Price Level.*

1928. *Money.*

1938. The Future of International Trade. *Economic Journal*, **48**, 1–14. Reprinted in American Economic Association, *Readings in the Theory of International Trade*, Homewood, Illinois, 1950, to which reference is made.

Robinson, E. A. G. 1951. The overall allocation of resources. In *Lessons of the British War Economy*, ed. D. N. Chester, pp. 34–57. Cambridge.

Robinson, J. 1956. *The Accumulation of Capital.*

Roderick, G. W. & Stephens, M. D. 1972. *Scientific and Technical Education in Nineteenth-Century England.* Newton Abbot.

Rose, M. E. 1971. *The English Poor Law, 1780–1930.* Newton Abbot.

1972. *The Relief of Poverty 1834–1914.*

Rosen, A. 1974. *Rise up Women.*

Rosenberg, N. 1972. *Technology and American Economic Growth.* New York.

1976. *Perspectives on Technology.* Cambridge.

Rostas, L. 1943. Industrial production, productivity and distribution in Britain, Germany and the United States, 1935–7. *Economic Journal*, **53**, 39–54.

1948. *Comparative Productivity in British and American Industry.* Cambridge.

Rostow, W. W. 1948. *British Economy of the Nineteenth Century; essays.* Oxford.

Rotha, P. 1960. *The Film Till Now.*

Rousiers, P. de. 1896. *The Labour Question.*

Routh, G. 1965. *Occupation and pay in Great Britain 1906–60.* Cambridge.

Rowe, J. W. F. 1923. *Wages in the Coal Industry.*

1928. *Wages in Practice and Theory.*

Rowntree, B. S. 1901. *Poverty. A Study of Town Life.*
    1922. *Poverty: A Study of Town Life.* (1st edition: 1901.)
    1941. *Poverty and Progress: A Second Social Survey of York.*
Rowntree, B. S. & Kendall, M. 1913. *How the Labourer Lives.*
Rubinstein, W. D. 1974. Men of property: some aspects of occupation, inheritance & power among top British wealthholders. In *Elites & Power in British Society*, ed. P. Stanworth & A. Giddens, pp. 144–69.
    1977a. Wealth, elites & the class structure of Modern Britain. *Past and Present*, **76**, 99–126.
    1977b, The Victorian middle classes: wealth, occupation and geography. *Econ. Hist. Rev. 2nd Ser.*, **30**, 602–23.
Runciman, W. G. 1966. *Relative Deprivation and Social Justice.*
Russell, A. K. 1973. *Liberal Landslide.* Newton Abbot.
Ryan, P. A. 1978. 'Poplarism' 1894–1930. In *The Origins of British Social Policy*, ed. P. Thane, pp. 56–83.

Salter, W. E. G. 1966. *Productivity and Technical Change.* Cambridge.
Samuel, R. ed. 1975. *Village Life and Labour.*
    ed. 1977. *Miners, Quarrymen and Saltworkers.*
Sandberg, L. 1974. *Lancashire in Decline.* Columbus, Ohio.
Sanderson, M. 1972. *The Universities & British Industry, 1850–1970.*
Saul, S. B. 1960. *Studies in British Overseas Trade, 1870–1914.* Liverpool.
    1962. House building in England, 1890–1914. *Econ. Hist. Rev. 2nd Ser.*, **15**, 119–37.
    1965. The export economy 1870–1914. *Yorkshire Bulletin of Economic and Social Research*, **17**, 5–18.
    1968. The engineering industry. In *The Development of British Industry and Foreign Competition 1875–1914*, ed. D. H. Aldcroft, pp. 186–237.
    1969. *The Myth of the Great Depression, 1873–96.*
Saville, J. 1957. *Rural Depopulation in England and Wales 1851–1951.*
    1974. Trade unions & free labour: The background to the Taff Vale decision. In *Essays in Social History*, ed. M. W. Flinn & T. C. Smout, pp. 251–76. Oxford.
Sayers, R. S. 1936. *Bank of England Operations 1890–1914.*
    1950. The springs of technical progress in Britain, 1919–39. *Economic Journal*, **60**, 275–91.
    1956. *Financial Policy 1939–45.*
    1958, *Modern Banking.* 4th edition. Oxford.
    1960. The return to gold, 1925. In *Studies in the Industrial Revolution*, ed. L. S. Pressnell, pp. 313–27. Also in *The Gold Standard and Employment Policies between the Wars*, ed. S. Pollard, pp. 85–98. 1970.
    1967. *A History of Economic Change in England 1880–1939.*
    1976. *The Bank of England 1891–1944.* Cambridge.
Schlöte, W. 1952. trans. W. O. Henderson & W. H. Chaloner. *British Overseas Trade from 1700 to the 1930s.* Oxford.
Schultz, T. W. 1964. *Transforming Traditional Agriculture.* New Haven.
Schuyler, R. L. 1945. *The Fall of the Old Colonial System.*
Scott-James, R. A. 1913. *The Influence of the Press.*
Searle, G. R. 1971. *The Quest for National Efficiency.* Oxford.

440

Shackle, G. L. S. 1973. *An Economic Querist.*
Shapiro, E. 1976. Cyclical fluctuations in prices and output in the United Kingdom, 1921–71. *Economic Journal*, **86**, 746–58.
Sharlin, H. I. 1963. *The Making of the Electrical Age.*
Shaw, G. B. 1930. *The Apple Cart.*
Sheppard, D. K. 1971. *The Growth and Role of U.K. Financial Institutions, 1880–1962.*
Sherrington, C. E. R. 1934. *A Hundred Years of Inland Transport, 1830–1933.*
Shils, E. 1962. The Theory of Mass Society. *Diogenes*, **39**, 45–66.
Shorter, E. & Tilly, C. 1974. *Strikes in France, 1863–1968.*
Simey, T. S. & M. B. 1960. *Charles Booth, Social Scientist.*
Simmons, J. 1962. *Transport: A Visual History of Modern Britain.*
Simon, B. 1974. *The Politics of Educational Reform, 1920–40.*
Simon. M. 1967. The pattern of new British portfolio foreign investment, 1865–1914. In *Capital Movements and Economic Development*, ed. J. H. Adler, pp. 33–70. Also in *The Export of Capital from Britain, 1870–1914*, ed. A. R. Hall, pp. 15–44, 1968.
Singer, H. W. 1940. *Unemployment and the Unemployed.*
Sissons, M. & French, P. eds. 1964. *Age of Austerity, 1945–51.* Harmondsworth.
Skidelsky, R. 1967. *Politicians and the Slump: the Labour Government of 1929–1931.* Reprinted Harmondsworth, 1970.
Slight, J. & Scott Burn, R. 1858. *The Book of Farm Implements & Machines.*
Smailes, A. E. 1953. *The Geography of Towns.*
Smiles, S. 1859. *Self-Help.*
Smith, A. 1776. *The Wealth of Nations.* New York, 1937.
Smith, S. 1820. Article in *The Edinburgh Review*, 19 January 1820.
Solow, B. L. 1971. *The Land Question and the Irish Economy 1870–1903.* Cambridge, Mass.
Soltow, L. 1968. Long-run changes in British income inequality. *Econ. Hist. Rev. 2nd Ser.*, **21**, 17–29.
Spearing, J. B. 1860. On the agriculture of Berkshire. *Journal of the Royal Agricultural Society of England*, **21**, 1–46.
Springhall, J. 1972. Boy scouts, class & militarism in relation to British youth movements 1908–30. *International Review of Social History*, **16**, 125–58.
Stedman Jones, G. 1971. *Outcast London.* Oxford.
   1974. Working-class culture and working-class politics in London 1870–1900. *Journal of Social History*, **7**, 460–508.
Stevenson, J. & Cook, C. 1977. *The Slump: society & politics during the depression.*
Stevenson, T. H. C. 1920. The fertility of various social classes in England and Wales from the middle of the nineteenth century to 1911. *Journal of the Royal Statistical Society*, **83**, 401–32.
Stone, I. 1977. British direct and portfolio investment in Latin America before 1914. *Journal of Economic History*, **37**, 690–722.
Stone, J. M. 1971. Financial panics: their implications for the mix of domestic and foreign investments of Great Britain, 1880–1913. *Quarterly Journal of Economics*, **85**, 304–26.
Stone, L. 1969. Literacy and Education in England 1640–1900, *Past and Present*, **42**, 69–139.
Stone, R. 1954. *The Measurement of Consumers' Expenditure and Behaviour in the United Kingdom, 1920–38.* Cambridge.
Stone, R. & W. M. 1938–39. The marginal propensity to consume and the multiplier: a statistical investigation. *Review of Economic Studies*, **6**, 1–24.

Svennilson, I. 1954. *Growth and Stagnation in the European Economy*. United Nations Economic Commission for Europe. Geneva.

Swingewood, A. 1977. *The Myth of Mass Culture*.

Tarn, J. N. 1973. *Five per cent philanthropy*.

Tawney, R. H. 1914. An experiment in democratic education. *Political Quarterly*, May 1914, 62–84.

    1943. The abolition of economic controls, 1918–21. *Econ. Hist. Rev. 2nd Ser.*, **13**, 1–30.

Taylor, A. J. 1961. Labour productivity and technological innovation in the British coal industry, 1850–1914. *Econ. Hist. Rev. 2nd Ser.*, **14**, 48–70.

    1968. The coal industry. In *The Development of British Industry and Foreign Competition 1875–1914*, ed. D. H. Aldcroft, pp. 37–70.

Taylor, A. J. P. 1965. *English History 1914–45*. Oxford.

Taylor, D. 1976. The English dairy industry, 1860–1930. *Econ. Hist. Rev. 2nd Ser.*, **29**, 585–601.

Taylor, P. 1971. *The Distant Magnet*.

Temin, P. 1966. The relative decline of the British steel industry, 1880–1913. In *Industrialization in Two Systems*, ed. H. Rosovsky, pp. 140–55. New York.

    ed. 1973. *The New Economic History*. Harmondsworth.

Thane, P. 1975. The working class and state 'welfare', 1880–1914. *Bulletin of the Society for the Study of Labour History No. 31*, 6–8.

    ed. 1978a. *The Origins of British Social Policy*.

    1978b. Non-contributory versus insurance pensions 1878–1908. In *The Origins of British Social Policy*, ed. P. Thane, pp. 84–106.

Thatcher, A. R. 1976. Statistics of unemployment in the United Kingdom. In *The Concept and Measurement of Involuntary Unemployment*, ed. G. D. N. Worswick, *pp. 83–94*.

Thernstrom, S. 1964. *Poverty & Progress; Social mobility in a nineteenth century city*. Cambridge, Mass.

Thomas, B. 1972. *Migration and Urban Development*.

    1973. *Migration and Economic Growth: a Study of Great Britain and the Atlantic Economy*. Cambridge.

Thomas, F. G. 1939. *The Changing Village. An essay on rural reconstruction*.

Thomas, T. J. 1975. Econometric history and the interwar period: could Lloyd George have done it? Econometric Society Third World Congress, August 1975. Mimeo.

    1976. Aspects of U.K. macroeconomic policy during the interwar period: a study in econometric history. PhD thesis (Cambridge).

Thomas, W. A. 1973. *The Provincial Stock Exchanges*.

Thompson, E. P. 1963. *The making of the English working class*.

    1977. *William Morris*.

Thompson, F. M. L. 1963. *English Landed Society in the Nineteenth Century*.

    1968. The second agricultural revolution 1815–80. *Econ. Hist. Rev. 2nd Ser.*, **21**, 62–77.

    1974. *Hampstead*.

Thompson, P. 1975. *The Edwardians: the remaking of British Society*.

Tilly, C. L. & R. 1975. *The Rebellious Century 1830–1930*. Cambridge, Mass.

Tinbergen, J. 1951. *Business Cycles in the United Kingdom, 1870–1914*. Amsterdam.

Titmuss, R. M. 1943. *Birth Poverty and Wealth. A study of infant mortality*.

    1950. *Problems of Social Policy*.

    1958. *Essays on 'The Welfare State'*.

Touraine, A. 1974. *The Post-Industrial Society*, trans. L. F. X. Mayhew.
Townsend, P. 1962. The Meaning of Poverty. *British Journal of Sociology*, **13**, 210–27.
Treble, J. H. 1978. Unemployment & unemployment policies in Glasgow, 1890–1905. In *The Origins of British Social Policy*, ed. P. Thane, pp. 147–72.
Trevelyan, G. M. 1952. *Illustrated English Social History*.
Tuchman, B. 1966. *The Proud Tower*.
Turner, E. S. 1952. *The Shocking History of Advertising!*
Turner, H. A. 1952. Trade unions, differentials and the levelling of wages. *Manchester School of Economic and Social Studies*, **20**, 227–82.
  1962. *Trade Union Growth, Structure and Policy*.
Turner, R. H. 1961. Modes of social ascent through education: sponsored and contest mobility. In *Education, Economy and Society*, eds. A. H. Halsey, J. Floud & C. A. Anderson. New York.

United Nations. 1953. *The Determinants and Consequences of Population Trends*. United Nations Department of Social Affairs. Population Studies No. 17. New York.

Vaizey, J. E. & Sheehan, J. 1968. *Resources for Education*.
Van Wyk Smith, M. (compiled by) 1978. *Drummer Hodge: The Poetry of the Anglo-Boer War, 1899–1902*. Oxford.
Von Tunzelmann, N. 1977. Britain's 'new industries' between the wars: a new 'development block'? Unpublished paper.

Waites, B. 1976. The effect of the first world war on class and status in England 1910–20. *Journal of Contemporary History*, **2**, 27–48.
Waller, W. ed. 1940. *War in the Twentieth Century*. New York.
Walters, A. A. 1971. *Money in Boom and Slump*.
Walters, R. 1975. Labour productivity in the South Wales steam-coal industry, 1870–1914. *Econ. Hist. Rev. 2nd Ser.*, **28**, 280–303.
Walton, J. 1973. *A Study in the Diffusion of Agricultural Machinery in the Nineteenth Century*. Oxford.
Walvin, J. 1975. *The People's Game: a social history of British football*.
Wan, H. Y. Jr. 1971. *Economic Growth*. New York.
Ware, R. G. 1974. The balance of payments in the inter-war period: further details. *Bank of England Quarterly Bulletin*, **14**, 47–52.
Webb, S. see Passfield, Lord.
Wehler, H. U. 1970. Bismarck's imperialism 1862–90. *Past and Present*, **48**, 119–55.
Wendt, P. F. 1962. *Housing Policy – the search for Solutions*. Berkeley & Los Angeles.
White, A. 1901. *Efficiency and Empire*.
Whitehead, F. 1964. Advertising. In *Discrimination and Popular Culture*, ed. D. Thompson, pp. 23–49. Harmondsworth.
Whybrow, J. & Waterhouse, R. 1976. *How Birmingham Became a Great City*. Birmingham.
Wilkins, M. 1970. *The Emergence of Multinational Enterprise: American Business Abroad from the Colonial Era to 1914*. Cambridge, Mass.
Wilkinson, E. C. 1939. *The Town that was Murdered. The life-story of Jarrow*.
Williams, J. B. 1972. *British Commercial Policy and Trade Expansion, 1750–1850*. Oxford.
Williams, R. 1961. *The Long Revolution*.

1968. *Communications.* Harmondsworth.

1976. *Keywords: A vocabulary of Culture and Society.*

Williamson, J. G. 1964. *American Growth and the Balance of Payments 1820–1913.* Chapel Hill, N.C.

1965. Regional inequality and the process of national development: a description of the patterns. *Economic Development and Cultural Change,* **13**, 3–84.

Willmott, P. & Young, M. 1960. *Family and Class in a London suburb.*

Wilson, B. 1966. *Religion in Secular Society.*

Wilson, G. B. 1940. *Alcohol and the Nation.*

Wilson J. 1864. Reaping machines. *Transactions of the Highland and Agricultural Society of Scotland N.S.,* **19**, 123–49.

Wilson, T. 1966. Instability and the rate of growth. *Lloyd's Bank Review No. 81*, 16–32.

Wilson Fox, A. 1903. Agricultural wages in England and Wales during the last half century. *Journal of the Royal Statistical Society,* **66**, 273–348. Also in *Essays in Agrarian History*, ed. W. A. Minchinton, pp. 121–98, Vol. 2. Newton Abbot, 1968.

Wilson Harris, H. 1946. *J. A. Spender.*

Winch, D. 1969. *Economics and Policy, A Historical Study. 1972.*

Winter, J. M. 1977. The impact of the First World War on civilian health in Britain. *Econ. Hist. Rev. 2nd Ser.,* **30**, 487–503.

Wohl, A. S. 1977. *The Eternal Slum: housing and social policy in Victorian London.*

Wood, G. H. 1903. The course of women's wages during the nineteenth century. In *A History of Factory Legislation*, ed. B. L. Hutchins & A. Harrison, Appendix A.

1909. Real wages and the standard of comfort since 1850. *Journal of the Royal Statistical Society,* **72**, 91–103. Reprinted in *Essays in Economic History*, vol. 3, ed. E. M. Carus Wilson, pp. 132–43. 1962.

Woodruff, W. 1966. *Impact of Western Man.*

Worswick, G. D. N. 1971. Fiscal policy and stabilization in Britain. In *Britain's Economic Prospects Reconsidered*, Ed. A. Cairncross, pp. 36–61.

ed. 1976. *The Concept and Measurement of Involuntary Unemployment.*

Wright, G. 1971. An econometric study of cotton production and trade, 1830–60. *Review of Economics and Statistics,* **53**, 111–20.

1974. Cotton consumption and the post-bellum recovery of the American South. *Journal of Economic History,* **34**, 610–35.

Wrightson, J. 1890. The agricultural lessons of 'The Eighties'. *Journal of the Royal Agricultural Society of England, Third Series,* **1**, 275–88.

1906. Comparative economy of different methods of harvesting corn crops. *Journal of the Royal Agricultural Society of England,* **67**, 98–106.

Young, A. 1928. Increasing returns and economic progress. *Economic Journal* **38**, 527–42.

Youngson Brown, A. J. 1953. Trade union policy in the Scots coalfields, 1855–85. *Econ. Hist. Rev. 2nd Ser.,* **6**, 35–50.

Zevin, R. B. 1968. The use of a 'long run' learning function: with applications to a Massachusetts cotton textile firm, 1823–60. Unpublished manuscript. Presented to the Workshop in Economic History, University of Chicago, 22 November 1968.

Index and glossary

Excess of government spending over tax receipts, as during wars. A budget deficit is financed either by borrowing or by printing money. Cf. balanced budget.

(1) Commodities used to make other commodities in future. Thus, bricks, steel, lathes, and mastery of the Latin fourth declension are not valued in themselves for direct consumption, but are all used to make things in the future that are: houses, motor cars, chairs, Latin poetry.

(2) The pile of existing capital, somehow added together into one number. The related but distinct idea is 'investment', i.e., the additions to the stock. The flow of water per minute into a bathtub added up over the number of minutes it has been flowing is the stock of water in the bathtub. Likewise, investment added up is the stock of capital.

(3) In business, the financial resources available for an enterprise; what is put into a project (see capital market).

capital deepening

Giving more machines to the same number of men; or, producing a given output with more capital. Contrast 'capital widening'. An assembly line producing automobiles is a deepening of capital relative to hand methods.

capital formation 70, 315–16

Investment (q.v.), i.e., using up resources now to get a return in the future, such as building a railway, educating the people, making ships.

capital gains and losses

Changes in the value of a long-lived asset caused by a rise or fall in its price. If the land tax is raised unexpectedly, for example, land becomes suddenly less desirable and landlords experience a capital loss.

capital goods

see capital

capital intensive

Using much capital (long-lived goods used to produce other goods) relative to labour or land. Relative to a blacksmith's forge, a fully-automated continuous processing mill is a

deepening of capital,
See capital deepening
defence expenditure, 95
deference, 203
deficit financing, 261–2
The act of financing government expenditure partially through borrowing from the public rather than taxing it.
deflation
(1) A condition of low aggregate demand (q.v.)
(2) A fall in prices, said sometimes to result from (1).
deflator
The index of prices used to express incomes earned in one year in terms of the prices of another year (the base year). The verb, 'deflation', is the use of such a price index. Cf. Consumer price index, base-year prices.
demand, aggregate, 269, 270, 271, 273, 279, 284, 332
The total demand for all goods and services in the economy. Its actual level will be identical to national income (q.v.). Its planned level depends on the consumption and investment plans of households, government, and firms, because consumption, government spending, and investment is what income can be used for. Aggregate demand in this second, planned sense is what drives the Keynesian model (q.v.) of the determination of the national income.
demand, consumption, Ch. 6 passim
demand-curve
The amounts of a commodity that people wish to buy at various different prices per unit of it. At a low price of labour, for example, businesses and other buyers of labour would like to buy much of it. Whether or not their wish is fulfilled depends on the supply curve (q.v.).
demand-deficient unemployment
Men out of work because the society does not wish to buy all of what it produces. Distinguish frictional unemployment, i.e., men out of work temporarily while moving from a job society does not now want to a job it does want. Identical to cyclical unemployment.
demand, effective, 17, 27, 29, 271, 330
Equilibrium (q.v.) aggregate demand (q.v.). It is, in other words, the national income, being the amount of spending by households, governments, and firms that they were able to effect.
demand, factors in, 1870–1914, 10, 11, 15, 27, 32, 75, Ch. 6 passim, 254
factors in, 1918–1945, Ch. 14 passim

demand for imports, 17
demand for labour, 268–9
The number of people businesses wish to hire at some wage. The lower the wage the larger the number demanded.
demand management, 245
The government's attempt to keep the society's spending at the level of full employment (q.v.), neither too high not too low, by manipulating its own expenditures. Since its expenditures are part of aggregate demand (q.v.), the attempt may theoretically achieve success. *See* full employment, surplus, fiscal policy, budget deficit.
demand-pull inflation
A rise in prices generally in the economy due to the society's desire to buy more than it has. Contrast cost-push inflation, cf. deflation.
demobilisation, 265, 274
demographic crisis, subsistence crisis
Overpopulation relative to the amount of land available for agriculture, and the misery that results.
demographic transition
The move experienced by all European countries in the 18th through 20th centuries from a roughly stable population brought about by high birth rates matched with equally high death rates to a roughly stable population brought about by low birth rates matched with equally low death rates. Cf. Vol. 2, p. 242.
Denison, E. F., 378
Denmark,
dairy imports from, 175
electricity, 318
dependency ratio, 150
The ratio of those who do not work for money (i.e., normally children, old people and some married women) to those who do work for money.
deposits, deposit liabilities, demand deposits
Cheque-drawing privileges; your chequing account.
depreciation, replacement investment
(1) The wearing-out of capital; (2) expenditure to replace the worn-out capital; (3) the fund accumulated to allow for the expenditure to replace the worn-out capital. The three need not be identical. Depreciation is subtracted from 'gross' income to get 'net' income because a fund used to maintain capital is not available for satisfying present wants.
depreciation
Of a currency, a fall in its value relative to other currencies.
Contrast appreciation, a rise in value.

depreciation (*cont.*)

Contrast devaluation, which entails some intent.

Depressed Condition of Agricultural Interests, Royal Commission on, 1880–2, 176, 187

Deptford, 352

devaluation

of 1931, 260, 298, 304, 310

of 1949, 370, 372, 389, 391, 392, 399, 400, 404, 406

of 1967, 373, 387, 389, 393, 404, 406

of 1972, 407

A fall in the value of a currency relative to another, with the connotation that the fall was intended and arranged (if not necessarily desired) by a nation's government. Contrast depreciation, which connotes an unintended fall in value.

deviation from trend, absolute and relative

Of a time-series, i.e., a statistic for a series of years, cases in which the statistics are higher or lower than a trend, i.e., higher or lower than what might be expected from a line fitted through the points. A harvest failure in 1816, for example, would be a deviation from the trend of the wheat crop 1800 to 1820. The absolute deviation is the number of bushels below the 1800–1820 trend that the crop fell; the relative deviation is the percentage fall. Cf. Vol. 2, p. 29–31.

diet, 133–4

differentials

Usually in reference to wages, differences between wages from one job to another or from one place to another. If the higher wage is compensation for worse conditions or higher skills the differentials have no tendency to disappear, and are called 'compensating' or 'equalizing'.

diminishing returns, 75, 86

The fall in the amount of additional output as additional doses of input are applied. The nation's agriculture is subject to diminishing returns as more workers and capital apply themselves to the fixed amount of land. Output does not fall: it merely rises less than it did from previous doses.

direct investment

An investment in one's own company by contrast with investment in the bonds of other companies ('portfolio investment'). Cunard Lines, Ltd. investing in port facilities for itself in Quebec would be an example of direct investment; investing in Canadian Pacific Railway bonds would be indirect or portfolio investment. Cf. Vol. 2, p. 73.

direct tax

Levied on the people on whom it is believed or intended to fall, such as the income tax. The distinction between direct and indirect taxes, however, 'is practically relegated to the mind of the legislator. What he proposes should be borne by the original payer is called a direct tax, what he intends to be borne by someone else than the original taxpayer is called indirect. Unfortunately, the intention of the legislator is not equivalent to the actual result' (E. R. A. Seligman, *On the Shifting and Incidence of Taxation*, 1892, p. 183). Cf. indirect tax.

discounted value, discounted present value, present value

The amount by which one down-values income earned in the future relative to income earned today. If the interest rate were 10 per cent, for example, one would down-value a pound earned next year to 90p relative to a pound earned today: the discounted value would be 10 per cent below the money value.

discount rate, market rate of discount

The percentage reduction of the price of a short-term IOU (e.g., a 90 day bill) now below its value when it falls due later. For example, a bill worth 100.00 pounds 90 days from now might sell for 99.00 pounds today. The rate is usually expressed as the annual percentage interest rate one would earn on buying such a bill for 99 pounds and holding it to maturity [approximately $(12/3) \times \$(£1/£99) = 4$ per cent; more exactly, allowing for compounding, 3·67 per cent].

discounting

See rediscounting

diseconomies of (managerial) scale

Rises in cost as an enterprise becomes too big for the abilities of its managers to manage. Cf. economies of scale.

disposable income

National income (q.v.) minus personal taxes plus subsidies and payments of interest on the government debt. It is the income available in someone's bank account or pocket for spending or saving, the government having taken its share of the product earlier.

distribution

of goods, 12

of income, 4, 254–5, 331

(1) By size: the frequency of rich and poor.

(2) Functional: how income is allotted to labour, to land, and to capital.

of industry, 245–8

of unemployment, 268–9

equilibrium
A much-used term in economics, meaning a condition in which no forces of self-interest, arithmetic, or whatever tend to change the situation. If the gap between urban and rural wages is an equilibrium, for instance, there is no natural tendency for it to disappear. A ball at the bottom of a bowl is in equilibrium.

equilibrium growth path for capital
The way capital would pile up in an economy if it grew neither too fast nor too slow (in the opinion of those supplying and demanding it).

equilibrium level of interest rate
The return on borrowing or lending that makes the amount people wish to borrow equal to the amount (other) people wish to lend.

equilibrium wage
The payment to workers that makes the amount of hours workers as a whole wish to supply equal to the amount buyers of labour (owners of cotton mills, buyers of haircuts, students at university) wish to buy. Cf. Vol. 2, p. 269.

equity
(1) Titles of ownership; stock certificates.
(2) The value of ownership in a company; the right of ownership.

equity interest
The value of a company. Both words are here used in uncommon senses: 'equity' to mean 'the value of ownership' (as in the phrase, 'I have £2,000 of equity in my house left after the mortgage is subtracted from the price of the house'); 'interest' to mean 'legally recognized concern or right'.

Ernle, Lord, 175
Essex, 189, 193, 194
Eton College, 216
euro-dollar market, 407
The business of offering outside the United States the right to draw on a checking account (usually paying interest) in dollars.

ex ante
The anticipated value; or from the point of view of before the event; or planned. For example, *ex ante* profits in a venture are always high – for why else would one embark on it? *Ex post*, alas, they may be low.

ex post
The realized value or from the point of view of after the event or attained.
See ex ante.

excess capacity
The amount less that one produces when producing less than one can. The British economy in 1933 had excess capacity, with millions of workers out of work and thousands of factories idle.

excess demand
(1) In microeconomics, a situation in a market in which the amount people wish to buy is at the existing price larger than the amount (other) people wish to sell.
(2) In macroeconomics, a condition in which aggregate demand (q.v., that is, what people wish to spend) is larger than aggregate supply (i.e., what they plan currently to produce).

exchange controls, 299, 306, 370, 387, 399, 400, 406
exchange equalisation account, 277, 304
exchange rate, 257, 258, 288, 289, 299, 301, 304–7, 386, 406–7
The value of one country's money in terms of another, such as \$4.86 per pound sterling (the rate during much of the past two centuries). An exchange rate is 'fixed' if the government of one of the countries is willing to buy and sell its currency at the fixed price, in the same way as it might fix the price of wheat.

Exhibition
Crystal Palace, 1851, 182, 184
South London Industrial, 1865, 208

exogenous
Caused outside the system being analyzed. The weather (except smog) is exogenous to the economy: it may cause things in the economy but is not in turn caused by them. The price of housing, in contrast, *is* caused inside the economy. Cf. autonomous spending; contrast endogenous; cf. Vol. 1, p. 35.

expected, expectation, expected value
Statistically speaking, the average of what one anticipates. If one anticipated that the profits on new cotton spindles, say, could be 4, 6, or 8 per cent, each equally likely, then the expected value would be 6 per cent.

expected lifetime income, 270
One's anticipated income over one's remaining life. The concept is useful because decisions by income earners depend presumably on their expected lifetime income, not merely the income they happen to have this year. A surgeon, for example, would be sensible to buy more than he earns early in his careeer, in anticipation of high income later. Identical to permanent income.

expenditure tax
Taxes imposed only on the amounts people spend, as distinct from taxes on income, which tax what they save out of the income as well as what they spend. A tax on food would be

exponential growth
Growth at a constant percentage rate per year, in the manner of compound interest. A straight line upward sloping on an ordinary graph against time has a falling percentage rate of growth, because the constant absolute rise per year is applied to a larger and larger base. An exponential curve would have to be curving up steeper and steeper to maintain the same rate.

externalities, external effects, external economies or diseconomies
Effects you did not directly pay for, such as the pain of smoke in your eye from the local factory or the pleasure of the council's flower garden. The weeds that spread from your neighbour's ill-kept plot in the village fields to your plot is a 'negative' (i.e., bad) externality. The quickening of trade that spreads from the new railway to your business is a positive (i.e., good) externality. An alternative terminology is that external economies are good, external diseconomies bad. Whatever terminology is used, the key idea is the external nature of the event, that is, outside your own control and not directly affected by your activities. Contrast internal economies of scale.

factor, factor of production
One of the inputs into making things, especially the tripartite division into the inputs, land, labour, and capital.
factor endowments
The inputs a nation has at its disposal, including labour, machinery, buildings and skills as well as coal, climate, and soil. Cf. classical vs. Hecksher–Ohlin.
factor income distribution
The incomes to each of the three classical 'factors' of productions, i.e., labour, land, and capital. Cf. Vol. 2, p. 122. It is also called the functional distribution of income.
factor shares
The fractions of income going to labour, capital, land and other inputs. Cf. Vol. 2, p. 176.

farming
See agriculture
final goods
Goods used for consumption, investment, government spending or exports, i.e., not used merely to make other goods. Contrast intermediate goods, compare aggregate demand.
financial intermediation
Transferring money from ultimate savers (in trade union pension funds, insurance policies, railway bonds, personal IOUs, etc.). Banks, insurance companies, and other financial institutions are engaged in intermediation: they borrow from the public, who get a secure place to put their funds and a reward in interest; and they loan to business, who get use of the funds.
fiscal policy
The plans by government for its own taxing and spending, which may achieve goals such as full employment, growth, and stable prices. Cf. monetary policy, demand management, full employment surplus.
fixed capital
Capital that cannot be varied in amount quickly to suit circumstances; opposite, therefore, of 'working capital', 'variable capital', 'goods in process', 'inventories', or any number of other similar ideas. A railway's lines and sidings are fixed capital; its stock of coal to burn in engines is variable.
fixed cost, overhead cost
Costs that do not rise as one makes more. The cost of digging the main shaft is a fixed cost for a coal mine, because it is given and unchanging whether the coal raised is much or little or nil. The costs of miners or of pit props, by contrast, do rise as the mine raises more coal. Contrast variable costs.

Goodhart, C. A. E., 47

goodwill

The reputation, trademark, employee morale, good collection of managers, or other distinctive feature of a firm. As an accounting idea it makes cost equal revenue when revenue is high: if revenue exceeds costs the excess can be called the income of goodwill. As an economic idea it serves a similar function, and is called 'entrepreneurial income'.

government debt, 259–61

Bonds, or IOUs, issued by government. Cf. budget deficit, consols.

government expenditure

and economic policy, 374

and private investment, 249–50

on public works, 249–50, 280

on social services, 138

reduction of, 275, 277

unemployment pay, 278

wartime, 263

For purposes of reckoning the national income, the purchases by the government of goods and services valued by consumers. Transfers of income that are not purchases of goods are not part of government spending in this sense: allowances under the Poor Law are not part of spending, nor under some conventions are interest payments on past government borrowings. Under some conventions of measuring national income, indeed, the provision of roads and police are taken to be depreciation, and are therefore not included in net income.

great depression

(1) The business slump of the 1930s which was in Britain a continuation of a slump in the 1920s.

(2) In an obsolete and exploded but still widely used sense, the slow growth of 1873–1896 – which was not in fact slow real growth but merely a fall in prices. Cf. Vol. 2, chapter 1.

gross

In economic terminology, 'inclusive of something', distinguished from 'net'. Thus gross exports of shipping services from Britain are all British sales of shipping services to foreigners, whereas net exports are all British sales to foreigners minus sales by foreigners to Britain.

gross barter terms of trade

The ratio of the amount of exports a country gains from trade to the amount of exports it must sacrifice to acquire the imports. The concept was introduced by the American econ-omist Frank Taussig (1859–1940) to allow for tribute payment and immigrants' remittances home as an element in trade. It has proven unsuccessful, and most modern studies focus attention on the net barter terms, simply called *the* terms of trade (q.v.).

gross domestic fixed capital formation

The expenditure to produce ('form') new machinery, buildings, and other slow-to-adjust assets ('fixed capital') located at home ('domestic', as opposed to foreign), and including ('gross') replacements of worn-out capital as well as entirely new capital.

gross domestic product

The sum of the value of everything produced in Britain, by contrast with things produced by British capital or labour abroad.

gross national income or gross national product

Gross national income or (what amounts to the same thing) product, or 'GNP', includes as output of the economy the costs of maintenance and replacement of the machinery buildings, railways, etc. that make up the nation's capital. Net national income or product subtracts out these costs, as not available for consumption or new investment. The difference is usually small. Cf. national product, depreciation.

gross reproduction rate

A measure of how many children the typical woman will have over her life. It eliminates the effect of varying proportions of women at various ages. Cf. Vol. 2, p. 147.

growth theory

A branch of economics dealing in an abstract (usually mathematical) form with certain of the causes of the wealth of nations. Despite its encouraging name, it is not empirically based, and is not therefore a theory of any actually achieved economic growth.

gun making, 162

G.K.N. (Guest, Keen and Nettlefolds), 327

Gurney family, 223

Habakkuk, H. J., 76, 185

Haggard, H. Rider, 191

Hancock, K. J., 274

Hannah, L., 253, 324

Hardie, Keir, 231, 237

Harrod–Domar Model

The extension of Keynesian thinking to the long-run, named in honour of the economists who developed it. The model contemplates the possiblity that the 'natural' growth of income necessary for full employment (given the growth of population) may be less or more

imports (*cont.*)
  of food, 70, 291, 303, 309
  of grain, 195
  of manufactures, 143
  of raw materials, 70, 291, 303
  price of, 393, 394
  prices of, 400
  quotas on, 300
  restriction of, 19
income
  See national income
income distribution, 17, 70, 75, Ch. 6 passim, 204, 408, 411
income effect
  The virtual increase in the income of consumers that takes place when a price of something they buy falls. The fall in the price of grain in the late 19th century, for example, had two effects on the consumption of grain: by the 'substitution' effect, cheaper grain was substituted for other goods, increasing the amount of grain consumed; by the income effect, less grain was consumed, for richer people (made richer by the price fall) buy proportionately less grain. Cf. Engel's Law; Vol. 2, p. 331.
income elasticity of demand
  How sensitive the demand for some particular product is to changes in the incomes of demanders. If a 10 per cent rise in income, for example, causes a 5 per cent rise in the quantity of food demanded, then food is said to have an income elasticity of 5/10 or 1/2. Cf. Vol. 2, p. 121.
  See elasticity.
income elasticity of expenditure
  How sensitive expenditure (i.e., non-savings) is to a rise of income. If expenditure rose in proportion to income the elasticity would be 1·0; if less than in proportion, less than 1·0. Cf. consumption function, propensity to consume.
incomes policy, 372, 392–3
increasing returns.
  See economies of scale
India, 87, 91–2, 94–5
  as creditor of Britain, 288
  as market for British exports, 291
  as market for British goods, 294
  benefits from, 89
  British investment in, 74
  competition from, 297
  cotton industry, 91, 294, 304
  exchange rate, 301
  exports of manufactures, 53
  exports to, 66

India Office, 350
  industrialisation of, 303
  investment in, 94
  investment in railways in, 63
  iron industry in, 91
  jute industry in, 91
  Mutiny of 1857, 75, 90
  population, 11
  public finance in, 95
  public finance of, 96
  railway building in, 38
  railway stock of, 83
  railway system of, 76
  railways in, 89, 91
  sterling balances of, 292
  tariffs, 294, 297–9
  taxation in, 90
  textile industry, 309
  war finance, 293
indirect tax
  Levied 'on' the goods, such as a tax on petrol levied on the station owner, 'in the expectation and intention (as Mill put it) that he shall indemnify himself at the expense of another', i.e., the motorist. Thus are import duties, excises, sales taxes, and so forth distinguished from 'direct' taxes, such as the income tax or the land tax. *See* direct tax.
Industrial Reconstruction Corporation, 409
Industrial Transference Board, 276
industry, staple.
  See staple
inflation, 6, 258, 272, 276, 369, 372, 390–5, 405, 413
  A sustained rise in money prices. The rise in one price – say, food – is not inflation, for it may represent merely a growing scarcity of food relative to other goods. Inflation is a growing scarcity of all goods relative to money. Cf. cost-push inflation.
inflationary finance
  The support of government by the printing of money, as distinct from taxing or borrowing from the public. Cf. budget deficit, government debt, balanced budget, fiscal policy, demand management.
inflationary gap
  An excess of desired expenditure in the nation over the capacity to produce it. In the Keynesian theory the gap is the cause of inflation.
informal empire
  The nations tied to Britain by commerce and foreign policy, especially in Latin America; 'the empire of free trade', as distinct from the literal empire in Canada, India, and so forth. Cf. Vol. 2, p. 71.

464

informational cost
Expense incurred in finding information, as for example the time spent looking up this definition. The cost of discovering the market price is an informational cost, which will be high across high barriers of distance and culture. Cf. adjustment costs.

infrastructure
The capital and the institutions needed for an economy to work well: good roads, fair and fast courts of law, honest (or predictably corrupt) government, and the like.

input–output analysis, 316
The use of input–output tables (q.v.) to reckon what flows among industries might be in various hypothetical circumstances.

input–output table, 63
An array of the flows of goods around the economy. One column in such an array might be, for example, the steel industry. The steel output is produced by other industries putting in coal, iron ore, railways, machinery, oil, electricity, paper, and so forth. One row in such an array might also be steel. The steel output is distributed to the machinery industry (which in turn sells machinery back to steel) to construction, to shipbuilding, to railways and so forth. The table includes only intermediate goods, i.e., goods used to make goods.

insurance
as export of services, 13, 66, 96, 256, 289
expenditure on, 136, 139
investment by companies, 320
life, 126
sickness and unemployment, 227, 361–2

interest rate
1860–1914, 44, 105
1920–1931, 258–9, 276, 283, 292
1931–1939, 283, 301, 304
1945–1977, 401–6
fluctuations in, 43, 47

intermediate goods
Goods used to make goods, as distinct from 'final' goods (q.v.). Steel ingots, railway freight, jet fuel, computer services are all examples. Cf. input–output table.

internal economies of scale
A fall in cost a firm may experience when it expands, as against 'external economies' (coming from outside the firm) or 'internal diseconomies' (a rise rather than a fall in cost). For example, the spreading of the fixed costs of a large building that occurs when more activity is crammed into it is an internal economy of scale.

inventories, stocks, goods in progress, working capital, variable capital
The physical amounts or money values of materials held for working up. 'Goods in process' is the most illuminating term. The shoemaker's holding of leather, the steelmaker's holding of finished steel, the publisher's holding of paper, ink and finished books are all 'goods in process'.

inventory costs
The expenditure to keep goods in storage awaiting sale, as on a shopkeeper's shelf or in a farmer's barn.

Inverness, 184

investment
investment bank, 83
A storehouse of funds that specializes in loaning out its funds to business for long-term projects. In European economic history the German investment banks of the late 19th century are said to have been especially bold and important in German growth, by contrast with the greater caution of British banks.
by landlords, 216
domestic, 1860–1914, 14–16, 27, 34–5, 37, 40–2, 63, 70
domestic, 1900–1939, 259, 276–7, 283, 319
domestic, 1945–1977, 379–80, 383
fluctuations in, 29, 32
foreign, 1860–1914, 2–4, 13–15, 34–9, 42, 46, 48, 50, 63, 66, Ch. 4 passim, 216, 222
foreign, 1900–1939, 244, 248–50, 256–7, Ch. 12 passim, 331, 345, 390
foreign, 1945–1977, 412–14
from abroad, 250, 257, 259, 345
investment good
A thing such as a railway or a university education purchased to satisfy human desires indirectly and later, not directly and now. Contrast consumption good. Cf. capital, which is the accumulated pile of investment goods.
in agriculture, 188, 193
in docks, 214, 215
in Keynesian economies, 250
in land, 214
in residential building, 251
overseas, 19, 47
residential, 202
return to, 15, 16, 35, Ch. 4 passim
role of city of London, 16, Ch. 4 passim, 222
share in output, 13
social return to, 379
Using up resources now to get a return in the future, such as buildings, railways, educating

national debt (*cont.*)
   nation but only those owed by the state. The chief source of such indebtedness since the 18th century has been the exigencies of war.

National Government, 261, 277

National Health Service, 263, 411

national income, national product, national value added
   The sum of the value of everything produced for the nation, taking care not to count the value of, say, coal twice, once when it is mined and again when it is burned to make iron. National income is the sum of every income earned in the nation: workers, capitalists, landlords, bureaucrats. As a first approximation it is equal to national product, for the cost of producing things is someone's income. The taxes on things such as sales tax on bread, however, make for a difference between what is paid ('at market prices') and what is earned ('at factor costs'). The national income at factor cost, then, is rather lower than national product (which itself may be lowered by removing depreciation; see gross national product). The national value added is the sum of all values added. The value added by each firm is the value of the labour and capital it uses, that is, the value of its goods in excess of its purchases from other industries. The sum of all these will be the sum value of labour and capital, i.e., national income.

National Institute of Economic and Social Research, 377, 381

National Insurance Act 1911, 266

National Plan 1964–5, 408

National Shipbuilders Securities Ltd, 248, 253

nationalisation, 221, 368, 407, 408, 410

nationalised industries, 374

natural price of labour
   The wage that would result in the long run if the number of labourers always increased (by birth) when they grew to some degree prosperous. Cf. Iron Law of Wages; Malthusian trap.

natural rate of growth
   In the Harrod–Domar model (q.v.) the percentage rate at which income would grow if it grew in accord with growing population.

natural rate of unemployment
   The percentage of people out of work in normal times, such as people between jobs, in the normal course of the economy. It is, therefore, the lowest possible rate of unemployment. Identical to frictional unemployment. Cf. Vol. 2, p. 273.

Navigation Acts
   A set of acts of Parliament from the 1660s through the 18th century meant to reserve the foreign trade of Britain and its colonies for British subjects. In particular, they protected the British shipping industry against European competition, protected other industries at home from colonial competition, and compelled the colonies to trade through British ports.

neo-classical economics
   The modern orthodoxy in economics, as distinct from classical economics (q.v.) before it and modern Marxian, institutionalist, or Austrian economics. It emphasizes mathematics in method and profit-maximizing in substance. In its simplest and most characteristic form it treats as given the technology, taste and resources of an economy, turning its attention to how these interact. The various schools may be distinguished by their respective forefathers: those of neo-classical economics are Adam Smith and his intellectual grandson, Alfred Marshall. Cf. Marshallian, classical economics.

net investment
   All investment minus the investment in depreciation; which is to say, the investment that results during a year in a net increase – allowing for replacement as it wears out – of the stock of capital.

net national product
   See gross national product. Briefly, it is what the nation makes excluding that used to repair old machines and buildings.

net output.
   See value added

net overseas assets
   The value of what foreigners owe Britain subtracting out what Britain owes them.

Netherlands, 3, 71, 72, 175, 318

new husbandry
   The system of agriculture introduced in England from the 16th to the 18th century (there is controversy about precisely when) involving the use of grasses, turnips, and other novelties. Cf. Norfolk rotation, mixed farming.

new industries, 353

new issues
   Fresh IOUs, as distinct from ones made in the past and now being traded.

New York, money market of, 292, 295, 296

New Zealand,
   agricultural exports of, 302
   as market for British exports, 291
   dairy imports from, 175, 181, 197

rediscounting, discounting

The purchase of IOU's before they are due, giving the original holder money immediately and giving the holder in due course the interest to be earned by holding them. The Bank of England, for example, commonly rediscounted bills (i.e., short term IOUs) for the banks. The banks had themselves bought the bills (discounted them), and the Bank bought the bills in turn from them (rediscounted the bills).

redistribution of income

A shift in who gets what as pay or other earnings.

re-exports

Goods imported into Britain and then immediately exported abroad without further processing. Under the Navigation Acts (q.v.) Britain was by law endowed with a large re-export trade of products from the colonies bound for foreign countries.

regression analysis, regression equation, curve fitting

Techniques for fitting straight lines through a scatter of points. In finding the straight line that would best summarize the relationship during 1921–1938 between consumption and income, for instance, one is said to 'regress consumption on income', i.e., fit a straight line through points on a graph of annual consumption and income for these years. The simplest and by far the most widely used of the techniques is called 'least squares' or 'ordinary least square'. The result will be, as it is (roughly) in Vol. 2, p. 342, eq. 1, an equation for a straight line, such as Consumption in £ million at 1938 prices equals £277 million plus 0·44 times income in £ million at 1938 prices. Symbolically, the equation is in general $C = \alpha + \beta Y$. The actual numerical result says that the line that best fits the scatter of combinations of consumption and income is a constant (£277 million) plus 44 per cent of whatever income happens to be. The 'slope' or 'slope coefficient' or 'regression coefficient' or 'beta' is in this case 0·44. Consumption here is called the 'dependent' variable, income the 'independent' variable, in accord with the notion that consumption is dependent on income. The technique generalizes easily to more than one independent variable, in which case it is called 'multiple regression' and amounts to fitting a plane (rather than a line) through points in space (rather than through points on a plane surface). In multiple regression the coefficient 'on' (i.e., multiplying) each independent variable measures the way each by itself influences the dependent variable. The equation fitted in the case mentioned above (Vol. 2, p. 342, eq. 1) was in fact Consumption = $277 + (0·44)$ Income + $(0·47)$ Consumption Last Year, which is a multiple regression of this year's consumption on this year's income and last year's consumption. It says that for a given consumption last year each £ of income raised consumption by £0·44; and for a given income each £ of consumption last year raised consumption this year by £0·47. The technique generalizes with rather more difficulty to more than one dependent variable, in which case it is called 'simultaneous equation estimation'.

regressive taxes

Taxes whose burden falls on the poor, as taxes on food are said to be relative to 'progressive' taxes such as those on mink coats and yachts.

relative income hypothesis

The notion that one's consumption (as distinct from savings) depends on one's relative economic position, not absolute wealth. According to the hypothesis the poor will save little (i.e., consume virtually all their income) even though they are in absolute terms as wealthy as, say, the high-saving middle class of a much poorer country. Cf. permanent income hypothesis; Vol. 2, p. 130.

relative price

As distinct from 'nominal' or 'money' or 'absolute' prices, the price of one good in terms of another good, rather than in terms of money. If farm labour earns 16 shillings a week when wheat sells for 8 shillings a bushel, then the price of a week of labour relative to a bushel of wheat is 2·0 bushels per week. Note the units: they are physical, not money, units. Relative prices are determined by the real effectiveness of the economy, whereas money prices are determined by relative prices and by the dearness of money. Cf. Vol. 2, p. 410.

rent, economic rent, pure rent

The return to specialized factors of production in an industry, i.e., those factors used in that industry alone. Agricultural land with no use outside of agriculture is the classic example. A coal seam is another. Economic rent need not correspond exactly to the amount earned in 'rent' in the ordinary sense of weekly rent for a flat, or even yearly rent for land. For definitions in slightly different terms, cf. economic rent, producers' surplus.

    The economics of finding the best deal, the logic of which has only recently been explored seriously. Its main significance is that it offers a rationale for conditions otherwise outside the traditional economic models of man. A condition of ignorance about who exactly will pay the highest price for one's product may be the best one can do, in view of the high costs of search. A condition of unemployment, likewise, may be the best one can do, in view of the high costs of search.

    A view associated in particular with the American Keynesian economist Alvin Hansen in the late 1930s and early 1940s that modern capitalism had exhausted its ability to grow. Circa 1940 the view was quite plausible, considering the recent experience of the Great Depression (q.v.) and a sharp fall in the growth rate of the population associated with the demographic transition (q.v.).

    A law of 1662, in effect with varying force for a century and a half after, that allowed local authorities to expel a newcomer to the parish within 40 days of his arrival if he seemed likely to become destitute. Theoretically a great obstacle to the mobility of working people, its practical effect is in doubt.

    The expenditure of a company or person to supply something before they have been permitted to adjust their affairs to supply it cheapest. For instance, the short run cost curve of steel shows what additional steel will cost if no new plants, iron mines, or marketing arrangements are permitted. In the long run the cost will be lower, for new plants will be built to service the additional quantity demanded. Cf. cost.

    The profile of how many people earn what yearly incomes, from the poorest to the richest, is known as the income distribution of the society. A graph of such a distribution, i.e. of how many people have each income (£100–£200, £200–£300, etc.), is not normally bell shaped, but squeezed over towards the low end. Such squeezing is known as skewness. Cf. Lorenz curve.

    The results of a meeting in Washington during December 1971 that fixed the prices of the world's currencies in terms of gold. The agreement lasted for less than a year, after which all major currencies 'floated', i.e., moved relative to each other in response to their market.

    The value of alternatives sacrificed by some decision, viewed from the entire society's point of view. A decision to pay one's rent of £100

  The value of one's sellable things. It may be
  defined narrowly to include only money,
  houses, bonds, jewels; or broadly to include
  the value (even if one cannot sell it for a sum
  now) of future earnings. The nation's wealth
  does not include bonds and other IOUs of one
  citizen to another, which cancel out when
  viewed as one man's debt.

  The typical value of some measure, adjusted
  for the relative importance of various items.
  Thus, the unweighted average of city sizes
  would count Camberley and London each as
  cities; the weighted average would count
  London more times than Camberley, perhaps
  in proportion to their sizes. Such a procedure
  would give the size of city in which the typical
  person lived while the unweighted procedure
  would give the average population of a list of
  places called cities.
  The capital (q.v.) of a firm in the form of
  materials to be worked on, cash in hand,
  inventories of finished products, and so forth
  that can be readily made into cash.